Affectionately | Marcel

The Selected Correspondence of Marcel Duchamp

*To
the memory of
Alexina
Duchamp*

Affectionately | Marcel

The Selected Correspondence of Marcel Duchamp

edited by **Francis M. Naumann** and **Hector Obalk**

translation by **Jill Taylor**

published by **Ludion Press** Ghent - Amsterdam

This book has been born out of the research conducted by **Francis M. Naumann**, who has been collecting photocopies of Marcel Duchamp's correspondence all over the world for some twenty years. Further research by Hector Obalk and André Gervais brought this exceptional corpus to over 1100 autograph letters.

Hector Obalk, who proposed the selection of the 285 letters published here, transcribed and organized these letters into fourteen chapters, putting them into context through lists of addresses, major works and major exhibitions. He also compiled the various indexes—thanks to the expertise and patience of **Florian Debraine**.

For the present volume, Francis M. Naumann wrote the 'Introduction' and is author of the individual biographies of major correspondents. He also provided the chronological data inserted between the letters, as well as the greater part of the information given in the one thousand sidenotes appearing in the margins of this edition.

Important contributions to the content of these invaluable sidenotes were also made by **Naomi Sawelson-Gorse**, whose familiarity with art history in the USA and the Arensberg circle proved enlightening, and above all by **André Gervais**, whose theoretical and historical knowledge of Dada and Surrealist French literature place him among the most eminent scholars in the field.

The final editing and synthesis of these notes, and, more generally, of this English edition, is the work of **Jill Taylor**—also author of the translation of the Obalk texts and the Duchamp letters.

The authors are grateful to the staff and administrators of the various libraries and museums listed on p.7, especially to: Linda Ashton, Laurence Camous, François Chapon, Aldo R. Cupo, Emmanuelle Etchecopar-Etchar, Donald Gallup, Anne d'Harnoncourt, Cathy Henderson, Margaret Kline, Carlton Lake, Garnett McCoy, Valérie Séguéla, Thomas F. Staley, Elizabeth Wrigley and Anne-Marie Zuchelli.

The authors are also deeply grateful to the following for their help and advice : André Buckles, Alice Buckles-Brown, William A. Camfield, Chantal Combes, Niki Ekstrom, David Fleiss, Richard Hamilton, Dona Hochart, Marie T. Keller, Billy Klüver and Julie Martin, Romain Lacroix, Carlton Lake, Anna Lamparska, Jean-Jacques Lebel, Patrice Lefrançois, Rona Millenaar, Peter Ruyffelaere, Michael Taylor, Calvin Tomkins, Paul van Calster, Beatrice Wood and Lisa Zeitz.

Finally, this book would not have been possible without the encouragement and generous cooperation of Alexina Duchamp (d. 1995) and her daughter Jacqueline Matisse Monnier.

table of contents

Transcription, typesetting and design **Hector Obalk**, Paris
  with the assistance of Florian Debraine, James Peach, Davis Xavier, Henri Bordes,
  Camille Courier de Méré and Céline Barre.

Typefaces **Martin Majoor** (Scala and Scala Sans)
  and **Robert Slimbach** (Adobe Garamond Semi Bold)

Jacket design **Anneke Germers**, Amsterdam
  front: photo by Man Ray
  back & front: letter to Suzanne Duchamp, 15 January 1916

Published in 2000 by **Ludion** Press, Muinkkaai 42, B-9000 Ghent, Belgium.

Distributed in the USA and Canada by **D.A.P.** / Distributed Art Publishers, Inc.,
  155 Sixth Avenue 2nd Floor, New York NY 10013-1507.

ISBN 90-5544-249-6

Printed and bound in Belgium.

repositories

of the letters

The majority of the 285 letters published in this volume have been transcribed from the original manuscript or, failing this, from a photocopy of the original letter.

The following abbreviations are used to identify the libraries and museums in the United States and Europe where Duchamp's letters are currently preserved:

AAA = Archives of American Art, Smithsonian Institution, Washington, D.C.
(Suzanne Duchamp and Jean Crotti, Walter Pach, Beatrice Wood)

BLJD = Bibliothèque littéraire Jacques Doucet, Université de Paris, France.
(André Breton, Jacques Doucet, Pierre de Massot, Francis Picabia, Tristan Tzara)

GRI = Getty Research Institute for the History of Art and the Humanities, Los Angeles, California.
(Yvonne Chastel/Crotti/Lyon, Helen Freeman, Man Ray)

HRHRC = Harry Ransom Humanities Research Center, University of Texas, Austin.
(Henri-Pierre Roché)

MNAM = Musée National d'Art Moderne, Centre Georges Pompidou, Paris.
(Constantin Brancusi, Man Ray)

Newberry Library = The Newberry Library, Chicago, Illinois.
(Alice Rouillier)

NYPL = The New York Public Library, Manuscript & Archives Division, Astor, Lenox & Tilden Foundations
(John Quinn)

PMA = The Philadelphia Museum of Art, Philadelphia, Pennsylvania.
(Walter and Louise Arensberg, Fiske Kimball)

YCAL = Yale Collection of American Literature, Beinecke Library, Yale University, New Haven, Connecticut
(Katherine S. Dreier, Henry McBride, Alfred Stieglitz, the Stettheimer sisters)

Twenty or so of the letters, whose location is unknown or to which access is now restricted, have been published thanks to transcriptions preserved in the archives of the late Yves Poupard-Lieussou or those of André Gervais—as in the case for certain letters to Michel Carrouges, Pierre de Massot, André Breton and Jehan Mayoux. In each case, the name of the author of the transcription is given after the word "source."

introduction

by Francis M. Naumann

In reading the letters of Marcel Duchamp, their casual and sometimes impersonal tone suggests that he wrote to his friends, relatives, and colleagues only when some other more engaging activity failed to attract his interests. He probably considered the process of written communication one of life's inevitable necessities, an activity he engaged in as an unavoidable part of his existence as (to use his own word) a *"respirateur."* Yet his letters have proven to be invaluable documents, providing crucial information on the subject of his art and life. Biographers and art historians are given the facts and details necessary for the compilation of a complete and accurate chronology, and some of the more personal letters provide rare but invaluable insight into his thinking at critical periods in his artistic development.

Duchamp wrote in a self-consciously efficient style, a method of communication that was also evident in other aspects of his everyday life, particularly in his artistic production. In a letter to Katherine Dreier—who was in the habit of writing long and somewhat exhausting letters to Duchamp—he replied: *"Can't write such letters as your nice last one—but in my telegraphic way I mean the same thing."*[1] A few months before this letter was sent, Duchamp had a rubber stamp prepared of his address, which was headed with the following declaration: *"style télégraphique / pour correspondance / en retard"* ["telegraphic style / for correspondence / late"]. Although he may have sounded somewhat apologetic in his letter to Dreier, Duchamp must have possessed a certain pride in his own efficiency, for the rubber stamp inscription was reprinted in facsimile form opposite the first page of text in Robert Lebel's *Sur Marcel Duchamp*, the first monograph on the artist and a book whose layout was approved in all of its details by Duchamp himself.[2]

As a personality, Duchamp was not by nature forthcoming. In conversation, he provided information about himself only when specifically requested, and in his letters, he relayed information about his daily activities only when he felt the subject was something that might be of interest to his correspondent. As a result, many letters contain little more than an update of his daily activities, from playing chess to his continued involvement within the world of art. Sundry and unexceptional though many of these activities may appear, some—such as his early thoughts on the formation of the readymade—affected not only the course of Duchamp's personal artistic future, but, as time would prove, the entire history of western art.[3] In expressing his opinion on the current art scene, Duchamp could—on occasion—be almost philo-

1. Marcel Duchamp to Katherine Dreier, November 4, 1952.
2. Robert Lebel, *Sur Marcel Duchamp* (Paris: Trianon, 1959); this declaration is printed above the facsimile of a handwritten note from Duchamp to Robert Lebel dated February 9, 1954.

sophical in his observations. In the first letter of the present publication, for example, he offers a friendly formal critique of his sister's painting, and almost exactly forty years later, he writes a long and thoughtful letter to his brother-in-law, Jean Crotti, advising him to resist evaluating his own position within the world of art and explaining why such an effort would be only futile.[4]

In his everyday life, Duchamp seemed somewhat reluctant to criticize interpretations of his work, but when solicited—as they were when Michel Carrouges sent him a manuscript that he had written comparing the *Large Glass* to the writings of Kafka— Duchamp could be surprisingly direct, yet always delicate in expressing his opinion.[5] When Carrouges's book finally appeared a few years later, the artist could be far more precise in his objections, as he was in a letter to André Breton, and in another letter written to a reviewer whose criticism of the book he supported.[6]

Readers already familiar with Duchamp's work and the events of his life—particularly those who have read Calvin Tomkins's beautifully-written biography of the artist[7]—may be disappointed not to discover in the present compilation examples of letters that Duchamp wrote to Maria Martins (1894-1973). While living in New York in the 1940s, Duchamp fell deeply in love with this woman, a beautiful and brilliant Brazilian sculptor who was married to the Brazilian Ambassador to the United States and who had two teenage daughters. Since Martins served as a model for the *Etant donnés*—a work that Duchamp worked on in secrecy during the last twenty years of his life—his love affair with her has developed into a subject of great interest among Duchamp scholars. Nevertheless, even though over a half century has passed since they were written, members of both the Duchamp and Martins families maintain that these letters contain passages that they consider still too personal and private for publication. It is in deference to their wishes that these letters have been withdrawn from the present publication. It is hoped that readers will retain their interest in this subject and patiently await future editions of this book, for it is inevitable that at some point in the future, these letters will be made public.[8]

Once Duchamp had become fairly well known for his artistic accomplishments— which was certainly the case after the notorious reception of his *Nude Descending a Staircase* at the Armory Show in 1913—virtually everyone who received a letter from him carefully preserved it (even his closest friends and relatives). By contrast, after having responded to a letter he received, Duchamp quickly discarded it, its disap-

---

3.   See, for example, his famous letter to his sister Suzanne explaining his concept of the readymade, dated 15 January [1916] (letter 11).

4.   See Duchamp to Suzanne, March 15, 1912 (letter 1) and Duchamp to Suzanne and Jean Crotti, August 17, 1952 (letter 216).

5.   Duchamp to Michel Carrouges, February 6, 1950 (letter 189).

6.   Duchamp to André Breton, October 4, 1954 (letter 235), and Duchamp to Jehan Mayoux, March 8, 1956 (letter 239).

7.   Calvin Tomkins, *Duchamp: A Biography* (New York: Henry Holt and Company, 1996).

8.   Meanwhile, for more information on Duchamp's relationship with Maria Martins, readers are advised to consult Tomkins's biography (see previous note) or my own writings on this subject: "The Bachelor's Quest," *Art in America*, vol. 81, no. 9 (September 1993), pp. 72-81, and "Don't Forget I Come From the Tropics," in *Maria: The Surrealist Sculpture of Maria Martins*, exh. cat., André Emmerich Gallery, New York, 19 March - 18 April 1998, pp. 8-38.

pearance representing a convenient and accurate filing system in its own right (if the letter was no longer in his possession, it indicated that he had responded). As a result, well over one thousand five hundred letters from his hand are extant, whereas the letters written to him only survive if they were composed on a typewriter, and only if the correspondent retained a carbon copy. For this reason, it was decided to publish only letters written *by* Duchamp, providing information relayed by the correspondent (if known) only when this was considered essential to the comprehension of Duchamp's letter. It was also decided that the individual letters should not be excerpted or edited in any way, but rather presented in their entirety, retaining—to the degree possible in typeset transcription—the appearance and sensitivity of the original document.

In the initial planning stages of this book, it was decided that the letters would be grouped according to correspondent, but as more and more letters were uncovered, it was determined that a chronological ordering system would be more informative and of greater interest to the general reader. Moreover, in order to encourage a pleasurable reading of these letters (as opposed to consulting them for reference purposes alone), it was decided to keep the extraneous information to a minimum. Essential chronological facts are interspersed among the letters, and footnotes are provided only to clarify information that might not otherwise be apparent from the context.

Since the book is arranged chronologically, efforts were made to find letters that provided as much information as possible on what Duchamp was doing at a particular time and place. Naturally, letters that revealed information about his artistic production were given priority, unless the information they contain was already provided in another document. In various archives that contain examples of Duchamp's correspondence, there are many notes, telegrams, postcards, *pneumatiques*[9], etc., of no more than one or two sentences in length, written to arrange (or confirm) the time and place of a meeting. In selecting letters for the present publication, these comparatively brief missives were often passed over, in favor of letters that were longer and, in most cases, more interesting and informative. Since the letters published here represent only a portion of the extant correspondence (less than one-fifth), interested readers are encouraged to consult the individual repositories in which Duchamp's original letters are preserved.

Finally, it should be noted that this compilation does not represent the first publication of Duchamp's letters. His correspondence has always been of great interest, not only among Duchamp scholars, but even to his friends and colleagues, a number of whom sought permission for their publication even within the artist's lifetime. An amusing letter that Duchamp wrote to Tristan Tzara in 1922, for example—about a Dada bracelet that he wanted to manufacture—was published in the form of a small booklet by Tzara in 1958. And the long letter of advice that he wrote to Jean Crotti in 1952 (mentioned above) was published as the foreword to a catalogue of his paintings at a gallery in Paris in 1959. Excerpts from Duchamp's letters were used by vir-

---

9.   A *pneumatique* is a message placed in a cylindrical container and sent from one post office to another in Paris by means of an elaborate underground network of pressurized tubes. This system is no longer used, having been replaced by the telegram and other more convenient and efficient delivery services.

tually every scholar who wrote about the artist, beginning with the presentation of seventeen letters written to the collector Jacques Doucet, which appeared for the first time in Michel Sanouillet's *Marchand du sel*, the first anthology of Duchamp's writings. More recently, Duchamp's complete correspondence with the artist and writer Marcel Jean was published in the form of a small book.[10]

I was first made aware of the importance of Duchamp's letters some twenty years ago, when a tip from Professor William A. Camfield of Rice University led me to the discovery of Duchamp's complete correspondence with his sister Suzanne and his brother-in-law Jean Crotti. I spent the next three years transcribing and translating these documents, and, with the permission of Alexina Duchamp, ten letters appeared in an issue of the *Archives of American Art Journal*. I repeated this process to publish ten more letters written to Louise and Walter Arensberg, and, a few years later, when the papers of Walter Pach were acquired by the Archives of American Art, I was granted permission to publish sixteen letters, representing his complete correspondence with Duchamp.[11]

Over time, I gained a minor reputation for my publication of this material, and scholars from all over the world began contacting me on a regular basis to inquire about the location of other letters. It was at this time that I approached Alexina Duchamp (whom I eventually got to know well enough to address her by her nickname: Teeny) and asked if she would consider participating in a joint venture to publish her husband's selected correspondence. She immediately agreed, and offered to give me whatever help she could. I shall remain forever indebted to Teeny for having provided me not only with the authorization necessary to proceed with this project, but also with the encouragement to continue it. I deeply regret that she did not live to see the final publication, but it is for this reason that—with great respect and affection—this book is dedicated to her memory.

August 1999
Yorktown Heights, New York

---

10. Herbert Molderings, ed., *Marcel Duchamp: Letters to Marcel Jean* (Munich: Silke Schreiber, 1987); Michel Sanouillet, ed., *Marchand du sel: Écrits de Marcel Duchamp* (Paris: Le Terrain Vague, 1958), in English as *Salt Seller: The Writings of Marcel Duchamp*, Michel Sanouillet and Elmer Peterson, eds. (New York: Oxford University Press, 1973); the letter to Tzara was published by PAB: Alès (Gard), and the letter to Crotti appeared in *Jean Crotti*, exh. cat., Musée Galliera, Paris, 11 December 1959 - 11 January 1960.

11. "Affectueusement, Marcel: Ten Letters from Marcel Duchamp to Suzanne Duchamp and Jean Crotti," *Archives of American Art Journal*, vol. 22, no. 4 (Spring 1983), pp.2-19; "Marcel Duchamp's Letters to Walter and Louise Arensberg: 1917-1921," *Dada/Surrealism*, no. 16 (1987), pp. 203-27 (repr. in Rudolf E. Kuenzli and Naumann, eds., *Marcel Duchamp: Artist of the Century* [Cambridge: MIT, 1989]); and "Amicalement, Marcel: Fourteen Letters from Marcel Duchamp to Walter Pach," *Archives of American Art Journal*, vol. 29, nos. 3 & 4 (1989), pp.36-50. These same letters have been retranslated and are included in the present volume.

preamble

by Hector Obalk

As this collection of letters aims to provide a kind of biography of Marcel Duchamp by the artist himself, the letters are grouped into chapters representing different periods in MD's life and generally corresponding to the different places in which he lived.

As the reader works his way through the abundance of information provided in the one thousand notes, he will be assisted by three short summaries in list form at the start of each of the 14 chapters: a list of addresses where Duchamp lived or sojourned at some time, a list of his major works (together with a brief description) and finally a list of the various exhibitions where his work was shown.[12]

Meanwhile, for the benefit of those who might feel daunted by lists of this kind, a narrative and critical synthesis of the life and work of Marcel Duchamp, roughly decade by decade, is provided below for the reader to refer to while going through the letters.

Henri Robert Marcel Duchamp is born in Blainville-Crevon (Normandy) 28 July 1887. His father is a notary public and mayor of the town and his grandfather is the engraver Emile Nicolle.

Aged 10, he is sent away to school—Ecole Bossuet in Rouen and then to the Lycée Corneille—until July 1904.

His two brothers, his elders by ten and twelve years, are both students in Paris, Raymond at Medical School and Gaston at the Law Faculty.

His first known paintings date from 1902: *Landscape at Blainville, Church at Blainville, Garden and Chapel at Blainville*—all of Impressionist influence.

In 1904, he goes to Paris to join his two brothers, who have both become artists, in Montmartre. Raymond is a sculptor and goes under the name of Raymond Duchamp-Villon. Gaston, with whom Marcel will live at first, is a painter and engraver and goes under the name of Jacques Villon.

Like his brothers, MD will embark on his career as an artist by drawing cartoons for newspapers ("**dessins d'humour**" in French), cartoons which are to be exhibited for two years running at the Salon des Artistes Humoristes, Palais de Glace (1907 and 1908) and published in French magazines such as *Le Rire, Le Courrier Français* or *Le Témoin* (until 1910).

---

12. These lists of residences and exhibitions appear almost, but not quite, entirely thanks to the impressive and irreplaceable *Ephemerides* by Jennifer Gough-Cooper and Jacques Caumont, published in the *Marcel Duchamp* catalogue (Palazzo Grassi, Venice, summer 1993).

In 1908, his two brothers share a studio with Frantisek Kupka in Puteaux (suburb to the West of Paris). Marcel takes part in the "**Puteaux Sundays**" where, in the wake of "Cubism," there are discussions on non-Euclidian geometry, chronophotography, the Golden Section and the fourth dimension—with artists and writers such as Apollinaire, Barzun, Duchamp-Villon, Le Fauconnier, la Fresnaye, Gleizes, Hourcade, Kupka, Léger, Metzinger, Pach, Raynal, Ribemont-Dessaignes, Villon...

As a **young painter** from a family of artists, Marcel Duchamp successively goes through the pictorial trends of his time: **Impressionnism** until 1909, **Fauvism** (in 1909-1910), **Symbolism** (end 1910-1911), **Cubism** and **Futurism** (from autumn 1911).

Like all future modern painters (with the exception of Braque and Picasso), he exhibits his work at the Salons where "Modern Art" is going on. He exhibits five years running at the **Salon d'Automne** (1908 to 1912) and four years running at the **Salon des Indépendants** (1909 to 1912).

While carrying out his Cubo-Futurist research—becoming increasingly original with *Yvonne and Magdeleine Torn in Tatters, Apropos of Little Sister, Sonata, Dulcinea, The Chess Players, Portrait of Chess Players, Coffee Mill, Sad Young Man on a Train, Nude Descending a Staircase, No.1 and No.2, The King and Queen Surrounded by Swift Nudes*—a great disappointment is to befall him on 18 March 1912, two days before the opening of the new Salon des Indépendants of the same year. MD receives a visit from his brothers who ask him to withdraw his **Nude Descending a Staircase**, *No.2*, as its title seems to make mockery of Cubism and Modern Art.

In June 1912, he sets out on a four-month trip: Basle, Constance, Vienna, Prague, Berlin, Dresden and above all **Munich** where he produces—a far cry from Cubism and Futurism—his first truly personal paintings, *Passage from Virgin to Bride* and *Bride*, which form the initial research for what eventually will be his Large Glass.

Upon his return, he takes two very surprising decisions which historians to date have tended to take as one single decision. Firstly, and in spite of the five or six masterpieces he has just completed, he gives up painting. Secondly, in spite of all the effort he has put into it so far, he decides not to be an artist "for a living," painter or otherwise.

Upon his return to Paris in October 1912, he looks for paid employment with the sole aim of having some *temps libre* (free time).

As a trainee at the Sainte-Geneviève Library, he consults treatises on perspective and the fourth dimension, forsaking all ambition in the "world of art."

The current volume of his letters begins in 1912, in the initial stages of this sudden about-turn.

For the next ten years, he is to devote his *temps libre* to his *magnum opus*, **The Bride Stripped Bare by her Bachelors, Even**—which is at the same time both a painting on glass, 3 meters high (the Large Glass), and a highly speculative literary œuvre (the future Green Box).

After his *Nude Descending a Staircase* No.2 is exhibited at the Armory Show in 1913, the unforseeable *succès de scandale* with which it is received provides MD with the opportunity to flee France, already at war, and go and live in New York, where he is welcomed like the Messiah from the moment he arrives in June 1915.

It is also in the 1910's that he buys, somewhat parsimoniously, a few ordinary objects, mainly industrially manufactured, arousing curiosity in their presence by inscribing them with a sibylline phrase and installing them at his place in very unusual ways (snow shovel hanging from the ceiling, coat rack nailed to the floor). These are his famous **readymades**, never exhibited at the time, which he thought of more as objects which ask questions (Is it art? Is it beautiful? Is it useless? Is it unique?) rather than things that had been christened art "through the mere choice of the artist."[13]

In the twenties, continuing to perfect his **chess** playing, he slowly relinquishes his Large Glass, which in 1923 he considers to be "definitively unfinished." In 1923, after a long stay in the United States and in Argentina, he moves back to France where he is to spend the next twenty years—interspersed with frequent trips to Brussels, London, Rouen, Nice and Monte Carlo.

Duchamp divides his time between making up **literary puns** of the crudest kind (signed Rrose Sélavy), limited production of truly **Dada objects** (mustachioed Mona Lisa, Wanted poster, fake check...), experimenting with **optical machines** (Rotatives, stereoscopic views, movie...) and international chess championships.

In the thirties, while pursuing his chess career, he comes back to his unfinished works of fifteen years earlier, concentrating on two retrospective presentations of his work: the *Green Box* and the *Box-in-a-Valise*. The **Green Box** (Sept 1934) is a collection in facsimile of a selection of rough notes published in true form—the paper torn in exactly the same place. These notes describe thoughts and projects concerning the *Bride Stripped Bare...* and also language, color, geometry, photography, readymades and other more philosophical topics. The **Box-in-a-Valise** is a sort of portable museum containing reproductions and replicas of the things Marcel did in his lifetime: traditional canvases, unfinished Large Glass, book covers, assemblages, readymades...

After 1935 and during the forties, Duchamp handles exhibitions in an advisory or coordinating capacity, notably with André Breton to whom he has always shown a kind of deference. He designs and installs windows and environments, notably for the Gradiva gallery, Brentano's bookshop and the big International Surrealist shows.

If he gave up painting around 1912—in actual fact in 1918 with *Tu m'*—Duchamp will spend a lifetime perfecting his incredible talent as a graphic designer, often demonstrating a pioneering inventiveness in an era where the Macintosh has not yet come to pass: layout for his chess treatise (1932), covers of *Minotaure* review (1935), *Transition* (1937), *First Papers of Surrealism* (1942), *View* (1945) and *Prière de toucher* (1947), posters for his shows at the Sidney Janis Gallery (1953), at the Pasadena Museum (1963) and at Galerie Givaudan (1967).

---

13. In support of this argument, see my essay *La notion de readymade*, to be published by *Les Cahiers du MNAM*, Pompidou Center. Short version published by *tout-fait.com* No. 2.

To get away from World War II, Marcel Duchamp settles permanently in the United States in 1942.

In his New York studio, he starts work, in the greatest secrecy, on a quasi-pornographic installation called **Given: 1. The Waterfall 2. The Illuminating Gas** (1946-1966), showing the Bride now fallen, lying naked on a pile of twigs in a waterfall landscape. In stark contrast to the transparency of the Large Glass and the incompleteness of the story it tells, *Given*, through its unequivocal realism, is a sort of final episode in the *Bride Stripped Bare* and will not be revealed to the public until after Marcel's death.

In the fifties, Duchamp sets to work on the manufacture of seven particularly strange and crypto-erotic sculptures, fake casts of bodily parts—*Not a Shoe, Female Fig Leaf, Objet-Dard, Wedge of Chastity, With My Tongue in My Cheek, Torture-morte, Sculpture-morte*—pointing the way to a new form of sculpture.

The sixties are notably the replica years—**replicas** of his own work, made by others and signed by MD: manufactured replicas, in eight copies, of each of his historical readymades for the famous Schwarz edition (1964); hand-made replicas of his Large Glass (1961 and 1966), as it can no longer be moved around, by Ulf Linde or Richard Hamilton, which he signs *pour copie conforme* ("certified true copy"). Paradoxically, the latter consists, in fact, of hyperrealist sculptures carved or cast after photos of readymades which, for the most part, had been lost. This is probably where the fallacy originated of a Marcel Duchamp—genius for some, charlatan for others, both wrong in this instance—who spent a lifetime turning anything and everything into works of art.

Duchamp's final creation is, like Picasso's and Renoir's last works, definitely voluptuous: a series of nine lithographs, all delicate tracings of fragments of works by Rodin, Courbet, Cranach, Ingres...

After Marcel's death, his family found a number of unpublished pieces of writing—notes on the infrathin, projects for artworks, puns—but not a single copy of the thousands of letters he wrote.

November 1999
Paris

transcription policy

by Hector Obalk

It is clear that the letters of Marcel Duchamp, unlike those of many writers, were in no way written to be published. For this reason, publication of these letters raises a number of editorial problems as to how faithful one should be to the original manuscript, on which decisions had to be reached.

The manuscript editor is always torn between the somewhat contradictory principles of being faithful to the original (*fidélité au manuscrit*) and making the text in question accessible to the reader (*confort de lecture*).

The approach finally adopted here is that of a *linear* transcription (and not a *diplomatic* one). In other words, the aim of the page layout is not to attempt to reproduce the way the words are set out in the manuscript (as in a diplomatic transcription), but rather to make the text as readable as possible by reconstructing its essential linearity.

In this way, the printed text does not start a new line every time there is a new line in the manuscript, but only when there is a new paragraph. The decision as to where a new paragraph begins can at times be tricky.

More precisely, the protocol of transcription is set out below.

• Words underlined by the author are underlined in the transcription

> ne pas alarmer Mary <u>si</u> elle ne <u>croit pas</u> être en danger

(Where a word is only partially underlined in the original letter, either towards the beginning or end of the word, that word is underlined completely).

• Words encircled by the author are encircled in the transcription

> if the price is (not) too high

• Words added subsequently by the author are given in italics in the transcription

> except Friday *and Saturday* in the afternoon

• Words scribbled out by the author are simply crossed out in the transcription

> Mary semble n'avoir pas ~~conscien~~ connaissance de la gravité

unless the word scribbled out is subsequently written out again.

Hence the sentence,

> Mary semble n'avoir pas ~~connaissance~~ connaissance de la gravité

will finally be transcribed as follows

> Mary semble n'avoir pas connaissance de la gravité

• "Unresolved alternatives" (which occur when the author leaves himself the choice between several words without taking a final decision) are between backslashes:

Danger *Crise*\\ en faveur de 2 fois.

• A break in the text, whether a large gap or a dividing line, is denoted as follows:

———

• It was necessary to invent a sign for the "extended periods at ground level," one of Marcel's specialties. These are a kind of dash along the baseline, transcribed as follows:

Donne moi un titre et l'année pour le catalogue s.v.p.——

They punctuate Duchamp's prose—something like "STOP" between words in a telegram—though it remains unclear whether they correspond to periods or commas. They are, however, semantically as well as visually different from ordinary dashes (printed *above* the baseline, half-way up the x-height) which, as we all know, serve as parentheses.

an impressive collection of paintings—old and new—which will be exhibited and sold

• English quotation marks (designed as hanging commas) are respected throughout

I am living in Nice "bachelorly"

even where they are closed on the baseline

J'en fais un "Readymade,, à distance

or where they ruffle the word

I don't want to start anything in the way of an „Art", museum

• Captions to sketches are printed in italics, preceded by a hyphen

- *cuivre*
- *velours*

• Word endings written in superscript are respected throughout

5th July, 2h ¼
Mlle Pogany, Me Bellier,
31bis rue, 51st St, 2nd floor,
13m sur 7m, 51inches, 125c.c., \$200.00, 700f, pour mon No de quota
Afft Affectt à tous deux de nous2 St Marcel c/o Peggy
Paris (Vme) St Cyr s/Loire Seine Inf. re

as are abbreviations

qqchose, c-à-d, càd, 32 frs, cinématg. ques, collect., en circul. tion

• Erroneous spelling is preserved

I will reimbourse you, the sides rooms, very durty,
the Conmittee, a very well know firm, a whif of fresh air, ecstacy

in English as in French—or German

> Chère Jean, j'attend, aucune nouvelles,
> côter, psychiâtrie, à propo, saoulographie,
> ammollir, missionaire, mastiquage, transcendental, évènement, rassi,
> mise-en-marche, dûe, éxécution, maquetee, frêt,
> zùm, Jüdenstrasse

as is the almost systematic absence of hyphens

> fais le, porte bouteilles,
> est il, peut être, chef d'œuvre,
> dois je, bien être, ce jour là, vis à vis,
> est ce, moi même, là bas

• Forgotten accents remain so

> cablé, aout, déja, dégoutée,
> connaitrai, entraineur, americain, diner, coté, reclame,
> j'acheterai, baton, platre, chateau, préfèrerais, hotel,
> théatre, eventuel, débacle, plait, hopital, coute

while "lazy spelling" causing letters to get swallowed up in the flow

> Affectmt, Affecmnt, Affemnt, Affemt, Afment...

are duly printed in full

> Affectueusement

unless it is a clear abbreviation

> Affect^t

And ambiguous strokes of the pen

> boite, càble, dèjà, dú

are generously given the benefit of the doubt.

> boîte, câble, déjà, dû

• The reader will appreciate Duchamp's neologisms

> chèrettie, j'ai beaucoup flemmé, cubifier Buenos Aires, libationner,
>   patArder,
> hotelwagramiens, Bonmarchéiques, Yvonnesques, ragotesque,
>   télégrammique, dadaïque, en à-quoi-bon
> réaccoutumance, dénigration, répareurs, phototypeur, patriotesses,
>   éberluement, embourbement, co-générationaires,
> affectionnément, intéressamment, conséquentemement, désolément

his spontaneous *Franglais*

> je ne feelerai, démonstrationer, bildinge, exhibiter, Stéréotyped trophy

and the idiosyncrasies of his prose

> profitez donc z'en, petit-enfant, une partie d'icelle, poëmes

- Finally, semi-bold Garamond is used to represent Marcel's handwriting

> Marcelavy

- Bold Courier for typewritten text

> **Marcel Duchamp**

- Scala Sans for information provided by the editors

> letterhead crossed out in pen | added on back of envelope:
> | allograph writing in pencil: | enclosure: | end of letter missing

Editorial information may also be inserted into the author's text, in square brackets

> "portrait,, dans Magdel[e]ine et Yvonne,,
> je viens de poser [pour] une petite scène
> l'ordre dans lequ[el = paper ripped]
> if you can accept my decease [sic for « disease »] to be unable to write
> I did not want to ask him [for] this change

- Allographic text (= not written in Marcel's hand) is printed in Garamond in a smaller type size and in gray

> Love Mary

(Allographic texts are transcribed only if they form part of the correspondence sent by MD: they are not transcribed if they were added after the addressee received the letter.)

- Finally, letterheads are denoted by a gray slabserif typeface

> LE HAVRE, le *27 Décembre* 1919

But all this goes without saying...

instructions for use

Sample transcription

location of original: AAA, BLJD, GRI, HRHCR, MNAM, NYPL, PMA, YCAL... are abbreviations used in the notes to identify institutions. See full description page 7.

ooo. Marcel Duchamp and X to correspondents Y and Z   format

date and place [in brackets when not written on letter]   location of original

15 Dec— 99
285 letters
from Marcel Duchamp or

or Morice or Totor or Duche or Dee—

———

Letters are published in the original— either English or French—
Transcription is ~~diplomatic~~ linear
— Crossed out words are crossed out ~~this way~~.
— Underlined words are underlined <u>this way</u> (even <u><u>twice</u></u>).
— Some encircled figures are (encircled).
Original spelling is maintained…

———

PS: manuscript inserts or lines added later are printed in italics *(because italics can never exist in handwriting!)*

▷TRANSLATION: *of letters from French into English. Underlinings, encirclings and carriage returns are left out (see above transcription). Punctuation is corrected. Abbreviations are spelled out in full. Words in* roman type *are in English in the original letter. Puns are translated both phonetically and literally. Translator's notes are* [in sans serif typeface]. *MD's signature and trademark,* Affectueusement, *meaning "with love," is systematically translated "Affectionately"—title role of this book.*   *Jill Taylor*

Neuilly, Munich, Paris | 1912-1915

lives in Neuilly, 9 rue Amiral-de-Joinville
after visiting Basel, stays in Munich, 65 Barerstrasse | 21 June to Aug 1912
visits Vienna, Prague, Leipzig, Dresden and Berlin | first 3 weeks of Sept 1912
*round trips to Etival (Jura) at Gabrielle Picabia's, to Herne Bay (England) with his sister Yvonne,
   and to Yport (Seine-Inférieure) by the sea, with his parents*
moves to Paris, 23 rue Saint-Hippolyte | Oct 1913 to June 1915

from 15 March 1912 to 5 June 1915

▶ MAJOR WORKS

The King and Queen Surrounded by Swift Nudes
   (oil on canvas, May 1912)
The Bride Stripped Bare by the Bachelors (pencil
   and wash on paper, July 1912)
The Passage from Virgin to Bride (oil on canvas,
   July-Aug 1912)
Bride (oil on canvas, Aug 1912)
Chocolate Grinder, No.1 (oil on canvas, Feb-
   Mar 1913)
Bachelor Apparatus: 1. Plan and 2. Elevation
   (pencil and red ink on paper, 1913)
Plan of Large Glass, scale 1:10 (pencil on tracing
   cloth, 1913)
Boxing Match (pencil and crayon on paper,
   1913)
Cemetery of Uniforms and Liveries, No.1 (pencil
   on paper, 1913)
Perspective Sketch for the Bachelor Machine
   (cardboard, 1913, lost)

Bicycle Wheel (bicycle wheel and fork mounted
   on a white kitchen stool, 1913)
3 Standard Stoppages (1 m thread glued with
   varnish on linen, 1913-14)
Pharmacy (drops of gouache on a commercial
   print, Jan 1914)
To Have the Apprentice in the Sun (India ink
   and pencil on music paper, Jan 1914)
The Box of 1914 (photographic facsimiles of
   16 manuscript notes, 1913-14)
Chocolate Grinder, No.2 (oil and thread on
   canvas, Feb 1914)
Network of Stoppages (oil on canvas, early
   1914)
Ready made (bottle dryer, 1914)
*Glider Containing a Water Mill in Neighboring
   Metals* (oil and lead wire on glass,
   Oct 1913-15)
9 Malic Moulds (oil, lead wire, and sheet lead
   on glass, 1914-15)

▶ EXHIBITIONS*

Société des Artistes indépendants (28th exh.), Quai d'Orsay, Paris. By MD: *Nu descendant l'escalier* [withdrawn]; *Dessin* — 20 Mar - 16 May 1912

Exposició d'Art Cubista, Galeries J. Dalmau, Barcelona, Spain. By MD: *Sonata*; *Desnú baixant una escala* — 20 Apr - 10 May 1912

Société Normande de Peinture Moderne (3rd exh.), Grand skating, Rouen, France. By MD: *Portraits*; *Portraits de joueurs d'échecs* — 15 June - 15 July 1912

10ᵉ Salon d'Automne, Grand Palais, Paris. By MD: *Vierge* — 1 Oct - 8 Nov 1912

La Section d'Or, [galerie de La Boëtie] 64, rue La Boëtie, Paris. By MD: *Portrait de joueurs d'échecs*; *Le roi et la reine entourés de nus vites*; *Nu descendant un escalier*; *Peinture*; *Aquarelle*; *Le Roi et la Reine traversés par des nus vites* — 10 Oct - 30 Oct 1912

---

* Wherever possible, titles of works are given as they appear in the catalog or price list of the respective exhibitions (See footnote 12).

International Exhibition of Modern Art (called "Armory Show"), Association of American Painters and Sculptors, Armory of the 69th Infantry Regiment, New York City (travels to Chicago and Boston). By MD: *King and Queen surrounded by nudes*; *Chess players*; *Nude figure descending a staircase*; *Sketch of a nude.* — 15 Feb - 15 Mar 1913

Post-Impressionist Exhibition, Art Museum, Portland. By MD: *Nude descending a staircase* — Oct -Nov 1913

Vickery Atkins & Torrey, San Francisco. By MD: *Nude descending a staircase* — 1914

First Exhibition of Works by Contemporary French Artists, Carroll Galleries, New York. By MD: *Virgin* — Dec 1914 - 2 Jan 1915

Second Exhibition: French Modernists and Odilon Redon, Carroll Galleries, New York City. By MD: *Nu descendant un escalier, n°1* — 1 Jan - 3 Feb 1915

Third Exhibition of Contemporary French Art, Carroll Galleries, New York City. By MD: *Portrait*; *Chocolate grinder I*; *Chocolate grinder II*; *Chess players*; *Study of a girl* — 8 Mar - 3 Apr 1915

Spring 1912
When Duchamp's sister Suzanne considers
submitting paintings for exhibition at the Salon des
Indépendants, she avidly seeks the advice of her
older, more experienced brother.
Duchamp responds by writing the following letter,
which conveys a carefully-phrased,
gentle critique of his sister's paintings.

1. Marcel Duchamp to Suzanne Duchamp[*]   autograph letter
[15 March 1912], Neuilly   collection AAA

Neuilly.

Vendredi

Ma chère Suzanne.

Je reçois tout à l'heure tes trois toiles en bon état.

Laisse moi ne pas te dire que je les aime, que je les trouve intéressantes
  (toutes locutions aussi inutiles que mitoyennes)

J'y vois ton dessin, celui de tes ~~autres~~ *anciennes* toiles, plus caché sous des
  harmonies de couleur. Ces harmonies de couleurs ont l'air de
  t'intéresser pour elles mêmes, pour le rapport (par ex dans ton portrait)
  entre le bleu de fond et le rose du corsage. et non pas pour créer une
  atmosphère : Là dessus je suis de ton avis.

Mais Je crois que le rapport de couleur à couleur, parce qu'il est optique
  seulement, exprime moins l'artiste, que le dessin.

(Voir les impressionnistes)

Justement tu dessines, inconsciemment peut être, avant tout.

Dans ton "portrait,, dans Magdel[e]ine et Yvonne,, il y a compositions et
  dessin.

Ce sont là, je crois, tes qualités et tu les développeras nécessairement.

Suzanne's **three paintings** are *Portrait, Intimité,* and *A des Esseintes (fleurs),* to be exhibited at the Salon des Indépendants.

---

* **Suzanne Duchamp** (1889-1963), was Marcel Duchamp's youngest sister, and the member of his family with whom he developed the closest and most enduring relationship. At the age of 16, Suzanne entered the Ecole des Beaux-Arts in Rouen, thus beginning her career as an artist, the same profession practiced by her three older brothers. As this first letter of their correspondence attests, she often sought Marcel's advice on her paintings, and it seems that he was always willing to provide a gentle critique. In 1911, Suzanne married Charles Desmares, a pharmacist from Rouen, but the couple separated a few years later. In 1916, she met and fell in love with Jean Crotti (see p.53), a Swiss painter who had just come from New York where he had shared a studio with Duchamp. They married in 1919, and, although they took part in some Dada activities in Paris, by 1920 they had begun their own two-person movement: *Tabu*, a mechanomorphic style of painting that was related to Dada, but which emphasized a more positive approach. Eventually, both artists would revert to more personal, figurative styles, yet throughout their lives, as a number of letters confirm, they continued to seek Duchamp's opinion and advice concerning their work.

Il n'y *a* pas de différence plastique entre le dessin sur papier et la peinture sur toile. La seconde est du dessin fait de couleurs qui sont les timbres différents de ton harmonie en noir et blanc (encore que ceux ci soient des couleurs) — fondamentale cette harmonie.

———

Evite de prendre tout ce que je te raconte pour des conseils.
Ce n'est que ce à quoi j'ai pensé devant tes toiles.

———

Charly m'a dit que vous veniez pour le vernissage.
Je demanderai tes cartes au secrétariat et te les enverrai à Rouen.

"Charly" = Charles Desmares, husband of MD's sister Suzanne.

———

Je trouve que tu peux mettre 200^f pour les 2 grands et 100^f pour la nature morte. Réponds moi <u>par retour</u>. Si je puis inscrire aussi les prix sur ta feuille.
J'irai Dimanche matin les porter aux Indépendants
    Affect. à Charly.
      à tous
      à toi
      Marcel.

28th Salon des **Indépendants**, 20 Mar - 16 May 1912, where MD plans to exhibit his famous *Nude Descending No. 2* [cat. 17].

▷ TRANSLATION: *Neuilly, Friday. My dear Suzanne, Your three canvases arrived earlier unharmed. Allow me not to tell you that I love them, that I find them interesting (all expressions as futile as they are meaningless). I spotted your drawing, the one from your earlier canvases, more hidden beneath color harmonies. These color harmonies seem to interest you for their own sake, for the relationship (e.g. in your portrait) between the blue of the background and the pink in the blouse and not for the sake of creating an atmosphere. In that respect, I agree with you. But I think that the relationship of color to color, because it is merely optical, expresses less the artist than the drawing. (See the impressionists). And precisely, what you do, subconsciously perhaps, is, above all, to draw. In your "portrait," in "Magdeline and Yvonne," there are compositions and drawing. These are, I think, your strengths and you'll develop them as a matter of course. There is no plastic difference between drawing on paper and painting on canvas. The latter is drawing made of colors which are the different shades of your harmony in black and white (though these are in color as it happens). Fundamental, this harmony. Don't take everything I say as advice. It's only what came to mind when I had your canvases in front of me. Charly told me you were coming for the opening. I'll ask the office for your invitations and send them to you in Rouen. I think you could say 200FF for the 2 big ones and 100FF for the still life. Let me know by return whether I may put these prices on your price list. I'll go on Sunday morning and take them to the Independents. Affectionately to Charly, to all, to you, Marcel.*

18 March 1912
Two days before the opening of the Salon des
Indépendants, Duchamp finds himself obliged to
withdraw his *Nude Descending No. 1* [cat. 16] from
the exhibition, for the title is interpreted by his
fellow artists as a mockery of Cubism and Modern
Art. The painting is exhibited for the first time at the
"Exposició d'Art Cubista," held at the Galerie
Dalmau, Barcelona, 20 April - 10 May 1912.

June-October 1912
Travels for four months: Basel, Constance, Vienna,
Prague, Berlin, Dresden and, above all, Munich.
From Berlin, he sends the following report about the
city to his brother and family back in Paris.

2. Marcel Duchamp to Jacques Villon and family   autograph letter
[26 September 1912], Berlin   Duchamp Archives, Villiers-sous-Grez

Gaston Duchamp
(1875-1963), painter
and etcher, elder
brother of MD, who
changed his name to
Jacques Villon.

Berlin— Jeudi—
    Chers vieux.
De nouveau, me voici habitué à la vie berlinoise— La seconde impression
est meilleure que le premier abord. Probablement parce que j'ai visité
quelques peintures : toujours les musées qui sont des merveilles
d'installation = Pourquoi le Louvre est il si mal "rangé„?—
Et puis la Sécession Berlinoise qui m'a enfin permis de voir la "gueule„ de
la jeune peinture française, à l'étranger. Une salle y est réservée à Friez,
Marquet, Valtat, Herbin, et 4 Picasso— J'ai eu très grand plaisir à
retrouver du cubisme, il y avait si longtemps que je n'en avais vu. Et cela
n'a pas ~~pe~~ contribué pour peu, ~~dans~~ à mon indulgence pour Berlin.
Je prends autobus, trams, comme si j'avais toujours vécu ici.
Le métro n'a pas ici la même importance qu'à Paris. ~~(ici~~ Il y a seulement
une grande ligne et une transversale— d'ailleurs très agréable—
Les omnibus à chevaux, car il y en a encore beaucoup ici, ressemblent par
leurs petites dimensions à notre Auteuil St Sulpice (avec une petite
exagération) =
Les Linden, oui, les Linden! Il y manque les tilleuls en question. C'est un
boulevard très large et pas très long.
Seul le Tiergarten est agréable
J'ai reçu l'annonce officielle que mon dessin avait plu au jury du Salon
d'Automne. Grand bien me fasse! J'ai enfin trouvé le Gil Blas et j'espère
suivre avec intérêt le vernissage de l'automne, sans doute décrites ami
Vxcll.
Je vous écris d'un Café dit "littéraire„. Il y a surtout beaucoup de femmes
qui n'ont rien de littéraire—

24th exh. of the **Berlin
Secession** held at the
*Ausstellungshaus am
Kurfürstendam*,
summer 1912.

"**Linden**" = lime trees
(in German). "Unter
den Linden" is a famous
avenue in Berlin.

"**drawing**" is *Virgin
No. 1* [cat. 20], at the
Salon d'Automne, Paris,
1 Sept - 8 Nov 1912.

"**Vxcll**" = Louis
Vauxcelles, art critic for
the newspaper *Gil Blas*.

J'espère que mon ami me retrouvera ici au commencement de la semaine prochaine. et me fera connaître la "vie de nuit„ à Berlin. C'est une spécialité.

J'espère rentrer vers le 10 à Paris. En revenant, je m'arrêterai sans doute à Cologne.

Mon vieux Raymond est sans doute un peu au repos maintenant. Et Gaston a t il fini son service—

Je commence à avoir bien besoin de revoir des têtes amies—

> Enfin à bientôt maintenant
> à tous très affectueusement
> Marcel

Hotel zùm Goldenen Löwen
Berlin
Jüdenstrasse 55

"mon ami" is probably **Max Bergmann** (1884-1955), a German painter who met MD while studying in Paris a few years earlier.

Raymond Duchamp (1876-1918), eldest brother of MD and sculptor, who changed his name to **Raymond Duchamp-Villon**.

▷ TRANSLATION: *Berlin, Thursday. Hello dears, Here I am again, back in the swing of Berlin life. My second impression is better than the first time around, probably because I've been to see a few paintings—without fail, the museums here are incredibly well set out. Why is the Louvre such a "mess"? And then the Berlin Secession which finally allowed me to see how young French painting was looking abroad. There's a special room for Friez, Marquet, Valtat, Herbin and 4 for Picasso. I was really pleased to find they have Cubism here, it was so long since I'd seen any. And that certainly played a part in my having a soft spot for Berlin. I take buses, trams, as if I'd lived here all my life. The underground is not as big as in Paris. (There's just one main line and one that runs across it—very pleasant in fact.) The horse-drawn buses, for there are still plenty of those here, are so small they look like our Auteuil St Sulpice (slight exaggeration). And then the Lindens, yes, the Lindens! Except without the lime trees in question. It's a very wide avenue and not very long. The Tiergarten is the only really pleasant place. I've been informed officially that the Jury at the Salon d'Automne liked my drawing. Much good may it do me! I finally found the Gil Blas and will be interested to follow, hopefully, the opening in the fall, no doubt with descriptions by our friend Vauxcelles. I'm writing to you from a so-called "literary" café. There are mainly a lot of women here who have nothing literary about them at all. I hope that my friend will meet me here at the beginning of next week and will show me "Berlin by night." It's a local speciality. I hope to return to Paris around the 10th. On my way back I'll most probably stop off in Cologne. My dear Raymond should have a bit of leave around now. What about Gaston, has he finished his military service yet? I'm beginning to feel the need to see old faces. See you soon now anyhow. Very affectionately to all, Marcel. Hotel zum Goldenen Löwen, Berlin, Jüdenstrasse 55.*

10 October 1912
Duchamp returns to Paris and begins
looking for a job. In December, he enrolls
on a course on bibliography
at the École des Chartes in Paris.

1913
Determined to withdraw from the artistic scene
in Paris, Duchamp decides to become a librarian.
At roughly the same time, the scandalous reception
of his work at the Armory Show in New York
makes him famous in America.

---

3. Marcel Duchamp to Walter Pach[*]   autograph letter
2 July [1913], Neuilly   collection AAA

Neuilly ⁵/Seine.
9 rue Amiral de Joinville.
Mercredi. 2 Juillet.
    Cher Monsieur Pach, J'ai appris par mes frères toutes les bonnes
nouvelles de l'exposition d'Amérique. Je suis très heureux; et vous
remercie du dévouement avec lequel vous avez défendu notre peinture.
Je voulais depuis longtemps vous écrire mais je suis tellement paresseux
que je ne cherche plus à m'en excuser.
    Et puis il y a une question économique : Le dernier chèque de 600 ᶠ a t il
été envoyé?__ ou bien est ce seulement un retard?__ Je ne l'ai pas

"America exhibition" =
Armory Show, NY,
5 Feb - 15 Mar 1913,
which is to make MD
famous for his *Nude
Descending No. 2*
[cat. 17].

---

* **Walter Pach** (1883-1958). Through his lectures, writings, and the art exhibitions he organized,
Walter Pach is clearly one of the most important and influential figures in the history of early
American modernism. Working behind the scenes—as was his style—for nearly fifty years he
labored tirelessly and selflessly as an artist, journalist, critic, historian, teacher, collector, lec-
turer, adviser, curator, connoisseur, translator and all-round spokesman for the most advanced
expressions of the new art. Pach and Duchamp met in Paris in the years just before the First
World War, at a time when both were still young men in their twenties. Pach later recalled having first noticed the quality of Duchamp's work at the *Section d'Or* exhibition of 1912, where
Duchamp's *Nude Descending a Staircase* was given its first Parisian showing. Pach, who had
been assigned the responsibility of selecting works for the Armory Show, chose this painting
and three others by Duchamp for inclusion in this important exhibition, a decision that would
not only solidify their friendship, but one that would have tremendous repercussions for
Duchamp's future in America. It was Pach who met Duchamp at the piers when he arrived in
New York in 1915, and it was Pach who helped him find a place to live and who introduced him
to important personalities in the art world of New York. Throughout these early years in America, Duchamp kept in frequent contact with Pach and his wife **Magda** (who was also a painter),
but as the years progressed, their exchange became more sporadic. Finally in 1943, when
Duchamp was living in New York, their correspondence ceased altogether, for occasional
meetings and telephone conversations probably eliminated a need to communicate by letter.
Nevertheless, they remained good friends, and although Pach does not seem to have accepted
the more radical aspects of Duchamp's art, whenever the opportunity presented itself, he
would continue to expound upon Duchamp's talent as a painter.

reçu— Y a t il une erreur de poste? Je vous demande une simple carte
postale de réponse—

Travaillez vous beaucoup?

Je suis très navré en ce moment et je ne fiche absolument rien. Ce sont de
petits moments désagréables.

Je vais partir au mois d'Août passer quelque temps en Angleterre.

Il fait très beau à Puteaux le dimanche, et vous devez regretter de ne pas
prendre part aux jeux dans le jardin—

Reviendrez vous bientôt parmi nous? Ne regrettez vous pas un peu Paris.
Nous avons eu la visite de Monsieur Torrey. qui est un excellent homme.

Il a paru très content de nous connaître—

Au Revoir, cher Monsieur Pach, et à bientôt de vos nouvelles.

très cordialement à vous,

Marcel Duchamp—

MD will spend the month of August at Lynton College, Herne Bay, England, with his sister Yvonne, who has gone there to prepare for a degree in English.

Puteaux, Paris suburb, where MD's brothers live.

Frederic C. Torrey (1864-1953), part-owner of an antiques firm in San Francisco, purchased by telegram MD's *Nude Descending No. 2* [cat. 17] from the Armory Show.

▷ TRANSLATION: *Neuilly s/Seine. 9 rue Amiral de Joinville. Wednesday 2 July. Dear Mr Pach, I heard all the good news about the America exhibition from my brothers. I am really pleased and thank you for having made such a devoted stand for our painting. I have been wanting to write to you for a long time but am so lazy that I don't even attempt to make excuses any more. And then there is a financial matter: has the last check for 600FF been sent? or is there simply some kind of hold up? I have not received it. Could the Post Office have made a mistake? Could you simply send me your reply on a postcard. Are you working hard? I am very down at the moment and doing absolutely nothing. It's very irritating when it's like this. I am going away in August to spend some time in England. It's always fine in Puteaux on a Sunday, and you must miss playing games in the garden with us. Will you come back to us soon? Don't you miss Paris just a little? We had a visit from Mr Torrey who is a fine man. He seemed very pleased to meet us. Farewell, dear Mr Pach, and look forward to hearing from you soon. Most sincerely yours, Marcel Duchamp.*

---

4. Marcel Duchamp to Walter Pach   autograph letter
19 January 1915, Paris   collection AAA

BIBLIOTHÈQUE Ste GENEVIÈVE
Paris le *19 Janvier* 1915

Mon cher ami.

Merci mille fois de votre si gentille lettre. Elle m'a fait vraiment plaisir Je
l'ai communiquée à la famille qui va vous écrire aussi.

D'abord, toutes mes félicitations pour votre paternité. Et je vous prie de
présenter à Madame Pach mes vœux de longue vie pour le jeune
Raymond— Vous devez être profondément heureux du bon
dénouement.

Pach married German painter **Magdaleine** (Magda) **Frohberg** in Feb 1914. Their son **Raymond** (named after MD's brother) was born 26 Dec 1914.

Jacques Villon doit vous avoir écrit ; il est toujours vers Amiens ; mais depuis 15 jours au repos. c-à-d. à 20 Km. en arrière des tranchées ; Rien n'est changé à la situation depuis votre départ. Toujours la lecture des communiqués de guerre 2 fois par jour. Moins d'impatience : une sorte d'hivernage du sang : De sorte que je m'en trouve bien, ayant moins à causer et à entendre causer de cette "affaire„

Raymond Duchamp-Villon is an assistant medical officer at Saint-Germain-en-Laye.

Raymond est toujours à St Germain. De temps en temps il parle d'un départ probable ; mais rien de définitif en ce moment. Yvonne est toujours à l'hôpital, enchantée de sa vie d'infirmière ; elle ne donnerait pas sa place pour un empire (d'Allemagne). J'y vais tous les 10 jours passer une soirée.

Yvonne Duchamp-Villon, née Bon (1895-1969) married Raymond Duchamp 9 Sept 1903.

A Paris, la vie est toujours aussi bête. Depuis hier, il faut éviter toutes lumières qui pourraient indiquer Paris aux Zeppelins ; à partir de 6^h boutiques à demi-closes, plus d'enseignes lumineuses. ; les rues juste éclairées et à la première alerte obscurité complète. On va au cinéma, car les théâtres sont encore moins intéressants.

Ma belle-sœur Villon va probablement partir comme infirmière dans le Nord et bientôt. Elle en est contente. Peut être pourra t elle voir son mari. Cela est moins probable—

Gaby Villon, née Gabrielle Bœuf (1879-1968) married Jacques Villon 22 Oct 1913.

J'ai passé le conseil de réforme : et je suis condamné à rester civil pendant toute la durée de la guerre. Ils m'ont trouvé trop <u>malade</u> pour être soldat. Je ne suis pas fâché de cette décision : vous le savez bien

MD went through the Medical Board 6 Jan.

Je continue donc à travailler régulièrement, peu d'heures par jour, très las en ce moment. Je n'ai pas encore fini mon machin rouge sur verre— Je pense le terminer fin février.

"red thing on glass" is *9 Malic Moulds* [cat. 31]

Je n'ai pas vu d'artistes depuis longtemps. Je ne sais pas si Brancusi a quitté Paris. Je ne crois pas. J'irai *le* voir un de ces jours.

Le Montparnasse est toujours semblable à lui même.

Montparnasse = left-bank district of Paris famed for its artistic community.

Je vous écris de la Bibliothèque où la vie est encore plus large qu'en temps de paix. C'est vous dire qu'on a peu de choses à faire.

Two-year internship Sainte Geneviève Library, Paris.

La nouvelle de la vente de l'aquarelle et des gravures nous a bien fait plaisir et nous sommes heureux si vos efforts n'ont pas été vains, mon cher Pach

Watercolor must be *Dark Skin* [cat. 8], purchased from the Carroll Galleries Jan 1915 by John Quinn.

La vie à New York a-t-elle ~~ree~~ encore un contre coup de la guerre ou bien cette crise est-elle passée ? Sans doute.

Merci aussi des catalogues. Ici pas d'exposition naturellement. Des drapeaux, c'est tout ce qu'on peut voir de couleur. Quelques concerts le Dimanche, bien maigres, sans musique allemande.

Écrivez un petit mot de temps en temps. Moi aussi j'ai une grande paresse à écrire.

Viendrez vous à Paris cet été comme vous m'en aviez parlé?
Présentez je vous prie à Madame Pach mes respectueuses salutations et
donnez un baiser pour moi au jeune Raymond.
       très amicalement vôtre
       Marcel Duchamp
23 rue St Hippolyte
Paris

▷ TRANSLATION: *Paris, 19th January 1915. My dear friend, Many thanks for your very kind letter which I was really pleased to receive. I passed it on to my family who are going to write to you also. First of all, my congratulations on your becoming a father. And please give my best wishes to Mrs Pach and young Raymond. You must be overjoyed with this happy ending. Jacques Villon must have written to you: he is still somewhere near Amiens , but on leave for the last fortnight. i.e. 30 miles behind the trenches. No change in the situation since you left. Still reading war communiqués twice a day. Less impatience, a sort of hibernation of the blood, which quite suits me—not having to talk about and hear so much talk about this "affair." Raymond is still in St Germain. Every so often he says he'll soon be on the move, but nothing definite as yet. Yvonne is still at the hospital, thrilled with life as a nurse. She wouldn't give up her job for a (German) empire. I go and spend an evening there every 10 days. In Paris, life is still as silly as ever. As from yesterday, we are not to use lights that could show up Paris for the Zeppelins. After 6 o'clock, shops half-closed, no signs lit, the streets are barely lit at all and at the slightest alert everything is in total darkness. We go to the movies as the theater here is even less interesting. My sister-in-law Villon will probably be going to the North as a nurse and soon. She is very pleased about it. Perhaps she'll get to see her husband. That's not so likely. I went through the Medical Board and am doomed to remain a civilian for the entire duration of the war. They said I was too sick to be a soldier. I am not too unhappy about this decision, as you'll well imagine. So I carry on working regularly, but few hours a day, weary at the moment. I still haven't finished my red thing on glass. I expect to finish it end of February. I haven't seen any artists for a long time. I don't know if Brancusi has left Paris. I don't think so. I'll go and see him one of these days. Montparnasse is still the same as it always was. I'm writing to you from the Library where life is even more extravagant than in peacetime. By which I mean how little we have to do. We were really pleased about the news that the watercolor and the engravings have been sold and happy if your efforts have not been in vain, my dear Pach. Is New York still suffering from repercussions of the war or is the crisis over now? No doubt. Thanks also for the catalogs. Here no exhibitions of course. Flags are the only things you get to see in color. A few concerts on Sundays, pretty thin with no German music. Drop me a line from time to time. I am also very lazy when it comes to writing. Will you be coming to Paris this summer as you mentioned before? Please give my regards to Mrs Pach and a big kiss from me to young Raymond. Your friend Marcel Duchamp. 23 rue St Hyppolyte Paris.*

5. Marcel Duchamp to Walter Pach   autograph letter
12 March [1915], Paris   collection AAA

St Hippolyte. Vendredi 12 ~~Février~~ Mars

    Mon Cher ami. J'ai bien lu votre lettre à Raymond et les bonnes   **Raymond** = Raymond
nouvelles de vous. J'ai eu aussi la reproduction dans le journal de mon   Duchamp-Villon
dessin.   **"drawing"** = Virgin No. 1
                    [cat. 20]

Je reçois votre catalogue de Matisse; cette exposition a dû être bien   **"Henri Matisse"** exh.
intéressante parce que nombreuse et diverse. Je me rappelle bien son   Montross Galleries, NY,
tableau des "poissons rouges,, et la reproduction est bonne.   20 Jan - 27 Feb 1915.

Ici la guerre dure, dure… De Villon toujours d'excellentes nouvelles;
bonne santé, bon moral presque gai : il nous épate tous par son
endurance; on parle du "grand coup de printemps,, qui doit être décisif;
une très grande confiance circule avec les premières pousses.— Je me
rappelle trop la même confiance du mois d'août et je ne vois là qu'une
imagination civile mal réglée. Enfin sans pessimisme aucun, on pense
voir la fin de la guerre cet été (avant les vacances).

Paris s'est seulement assombri depuis votre départ. Les promenades du   MD's parents living at
soir sont devenues tristes parce que l'éclairage est tout à fait bas.   71 rue Jeanne d'Arc,
                    Rouen.

J'ai été passer un ½ mois à Rouen dans la famille pour changer d'air.

Depuis mon retour je travaille beaucoup; je termine mes bouts de verre   Top section of the
commencés et je prépare le haut de mon tableau. Je suis surtout content   Large Glass [cat. 2].
de finir ces quelques petites choses avant de recommencer une autre
partie.

Raymond est toujours heureux à St Germain; sa femme y est infirmière à   **Raymond** = Raymond
l'hopital vous le savez; J'y vais assez souvent on fait des parties de poker   Duchamp-Villon
et on se croit bien loin des évènements.

— D'ailleurs ici on a très peu l'impression de guerre; au contraire dans les
petites villes de province.

J'ai entendu dire que Delaunay était ou partait en Amérique. Le savez   **Robert Delaunay** (1885-
vous?   1941), French modern
                    painter.

La vie artistique du Mont Parnasse est toujours égale. quoique je sois bien
peu au courant. Je n'ai rencontré aucun peintre de connaissance. Je ne
suis pas retourné à l'atelier russe de l'avenue du Maine (où nous devions
dîner.). Il faut absolument que j'aille voir Brancusi.

De Picasso, de Braque, de Derain je n'ai pas de nouvelles.

~~La~~ Ma belle sœur Villon et ma sœur sont infirmières à l'hopital des Jeunes
Aveugles (Boulevard des Invalides, coin de la rue de Sèvres). Elles sont   in Paris, left bank
enchantées de leur métier

Comment vont Madame Pach et le jeune Raymond. Heureusement pour   Raymond =
lui, il n'aura pas souvenir des mauvais moments qui l'ont vu naître. Il   Raymond Pach
est déjà grand maintenant, et vous devez être bien heureux
Donc au revoir, mon cher ami, je vous promets de vous écrire plus
souvent. J'ai peur que vous ayez cette lettre bien tard à cause des
sous marins allemands
Je vous charge de tous mes respects pour Madame Pach, de beaucoup de
baisers pour Raymond et pour vous mille amitiés les meilleures—
    Marcel Duchamp—
23 r. St Hippolyte

▷ TRANSLATION: *St Hyppolyte. Friday 12th March. My dear friend, Thank you for
your letter to Raymond which I read and your own good news. I also got the reproduction of my drawing in the journal. I've just received your Matisse catalog; this
exhibition must have been very interesting since large and varied. I have a very
clear recollection of his painting of the "goldfish" and the reproduction is good. Here
the war goes on and on... News of Villon excellent as always: in good health, good
spirits, almost jolly—he amazes us all with his endurance. There is talk of the
"great spring attack" supposed to be decisive. There's a lot of confidence in the air
with the first buds of spring. I remember only too well the same confidence in the
month of August and it just seems to me that civilians are getting carried away.
Anyway, with not a hint of pessimism, they think the war will end this summer (before the vacation). Paris just started to get darker after you left. Evening strolls are
miserable now because the lighting is so low. I went to spend ½ month in Rouen
with my family just to get a change of scene. Since I got back, I've been working a
lot. I'm about to finish the bits of glass I started and am getting ready to work on
the top of my painting. Most of all I'm happy to be finishing these few minor things
before starting again on another part. Raymond is still happy in St Germain. His
wife is a nurse at the hospital, as you know. I go there quite often. We play poker
and feel like we are far away from all that is going on. In any case we don't feel the
war very much here—quite the opposite in small provincial towns. I heard that
Delaunay was in, or was going to, America. Do you know if it's true? Artistic life
in Montparnasse is still the same. Except I'm hardly in touch with it. I haven't met
a single artist I know. I didn't go back to the Russian studio of the avenue du Maine
(where we were to have dinner). I absolutely must go and see Brancusi. Of Picasso,
Braque, Derain, I have no news. My sister-in-law Villon and my sister are nurses
at the "Jeunes Aveugles" hospital for the young blind (Boulevard des Invalides, corner of the rue de Sèvres). They are thrilled with their job. How is Mrs Pach? and
young Raymond? Thankfully for him, he will have no recollection of the unpleasant
times into which he was born. He's already a big boy now, and you must be very
happy. So farewell my dear friend, I promise to write more often. I'm afraid this
letter might be pretty late on account of the German submarines. Please give my
regards to Mrs Pach, and lots of kisses to Raymond and all my very best wishes to
you dear friend, Marcel Duchamp. 23 rue St Hippolyte.*

6. Marcel Duchamp to Walter Pach   autograph letter
2 April [1915], Paris   collection AAA

Paris. Vendredi. 2 avril
    Mon cher ami.

J'ai bien reçu votre lettre du 9 mars nous apportant les bonnes nouvelles
de vente à l'exposition. Raymond et Villon me chargent de vous
transmettre leur joie.

Les bois de Raymond sont chez Pottier. Nous avons été au consulat; tous
les papiers sont en règle. Et je vous *les* envoie ci joint.— Dans le même
emballage j'ai donné à Pottier 2 peintures et un grand dessin sur carton
qui étaient chez Picabia et que je devais vous faire emporter en
novembre. Ceci est pour que vous choisissiez ce qui vous plaira mieux
que la petite étude de girl. Si non gardez la et faites affaire avec mon
envoi si l'occasion se présente. Il reste bien entendu que je garde à ma
charge les frais de ce transport (Si vous faites affaire de la girl, comptez
600^f.)— Cet envoi doit partir de Bordeaux à bord de "l'Espagne„ le 10
avril.

Mme Villon doit faire un envoi à votre adresse (Beekman Place) de
gravures qui ne pourra, je crois, partir le 10. Peut être aussi Ribemont-
Dessaignes joindra quelques petites toiles à cet envoi. Ce dernier est très
déprimé et je l'estime beaucoup : j'espère ne pas vous ennuyer en lui
faisant ce plaisir.

Et maintenant une chose qui m'intéresse particulièrement : Je suis tout à
fait décidé à quitter la France— Et comme je vous l'avais dit en
Novembre dernier, j'irais volontiers vivre à New York. Mais à la
condition que j'y gagne ma vie. Donc 1° Pensez vous que je puisse
trouver facilement un emploi de bibliothécaire ou analogue me laissant
une grande liberté pour travailler (Renseignements : je ne sais pas
l'anglais, grade universitaire bachelier ès lettres (ne riez pas!!), j'ai passé
2 ans à la Bibliothèque Ste Geneviève comme stagiaire— 2° Je partirais
d'ici au plus tôt fin mai. Pensez vous que cette époque soit favorable ou
qu'au contraire il vaille mieux attendre Septembre.

Je n'ai parlé à personne de cette intention. Je vous demande donc de me
répondre ~~sur~~ à ce sujet sur une feuille séparée de votre lettre afin que mes
frères ne sachent rien avant que mon intention soit nettement arrêtée.

De la guerre, des nouvelles insignifiantes. Pas d'avance importante, pas de
recul. Un équilibre désespérant.

Villon est gai dans ses lettres, il est au bureau de sa compagnie un peu en
arrière des tranchées et fait des écritures. Il dessine et je crois qu'il nous
enverra des dessins documentaires des tranchées.

J'ai quitté Raymond tout à l'heure après le consulat. Il retourne à
St Germain où Yvonne et lui continuent leur vie.

Probably "Third Exhibition of Contemporary French Art," Carroll Gallery, NY, 8 Mar - 3 Apr 1915.

Pottier, French packer and shipping agent

Francis Picabia, see p.58.

Georges Ribemont-Dessaignes (1884-1974), French poet and artist.

Raymond and Yvonne Duchamp-Villon

Je travaille un peu, bien dérangé par des tas de gens qu'on ne voit jamais
en temps de paix et que la guerre oblige à rencontrer.

Voilà mon cher ami, peu de nouvelles. Je vous charge de tous mes respects
pour Mme Pach et de baisers pour le jeune Raymond.

tout cordialemnt à vous.

Marcel Duchamp—

23 St Hippolyte

[allograph writing in pencil (probably Walter Pach's) on letter after receiving it:]

prices on invoice:

carton peint —	600 *francs* nu descendant
carton dessiné	1000 machine célibataire
toile Vierge et mariée	600
————	
Sculptures	each 1000

"nu descendant" = *Nude
Descending No. 1* [cat. 16].

"machine célibataire" = probab
Bachelor Machine [cat. 26].

"Vierge et mariée" = *Passage..
[cat. 22].

▷ TRANSLATION: *Paris, Friday 2nd April. My dear friend, Thank you for your letter
of 9th March bringing us the good news about sales at the exhibition. Raymond
and Villon asked me to tell you how thrilled they were. Raymond's woods are at
Pottier's. We went to the Consulate: all the papers are in order and I'm enclosing
them here. In the same package, I gave Pottier 2 paintings and a large drawing on
cardboard which were at Picabia's and which I was to let you take away in November. This is so you can choose which one you would like better than the small study
of a girl. Otherwise keep her and get a good deal with what I've sent you if you get
the chance. It remains to say that I will bear the transport costs naturally. (If you
do get a good deal with the girl, reckon 600FF.) This shipment will leave Bordeaux
on the "Espagne" 10th April. Mrs Villon will be sending to your address (Beekman
Place) a shipment of engravings which, I think, cannot leave until the 10th.
Ribemont-Dessaignes might also add a few small canvases to this shipment. He is
very depressed and I hold him in very high esteem: I hope you don't mind me doing
him this service. And now something that concerns me in particular: I have made
up my mind to leave France. And as I told you last November, I would happily go
and live in New York. But only on condition that I could earn my living there. So
1/ Do you think it would be easy for me to find a job as a librarian there or something similar that would leave me plenty of freedom to work? (For information: I
know no English, university entrance exam in arts [Baccalauréat] (don't laugh!!),
I spent 2 years at the Sainte Geneviève Library as a trainee. 2/ I would leave here
at the earliest end of May. Do you think this would be the right time or on the contrary that it would be better to wait until September? I have told nobody about this
plan. Could you please, therefore, reply to these questions on a separate sheet of paper in your letter so that my brothers don't find out until my plans have been final-
ized. About the war, no important news. No significant steps forward, or
backwards. An exasperating equilibrium. Villon is cheerful in his letters, he's in his
army unit's office some way behind the trenches and pen-pushing. He draws and I
think will send us some documentary drawings of the trenches. I left Raymond a
short while ago after the Consulate. He's going back to St Germain where he and*

Yvonne go on with their life together. I'm doing some work, pretty well interrupted by a bunch of people one never sees in peacetime but whom one is forced to see by the war. There we are then, my friend, not much news. My regards as always to Mrs Pach and kisses to young Raymond. Most sincerely yours, Marcel Duchamp. 23 St Hippolyte.

[allograph writing, see price list:] prices on invoice / *painting on cardboard* / *drawing on cardboard / canvas / Sculptures*

---

7. Marcel Duchamp to Walter Pach   autograph letter
27 April [1915], Paris   collection AAA

CAFÉ-RESTAURANT
L. MOLLARD
HOTEL ANGLO AMÉRICAIN
113-115-117, RUE ST-LAZARE
PARIS (VIII⁶)

27 avril
   Mon cher ami

Je reçois ce matin votre lettre double__ Elle m'a bien fait plaisir. J'ai en effet reçu ce catalogue de la Galerie Montross et j'étais très étonné de ne pas vous voir à côté de M.M. Davies et Kuhn. aussi je sens beaucoup de découragement dans votre lettre!

Vous regrettez Paris. oui, je comprends bien votre regret parce que vous y avez vécu une vie d'artiste libre avec toutes les joies et tous les sales moments qu'on aime à se rappeler__

Pour mon séjour à New York, c'est tout différent. Je n'y vais pas chercher ce qui me manque à Paris. Je n'espère ~~tro~~ pas trouver là bas autre chose que des individus

— Si vous vous rappelez nos conversations du Boulevard Sᵗ Michel et Raspail, vous verrez dans mon intention de départ la suite nécessaire de ces conversations,

— Je ne vais pas à New York, je pars de Paris. C'est tout différent.

Depuis longtemps déjà avant la guerre, je n'aimais pas la "vie artistique„ dans laquelle j'étais engagé.__ Elle est tout à fait contraire à mes désirs.__ J'avais donc essayé par la Bibliothèque de m'évader un peu des artistes.

Puis avec la guerre mon incompatibilité *avec ce milieu* a augmenté. Je voulais absolument partir. Où? ~~où~~ Je n'avais que New York où je vous connaissais. où j'espère pouvoir éviter une vie artistique, au besoin par un travail qui m'occuperait beaucoup.

Je vous ai demandé le secret vis à vis de mes frères parce que je sais que ce départ leur sera très pénible.

— De même pour mon père et mes sœurs.

Montross Gallery, NY, exh. "Exhibition of Paintings, Drawings and Sculpture," 31 Mar - 24 Apr 1915.

Arthur B. Davies (1862-1928) and **Walt Kuhn** (1877-1949), both painters and organizers of the *Armory Show*.

in Paris, left bank

Sainte Geneviève Library, Paris, where he has been working since circa May 1913.

Mais en somme, puisque vous me mettez en garde contre New York; si je
n'y puis vivre plus qu'à Paris, je pourrai revenir ~~où~~ ou aller ailleurs.__
— J'ai insisté auprès de vous pour ma préoccup~~p~~ation de gagner de
l'argent pour vivre en sécurité là bas. C'est une conséquence nécessaire.
Je considère que mon père a assez fait pour moi. Et je ne veux pas
entrevoir une vie d'artiste en quête de gloire et d'argent. Je suis très
heureux lorsque j'apprends que vous m'avez vendu ces toiles et je vous
remercie très sincèrement de votre amitié. Mais j'ai peur d'en arriver à
avoir besoin de vendre des toiles, en un mot d'être artiste peintre.
— Donc je partirai probablement le 22 ou plutôt le 29 Mai. Si la
Préfecture de Police m'autorise à prendre le paquebot. Je vous
télégraphierai de Bordeaux.

J'espère (?) ici trouver une promesse de situation. (ceci est problématique).
En tout cas, je vous supplie de ne pas croire que mes frères puissent
croire à une pression de votre part.

Nous avons tous les trois trop de confiance et d'amitié pour vous.

Et je suis sûr qu'ils seront au moins consolés de savoir que je vous
retrouverai là bas.

Je vais à St Germain. Je leur donnerai votre lettre et les bonnes nouvelles
de vous.

Je vous quitte et j'espère à bientôt. Je vous charge de tous mes
remerciements pour Madame Pach au sujet de la Maison Brentano__
Mais n'oubliez pas que je ne sais pas un mot d'anglais ce qui est je crois
le plus ennuyeux de cette histoire.

    Tous mes respects donc, mille amitiés pour vous et un salut militaire
pour le jeune Raymond.

    M. Duchamp__

> MD will in fact leave on 6 June 1915.

> Mrs Pach worked for **Brentano**'s bookstore on Fifth Avenue.

▷ TRANSLATION: *27th April. My dear friend, I got your double letter this morning. I
was really delighted. I have, indeed, received the catalog from the Montross Gallery
and was very surprised not to see you next to Messrs Davies and Kuhn. Also, you
seem to me somewhat demoralized in your letter! You miss Paris. Yes, I can understand that because you were living the free life of an artist with all the joys and all
the bad times one so likes to recall. As for my time in New York, that's altogether
different. I'm not looking for anything there except individuals. If you remember
our conversations of the boulevard St Michel or Raspail, you will see that my intention to leave is the unavoidable consequence of these conversations. I am not going
to New York, I am leaving Paris. That's quite different. Long before the war, I already had a distaste for the artistic life I was involved in. It's quite the opposite of
what I'm looking for. And so I tried, through the Library, to escape from artists
somewhat. Then, with the war, my incompatibility with this milieu grew. I wanted
to go away at all costs. Where to? My only option was New York where I knew you
and where I hope to be able to escape leading the artistic life, if needs be through a*

job which will keep me very busy. I asked you to keep all this secret from my brothers because I know my leaving will be very painful for them. The same goes for my father and sisters. But at the end of the day, as you guard me against New York, if I can't live there any more than in Paris, I can always come back or go elsewhere. I have impressed upon you my preoccupation with earning money so as to have a secure existence over there. That's the way it has to be. I consider that my father has done enough for me already. And I'm not after leading the life of an artist in search of fame and fortune. I am very happy to hear that you sold these canvases for me and thank you very sincerely for your friendship. But I am afraid of getting to the stage of needing to sell canvases, in a word, of being a painter for a living. So I'll be leaving probably on the 22nd or rather 29th May, if the police authorities allow me to take the steamer. I will send you a telegram from Bordeaux. I hope to find the offer of a job here (this is problematic). In any case, please on no account think that my brothers could think that there was any pressure from you. All three of us trust you far too much and you are far too much of a friend for that. And I'm sure that they will be comforted at least to know that I have you there. I'm going to Saint-Germain. I will give them your letter and your good news. I'll leave you now and hope to see you soon. Please give my sincere thanks to Mrs Pach regarding Brentano's. But don't forget I can't speak a word of English which is, I think, the biggest problem in all of this. Best regards then, all good wishes to you, dear friend, and a military salute to Raymond, M. Duchamp.

---

8. Marcel Duchamp to Walter Pach   autograph letter
21 May 1915, Paris   collection AAA

Paris. 21 mai. 1915.
    Mon cher ami.
Je reçois votre lettre du 7. Mai.
En effet je comprends votre incertitude. Et il faut prendre ces moments là,
    le plus doucement possible et espérer
J'ai vu Raymond à St Germain. Je lui ai parlé de mon départ. Il trouve
    l'idée bonne mais il déplore la date. Il trouve que je devrais attendre.
    Comme je le pensais, il y a chez lui une raison sentimentale et familiale
    que je partage.
Mais j'ai suffisamment pesé tout pour *ne pas* changer mon intention
J'ai été à la Cie transatlantique il n'y a pas de départ le 29 mai. Le
    "Rochambeau„ partira le 5 Juin. Et il est à peu près certain que je
    partirai ce jour là.__
Je lui ai parlé aussi pour la revue d'Arensberg.__ Voici : Je verrai
    Mme Ricou demain qui aura peut être des articles de Mercereau.__

"revue d'Arensberg"= probably poetry journal *Others*, ed. by Alfred Kreymborg, sponsored initially by Walter Arensberg.

Alexandre Mercereau (b.1884), French symbolist poet and literary critic.

De même Gleizes aura peut être des articles.

En un mot je vais tâcher d'amorcer q une entente avec quelques amis qui pourraient alimenter de poëmes ou de proses. Il me suffit de trouver quelqu'un *de confiance* ici qui s'occuperait de correspondre régulièrement avec Arensberg—

En partant le 5 j'espère vous apporter quelque chose pour la revue.

(La difficulté est qu'ils sont tous à la guerre).

Je ne crains pas de trouver trop d'écrits.

Au sujet de mon séjour là bas Je suis décidé à faire un travail qui m'empêcherait même de faire ma peinture. Tant pis! Surtout "ne vous faites pas de bile" mon cher ami

Je suis assez ennuyé de vous occasionner tant d'ennuis.

Mais j'espère rattraper tout cela.

Tous mes hommages à Madame Pach et un baiser au petit Raymond
    pour vous mille amitiés
    Marcel Duchamp

Albert Gleizes (1881-1953), French Cubist painter and theoretician.

▷ TRANSLATION: *Paris, 21st May 1915. My dear friend. I have just got your letter of 7th May. I can well understand your feelings of uncertainty. In moments like these, you have to take things as calmly as possible and hope for the best. I saw Raymond in St Germain. I spoke to him about my leaving. He finds the idea all right, but is appalled by the date. He thinks I should wait. As I had expected, he is sentimental and looks at things from a family point of view, as I do. But I've weighed it all up sufficiently not to change my mind. I've been to the Transatlantic Co.—nothing leaving on 29th May. The "Rochambeau" leaves on 5th June. And I'm almost certain I'll be leaving on that date. I also spoke to him about the Arensberg review. This is the plan: I will see Mrs Ricou tomorrow who might have some articles by Mercereau. Likewise Gleizes might also have some articles. I will try to work something out with some friends who could contribute poems or prose. I just need to find someone I trust here to take care of corresponding regularly with Arensberg. When I leave on the 5th, I hope to bring you something for the review. (The problem is they're all at war). I'm in no danger of finding too much writing. About my stay over there, I have made up my mind to take a job, even one which would actually prevent me from doing my painting. Too bad! Above all, don't lose any sleep over it, my dear friend. I am put out as it is, for putting you out so much. But I hope to make it all up to you. My compliments to Mrs Pach and give little Raymond a kiss from me. All good wishes to you, dearest friend, Marcel Duchamp.*

6 June 1915
Duchamp boards the "Rochambeau"
at Bordeaux headed for New York.
It is his first trans-Atlantic crossing.
He brings with him *9 Malic Moulds* [cat. 31] and the
notes he has compiled over the course of the
previous three years for the *Large Glass* [cat. 2].

move to USA: New York | 1915-1918

chapter 2

aboard ship for USA, on the S.S. "Rochambeau" | 6 June 1915
lives in New York: 33 West 67th Street, 34 Beekman Place and 1947 Broadway

from 6 June 1915 to 13 August 1918

▶ MAJOR WORKS

In Advance of the Broken Arm (snow shovel,
 Nov 1915)
Rendez-vous du Dimanche 6 Février 1916...
 (typewritten text on four postcards,
 Feb 1916)
Comb (readymade, Feb 1916)
A bruit secret / With Hidden Noise (brass plates
 and ball of twine, Easter 1916)
... pliant... de voyage / Traveler's Folding Item
 (typewriter cover, 1916)
Nude Descending a Staircase, No.3
 (watercolor, ink, pencil, and pastel on
 photograph, 1916)
Apolinère Enameled (rectified readymade:
 advertising sign for Sapolin paints, 1917)
Fountain (urinal signed R. Mutt, 1917)
The Blind Man No.1: "Independents'
 Number" (review, 10 Apr 1917)
The Blind Man No.2: "P.B.T." (review, May
 1917)
Rongwrong (review, single issue July 1917)
Trébuchet / Trap (coat rack, 1917)
Hat Rack (1917)

Tu m' (oil and pencil on canvas, with bottle
 brush, three safety pins, and a bolt, 1918)
Sculpture for Traveling (strips cut out of rubber
 bathing caps, 1918)

▶ EXHIBITIONS

Modern Art after Cézanne, Bourgeois Gallery, New York.
 By MD: *The King and Queen surrounded by swift
 nudes*; *Celibated utensil*; *Chocolate grinder*;
 Chocolate grinder; *2 Ready Mades* [listed under
 "Sculptures"]; *Boxing match* — **3 Apr - 29 Apr 1916**
**Exhibition of Pictures by Jean Crotti, Marcel Duchamp,
 Albert Gleizes, Jean Metzinger**, Montross Galleries,
 550 Fifth Avenue above 55th St, New York. By MD,
 listed under "Paintings": *Landscape*; *Yvonne et
 Magdeleine déchiquetées* (lent); listed under
 "Drawings": *Virgin*; *Portrait*; *Pharmacie*
 — **4 Apr - 22 Apr 1916**
Advanced Modern Art, McClaes Galleries, Philadelphia,
 USA. By MD: *The King and the Queen surrounded
 by Swift Nudes* — **17 May - 15 June 1916**
The Society of Independent Artists, 20 West 31a Street,
 New York. By Richard Mutt: *Fountain* (not
 included in the catalog, not exhibited in the show)
 — **9 Apr - 6 May 1917**

15 June 1915
The "Rochambeau" arrives in New York. Duchamp
is probably met at the piers by Walter Pach.
After spending a few weeks in relatively cramped
quarters with the Pach family, arrangements are
made for him to stay in the large duplex apartment
of Walter and Louise Arensberg, wealthy collectors
of modern art, then vacationing at their
country home in Pomfret, Connecticut.

9. Marcel Duchamp to Walter Pach   autograph letter
[28 July 1915, New York]   collection AAA

Mercredi―

    Mon cher Pach―

Avez vous eu votre paquet? J'ai demandé une palette carrée. Il m'a
répondu qu'il n'en avait pas d'autres. J'ai peur que vous ne soyez pas
satisfait. Dites le moi. J'en trouverai facilement chez Montross ou
ailleurs. Pour vous contenter aussi : j'ai payé 79 Cents.

―――――

J'ai vu votre père chez "Nicholas„ : Il m'a dit de venir chercher
l'exemplaire de ma photo. Elle est très bien. Mais dites moi : est ce pour
le Vanity Fair, ou pour moi? et dois je la porter à cette publication?
Donnez moi instructions. ~~Si~~

Une chose qui vous intéressera plus : Mr. Quinn m'a téléphoné Samedi
matin 11^h. J'ai été le voir 2 minutes chez lui et il m'a invité pour le
même soir, 4 heures, à aller avec lui, Mr. Gregg et Mr. Kuhn et une
demoiselle (dont je ne sais plus le nom) à Coney Island. Nous avons
passé là une soirée très amusante : Luna Park, Steeple Chase, dîner chez
Feltman, retour en auto : vous voyez cela.

    Mr. Gregg est, de seconde impression, très très sympathique. Kuhn a été
<u>charmant</u> avec moi. Et j'ai pu comprendre mieux tout ce que vous
m'avez dit. D'ailleurs notre conversation a été générale, d'autant plus
difficile pour moi qu'on ne disait pas un mot de français. Mais je m'en
suis tiré― Pas un mot de vous, bien entendu― Discrétion― Pas un
mot de Davies.

― Mr. Quinn, en effet, peut être pour moi un appui de cordialité. Je l'ai
mieux apprécié encore que la première fois. Il est fort inquiet de savoir si
le cubisme est tué par la guerre et des questions d'ordre général sur l'art
d'Europe pendant ces 3 prochaines années. Dès que mon anglais me le
permettra je me promets de lui faire abandonner cette vision politique
"politicale„ de l'art; et je tâcherai de lui bien exprimer nos idées ~~en~~ qui
sont en dehors de toute influence de milieu ou d'époque― jusqu'à un

Photograph by Pach
Brothers Studio
(Walter's father's firm),
published in *Vanity
Fair*, Sept 1915, p.57.

John Quinn, see p.42.

Frederick James Gregg,
art critic, chairman of
the Armory Show's
press committee, wrote
the introduction to the
catalog.

certain point évidemment. Il pourra y avoir un profit pour lui et pour moi à remuer ces 2 points de vue dans le même panier.—

J'ai eu un téléphone de Friedmann pour un soir de la semaine dernière et je ne pouvais pas y aller. Je leur ai écrit pour aller voir Of un de ces jours, j'attends la réponse

Aussi, une lettre de Miss Junghaus, à New York. Je lui ai répondu.

J'attends un téléphone d'elle.

Je dois aller prendre un breakfast chez Mr Quinn un matin prochain—

Je travaille toujours très content. Vous écrirai en anglais bientôt—

> Tous mes respects à Madame Pach
> Baiser au petit.
> Cordialemnt vôtre
> M. Duchamp—

George Of (1876-1954), painter, owns and runs a framemaking shop W 56th St., Manhattan.

▷ TRANSLATION: *Wednesday. My dear Pach, Did you get your parcel? I asked for a square palette. He told me he didn't have any more. I think this may not do for you. Let me know. I can easily get one from Montross or somewhere. This will make you happy also: I paid 79 cents. I saw your father at "Nicholas'": he told me to come and pick up the copy of my photo. It's really good. But tell me something: is it for Vanity Fair or for me? and am I supposed to take it to this publication? Instructions please. Something of more interest to you: Mr Quinn telephoned me Saturday morning, 11 o'clock. I stopped by to see him for just a few moments and he invited me—4 hours—to go that same evening with him, Mr Gregg and Mr Kuhn and a young lady (whose name I've forgotten), to Coney Island. We spent a very entertaining evening there: Luna Park, Steeple Chase, dinner at Feltman's, came back by car—you can imagine. Mr Gregg is, on second impression, very very nice. Kuhn was charming to me. And I understood better all that you'd said to me. What's more, the conversation was general, all the more difficult for me as not a single word of French was spoken. But I got by. Not a word about you, naturally. Discretion. Not a word about Davies. Mr Quinn, it's true, could turn out to be a very congenial ally for me. I liked him better than the first time. He's extremely anxious to know whether Cubism has been killed by the war and about other general questions on art in Europe in next three years. As soon as my English will let me, I've promised myself I'll get him to let go of this "political" vision of art and I will endeavour to convey our ideas to him which are outside the influence of any milieu or era, up to a certain point obviously. It could be beneficial both for him and for me to shake these two ideas about together. I got a telephone call from Friedmann about something one evening last week and couldn't go. I wrote to them about going to see Of one of these days. I'm waiting for a reply. Also, a letter from Miss Junghaus, in New York. I have replied. I'm expecting a telephone call from her. I have to go to Mr Quinn's for a breakfast one morning soon. I'm still working away quite happily. Will write to you in English soon. My regards as always to Mrs Pach. Kiss for the little one. Sincerely yours, M. Duchamp.*

10. Marcel Duchamp to John Quinn[*]
5 November 1915, [New York]

autograph letter
collection NYPL

Friday Nov. 5th 1915

    Dear Mr. Quinn,

I met Miss Bella Greene at the Library at 3.45 P.M.

She asked me my wishes, as number (how many) of working hours, and as remuneration.__

She decided to ask to the President of the French Institute for : 4 hours in the afternoon every day (from 2 o'clock to 6.) and $100 a month.

My hope is surpassed : I assure you, instead this work will be an obstacle for my own work, I will have ~~my~~ the entire freedom which I need.

Now I am beginning my english translation. I wish you will be pleased by it.

    Very sincerely yours
    Marcel Duchamp__

Bella Greene works at the French Institute; librarian at the Pierpont Morgan Library.

---

* **John Quinn** (1870-1924), a successful New York lawyer and important early collector of modern art in the years before World War I, amassed the single largest and most comprehensive collection of modern French and American art to exist anywhere in the world. Duchamp met Quinn during the summer of 1915, but even before they met, Quinn had demonstrated a keen interest in the artist's work, having acquired *The Chess Game* (1910) and *Apropos of Little Sister* (1911) from exhibitions of Contemporary French Art that were held at the Carroll Galleries in New York. Duchamp was probably introduced to Quinn by Walter Pach (p.27), who was a strong early advocate of the Cubist sculpture of Duchamp's brother, Raymond Duchamp-Villon. Quinn began to collect Duchamp-Villon's work from the time he first saw it at the Armory Show in 1913, and he would go on to acquire examples of virtually every known sculpture by the artist. During the time of Duchamp's first sojourn in New York, Quinn often asked him to translate letters that he received from artists in France. Quinn paid a modest fee for this service, but to further convey his gratitude, in August of 1915 he invited Duchamp and the journalist Frederic James Gregg to join him for a week vacation in Spring Lake, a summer resort community on the Jersey Shore about two and one-half hours (by boat) directly south of Manhattan. Duchamp repaid Quinn's generosity by making a quick little portrait sketch, which he presented to his patron as a gift. A few months later, Quinn purchased the first version of Duchamp's *Nude Descending a Staircase* (1911), which he acquired directly from the artist for $120. Quinn's cordial relationship with Duchamp continued throughout the early years he spent in New York. The artist's new mechanical and intellectual expressions, however, held little appeal for the veteran collector, whose taste, by then, was obviously more securely rooted in the mainstream tradition of modern European art.

11. Marcel Duchamp to Suzanne Duchamp   autograph letter
15 January [1916], New York   collection AAA

15 Janvier environ.

    Ma chère Suzanne

Merci énormément pour t'occuper de toutes mes affaires— Mais
pourquoi n'aurais tu pas pris ~~cette~~ mon atelier pour habiter. J'y pense
juste maintenant— Mais je pense que peut-être ça ne t'irait pas.

En tout cas, le bail finit 15 juillet et si tu reprenais, ne le fais qu'en
proposant à mon proprio. de louer 3 mois par 3 mois, comme cela se
passe ordinairement; il acceptera sûrement. Peut être père ne serait *pas*
mécontent de regagner un terme si c'est possible que tu quittes La
Condamine pour 15 Avril.— But I don't know anything about your   Rue de **La Condamine**,
intentions et je ne veux que te suggérer quelque chose.—   in the north of Paris.

Maintenant si tu es montée *chez moi* tu as vu dans l'atelier une roue de   *Bicycle Wheel* [cat. 33]
bicyclette et un <u>porte bouteilles</u>.— J'avais acheté cela comme une   and *Readymade (bottle
sculpture toute faite. Et j'ai une intention à propos de ce dit porte   dryer)* [cat. 35]
bouteilles : Ecoute.

Ici, à N.Y., j'ai acheté des objets dans le même goût et je les traite comme
des "readymade„ tu sais assez d'anglais pour comprendre le sens de
"<u>tout fait</u>" que je donne à ces objets— Je les signe et je leur donne une
inscription en anglais. Je te donne qques exemples :

J'ai par exemple une grande pelle à neige sur laquelle j'ai inscrit en bas : <u>In
advance of the broken arm</u>. traduction française : <u>En avance du bras</u>   *In Advance...* [cat. 36]
<u>cassé</u>— Ne t'escrime pas trop à comprendre dans le sens romantique ou
impressionniste ou cubiste — cela n'a aucun rapport avec;

Un autre "readymade" s'appelle : <u>Emergency in favor of twice</u>. traduction   *Emergency...* [cat. 37]
française possible : <u>Danger *Crise*\ en faveur de 2 fois</u>.

Tout ce préambule pour te dire :

Prends pour toi ce porte bouteilles. J'en fais un "Readymade„ à distance.   *Readymade (bottle
Tu inscriras en bas et <u>à l'intérieur</u> du cercle du bas. en petites lettres   dryer)* [cat. 35]
peintes avec un pinceau à l'huile en couleur blanc d'argent la ~~phr~~
inscription que je vais te donner ci après. et tu signeras de la même
écriture comme suit :

    [d'après] Marcel Duchamp.

[end of letter could very well be missing]

▷ TRANSLATION: *15th January approximately. My dear Suzanne, A huge thank you
for having taken care of everything for me. But why didn't you take my studio and
go and live there? I've only just thought of it. Though I think, perhaps, it wouldn't
do for you. In any case, the lease is up 15th July and if you were to renew it, make
sure you ask the landlord to let it 3 months at a time, the usual way. He's bound to
agree. Perhaps Father wouldn't mind getting a term's rent back if there's a possibil-*

ity you'll be leaving La Condamine by 15th April. But I don't know anything about your plans and I'm only making a suggestion. Now, if you have been up to my place, you will have seen, in the studio, a bicycle wheel and a bottle rack. I bought this as a ready-made sculpture. And I have a plan concerning this so-called bottle rack. Listen to this: here, in N.Y., I have bought various objects in the same taste and I treat them as "readymades." You know enough English to understand the meaning of "ready-made" that I give these objects. I sign them and I think of an inscription for them in English. I'll give you a few examples. I have, for example, a large snow shovel on which I have inscribed at the bottom: In advance of the broken arm, *French translation:* En avance du bras cassé. *Don't tear your hair out trying to understand this in the Romantic or Impressionist or Cubist sense—it has nothing to do with all that. Another "readymade" is called:* Emergency in favor of twice, *possible French translation:* Danger \Crise\ en faveur de 2 fois. *This long preamble just to say: take this bottle rack for yourself. I'm making it a "Readymade," remotely. You are to inscribe it at the bottom and on the inside of the bottom circle, in small letters painted with a brush in oil, silver white color, with an inscription which I will give you herewith, and then sign it, in the same handwriting, as follows: [after] Marcel Duchamp.*

---

12. Marcel Duchamp to John Quinn   autograph letter
15 March 1916, New York   collection NYPL

> 1947 Broadway. N.Y.
> March. 15th 1916.
>   Dear Mr. Quinn
> Do you know we are going to have an exhibition on the 1st of April at
>   Bourgeois Galleries. There will be some paintings by Seurat, Cézanne,
>   Van Gogh, Rouault, Dufy, Villon.
> Would you be pleased by exhibiting one of the two bronzes (woman
>   seated) by my brother Duchamp-Villon. If you are interested in selling
>   the first one (without the marble base) or if you simply like to loan one
>   of those sculptures, I would thank you very much for helping me to put
>   a sculpture by my brother in this exhibition_
> I work very much, for the present, and I want you to come here and see
>   my things.
>   Very sincerely yours.
>   Marcel Duchamp_

"Modern Art After Cézanne," **Bourgeois Galleries**, NY, 3 Apr - 29 May 1916.

13. Marcel Duchamp to Suzanne Duchamp   autograph letter
17 October 1916, New York   collection AAA

> N.Y. 17 Octobre 1916
>> Ma chère Suzanne
> Première chose, je change d'adresse
> Je vais avoir un petit atelier, une pièce et bain dans une très jolie maison
>> d'ateliers. C'est par un arrangement avec un de mes amis.
>>> 33 West 67th Street
>>> New York City
> J'ai déjà habité là l'année dernière mais chez des amis.—
> Merci pour mon déménagement. Je pense que tu t'es adressée à Père pour
>> tous les frais. Sinon dis moi ce que tu as dépensé je serais très content de
>> t'adresser un "chèque sur Paris"—
> Oui Crotti nous a quittés. Sa femme qui était restée ici cet été est repartie
>> à Paris tu la rencontreras un jour—
> Je travaille un peu. Mais j'ai une vie un peu déréglée.
> Naturellement prends cette gravure de Naudin. As tu écrit la phrase sur le
>> ready made. fais le.— et envoie la moi (la phrase). en m'indiquant
>> comment tu as fait
> J'écris un peu à tout le monde en ce moment. C'est la chose qui
>> m'assomme le plus c'est dommage que les cables coûtent si cher
> C'est si commode.
> Au revoir ma chère Suzanne, dis mes bonnes amitiés à Henriette, à tous
>> les amis et amies de l'hôpital.
>>> Affectueusement à toi
>>> Marcel

Same building as where the Arensbergs are living. MD's rent is paid by W. Arensberg in exchange for ownership of the *Large Glass* [cat. 2].

Jean Crotti (see p.53), was MD's studio mate in NY, 1915-16. Crotti's wife is Yvonne Chastel.

Bernard Naudin (1876-1946), French engraver and illustrator.

▷ TRANSLATION: *N.Y. 17th October 1916. My dear Suzanne, First of all, I'm moving. I'm getting a little studio, one room with bath in a very pretty block of studios. It's through an arrangement with a friend of mine, 33 West 67th Street, New York City. I already lived there last year but staying with friends. Thank you for moving my stuff. I'm assuming you went to Father for all the expenses. Otherwise tell me what you spent and I'll be happy to send you a "check drawn on Paris." Yes, Crotti has left us. His wife, who'd stayed here for the summer, has gone back to Paris. You'll meet her one day. I'm working a bit. But my life is somewhat erratic. Of course you can take that engraving by Naudin. Did you write the inscription on the ready made? Do it. And send it to me (the inscription) and let me know exactly what you did. I'm writing to more or less everybody at the moment. That's what's most crippling. It's a pity cables are so expensive. It's so convenient. Farewell, my dear Suzanne. Give my best wishes to Henriette and to all friends, male and female, at the hospital. Affectionately yours, Marcel.*

14. Marcel Duchamp to Katherine S. Dreier*   autograph letter
11 April [1917], New York   collection YCAL

N.Y. 33 W. 67.th Street—

April 11th.

Dear Miss Dreier

I am extremely sorry, after having promised to help you decorate the tea room, to have to withdraw my promise. As you know, I have resigned from the board of Directors on account of a serious disagreement with the ruling spirit of the Society.

With best wishes.

Sincerely yours

Marcel Duchamp

The **Society** of Independent Artists refused to show *Fountain* [cat. 38], a urinal submitted to the exhibition by a certain Richard Mutt.

* **Katherine S. Dreier** (1877-1952) was an artist and collector, who, with Man Ray (p.106) and Marcel Duchamp, founded the Société Anonyme, the first museum in America devoted exclusively to the display and promotion of modern art. She probably met Duchamp in the fall of 1916, in meetings held at the apartment of Walter and Louise Arensberg (p.50) to establish the Society of Independent Artists (both Duchamp and Dreier served on its founding Board of Directors). Although she failed to fully comprehend the more profound philosophical implications of Duchamp's work, that did not prevent her from admiring and collecting it, and on at least one occasion, of offering Duchamp a lucrative commission. "*His charming personality and extreme good looks as a young man,*" she recalled years later, "*won the interest and hearts of everybody there*" (including, we can be relatively safe in assuming, Dreier's as well). Dreier's letters to Duchamp were almost always long and tedious, whereas his responses were, as he confessed in one letter, comparatively brief and "telegraphic." There can be no doubt that Duchamp had a great deal of respect for Dreier's steadfast commitment to modern art. Throughout the years of their friendship, he willingly lent his assistance in the various exhibitions she organized (particularly the International survey of modern art at the Brooklyn Museum in 1926), and he served as a loyal and trusted adviser on the many works of art she acquired. For her part, Dreier seems to have been fascinated by Duchamp both as an artist and as a man. Yet there is no indication that their professional relationship ever exceeded the bounds of a strong platonic friendship, one which endured for over thirty-five years, until the time of Dreier's death in 1952.

---

15. Marcel Duchamp to Suzanne Duchamp   autograph letter
11 April [1917, New York]   collection AAA

> 11 avril
>   Ma chère Suzanne—
> Impossible d'écrire—
> J'ai su par Crotti que tu travaillais beaucoup.
> Dis moi ce que tu fais— et si ce n'est pas trop difficile à envoyer. Je
>   pourrais peut être t'exposer au mois d'Octobre ou Novembre—
>   prochain— ici.
> Mais dis moi ce que tu fais—
> Raconte ce détail à la famille : Les Indépendants sont ouverts ici avec gros
>   succès.
> Une de mes amies ~~sous~~ sous un pseudonyme masculin, Richard Mutt,
>   avait envoyé une pissotière en porcelaine comme sculpture;
> Ce n'était pas du tout indécent. aucune raison pour la refuser. Le comité
>   a décidé de refuser d'exposer cette chose. J'ai donné ma démission et
>   c'est un potin qui aura sa valeur dans New York— ~~j'av~~
> J'avais envie de faire une exposition spéciale des refusés aux
>   Indépendants— mais ce serait un pléonasme!—
> Et la pissotière aurait été lonely—
> A bientôt.
>   Affect.
>   Marcel

Fountain [cat. 38]. Address on admission label attached to urinal, suggests the "female friend" is probably **Louise Norton**, née McCutcheon (1890-1988), married to Allen Norton and later to marry composer Edgard Varèse.

▷ TRANSLATION: *11th April. My dear Suzanne, Impossible to write. I heard from Crotti that you're working a lot. Let me know what you're doing—and if it's not too difficult to ship. I might in fact be able to exhibit you next October or November— over here. But let me know what it is you're doing. Tell the family this snippet: the Independents opened here with enormous success. A female friend of mine, using a male pseudonym, Richard Mutt, submitted a porcelain urinal as a sculpture. It wasn't at all indecent. No reason to refuse it. The committee decided to refuse to exhibit this thing. I handed in my resignation and it'll be a juicy piece of gossip in New York. I felt like organizing a special exhibition for things refused at the Independents, but that would be a pleonasm! And the urinal would have been* lonely. *Bye for now. Affectionately, Marcel.*

16. Marcel Duchamp to Ettie Stettheimer*   autograph letter
[9 August 1917], New York   collection YCAL

33 W. 67.
entre Jeudi et Vendredi.

J'ai été hier à Tarry. et nous avons mangé du "corn" délicieux, sucré.
Moi qui n'ai pas un goût très marqué pour ce genre de légume à cause
de la difficulté gymnastique à le manger, ai été émerveillé et en conserve
encore maintenant le souvenir.

Evidemment la maison n'était pas complète, sans vous. Il y manquait cette
voix définitive qu'on entend partir de la terrasse, sans jamais d'écho qui
oserait mettre en balance une solution un peu différente.

J'ai proposé à vos sœurs de les faire poser. Mlle Carrie n'est pas du tout
enthousiaste.

Elle trouve que j'ai l'esprit trop caricaturiste (ce que j'ai du mal à admettre,
mais je *le* crois, ne me connaissant pas du tout).

Je lui ai proposé un marché : déchirer le portrait s'il ne lui plaît pas. Je ne
feelerai pas offensé.

Tarrytown, about 20 miles north of NYC along the Hudson River. The Stettheimers rented a house there for the summer.

---

* **Carrie** (1870-1944), **Ettie** (1874-1955) and **Florine** (1871-1944) **Stettheimer** were three well-to-do, unmarried sisters, who lived with their mother in a lavishly decorated apartment on West Seventy-Sixth Street in Manhattan. The Stettheimers often hosted formal dinner parties at their apartment, festive evenings that were attended by some of New York's most important vanguard artists, writers and composers, including, among others, Francis Picabia (p.58), Carl Van Vechten, Henri-Pierre Roché (p.57), Edgard Varèse, and Henry McBride (p.110). Duchamp probably met the Stettheimers in the fall of 1916, when all three sisters began taking French lessons from him (which none of them really needed, since they all had lived in France for a number of years before the war and spoke the language with considerable fluency). Duchamp had the most in common with **Florine**, a painter and poet who specialized in the depiction of genre scenes based on personal experiences, such as her *La Fête à Duchamp*, which recorded a party that the Stettheimers hosted at their summer home in Tarrytown, New York, on the occasion of Duchamp's 30th birthday in 1917. **Carrie** Stettheimer spent much of her time working on the construction of a large dolls house, the main room of which was decorated by paintings made by artists in their circle, including Duchamp, who painted a miniature version of his *Nude Descending a Staircase*. Duchamp seems to have formed the strongest emotional attachment to **Ettie** Stettheimer, who, among the three sisters, was the most intellectual and educated (she held a Ph.D. in philosophy). Moreover, she openly flirted with Duchamp, and when he left for Buenos Aires in 1918, he invited her to join him, but she declined (years later, Duchamp ended up being a character in one of her novels, a man she described as "a charming and rare creature, sensitive, delicate and with a rare polished finish"). After Duchamp returned to Paris in 1923, he saw the Stettheimers only on rare and infrequent trips to the United States, but they remained in contact through an occasional exchange of letters.

Quant à Mlle Florine elle va se procurer du papier pour la prochaine fois. Son manque d'enthousiasme est moins apparent.

Nous avons fait une ballade à Nikko Inn avec Avery Hapwood. J'ai énormément de sympathie pour lui.

Je ne fais rien de différent. J'ai une sorte de diminution d'intérêt pour les quelques rares choses qui m'attiraient. Ceci pour vous permettre de mépriser un peu plus, du haut de votre bonne santé, de vos montagnes—

J'ai fait de mon mieux je vous ai écrit une lettre bien vide. Ne m'en veuillez pas, c'est la plus sincère expression de mes sentiments à l'heure actuelle—

A bientôt de vos nouvelles
    très affectueusement
    Marcel Duchamp

Nikko Inn = restaurant overlooking the Hudson River.

"Hapwood" = in fact **Avery Hopwood** (1882-1928), successful NY playwright and frequent guest at the Stettheimer soirées.

▷ TRANSLATION: *33 W. 67. Thursday / Friday. I was in Tarry yesterday and we had "corn," delicious and sweet. I've never been particularly partial to this kind of vegetable on account of the gymnastics involved in eating them but I was absolutely amazed and can still remember the taste even now. Naturally the house was empty without you. I missed the firm voice that comes ringing from the terrace with ne'er a peep in reply daring to propose even a slightly different point of view. I've asked your sisters to sit for me. Miss Carrie is not at all keen. She thinks I am too much of a cartoonist (which I find hard to accept, but I can believe it, not knowing myself at all). I've offered her a deal: to tear up the portrait if she doesn't like it. I won't feel offended. As for Miss Florine, she's going to bring some paper along next time. Her lack of enthusiasm is less apparent. We had a stroll to the Nikko Inn with Avery Hapwood. I like him tremendously. I'm not doing anything new. I seem to be losing interest in the few rare things that did appeal to me. So you can feel a little more contempt, look down from the heights of your wholesomeness, from your mountains. I've done my best—I've written you a perfectly empty letter. Don't be cross with me—it's the most sincere expression of my feelings right now. Look forward to hearing from you soon. Very affectionately, Marcel Duchamp.*

17. Marcel Duchamp to Louise Arensberg[*]   autograph letter
Friday [24 August 1917], New York   collection PMA

Vendredi
    Chère Lou.
Il y a bien longtemps que je veux vous écrire...
Vous recevrez par le même courrier un RongwRong qui se décide à   *Rongwrong* = single-
paraître.   issue Dada magazine
                                                                         edited by MD, July 1917.
L'été ici se passe absolument comme l'hiver. On boit un peu, j'ai pris
quelques cuites; et hier soir, chez Joel's où nous étions avec Aileen et 3   Probably **Aileen
ou 4 de ses amis, ~~m~~ la soirée s'est terminée par une bataille.   Dresser** (b.1890),
                                                                            Beatrice Wood's
— Des brutes d'une autre table à côté sont venues chanter un peu trop fort landlady and an
près de nous, ils ont aussi voulu embrasser "nos femmes"— Petite   occasional visitor at the
                                                                            Arensberg gatherings.
discussion d'abord, puis, plus saouls que nous, ils ont flanqué Walter   **Walter** = Walter
par terre, sans blessure et moi j'ai reçu un formidable coup de poing   Arensberg
dans l'oreille, je saigne encore, et c'est enflé— Pas grave—

* **Louise** (1879-1953) and **Walter** (1878-1954) **Arensberg** were wealthy collectors of modern art
who, for a five year period—from 1915 through 1920—opened their large duplex apartment on
West 67th Street in Manhattan to nearly nightly gatherings of the avant-garde, artists and writers from both sides of the Atlantic whose activities during these years have been characterized
as "the nexus of New York Dada." Walter Arensberg attended Harvard, where he majored in
English literature and graduated with honors in 1900. In 1907, he married Louise Stevens, a
music student who was born in Dresden, Germany, but raised in Ludlow, Massachusetts, she
was heir to the Stevenses' textile fortune. The Arensbergs moved to New York in 1914, and met
Duchamp shortly after he arrived in America during the summer of 1915. Soon, Duchamp
became their new "star boarder," for he attended the nightly soirées, and eventually took a
small studio in the same building (connected to the Arensberg apartment by a short hallway).
During these years, Duchamp often provided the Arensbergs with advice on their growing collection of modern art, and after they moved to California in 1921 (and he returned to Paris in
1923), he would frequently act as their European liaison in locating and acquiring important
paintings and sculptures for their collection. Eventually, the Arensbergs would amass the single largest and most comprehensive collection of Duchamp's work, which, along with their
entire collection of modern art (including nearly 200 pieces of Pre-Columbian Art they assembled while living in California), they gave to the Philadelphia Museum of Art. Duchamp not
only served as the Arensbergs' principal representative in the delicate negotiations that took
place in arranging for the terms of this gift, but after Louise Arensberg's death in 1953, followed
two months later by her husband's, Duchamp oversaw the installation of their collection in the
galleries of the Philadelphia Museum, where the Arensberg Collection remains on display to
this very day.

A part cela, je ne travaille presque pas.

J'ai quelques leçons.

Nous nous couchons plus tôt. (3h. au lieu de 5.).

Les Picabia sont dans les Catskills.

Francis Picabia, see p.58.

Les Gleizes à N.Y.

Helen Freeman m'avait dit qu'elle vous écrirait pour aller vous voir.
  L'a t elle fait?—

Helen Freeman, see p.308

Walter a bonne mine.

Mon atelier a été peint en blanc— C'est très bien.

Walter = Walter Arensberg

Et vous que faites vous? Si loin, êtes vous tellement dégoutée de N.Y.

Jouez vous au tennis? Faites vous de l'auto. Racontez moi un peu des
  histoires.

Et quand revenez vous parmi nous?

Ecrivez moi une petite lettre.

Je serais si content.

A bientôt chère Lou
      et très affectueusement
      Marcel.

▷ TRANSLATION: *Friday. Dear Lou, I've been wanting to write to you for some time now... You will also receive in the same mail a copy of a RongwRong which is finally ready to appear in print. Summer here is exactly the same as winter. We drink a bit, I've been plastered a few times and last night, at Joel's place where we'd been with Aileen and three or four of her friends, the evening ended in a brawl. Some brutes from another table nearby came over singing a bit too loudly right by us, also wanting to kiss "our women." Slight argument for starters, then, even drunker than we were, they floored Walter, who is unhurt while I sustained a great blow to the ear and it's still bleeding and swollen. Nothing to worry about. Apart from that, I'm hardly doing any work at all. I have a few lessons. We go to bed earlier now (3 a.m. instead of 5.) The Picabias are in the Catskills. The Gleizeses in New York. Helen Freeman told me she was going to write to you about going to see you. Has she done so? Walter looks well. My studio has been painted white—it's really good. And what about you, what are you up to? So far away, are you utterly fed up with New York? Do you play tennis? Do you drive? Please let me have some news. And when are you coming back to us? Drop me a line or two. I should be so pleased. So long, dear Lou, and very affectionately, Marcel.*

18. Marcel Duchamp to Carrie, Ettie and Florine Stettheimer   autograph letter
[8 October 1917], New York   collection YCAL

Avez vous reçu Sev. Arts Chère Miss Ettie.

Lundi

Un grand changement depuis ce matin. Je vais, à partir de demain, travailler à une mission française pour la guerre— downtown, de 9^h ½ du matin à 5 heures du soir tous les jours—

J'avais été voir ces gens à la fin de la semaine dernière. Et ils m'ont proposé d'être secrétaire particulier d'un capitaine, à des appointements faibles d'abord mais qui augmenteront si je suis l'homme qu'il leur faut. Je vous demande donc d'abandonner mes leçons jusqu'à ce qu'ils me mettent à la porte—

Ce sera peut être dans huit jours ou dans 8 ans—

Je vais être utile à mon pays moi aussi.

Je ne sais pas ce que je vais avoir à faire exactement.

Venez vous à N.Y. un de ces jours. Je pourrais vous voir le soir et causer de tout cela avec vous.

Mes regrets du mercredi. Mes regrets de n'être plus digne de votre accueil, un misérable bureaucrate qui abandonne tout ce qu'il avait aimé et aime à N.Y. depuis 2 ans.—

A bientôt à N.Y. = et veuillez présenter mes hommages respectueux à Mrs Stettheimer

　　　Très affectueusement à toutes trois

　　　M. Duch

Seven Arts, an extremely influential NY magazine edited by James Oppenheim, appeared for only one year, Nov 1916 - Oct 1917.

MD's Wednesday French lessons to the Stettheimers.

▷ TRANSLATION: *Have you received Seven Arts dear Miss Ettie?*
Monday. A great change from this morning on. As from tomorrow, I will be working at a French war mission—downtown, from 9.30 in the morning till 5 in the afternoon every day. I went to see these people last week. They've offered me the position of personal secretary to a captain, for a modest salary to begin but which will increase if I prove to be the man for the job. I must ask you therefore to forget about my lessons until they throw me out. That could be in eight days or in eight years from now. I too am to be of service to my country. I don't know exactly what I will have to do as yet. Will you come to New York one of these days? I could see you in the evenings and chat to you about all of this. My apologies for Wednesday. My apologies for no longer being worthy of your hospitality, a wretched bureaucrat who has been forsaking all he had loved and loves in N.Y. for two years now. See you soon in N.Y. and please pass on my esteemed regards to Mrs. Stettheimer. Very affectionately to all three of you, M. Duch.

19. Marcel Duchamp to Jean Crotti[*]   autograph letter
8 July [1918], New York   collection AAA

N.Y. 8 juillet. 33 W. 67

Mon cher Jean, Yvonne t'a écrit et tu as reçu le cable que j'allais et probablement Yvonne aussi partir pour Buenos Aires— Plusieurs raisons que tu connais : Rien de grave; seulement une sorte de fatigue de la part des A.— Des gens malintentionnés ont probablement arrangé les choses ainsi— J'ai vu dernièrement Lou qui a été très gentille— Walter vient de perdre sa mère. Il est à Pittsburgh et je ne l'ai pas vu depuis un mois. J'ai fini le grand panneau pour Miss Dreier et j'ai recommencé une autre chose plus intéressante pour elle aussi : tu te rappelles les ~~capes de~~ coiffures de bain en caoutchouc de toutes couleurs =

J'en ai acheté, les ai découpées en petites bandes irrégulières, *les ai* collées ensemble, pas à plat, au milieu (en l'air) de mon atelier, et attaché par des ficelles aux différents murs et clous de mon atelier
Ça fait une sorte de toile d'araignée de toutes les couleurs.

Yvonne Chastel (1884-1968) who divorced from Jean Crotti Dec 1917.

"A." = Arensberg

Arensberg family home in Oakmont, PA, a suburb of Pittsburgh.

"large panel" = *Tu m'* [cat. 29]

"rubber bathing caps" = *Sculpture for Traveling* [cat. 39]

* **Jean Crotti** (1878-1958), a Swiss-born painter who lived in Paris and, upon the outbreak of World War I, moved to New York with his wife Yvonne. Shortly after his arrival, he met Duchamp and shared a studio with him in the Lincoln Arcade Building on Broadway at 66th Street. There, he radically departed from his earlier Orphist/Cubist style to begin painting—like his studio-mate—on glass and in a machinist style. In 1916, he showed some of these works in an exhibition at the Montross Gallery, a show that included paintings by Albert Gleizes, Jean Metzinger, and Duchamp, dubbed by the press "The Four Musketeers Exhibition." Crotti also submitted a sculpture of wire and cast metal entitled *Portrait of Marcel Duchamp (Sculpture Made to Measure)*, a work that was singled out by reviewers for its unusual use of materials. Crotti returned to Paris in 1916, and it was probably then that he met and fell in love with Duchamp's sister Suzanne (p.23). They were married in 1919 and, shortly thereafter, developed the principles of their own artistic movement, Tabu, an off-shoot of Dada. In the 1940's, Crotti would become fairly well known in Parisian artistic circles for his invention of something he called "*les gemmaux*," a technique of working in colored glass. The subjects of his paintings were often religious, a commitment to a deep-rooted Christian faith that he retained from childhood and never abandoned. Throughout the years of their marriage, both Suzanne Duchamp and Jean Crotti would keep in frequent contact with Duchamp, not only to exchange information about personal and professional activities, but to occasionally seek his advice on their own artistic careers.

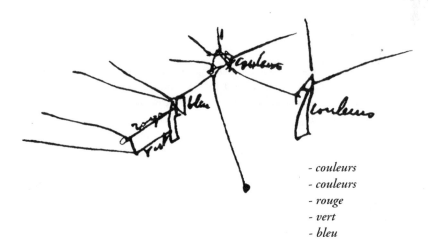

- *couleurs*
- *couleurs*
- *rouge*
- *vert*
- *bleu*

J'ai presque fini ça__

Si tout se passe comme je l'espère, il y a un bateau partant le 3 aout__ ou
   bien un autre vers le 14 aout__ Si le bateau du 4 aout n'est pas
   réquisitionné par les Etats Unis, nous devons le prendre; il est beaucoup
   moins cher : $200 jusqu'à Buenos Aires direct__ L'autre, le 14 va par
   Panama, le Pacifique et Valparaiso Chili où nous prendrions un train
   qui traverse jusqu'à Buenos Aires en 2 jours. Ce second est plus cher; le
   voyage coûte près de $400__

Le premier met 27 jours

Le second met 21 - - - train compris.

De sur le bateau je t'enverrai un petit mot t'annonçant que nous avons
   quitté N.Y. et comment!

Nous avons eu le cable de Suzanne et Yvonne je crois est contente de
   partir__ car comme tu l'avais déjà constaté ici est bien changé,
   atmosphère et tout. Contrainte règne__ Je n'ai pas travaillé à mon verre
   depuis que tu es venu ici et n'ai pas grande envie.

Probablement une autre at terre me permettra d'avoir un peu plus
   d'entrain__

Ne parle pas à ma famille de ce départ, que je ne veux annoncer que du
   bateau__ En même temps qu'à toi j'écrirai à Rouen et à Puteaux. Mon
   intention très vague est de rester longtemps là bas, plusieurs années
   vraisemblablement__ c-à-d. au fond couper entièrement avec eet cette
   partie ci du monde__

Tu pourrais avoir envie de venir à Buenos Aires__ Peut être t'y verrai je
   plus tôt que nous ne le croyons tous les deux.

= **Suzanne** Duchamp
and **Yvonne** Chastel

Large Glass [cat. 2]

— Ce soir je viens de poser [pour] une petite scène de blessé soigné par une
superbe nurse dans un film de Perret qui s'appelle : <u>Lafayette, we come</u>.
Si par hasard ce film est donné à Paris va le voir uniquement pour ma
petite scène de 2 minutes.

Yvonne espère pouvoir arranger ses affaires avec ta maison qui a un
correspondant à Buenos Aires, de sorte qu'elle est je crois contente de
voir un soleil un peu moins humide que celui de N.Y.__

Je vais chercher des leçons de français là-bas, car je n'espère pas trouver
d'amateurs d'art moderne et n'ai pas l'intention d'exhibiter quoique
probablement le pays doive être amusant à cultiver dans ce sens__

J'emporte tous mes papiers pour travailler à mon verre pour finir sur
papier tous les dessins__ de sorte que si un jour je repasse par N.Y. je
pourrai finir assez rapidement cette grande saloperie.__

Au revoir, vieux. embrasse Suzanne pour moi dis lui mes excuses de ne lui
avoir pas écrit, prends en ta part__

Quand tu me reverras, j'aurai beaucoup changé!

           très affectueusement à vous deux.

           Marcel

*En principe tu peux écrire Poste Restante Buenos Aires__ J'irai de temps en
temps à la poste dans les premiers temps jusqu'à ce que j'aie une adresse
fixe que je puisse t'envoyer__*

La Fayette! We come!,
by Léonce Perret, 1918
(1800 meters).

Jean Crotti has a
business involved with
the sale of coal.

*The Bride Stripped
Bare...* [cat. 1]

▷ TRANSLATION: *N.Y. 8th July. 33 W. 67. My dear Jean, Yvonne has written to you
and you'll have got the cable saying that I was leaving (and probably Yvonne, too)
for Buenos Aires. Several reasons you already know about. Nothing serious, just a
sort of fatigue on the part of the A's. Probably been engineered this way by spiteful
people. I saw Lou recently who was very sweet. Walter has just lost his mother. He's
in Pittsburgh and I haven't seen him for a month. I've finished the large panel for
Miss Dreier and started afresh on something else more interesting, also for her. Do
you remember those rubber bathing caps that come in all colors? I bought some, cut
them up into uneven little strips, stuck them together, not flat, in the middle of my
studio (in the air) and attached them with string to the various walls and nails in
my studio. It looks like a kind of multicolored spider's web. [sketch captions: colors;
colors; red; green; blue] I've almost got it finished. If everything goes the way I hope
it will, there's a ship sailing on 3rd August, and then another around 14th August.
If the ship of 4th August is not requisitioned by the United States, we should be on
it. It's a lot cheaper: $200 to Buenos Aires direct. The other one goes through
Panama, the Pacific and Valparaiso, Chile, then we would take a train across to
Buenos Aires taking 2 days. The second option is more expensive, the trip costing
almost $400. The first takes 27 days. The second takes 21, train included. From the
boat, I'll drop you a line letting you know we've left N.Y. and how! We got
Suzanne's cable and Yvonne, I think, is glad to be leaving, for, as you rightly ob-*

served, things are much changed here, atmosphere and everything. Constraint the order of the day. I haven't worked on my glass since you came and haven't much felt like it. Don't speak to my family about my leaving. I only want to tell them from on the boat. At the same time as writing to you, I'll also write to Rouen and Puteaux. My plan, as yet very vague, is to stay there for a long time, several years probably, i.e. really make a clean break with this part of the world. You might feel like coming to Buenos Aires. Perhaps I'll see you sooner than either of us think. This evening, I've just acted a short scene as a wounded man being tended by a superb nurse in a film by Perret called Lafayette, we come. *If, by any chance, this film gets shown in Paris, go and see it just for my little 2-minute scene. Yvonne hopes to be able to sort out her business with your company, with it having a correspondent in Buenos Aires, and is, I think, looking forward to seeing a less watery sun than in N.Y. I will try to give some French lessons over there, as I don't expect to find modern-art lovers and have no intention of exhibiting anything, although it would no doubt be an entertaining country to cultivate in that sense. I'm taking with me all my papers for working on the glass so I can finish, on paper, all the drawings, so that if, one day, I stop by N.Y., I'll be able to have done quite quickly with this big piece of trash. Farewell, old man. Give my love to Suzanne and apologize to her on my behalf for not having written—you can take your share of the blame. The next time you see me, I will have changed a lot! Very affectionately to you both, Marcel. In theory, you can write Poste Restante Buenos Aires. I'll go to the Post Office from time to time in the beginning until I've got a proper address I can send you.*

20. Marcel Duchamp to Henri-Pierre Roché[*]   autograph letter
[11 August 1918], New York   collection HRHRC

> N. Y. 33 W. 67. Dimanche
>   Mon cher vieux
> Mon bateau pour B. A. part mardi matin très probablement
> Donc ceci sont mes adieux. Peut être la mission t'enverra en Argentine et
>   là nous nous reverrons.
> Je m'éloigne encore, ça devient une manie chez moi.
> J'ai laissé *pour toi* chez Walter sur le balcon, le tableau d'Eilsheimius et un
>   paquet de Blindmen et autres dessins de Béa que je te demande de lui
>   remettre quand tu la verras__ (en même *temps* que tu l'embrasses au
>   revoir pour moi)
> Good bye dear, à bientôt dans 2 ans__ ou moins.
>   Affectueux Marcel__
> Poste Restante
> Buenos Aires.

Louis Michel **Eilshemius** (1864-1941), American painter whose work MD discovered at the Independents, 1917.

The Blindman, review edited by MD, Roché and Beatrice Wood (**Béa**, see p.222), appeared in 2 issues only: April and May 1917.

▷ TRANSLATION: *N.Y. 33 W. 67, Sunday. Hello old man. My ship sails for Buenos Aires Tuesday morning, most probably. So I'll say my adieus. Perhaps the mission will send you to Argentina and it'll be there that we'll meet up. Off I go again, it's getting to be a habit. I've left for you at Walter's, on the balcony, the Eilsheimius*

---

* **Henri-Pierre Roché** (1879-1959) was one of Marcel Duchamp's closest friends. From the time they met in New York during the years of World War I and throughout their lives they remained in almost continuous contact. Roché was an author and art critic in Paris; equipped with an innate intelligence and natural charm, he formed easy friendships with the most important Parisian artists and writers of his day (Gertrude Stein once called him "a general introducer"). In 1916, he was sent to New York on a diplomatic mission, and within a few weeks, he met Duchamp at a dinner in the Brevoort Hotel. They later attended a fancy costume ball, where Roché thought that Duchamp was so naturally victorious (probably in his ability to attract young women) that he started calling him "Victor," a name eventually shortened affectionately to "Totor." Through Duchamp, Roché met Beatrice Wood and, for about a year, the three were inseparable, a sort of *ménage à trois* that bonded them in friendship for life. Under the code name P.B.T. ("P" = Pierre; "B" = Beatrice; "T" = Totor), they published *The Blind Man*, the second and last issue of a magazine that was devoted to the defense of Richard Mutt's rejected *Fountain*. After a three-year stint in New York, Roché was back in Paris, and when Duchamp returned in 1923, their exploits as bachelors continued. In 1926, they formed a partnership in the ownership of works by Brancusi (p.90) that they purchased from the estate of John Quinn (p.42), and Roché would often assist Duchamp in financing his various artistic ventures, such as the manufacture of his *rotoreliefs* (1935) and the production of his *valise* (1941). During the last decades of his life, Roché became a celebrated author, publishing two novels (1953, 1956) that were made into films by François Truffaut. He welcomed the opportunity to write about Duchamp, and did so in a series of articles (1953-1955), including one where he perceptively observed: "His [Duchamp's] finest work is his use of time." Roché died at the age of 79 in 1959, leaving unfinished the manuscript for a third novel that he wanted to call *Victor*, which, as its title suggests, was based on his lifelong friendship with Duchamp.

picture and a batch of Blindmen *and various drawings of Béa's which I would like you to give back to her when you see her (and kiss her goodbye for me at the same time). Good bye dear, see you soon, in two years' time or less. Yours affectionately, Marcel. Poste Restante. Buenos Aires.*

---

21. Marcel Duchamp to Francis Picabia*   autograph letter
13 August [1918], New York   collection BLJD

N.Y. 13 Aout
    Je pars demain pour Buenos Aires pour un an ou 2, sans mission, sans connaitre personne là bas—
C'est une suite à notre conservation de l'année dernière.
Tachez de venir—
Je ne vous *ai* pas écrit du tout, j'ai reçu des cartes postales de vous.
Que faites vous? Etes vous tous deux en Suisse pouvez vous voyager.
Ici, rien, Varèse est un homme rangé qui va réussir l'hiver prochain. Plus de Brevoort.
Tout est changé et [il y a] moins moyen de s'amuser—
Arensberg n'a pas écrit un mot depuis 391.
Je n'ai pas vu Stieglitz

Edgard Varèse (1883-1965), vanguard French composer, moved to NY during the war.

Hotel Brevoort, Greenwich Village, favorite gathering place for French artists and writers during the war.

391, ephemeral magazine (19 issues, 1917 - 1924) published by Francis Picabia.

Alfred Stieglitz, see p.109.

---

* **Francis Picabia** (1879-1953) French-born Cuban pioneer of abstract painting. Picabia and Duchamp met in Paris in 1910 or 1911. After Picabia returned from his first trip to the United States in 1913 (to attend the Armory Show), he convinced Duchamp that the art of the future was in New York. When Duchamp arrived in America during the summer of 1915, Picabia and his wife Gabrielle Buffet were already there (having arrived only a few days earlier). It was during this trip that Picabia forged his so-called machinist style, an art based on the most recent advancements in machine technology (which, it could be argued, had been anticipated by Duchamp's depiction of an ordinary chocolate grinder two years earlier). Their camaraderie intensified when they engaged in a number of wild escapades together during the time of Picabia's third and last visit to the United States in 1917. To variant degrees, they participated in Dada activities in New York and Paris during and just after the years of World War I, and even after Duchamp ceased his own artistic production, he continued to consider Picabia an important painter. After his father's death in 1925, Duchamp invested a portion of his inheritance in paintings by Picabia, works that he purchased directly from the artist. These paintings—which reflected various periods in Picabia's artistic development—sold in a very successful public auction at the Hotel Drouet in 1926. Duchamp always held his colleague's work in high regard, in part, because Picabia refused to adhere to a single style. *"He could be called the greatest exponent of freedom in art,"* Duchamp wrote in 1949, *"not only against academic slavery, but also against slavery to any given dogma."* Picabia died at his home in Paris in 1953, exactly one week before his two-person show with Duchamp was scheduled to open at the Rose Fried Gallery in New York. Duchamp sent a telegram to his old friend, saying only: *"See you soon."*

De Zayas quelquefois—

J'ai travaillé un peu.

Rien fini—

J'aimerais bien rejouer aux échecs avec vous.

Venez là bas tous les deux et si on s'y embête on trouvera bien une île.

L'avantage c'est que c'est loin. Je ne vous vois pas très bien à Gstaad depuis
    1 an presque.

Il y a des potins je ne les sais pas— Roché est le mieux informé il est à
    Washington définitivement

    Au revoir très affectueusement à tous deux.

    Marcel Duchamp

Les Gleizes ont envie de descendre à B.A.

Regardez les lignes d'Espagne— Ce n'est pas très long—

Je reste 27 jours en mer—

*J'ai vu Bordelongue à son passage à N.Y. pour la France— Il doit rester peu
    de temps à Paris et revenir.*

Marius de Zayas (1880-1961), Mexican caricaturist, director of The Modern Gallery, 500 Fifth Avenue, Manhattan (where Picabia was given a show in 1916).

Gstaad, Switzerland, where the Picabias are living.

▷ TRANSLATION: *N.Y. 13th August. I leave tomorrow for Buenos Aires for a year or 2, with no particular goal and without knowing a soul over there. It's a follow-up to our conversation last year. Try to come over. I did not write to you once. I received postcards from you. What are you up to? Are you both in Switzerland? Can you travel? Here, nothing. Varèse is a steady chap, he's going to make it next winter. No more Brevoort. Everything has changed and there's less fun to be had. Arensberg has not written a single line since 391. I haven't seen Stieglitz. De Zayas occasionally. I've worked a little bit. Finished nothing. I would really like to play chess with you again. Come over, both of you and if we get fed up we'll find ourselves an island. The good thing is, it's far away. You haven't seemed happy to me in Gstaad for almost a year. There is gossip, I'm not in on it. Roché is the most clued up and he's in Washington for good. Farewell, very affectionately to you both, Marcel Duchamp. The Gleizeses want to go down to B.A. Have a look at the shipping lines out of Spain. It doesn't take very long. I'll be at sea for 27 days. I saw Bordelongue passing through New York on his way to France. He's to stop in Paris for a short time and come back.*

14 August 1918
Duchamp and Yvonne Crotti, recently divorced from Jean Crotti, set out for Buenos Aires aboard the S.S. "Crofton Hall." Duchamp takes with him the notes he has compiled for the *Large Glass* [cat. 2].

Buenos Aires | 1918-1919

aboard ship for Argentina on the "Crofton Hall" | 14 Aug 1918
lives in Buenos Aires, at 1743 Alsina, with Yvonne Chastel
has a studio at 1507 Sarmiento

from 14 August 1918 to 22 June 1919

▶   MAJOR WORKS

To Be Looked at…(oil, silver leaf, lead wire and
   magnifying lens on glass, 1918)
Handmade Stereopticon Slide (pencil on
   photographic stereopticon slide, 1918-19)
Chess Pieces (set of wooden chess pieces,
   1918-19)
Unhappy Readymade (assisted readymade:
   geometry textbook, 1919)

▶   EXHIBITION

The Evolution of French Art, Arden Gallery, New York
   City. By MD: *Nude Descending a Staircase*;
   Combat de boxe; *The King and the Queen*
   — **29 Apr - 24 May 1919**

22. Marcel Duchamp to Louise and Walter Arensberg   autograph letter
[circa 21 August 1918], aboard ship for Buenos Aires (posted from Barbados)   collection PMA

on board S.S. "Crofton Hall"
NORTON LINE

    Chers Walter Lou
En route depuis une semaine. Ce petit mot repartira pour New York de
    Barbados le 23— *(on s'y arrête quelques heures pour charbon)*
La mer est très calme, et on ne me donne ~~que~~ de la lumière le soir que dans
    une smoking room très chaude et pas aérée à cause des sous marins—
On a vaguement parlé il y a 3 jours d'un oil tanker qu'un sous marin aurait
    fait sauter à quelques miles de nous en face Atlantic City— Mais je n'ai
    rien vu—
Pas d'échecs, personne pour jouer—
Je travaille avec mes papiers que j'arrange.
Vous cablerai de Buenos Aires dès arrivé (14 Septembre environ)
Pas de mal de mer encore—
    Affectueusement à tous deux
    Marcel
    Envoyé de Barbados 24 Août très chaud

▷ TRANSLATION: *Dears Walter/Lou, Under way for a week now. These few lines will
leave for New York from Barbados on the 23rd. (We are stopping there for a few
hours for coal). The sea is very calm, and in the evenings, they only let me have light
in a smoking room that is very hot and stuffy, on account of the submarines. There
was some talk three days ago about an oil tanker said to have been blown up a few
miles from us not far from Atlantic City. I didn't see a thing. No chess, nobody to
play. I'm working on my papers, sorting them out. Will wire you from Buenos Aires
moment I arrive (14th September approximately). Not seasick yet. Affectionately
to you both, Marcel. From Barbados, 24th August, very hot.*

9 September 1918
After three weeks at sea, the S.S. "Crofton Hall"
finally arrives safely in Buenos Aires.
Duchamp and Yvonne immediately begin searching
for a studio and a place to live.

---

23. Marcel Duchamp to Carrie, Ettie and Florine Stettheimer   autograph letter
20 September [1918], Buenos Aires   collection YCAL

N'ai pas d'adresse fixe. Ecrivez Poste Restante

Buenos Aires

20 septembre__

    Chères 3 sœurs,

un télégramme plutôt qu'une lettre *car* j'apprends qu'un bateau part
    demain pour New York.

Depuis 5 jours ici, content en général, ne connais rien ni personne, pas
    même un mot d'espagnol, amusant quand même. Cherche un
    appartement pour travailler.

Tous ces hommes noirs et ces femmes noires n'ont rien qui me rappelle
    New York.

Ne croyez pas les gens qui vous disent que Buenos Aires est très cher.
    Beaucoup moins cher que New York.

Nourriture splendide, un beurre comme on n'en vend pas Columbus
    Avenue chère Carrie.

Des petites rues comme derrière la Madeleine à Paris__

Une grande avenue pas bien longue, aspect général européen.
    ("<u>Continental</u>").

Le voyage a été très "pericoloso" paraît il__ je ne m'en suis guère aperçu,
    excepté le soir où le manque absolu de lumière était gênant. L'équateur
    n'est pas très chaud même au mois d'Août

Printemps ici. J'aurai 2 étés cette année

A bientôt donc une plus longue lettre

Mes hommages à Madame Stettheimer

    très affectueusement à toutes.

    Marcel Duchamp

▷ TRANSLATION: *No fixed address. Write Poste Restante. Buenos Aires. 20th September. Dear 3 sisters, Telegram rather than letter as have just learnt a ship sailing for New York tomorrow. Been here for 5 days, content on the whole, know nothing and nobody, not a single word of Spanish, fun though. Looking for an apartment to work in. All these black men and black women make me realize I'm a long long way from New York. Don't believe people who tell you Buenos Aires is expensive. Much less expensive than New York. Wonderful food and butter like you can't get on Columbus Avenue, dear Carrie. Narrow streets like at the back of the Madeleine in Paris. One wide avenue, not very long, European style overall. ("Continental"). The trip was very "pericoloso," it would seem. I barely noticed, except for the evening when having no light whatsoever was a nuisance. The equator isn't very hot even in the month of August. Springtime here. I'll have two summers this year. I'll write at greater length very soon. My regards to Mrs Stettheimer. Very affectionately to you all, Marcel Duchamp.*

October 1918
Duchamp finds a studio at 1507 Sarmiento, and Yvonne moves into an apartment a few blocks away, at 1743 Alsina Street.

---

24. Marcel Duchamp to Louise and Walter Arensberg
8 November 1918, Buenos Aires

autograph letter
collection PMA

Buenos Aires.
8 novembre. 1918—
        Cher Walter. Chère Lou—
Déjà un vieux Buenos Airien! 2 mois ici. Connais la ville par cœur.— Très province très famille. La société très importante et très fermée; Pas d'Healys ou de Reisenwebers et encore moins de Follies—
L̶e̶ Au "Casino" = genre Arcade Building Theatre = on ne voit que des hommes— Les dames bien élevées ne vont pas à ces théatres gais (ô combien)— Pas de vie d'hôtels comme à N.Y. Le "Plaza" ici est un prétexte à réunions familiales du Dimanche pour la Croix Rouge de diverses nations.
Il y a bien l'odeur de paix qui est épatante à respirer et une tranquillité provinciale qui me permettent et forcent même à travailler— De sorte que j'ai loué une chambre loin du confort auquel je fus habitué 67me rue et j'y travaille.

33 W 67th St., NY.

J'ai commencé la partie g̶a̶u̶c̶h̶e̶ *droite* du Verre et j'espère que quelques mois vont me suffire pour terminer entièrement les dessins que je veux rapporter un jour à N.Y. pour finir le Verre—

MD refers to his little study on glass, *To Be Looked at...* [cat. 32].

Large Glass [cat. 2]

Je pense souvent à vous et à mes 3 bonnes années près de vous— Mon seul plaisir ici est de travailler, ce n'est pas plus mal qu'autre chose, pour un flemmard comme moi—
Mais les bonnes nouvelles m'enchantent
Hier 7 novembre— Nous avons eu la fausse nouvelle que l'armistice était signé— Aujourd'hui la nouvelle a été démentie—
Mais quand même, c'est une question de jours maintenant—
Et je pense à vous Walter, à tout ce que paix means to you. Et Allen, j'espère, ne connaitra pas la France.

Probably **Allen Norton** (c.1890-1944), poet, friend of W. Arensberg.

Vous avez sans doute appris à N.Y. déja la mort de mon frère Raymond— J'ai reçu ici un câble de ma famille vers le 27 octobre. C'est une chose affreuse car vous savez combien il m'était proche et cher—

MD's brother died of blood poisoning in a military hospital, Cannes, 9 Oct 1918.

J'ai écrit il y a quelques jours à Barzun lui demandant de réunir des toiles pour une exposition cubiste ici où les gens sont aussi bêtes

Henri-Martin Barzun (1881-1973), French poet MD knows from Puteaux.

qu'ignorants— Barzun vous en causera et dîtes bien à de Zayas, qui en somme serait le plus gros envoyeur, de choisir de bonnes choses, conseillez le même dans son choix. J'aimerais tant réunir 30 <u>bonnes</u> choses. J'ai trouvé des galeries ici, qui à cause de la nouveauté de la chose, donneraient les salles pour rien =

Comprenez bien que je vous demande de ne rien envoyer de vos toiles, car j'ai recommandé à Barzun qu'il ne soit envoyé que des choses à vendre— Il est très possible que ce soit un débouché important pour eux, les marchands.

Moi-même n'exposerai rien, selon mes principes.

(Il est entendu aussi, n'est-ce pas, que vous n'exposerez rien de moi, si vous tenez à me faire plaisir, au cas où on vous demanderait de prêter quelque chose à N.Y. Ceci entre parenthèses)—

Mes projets : si la guerre se termine, je resterai ici jusqu'en Juin Juillet. et pense partir en France à ce moment. J'y passerais quelques mois et reviendrais à New York ensuite.

Ce sont des projets!!

Un mot de vous me ferait plaisir, sur vos projets et sur ce que deviennent N.Y. et les amis.

Miss Dreier est ici depuis un mois. Elle s'occupe d'articles pour le Studio et différentes autres choses mais elle a à souffrir de la ville = Je veux dire Buenos Aires n'admet pas de femmes seules. C'est insensé, l'insolence et la bêtise des hommes ici—

Au revoir, chère Lou et cher Walter ne m'oubliez pas trop— Maintenant que les évènements guerriers se précipitent, le temps ne sera pas long avant que nous nous revoyions

très affectueusement à tous deux

Marcel

1507 Sarmiento

Buenos Aires Argentina

Katherine Dreier arrived in Buenos Aires 14 Sept 1918, with the intention of writing articles on Argentinian life.

▷ TRANSLATION: *Buenos Aires. 8th November 1918. Dear Walter, Dear Lou, Already a real Buenos Airean! Been here for 2 months. Know the town like the back of my hand. Very provinces, very family. Society life a big thing here and very closed: none of your Healys or your Reisenwebers and still less the Follies. At the "Casino" = Arcade Building Theater type of thing = nothing but men. Well brought-up ladies do not frequent such swinging places (and aren't they just!) No hotel scene like in N.Y. The "Plaza" here is just a place for family gatherings on a Sunday in aid of the Red Cross in various nations of the world. You can smell peace here and it's a joy to breathe it in and, with the tranquillity of the provinces, all this allows and also forces me to work. So much so that I have rented a room—a far cry from the comforts I was accustomed to in 67th Street and I am working. I have started the right side of the Glass and hope that a few months will suffice to conclude my work on the drawings that I want to bring back one day to N.Y. to finish the Glass. I think of you often and the three good years I spent with you. Working is my only pleasure here, it's no worse than anything else for a loafer like me. But I was delighted at the good news. Yesterday, 7th November, we were wrongly informed that the Armistice had been signed. Today the news has been refuted. But still, it's only a matter of days now. And I think of you, Walter, and all that peace means to you. And Allen, I hope, will not have to go through France. You have no doubt already learnt in N.Y. of the death of my brother Raymond. I had a cable from my family around 27th October. It's a really dreadful thing, for you know how close we were and how dear he was to me. I wrote to Barzun a few days ago asking him to get some canvases together for a Cubist exhibition here where the people are as stupid as they are ignorant. Barzun will give you the low-down, and make sure you tell de Zayas, who, in short, will be the largest supplier, to choose good things and you could even give him some guidance. I would really like to get together 30 good things. I have found galleries here which, because of the newness of the thing, would be prepared to let us have the rooms for free = Let me make it clear that I am not asking you to send any of your own canvases because I told Barzun that I think only things that are for sale should be sent. It could be a good break for them, the dealers. I will not exhibit anything myself, as is my principle. (It is also understood, naturally, that you will not exhibit anything of mine, if you don't mind, should anyone ask you to lend anything in N.Y. Just an aside). My plans: if the war ends, I shall stay here until June/July and then probably go to France at that point. I'd spend a few months there and then return to New York. That's the plan!! It would be good to hear from you, about your plans and what's going on in N.Y. and with friends. Miss Dreier has been here for a month. She takes care of articles for the Studio and various other things but this town is very hard for her, I mean women on their own are not accepted in Buenos Aires. It is crazy, the insolence and stupidity of the men here. So long dear Lou and dear Walter. Think of me from time to time. Now that the war is coming to a close, it won't be long before we see each other again. Very affectionately to you both, Marcel. 1507 Sarmiento. Buenos Aires. Argentina.*

---

25. Marcel Duchamp to Carrie, Ettie and Florine Stettheimer   autograph letter
12 November 1918, Buenos Aires   collection YCAL

Buenos Aires 12 novembre 1918
Ma chère Ettie
Merci de votre carte qui, quoique lointaine dans le temps et dans l'espace m'a replacé parmi vous à Bedford Hills.

Buenos Aires n'existe pas. Rien qu'une grande ville de province avec des gens très riches sans aucun goût, tout acheté en Europe, la pierre de leurs maisons comprise. On ne fabrique rien ici : de sorte que j'ai retrouvé des

The Stettheimers rented the Rupert Hughes Estate, **Bedford Hills**, NY, summer 1918.

pâtes dentifrices françaises que j'avais complètement oubliées à New York—

Pas de sorties le soir : les gens "bien" se voient entre eux, n'ont aucune envie de connaître d'autres personnes que celles de leurs habitudes—

Ils ont beaucoup d'arrogance dans leurs façons de faire. Ils pensent que New York est construit tout en or et respectent beaucoup les gens qui parlent anglais même mal.

Il y a une colonie anglaise

‑ ‑ ‑ ‑ ‑ ‑ ‑ ‑ ‑ ‑ américaine

‑ ‑ ‑ ‑ ‑ ‑ ‑ ‑ ‑ ‑ italienne

Il n'y a pas de colonie française. Les Français d'ici plus nombreux qu'à New York peut-être sont affreux à voir.

Les susdites colonies sont fermées.

La vie est moins chère qu'à New York— Une nourriture étonnante et saine (Je n'engraisse pas pour cela).

<u>Mais</u>. tout cela fait que j'ai travaillé et que je travaille avec plaisir. (La nuit beaucoup, et mes yeux ne me font pas mal) Je suis très heureux au fond, d'avoir trouvé cette vie différente entièrement = Je me sens un peu revenu à la campagne où on trouve du plaisir à travailler.

La ville, depuis 3 jours, n'arrête pas de "libationner", manifester, "démonstrationer"— Le jour de gloire est arrivé—

"V Day" = 11 Nov 1918, Armistice Day and end of World War I.

J'imagine ce que doit être New York en ce moment et, quoique je déteste ces manifestations, je sais que vous toutes les aimez et suis heureux que vous y participez. Si tôt...... Star Spangled banner ♫♪ etc.

Mes projets ?

J'ai écrit à Barzun de me faire envoyer une exposition cubiste pour le mois de Mai Juin prochain (~~ab~~ début de l'hiver ici)— Donc si cela se passe normalement, je resterais ici jusqu'en Juillet Août et peut être à ce moment là, repartirais je en France— pour quelques mois.

Retour à New York ensuite— Serez vous en Europe vers Aout Septembre— Si oui, je vous donne ici mon adresse familiale de sorte que si vous me "dropez" un mot je courrai vous voir n'importe où que vous soyez.

M. Duchamp

71 rue Jeanne d'Arc

<u>Rouen</u> Seine Inf. ^{re}

Maintenant, une très mauvaise nouvelle que vous savez déjà sans doute : mon frère Raymond est mort, à la suite de nombreuses rechutes, de son empoisonnement du sang qu'il avait traîné pendant 2 ans = C'est une chose terrible pour ma famille et pour moi—

Raymond Duchamp-Villon died 9 Oct, see p.64.

——————

Ma Chère Carrie,

    Avez vous continué votre maison de poupées? je ne dis pas : fini_

Ce serait une injure. Où en sont les tapissiers?

Mes maisons de poupée avancent aussi.

Loin des yeux, près du cœur; quoique vous en ayez dit souvent.

Voilà ce que je constate en ce moment_

Carrie working on her doll's house.

——————

Ma chère Florine peintresse du Roi.

    Rien ici; Pas même d'ateliers. Les peintres ici sont des jeunes gens

bien sages qui habitent dans leur famille et utilisent le grenier ou une

cour vitrée comme atelier_

Aucun peintre intéressant_ Règne de Zuloaga et d'Anglada Camarosa_

Galeries ridicules.

Au milieu de tout cela, je suis content parce que je travaille_

Vous envoie à toutes trois mes affectueux souvenirs et vous prie de

présenter à Madame Stettheimer mes respectueux hommages_

    Marcel Duchamp 1507 Sarmiento

    Buenos Aires

Je comprends un peu d'espagnol et le parle moins

Miss Dreier est venue ici. Ceci vous amusera sans doute. Elle prépare des

articles pour l'International Studio.

Florine working on her paintings.

*Ignacio **Zuloaga y Zaboleta** (1870-1945) and Hermenegildo **Anglada-Camarasa** (1873-1959), popular Spanish painters.*

▷ TRANSLATION: *Buenos Aires, 12th November 1918. My dear Ettie, Thank you for your card which, though far away in time and space, brought me back in your midst at Bedford Hills. Buenos Aires does not exist—just a large provincial town full of very rich people with absolutely no taste, and everything bought in Europe, right down to the stone they build their houses with. Nothing is manufactured here: to the extent that I found French toothpaste here I'd completely forgotten about in New York. No evenings out: "nice" people here keep to themselves and have no desire whatsoever to make the acquaintance of those outside their own circles. They are extremely arrogant in their ways. They think the streets of New York are paved with gold and have automatic respect for people who speak English, even badly. There's an English colony, there's an American colony, there's an Italian colony. There's no French colony. The French here, perhaps more numerous than in New York, revolting. The above-mentioned colonies are closed. It's cheaper here than in New York. Amazing food and healthy too (I'm not getting fat for that). But the result of all this is that I'm working and enjoying working (especially at night, and my eyes are not hurting). In actual fact, I am very happy to have found such a different way of life = It feels a bit like being back in the countryside where it is enjoyable to work. The city has not stopped "libationating," demonstrating, "demonstra-tionating" for 3 days. V day is here. I can imagine what New York must be like right now and, while I hate pageantry, I know you all like it and am glad you can join in. As soon as* Star spangled banner [sketch] *etc. My plans? I've written to Barzun to ask him to send me a Cubist exhibition for May/June (beginning of winter here). So, if all goes according to plan, I'll stay here until July/August and then perhaps go back to France for a few months. Then back to New York. Will you be in Europe around August/September? If so, I'll give you my family's address and if you "drop" me a line, I will rush to be by your side wherever you are: M. Duchamp, 71 rue Jeanne d'Arc, Rouen, Seine Inférieure.*

Now some very bad news which you probably already know about: my brother Raymond has died, following several relapses, of blood poisoning he'd been suffering from for two years = It's a most awful thing for my family and for myself.

My dear Carrie, Have you continued work on your doll's house? I didn't say finished, that would be an insult. How far have the upholsterers got? My doll's houses are also coming along. Out of sight, but very much on my mind, in spite of what you have often said. That's the way I see it right now.

My dear Florine, painteress to the King. Nothing here, not even studios. The painters here are all very well-behaved young people who live at home with their families and use the attic or a glassed-in courtyard as their studio. Not a single interesting painter. Zuloaga and Anglada Camarosa rule. Galleries ridiculous. Amidst all this, I am happy because I am working. I remember all of you with great affection and beg you to convey my regards to Mrs Stettheimer, Marcel Duchamp. 1507 Sarmiento, Buenos Aires. I am beginning to understand Spanish a bit, but speak it less. Miss Dreier is here. This will no doubt amuse you. She is writing articles for the International Studio.

---

26. Marcel Duchamp to Walter Pach　　　　　autograph letter
15 November [1918], Buenos Aires　　　　　collection AAA

Buenos Aires. 15 Novembre—
　　　Mon cher Walter, chère Magda.
Je reçois seulement il y a quelques jours, vos deux lettres et vous en
　　remercie bien—
Vous savez sans doute que notre cher Raymond est mort vers le 27
　　Octobre— Un cable de ma famille me l'a annoncé ici— Je sais que vous
　　en sentirez plus de douleur qu'aucun autre, je sais la profonde amitié et
　　admiration que vous aviez pour lui— Je n'ai pas eu de détails encore. Ç'a
　　dû être une agonie terrible après 2 ans de souffrances—
A côté de cela, la nouvelle de l'armistice a été la bonne nouvelle—
　　Démonstrations ici, parades etc. Buenos Aires est une grande ville de
　　province— et n'est pas intéressant. Il y a une ~~vill~~ vie calme de province
　　qui m'a changé et fait regretter New York. Mais j'y suis habitué
　　maintenant et je travaille beaucoup = J'ai emporté toutes mes notes
　　pour le verre de sorte que je puis le continuer ici et espère en finir les　　　*Large Glass* [cat. 2]
　　dessins. en quelques mois—

La gent "peintresse" n'a aucun intérêt__ Zuloagas et Anglada Camarosas : Tous élèves plus ou moins__

Quelques galeries importantes vendant cher et ferme__ Les quelques gens que j'ai rencontrés ont "entendu parler" de cubisme mais ignorent tout de ce que peut signifier mouvement moderne__

J'ai tout de suite pensé faire une exposition ici l'hiver prochain (qui, ici, commence en Mai-Juin)__ J'ai écrit à *H.M.* Barzun à N.Y. qui, par sa position indépendante, pourra réunir, j'espère, une ~~3~~ trentaine de bonnes choses__ Je lui dis de s'adresser à vous d'avoir votre avis, et je vous demande de l'aider un peu si votre temps vous le permet. Je lui ai envoyé une longue lettre avec tous détails : Comme il vous le dira sans doute, j'ai demandé des marchands-intermédiaires ou *des* peintres eux mêmes, l'encadrement de leurs choses, et le paiement de l'assurance *(aller et retour)* ce qui, en somme, n'est pas exagéré; le reste je m'arrangerai ici__ Voyez donc de Zayas qui sera le plus gros envoyeur et ~~et~~ décidez le à participer dans ces conditions à l'envoi.

Mes projets =

Je compte rester ici jusqu'à ~~Juin~~ Juillet après l'exposition si elle a lieu__ Et puis je repartirais en Europe vers cette époque__ où je resterais quelques mois et reviendrais à N.Y. ensuite.

Projets, projets__

En tout cas, je trouve inutile de partir en France maintenant__

Le réajustement à la paix demandera autant de temps (6 mois à un an) que ~~la~~ celui à la guerre__

Voilà, je suis content. en somme.

J'espère que Magda et le petit vont bien que vous avez retrouvé N.Y. avec plaisir et que votre hiver n'est pas trop dur__

Je vous écris les portes ouvertes. C'est l'été presque ici__ Moustiques et mouches en quantité__

Adieu. au revoir, à bientôt__

     très affectueusement à tous trois

     Marcel Duchamp

1507 Sarmiento

Buenos Aires

Spanish painters, see note on previous letter.

MD in fact leaves Argentina 22 June 1919 and stays mainly in Paris until 27 Dec.

▷ TRANSLATION: *Buenos Aires, 15th November. My dear Walter, dear Magda, I received only a few days ago your two letters and thank you very much. You will no doubt know that our dear Raymond died around 27th October. A cable from my family brought me the news here. I know that you will be more upset than anybody. I know what a true friend you were and what admiration you had for him. I don't have the details yet. He must have gone through terrible agony after 2 years of suffering. Aside from that, the good news is the armistice. Demonstrations here, parades etc. Buenos Aires is a large provincial town and is of no interest. Life is quiet and provincial which has been a big change for me and made me miss New York. But I'm used to it and working a lot. = I brought all my notes for the glass with me so that I can carry on with it here and hope to finish the drawings for it in a few months. The "painter species" is of no interest whatsoever. Zuloagas and Anglada Camarosas. All students, more or less. One or two galleries of significance, with sure sales and high prices. The few people I have met have "heard of" Cubism, but have no idea of the meaning of modern movement. I immediately thought of holding an exhibition here next winter (which starts in May/June here). I wrote to H.M. Barzun in N.Y. who, thanks to his independent position, I hope could get together thirty or so good things. I told him to get in touch with you and ask your opinion und I would be grateful if you could help him a little, your schedule permitting. I sent him a long letter with all details. As he will no doubt tell you, I've asked the go-between dealers or the painters themselves to frame their things and to take out insurance (round trip) which, all in all, is not too much to ask. I will take care of all the rest here. Go and see de Zayas who will be the largest contributor and convince him to send his things on these terms. My plans = I'm planning to stay here until June/July after the exhibition, if it takes place. And then I'll leave for Europe around that time, stay there for a few months and then come back to N.Y. Plans, plans. In any case, I see no point in going to France just now. Getting used to peacetime will take as long (6 months to a year) as it did to get used to the war. So there you are, I'm quite contented. On the whole. I hope that Magda and the little one are well and that you were pleased to get back to New York and that your winter is not too harsh. I have the doors open as I write. It's almost summer here. Mosquitoes and flies in abundance. Farewell, goodbye, so long. Very affectionately to all three, Marcel Duchamp. 1507 Sarmiento Buenos Aires.*

---

27. Marcel Duchamp to Louise Arensberg   autograph letter
7 and 10 January [1919], Buenos Aires   collection PMA

Buenos Aires. 7 Janvier.
    Chère Lou. J'ai reçu il y a quelque temps déja votre lettre datée 7 octobre et vous remercie de la lettre incluse—
J'ai été aussi très heureux d'apprendre quelques "happenings" de New York. et espère que vous avez un hiver pas trop rigoureux et beaucoup de théatre et musique—
Ici Noël et Jour de l'an par 90° de chaleur. sont une nouveauté. Je joins ici pour vous et Walter mes meilleurs souhaits—
Comme mes lettres vous l'ont indiqué, je travaille ici car il n'y a pas moyen de beaucoup s'amuser.
A part quelques tangos, il n'y a rien, ou alors le théatre avec troupes étrangères souvent françaises (qui me rappellent un peu trop que je comprends bien le français).

Je joue aux échecs seul pour l'instant; j'ai trouvé des revues dans lesquelles j'ai
découpé une quarantaine de parties de Capablanca que je vais to play over—

Je vais aussi probablement entrer au Chess Club d'ici, pour m'essayer de
nouveau.

Je me suis fait faire un "set" de tampons en caoutchouc (que j'ai dessinés)
avec lesquels je marque des parties. J'en envoie ici un exemplaire pour
Walter.

Par le même courrier, Walter recevra un tableau d'oculiste (avec lequel les
oculistes "test" les yeux). Je me suis servi de tableaux d'oculistes ces
temps derniers. Et j'espère que celui ci pourra servir à Walter.

Je reçois peu de nouvelles— De ma famille un peu— à cause de la mort de
mon frère—

Avez-vous vu Barzun, qui maintenant doit avoir ma lettre, à propo [sic]
d'une exposition possible ici. J'attend [sic] de ses nouvelles vers 15
Février—

Miss Dreier a passé ici 4 3 mois et pense repartir à New York en Février

Je compte rester ici jusqu'en Juin et ensuite partir en France. (Je vous
donne ici mon adresse en France au cas d'un évènement imprévu :

> M.D.
> 71 rue Jeanne d'Arc
> Rouen (S.I.)

Ne me laissez pas sans nouvelles de vous. Avez-vous l'intention de voyager
l'été prochain. J'aimerais vous voir à Paris.

J'imagine que Walter est devenu Champion d'échecs, et qu'Allen doit être
de retour du camp et lui sert d'entraineur.

A tous deux mes affectueuses amitiés et à bientôt.

Marcel Duchamp
1507 Sarmiento
Buenos aires

Marcel Duchamp
1507 Sarmiento
Buenos Aires

10 Janvier.

Avant de mettre la lettre à la poste, je reçois votre lettre du 5
Novembre.

Je suis vraiment navré de la mort de Schamberg et je me demande d'où
vient cette vague de mort. Apollinaire, j'ai appris de France, est mort de
la grippe il y a quelques mois déja.

Cuban **José Raul Capablanca** (1888-1942), world chess champion, 1921-1927.

See samples of **rubber stamps** on the two illustrations following.

One such **eye chart**, is preserved among the Arensberg Papers at the PMA.

"S.I." = Seine Inférieure (in Normandy).

Surely **Allen Norton**.

Morton Schamberg (1881-1918), painter, died 13 Oct 1918.

Guillaume Apollinaire (1880-1918), French poet, died 9 Nov 1918.

C'est désolant.

Non je n'ai pas vu Mina et Cravan. Je serais bien étonné qu'ils soient ici sans les avoir rencontrés

Charlie est très applaudi ici et j'ai revu plusieurs de ses anciens films et j'attends avec impatience Charlie in "Soldier's life".

Mes amitiés à Dr. Southard et regrets pour lui de n'avoir pas worn out son uniforme.

Amitiés aussi pour la jolie Béatrice que je verrai sans doute un jour ici sur l'écran.

    Affectueusement à tous deux

    Marcel

Toutes mes féliciltations pour votre français qui est excellent—

Mina and Cravan, see p.85.

"Soldier's life" must be Chaplin's *Shoulder Arms*, 20 Oct 1918.

Dr Elmer Ernest Southard (1876-1920) director of Boston Psychopathic Hospital, old college friend of Walter's.

"jolie Béatrice" = Beatrice Wood (p.222).

Red diagram (with red and black chess stamps) probably enclosed in letter:

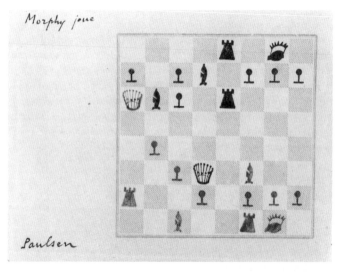

▷ TRANSLATION: *Buenos Aires, 7th January. Dear Lou, I received your letter dated 7th October some time ago now and thank you also for the enclosed letter. I was also very pleased to have news of "happenings" in New York and hope the winter's not too harsh your end and that you are getting plenty of theater and music. Here Christmas and New Year in 90° heat is something of a novelty. With this letter, I also send my very best wishes to you and Walter. As you can see from my letters, I am doing some work here as there isn't much in the way of entertainment. Apart from a few tango bars, there's nothing at all, or else the theater with its foreign companies, often French (a sorry reminder I actually speak the language). I play chess alone for the time being: I came across some magazines and cut out about 40 of Capablanca's games that I'm going to play over. I will probably also join the Chess Club here, to try my hand again. I've had a "set" of rubber stamps made (which I*

*designed) that I mark out games with. I'm sending a copy to Walter with this letter.
In the same mail, Walter will also receive an eye chart (the ones oculists use to
"test" eyes). I have been using eye charts lately and hope it will be of some use to
Walter. I don't get very much news. A little from my family on account of my brother's death. Have you seen Barzun? He must have my letter by now, regarding an
exhibition which might take place here. I'm expecting word from him around 15th
February. Miss Dreier has been here for 3 months now and is thinking of leaving
for New York in February. I plan to stay here until June and then leave for France.
(I'll give you my address in France now in case of anything unforeseen: M.D. 71
rue Jeanne d'Arc, Rouen (Seine Inférieure). Please send me your news soon. Do
you intend traveling next summer? I would love to see you in Paris. I expect Walter
has become a chess champion, and that Allen is back from camp to coach him.
Affectionately to you both, dear friends, and so long. [sketch] Marcel Duchamp. 1507
Sarmiento, Buenos Aires.*

*10th January. Before posting my letter, I have just received yours dated 5th No-
vember. I am really upset about the death of Schamberg and wonder where this
wave of death is coming from. Apollinaire, I heard from France, died of the flu several months ago now. It's so distressing. No, I haven't seen Mina and Cravan. I
would be really surprised they were here without my having seen them. Charlie is
much appreciated here and I have seen several of his old films again and can't wait
to see Charlie in "Soldier's life." My regards to Dr. Southard and apologies to him
for not having worn out his uniform. Best wishes also to the lovely Béatrice whom
I shall no doubt see on the screen one of these days. Affectionately to you both,
Marcel. My congratulations on your French which is really excellent.*

---

28. Marcel Duchamp to Carrie, Ettie and Florine Stettheimer   autograph letter
[circa 13 January 1919], Buenos Aires   collection YCAL

Buenos Aires.

Vous m'avez fait très plaisir, chère Florine avec votre longue lettre à
propos d'une exposition que je vous aurais aidé à détester.
Naturellement, je suis de votre avis― Anisfeld est un très mauvais   **Boris Anisfield** (1879-
peintre (je n'ai jamais vu son nom ni sa peinture). Il n'arrivera à la   1973), Russian painter
célébrité que s'il peint 3 000 autres peintures du même genre―   active in US.
  " A toutes les trois j'envoie mes meilleurs souhaits pour l'année
  19 (répété 2 fois) que nous appellerons l'année de délivrance par les
  Américains. „
Ceci dit (pour qu'au moins vous ne me reprochiez pas mon indifférence
  vis à vis du temps).
13 janvier― Je crains bien que vous ne me remplaciez pas et ceci est ennuyeux
  pour votre français : mais pourquoi n'écrivez[-vous] pas en français.
  Surtout Carrie qui a tant écrit à ses "poilus filleuls" pourrait bien
  s'amuser à me dire en excellent français ce que l'Amérique a fait dans

cette guerre et ses espoirs dans la victoire finale etc etc. (comme il y a un an).

Le diner dont vous me parlez j'y ai un peu assisté avec votre lettre : je vois Sidès et Nadelman rivalisant à qui danserait le plus souvent avec Ettie à la fin de la soirée_

Dites je vous prie à Carl *V. Vcht.* que je m'occupe de lui trouver des photos et que je *les* lui enverrai très bientôt.

Je passe mes nuits à travailler et à jouer aux échecs. Tout comme à N.Y.

J'ai peu ou pas d'amis

Le beurre continue à être bon_ mais on s'y habitue

90° pour Noël et Jour de l'an.

Les soldats ici sont habillés à l'Allemande. de sorte qu'une de mes premières impressions ici a été de me croire prisonnier de guerre_

(Quoique la conférence de la paix ne soit pas encore "actually" commencée. je me transporte avec cette lettre près de vous :

" Dans quelques jours les dernières questions vont être réglées. La paix avec l'Allemagne a été signée il y a 3 semaines déjà et la Ligue des Nations sera scellée quand l'Angleterre aura fini de réserver ses réponses. Mais l'esprit de la conférence est excellent et je crois qu'avec ce second voyage de Wilson (arrivé pour la seconde fois en France la semaine dernière) tout va être terminé (POUR CINQUANTE ANS) et nous pourrons jouir en paix de l'équilibre d'une Europe en petits morceaux. „

———

Ma chère Ett

Avez vous entendu parler de "ready mades"_?

Sinon adressez vous à Roché pour l'information.

L'article *de la Tribune* si rigolo dont vous me parlez est un "Ready made."_ Je l'ai signé mais pas écrit_ Je regrette de n'avoir pas gardé quelques autres articles du même genre qui vous auraient bien amusée.

Besides which, je n'ai jamais eu de cheveux ondulés (excepté à l'âge de 5 ans) et votre lotion me manque ici.

your immune baby

———

Et la maison de poupée : à quelle pièce en sommes nous chère Carrie?

Rez de chaussée, ascenseur, ou premier étage? a t elle été peinte extérieurement?

Une photo de l'état de la construction me ferait plaisir_

Qu'allez vous faire de tous vos filleuls? Maintenant. Allez vous les lâcher dans la paix? C'est une question grave à décider, âme compatissante!

Alfredo Sidès, Lebanese rug salesman, a regular at soirées at both the Stettheimer and the Arensberg apartments.

Elie Nadelman (1882-1946), Polish-born sculptor, emigrated to US in 1914.

Carl V. Vcht = Carl Van Vechten (1880-1964), music critic and novelist turned photographer, literary associate of Arensberg's.

Thomas Woodrow Wilson (1856-1924), US President 1913-1921.

"Ett" = Ettie Stettheimer.

"The Nude-Descending-a Staircase Man Surveys Us," written by Henry McBride, *The New York Tribune*, 12 Sept 1915, p.2.

Je regrette de n'être plus là pour trouver les formules (qui n'étaient jamais exactement l'expression de votre pensée, mais enfin!) par lesquelles vous les avez réconfortés. C'était bien amusant quelquefois.

Irez vous en Europe cet été?

Moi j'y serai vers juillet et pense rester seulement quelques mois là bas.

Je retournerai ensuite travailler à N.Y.

Vous ai je déjà donné mon adresse en France? je crois que oui. Ecrivez moi là à partir de juillet

      M.D. 71 rue Jeanne d'Arc

      Rouen.

Et votre nouveau chauffeur : Quel genre?

Vous êtes contente de lui et la maison marche bien. La poissonnerie de Columbus Ave est toujours bien achalandée?

Je vous prie de transmettre à Madame Stettheimer l'expression de mes meilleurs vœux de nouvelle année

      Affectueusement à toutes trois

      Duch'

1507 Sarmiento

Buenos Aires.

▷ TRANSLATION: *Buenos Aires. I was so pleased, dear Florine, to get your long letter about an exhibition I apparently helped you to hate. Naturally I am of the same opinion as yourself. Anisfield is a very bad painter (I have never seen either his name or his painting). He will have to paint another 3,000 paintings of the same kind if he is to achieve fame. "To all three of you, I send my best wishes for 19 (twice over), the year of deliverance for Americans." This said (so that at least you don't reproach me for my indifference about our times), 13th January. I'm rather worried you're not finding anyone to take my place and this is unfortunate for your French: but why not write to me in French? Carrie, especially, who has written so many letters to her "hairy godsons," might find it quite enjoyable to write and tell me in excellent French what America did during the war and what her hopes are for the final victory etc. etc. (like a year ago). The dinner you mention, I almost feel like I had been there through your letter: I can picture Sidès and Nadelman competing over who would have the most dances with Ettie at the end of the evening. Please tell Carl V. Vcht that I will see to finding photos for him and send them to him very soon. I spend my nights working and playing chess. Just like in N.Y. I have few or no friends. The butter is still good, but one gets used to it. 90° for Christmas and New Year's Day. The soldiers here are dressed like Germans so that one of my first impressions here was to feel like I was a prisoner of war. (Although the peace conference hasn't "actually" begun, with this letter I am transported to your side: "In a few days the final questions will be settled. Peace with Germany was signed three weeks ago already and the League of Nations will become official as soon as England stops stalling. But there is an excellent conference spirit and I think that with Wilson's second visit (he went to France for the second time last week) it will all be over (FOR FIFTY YEARS) and we will be able to enjoy in peace a stable Europe in little pieces." My dear Ett., Have you heard about "ready mades"? If not, ask Roché about them. That very funny article in the* Tribune *that you mention is a "Ready made." I signed it, but didn't write it. I'm sorry I didn't keep some other articles of the same type which you would have really enjoyed.* Besides which, I have never had wavy hair (apart from when I was 5) and I miss your lotion here, your immune baby. *And the doll's house: which room are we on, dear Carrie? Ground floor, elevator, or first floor? has it been painted on the outside? I would really like to have a photo of its current state of construction. What are you going to do with all your godsons—now? Are you going to leave them in peace time? It's a serious decision, compassionate soul you! I am sorry I am no longer there to find the words (which were never really the exact expression of your thoughts, but still!) you used to comfort them. It was quite fun sometimes. Will you go to Europe this summer? I will be there around July and expect to stay only a few months. I will then return to work in N.Y. Have I already given you my address in France? I think I did. Write to me there from July onwards: M.D. 71 rue Jeanne d'Arc, Rouen. And your new chauffeur: what like? Are you happy with him and is the house working out? Is the fishmonger's on Columbus Avenue still as well stocked? Please convey to Mrs Stettheimer my very best wishes for the new year. Affectionately to all three of you. Duch'. 1507 Sarmiento, Buenos Aires.*

---

29. Marcel Duchamp to Louise and Walter Arensberg   autograph letter
End-March 1919, Buenos Aires   collection PMA

Buenos Aires. fin Mars —19.

Chère Lou, Cher Walter, Il y a longtemps que j'ai reçu votre lettre contenant le chèque que vous avez été si gentils de me faire parvenir. Je vous ai câblé immédiatement, accusant réception de la lettre et répondant à votre "exhibit or not exhibit„ ultimatum— Je pense que maintenant l'exposition est ouverte et serais heureux que vous me donniez quelques détails amusants sur l'accueil fait à cette officialisation du cubisme.

Comme vous le savez j'avais trouvé des galeries ici où une exposition aurait pu avoir lieu. Mais l'indifférence de Gleizes et Barzun dont je n'ai ai eu aucune nouvelles (*et* à qui j'ai câblé en Février) me font penser qu'elle n'aura pas lieu— L'idée de De Zayas est possible mais il faudrait que je voie les officiels d'ici et je le ferai volontiers (ayant de bonnes "connections" pour leur être présenté convenablement)— Dans le cas où l'idée de faire une *F suivre l*'exposition ici, continuerait, faites moi câbler par De Zayas des instructions. J'irais voir les officiels et ni vous tiendrais au courant. Mais dans tous les cas mon impression est que personne ici ne voudra aider pécuniairement et que les chances de ventes sont infinitésimales.

"The Evolution of French Art," Arden Gallery, NY, 29 Apr - 24 May 1919. MD will show three works, *Nude Descending No. 1* [cat. 16], *Boxing Match* [cat. 24], *King and Queen... (on paper)* [cat. 18].

J'ai l'intention de quitter B.A. en Juin (première partie de Juin)— Donc
mes démarches ne pourraient aboutir qu'à mettre de Zayas ou autres
officiels en rapport avec ceux de~~ici. et~~

En plus, les meilleurs mois ici sont Juin Juillet et Août—

— Je fais des échecs en masse. Je fais partie du Club ici où il y a de très forts
joueurs classés par catégories. Je n'ai pas eu l'honneur d'être classé encore
et je joue avec différents joueurs de 2me catégorie et 3me perdant et
gagnant de temps en temps.

Je prends des leçons d'échecs avec le meilleur joueur du club qui enseigne
admirablement et me fait faire des progrès "théoriques"—

Donc j'avais pensé qu'à mon retour en France je pourrais peut-être jouer
par câble avec Walter—

~~Si~~ J'ai trouvé dans un livre, la f manière de jouer par câble réduisant les
frais ~~tél~~ d'envoi—

Je vous en fais une description et vous demande de garder ce papier jusqu'à
Juillet— Si vous receviez un cable bizarre de France, ce serait le début
d'une partie d'échecs.

— Nous jouerons deux parties simultanées. Dans mon premier
télégramme j'enverrai mon premier coup de la première partie par
exemple :

~~P4R PK4~~ sera cablé :

    one GEGO

Walter me répondra sa réponse comme suit :

    one SESOFEFO.

Ce qui veut dire 1er coup des Noirs *(Walter)* de la première partie est
SESO (P4R). et qu'il joue FEFO *PQ4* comme premier coup de la 2me
partie. (ayant les Blancs).

Je crois indispensable de mettre le numéro one, two, three etc, indiquant
à quel coup on est et évitant les erreurs.

(On a droit à un mot de 8 lettres; c'est sur cette base qu'a été construit ce
système de transmission).

Avant d'envoyer je m'informerai si la censure permet l'envoi de cette
littérature par câble.

Cette notation est la notation Gringmuth.

Notation introduced
in the 19th century by
D.A. Gringmuth of
St. Petersburg.

— Voici une adresse *à Paris* où vous pourrez toujours m'envoyer les câbles :

    Duchamp

    ~~22, rue Cond~~

    22 rue Lacondamine Paris

Quant au reste, je travaille— Il a fait très chaud, et maintenant l'indian
Summer est merveilleux.

Miss Dreier a été retardée pour son retour. Son bateau *Le Vauban* part le
3 avril et vous apportera probablement cette lettre. Elle vous racontera
probablement les côtés amusants de B.A.

Au revoir donc, à bientôt; dans 6 ou 8 mois je pense être à New York.

Je viens de recevoir le magazine de Man Ray TNT, que j'ai enjoyed very
much. J'ai beaucoup aimé la composition de Walter qui, j'espère,
continue à produire quelques bonnes choses comme ça, les seules qu'on
puisse lire aujourd'hui. (Les autres sont littérature).

Remerciez Man Ray de m'avoir reproduit le dessin; j'ai l'intention de lui
envoyer un petit mot.

> *TNT* (Mar 1919), ed. by Man Ray and Adolf Wolff, published Arensberg's "Vacuum Tires: A Formula for the Digestion of Figments," and MD's *Boxing Match* [cat. 24].

    Affectueusement à tous deux Marcel.

1507 Sarmiento B.A.

———

[Enclosure:]

Pour "castles"— indiquer seulement le déplacement du Roi
par exemple : GAKA
      ou GADA
      ou SAWA
      ou SAPA

▷ TRANSLATION: *Buenos Aires, end March '19. Dear Lou, dear Walter, It's already
some time since I received your last letter with the check you so kindly sent me. I
wired you immediately, acknowledging receipt of the letter and to reply to your "ex-*

hibit or not exhibit" ultimatum. I think the exhibition must be open by now and I would be amused to hear how this officialization of Cubism actually went down. As you know, I have found galleries here where an exhibition could be held. But Gleizes and Barzun are so indifferent, I have no word (and I sent a cable in February), it makes me think it will not happen. De Zayas' idea is a possiblility, but I would need to see the officials here and would do so with pleasure (having the right "connections" to be properly introduced). If the idea of bringing the exhibition over here still applies, have instructions cabled to me through de Zayas. I could go and see the officials and keep you posted. But in any case, my impression is that nobody here would be willing to help financially and that the chances of selling anything are microscopic. I plan to leave Buenos Aires in June (first part of June), so the most I could do now would be to put de Zayas or other officials in touch with the ones over here. What's more, the best months here are June, July and August. I'm playing chess in a big way. I'm a member of the Club here where there are some very good players ranked according to their standard. I haven't had the honor of being ranked yet and play with various players in Categories 2 and 3, losing and winning every now and then. I'm taking chess lessons with the best player in the club who is a wonderful teacher and makes me make "theoretical" progress. So I've been thinking that after I return to France I could play by cable with Walter. I read it in a book—how to play by cable without incurring huge cable costs. I'll write it down for you and ask you to keep it until July. If you get a strange cable from France, it'll be the opening of a game of chess. We will play two games simultaneously. In my first telegram, I will send my first move in the first game, for example: PK4 will be wired: one GEGO. Walter will send me his reply as follows: one SESOFEFO, which means the first move of the Blacks (Walter) in the first game is SESO (PK4) and that his first move in the second game is FEFO PQ4 (he has the Whites). I think it imperative to specify numbers one, two, three, etc, indicating exact position to avoid errors. (An 8-letter word is the maximum we are allowed, that is how the transmission system was designed). Before I send it, I will find out whether sending literature of this kind by cable is permitted by the censors. This system of notation is the Gringmuth notation system. You can send me these cables in Paris at this address: Duchamp, 22 rue Lacondamine, Paris. Apart from that, I am working. It has been very hot, and now the Indian summer is marvelous. Miss Dreier has been held up in her plans to go back. Her ship, Le Vauban, is leaving on 3rd April and will probably also bring you this letter. She will no doubt give you her version of the more amusing side to B.A. So long then, for now at least; in 6 to 8 months I expect to be in New York. I have just received Man Ray's magazine TNT, which I enjoyed very much. I very much liked Walter's piece and I trust he will go on producing good things like that, the only thing you can actually read these days. (The rest is literature). Do thank Man Ray for having reproduced the drawing—I will be dropping him a line. Affectionately to you both, Marcel. 1507 Sarmiento Buenos Aires. [sketch] *For "castles," specify only the King's move. For example GAKA or GADA or SAWA or SAPA.*

30. Marcel Duchamp to Carrie, Ettie and Florine Stettheimer   autograph letter
3 May [1919], Buenos Aires   Estate of Joseph Solomon

Buenos Aires 3 mai.
    Dear three.
Il y a bien longtemps que je veux vous écrire; mais je n'en trouve pas le
    temps tellement les échecs absorbent mon attention. Je joue jour et nuit
    et rien ne m'intéresse dans le monde plus que de trouver le coup juste.
Aussi pardonnez à un pauvre idiot, maniaque. Je vous sais assez bonnes
    pour pardonner⸺
Rien ne se passe ici de transcendental; des grèves, beaucoup de grèves, le
    peuple bouge.
La peinture me plaît de moins en moins⸺
Je ne vous demanderai même pas ce que vous pensez de votre Mr. Wilson
J'ai rencontré ici un certain Robert C. Brown dont vous connaissez peut-
    être le nom, Ettie; il faisait partie de la Bande Max Eastman et écrivait
    dans le temps. Nous causons de New York
En résumé rien à vous dire qui puisse vous amuser⸺ Je quitte B.A. le 15
    Juin pour la France⸺ sur un bateau anglais dont je ne sais pas encore le
    nom.
J'espère arriver là bas vers le 15 Juillet. embrasser ma famille pendant 2 ou
    3 mois et revenir à New York pour exécuter des dessins que j'ai faits ici.
J'aimerais tant recevoir de vos nouvelles mais naturellement "loin des yeux
    loin du cœur". Retenez cela (le professeur de français parle) c'est une
    excellente bromide.
Avez vous eu beaucoup de "diners" cet hiver. De nouvelles têtes
Ettie, vous me parliez de Lachaise dans votre dernière lettre; c'est un
    excellent sculpteur, au sens Nadelman du mot;
De plus un charmant garçon que je n'ai vu que 2 ou 3 fois. Il y a un côté
    foi dans sa sculpture avec lequel je suis en désaccord mais cela n'a pas
    d'importance
Généralement les sculpteurs et les musiciens ont ce côté religieux qui gâte,
    à mon point de vue, la manufacture de leurs œuvres. Silence et
    recueillement sont leurs mots d'ordre; quelque chose de grand va naître
    etc.
Et la maison de poupée? Je crois qu'elle sera bientôt terminée et que l'hiver
    prochain aura lieu la tombola à laquelle j'espère participer
Parlez moi Carrie, de l'ascenseur
Voyez vous Roché de temps en temps? Ou bien a t il cessé de vous plaire?
    Car vous êtes très difficiles. Et je puis m'estimer très heureux d'avoir pu
    ne pas vous déplaire ou vous fatiguer.
Et ce cher Leo Stein? Où en est il de ses investigations esthétiques?

Robert Carlton Brown (1886-1959), experimental poet contributing to *Others* and *The Blind Man* No.2

Max Eastman (1883-1969), editor of *The Masses* and *Liberator*.

Gaston Lachaise (1882-1935), French sculptor, emigrated to US during the war.

Leo Stein (1872-1946) collector, aesthetician and older brother of Gertrude Stein.

Je ne puis que vous poser des questions. Je n'ai autour de moi que des points d'interrogation.

Je voudrais bien aussi savoir quels "groupes" Florine a faits depuis mon départ.__ Le "groupe" est une excellente dénomination pour le genre de toiles que vous avez faites. Le groupe n'a rien de l'assommante "composition" et est mobile c.à.d. qu'au lieu de ne considérer que les différentes situations ~~dan~~ colorées ou formelles dans la toile, il faut joindre [ensemble] ce que les différents points donneraient si changés de place, et ce qu'une multiplication virtuelle par la couleur ajoute à la mobilité de ces points__

Le tout non pas laissé à l'imagination mais régularisé par des nécessités optiques, ~~à peu pr~~ communes à à peu près tous les individus__

Sur ce le Duche va vous dire au revoir et vous demande un petit mot adressé
    71 rue Jeanne d'Arc Rouen__

car il ne sera plus à B.A. quand vous recevrez ce mot__
    N'oubliez de faire mes hommages à Mrs. Stettheimer
    et très affectueusement à toutes trois
    M. Duchamp

▷ TRANSLATION: *Buenos Aires, 3rd May.* Dear three, *I have been wanting to write to you for some time, but never have time, so absorbed am I in playing chess. I play night and day and nothing in the whole world interests me more than finding the right move. Therefore please find it in you to forgive a poor fool, a maniac. I know that you have enough natural goodness in you to forgive. Nothing transcendental going on here—strikes, a lot of strikes, the people are on the move. Painting interests me less and less. I'm not even going to ask you what you think of your Mr Wilson. I met here a certain Robert C. Brown whom you probably know by name, Ettie: He belonged to the Max Eastman Gang and used to write at one time. We chat about New York. In short, nothing entertaining to tell you. I'm leaving B.A. 15th June for France on an English ship of which I don't yet know the name. I hope to arrive over there toward 15th July, say hello to my family for a few months and come back to New York to execute some drawings I've been doing here. I would be so pleased to hear from you, but naturally, "out of sight out of mind." Remember (French professor speaking) that it's an excellent form of* bromide. *Have you had a lot of "diners" this winter? New faces? Ettie, you talked about Lachaise in your last letter: he's an excellent sculptor in the Nadelman sense of the word. What's more, a delightful young man whom I've only seen 2 or 3 times. There's a faith aspect to his sculpture with which I don't resonate, but that is of no importance. Generally sculptors and musicians have this religious side which spoils, in my view, the execution of their works. Silence and comtemplation are the words they live by—something great is about to be born etc. And the doll's house? I think it must be almost finished and that the raffle I so want to enter will take place next winter. Tell me about the elevator, Carrie. Do you see Roché from time to time? Or has he fallen from favor with you? For you are very demanding. And I consider myself fortunate to have managed not to displease you and that you have not tired of me. And what about dear Leo Stein? How far has he got with his research into aesthetics? All I can do is ask you questions. I have nothing but question marks all around me. I am also keen to know what "groups" Florine has done since I left. "Group" is an excellent denomination for the kind of canvases you have been producing. There is nothing boring in "group" the way there is in "composition" and it's mobile, i.e. instead of seeing only a series of colored or formal situations on the canvas, you have to consider the effect of the different points joining up were they to change place, and what virtual multiplication through color would add to the mobility of these points. All this, not left to the imagination, but customized by optical requirements common to almost all individuals. On this note, the Duche will bid you farewell and asks that you might drop him a line at 71 rue Jeanne d'Arc, Rouen, for he will no longer be in B.A. by the time you receive this note. Be sure to give my respects to Mrs Stettheimer and very affectionately to all three of you.*

---

31. Marcel Duchamp to Walter Pach   autograph letter
6 June 1919, Buenos Aires   collection AAA

Buenos Aires 6 Juin 19

Mon cher Walter. Chère Magda. J'ai été bien négligent. J'aurai dû répondre depuis longtemps à votre lettre, la dernière celle où vous me demandiez de télégraphier— Naturellement en même temps que votre lettre, j'en attendais une de Barzun = N'ayant rien reçu de lui et *avec* vos indications plutôt pessimistes sur l'exposition, j'ai décidé d'abandonner le projet, dans lequel d'ailleurs, il n'y avait qu'embêtements pour moi— Ç'a été un tort = au point de vue monétaire, B.A. est une ville où tout ce qui est nouveau (pour eux) a un succès financier = Et même en peinture moderne, il y a un marché à créer. Je ne vous dis pas avoir rencontré ~~de~~ personne qui semble s'intéresser à la question mais je suis sûr qu'une exposition ferait naître des amateurs = New York à ce ~~pt d~~ point de vue est une ville pleine de traditions dans ce domaine à côté de B.A = Naturellement, ici aussi, il y a le peintre européen qui arrive, annoncé comme un cabot, fait une dizaine de portraits dans son année et retourne en Europe ensuite vivre à la campagne et pêcher à la ligne (voir Guirand de Scévola).

En dehors de tout cela, j'ai travaillé un peu, joué beaucoup aux échecs, et repars en France le 20 Juin, sur une ligne anglaise débarquant à Londres. vers le 19 ou 20 Juillet— Donc écrivez moi à Rouen 71 rue Jeanne d'arc je trouverai j'espère un mot de vous en arrivant là-bas.

Quoiqu'il n'y ait pas de comparaison à établir entre N.Y. et B.A. j'ai beaucoup aimé les 10 mois que j'ai passés ici. J'ai beaucoup flemmé, et c'est probablement pour cela que j'en garderai un bon souvenir—

Lucien Guirand de Scévola (1874-1950), French painter, best known for his portraits, genre scenes, and landscapes of Versailles.

Et vous deux, que faites vous? Les Indépendants sont finis maintenant
l'été de nouveau, allez vous à la campagne— Racontez moi quelques
potins—

J'appréhende beaucoup mon arrivée à Puteaux, où ce pauvre Raymond va
manquer— C'est réellement une chose affreuse ~~qu'on~~ dont on se rend
compte de plus en plus exactement à mesure que le pur évènement
s'éloigne dans le temps—

Pensez vous vous même aller en Europe? Si oui naturellement nous nous
verrons là-bas. Je doute que vous veniez à cette époque de l'année—

Au revoir donc, embrassez le petit Raymond pour moi
    et très affectueusement à tous deux
    Marcel

71 rue Jeanne d'Arc
Rouen
J'espère être de retour à N.Y. en Octobre Novembre—

Raymond = Raymond Duchamp-Villon

Raymond = Raymond Pach

▷ TRANSLATION: *Buenos Aires. 6th June 1919. My dear Walter, dear Magda, I have been extremely remiss. I should have replied to your letter a long time ago, the last one in which you ask me to send you a telegram. Naturally, at the same time as your letter, I was waiting for one from Barzun. = Having received nothing from him and after your rather pessimistic comments about the exhibition, I decided to give up on this project which was in fact nothing but trouble for me. That was a mistake = from a financial point of view. B.A. is a city where anything that's new (to them) is a financial success. = And even in modern painting, there's a market to be made. I'm not saying I've actually met anybody who's shown any interest in the matter, but I'm sure that an exhibition would produce new enthusiasts. = New York from this point of view is a city with a great tradition in this area next to Buenos Aires. Naturally, here too, you get your European painter with the reputation of being third rate who does his ten portraits in a year and then goes back to Europe to live in the country and go fishing (see Guirand de Scévola). Outside all that, I've done a little work, played a lot of chess and am leaving for France on the 20th June on an English liner landing in London around 19th or 20th July. So write to me in Rouen, 71 rue Jeanne d'Arc, and I'll hope to find a letter from you when I get there. While there is no comparison whatsover between N.Y. and B.A., I've really enjoyed the 10 months I spent here. I've loafed around a lot, and that's probably why I'll have fond memories of the place. How about you two, what are you up to? The Independents is over now. Summer again. Are you going to the country? Give me some gossip. I'm very apprehensive about my arrival in Puteaux where poor Raymond will be much missed. It really is such a dreadful thing which only properly starts to sink in as you get some distance from the event itself with the passing of time. Do you think you might go to Europe yourself? If so, we'll meet up over there of course. I don't suppose you will come at this time of year. Farewell then, give my love to little Raymond and very affectionately to the two of you, Marcel. 71 rue Jeanne d'Arc, Rouen. I hope to be back in N.Y. in October / November.*

32. Marcel Duchamp to Louise and Walter Arensberg
15 and 20 June [1919], Buenos Aires

autograph letter
collection PMA

B.A.   15 Juin
    Chère Lou cher Walter
Sur mon départ, je commence mes malles__ Si tout se passe comme prévu,
    mon bateau ("Highland Pride" Nelson line) part le 22 Juin et doit
    arriver à Londres vers 18 ou 19 Juillet__
Je n'ai presque rien fait ces derniers temps, plus préoccupé par le départ;
    je continue à jouer beaucoup aux échecs
Vous ai-je dit dans ma dernière lettre que j'avais rencontré Bobby Brown
    et Rose Watson__ Ils m'ont dit que Mina Loy a passé quelques mois ici
    et est repartie en Angleterre depuis Mars ou Avril__ Elle n'avait pas de
    nouvelles de Cravan depuis son départ du Mexique__

    —

20 Juin La paix va être signée quand je serai en mer__ et j'espère après 2 ou
    3 mois de séjour en France reprendre un bateau pour New York
Mes malles sont finies. Dimanche 22 à 3 heures je quitte Buenos Aires où
    l'on travaille très bien si on ne s'y amuse pas beaucoup.
Je me sens tout à fait prêt à devenir le chess maniaque__ Tout autour de
    moi prend la forme de cavalier ou de dame et le monde extérieur n'a pas
    d'autre intérêt pour moi que *dans* sa transposition en positions
    gagnantes ou perdantes__
Au revoir donc de B.A.__ Je vous écrirai dès en arrivant en France__
Donnez-moi un peu de vos nouvelles. Je n'ai rien reçu de vous depuis 3
    mois.
    A bientôt donc et très affectueusement à tous deux
    Marcel.
M. Duchamp   71 rue Jeanne d'Arc   Rouen   Seine Inférieure

Robert C. Brown (see
p.81), married to **Rose
Johnson** (d.1925), not
Rose Watson.

Arthur Cravan,
pseudonym of Fabian
Lloyd (1887-1918?),
English poet and boxer
married to **Mina Loy**
(1882-1966), English
poet. He mysteriously
disappeared off the
coast of Mexico in 1918.

Treaty of Versailles,
signed 28 June 1919.

▷ TRANSLATION: *Buenos Aires, 5th June. Dear Lou, dear Walter, Departure immi-
nent, I'm starting to pack my trunks. If all goes according to plan, my ship ("Highland Pride" Nelson line) leaves 22nd June and should arrive in London around
18th or 19th July. I've hardly done a thing lately, more wrapped up in my departure. I still play chess a lot. Did I tell you in my last letter that I ran into Bobby
Brown and Rose Watson? They told me that Mina Loy was here for several months
and then went back to England in March or April. She hadn't heard from Cravan
since he left Mexico.*
    *20th June. The peace is going to be signed while I'm at sea. And I hope, after 2
or 3 months in France, I'll be able to take a boat for New York. My trunks are
packed. Sunday 22nd at 3 o'clock I leave Buenos Aires, a very good place for work
even if you don't have a lot of fun. I am all set to become chess maniac. I find all*

around me transformed into knight or queen and the outside world holds no other interest for me than in its transposition into winning or losing scenarios. So long then from B.A. I will write you moment I reach France. Do drop me a line with your news. I have heard nothing from you in three months. So long then and very affectionately to you both, Marcel. M. Duchamp, 71 rue Jeanne d'Arc, Rouen, Seine Inférieure.

22 June 1919
After just over nine months in Buenos Aires,
Duchamp boards the S.S. "Highland Pride"
and returns to Europe.

New York, Paris, Rouen | 1919-1923

aboard ship for Europe, on the "Highland Pride" | 22 June 1919
lives in Paris: 32 avenue Charles-Floquet at Gabrielle Picabia's, and 22 rue de la Condamine
lives in New York: 246 West 73rd Street, then 1947 Broadway
round trips to Rouen, 71 rue Jeanne d'Arc, at his parents'

from 22 June 1919 to 10 February 1923

▶ MAJOR WORKS

L.H.O.O.Q. (Mona Lisa postcard with mustache and goatee added in pencil, 1919)
Duchamp with Shaved Head (photograph, 1919)
Tzanck Check (counterfeit check from an imaginary bank, ink on paper, Dec 1919)
Air de Paris / Paris Air (glass ampoule of air, Dec 1919)
Rotary Glass Plates (motorized optical device, 1920)
Fresh Widow (miniature French window, 1920)
Letterhead of the Société Anonyme (India ink on paper; 1920)
Elevage de poussière / Dust Breeding (photograph by Man Ray and MD, 1920)
Témoins oculistes / Oculist Witnesses (pencil on reverse of carbon paper, 1920)
Belle Haleine (perfume bottle, 1921)
Why not sneeze Rose Sélavy? (birdcage, marble cubes, thermometer, cuttlebone, 1921)

Marcel Duchamp as Rrose Sélavy (photograph by Man Ray, reworked by MD, 1921)
La bagarre d'Austerlitz / The Brawl at Austerlitz (miniature window, 1921)
Layout for "Some French Moderns, Says McBride" (enclosed in three-ring binder, 1922)
The Non-Dada (religious pamphlet enclosed in envelope, 1922)
Wanted $2,000 ("Wanted" poster, with photographs, 1923)
Large Glass (oil, varnish, lead on glass panels, 1915-23)

▶ EXHIBITIONS

International Exhibition of Modern Art (inaugural), Société Anonyme, Inc. Gallery, New York City. By MD: *Disturbed balance [To Be Looked at...]*
— 30 Apr - 15 June 1920
Third Exhibition, Société Anonyme, Inc. Gallery, New York City. By MD: *With hidden Noise*
— 2 Aug - 11 Sept 1920
Salon Dada, Exposition Internationale, Galerie Montaigne (Théâtre des Champs-Elysées), Paris.

MD did not send anything: places Nos. 28 to 31 remained empty — 6 June - 30 June 1921

Salon d'Automne, Grand Palais, Paris. By MD: contribution to *L'Œil Cacodylate* by Francis Picabia — 1 Nov - 20 Nov 1921

Exhibition of Paintings from the collection of the late Arthur Jerome Eddy, The Art Institute, Chicago. By MD: *Chess players* — 19 Sept - 22 Oct 1922

26 July 1919
After a three-day stop over in London, Duchamp
returns to France where he has not been for over
four years. He spends the fall months in Paris, for a
time as houseguest of the Picabias, and makes
intermittent trips to Rouen to visit his family.

---

33. Marcel Duchamp to Walter Pach   letter
"late August" [1919], Paris   collection AAA

Paris Fin Août
   Mon cher Walter
   Chère Magda
Depuis un mois ici je revois tous les amis un à un— Personne n'a changé,
   ils habitent tous dans les mêmes appartements avec les mêmes
   poussières qu'il y a cinq ans.
Je vois peu les peintres (air connu), n'ai rien vu en peinture qui m'intéresse
   excepté les choses de Ribemont Dessaignes, Picabia et mon frère qui a
   travaillé. beaucoup depuis sa démobilisation
Paris l'été est décidément très joli à cause du manque de gens.
Il fait juste chaud et je me prépare à passer l'hiver à N.Y.
Je repartirai en Décembre pour là-bas— Espère que vous êtes contents que
   l'enfant grandit;
J'ai vu Yvonne la femme de Raymond qui n'est pas encore démobilisée—
   Je suis allé à Laon la voir.
Villon et Gaby toujours à Puteaux vous envoient leurs bonnes amitiés
Écrivez moi un petit mot :
      ^c/o Francis Picabia
      32 avenue Charles Floquet
      Paris
J'habite là et y resterai les 3 mois que je passe en France
      Bien affectueusement à tous trois
      Marcel.

Yvonne (née Bon),
widow of **Raymond**
Duchamp-Villon.

Jacques and **Gaby**
Villon

Address in fact that of
Gabrielle Buffet, wife of
Picabia (as Picabia is
then living with his
mistress, Germaine
Everling).

▷ TRANSLATION: *Paris, late August. My dear Walter, dear Magda, For a month now
I've been seeing all my friends here one by one. Nobody has changed, they're all still
living in the same apartments with the same dust as five years ago. I don't see much
of the painters (same old tune) and have seen nothing of any interest in painting
except for things by Ribemont-Dessaignes, Picabia and my brother who has done a
lot of work since he was demobbed. Paris in summer is really very pretty on account
of the lack of people. It's just warm and I'm trying to get used to the idea of spending
the winter in N.Y. I'll be on my way back over there in December. You must be happy the child is getting bigger. I saw Yvonne, Raymond's wife, who hasn't been demobbed yet. I went to Laon to see her. Villon and Gaby still in Puteaux and send*

you their best wishes. Drop me a line c/o Francis Picabia, 32 avenue Charles Floquet, Paris. This is where I'm living and where I will stay for the whole three months I am in France. Very affectionately to the three of you, Marcel.

---

34. Marcel Duchamp to Constantin Brancusi[*]
[between 9 Aug and 27 Dec 1919], Paris

autograph letter
collection MNAM

32 avenue Charles Floquet
    Cher Brancusi J'ai bien envie de vous voir__ Puis je venir Mercredi 5^h ½ à votre atelier? J'amènerai avec moi une amie américaine Miss Dreier, qui vous connait de réputation et serait enchantée de voir vos choses nouvelles__
Ne répondez pas__ Nous viendrons. Mercredi 5^h ½__
très affectueusement
    Marcel Duchamp

Brancusi's home and studio, 8 Impasse Ronsin, Paris.

Dreier is staying in Paris for a few weeks at the Hotel Brighton. MD escorts her around to various artists' studios.

▷ TRANSLATION: *32 avenue Charles Floquet. Dear Brancusi, I would really like to see you. May I come by your studio Wednesday 5.30? I'll be bringing an American friend with me, Miss Dreier, who knows you by reputation and would be delighted to see your new things. No need to reply—we'll just come. Wednesday 5.30. Very affectionately, Marcel Duchamp.*

27 December 1919
After only five months in France, Duchamp boards the "Touraine" in Le Havre headed for New York.

6 January 1920
Duchamp arrives in New York, where he is to remain for about a year and a half.

---

* **Constantin Brancusi** (1876-1957), considered by many to be the greatest modern sculptor of the twentieth century, was born and raised in Romania but moved to Paris in 1904. Brancusi and Duchamp met before World War I; with the painter Fernand Léger, in 1912 they attended the Paris Air Show, where, when they came upon an airplane, Duchamp turned to Brancusi and said: "*It's all over for painting. Who could better that propeller? Tell me, can you do that?*" This was a remarkably prophetic exchange, considering the fact that Duchamp would eventually cease his activities as a painter, and Brancusi would become known for the linear refinement of his sculptural form, an aspect of his work that was often compared to the newest advancements in machinist technology. In the mid-1920's, with Henri-Pierre Roché (p.57) and another silent business partner, Duchamp became part-owner of nearly 30 sculptures by the artist that were acquired from the estate of John Quinn (p.42), and he subsequently oversaw the installation of several Brancusi exhibitions in the United States. In addition to these professional associations, Duchamp and Brancusi remained exceptionally close friends throughout their lives, a fact that is confirmed by the way in which they began to address one another after 1926, each calling the other "Morice" (or occasionally "Maurice"), likely meant as a name of endearment.

35. Marcel Duchamp to Jean Crotti and Suzanne Duchamp   autograph letter
circa 20 Oct [1920], New York   collection AAA

N.Y. 20 Oct. environ— Il faut que j'aie qqchose à te demander pour t'écrire— (Ceci pour t'éviter de le constater.)

Cher vieux cher Suzanne— Je n'ai fait que vouloir vous écrire depuis 6 mois. Mais ça me fait chier d'écrire… etc. etc.

Peu de choses nouvelles ici.—

La Société Anonyme est une galerie où on expose sans vendre— Ça coûte 25 cents d'entrée— Les gens ont du mal à payer 25 cents— Ma première idée était de faire payer 50 cents aux critiques. Mais ils ne viennent même pas. A part cela, c'est la seule chose intéressante à N.Y.— Rien autre, De Zayas est devenu Commercial traveler en tableaux. (Toutes époques, tous genres). Notre ami Caudy a disparu de la circul.^{tion}

Montross je n'ai pas vu depuis 2 ans— les Indépendants ont leur exposition annuelle—

En tout cas, la peinture n'est pas une chose si intéressante qu'on doive y consacrer plus que je viens de le faire.

Walter va bien travaille comme un fou à son Dante qui menace de n'être jamais fini— J'y vais moins souvent qu'autrefois. Moins ou pas de réunions comme celles célèbres.— On boit de temps en temps, beaucoup si on veut, mais trop cher pour moi. (By the way. j'ai vu Bibily il y a un mois, seulement pour la première fois depuis le fameux envoi. Il m'a juré ses grands Dieux qu'il n'avait jamais rien reçu— Probablement c'est vrai—

En tout cas je te remercie cher vieux et toi aussi Suzanne d'avoir envoyé la "liqueur" et m'excuse un peu tard de vous avoir tant emmerdé avec ça.

Je ne bois réellement plus, mais n'engraisse *pas* pour cela; me couche entre 4 et 5^h— ai beaucoup de mal à me lever avant 1 : P.M.

Ai beaucoup de leçons [La saison d'hiver recommence,]

J'ai fait un "monocle"— C'est une chose qui tourne à toute vitesse avec un moteur électrique— très dangereuse— ai failli tuer Man Ray avec. J'espère en faire des photos et vous en envoyer—

— J'ai une "Moving Picture Camera„ depuis déja six mois. Mais ça coûte tellement cher (le film) que je suis obligé d'espacer mes épanchements cinématg^{ques}

Je m'emmerde moins aujourd'hui que les jours ordinaires. Profitez donc z'en—

Alice est à Long Beach (ou était) avec son mari que je ne connais pas. Béatrice aussi mariée, est quelquefois bien emmerdée—

Caudy – Robert J. Coady (1876-1921), gallery director and editor of The Soil.

Newman Emerson Montross (1849-1932), art dealer whose gallery at 500 Fifth Avenue held the "Four Muskateers Exhibition" in Apr 1916.

W. Arensberg working on The Cryptography of Dante (NY, Alfred A. Knopf, 1921).

Bibily, believed to be a man working at the French Embassy, NY.

Rotary Glass Plates [cat. 50]

Béatrice = Beatrice Wood (p.222)

J'ai beaucoup aimé la photo du Ready Made qui s'ennuie sur le balcon⎯ S'il est complètement déchiqueté vous pouvez le remplacer (Ah! c'est vrai vous avez déménagé

Je travaille aussi à mon grand verre (j'y gratte du miroir en dessin d'après la planche qu'Yvonne a chez elle)⎯

Et les échecs? Superbe Superbe!⎯ J'ai joué beaucoup dans des exhibitions simultanées données par Marshall jouant 12 échiquiers à la fois⎯ Et j'ai gagné 2 fois ma partie⎯

J'ai fait des progrès énormes et je travaille comme un nègre. Non pas que j'aie des chances de devenir le Champion de France mais j'aurai le plaisir de pouvoir jouer avec presque n'importe quel joueur, dans un an ou deux.

C'est naturellement la partie de ma vie qui m'amuse le plus⎯

Cet hiver je ~~fa~~ vais faire partie de l'équipe Marshall (ses 8 meilleurs joueurs) contre les autres équipes de N.Y. comme je l'avais déja fait l'hiver dernier.⎯ Mais j'espère gagner quelques parties cette fois (Ce que je n'avais pas fait)⎯ Je suis crazy about it⎯

Autre chose⎯ je vais lancer sur le marché une nouvelle forme d'échecs dont suivent les principales caractéristiques :

La Dame est faite d'une tour et un fou combinés⎯ Le Cavalier est le même que celui que j'avais en Amérique du Sud. ~~la~~ Le Pion aussi Le Roi aussi

2° Ils seront coloriés. c.à.d.

La dame Blanche sera vert clair

- - - - - - Noire - - - - - - foncé

Les tours seront Bleu clair et foncé

Les fous - - - - jaune - - - - - - - -

Cavaliers Rouge$ clair et foncé

Roi Blanc et Roi Noir

Pions Blancs et Noirs.

Please notice que la dame dans sa couleur est une combinaison du fou et de la Tour (comme elle l'est dans sa marche)⎯

3° Je vais demander à Marshall de me donner son nom pour les appeler Marshall's Chessmen⎯

Je lui donnerai 10 % des recettes.

4° Ils seront faits en plâtre moulé et combiné avec de la colle ce qui en fera des pièces aussi solides qu'en bois.

(Peut-être que ta pierre serait utile; je t'enverrai un set dès que ce sera prêt et tu pourras faire des expériences si ça t'amuse)⎯

Je ne t'ai pas parlé de toi; comment vas tu mon vieux, tu ne m'en veux pas d'avoir été si long à t'écrire mais ça me fait tellement chier d'écrire.

Au revoir mes enfants; je vais écrire à Puteaux.

Unhappy Readymade [cat. 40]

"Oculist Witnesses," detail of the *Large Glass* [cat. 2].

Yvonne is either his ex-mistress, Yvonne Chastel, or his sister, Yvonne Duchamp.

Frank J. Marshall (1877-1944), US chess champion 1900 - 1936 and founder of The Marshall Chess Club.

Pense toujours aller en France en Juillet 1921.

Dites moi un peu ce que vous fabriquez—

Ah! j'allais oublier l'objet pratique de ma lettre :

Carl Van Vechten a acheté un livre qui s'appelle :

> G. de Cherville :
> "Chiens et chats d'Eugène Lambert.

Il a payé 30 fr. pour le livre et on lui demande 32 fr. pour l'envoyer

— S'il est possible de l'envoyer par la poste, veux tu t'en occuper, aller chez Albert Lefrançois 8 rue de Rome. (La lettre qu'il avait écrite à Carl est jointe ici) Si pas possible par la poste, veux tu le donner à quelqu'un qui vient ici pour lui éviter ces 32 frs de transport. Il te remboursera naturellement tes "débours"—

Carl a écrit déja à Lefrançois pour que celui ci donne le livre (par lui payé) au porteur de la lettre ci jointe— Donc tu vois ce n'est pas trop compliqué; et moins que la bouteille de Whisky

Un de ces jours je vais prendre une cuite.

>   Affectueusement à tous deux
>   Marcel

1947 Broadway

Room 316

N.Y. City

Le vieux bildinge va toujours bien et t'envoie ses amitiés.

▷ TRANSLATION: *N.Y. 20th Oct. approx. I must be after something if I'm writing to you. (So that you don't say it first). Dear old man, dear Suzanne, I have wanted nothing but to write to you for 6 months. But writing's a pain in the ass for me... etc. etc. Nothing much new here. The Société Anonyme is a gallery where you exhibit but don't sell. It costs 25 cents to go in. People find it hard to part with their 25 cents. My first idea was to charge critics 50 cents. But they don't come at all. Apart from that, it's the only thing of any interest in N.Y. Nothing else. De Zayas has become a traveling salesman for paintings (all eras, all genres). Our friend Caudy has disappeared from circulation. Montross I haven't seen for 2 years. The Independents hold their annual exhibition. In any case, painting is not such an interesting thing that one should devote any more time to it than I've just done. Walter is fine, working like a maniac on his Dante which threatens never to be finished. I don't go as often as I used to. Fewer meetings like the celebrated ones of the past or none at all. We drink from time to time, quite a lot if you like, but too expensive for me. (By the way, I saw Bibily a month ago, for the first time, in fact, since the famous shipment. He swore to God he had not received a thing. It's probably true.) In any case, thank you, dear boy and you too, Suzanne, for sending the "liqueur" and I apologize a little late for having been such a pain in the ass about that. I actually don't drink any more, but it's not for all that that I'm getting fat.*

Go to bed between 4 and 5am and find it very hard to get up before 1pm. Have a lot of lessons. (The winter season is just starting up again.) I've made a "monocle." It's a thing that rotates at top speed driven by an electric motor—highly dangerous—I almost killed Man Ray with it. I hope to take some photos of it and send them to you. I've had a "Moving Picture Camera" *for six months now, but it's so expensive (the film) that I have to space out my cinematographic outpourings. I'm less bored bloody rigid today than on ordinary days, so make the most of it. Alice is in Long Beach (or was) with her husband whom I don't know. Béatrice married also and sometimes it's a pain in the ass for her. I really liked the photo of the Ready Made getting bored on the balcony. If it's completely torn to shreds, you can replace it (Ah! it's true, you've moved!) I'm also working on my large glass (scraping a drawing onto a mirror after a plate Yvonne had at her place). And chess? Superb, absolutely superb. I played a lot in the simultaneous exhibitions given by Marshall, playing 12 players at a time. And I won my match twice. I've made enormous progress and work like a black. Not that I have any chance of becoming Champion of France, but I will have the pleasure of being able to play with almost anybody in a year or two. This is naturally the part of my life I enjoy the most. This winter, I'm going to be on Marshall's team (his 8 best players) against all the other teams in N.Y. like I already did last year. But I hope to win a few matches this time round! (Something I didn't do last time). I am* crazy *about it! Another thing: I'm going to launch on the market a new form of chess, of which the main features are as follows: the queen is made of a castle and a bishop combined. The knight is the same as the one I had in South America, the pawn as well, the king as well. 2nd They'll be colored, i.e. the white queen will be pale green, the black queen, dark green. The castles will be pale and dark blue. The bishops, pale and dark yellow. Knights, pale and dark red. Black king and white king. Pawns, black and white. Please notice that the queen in her coloring is a combination of the bishop and the castle (as she is in the way she moves). 3rd I am going to ask Marshall to give me his name so I can call them* Marshall's Chessmen. *I will give him 10% of takings. 4th They'll be made in plaster moulds and bound with glue which will make them as sturdy as wooden pieces. (Your stone might be useful. I'll send you a set as soon as one's ready and you can try it out if you want to.) I haven't mentioned you at all. How are you my friend? Not mad at me for having taken so long to write but writing's such a pain in the ass for me. So long kids. I'm going to write to Puteaux now. Still expect to go to France in July 1921. Let me know what you're getting up to. Ah! I was forgetting the practical purpose of my letter. Carl Van Lechtern has bought a book called "Chiens et chats d'Eugène Lambert," G. de Cherville. He paid 30 francs for the book and they're asking him for 32 francs to send it. If it's possible to send it by post, could you take care of it and go to Albert Lefrançois's,* 8 rue de Rome. *(I've enclosed the letter he wrote to Carl here.) If not possible by post, could you give it to somebody who's coming over here so he doesn't have to pay the 32 francs shipping costs? He will, of course, reimburse your "expenses." Carl has already written to Lefrançois telling him to give the book (which he has paid for) to the bearer of this letter. So you see it's not that complicated. And less so than the bottle of whisky. One*

*of these days I'm going to get plastered. Affectionately to you both, Marcel. 1947
Broadway, Room 316, N.Y. City. The old building is fine still and sends its best
wishes.*

---

36. Marcel Duchamp to Francis Picabia   autograph letter
[20 January 1921], New York   collection BLJD

Mâcheur Fran[cfort sau]cisse Pis qu[e quand elle s']habilla,
  Je me suis enfin un peu occupé de vendre des Dadas, 391 et des livres.
  Ci inclus un chèque pour quelques ventes— Man Ray s'en ~~oe~~ est occupé
  ces jours derniers et la vente a mieux marché— J'espère vous envoyer
  bientôt un autre chèque aussi important
  Man Ray et une de nos amies Bessie Breuer, vont faire paraitre un New
  York Dada—
  Voulez vous être assez gentil pour demander à Tzara de faire une courte
  autorisation d'imprimer, qu'on mettrait sur le magazine—
  Ici Rien, toujours Rien, très Dada—
Si vous voulez une règle de grammaire :
  Le ~~sujet~~ *verbe* s'accorde avec le sujet consonnamment :
  Par exemple :
        Le nègre aigrit
        Les négresses s'aigrissent ou maigrissent.
  Comment va Emile Augier? Bonjour ma chère Germaine, avez vous
  toujours le petit poêle électrique qui chauffe si localement?
  J'espère aller en France vers Juin. pour quelques mois—
  On boit quand même ici. Ça ne se fait pas de la même façon qu'avant. Il
  s'y ajoute maintenant la peur d'être empoisonné.
  Comment va G.R.D.? Affections ainsi qu'à Tzara.
  Y a t il toujours des échecs dans la famille? Le Docteur j'espère jouer avec
  lui en été.—
  Je passe mon temps en échecs naturellement.
  N'oubliez pas des amitiés à la petite Russe *Rouchka* qui s'était fâchée avec
  moi pour je ne sais quelle raison—
        Affectueusement à tous—
        Marcel
  1947 Broadway
  Room 316
  New York City

Dada = Tzara review,
7 issues 1917-1920.
391 = Picabia review
(see p.58).

Bessie Breuer (1893-1975), American
journalist, and future
novelist, who met MD
shortly after he arrived
in US in 1915.

Rue **Emile Augier**,
where Picabia lives.
Germaine Everling
(1886-1976), after
meeting Picabia in 1917,
lives with him for 20 years.

Reference to the
Prohibition in the US
1920 - 1933.
"G.R.D." = Georges
Ribemont-Dessaignes

▷ TRANSLATION: [adaptation:] *Mast[icat]er Fran[cfurter] sizz[ling] Peak-a [when she]
be-a [dressing].* [literally: Masticater Frankfurt sausage worse than when she dressed /
Francis Picabia].

I finally got round to doing something about selling the 391 Dadas and the books. Enclosed a check for a few sales. Man Ray took over the last few days and sales went better. I hope soon to send you another check for as much. Man Ray and a friend of ours, Bessie Breuer, are going to bring out a New York Dada. Would you be kind enough to ask Tzara for a short publishing authorization that we could put on the magazine? Here, Nothing, eternally Nothing, very Dada. If you please, a grammar lesson: The verb agrees with the subject consonantly. For example, The negro grows bitter. The negresses grow bitter or grow thinner. How is Emile Augier? Hello my dear Germaine, Do you still have the little electric stove that heats in just the right places? I hope to go to France around June, for a few months. Still some drinking going on here. But not in the same way as before. You've got the fear of being poisoned to reckon with now, too. How is G.R.D.? Affections and to Tzara also. Is there still chess in the family?—The Doctor: I hope to play with him this summer. I spend all my time at chess, naturally. Don't forget to give my regards to Rouchka the little Russian girl who got mad at me, I don't know why. Affectionately to all, Marcel. 1947 Broadway, Room 316, New York City.

---

37. Marcel Duchamp to Tristan Tzara[*], Francis Picabia and Germaine Everling   letter
8 February [1921, New York]   collection BLJD

8 Fév.

   Mon chèque n'était pas une blague =
J'avais simplement oublié de le regarder avant de vous l'envoyer—
Ci joint un duplicata à votre nom cette fois ci— Voulez vous me renvoyer
   le 1er chèque *pour* que je puisse me faire rembourser—
Je crois ma chère Germaine que je boirai du vin, cett été; je ne pense être
   à Paris avant Juin—
Tzara, je vais probablement faire traduire votre autorisation pour que tout
   le monde ici puis[se] "comprendre" —

MD's check is for book sales in NY (see previous letter).

Germaine = Germaine Everling

Tzara's letter published under the heading "Authorization" in *New York Dada*, Apr 1921.

---

* **Tristan Tzara** (1896-1963) was a Romanian-born poet who, with Hugo Ball, Emmy Hennings, Marcel Janco and Richard Huelsenbeck, founded the Dada Movement in Zurich, Switzerland, in 1916. Duchamp first heard about Dada in late 1916 or early 1917, when he saw a copy of Tzara's Dada novelette, *The First Celestial Adventure of Mr. Fire Extinguisher*, which was probably sent by Tzara to Francis Picabia. Eventually, Duchamp would enter into a direct communication with Tzara, when he sought his authorization to publish *New York Dada* in 1921. Tzara had moved to Paris in 1920, where he had tried to promote the Dada movement internationally, an effort that failed when most vanguard European artists switched their artistic allegiances to Surrealism, a new movement in art and literature spearheaded by André Breton (p.196). It was probably during Duchamp's visit to Paris in 1921-22 that he met Tzara for the first time. Although Duchamp never officially joined any artistic enterprise, he shared much in common with the revolutionary and nihilistic aspects of Dada. For these reasons, he admired Tzara and they remained colleagues and fairly good friends for the remaining years of their lives.

Mon ambition est d'être joueur d'échecs professionnel (ou anti fesses
Lionel)__ Je ne sais pas exactement en quoi ça consiste.
    Affectueusement à tous
    M. Duchamp
Francis, sur votre Rastaquouère, vous avez mis une inscription : dont voici
une bonne traduction :
    Les cirages les plus lymphatiques
    jonchent ceux : conne, colle et pâte.

Jésus-Christ Rastaquouère = Picabia's novel (Paris, Au Sans Pareil, 1920).

▷ TRANSLATION: *8th Feb. My check was not a joke. I simply forgot to take a look at it
before sending it to you. Enclosed a duplicate, in your name this time. Would you
return the first check to me so that I can claim the money back? I think, my dear
Germaine, that it will be summer before I am drinking wine—I don't expect to be
in Paris before June. Tzara, I'm probably going to have your authorization translated so that everybody can "understand" it. My ambition is to be a professional
chess player (anti-fesses Lionel). [A wordplay on pro-/anti-, fessional/ass Lionel] I don't
know exactly what it entails. Affectionately to all, M. Duchamp. Francis, about
your* Rastaquouère, *you put an inscription on it and this is a good translation:*
[literally:] *The most lymphatic shoe-shines strew these: sex, glue and paste.* [see margin
note for this pun]

The original Picabia dedication can be reconstructed: *Les virages les plus sympathiques sont ceux qu'on ne connaît pas.* (The nicest bends in the road are those we don't yet know.)

---

38. Marcel Duchamp to Jean Crotti   letter
19 May [1921], New York   collection AAA

19 Mai N.Y.
    Merci d'envoyer le livre. Je l'attends.
Tu sais très bien que je n'ai rien à exposer__ que le mot exposer ressemble
    au mot épouser__
Conséquentemement, n'attends rien et ne t'inquiète pas__
Merci tout de même d'avoir pensé à moi__
Ça va être très amusant pour moi cette exposition Dada__ ici Rien du tout
    que la ville elle même. Le moindre plaisir coûte cher maintenant, et la
    saoulographie est devenue très high brow.
J'attends d'être en mer (3 miles out) pour boire un cocktail à des prix
    normaux. ou des cocktails à un prix normal.
Je pars sur "la France" le 9 Juin et pense passer un jour ou 2 à Rouen avant
    de visiter Paris__
J'ai vu Peter Juley et j'ai 2 clichés de la tête__ Je vais voir Sheeler pour
    le Clown

Peter Juley (1862-1937), American photographer.

"la tête" (the head) = probably MD's *Portrait of Marcel Duchamp (Sculpture Made to Measure)*, repro. in *Vanity Fair*, June 1916.

Charles Sheeler (1883-1965), American painter, photographer, working at this time for Marius de Zayas.

Jean Crotti, *The Clown*, 1916 (Musée d'Art Moderne de la Ville de Paris, Paris).

Vais m'occuper des disques pour toi et Mad＿

Votre catalogue est superbe＿ quel genre de succès avez vous eu?＿ Je regrette de n'avoir pas été là? Quels genres de tableaux achètes et vends tu? Es tu en rapport avec de Zayas＿ C'est un des grands manie tout du moderne et de l'ancien ici.

Si tu as besoin d'un employé je pourrais peut-être faire ton affaire＿

    A bientôt tous deux＿

    Affect.

    Marcel.

"Mad" = Madeleine Turban, a friend of MD's in Paris.

▷ TRANSLATION: *19th May N.Y. Please send the book. I'm waiting for it. You know very well that I have nothing to exhibit—that the word exhibit is like the word marriage for me. Consequently, don't expect anything and don't worry. Thanks all the same for having thought of me. It's going to be great fun for me, this Dada exhibition: Here, Nothing at all but the city itself. The least pleasure is really expensive now and boozology has become very high brow. I'll wait until I'm at sea (3 miles out) to have a cocktail at normal prices, or cocktails at a normal price. I leave on "The France" on the 9th June and I plan to spend a day or two in Rouen before going to Paris. I saw Peter Juley and have 2 photos of the Head—I'm going to see Sheeler about the Clown. Will attend to the records for you and Mad. Your catalog is superb. What sort of success have you had with it? I'm sorry not to have been there. What kind of paintings do you buy and sell? Are you in touch with de Zayas? He's one of the big handlers here—everything in ancient and modern art. If you need an employee, I could perhaps be the man for the job. So long the two of you, Affectionately, Marcel.*

---

39. Marcel Duchamp to Jean Crotti   telegram
[1 June 1921, New York]   collection BLJD

    = DE NEVV YORK 461 10 = V VVESTERN UNION =

    = PODE BAL = DUCHAMP =

    LCD CROTTI 5 RUE PARMENTIER NEUILLYSSEINE

▷ TRANSLATION: The French "Peau de balle et balai de crin" means: *bollocks to you.*

Telegram sent in reply to Crotti's request (on Tzara's behalf) to show at the "Salon Dada," held at the Galerie Montaigne, Paris, 6-30 June 1921.

9 June 1921
Duchamp departs for Europe aboard the "France."

16 June 1921
The "France" docks in Le Havre. Before going to Paris, Duchamp stops in Rouen to visit his parents.

40. Marcel Duchamp to Ettie Stettheimer
circa 6 July [1921], Rouen

autograph letter
collection YCAL

6 Juillet environ

Rouen— 71 rue Jeanne d'Arc

   Merci de vos 2 lettres chèrettie.

Rien de changé ici. C'est désespérément la même chose—

Les Dadas ont fait trop de bruit *(contre)* à une représentation *de bruiteurs*
   futuristes— Pour les punir on a fermé leur exposition—

De loin ces choses, ces Mouvements s'enjolivent d'un charme qu'ils n'ont
   pas de près je vous assure— Mais après tout je commence à être habitué
   aux -Ismes—

J'ai vu Gleizes 2 minutes, je lui ai immédiatement parlé d'une exposition
   pour Florine—

Il va s'en occuper et voit la chose très possible— Je vais lui donner les
   photos et il écrira directement à Florine pour lui dire ce qu'il a fait.

Je n'ai pas encore été au Bon Marché ni à l'hôtel Wagram— Ceci va se
   faire bientôt— Je rentre à Paris demain et vais m'occuper de la flanelle
   mauve—

Carpentier m'a fait perdre tous mes paris c'est un imbécile— Nous avons
   su la nouvelle quelques minutes après—

Sidès, je n'ai pas vu—

Tout est *trop* silencieux en Europe—

Où est ce bon "elevated" bien bruyant?— Columbus AVE— qu'il est bon
   de penser à toi.

Temps remarquablement délicieux ici—

Dites bien à Carrie que je compte voir sa maison finie à mon retour—

Où en sont vos \tes\ chapitres Ettie? Moi qui ne fiche rien, je voudrais que
   tu travailles— Logique Dada.

J'ai eu très grand plaisir à revoir Tarrytown où toi et moi avons passé de si
   bons moments sans flirter cependant.

Ne pas flirter n'est pas donné à tout le monde— Les Dieux donc ont l'œil
   sur nous—

J'espère te donner de meilleures nouvelles de mes résultats
   hotelwagramiens et Bonmarchéiques bientôt

      Vous embrasse toutes trois
      et te charge de hommages pour Mme Stettheimer
      Rose-Mar-cel.

"Concert bruitiste,"
17 June 1921, resulted in
the closure of Tzara's
"Salon Dada" next day.

Florine = Florine
Stettheimer

MD may be referring to
Georges Carpentier
(1894-1975), French
boxer with a striking
resemblance to MD
(see profile portrait on
cover of *391*, No.XIX,
Oct 1924).

= **elevated** railway, NY.

Carrie = Carrie
Stettheimer

Tarrytown, see p.48.

▷ TRANSLATION: *6th July or thereabouts, Rouen, 71 rue Jeanne d'Arc. Thank you for
your 2 letters, dearettie. No change here. Depressingly the same thing. The Dadas
made too much noise at a Futurist (sound effects) show. As a punishment, they had
their exhibition closed down. From afar, these things, these Movements take on a*

kind of appeal they don't have close up, I can assure you. But, after all, I'm begin-
ning to get used to the -isms. I saw Gleizes for 2 minutes. I immediately spoke to
him about an exhibition for Florine. He's going to attend to it and sees it as a real
possibility. I'm going to give him the photos and he'll write to Florine himself to let
her know what he's done. I haven't been to the Bon Marché yet or the Hôtel
Wagram. But I will. I'm going back to Paris and will get on to the mauve flannel
skirt. Carpentier made me lose all my bets—he's a fool. We found out a few minutes
later. Have not seen Sidès. Everything is too quiet in Europe. Where is the good old
"elevated" with all its clatter? Columbus Ave—how good it is to think of you! Re-
markably fine weather here. Make sure you tell Carrie that I expect to see her house
finished when I get back. How far have you all got, have you got, Ettie, with your
chapters? As I don't lift a finger, I want you to work. Dada Logic. I was really
pleased to go to Tarrytown again where you and I spent such happy times together,
without flirting however. It's not easy, not flirting, not everyone can manage it. The
gods must be watching over us. I hope to have better news for you soon of my hotel-
wagramian and bonmarcheic investigations. Love to you all three and give my re-
gards to Mrs Stettheimer, Rose-Mar-cel.

---

41. Marcel Duchamp to Carrie, Ettie and Florine Stettheimer   autograph letter
1 September [1921, Paris]   Estate of Joseph Solomon

Sept. 1st
    Chère Florine
Avec un peu de retard, il y a beaucoup de travail de fait.
Gleizes vous aura la galerie Povolozky 13 rue Bonaparte, où lui, Lhote,   **André Lhote**
    Picabia ont fait des expositions l'année dernière.   (1885-1962), French
                                                              Cubist painter and
Il pense l'avoir pour rien et me dit que vous devez compter 1000 ou 1200   theoretician.
    francs de frais pour le catalogue et détails.
Il est parti ce soir pour la campagne jusqu'au 25 Sept. mais m'a chargé de
    vous dire de faire l'envoi d'une ~~15~~ quinzaine de tableaux ou plus. Tout
    de suite à l'adresse :
    Robinot
    Emballeur
    Grand Palais des Champs Elysées Porte D
    Paris
Mettez aussi sur l'adresse entre parenthèses (pour Mr. Albert Gleizes)
Dès qu'ils seront arrivés il s'en occupera et peut être même pourrait vous
    faire accepter quelque chose au Salon d'Automne qui ouvre fin
    Septembre—
Il doit d'ailleurs vous écrire ces jours ci.—

———

Chère Ettie chère Carrie
il fait bien bon ici, quoique ce soit ma patrie.
Je cherche quelques effets de cinéma avec ma camera—
J'espère rapporter quelques feet à N.Y.
J'ai appris aussi il y a quelque temps la mort de ce pauvre Thévenaz—.
Je n'ai pas vu Sidès qui est ici cependant.
Hartley. Man Ray— j'ai vus.
Tout Greenwich Village se promène sur Montparnasse— McBride
    rencontré par hasard au Rond Point des Champs Elysées—
Et vous? quelques détails *sur* la vie en plein air à Tarrytown—
L'ibsenienne Carrie a t elle mis l'ascenseur?
Le vin ici me plaît beaucoup.
J'espère rentrer à N.Y. en Décembre— quoiqu'au fond je ne sache pas
    pourquoi.
Paris est bien assommant au bout de quelque temps—
    Affectueusement à toutes trois et
    Mes hommages à Madame Stettheimer
    Rrose Sélavy
7 rue Lemaitre Puteaux (Seine)
ou à Rouen 71 rue Jeanne d'Arc

In Puteaux, end July, MD fixed, onto a bicycle wheel, sketches of spirals he filmed with the camera bought in NY, April 1920. (info from J. Caumont)

Paul Thévenaz (1891-1921), Swiss Art Deco painter and friend of the Stettheimers'.

Marsden Hartley (1877-1943), American painter, spends summer and fall of 1921 in Europe.

Tarrytown, see p.48.

▷ TRANSLATION: Sept. 1st. *Dear Florine, A little slow but much work done. Gleizes will get you the Povolozky Gallery, 13 rue Bonaparte, where he, Lhote and Picabia held exhibitions last year. He thinks he can get it for nothing and says you should expect to put up 1,000 to 1,200 francs for the catalog and minor expenses. He left for the country this evening until 25th Sept. but asked me to tell you to go ahead and send fifteen or so pictures or more. At once to: Robinot, Emballeur, Grand Palais des Champs Elysées, Porte D, Paris. Also put on the address in brackets (for Mr Albert Gleizes). As soon as they arrive he will attend to them and might even be able to get something of yours accepted at the Salon d'Automne opening end September. Furthermore, he will be writing to you in the next few days. Dear Ettie, dear Carrie, Pleasant weather here, even if it is my homeland. I'm trying to get some cinema effects with my camera. I hope to bring back a few feet to N.Y. I also learnt, some time ago now, of the death of poor Thévenaz. I haven't seen Sidès although he is here. Seen Hartley, Man Ray. All of Greenwich Village is out strolling in Montparnasse. Ran into McBride quite by chance at the Rond Point des Champs Elysées. And you?—News of life in the open air in Tarrytown please. Has our Ibsenian Carrie put the elevator in? I like the wine here very much. I hope to return to New York in December, although deep down I don't really know why. Paris is deadly boring after a while. Affectionately to the three of you and my respects to Mrs Stettheimer, Rrose Sélavy. 7 rue Lemaitre, Puteaux, (Seine) or in Rouen, 71 rue Jeanne d'Arc.*

42. Marcel Duchamp to Louise and Walter Arensberg   autograph letter
15 November 1921, Rouen   collection PMA

Paris 15 Novembre.
      Chère Lou Cher Walter
Votre lettre annonce de bien tristes choses. N'allez vous pas revenir à N.Y.
   du tout? Rester en Californie?—
Ça me navre—
J'ai déjà assez de Paris et de la France en général— Je dois prendre un
   bateau dans le milieu de Janvier— je ne sais pas encore lequel, étant à la
   recherche d'une traversée économique—
A N.Y. j'ai l'intention de trouver un "job" dans le cinéma— pas comme
   acteur, plutôt comme assistant cameraman.
J'ai correspondu avec Sheeler à qui j'avais demandé de m'envoyer des
   photos du Nu—   *Nude Descending*
                                                          No. 1 [cat. 16] or *No. 2*
J'ai fait un bout de film, court, que j'emporterai avec moi—   [cat. 17]
Je continue les échecs, joue avec quelques forts joueurs d'ici et "tiens le
   coup"—
Que pouvez vous faire pendant 24 heures tous les jours en Californie. La
   nature doit se répéter bien souvent—
J'espère avancer mon verre encore un peu et peut-être le finir, si ça marche   *Large Glass* [cat. 2]
   comme je veux. Il ne me reste qu'un travail de fils de plomb sans choses
   extraordinaires. Peut être ne mourrai je pas avant qu'il soit fini.   The Comte de
                                                                          Lautréamont's *Poésies*,
Je vais vous envoyer la petite brochure des poésies de Lautréamont.   posthumously edited
Peut être aussi je pourrais vous être utile ici pour vendre les Picassos— Je   by Breton (Paris, Au
   connais Rosenberg et pourrais lui en parler si vous m'écrivez de le faire.   Sans-Pareil, 1920).
Donc pas à bientôt mais il n'y aura que 4000 miles entre nous au lieu de   **Léonce Rosenberg**
   8000 en Janvier   (1879-1947), owner of
                                                          the Galerie de l'Effort
      Affectueusement à tous deux   Moderne in Paris,
      Marcel   where many Cubists
71 rue Jeanne d'Arc Rouen   (including Picasso)
                                                          showed their work.

▷ TRANSLATION: *Paris 15th November. Dear Lou, dear Walter. What sad news your
letter brings. Won't you be coming back to New York at all? Staying in California?
It breaks my heart. I have already had enough of Paris and of France in general. I
am to take a boat mid-January. I don't know which as yet as I am looking for an
inexpensive passage. In New York I'm planning on getting a "job" in the cinema—
not as an actor, rather as an assistant cameraman. I've been in correspondance
with Sheeler whom I've asked to send me some photos of the Nude. I've made a bit
of film, a short, which I will bring with me. I'm keeping up my chess, playing with
some of the very good players here and "holding my own." Whatever can you find
to do 24 hours a day in California? The countryside must get quite repetitive after*

a while. I'm hoping to make a little more headway with my glass and possibly finish it, if things turn out as I would like. I just have some work to do with a lead wire, nothing out of the ordinary. Perhaps I won't die before it's finished, then. I'm going to send you the little book of Lautréamont's poetry. Perhaps I could also be of service to you with the sale of the Picassos. I know Rosenberg and could talk to him if you write and tell me to. So, not quite see you soon, but there will only be 4,000 miles between us in January instead of 8,000. Affectionately to you both, Marcel, 71 rue Jeanne d'Arc, Rouen.

---

43. Marcel Duchamp to Louise and Walter Arensberg   letter
[fall 1921], Rouen   original lost: photocopy collection PMA

[2 first pages are missing. Page 3:]
    Les Crotti de toute sorte vont bien et vous envoient des souvenirs
    Avez-vous les ~~poésies~~ *Poésies* du Comte de Lautréamont ?
    Ça a été réédité l'année dernière. Ce ne sont d'ailleurs pas les Poésies. Ce
        n'est qu'une longue préface aux Poésies— qui n'ont jamais été écrites,
        (car il a dû mourir avant) Je l vous l'enverrai.
    Vous y verrez toute la semence dadaïque.
        Ecrivez un peu— Affectueusement à tous deux
        Marcel
    71 rue Jeanne d'Arc Rouen

▷ TRANSLATION: *The Crottis of all varieties are well and wish to be remembered to you. Do you have the Comte de Lautréamont's Poems ? A new edition came out last year. In fact they aren't the Poems at all. Just a long preface to the Poems— which he never in fact wrote (as he must have died before). I'll send it to you. You'll see the whole Dadaic seed is in it. Drop me a line. Affectionately to you both, Marcel. 71 rue Jeanne d'Arc, Rouen.*

44. Marcel Duchamp to Ettie Stettheimer   autograph letter
3 January [1922], Rouen   collection YCAL

[written with left hand:]

Rouen 3 janvier
C'est très difficile d'écrire même de la main gauche.

[written with right hand:]

Je reprends ma droite.

Souhaits de saison pour toute la famille Stettheimer. Merci chère Ettie de
toutes les nouvelles que vous me donnez.

J'ai été à l'hotel Wagram. le manager, qui est au courant de votre histoire
m'a dit qu'on ne savait vraiment pas où étaient les chapeaux et plumes.
On sait où est votre buste. Je crains que la boîte de vues d'optique ne
soit dans un coin perdu de garde meuble—

En tout cas je rentre à Paris dans 2 jours et je vais tâcher de voir Mr.
Duhamel qui n'est visible qu'à des heures bien matutinales pour moi =
Si je peux dénicher la boîte de vues d'optique je la rapporterai comme le
dit Florine— Le reste reste—

L'Aquitania part le 28 janvier avec moi— Je serai dans vos murs (quelle
expression européenne!) le 2 ou 3 Février—

Gleizes et moi avons déploré la non venue de Florine à Paris— A t elle au
moins fait le nécessaire pour exposer aux Indépendants?

Et la House Keeperin? M'en veut elle de ne pas lui avoir écrit? Pardonnez
moi chère Carrie = je n'ai pas voulu vous rappeler les dures heures de la
guerre qui et ses lettres de filleuls.

J'ai vu le Dial— Il y a dada de génie j'aime mieux ça que génie de dada—
Ça me rappelle la bonne nouvelle et la nouvelle bonne—

Henry McBride, "The
Walter Arenbergs [sic],"
The Dial, July 1920.

Au revoir et cette fois ci, ce n'est pas du papier mais ma main que vous
toucherez. Encore un mois et je longerai Columbus AVENUE à l'ombre
de l'Elevated⎯

= **elevated** railway, NY.

Affectueusement à toutes

~~Marcel~~

Duche

▷ TRANSLATION: *Rouen, 3rd January. Writing is really difficult even with your left
hand. I'm going back to my right hand now. Season's greetings to all the
Stettheimer family. Thank you, dear Ettie, for all the news you send me. I went to
the Hotel Wagram. The manager, who knows the whole story, told me they really
didn't know where the hats and the feathers were. They know where your bust is. I
fear the optical viewing box must be lying around in some warehouse somewhere.
In any case, I'll be back in Paris in two days and will try to see Mr Duhamel who
is only available first thing in the morning—it is for me anyway. = If I can fish out
the optical viewing box, I'll bring it back as Florine says. Whatever's left gets left
here. The Aquitania leaves on 28th January with me on it. I will be within your
walls (what a European expression!) by 2nd or 3rd February. Gleizes and I were
appalled at Florine's not coming to Paris. Has she at least done the necessary so
that she can exhibit at the Independents? And the House Keeperin? Is she mad
at me for not having written her? Forgive me, my dear Carrie = I did not mean to
remind you of the hard times in the war and its letters from godsons. I've seen the
Dial. It has genius Dada. I prefer that to Dada genius. That reminds me of "made
good news" and "good new maid." Goodbye and this time it will not be paper but
my hand you will touch. One more month and I'll be walking down Columbus
Avenue in the shade of the Elevated. Affectionately to you all, Duche.*

28 January 1922
Duchamp sails for New York aboard the S.S.
"Aquitania," arriving approximately one week later.
He takes a studio in the Lincoln Arcade Building.

---

45. Marcel Duchamp to Henri-Pierre Roché   autograph letter
circa 15 February [1922], New York   collection HRHRC

15 Février environ
Non je n'ai vraiment pas envie d'ouvrir des horizons.
Quand j'aurai un peu d'argent, je ferai d'autres choses⎯ Mais je ne crois
pas *que* les quelques centaines de francs ou de thunes que j'en tirerais me
dédommageraient de l'emmerdement de voir cela reproduit
publiquement.⎯
J'en ai plein le dos d'être peintre ou cinématographiste. La seule chose qui
puisse m'intéresser maintenant c'est une potion qui me ferait jouer
divinement aux échecs⎯
Cela m'exciterait.

Au revoir vieux, bonjour aux Couraux. et écris encore.
Duchamp
1947 Broadway Room 312 N. Y City

▷ TRANSLATION: *15th February approximately. No, I really don't feel like broadening my horizons. When I get a little money, I will do different things. But I don't think that the few hundred francs or whatever cash I would get out of it could make up for the hassle of seeing this reproduced for the public. I've had it up to here with being a painter or a cinematographer. The only thing that could arouse my interest right now is a wonder drug that would make me play chess divinely. That would really turn me on. Goodbye old chap, say hello to the Coraux and write again, Duchamp. 1947 Broadway. Room 312. N.Y. City.*

---

46. Marcel Duchamp to Man Ray[*]
[April or May 1922], New York

autograph letter
collection HRHRC

Merci de ta lettre et de la photo
Embrasse Kiki pour moi— Je suis enchanté de savoir que tu t'amuses bien
et que surtout tu as lâché la peinture

Kiki, called Kiki de Montparnasse, pseudonym of Alice Prin (1901-1953), girlfriend of Man Ray.

---

[*] **Man Ray** (1890-1976) and Duchamp met in 1915, shortly after Duchamp's arrival in America. Man Ray was living in an artist's colony in Ridgefield, New Jersey, where Walter Arensberg (p.50) took Duchamp out for a Sunday afternoon visit. According to Man Ray, he and Duchamp played tennis, communication kept to a minimum, for Man Ray hardly spoke a word of French. During the next three or four years, the two artists saw one another occasionally at various art events in New York, or at gatherings at the Arensberg apartment. But their friendship intensified in 1920, when Man Ray separated from his wife and lived alone in a studio on Eighth Street in Greenwich Village. Since Man Ray developed a proficiency with his camera, Duchamp enlisted his assistance in recording several of his works, from the piles of dust that accumulated on the surface of his *Large Glass*, to his famous female alter ego, Rrose Sélavy. These contacts led to many artistic collaborations, such as their publication of the single-issue magazine, *New York Dada*, the making of a Dada film (which was accidentally destroyed in the developing process) and, together with Katherine Dreier (p.46), the formation of the Société Anonyme. During the 1920's and 1930's, when they both lived in Paris, Man Ray and MD saw one another often, virtually eliminating the need for correspondence. But when Man Ray moved to Hollywood in the 1940's (and Duchamp lived in New York), they exchanged letters quite frequently. Duchamp designed the cover of Man Ray's catalog for an exhibition of his objects at the Julien Levy Gallery in 1945, and when Man Ray was passing through New York on his way back to Europe, Duchamp gave him an example of his *Female Fig Leaf*, an erotic object that he entrusted Man Ray to cast in a limited edition. When Duchamp wanted an example of his *Bottle Rack* for a show in New York, he would write and ask Man Ray to purchase one from a department store in Paris and ship it to him. During the last decades of their lives, whenever Duchamp returned to Paris, he would be certain to visit his old friend and fellow Dada co-conspirator; indeed, Man Ray and his wife Juliet were among the last people to see Duchamp, for with the art critic Robert Lebel and his wife, they dined with Duchamp and his wife Teeny at their apartment in Neuilly on the evening he died.

Oui j'ai été souffrant c.à.d. sortes de palpitations dans la région du cœur
mais rien d'organique dit le docteur "glandular" if you know what that
means— Tout est "glandular" cette année ici— Il m'a donné une potion
et des capsules brunes qui doivent activer la sécrétion de ma glande
surrénale
"Say it with music" est la chanson à la mode ici—
Avais tu vu "Shuffle Along" avant de quitter N.Y.? On le joue encore et
c'est un show nègre épatant.
J'ai vu un dernier Charlie Chaplin "Pay day" qui est amusant mais trop
court.
Vu Daniel qui m'a demandé de tes nouvelles, mais semble avoir oublié
qu'il t'avait promis quelque chose—
Stella a eu une "affaire" de queue importante, collage sérieux, qu'il vient
de rompre enchanté de retrouver sa liberté
Rien à la S.A.
Je donne mes leçons de français et fais juste assez pour vivre—
J'ai fait revenir mon verre et je travaille un peu dessus. Quelle barbe!—
Pas de cinéma— Pas de fonds—
Echecs beaucoup mais théoriques— Je descends moins au Club.— je
"travaille" chez moi— classifie, compile—
Marshall Club va être champion cette année. Nous avons encore Samedi
prochain à jouer contre "Swedish Club"— que nous devons battre
facilement et ce sera fini—
Nous avons battu Rice, Manhattan et tous les autres excepté Brooklyn
avec lequel nous avons fait match nul—
J'ai joué dans la plupart des parties mais pas tous— Un ou 2 nouveaux
bons joueurs au Club—
Hazel va bien et t'envoie ses amitiés—
Merci pour la photo de Brancusi Tzara et toi— *(et celle de Kiki et toi
épatante)*
Dis à Tzara que j'ai donné la photo de lui que tu avais faite à Little Review
pour qu'ils la reproduisent dans un prochain numéro. Mais je doute que
ce numéro paraissent parce que argent—
Embrasse Tzara pour moi. et à bientôt—
    J'écris un mot à G.R.D.
    Marcel à vie
1947 B'way—

"Shuffle Along" = a ballet playing in NY, spring 1922.

"Pay Day" released in NY 2 Apr 1922.

Charles Daniel (1856-1934) owner of the Daniel Gallery, NY, where Man Ray showed when living in NY.

Joseph Stella (1877-1946), Italian-born Futurist painter, emigrated to US 1896.

"S.A." = Société Anonyme, first "museum" of Modern Art, founded by Miss Dreier, MD and Man Ray, 29 Apr 1920.

Marshall Club = Chess club in NY, Miss Dreier is a member.

Hazel, ex-companion of Man Ray in NY.

Photograph published, with the images of Tzara and Man Ray cut, in the *Little Review* (spring 1922), p.29.

G.R.D. = Georges Ribemont-Dessaignes

▷ TRANSLATION: *Thank you for your letter and the photo. Give Kiki my love. I am
delighted to know that you're having fun and most of all that you're through with
painting. Yes, I have been sick, i.e. kind of palpitations around the heart but nothing organic the doctor says "glandular" if you know what that means. Everything*

is "glandular" this year. He's given me a potion and some brown capsules supposed to stimulate secretion of my suprarenal gland. "Say it with music" is the hit song here. Did you get to see "Shuffle Along" before leaving N.Y.? It's still playing and a wonderful negro show. I saw a recent Charlie Chaplin, "Pay day," which is funny but too short. Saw Daniel who asked after you, but seemed to have forgotten he'd promised you something. Stella had a big "lust affair," serious stuff, that he's just broken off—delighted to have his freedom again. Nothing at the S.A. I'm giving my French lessons and making just enough to get by. I had my glass brought back and am working on it a little. What a drag! No movies—no money. Lot of chess, but theoretical. I go down to the Club less now. I "work" at home, classifying, compiling. The Marshall Club is going to win the championship this year. We still have next Saturday to play against the "Swedish Club" which we should beat quite easily and that'll be that. We beat Rice, Manhattan and all the rest, except Brooklyn which was a draw. I played in most of the matches but not all. One or two good new players at the Club. Hazel is well and sends her best wishes. Thanks for the photo of Brancusi, Tzara and you (and the one of you and Kiki, amazing). Tell Tzara that I've given the photo you took of him to Little Review for them to reproduce it in a forthcoming issue. But I doubt this issue will come out because—money. Give my love to Tzara. So long. I'll drop a line to G.R.D. Yours ever, Marcel. 1947 Broadway.

47. Marcel Duchamp to Alfred Stieglitz[*]   autograph letter
[17 May 1922, New York]   collection YCAL

> Dear Stieglitz__
> Even a few ŷ words I don't feel like writing.
> You know exactly what I think about photography
> I would like to see it make people despise painting until something else
>   will make photography unbearable__
> There we are.
>   Affectueusement
>   Marcel Duchamp

Reply to Stieglitz's question, *"Can a photograph have the significance of art?"* All responses, including this one, appear in *MSS* [Manuscripts] No. 4, Dec 1922.

---

* **Alfred Stieglitz** (1864-1946), the acclaimed photographer and gallery owner, probably met Duchamp in 1915. Even before Duchamp came to New York, he would have heard about Stieglitz's Little Galleries of the Photo-Session, better known as "291" (from its address on Fifth Avenue), because his friend in Paris, Francis Picabia (p.58), had been given his first one-person show in America there two years earlier. When Picabia arrived for his second visit to New York in 1915, Duchamp would have had greater reason to encounter Stieglitz, even though—disgruntled by the lack of acceptance of modern art and by mounting financial difficulties—he was in the process of contemplating the closure of his gallery. How well Stieglitz and Duchamp got along is a matter open to question, since they differed so vastly in personality and temperament. Stieglitz could be rigid and formal in demeanor, and he was prone to lecturing anyone who was willing to listen on his particular point of view, no matter what the subject. Nevertheless, Duchamp recognized Stieglitz's important position within the New York art world, so it was he whom he approached in 1917 to take a photograph of the urinal that had been refused from display at the Independents. It was also Stieglitz's photograph of a woman's leg in high heels superimposed over a faint portrait that served as the frontispiece to *New York Dada.* In a public lecture delivered at the Brooklyn Museum in 1926, Stieglitz called *The Large Glass "one of the grandest works in the art of all time,"* and a few weeks later, after a viewing of Duchamp's *Anémic Cinéma,* he confessed that it *"was the first thing made by another person which he had ever wished he had done himself."* Stieglitz was disillusioned with Duchamp, however, when he heard that he had become involved in the art market (in a letter to Ettie Stettheimer he called Duchamp a *"Salesman of Art"*). In a letter to Katherine Dreier (letter 98.), Duchamp explained that he never really considered Stieglitz *"a friend of mine"* (but, then again, he confessed, there really weren't too many people whom he could call real friends).

48. Marcel Duchamp to Henry McBride[*]
[14 June 1922, New York]

autograph letter
collection YCAL

Mercredi
  Dear McBride
J'ai reçu les coupures. Merci
Je vais tâcher de trouver 5 photos__
  Matisse
  Picasso
  Marie Laurencin
  Picabia
  Brancusi
Croyez vous qu'il vous serait impossible de retrouver à l'Herald le Marie
  Laurencin du 6 Mai 1917 (paru à cette date)
Je vais demander à Sheeler s'il a des photos de Matisse, Picasso et
  Brancusi.
A propos de Picabia j'ai un numéro de 391 dans lequel il y a un dessin de
  lui qui est simplement une tache d'encre faite par un encrier renversé (et
  qu'il appelle *la* Sainte Vierge)__ Pensez vous que ce soit trop Dada?
Je pourrais probablement trouver autre chose de lui chez de Zayas.

Clippings for anthology of McBride's articles (written 1915 - 1922), designed by MD, under the title *"Some French Moderns... [cat. 56]"* (idem for subsequent letters to McBride).

Marie Laurencin (1885-1956), French painter.

La Sainte-Vierge, basically an **ink splash**, appears as the cover illustration to Picabia's *391*, March 1920.

---

* **Henry McBride** (1867-1962). When Duchamp arrived in America in 1915, Henry McBride was art editor of *The New York Sun*, and, throughout his long career as a journalist, he remained one of the most committed and dedicated supporters of modern art on the American scene. McBride probably first learned about Duchamp through the scandal that had resulted from the display of his *Nude Descending a Staircase* at the Armory Show in 1913. And because of his interest and support for modern French art, it is likely that he met Duchamp shortly after his arrival in the United States in 1915. McBride was the first to report upon Duchamp's discovery of Eilshemius at the 1917 Independents Exhibition, and it was McBride's writings on modern French art that Duchamp selected and published in *Some French Moderns Says McBride*, a book that he designed (with a somewhat eccentric layout) and published through the Société Anonyme in 1922. After Duchamp returned to Paris in 1923, McBride actually felt that his absence served to hinder the progress of modern art. *"When Marcel was here we almost got to the point of thinking that art consists of things rather than the painted reflection of them,"* he wrote in 1932. *"Now, it seems, we shall have to begin all over again."* After World War II, Duchamp returned to the United States and his friendship with McBride resumed. In 1952, when an exhibition of the Duchamp family opened at the Rose Fried Gallery in New York ("Duchamp Frères & Sœur: Œuvres d'Art"), McBride wrote for a last time on the artist whose work he had known for over forty years. *"From the moment of his arrival in America he began mystifying us,"* McBride observed, *"and he will go on mystifying us, I believe, to the end of the chapter."*

Now
Voici mon idée pour la couverture :

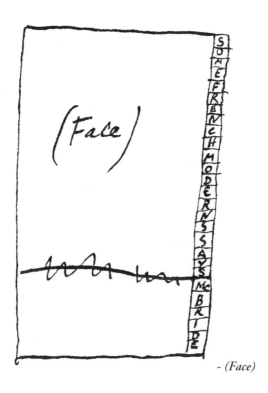

- *(Face)*

SOMEFRENCHMODERNSSAYSMcBRIDE

SOME FRENCH MODERNS SAYS MCBRIDE (présenté comme
l'alphabet de ces Dust proof files dans les bureaux)

Rien autre sur la couverture qui serait jaune crème et comme le papier
commercial.
De l'autre côté de chaque lettre
Société Anon. Incorp

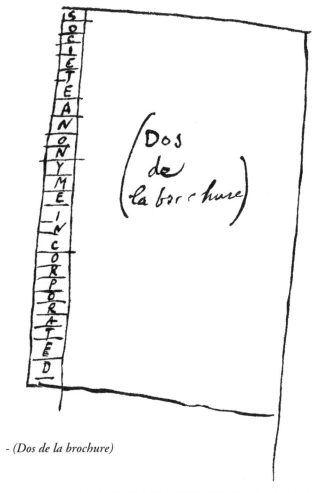

- (Dos de la brochure)

SOCIETEANONYMEINCORPORATED

Comme vous le voyez la brochure aurait 26 ou 27 pages (verso et recto)
puisque chaque lettre est attachée à une page différente.

Maintenant si j'ai assez de place je vous propose ceci : de partir à la
   première page avec des caractères infiniment petits, pour finir à la
   dernière page par de gros caractères, changeant la grandeur progressante
   des caractères à chaque page.
Je ne sais pas encore où je mettrai les illustrations
Dites moi d'abord ce que vous pensez de l'idée en général.
   Affectueusement
   Marcel
1947 B'way

▷ TRANSLATION: *Wednesday. Dear McBride, I got the clippings. Thank you. I will try to find 5 photos: Matisse, Picasso, Marie Laurencin, Picabia, Brancusi. Do you think it would be impossible for you to find, at the Herald, the Marie Laurencin dated 6th May 1917 (came out on that date)? I will ask Sheeler if he has photos of things by Matisse, Picasso and Brancusi. As far as Picabia is concerned, I have an issue of 391 in which there is a drawing by him. It is a simple ink stain made by an ink well, tipped over, (that he calls the Virgin Mary). Do you think this is too Dada? I could probably find something else by him at de Zayas'. Now—This is my idea for the cover:* [sketch caption: *front*] SOME FRENCH MODERNS SAYS MCBRIDE *(set out like the alphabet on those* Dust *proof files in offices). Nothing else on the cover, which would be creamy yellow and like business stationery. On the back of each letter, Société Anon. Incorp.* [sketch caption: *back of the brochure*]. *As you can see, the brochure would have 26 or 27 pages (front-back) since each letter is on a page of its own. Now, if I have enough room, I propose the following: Set off on the first page with minute characters, ending up on the last page with big characters, making the characters progressively larger with each page. I don't know where I'll put the illustrations yet. First, tell me what you think of the idea overall. Affectionately, Marcel. 1947 B'way.*

---

49. Marcel Duchamp to Henry McBride   autograph letter
[15 June 1922, New York]   collection YCAL

Jeudi
      Je vous envoie par le même courrier les photos que j'ai trouvées chez
De Zayas.
Sheeler m'a promis encore un Rousseau et un Brancusi (genre Mlle
   Pogany)—
Voulez *vous* me hiérarchiser par des numéros 1. 2. [paper ripped] etc. l'ordre
   dans lequ[el = paper ripped] vous les préférez— de façon à ce que si c'est
   trop cher je puisse supprimer les derniers numéros

Henri Rousseau
(1844-1910) alias *le Douanier*, French "naïve" painter.

Dans votre hiérarchie n'oubliez pas le Rousseau et Brancusi et renvoyez le tout vite—

Merci Marcel

▷ TRANSLATION: *Thursday. I am sending you, in the same mail, the photos that I found at De Zayas'. Sheeler has promised me another Rousseau and a Brancusi (Mademoiselle Pogany style). Could you list them for me, numbering them 1, 2, etc. according to your order of preference, so that I can take out the bottom numbers if it gets too expensive. Don't forget the Rousseau and the Brancusi in your list and send the whole thing back quickly. Thanks, Marcel.*

---

50. Marcel Duchamp to Henry McBride   autograph letter
[30 June 1922], New York   collection YCAL

J'ai enfin trouvé un Picabia convenable. C'est la photo d'une des choses qu'il avait à l'exposition dont vous parlez dans le numéro du Sun (à propos de lui).—

J'ai aussi trouvé un imprimeur qui me fera des prix raisonnables j'espère—

Si possible donc, nous aurons Brancusi

Bronze foncé

Sun = *The New York Sun*, newspaper where McBride is leading art critic.

Matisse (que vous avez vu)

Rousseau (les singes et la bouteille de lait) qui appartient à Arensberg.)

Picasso (ovale) dont j'espère avoir un bon cliché

Braque que je vous ai envoyé

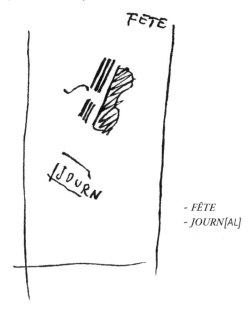

- *FÊTE*
- *JOURN[AL]*

Picabia (tableau peint pour raconter non pour prouver). Machine—
Derain que je vous ai envoyé Tête un peu penchée.
et le Marie Laurencin si vous pouvez l'avoir bientôt—

———

Je pense que c'est une bonne idée de mettre un Derain, un Braque,
   Brancusi et Rousseau quoique leurs noms ne soient pas mentionnés
   dans les articles— n'est-ce pas?
Dites moi si vous voulez que je mentionne les dates de chaque article— Je
   ne pense pas que ce soit nécessaire— J'avais pensé mettre les 2 premiers
   articles sur Cézanne ensemble ou tout au moins avec une petite
   séparation.
Dites moi aussi si vous préférez que les reproductions soient incorporées
   dans les articles ou toutes rejetées à la fin— je n'ai pas encore d'opinion
   à ce sujet

———

J'espère avoir 16 différents ~~types~~ *caractères* d'imprimerie (en grandeur et
   de la même famille)
Dès le 5 juillet je vais me mettre à l'exécution et j'espère avoir fini un mois
   après—

Dites moi bien vos dernières volontés, car comme vous me le dites, il n'est pas facile d'échanger des idées typographiques par lettre.

affect[t]

Marcel

1947 B'way—

30 juin

▷ TRANSLATION: *I've finally found a suitable Picabia. It's the photo of one of the things from the exhibition you talk about in that issue of the Sun (about him). I've also found a printer who will give me reasonable rates, I hope. If possible then, we will have Brancusi* [sketch]; *Matisse (which you've seen) dark bronze; Rousseau (the monkeys and the milk bottle—which belongs to Arensberg); Picasso (oval) of which I hope to get a good print; Braque which I sent you* [sketch caption: *Celebration; Newspaper*]; *Picabia (painting made to tell and not to prove). Machine; Derain which I sent you (Head slightly inclined) and the Marie Laurencin if you can get it soon. I think it is a good idea to put a Derain, a Braque, Brancusi and Rousseau even though their names are not mentioned in the articles, don't you? Tell me if you want me to put in the dates of each article. I don't think it is necessary. I thought I would put the two first articles on Cézanne together or at least with just a small gap. Tell me also whether you would prefer to have the reproductions inserted amongst the articles or at the end. I don't have an opinion on this point yet. I hope to have 16 different fonts (in terms of size—all the same family) I will get started on the execution by 5th July and hope to be finished a month later. Be sure and tell me your last wishes, because as you yourself say, it is not easy to exchange typographic ideas by letter. Affectionately, Marcel 1947 B'way 30th June.*

---

51. Marcel Duchamp to Henry McBride   autograph letter
[July? 1922, New York]   collection YCAL

Dear Henry (how do you like that?)

Tout va bien.— J'ai commencé Mercredi le travail d'exécution.

7 illustrations de la grandeur originale (les photos que je vous ai envoyées) : Brancusi, Derain Picasso, Braque, Rousseau, Matisse. Picabia.

Mon idée est de les encarter dans le texte collées sur un onglet.

Je pense donc qu'il sera mieux de les disperser— En première page je pourrais mettre Brancusi si vous voulez.

La brochure aura à peu près 30 pages__ et j'ai déjà choisi les caractères qui vont de 5 Pt. pour la première page à 120 ou plus pt. pour la dernière page qui aura 5 mots je crois)__ A chaque page le caractère, quoique de la même famille, changera en augmentant.

~~de~~ Les deux premiers articles sur Cézanne devront être lus à la loupe. Sur le verso de la première page de couverture je voudrais mettre

- *certified* [?]
- *copyright*

l'acknowledgment dont vous parlez.__ Mais voulez vous le formuler : Quelque chose comme cela :

> These Articles (?) appeared in the *N.Y.* Sun and N.Y. Herald *during the last seven years or* between 1915 and 1918
> Copyright 1922 by Rrose Sélavy

Cette dernière phrase est ma signature__ Rrose Sélavy, si vous ne le savez pas, est née en 1920.

Mais je voudrais que vous m'envoyiez une formule exacte d'acknowledgment comme vous la voulez.

A bientôt d'autres nouvelles je vais avoir Lundi ~~des~~ les "cuts" et je vous *en* enverrai les épreuves.

Rrose Sélavy

▷ TRANSLATION: Dear Henry, (how do you like that?) *Everything's fine. I started work on the execution on Wednesday. 7 illustrations true to their original size (the photos I sent you): Brancusi, Derain, Picasso, Braque, Rousseau, Matisse, Picabia. My idea is to incorporate them into the text by gluing them onto the binding strip* [sketch]. *I think it will be better to spread them out. I could, if you want, put Brancusi on the first page. The brochure will have about 30 pages and I have already chosen the typeface ranging from 5 pt. for the first page to 12 or more for the last page which will have 5 words (I think). With each page, the typeface, from the same family, will gradually increase in size. The first two articles on Cézanne will have to be read with a magnifying glass. On the back of the cover* [sketch] *I would like to put the* acknowledgment *you've been talking about. But can you draft it?— something like this:* These articles (?) appeared in the N.Y. Sun and N.Y. Herald during the last seven years or between 1915 and 1918 Copyright 1922 by Rrose Sélavy. *This last sentence is my signature. Rrose Sélavy, in case you didn't know, was born in 1920. But I would like you to send me a precise draft of the* acknowledgment *the way you want it. More news soon. I am getting the "cuts" Monday and will send you the proofs. Rrose Sélavy.*

---

52. Marcel Duchamp to Ettie Stettheimer   autograph letter
[9 July 1922, New York]   collection YCAL

Je suis parti les larmes dans les yeux. (Pourquoi pas?).

à Vous qui n'aimez pas les hommes qui pleurent, je n'ai pas voulu le
montrer__   **Poem** about

Merci à Florine pour le poëme. Mais ne veut elle pas le signer si je le fais   mosquitoes,
paraître à Paris dans un magazine Dada. R.S.V.P. (qu'elle signe <u>Florine</u>   apparently.
si elle ne veut pas compromettre la famille).

"J'en suis bien aise"__ est une vieille forme immortalisée dans une
chanson populaire "Je suis bien aise" (non pas "je suis aise") est encore
employé; mi-littéraire et mi-paysan__

Si vous avez l'intention de l'employer dites moi toute la phrase, parce que
c'est plutôt difficile à placer.

En tous cas cela veut dire : je suis heureux ou heureuse.   **Fania Marinoff** (1890-
                                                                            1971), Russian-born
Je suis bien aise d'apprendre que Fania est toujours la même petite fille   actress, wife of Carl
folle, que les pétards du 4 juillet ont réveillé ~~vous~~ vos sentiments de   Van Vechten (see p.75).
patriotesses et que vous avez acheté des aiguilles pour le Victrola.
                                                                            "**Victrola**" is a type of
Chaleur et morte saison.   gramophone, used
                                                                            later by MD for
C'est tout ce que j'ai à vous dire sur N.Y. City   *Rotoreliefs.*

Kan Karri vient elle?

        Baisers généreux et généraux pour toute la famille.

        Rrrose

Vendredi   **Suzanne Lenglen**
                                                                            (1899-1938), French
Je parie pour Lenglen.   tennis champion.

▷ TRANSLATION: *I had tears in my eyes when I left. (Why not?) Though as you don't
like men who cry, I did not want to show it. Thanks to Florine for the poem. But
won't she sign it if I publish it in Paris in a Dada magazine? R.S.V.P. (She can
sign it Florine if she doesn't want the family to be compromised). "J'en suis bien
aise" is an old expression that has been immortalized in a popular song "Je suis
bien aise" (and not "je suis aise") and is still in usage—part-literary and part-
uneducated. If you intend using it, give me the complete sentence because it's rather
hard to know when to use it. In any case it means I am a happy man or woman. I
am happy to learn that Fania is still the same crazy little girl, that the 4th July fire-
works aroused the patriotic woman in you all and that you bought needles for the
Victrola. Heat and slack season. That's all I have to tell you about N.Y. City. Kan
Karri come? A whole lot of kisses for the whole family, Rrose. Friday. I'm betting
on Lenglen.*

53. Marcel Duchamp to Yvonne Chastel   autograph letter
15 July [1922?], New York   collection GRI

N.Y. 15 Juillet

Ma chère petite Yvonne J'ai reçu le mot de Mad me demandant de   Madeleine Turban
renvoyer ces lettres à toi et 2 autres comme si elle était à N.Y. Quel
numéro! Où est-elle partie? J'ai aussi fait la connaissance d'une amie à
elle, Edna Nicolle qui est bien gentille mais vraiment un peu jeune et   Y.W.C.A. = Young
Y.W.C.A.—   Women's Christian
                                                                              Association.
Je reçois à l'instant une lettre de Gaby P— me disant que tu es changée en   "Gaby P" = Gabrielle
bien dis tu—   Picabia née Buffet
                                                                              (1881-1985), Francis
En tout cas tâchez de vous débarrasser toutes les deux de cette manie de   Picabia's first wife,
persécution que j'ai aussi mais dont je ne souffre pas—   music student who
                                                                              travels back and forth
Elle te racontera les potins de N.Y. Les Arensberg après avoir donné congé   between NY and Paris
de leur appartement vont rester je crois à N.Y— C'est un peu lugubre   to promote the French
et plein de potins dont je suis tout à fait en dehors.   fashion industry.

Je vois tout le monde mais réellement n'ai de relations intimes avec
personne—

C'est un des avantages de ma situation de mac— Les gens ont beaucoup
plus de respect pour moi qu'avant. Je rigole profondément de leur
attitude

J'ai déménagé et suis revenu au vieux Lincoln Arcade que tu connus—   Yvonne Chastel was
dans une chambre moitié moins grande que celle que tu connaissais et   indeed familiar with
je paie 35 dollars par mois.   Room 512; MD living in
                                                                              Room 312 since
J'arrange en ce moment cette pièce, blanchis   Feb 1922.

J'ai un appareil de cinéma et vais commencer à en faire sérieusement—

Eté délicieux assez chaud mais je ne semble bien vivre que dans cette
chaleur de N.Y.— Je vais vraiment mieux. Bois du lait par gallons.

Aimes tu le lait, bois ~~be~~ en beaucoup c'est excellent et simple à prendre—   Nicole Groult (b.1889),
                                                                              dress designer, sister
Je trouve que si l'affaire Groult s'établit sur un grand pied tu devrais venir   of Paul Poiret and close
avec Gaby— et tu y trouverais ton beurre—   friend of H.-P. Roché
                                                                              and Marie Laurencin.
Stella a été volé chez lui— on lui a pris tes mouchoirs c'est ce qu'il regrette
le plus.

De Journo va bien et s'occupe beaucoup de l'affaire Groult.

Dis aussi à Gaby que O'Gilvie n'a pas revu sa cliente et je pense qu'on va
incorporer avec 15 ou 20 000 dollars quitte à joindre ensuite l'apport des
autres.

Au revoir ma petite Yvonne, je sais que tu es bien dans ton atelier mais
raconte moi un peu tes histoires si tu en as envie—
J'espère aussi que tout s'arrangera pour [que] tu puisses venir à N.Y.
    Affectueusement
    Marcel.
1947 Broadway
Room 316
New York City

▷ TRANSLATION: *N.Y. 15th July. My dear little Yvonne, I got Mad's note asking me to
send you these letters and two others as if she were in N.Y. What a character!
Where's she gone? I also met a friend of hers, Edna Nicolle, who is very nice but
really rather young and Y.W.C.A. I've just this minute got a letter from Gaby P.
saying you are changed for the better, you say. Try, the pair of you, to get rid of this
persecution mania, which I also have, though I don't let it make me suffer. She'll
tell you the gossip from N.Y. The Arensbergs have taken leave of their apartment
but are going to stay in N.Y., I think. It's pretty gloomy and full of gossip but I'm
outside all that. I see everybody, but in reality, am close to nobody. It's one of the
advantages of my being a pimp. People have a lot more respect for me than before.
Their attitude really makes me laugh. I have moved house and come back to the old
Lincoln Arcade which you once knew, in a room half the size of the one you knew
and I'm paying 35 dollars a month. I'm fixing it up at the moment, this room,
whitewashing. I have a movie camera and am going to start using it seriously. Gorgeous summer, quite hot, but it's only in this N.Y. heat that I seem to really enjoy
life. I'm really much better. Drinking milk by the gallon. Do you like milk? You
should drink plenty of it—it's excellent and easy to drink. I think that if the Groult
affair takes off in a big way, you should come over with Gaby, and you'll make a
packet. Stella got burgled at his home. They stole your handkerchiefs which he's
more upset about than anything else. De Journo is fine and very involved with the
Groult matter. Tell Gaby also that O'Gilvie hasn't seen his client again and I think
we're incorporating with 15 or 20,000 dollars as we can always put in the deposit
from the others later. Farewell, my little Yvonne, I know that you are fine in your
studio, but do tell me a little about what's going on in your life, if you care to. I also
hope that things will work out so that you can come to N.Y. Affectionately, Marcel.
1947 Broadway, Room 316, New York City.*

---

54. Marcel Duchamp to Henry McBride   autograph letter
[after July, 1922, New York]   collection YCAL

> Cher Henry
> Une éternité depuis votre et ma dernières lettres.
> Où êtes-vous?
> Si vous êtes ici, je voudrais que vous veniez un jour à l'imprimerie avec
>   moi : je vous montrerais votre brochure presque finie
> Tout est imprimé__
> Nous finissons de coller les illustrations__ et pour satisfaire notre
>   curiosité, nous allons finir complètement d'abord 50 exemplaires, de
>   façon à pouvoir commencer à les distribuer__
> Ecrivez vite
>   Affect^t
>   Marcel Rrose

▷ TRANSLATION: *Dear Henry, An eternity since your last letter and mine. Where are you? If you are here, I would like you to come with me to the printer's one day and I'll show you your brochure—almost done. Everything's printed. We've almost finished gluing in the illustrations and, just to satisfy our curiosity, we're going to finish the first 50 copies completely, so that we can start to circulate them. Write soon. Affectionately, Marcel Rrose.*

---

55. Marcel Duchamp to Man Ray   autograph letter
[Summer 1922, New York]   Collection Attilio Codognato, Venice

> Dear Man
> I am a businessman__ Hart and I bought a dye shop__ He dyes and I keep
>   books__ If we are successful, we don't know what we will do.
> I received your 2 Rayographs which, I think, are wonderful. Got also the
>   magazine with the reproductions of your‡ photo__
> Keep on, dear old Man__
> Stella is sorry that he did not leave at the same time you did and is
>   planning to get away
> Nothing here of course__
> I am not even chessing. Got a little disgusted__
> Vanity Fair is full of portraits by you__ You are becoming a very well
>   know [sic] firm__
> No movies, no money__ or the other way around__
> Give that letter to Tzara and also the yellow one from the Baronness
>   affect^t
>   Marcelavy

Hart = Léon Hartl, French painter, opened a fabric-dyeing shop with MD, spring 1922, which was to close 6 months later.

Rayograph = photography without a camera (photographic paper is covered by an object, exposed to light and developed).

Vanity Fair, June 1922, p.76, "We Nominate for the Hall of Fame."

"Baroness" = Elsa von Freytag-Loringhoven (1874-1927), better known simply as "The Baroness," eccentric German artist and poet.

56. Marcel Duchamp to Ettie and Carrie Stettheimer
[11 August 1922, New York]

autograph letter
collection YCAL

Share Ettie, 2 longues semaines ont passé depuis notre birthday.
C'est le commencement des "nombreux heureux retours"— Je voudrais
avoir des boîtes de ce papier à lettres.

J'ai fait teindre ma chemise d'un vert bouteille foncé, genre raincoat,
merveilleux. J'attends avec impatience que vous veniez à N.Y. pour
m² exhiber Rrose Sélavy dans le vert bouteille.

Ma vie décousue continue.

Leçons par ci, leçons par là un peu de la brochure McBride qui n'en finit
pas.

Demandez à Florine de me renvoyer les mosquitoes avec la <u>nouvelle</u> fin et
sa <u>signature</u> et dites lui d'écrire et d'envoyer ses toiles à Paris car je suis
sûr qu'elle ne l'a pas encore fait.

Savez vous qu'on a failli ouvrir un restaurant Carrie-Rose

Je regrette bien de ne pas m'être levé une heure plus tôt ce matin là, ma
chère Carrie, pour m'être vu en garçon de café (ce qui est la
caractéristique des Français à l'étranger quand ils ne sont pas décorés de
la Légion d'honneur)

Je vous envoie par le même courrier une brochure que je me suis chargé de
propager ici— De Massot a 20 ans et vous amusera peut être un peu.

Evitez peut-être de la montrer à Mrs. Stettheimer qui ne veut pas que je
regarde "Jügend"—

A toutes affections multipliées

Rrose. Jeudi soir.

MD's perfume bottle
Beautiful Breath...
[cat. 45].

McBride brochure
*Some French
Moderns...* [cat. 56].

Mosquitoes, see p.118.

Reference to *Essai de
critique théâtrale,*
Paris, h.c., [May] 1922.

Pierre de Massot
(1900-1969), French
writer.

= "Jugend" = youth, in
German.

▷ TRANSLATION: Share *Ettie, 2 long weeks have gone by since our birthday. It's the
start of "many happy returns." I would like to have some boxes of stationery like
this. I've had my shirt dyed dark bottle green, like a raincoat, marvellous. I can't
wait for you to come to N.Y. so I can exhibit Rrose Sélavy in the bottle green. My
disjointed life goes on. Lessons here, lessons there and a bit of the McBride brochure
which is never-ending. Ask Florine to send me the mosquitoes with the new ending
and her signature and tell her to write and send her canvases to Paris because I'm
sure she hasn't yet done so. Do you know we just missed the opening of a restaurant
called Carrie-Rose? I'm really sorry I didn't get up an hour earlier that morning,
my dear Carrie, to have seen what I looked like as a waiter (which is the caricature
of the French abroad unless they have been awarded the Legion of Honor). I'm
sending you, in the same mail, a brochure I took it upon myself to distribute here.
De Massot is 20, you might find him amusing. Perhaps you'd better not show it to
Mrs Stettheimer who doesn't like me looking at "Jügend." To you all, affections
times over, Rrose. Thursday evening.*

57. Marcel Duchamp to Man Ray   autograph letter
[October (?) 1922], New York   collection Timothy Baum, New York

Thanks for the inventeur Constructeur— Simplement merveilleux—
Non cette chose que je vous ai envoyée est un "pamphlet" (réel) que j'ai
trouvé chez des amis. J'ai aussi bien reçu votre lettre me parlant du
changement important = un atelier dans cette maison (31bis Campagne
Première) est une chose remarquable.
Dans le même immeuble au 31bis ou au 31. j'ai des amis, Mr et Mme Haas
Du Rieux qui seraient sûrement contents de vous connaître et ~~de~~
probablement de vous demander des photos. Allez les voir de ma part,
ils sont très gentils = Ils ont un des petits hôtels derrière dans la cour
avec une entrée passage Denfert n°27.
Allez y de ma part—
Je joins ici une lettre pour Tzara qui est peut-être de retour à Paris. Lisez
la : elle contient un projet financier et peut être y verrez *vous* des moyens
pratiques d'opérer que Tzara ne verrait pas.—
Dites à Brancusi que je regrette de lui avoir fait de la peine, mais que les
girls Jane Heap et Margaret Anderson l'adorent : Ça, il ne peut pas
l'éviter.
Ci joint aussi un petit quatrain de Florine Stettheimer, que vous devriez
tâcher d'insérer dans une production de Tzara (Le cœur à Barbe ou
autre)—
Stella va bien, habite Brooklyn, fait une série de 5 toiles qui vont ensemble
et "expriment" New York— Il a l'intention d'exposer cela à la S.A.— Si
les salles sont assez grandes— (7^{m} de large)—
C'est lui qui a votre *grande* peinture qui est revenue de la tournée S.A.—
Peut-être aimeriez vous l'avoir à Paris. Si oui, on pourrait peut-être la
rouler et vous l'envoyer— Dites ce que vous voulez en faire.
Au revoir vieux. écrivez encore. Hazelle vous envoie ses amitiés elle va
partir en tournée vaudeville avec une amie—
Je n'ai pas vu les Locher depuis 2 mois. La teinture marche mais pas encore
assez pour me permettre d'acheter des cigares—
          Rrose Sélavy
1947 B'way.

The "**pamphlet**" is *The Non-Dada* [cat. 48].

"**letter for Tzara**" is next letter.

Brancusi upset apparently with the way he appears "sitting alone," as Man Ray is later to recall, "with the rubber bulb held in his crotch in a most suggestive attitude."

Jane Heap (1883-1964) and **Margaret Anderson** (1886-1973), editors of *The Little Review* (1914-1929).

Le Cœur à Barbe, eight-page Paris Dada publication by Tristan Tzara, April 1922.

S.A. = Société Anonyme

Big painting is Man Ray's *The Rope Dancer Accompanies Herself With Her Shadows*, 1916 (MoMA, NY).

Hazelle = Hazel (p.107)

Robert Evans Locher (1888-1956), an illustrator living with his wife, **Beatrice Howard**, in a large house on Staten Island where MD stays Dec 1926.

On "**la teinture**" (dyeing): see p.121.

▷ TRANSLATION: Thanks for the *Inventor Constructor. Simply marvellous. No, this
thing I sent you is a (real) "pamphlet" that I found at some friends' place. I also
got your letter telling me about the big change = a studio in this house (31 bis
Campagne Premier) is a remarkable thing. In the same building at 31 bis or at 31,
I have some friends, Mr and Mrs Haas du Rieux who would certainly be very
pleased to meet you and probably ask you for some photos. Go and see them on my
behalf, they're very nice.=They have one of the small hotels at the back, off the court-*

yard, with an entrance in passage Denfert no 27. Say I sent you. I enclose a letter for Tzara, perhaps he's back in Paris. Read it, there's a financial project in it—you might see a practical way to proceed that Tzara wouldn't. Tell Brancusi that I'm really sorry I upset him, but that the girls Jane Heap and Margaret Anderson are crazy about him. Nothing he can do about it. Also enclosed, a little poem by Florine Stettheimer which you should try to squeeze into one of Tzara's numbers (Le Cœur à barbe or something). Stella is fine, living in Brooklyn, making a series of 5 canvases that go together and "express" New York. He's planning on exhibiting it at the S.A. if the rooms are large enough (7m wide). He in fact has your big painting which has come back from the S.A. tour. Maybe you would like to have it in Paris? If so, maybe it could be rolled and sent to you. Let me know what you want to do. Goodbye old chap, write some more. Hazel sends her best wishes—she's going off on a vaudeville tour with a friend. I haven't seen the Lochers for 2 months. The dyeing's going well, but not well enough for me to buy cigars yet. Rrose Sélavy. 1947 Broadway.

---

58. Marcel Duchamp to Tristan Tzara   autograph letter
[October (?) 1922], New York   collection BLJD
published by P.A.B. (Alès, France) in 1959. See letters 253 and 254.

Tzara

    Cher vieux. J'ai vu vos articles dans Vanity Fair et aussi Secession. Mais pas encore Munson—

Il y aurait un grand projet possible qui rapporterait vraisemblablement de l'argent—

Ce serait de faire frapper ou faire 4 lettres DADA en métal séparées et réunies par une petite chaîne. Puis faire un prospectus pas très long (3 pages environ dans toutes les langues)— Dans ce prospectus, on énumérerait les vertus de Dada : En un mot pour faire acheter les'insigne à touts les gens de province de tous les pays, au prix d'un dollar ou l'équivalent en autres monnaies.— Le fait d'acheter cet insigne sacrerait l'acheteur Dada = on lui expliquerait naturellement qu'il y a 3 sortes de Dadas, les Dadas anti— les Dadas pro— et les Dadas neutres. Mais que quelles que soient ses opinions, l'insigne ~~lui permettrait d'éviter~~ le protégerait contre certaines maladies, contre les ennuis multiples de la vie, quelque chose comme les pilules Pink pour tout;— Naturellement l'objection première et la seule est la mise à la poste de 100 000 prospectus à 1 sou— La frappe des lettres en métal ne coûterait pas cher = Le secret de la réussite financière serait dans la rédaction alléchante du prospectus (qui à mon avis ne devrait être que ~~un~~ le résumé d'une brochure plus longue avec photos qui serait envoyée avec

Vanity Fair article by Tzara, "Some Memoirs of Dadaism," July 1922: his denial of having written the introduction to this article is reported in *Secession 3*, Aug 1922.

Gordham B. Munson (1896-1969), critic and educator, editor of *Secession*.

l'insigne). On recommanderait de porter l'insigne en bracelet
scapulaire, boutons de manchettes, épingle de cravate,
— Il y aurait des modèles en argent, or, platine. qui naturellement
coûteraient plus d'1 dollar.
— Il y aurait un agent dans chaque ville importante = et si vous pouviez
diviser le travail en Europe, je pourrais m'occuper des Etats Unis.
Naturellement je pense que ça amènerait toute une polémique de la part
de bien des Vrais Dadas; mais tout cela ne ferait que du bien au
rendement financier—
Si cela vous intéresse, vous devriez tâcher d'écrire un brouillon de
prospectus, je vous enverrai des idées si j'en ai.
Peut être pourrions nous commencer en petit—
Aussi sous forme de réclame dans les journaux revues, de province—
Vous comprenez bien mon idée : rien de "littéraire", "artistique". pure
médecine, panacée universelle, fétiche; dans ce sens : si vous avez mal
aux dents allez chez votre dentiste, et demandez lui s'il est Dada =
Si vous êtes à bout d'arguments dans une discussion : Dada est la meilleure
réponse à n'importe quel "pourquoi".— etc.

———

Si l'idée ne vous intéresse pas dites le moi quand même— parlez en à Man
Ray ça l'amusera. J'y penserai plus longuement si vous trouvez que ça en
vaille la peine.

———

Je vais aller voir Shadowland dans lequel Kreymborg a écrit un article sur
Dada— Peut être prendront ils un article de vous—
    Marcel Duchamp
1947 Broadway N. Y. City

Alfred Kreymborg
(1883-1966), poet and
literary critic, editor of
Others and *Glebe*,
his article, "Dada and
the dadas," appears in
Shadowland, Sept 1922

▷ TRANSLATION: *Tzara, I've read your articles in Vanity Fair and also Secession but
not Munson yet. There's a possibility of a big project which might well make some
money. This would be to have the 4 letters DADA punched or fashioned in metal
separately and then linked together by a little chain. Then make a leaflet, just a
short one (about 3 pages in each language). In this leaflet, we would spell out the
virtues of Dada, basically to get people from the provinces from all different coun-
tries to buy the insignia for a dollar or equivalent in other currencies. The act of buying the insignia amounts to a rite of passage to Dada status for the purchaser. We
would of course explain to him that there are 3 types of Dada—the anti-Dadas, the
pro-Dadas and the neutral Dadas. But that whatever their point of view, the insignia would protect them against certain illnesses, against many of life's problems,
something like Pink pills that cure anything. Naturally, the first and only argument against is having to put 100,000 penny leaflets in the post. Making the metal
letters wouldn't cost a lot. The trick to make it a financial success lies in writing a
mouth-watering leaflet (which in my view should just be a resumé of some longer*

brochure with photos to be sent out with the insignia). We would recommend wearing the insignia around the neck, as cufflinks or a tie-pin. There would be silver, gold and platinum models which would naturally cost more than 1 dollar. There would be an agent in every large town and if you could share out the work in Europe, I could take care of the United States. Of course I expect it would cause a good deal of controversy among Real Dadas, but all this can only do good to the coffers. If you are interested, you should start drafting a rough leaflet. I'll send you some ideas if I have any. Maybe we could start small, also as a kind of advertisement in newspapers and reviews—in the provinces. You'll get the idea: nothing "literary," "artistic"—pure medicine, universal panacea, fetish, so that if you have toothache, go to your dentist and ask him if he's Dada. If you run out of arguments in a discussion, Dada is the best answer to the question "why" etc. If you are not interested in the idea let me know all the same. Tell Man Ray about it, he'll find it amusing. I'll give it some more thought if you think the idea's worthwhile. I'm going to see Shadowland in which Kreymburg has written an article on Dada. Perhaps they'd take one of your articles. Marcel Duchamp. 1947 Broadway, N.Y. City.

---

59. Marcel Duchamp to Francis Picabia   autograph letter
[November 1922]   collection BLJD

> **Rrose Sélavy trouve qu'un incesticide doit coucher avec sa mère avant de la tuer; les punaises sont de rigueur.**

――――

Envoyer quelques numéros de Litté. (Lits et ratures)――   Refers to magazine
Etes vous à Montfort pour l'hiver?   *Littérature*, new series
Je rebois.   No.5, 1 Oct 1922, where
Ne fais rien.   MD published 6
Ai peu fait d'échecs depuis 4 mois   aphorisms signed
Vais recommencer mon entraînement.   Rrose Sélavy.
Rien ne se passe ici―― Vu De Journo deux ou 3 fois―― Ai une teinturerie
   qui va marcher――
Me couche beaucoup moins tard
    à Germaine des baisers à vous des fleurs   **Germaine** = Germaine
    Rrose Sélavy.   Everling

▷ TRANSLATION: *Rrose Sélavy feels that an incesticide should lie with its mother before killing her—bugs are a must. Send some issues of Litté. (read and red-inked). Are you in Montfort for the winter? I've started drinking again. Doing nothing. Hardly played chess in 4 months. Going to start my training again. Nothing ever happens here. Seen de Journo two or 3 times. Got a dye shop that's going to work. Going to bed much earlier. Kisses to Germaine and flowers for you, Rrose Sélavy.*

60. Marcel Duchamp to Francis Picabia
8 December 1922, New York

telegram
collection BLJD

Telegram in response
to a request from
Picabia that MD
collaborate on a film.

NEW YORK - 8.12 1922. 15 H.

PICABIA TREMBLAY

NON BOURDELLE DIEU

SELATZ

Tremblay-sur-Mauldre
(Seine-et-Oise), village
where Picabia lives.

▷ TRANSLATION: *Good God, not bloody likely. Selatz.* [Pun on the name Bourdelle (classic French sculptor) reminiscent of the French "bordel" (brothel). "Selatz" must be a new nickname for Sélavy.]

---

61. Marcel Duchamp to Jacques and Gabrielle Villon
25 December [1922, New York]

autograph letter
Duchamp Archives, Villiers-sous-Grez

HOTEL BREVOORT
anciennement Brevoort House
Coin de la 5me avenue et de la 8me rue
cable address, LAFBREVORT.
New York, *25 Déc.*

      Cher Gaston chère Gaby—

    Ton exposition est ouverte depuis le 16 à la Société Anonyme—
    L'ensemble fait très bien surtout à cause des murs qui sont en toile cirée
    bleu vert pâle presque blanc— neutre— J'ai transmis tes instructions de
    vente à Miss Dreier.

    Pach écrit une brochure sur toi avec 2 reproductions— et il va faire une
    conférence sur toi le 28 Décembre. Je trouve le Picasso épatant— Vais
    essayer de le faire "exclusiver" par ~~une~~ un autre marchand qui a plus de
    marché que de Zayas dans ce genre de choses.

    Miss Dreier a été enchantée de vous voir tous les deux à son passage à
    Paris—

    Vie monotone ici, quelques cuites car on reboit sérieusement— la
    Prohibition n'est qu'un mythe cette année—

    J'ai oublié de dire à Jean dans ma dernière lettre que j'avais répondu à
    Breton au sujet des jeux de mots de "Desnos en sommeil"—

    Quelques uns étaient vraiment très bien mais la plupart sentaient la rime
    un peu trop et étaient beaucoup plus Desnos que moi—

Gaston = Jacques
Villon, his one-man
show is held in the
gallery of the Société
Anonyme (16 Dec
1922 - 10 Jan 1923).

Jean = Jean Crotti

Robert Desnos
(1900-1945), French
poet, writes 199 puns in
1922-23 saying these
had been telepathically
dictated to him across
the Atlantic by Rrose
Sélavy, published in
Littérature No. 7,
Dec 1922 and in *Corps
et biens*, Paris,
Gallimard, 1930.

Je connais ici un photographe qui fait des photos ~~de~~ d'ectoplasme sur un
médium homme— je lui avais promis d'assister à des séances et j'ai eu
la flemme mais cela m'amuserait beaucoup—
        Au revoir vieux. amusez vous bien— Ne sais quand reviendrai—
        Marcel
1947 Broadway
N. Y. City

ectoplasm = a
mysterious substance
believed to flow
through the bodies of
mediums.

▷ TRANSLATION: *25th Dec. Dear Gaston, dear Gaby, Your exhibition has been open
since the 16th at the Société Anonyme. The overall thing looks very good especially
with these walls made of pale blue green almost white oilcloth—neutral. I passed
on your sales instructions to Miss Dreier. Pach is writing a brochure on you with 2
reproductions and he's going to give a talk on you 28th December. I find the Picasso
amazing. Will try to get it "exclusivized" by another dealer who has a better market
than de Zayas for this kind of thing. Miss Dreier was thrilled to see you both when
she was passing through Paris. Life dull here. Been plastered a few times as we've
started drinking seriously again—Prohibition is just a myth this year. I forgot to
tell Jean in my last letter that I'd replied to Breton about the puns in "Desnos
asleep." Some were really very good but, in most of them, the rhymes were too obvi-
ous and sounded much more like Desnos than me. I know a photographer here who
takes pictures of ectoplasm on a male medium: I promised I would go along to his
sessions, then I couldn't be bothered, but I would find it most amusing. Goodbye
old chum, have fun. Don't know when I'll be back. Marcel. 1947 Broadway, N.Y.
City.*

---

62. Marcel Duchamp to Francis Picabia   autograph letter
20 January [1923, New York]   collection BLJD

20 Janvier
        Naturellement ça m'ennuie— je vous ai câblé pour que vous n'ayez
        pas à préparer inutilement— Evitez je vous en prie—
Je n'ai rien fait depuis que je vous ai quitté excepté une sorte d'album,
        brochure arrangement extérieur d'une série de critiques par McBride
— Il y a dedans une page *à propos* et une reproduction *d'une chose* de
        vous—
Je vous l'enverrai.
Vu Milhaud ici qui a beaucoup de succès—
a bientôt affections à Germaine et Breton
        MarSélavy
Merci quand même.

"album" = *Some
French Moderns...*
[cat. 56], see p.110.

Darius Milhaud
(1892-1974), French
composer using
rhythmic structures
based on Brazilian
music and jazz.

▷ TRANSLATION: *20th January. Naturally, I feel put out. I wired you so that you wouldn't go to the trouble of preparing something for nothing. Please don't. I haven't done a thing since I left you, except a sort of album, brochure arrangement on the outside, of a series of reviews by McBride. Inside there's a one-page foreword and a reproduction of a piece by you. I'll send it to you. Saw Milhaud who is very succesful here. So long, affections to Germaine and Breton, MarSélavy. Thanks all the same.*

10 February 1923
Duchamp returns to Europe aboard the "Noordam,"
a Dutch liner that will take him to Rotterdam.

back to Europe: Brussels, Paris | 1923-1927

aboard ship for Europe, on the "Noordam" | 10 Feb 1923
lives in Brussels, 22 rue de la Madeleine, with Madge Lipton
lives in Paris: 37 rue Froidevaux, 29 rue Campagne-Première and 82 rue des Petits-Champs
*trips to Rouen, Monte Carlo, Nice, Vale de la Haye, Strasbourg, Venice—mostly for
  chess tournaments*
aboard ship for USA on the "Paris" | 13 to 20 Oct. 1926
lives in New York, 111 West 16th Street at Allen Norton's
trip to Staten Island, staying at the Locher's
trip to Chicago for Brancusi show, staying at the Racquet Club

from 10 February 1923 to 26 February 1927

▶ MAJOR WORKS

Monte Carlo Bond (photocollage on
  cardboard, for a roulette martingale, 1924)
Rotary Demisphere (motorized optical device,
  1925)
Poster for the Third French Chess Championship
  (Nice, 1925)
Nous nous cajolions (violet ink on paper, with
  photographic collage, circa 1925)
Disks Inscribed with Puns for Anémic Cinéma
  (white letters pasted on cardboard disks,
  1926)
Anémic cinéma (7-minute film made with Man
  Ray and Marc Allégret, 1925-autumn 1926)

▶ EXHIBITIONS

American Show, Belmaison, New York City — **1923**
Exhibition (selected by Sheeler), Works by Duchamp,
  Picasso, Braque, de Zayas, African Sculptures and,
  next door, photos by Sheeler, Whitney Studio Club
  Exhibition, New York City. By MD: *Nude*

*Descending a Staircase; The King and Queen
surrounded by Swift Nudes; A propos of little
Sister; Chocolate grinder No.2; The King and
Queen traversed by Swift Nudes*
  — **10 Mar - 31 Mar 1924**
**An Exhibition of
Modern French Art**, Museum of Art, Baltimore. By
  MD: *Le Passage* — **9 Jan - 1 Feb 1925**
The John Quinn Collection of Paintings, Watercolors,
  Drawings & Sculpture, Art Center, New York City.
  By MD: *Study of a Girl; Study for Nude
  Descending the Stairs; The Chess Players; Peau
  Brune* — **7 - 30 Jan 1926**
**International Exhibition of Modern Art assembled by
  Société Anonyme**, Brooklyn Museum, Brooklyn
  (travels to New York City). By MD: *Disturbed
  Balance* [*To Be Looked at...*]; *Glass* [Large Glass]
  — **19 Nov 1926 - 1 Jan 1927**
The John Quinn Collection, American Art Galleries,
  New York. By MD: *Peau Brune* — **5 - 8 Feb 1927**

21 February 1923
Duchamp disembarks in Rotterdam and,
rather than returning immediately to Paris,
goes straight to Brussels
where he intends to live for a few months
and begin playing chess professionally.
He makes occasional trips to Paris and Rouen
to visit family and friends.

---

63. Marcel Duchamp to Francis Picabia   postcard
[10 March 1923, Brussels]   collection BLJD

> J'habite 22 rue de la Madeleine et si vous ne l'écrivez pas à 9 de vos amis

MD's residence in
Brussels Feb - July 1923.

> dans les 24 heures un grand malheur vous tombera dessus—
> Affectueusement à Germaine et vous
>   Duchamp

Germaine = Germaine
Everling

▷ TRANSLATION: *I live at 22 rue de la Madeleine and if you do not write and tell to 9 of your friends in the next 24 hours, a great misfortune will befall you. Affectionately to Germaine and to you, Duchamp.*

---

64. Marcel Duchamp to Carrie, Ettie and Florine Stettheimer   autograph letter
15 March [1923], Brussels   collection YCAL

TAVERNE ROYALE
Bruxelles, le *15 mars*

> J'arrive de Paris et je trouve enfin un peu de temps—
> Florine j'ai vu la galerie en question : no good—
> Pas de lumière, sous les arcades de la Rue des Pyramides. Pas d'expositions
>   intéressantes.

Juliette Roche (1884-
1980), poet and
vanguard writer,
married to Albert
Gleizes (see p.38).

> J'ai vu Gleizes et Juliette. Bonne santé.— Contents—
> Votre tableau doit être reparti pour N.Y.— Ils n'ont rien payé à Robineau.
>   Il a été très remarqué au Salon— et Juliette regrettait infiniment que
>   vous exigiez une telle somme pour l'abandonner— Si vous n'avez pas de
>   nouvelles du tableau, j'irai voir Robineau—

"Salon" = Salon
d'Automne, 1922, where
Stettheimer's *Ashbury
Park South*, 1920 (Fiske
University, Nashville),
is shown, through the
auspices of Albert
Gleizes.

> J'ai passé quelques jours à Rouen quelques autres à Paris (bien morne) ~~en~~
>   et je suis ici en quête d'un job possible—
> Si vous insistez je vous enverrai des cartes postales de la Grand' Place et de
>   Ste. Gudule—
> Racontez moi un peu. Comment est N.Y. sans moi— indolente Ettie =
> Carrie voulez vous que je vous mette en rapport avec des filleuls belges
>   dans la Ruhr?—

De vous trois je crois que c'est Ettie que je verrai la première à Paris cet été—

Au revoir affectueux.

et hommages à Madame Stettheimer

Le voyage fut délicieux—

et les gâteaux de chez Dean aussi— Rrose Sélavy

▷ TRANSLATION: *Brussels, 15th March. Just back from Paris and finally have some time. Florine, I've seen the gallery in question: no good—no light, under the arcades of the rue des Pyramides. No interesting exhibitions. I've seen Gleizes and Juliette. Both well. Happy. Your painting must be on its way back to N.Y. They didn't pay Robineau any money. It received a lot of attention at the Salon and Juliette was very disappointed that you were insisting on such a large sum to give it up. If you don't hear anything about the painting, I'll go and see Robineau. I spent a few days in Rouen and another few days in Paris (so dreary) and I am in search of a possible job. If you really insist, I will send you some postcards of the Grand'Place and of Ste. Gudule. Send me some news. What is N.Y. like without me, Ettie, indolent thing? Carrie, would you like me to put you in touch with some Belgian godsons in the Ruhr? Of the three of you, I think Ettie's the one I'll see in Paris first this summer. Affectionate farewell and respects to Mrs Stettheimer. The trip was gorgeous, the cakes from Dean's too. Rrose Sélavy.*

---

65. Marcel Duchamp to Pierre de Massot   autograph letter
25 March [1923], Brussels   source: from André Gervais transcript

25 Mars

Reçu ton mot allé à N.Y. et retour ici à Bxelles—

La plupart de tes jeux sont excellents et m'ont amusé follement— Je serai à Paris fin Avril pour une sœur qui épouse— (celle entre les deux)—

Je joue énormément aux échecs ici.

Ne connaissant personne que Madge— la vie est délicieuse je n'entends pas parler arrhes— Pourvu que ça dure—

"Bxelles" = Brussels

MD's sister **Yvonne Duchamp** (1895-1969) marries Alphonse Duvernoy 28 Apr 1923, in Neuilly.

Madge Lipton, companion of Duchamp and friend of Germaine Everling.

Écris et raconte moi car je ne peux pas écrire— à moins que je ne t'envoie
de longues solutions de problèmes d'échecs qui ne t'intéresseraient pas
même vues de loin—
affections à Gabrielle Picabia et toi
Rrose
Bxelles.
22 rue de la Madeleine

▷ TRANSLATION: *25th March. Received your letter—had gone to N.Y. and back here
to Brussels. Most of your games are excellent and I enjoyed them like crazy. I'll be
in Paris end of April for a sister getting married (the middle one). I play masses of
chess here. Knowing nobody but Madge, life is gorgeous: I don't hear a thing about
deposits. Long may it last. Write and tell me about things as I cannot write—unless
I were to send you long solutions to chess problems which you wouldn't be interested
in, not even from afar. Affections to Gabrielle Picabia and to you, Rrose. Brussels,
22 rue de la Madeleine.*

---

66. Marcel Duchamp to Ettie and Carrie Stettheimer   autograph letter
26 July [1923], Rouen   collection YCAL

Famille 26 juillet
Anniversaire de quelqu'un
Le mien est après demain.
    Chère Ettie, merci de votre mouchoir télégrammique et honte pour
moi de n'avoir pas câblé une dentelle de Bruxelles—
Mais je croyais tellement que j'allais vous voir descendre du bateau avec
McBride—
Il repart ces jours ci— Nous avons dîné chez Brancusi qui nous avait fait
une sauce de lapin délicieuse— Il vous en parlera—
Je reviens habiter Paris ce qui m'ennuie profondément— et j'y cherche un
job—
Ai je dit à Florine que j'étais membre du jury au Salon d'automne cette
année (tirage au sort) et que par conséquent ma voix acquise pourrait
peut-être l'induire à envoyer quelque chose—
D'après Juliette et Gleizes, la toile est repartie ou en tout cas ~~sans danger~~
à l'abri chez Robineau— Malgré mes nombreuses promesses, je n'ai pas
encore vu ce Seigneur— mais ce me sera plus commode maintenant et
bientôt—
Gleizes, ayant perdu son beau père, se promène en auto (à lui) et apprend
à conduire.

Juliette = Juliette Roche

The "**canvas**" is
probably Stettheimer's
Ashbury Park South,
see p.132.

D'innombrables New yorkais ont peuplé Paris et continuent cet été.
Montparnasse ressemblait à un Greenwich village avec des avenues plus
larges que la 6me— Même la température a voulu imiter les
thermomètres de N.Y.—

Inutile d'ajouter à tout cela que j'ai beaucoup joué aux échecs à Bruxelles
et suis classé comme un des bons joueurs de Belgique— Je commence
par les petites nations—

Peut-être un jour me déciderai je à être champion de France ce qui *ne*
serait vraiment pas très remarquable—

Et Carrie à qui je n'ai encore rien dit— Elle est d'ailleurs toujours la plus
silencieuse de vous trois—

Dans quelle campagne dirigez vous le bien être de votre famille? ô Carrie
(ça ressemble à Criton)

McBride adore mon portrait par Florine— Il m'en a parlé—

Il y a eu une séance Dada (à laquelle je n'assistais pas) et où des coups de
poing ont été échangés, très amusant paraît il—

Je ne pense pas repartir en Amérique, maintenant— Plus tard mais
quand? Je n'ai aucune idée— Je crois décidément que je vous verrai ici
ou au moins une section du quatuor—

Mes hommages à Madame Stettheimer très affectionnément à vous
trois et j'attends quelques nouvelles de vos santés au moins.

Portrait of Marcel
Duchamp, 1923
(William Kelley
Simpson, NY).

Soirée du cœur à barbe,
organized by Tzara, at
the Théâtre Michel,
Paris, nights of 6 and 7
July 1923. Pierre de
Massot got his left arm
broken on stage by
André Breton's cane.

Marcel Duchamp [signed in mirror script]
71 rue Jeanne d'Arc
Rouen

▷ TRANSLATION: *Family, 26th July. Somebody's birthday. Mine is day after tomorrow. Dear Ettie, thank you for your telegramic handkerchief and shame on me for not having wired a piece of lace from Brussels. But I was so sure I would see you getting off the boat with McBride. He's leaving any day now. We dined at Brancusi's who made us a delicious rabbit sauce. He'll tell you about it. I'm coming back to live in Paris which I'm seriously fed up about and am looking for a job there. Did I tell Florine that I am on the jury at the Salon d'Automne this year (they drew lots) and that consequently having my vote might perhaps induce her to send something. According to Juliette and Gleizes, the canvas has left or, in any case, is safe and sound at Robineau's. In spite of my many promises, I still haven't seen this Master, but it'll be easier for me now and soon. Gleizes, now that he's lost his father-in-law, is driving around in a car (his own) and taking driving lessons. Hoards of New Yorkers have invaded Paris and are still coming this summer. Montparnasse looks like a kind of Greenwich Village with its avenues that are wider than 6th. Even the temperature has been trying to imitate thermometers in N.Y.*

Needless to say, in addition to all this I played a lot of chess in Brussels and am ranked among the good players in Belgium. I'm starting with the small nations. Maybe one day I'll just decide to become champion of France which would not be so remarkable after all. And Carrie, to whom I haven't said a word yet? Actually, she is the quietest of the three of you. What now your campaign for overseeing the well-being of your family? ô Carrie (sounds like Criton). McBride adores my portrait by Florine. He spoke to me about it. There was a Dada session (which I did not attend) where fisticuffs were exchanged, very amusing apparently. I'm not thinking of going back to America at the moment. Later, but when? I have no idea. It looks for certain like I will see you here or at least one section of the quartet. My respects to Mrs Stettheimer, very affectionately to you three and I look forward to hearing how you are keeping at least. Marcel Duchamp. 71 rue Jeanne d'Arc, Rouen.

---

67. Marcel Duchamp to Pierre de Massot   autograph letter
[on or around 26 July 1923], Rouen   source: from André Gervais transcript

Rouen
    Cher franc Massot—
Il a fallu un mot de toi pour me décider—
Je suppose que tu m'as écrit à Bruxelles et que je n'ai pas reçu la lettre
    comme beaucoup d'autres—

Address of studio MD rents 15 July 1923 - 1 Jan 1924.

J'ai un atelier pour cet hiver 37 rue Froidevaux où je vais habiter à partir
de jeudi—
Je viens ici à Rouen pour prendre un lit.
Vais tâcher d'y être très confortable

Jacques Doucet, see biography next letter.

— autre nouvelle importante au point de vue pécuniaire. Doucet a acheté
un verre qui était chez mon frère et me le paie 8 000, ce qui me ravit et
me permettra de payer qques dettes et de vivre jusqu'au 1ᵉʳ Janvier à peu
près convenablement.

Glider... [cat. 30], MD stored at his brother Raymond's before leaving for the US 1915.

— ceci par l'intermédiaire de Francis qui a invité Doucet au Tremblay et
lui a montré ledit verre.

Francis Picabia's house, called "Maison Rose," at Le Tremblay-sur-Mauldre.

À part cela je cherche un turbin régulier (dans les 1000 par mois)
Je ne peux vraiment pas me déplacer— Je suis resté à Paris tout le temps
et le trouve charmant vide—
Tâche de rentrer à Paris en Octobre—

"fossettes d'aisance" = one of MD's puns, first published in 1924 by Pierre de Massot.

quelques mots de temps à autre—
    fossettes d'aisances
est charmant

La Baule = well-known French seaside resort

Francis est à La Baule va rentrer incessamment et doit faire un film avec
    Georgette Leblanc—
        à bientôt vieux lapin
        Rrose Sélavy

Picabia's film never materializes, but the actress **Georgette Leblanc** (1869-1941) will act in *L'inhumaine* (1923), film directed by Marcel L'Herbier.

▷ TRANSLATION: *Rouen, Dear free Massot, It took your note to get me moving. I expect you wrote to me in Brussels and that I didn't get your letter like so many others. I have a studio for this winter—37 rue Froidevaux—where I will be staying as from Thursday. I've come here to Rouen to get a bed. Am going to try to be very comfortable. Another important piece of news from a financial point of view. Doucet bought a glass which was at my brother's and is paying me 8,000 for it, which I am delighted about as this will allow me to pay off a few debts and live more or less decently until 1st January. All this through Francis, as he invited Doucet to Tremblay and showed him the above-said glass. Apart from that, I'm looking for some regular graft (1,000 a month). I really can't move anywhere else. I've stayed in Paris the whole time and find it delightful when deserted. Try to come back to Paris in October. A pun or two from time to time:* Fossettes d'aisance [contraction of "fossettes" (= dimples) with fosses d'aisance (=septic tanks)]. *Francis is in La Baule, is coming back any moment and going to be making a movie with Georgette Leblanc. So long you old rascal, Rose Sélavy.*

---

68. Marcel Duchamp to Jacques Doucet[*]
[26 October 1923, Brussels]

postcard
collection BLJD

    Cher Monsieur Doucet
    D'un homme parfaitement heureux : je me classe très bien dans ce tournoi qui est mon premier important. Rrose Sélavy a un côté "femmes savantes" qui n'est pas désagréable. Je rentre Vendredi pour quelques heures et repars pour Rouen où je passerai 2 jours seulement. J'espère que je ne suis pas en retard pour le cadre— Mes hommages à Madame Doucet et bien affectueusement
    Marcel Duchamp
    Hotel Parisiana rue de la Fourche Bruxelles

During his stay in Brussels (19 Oct - 2 Nov 1923), MD gaines a respectable 3rd place in the National Tournament of Belgium.

Painting to be framed is MD's *Two Nudes* [cat. 7].

---

* **Jacques Doucet** (1853-1929), a wealthy French couturier and bibliophile, had amassed an impressive collection of eighteenth-century French art (which he sold in 1912), but went on to assemble an even more important collection of modern art. In 1920, he hired André Breton (p.196) to catalog his literary library, but soon Breton began to direct Doucet's interests toward collecting the art of living artists. Upon Breton's advice, in 1924 he acquired Picasso's *Les Demoiselles d'Avignon*, and a few months earlier—again through Breton's urging—he purchased two works by Duchamp: *Two Nudes* (a Fauve painting) and *Glider Containing a Water Mill in Neighboring Metals*, a large semi-circular study on glass for a detail of *The Large Glass*. In that same year, Doucet commissioned Duchamp's *Rotary Demisphere (Precision Optics)*, and much of their correspondence from this period provides periodic updates on the fabrication of this, as well as reports on Duchamp's scheme to win at the gambling tables of Monte Carlo (an enterprise in which Doucet had also invested some money). Doucet died in 1929 at the age of seventy-six, and although his art collection was dispersed, his great literary and manuscript library—which includes his correspondence with Duchamp, as well as the archives of Francis Picabia (p.58) and Tristan Tzara (p.96)—became a part of the Bibliothèque Sainte-Geneviève in Paris.

▷ TRANSLATION: *Dear Mr Doucet, From a man utterly contented. I am ranking very high in this tournament which is my first important one. Rrose Sélavy has something of the "blue stocking" about her which is not unpleasant. I'll be back for a few hours on Friday then leave for Rouen where I'll spend just two days. I hope I am not late as far as the frame is concerned. My respects to Mrs Doucet and very affectionately, Marcel Duchamp. Hotel Parisiana, rue de la Fourche, Brussels.*

---

69. Marcel Duchamp to Francis Picabia   postcard
[29 October 1923], Brussels   collection BLJD

à Bruxelles depuis 8 jours. Me classe très bien dans ce tournoi. 3me place vraisemblablement. Enchanté du séjour. Jouant tous les jours de 6 à 10 du soir— me reposant comme un poulain dans la journée. Rentrerai Paris Vendredi pour repartir à Rouen 2 jours. Affection Germaine
   Marcel

▷ TRANSLATION: *Been in Brussels for 8 days. Ranking very high in this tournament, 3rd place probably. Delighted with my trip here. Playing every day from 6 until 10 in the evening. Sleeping like a prize colt during the day. Will return Paris Friday to leave for Rouen for 2 days. Affectionately to Germaine, Marcel.*

---

70. Marcel Duchamp to Jacques Doucet   autograph letter
[22 December 1923], Paris   collection BLJD

29 Camp. Prem.
Samedi
   Cher Monsieur Doucet— Votre petit mot m'a fait bien plaisir—
De Seurat je ne sais rien : Sa poudreuse je crois appartient à une collection américaine— Le Chahut qui est, je trouve, son meilleur— je n'ai aucune idée où il est—
Il m'avait semblé entendre dire que Signac ou Cousturier (ses infâmes p$_o^a$sticheurs) ~~les~~ en avaient dans leurs collections—
Mais d'un autre côté je ne pense pas que *parmi* les dix ou 12 ~~grandes~~ choses importantes qu'il ait faites, aucune soit dans un musée. Si j'entends parler de quelque chose de plus précis je vous le dirai.
Man Ray *avec* qui je viens de déjeuner se fera un grand plaisir d'aller vous voir et vous apporter le portrait— Dites lui ou dites moi à quelle heure et quel jour sont le plus agréables pour vous
   Bien affectueusement
   M. Duchamp

La Poudreuse, today called *Young Woman Powdering Herself*, 1890 (Courtauld Institute Galleries, London).

Le Chahut, 1889-1890 (Rijksmuseum Kröller-Müller, Otterlo).

Paul Signac (1863-1935), neo-Impressionist painter. His student, **Lucie Cousturier** (1876-1925), author of monographs on Seurat and Signac.

▷ TRANSLATION: *29 Campagne Première, Saturday. Dear Mr Doucet, I was very pleased to get your note. As to Seurat, I don't know. His Poudreuse, I think, belongs to an American collection. The Chahut, which, in my view, is his best, I've no idea where it is. I seem to remember hearing that Signac or Cousturier (his vile imitators/wig-makers) had them in their collections. But on the other hand, I don't think that out of the ten or twelve important things he did, a single one of them is in a museum. If I get to hear of anything more specific, I'll let you know. Man Ray, with whom I've just had lunch, would be delighted to come and see you and bring you the portrait. Let him know or let me know what would be the best time and day for you. Very affectionately, M. Duchamp.*

---

71. Marcel Duchamp to Ettie Stettheimer   autograph letter
[1 January 1924], Rouen   collection YCAL

En villégiature de Circoncision à Rouen 1923-24
     J'ai déjeuné chez Turro il y a 10 jours. Charmant appartement meublé à la Alavoine avec Notre Dame à droite.— Mal, non pas mal chauffé. Il m'a dit que vous vouliez savoir ce que je devenais
          Ma chère Ettie.
Je le savais—
Donc ne vous attendez pas à de l'autobiographie = Car Rien Rien ne m'est arrivé.
J'ai des cheveux et vous ne dirai pas pourquoi—
Je m'embête très respectablement. J'ai habité un atelier affreusement froid que je viens d'abandonner et j'habite dans un petit hôtel très confortable 29 rue Campagne Première.
Je n'ai pas lu votre livre, seulement la partie qui me concernait = C'est toujours adorable d'avoir un portrait de soi même, même quand on ne sert que de second plan— Ce n'est pas moi qui puis vous dire s'il est ou n'est pas juste— (Vous prétendiez ne m'avoir pas *traité* assez gentiment). et c'est de seconde importance. Mais je suppose que vous vous servez de Susanna comme d'un sosie incomplet ou intentionnellement trompeur afin que votre réel self soit plus mystérieux encore.
Quelles drôles de confessions vous écririez!
Grodz sera certainement tres intrigué. Turro avait l'air enchanté.
Je fais peu de jeux de mots— Il semble y avoir un ralentissement dans la production.
Pas d'activité nouvelle à Paris que je sache.
Et même s il y en avait une, je ne crois *pas* que je puisse m'y intéresser—
Où que je sois j'ai l'impression d'être dans une salle d'attente. C'est fatiguant parce que le train a toujours beaucoup de retard.

MD moves from the rue Froidevaux to the Hotel Istria.

Love Days (NY, Alfred A. Knopf, [Oct] 1923), novel by Henrie Waste, pseudonym of Henrietta (or Ettie) Stettheimer, in which MD is thinly disguised as the painter Pierre Delaire.

Susanna = Susanna Moore, the protagonist of *Love Days*, in which her relationship with Pierre Delaire is explored.

J'aperçois quelquefois Leo Stein au Dôme mais ne lui cause pas. Il me
connait peu—

Je donne quelques leçons de français à des Américaines ici. Que faire
d'autre?

Les échecs naturellement beaucoup. Je me suis assez bien classé *(3me)* dans
un tournoi à Bruxelles— Je mourrai avant d'être fatigué de ce dada—
C'est une excellente chose—

J'ai naturellement une impossibilité absolue d'écrire, maladie qui
s'aggrave tous les jours—

Dans le repos de Rouen j'aime à penser à vous et j'en profite pour vous en
faire part.

Peut être viendrez vous ici—

Peut être irai je à N.Y.—

Je rêve constamment de voyages à N.Y.

Je crois que Florine fait des portraits payés maintenant. Est ce que mon
impression est juste— Ou bien alors demande t elle trop cher??

En tout cas elle arrivera à ce qu'elle veut.

Si elle avait une photo du mien j'aimerais qu'elle me l'envoie.

Et que fait Carrie? Je lui envoie des souhaits extraordinaires pour 1924

N'oubliez pas mon affectueux souvenir pour Mme Stettheimer.

A bientôt
Affectueusement

Stone of Air
29 rue Campagne Première Paris.

Le Dôme, café in Montparnasse, frequented by American artists and writers.

Portrait of Marcel Duchamp, see p.135.

"Stone of Air" is the translation of a pun: *Pierre / pierre* (stone), *Delaire / de l'air* (of air).

▷ TRANSLATION: *On circumcision vacation in Rouen 1923-24. I had lunch at Turro's ten days ago. Charming apartment, furnished in the Alavoine style, with Notre Dame on the right. Badly—no not badly heated. He told me you were asking what had become of me. My dear Ettie. I knew it. Now don't expect an autobiography because Nothing but Nothing has happened with me. I have hair and won't tell you why. I am respectably bored. I was living in a frightfully cold studio which I have forsaken for a small but very comfortable hotel, 29 rue Campagne Première. I have not read your book, just the part about me. = It's always adorable to have a portrait of oneself, even if one is only there as a backdrop. I'm not the right person to tell you whether it's accurate or not. (You say you didn't treat me very kindly: it's not important.) But I suppose you're using Susanna as an imperfect double or one that's deliberately misleading to make your real self seem all the more mysterious. What odd confessions you are inclined to make in your writing! Grodz will certainly be very intrigued. Turro seemed delighted. I make very few puns nowadays. There seems to be a slow-down in production. No new activity in Paris as far as I can tell. And even if there were one, I don't think I could get very interested in it. Wherever I am, I feel like I'm in a waiting room. It's tiring because the train is always very late. I sometimes catch sight of Leo Stein at the Dôme, but don't speak to him. He scarcely knows me. I'm giving a few French lessons to Americans here. What else is there to do? Chess a lot, naturally. I got ranked quite high (3rd) at a tournament in Brussels. I will die before tiring of this hobby. It's an excellent thing. I am naturally totally incapable of writing, an infliction that gets worse by the day. In the restfulness of Rouen I like to think of you and take the opportunity of sharing that with you. Perhaps you will come here. Perhaps I will go to N.Y. I dream of traveling to N.Y. all the time. I believe Florine is doing portraits for money now. Is my impression correct or does she ask for too high prices?? In any case, she'll get what she wants. If she had a photo of my portrait I should like her to send it to me. And what is Carrie up to? I wish her extraordinary things for 1924. Don't forget to remember me affectionately to Mrs Stettheimer. So long, affectionately,* Stone of Air. *29 rue Campagne Première, Paris.*

---

72. Marcel Duchamp to Jacques Doucet   autograph letter
28 February 1924, Paris   collection BLJD

Paris. 28 Février 1924
    Monsieur Doucet
J'ai téléphoné à Francis ce matin après votre premier pneu— Et je suis très
    heureux que vous ayez arrangé la question argent avec lui.
Il m'était difficile de vous dire que j'avais besoin d'à peu près 6 000 frcs—
    car je considère ceci comme un échange et non pas un paiement—
    J'aimerais pouvoir vous faire cadeau de cet hémisphère.
Donc je suis tout à votre disposition pour m'occuper du montage et
    présentation—
Et après votre second pneu je serai chez Man Ray vers 2 heures ½
    demain— Vendredi—
J'ai d'ailleurs téléphoné cet après midi—
    Bien cordialement à vous
    Marcel Duchamp.

Francis =
Francis Picabia

"hémisphère"= *Rotary Demisphere* [cat. 51]. Many of MD's subsequent letters to Doucet include details about its construction.

▷ TRANSLATION: *Paris, 28th February 1924. Dear Mr Doucet, I telephoned Francis this morning after your first local wire and I'm very happy that you've sorted out*

*the money matter with him. It was hard for me to tell you that I needed about
6,000 francs as I think of this as an exchange and not a payment. I would like to
be able to give you this hemisphere as a present. And I am at your complete disposal
for the setting up and presentation. Then after your second local wire, I'll be at Man
Ray's place around 2.30 tomorrow, Friday. In fact I telephoned this afternoon.
Yours most sincerely, Marcel Duchamp.*

---

73. Marcel Duchamp to Jacques Doucet   "pneumatique" letter
[6 March 1924], Paris   collection BLJD

> Montparnasse minuit. Jeudi
> Cher Monsieur Doucet.
> J'ai trouvé et acheté un pied aujourd'hui— chez Ruppaley fournisseur
> de'appareils d'électricité médicale =
> De là j'ai été chez Mildé et j'ai rendez vous Samedi 3 heures chez Man Ray
> avec un "ingénieur" qui me fera un devis après avoir entendu mes
> désirs = Je ne partirai donc pas avant Mercredi ou Jeudi et j'aimerais
> vous voir avant—
> Affectueusement à vous
> Marcel Duchamp.

▷ TRANSLATION: *Montparnasse. Midnight, Thursday. Dear Mr Doucet, I found and
bought a foot today, at Ruppaley's, supplier of electrical medical apparatus. From
there, I went on to Mildé's and have an appointment at 3 o'clock on Saturday at
Man Ray's with an "engineer" who will give me an estimate once he's acquainted
with my desires. So I won't be leaving before Wednesday or Thursday and would
like to see you before then. Affectionately yours, Marcel Duchamp.*

---

74. Marcel Duchamp to Jacques Doucet   autograph letter
31 March 1924, Nice   collection BLJD

> Nice 31 Mars 1924
> Cher Monsieur Doucet
> Merci de votre mot = Le climat me convient parfaitement et j'aimerais
> vivre ici.—
> Un tournoi d'échecs va être organisé ici (international) auquel je dois
> prendre part du 5 au 15 avril environ— Je compte donc rester ici jusqu'à
> cette date et rentrer à Paris vers le 20 au plus tard.
> Mais en dehors des échecs je m'occupe beaucoup de 30 et 40. J'ai essayé   **"30 et 40"** = Trente-et-
> maint système et perdu comme un novice—   Quarante, a casino game.
> Depuis j'ai de l'expérience et je suis parvenu à un résultat meilleur— Je
> joue à blanc et me défends parfaitement—

Tout cela naturellement amène la conclusion attendue— J'ai bien besoin de mes 2 derniers mille.

ᛋLe meilleur résultat obtenu est celui ci = Je ne suis pas joueur pour un sou— Je passe des après midis dans les salles de jeu et n'ai pas la moindre tentation.

Tout ce que j'ai perdu l'a été en pleine bonne volonté— et je n'ai pas encore été atteint par l'"échauffement" de la salle de jeu.

Toute cette vie m'amuse beaucoup.

et je vous expliquerai un de mes systèmes en rentrant.

Francis a quitté Cannes aujourd'hui rentrant. Vous les verrez bientôt sans doute.

     A bientôt donc et bien affectueusement à vous
     Marcel Duchamp
Hotel des Etrangers
rue du Palais
Nice A.M.

2,000 French francs = sum remaining after 6,000 [see letter 72] is taken from 8,000 [see letter 67].

Francis Picabia and Germaine Everling

▷ TRANSLATION: *Nice, 31st March 1924. Dear Mr Doucet, Thank you for your note. The climate suits me to a tee and I would like to live here. They are going to hold a chess tournament here (international) which I am to take part in, from 5th to 15th April approximately. So I expect to stay here until that date and then go back to Paris around 20th at the latest. But outside chess, I'm very involved in 30 and 40. I've tried umpteen systems and lost like a complete beginner. I've since got some experience and am achieving better results. I play blind and hold my own perfectly well. You can of course guess what all this is leading up to—I really need my last 2,000. The best result to come out of it all is this = I'm not a gambler by any means. I can spend entire afternoons in the gaming rooms without feeling the slightest bit tempted. Whatever I lost, I lost perfectly willingly and I haven't yet been smitten by gaming room "fever." I find this whole way of life very entertaining and I'll go through one of my systems with you when I get back. Francis left Cannes today— on his way home. You'll no doubt see them soon. So long then and yours affectionately, Marcel Duchamp. Hotel des Etrangers, rue du Palais, Nice A.M.*

---

75. Marcel Duchamp to Francis Picabia
[17 April 1924], Monte-Carlo

autograph letter
collection BLJD

CAFÉ DE PARIS
Monte-Carlo
Téléphone : 2-50

    Le *Jeudi*.........192

Avec un tout petit capital j'expérimente ma combinaison depuis 5 jours—

J'ai gagné régulièrement tous les jours de petites sommes— en 1 heure
ou 2—
Je perfectionne encore et j'espère rentrer à Paris avec le système tout à fait
au point.
C'est d'une monotonie délicieuse. Pas la moindre émotion
Le problème consiste d'ailleurs à trouver la figure rouge et noir à opposer
à la roulette—
La martingale n'a pas d'importance
Elles sont toutes bonnes et toutes mauvaises—
Mais avec la bonne figure— même une mauvaise martingale pourra
tenir—
Et je crois avoir trouvé une bonne figure—
Vous voyez que je n'ai pas cessé d'être peintre
je dessine maintenant sur le hasard—
    Affectueusement
    Rrose Sélavy
Je rentre Dimanche de Pâques— Serai Paris Lundi Pâques midi
Affectueusement à Germaine

▷ TRANSLATION: *Thursday. With a tiny budget, I've been trying out my system for the last 5 days. I've been winning regularly every day, small amounts, in an hour or 2. I'm still perfecting it and hope to come back to Paris with the system completely spot on. It is deliciously monotonous. Not a trace of emotion. The problem actually lies in finding the right red and black combination to play against the roulette wheel. The winning formula is of no importance. All of them are right and all of them are wrong. But with the right combination, even the wrong winning formula can hold up. And I think I've found the right combination. As you can see, I haven't quit being a painter. I'm drawing on Fortune now. Affectionately, Rrose Sélavy. I'll be coming back Easter Sunday. In Paris Easter Monday noon. Affectionately to Germaine.*

---

76. Marcel Duchamp to Jacques Doucet   envelope-letter
[14 September 1924], Paris   collection BLJD

Paris Dimanche—
    Cher Monsieur Doucet
Rentré depuis Dimanche avec un piètre résultat. J'ai essayé de talonner
notre mécanicien— J'ai presque (!) fini de monter le globe à raies sur la *Rotary Demisphere*
1ère plaque.— Il s'occupe (!) du moteur— Il a fait faire un triangle en [cat. 51]
bois pour donner plus d'assise à l'ensemble. En somme je suis sûr d'y
arriver— Il faudra votre patience et la mienne—

Non pas qu'il y mette aucune mauvaise volonté— Mais... vous savez le reste.

Dès que j'aurai obtenu quelque chose de montrable je vous demanderai de venir chez Man Ray—

    à bientôt donc et bien affectueusement
    M. Duchamp
29 rue Campagne Première

▷ TRANSLATION: *Paris. Sunday. Dear Mr Doucet, Back since Sunday with nothing much to show. I had a go at hounding our mechanic. I've almost finished mounting the striped globe on the 1st plate. He's taking care of the motor. He's had a wooden triangle made to make the whole thing steadier. All in all, I'm sure we'll get there. It'll take all your patience and mine. Not that he's unwilling in any way but... you know how it goes. As soon as I get something worth looking at, I'll ask you to come over to Man Ray's. See you soon then and affectionately, M. Duchamp. 29 rue Campagne Première.*

---

77. Marcel Duchamp to Jacques Doucet   envelope-letter
[14 September 1924, Paris]   collection BLJD

J'oubliais dans le mot qui vous arrivera en même temps que celui ci :
Je voudrais coller un velours comme fond sur la plaque de tôle qui soutient la spirale. Un velours anglais un velours de soie??— un velours qui rappelle les fonds absolument mats que l'on voit dans les studios de cinéma— 70^{cm} de large sur la même longueur. Peut être pourriez vous m'aider à trouver cela?

    Toujours affectueusement
    Marcel Duchamp

▷ TRANSLATION: *I was forgetting in the note which will reach you at the same time as this one. I wanted to stick a velvet backgound on the metal plate holding up the spiral. English velvet or silk velvet?? The kind of velvet reminiscent of the totally matt backgrounds in cinema studios. 70 cm wide by the same length. Perhaps you could help me to find this? Ever affectionately, Marcel Duchamp.*

---

78. Marcel Duchamp to Jacques Doucet   envelope-letter
[22 September 1924, Rouen]   collection BLJD

    Cher Mons Doucet
Votre lettre semble avoir eu un effet magique = Le mécanicien a fait en 1 jour ce ~~qu'il~~ qui me semblait devoir prendre huit.
Nous en sommes maintenant à prévoir une expérience de rotation pour la   *Rotary Demisphere*
semaine prochaine. Nous ne sommes. pas d'accord sur la question   [cat. 51]

velours. Car c'est le seul moyen d'obtenir une surface absolument mate
et vraiment noire en même temps— Mais nous pourrons faire des
essais =
à bientôt donc si vous le voulez bien, un rendez vous chez Man Ray pour
voir la chose tourner. Sinon finie—
         très affectueusement Duchamp

[added on back of envelope:]
      Oubliée dans ma poche— Rentre Mercredi soir

▷ TRANSLATION: *Dear Mr Doucet, Your letter seems to have had a magical effect =
the mechanic has done in one day what seems to me should have taken a week. We
are now ready to envisage a rotation experiment next week. We do not agree on the
question of velvet. It's the only way to obtain a totally matt surface that is really
black at the same time. But we can do some tests. See you soon, then, if you like—
meeting at Man Ray's to see the thing going round. Very affectionately, Duchamp.
Just found this in my pocket. Back Wednesday evening.*

---

79. Marcel Duchamp to Jacques Doucet	autograph letter
no date [between 14 Sept and 2 Oct 1924]	collection BLJD

       Cher Monsieur Doucet
Je vous envoie mon nouveau choix (sur les derniers trois).
Je préfère le plus noir des deux. Le plus grossier donnerait un gris, ~~en~~
      comparé à l'autre qui donne un noir rouge—
Arrêtons nous donc. et faisons un essai.
Je ferai faire, quand le tout sera fini, des fonds en aluminium *peint* qu'on
      pourra appliquer sur le velours et retirer. chacun donnant un fond
      différent—
         Bien affectueusement
         M. Duchamp

▷ TRANSLATION: *Dear Mr Doucet, I'm sending you my latest choice (out of the last
three). I prefer the blacker of the two. The roughest one would look gray compared
to the other one which looks a kind of reddish black. Let's take a decision then and
do a test. Once the whole thing's finished, I'll have painted aluminium backgrounds made that can be put onto the velvet and taken off, each giving a different
background. Affectionately, M. Duchamp.*

---

80. Marcel Duchamp to Jacques Doucet   envelope-letter
[20 October 1924], Paris   collection BLJD

Montparnasse Lundi.
    Cher Monsieur Doucet.
J'ai porté aujourd'hui la plaque de cuivre extérieure au graveur qui doit *y*
graver en cercle une phrase. ~~en~~ Cela et un travail de marbrure que je ferai
moi même sur le cuivre donneront à l'objet, même au repos un aspect
curieux. Car comme vous le dites fort bien, il pourrait devenir fastidieux
de le voir tourner trop souvent— Le graveur m'a fait un prix
approximatif de 300 francs— Le travail sera fini dans 5 ou 6 jours—
Je crois indispensable ce travail de lettres et de marbrures, surtout pour
éviter le côté batterie de cuisine qu'a toujours le cuivre rouge— Le reste
s'arrange~~ra~~ vous demanderai bientôt de venir chez Man Ray
    Bien affectueusement
    M. Duchamp

Rotary Demisphere
[cat. 51]

[written in top right-hand corner]
    Je n'ai pas encore placé le velours, j'attends que tout le côté construction soit
    fini.

▷ TRANSLATION: *Montparnasse. Monday. Dear Mr Doucet, I delivered today the out-*
er copper plate to the engraver who is to engrave one sentence on it in a circle. This,
along with some mottling that I will do myself, will make the object look curious
even when still. For as you so rightly say, it could become tedious to see it rotating
too many times. The engraver estimated it would cost 300 francs. The work will be
finished in 5 or 6 days. I think this lettering and mottling work is imperative above
all to avoid the kitchen drum kit effect that red copper always has. The rest is sorting
itself out. Will ask you to come to Man Ray's soon. Affectionately, M. Duchamp. I
haven't yet put the velvet on—I'm waiting until all the construction part is over.

---

81. Marcel Duchamp to Jacques Doucet   autograph letter
[31 October 1924], Paris   collection BLJD

Montparnasse Vendredi—
    Cher Monsieur Doucet
    Evidemment ma lettre était un peu confuse :

Par dessus ce que vous avez vu tourner chez Man Ray vient un¢ disque en
cuivre rouge supportant le globe en verre :

Rotary Demisphere
[cat. 51]

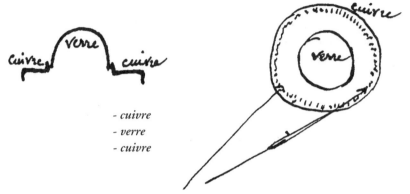

- *cuivre*
- *verre*
- *cuivre*

Sur ce disque en cuivre, au bord et tout autour, j'ai fait graver une légende par
un graveur— géographe— qui m'a fait un travail remarquable. Je l'ai vu
aujourd'hui et je joins ici sa facture de 300 francs.
Je peux m'occuper du règlement de cette facture et terminer le montage :
J'espère pouvoir vous demander de venir chez Man Ray vers le milieu de la
semaine prochaine— Tout sera fini—
    A bientôt donc de vos nouvelles et très affectueusement à vous
    M. Duchamp

▷ TRANSLATION: *Montparnasse. Friday. Dear Mr Doucet, Clearly my letter was a bit
confused. On top of what you saw rotating at Man Ray's, there's a red copper disk
supporting the glass globe.* [sketch caption: *copper; glass; copper*] *On this copper disk,
all the way around the edge, I've had a legend engraved by un engraver—geogra-
pher—who has done a remarkable piece of work for me. I saw him today and enclose his bill of 300 francs. I can take care of settling this bill and get the mounting
finished. I hope to be able to ask you to Man Ray's toward the middle of next week.
It'll all be finished. So look forward to your news and very affectionately yours,
M. Duchamp.*

---

82. Marcel Duchamp to Jacques Doucet   autograph letter
16 January 1925, Paris   collection BLJD

Paris 16 Janvier 1925
    Cher Monsieur Doucet.
J'ai mis à la poste tout à l'heure l'obligation dont nous avons parlé hier =
    Elle s'expliquera d'elle même.— J'ai beaucoup travaillé le système,
    appuyé de ma mauvaise expérience de l'année dernière— Ne soyez pas

Monte Carlo Bond
[cat. 49]

trop sceptique car il s'agit dans ce cas d'avoir cru éliminer le mot
hasard— Je voudrais avoir forcé la roulette à devenir un jeu d'échecs.—
Prétention et sa suite = mais j'aimerais tant payer mes dividendes.
J'irai vous voir avant de partir. Je vous téléphonerai et nous conviendrons
d'une heure.

    à bientôt donc, et mes hommages à Madame Doucet
    très affectueusement à vous
    M. Duchamp
29 rue Campagne Première
Paris

▷ TRANSLATION: *Dear Mr Doucet, I posted earlier this evening the gambling debt we
discussed yesterday. It is self-explanatory. I've done a lot of work on the system,
spurred on by the unfortunate experience of last year. Don't be too skeptical because
this time I believe I have eliminated the word chance. I would like to think I have
forced roulette to become a game of chess. Pretentiousness and its consequences. But
I really would like to pay my dividends. I will come and see you before leaving. I
will telephone you and we will fix up a time. See you soon then, and my respects to
Mrs Doucet, yours very affectionately, M. Duchamp. 29 rue Campagne Première,
Paris.*

---

83. Marcel Duchamp to Ettie Stettheimer   autograph letter
27 March [or May?] [1925], Paris   collection YCAL

Paris 27 mars [or "mai"?]
    Chère Ettie, quelle surprise de recevoir votre chèque laconique
Et quelle honte pour moi—
Depuis plusieurs années je vous écris en pensée bien souvent. Ne m'en
  tenez pas rigueur—
D'abord affaires : merci d'entrer dans ma combinaison : je vous ai envoyé
  hier une obligation recommandée qui est la seule valable de celles que   *Monte Carlo Bond*
  vous avez vues.— parce qu'elle est timbrée—   [cat. 49]
Si vous en avez une autre (par Jane Heap je présume) gardez la comme
  œuvre d'art mais les 20% vous seront payés sur celle que je vous adresse
  en même temps que cette lettre—
Et maintenant autre chose plus grave : mon père et ma mère sont morts   MD's mother died
  au mois de Février à 8 jours d'intervalle = Ce sont vraiment des   29 Jan 1925 and his
  moments épouvantables surtout lorsqu'ils se plaisent à la   father died five days
  multiplication.—   later, 3 Feb 1925.
Je suis donc obligé de rester à Paris jusqu'en Juin pour finir les partages de
  toutes sortes (meubles et titres).—

Je ne pense donc aller m'installer à Monte Carlo pour 3 mois qu'en Juin__ *MD will indeed be in Monte Carlo 3 June - 11 Sept.*
L'été y est délicieux parait il.

Rien d'autre ne m'est arrivé depuis mon retour à Paris. Je pense à NY. de façon rêveuse car je ne vois *pas* de possibilité pour moi d'y habiter comme je l'ai fait.

Il faudra donc bien que vous vous décidiez l'une ou l'autre ou toutes ensemble, à venir ici.

Je ne comprends vraiment pas votre paresse à prendre un bateau pour 3 mois__

Je suppose que Florine a produit d'innombrables portraits et qu'elle pense *à* les exposer à Paris.

Carrie je suis sûr, en a assez de s'occuper de la maison__

Je viens de voir un petit hotel tout meublé qui aurait fait splendidement votre affaire.

En plus petit la reproduction de votre maison (76th St.)__ Grand atelier en-bas__ 2500 francs par mois. Cela vous fera peut être venir__

Je fais peu d'échecs car je suis tout à la roulette__ J'y travaille depuis un an__ et mes statistiques me donnent pleine confiance__ J'ai passé un mois l'année dernière à Monte Carlo et j'ai pu constater que je n'étais *End Mar - 20 Apr 1924.* pas joueur = Je vais donc jouer là bas dans cet esprit : un esprit mécanisé contre une machine. Rien de romantique dans l'affaire, pas plus que de chance.__ Inutile d'ajouter que je ne crains pas d'être traduit en *Monte Carlo Bond* correctionnelle pour émission d'obligations trompeuses = Elles ne sont *[cat. 49]* pas sur le marché et seuls mes amis en ont__

Dites bien mes bonnes amitiés à votre mère et embrassez Carrie et Florine pour moi et à bientôt peut-être

　　　Affectueusement à vous
　　　Rrose Marcel
29 rue Campagne Première.
Paris

▷ TRANSLATION: *Paris, 27th March [or May]. Dear Ettie, What a surprise to receive your laconical check. And how shameful for me. For several years I have been writing to you in my mind very often. Don't hold it against me. First to business. Thank you for joining in my scheme. I sent you a bond, registered delivery yesterday, which is the only one of value among the ones you have seen because it's stamped. If you have another one (by Jane Heap, I presume) keep it as a work of art but the 20% will be paid to you on the one I'm sending you with this letter. And now to something more serious. My mother and my father died in the month of February only one week apart. = It really is a horrific thing to go through especially when events decide to accumulate. I have to stay in Paris, therefore, until June, to finish sharing out various things (furniture and shares). I don't think I'll be setting myself up in Monte Carlo for 3 months until June. Summer there is gorgeous, apparently. Noth-*

ing else since my return to Paris. I think about N.Y. in a dreamy way as I can't see any way I could possibly live there the way I did in the past. You'll just have to make up your minds—one or the other or all of you together—to come here. I simply can't understand why you are so lazy when it comes to taking a boat for three months. I expect Florine has produced hundreds of portraits and that she is going to exhibit them in Paris. Carrie, I am sure, has had enough of taking care of the house. I have just seen a small furnished hotel which would have suited you splendidly. A smaller scale replica of your house (76th St.). Large studio downstairs—2500 Francs a month. Maybe that will get you to come over. I'm doing very little chess as I'm all roulette. I've been working on it for a year and my statistics give me total confidence. I spent a month last year in Monte Carlo und was able to establish that I am not a gambler = So I am going to play over there in this frame of mind: a mechanical mind against a machine. Nothing romantic in this endeavour, no more than there is luck. Needless to say I'm not afraid to be brought before a court for issuing fake bonds. = They are not on the market and my friends are the only ones who have any. Give my very best wishes to your mother and my love to Carrie and Florine and see you soon perhaps. Yours affectionately, Rrose Marcel. 29 rue Campagne Première, Paris.

---

84. Marcel Duchamp to Jacques Doucet   autograph letter
[9, 16, 23 or 30 June 1925], Monaco   collection BLJD

> ### Monaco Mardi
> #### Cher Monsieur Doucet
> J'ai vu Francis il y a quelques jours— J'ai vu sa bâtisse s'annonçant ma foi fort belle—
> Il est entendu qu'il me fera signe dès qu'il saura quel jour vous irez à Mougins. et je vous y rencontrerai.
> La température que les gens du pays trouvent chaude est simplement supportable. Du bon soleil brisé à souhait—
> J'espère donc passer 3 mois ici.
> J'ai commencé à jouer : et la lenteur des progrès en plus ou moins ~~sont~~ est une épreuve de patience— Je me promène dans l'égalité, où je marque le pas de façon inquiétante pour la dite patience.
>   Mais enfin faire cela ou autre chose.
> Je ne suis ni ruiné ni milliardaire et ne serai jamais ni l'un ni l'autre
>   A bientôt mes hommages à Madame Doucet
>   Affectueusement à vous
>   Marcel Duchamp
> Hotel de Marseille Monaco

Mougins (Maritime Alps), Le Château de mai, where Picabia is setting up home with Germaine Everling.

▷ TRANSLATION: *Monaco. Tuesday. Dear Mr Doucet, I saw Francis a few days ago. I saw his building which, my goodness, looks like it is going to be very beautiful in-*

deed. Naturally he will get in touch with me as soon as he knows what day you're going to Mougins and I'll come and meet you. The temperature the local people find hot is, in fact, quite simply tolerable. Jolly good sunshine with as much breeze as you like. I'm hoping then to spend three months here. And what passes for progress is so slow, it tries ones patience. I stroll along evenly, marking time in a manner that is worrying for the above-said patience. But in the end, it's no worse than anything else. I'm neither bankrupt nor a millionaire and will never be either. See you soon. My respects to Mrs Doucet. Yours affectionately, Marcel Duchamp.

---

85. Marcel Duchamp to Jacques Doucet   autograph letter
19 October [1925], Paris   collection BLJD

> Paris. 19. Octobre
>   Cher Monsieur Doucet.
> Rentré depuis bien longtemps. j'ai remis cette lettre tous les jours—
> Je voudrais bien aller vous voir un ~~de~~ après midi vers 3^h si cela vous
>   convient. Sauf Jeudi choisissez le jour.
> Desnos m'a demandé, de la part de Breton, d'exposer le globe que vous
>   avez = me disant que vous aviez accepté de le prêter—
> Pour vous dire vrai, je n'y tiens pas— Et je le ne ferai que si vous y tenez—
> Toutes les expositions de peinture ou sculpture me font mal au cœur— Et
>   je voudrais éviter de m'y associer—
> Je regretterais aussi qu'on voie dans ce globe autre chose que de
>   "l'optique"—
> Nous pourrons décider quand je vous verrai—
>   Bien affectueusement à vous—
>   Marcel Duchamp—

In spite of **Breton**'s wishes, *Rotary Demisphere* [cat. 51] is finally not exhibited at the "Exposition Surréaliste," Galerie Pierre, Paris, opening 13 Nov 1925.

▷ TRANSLATION: *Paris, 19th October. Dear Mr Doucet, Back for some time now. I've been putting off this letter every day. I would very much like to come and see you one afternoon around 3pm if that suits you. Except Thursday, pick any day. Desnos has asked me, on behalf of Breton, to exhibit the globe you have, saying that you have agreed to lend it. To tell you the truth, I'm not keen on the idea and I'll only do it if you really want to. All painting and sculpture exhibitions make me sick. And I would like to avoid being associated with them. I would also be sorry if people saw in this globe anything other than "the optical." We can take a decision when we meet. Very affectionately to you, Marcel Duchamp.*

---

86. Marcel Duchamp to Constantin Brancusi   autograph letter
[between 4 and 28 December 1925], Monaco   collection MNAM

Monaco
Samedi
    J'ai bien tardé pour te dire qu'il y a beaucoup de soleil mais qu'il fait
    froid.
Je suis quand même enchanté : Je viens d'écrire mon système *de roulette*
    c.à.d. que tout y ~~mi~~ est mis au point— et j'ai l'intention de jouer ferme
    cet hiver.
Je rentre le 28 au matin à Paris. J'ai vu Francis qui m'a dit t'avoir écrit au   **Francis** =
    sujet de l'article.   Francis Picabia
Il est beaucoup moins militant qu'avant et semble se contenter de soleil et
    de confort. C'*est* le meilleur moyen de vraiment dire merde aux cons.
Te verrai bientôt— Je continue par télégramme mes transactions en
    Bourse
        Affectueusement
        Marcel Duchamp
Hotel de Marseille Monaco

Cherche un terrain.
[Serai à l'hotel] **Istria après.**

▷ TRANSLATION: *Monaco, Saturday. It's taken me quite a while just to say it's very
sunny here but cold. In any case, I'm quite thrilled: I've just finished writing my
system for roulette i.e. I've got it all off to a tee and I intend to do some serious playing this winter. I'll be back in Paris on the morning of 28th. I saw Francis who said
he'd written to you about the article. He's far less militant than before and seems
contented with sunshine and the easy life. It is the best way of telling the bastards
to go to hell. Will see you soon. Am still doing my Stock Exchange transactions by
telegram. Affectionately, Marcel Duchamp, Hotel de Marseille, Monaco. On the
lookout for a plot of land.* [Will be at] *Hotel Istria next.*

---

87. Marcel Duchamp to Jacques Doucet   autograph letter
27 January 1926, Paris   collection BLJD

29 rue Campagne Première
27 Janvier 1926   80 "Tableaux,
    Cher Monsieur Doucet   aquarelles et dessins
Je suis en pourparlers avec Me Bellier pour faire une vente des Picabias à   par Francis Picabia
    la Salle Drouot en Mairs.   appartenant à M.
                                                                      Marcel Duchamp"
                                                                      auction sale organized
                                                                      by MD and held at the
                                                                      Hotel Drouot, 8 March
                                                                      1926.

Je les ai tous réunis à Istria, retour de l'encadrement, et j'aimerais vous les
montrer.

Veuillez donc me donner un rendez vous dès que vous le pourrez, sauf
Samedi après midi—

J'ai vu Francis ici qui m'a donné de vos nouvelles—

    Bien affectueusement à vous

    Marcel Duchamp

Francis =
Francis Picabia

▷ TRANSLATION: *29 rue Campagne Première, 27th January 1926. Dear Mr Doucet,
I've started negotiations with Ms Bellier about organizing a sale of Picabias at the
Salle Drouot in March. I've gathered them all together at the Istria, back from
framing, and I would like to show them to you. Could you please then give me an
appointment as soon as you can, except Saturday afternoon? I saw Francis who
gave me news of you. Yours affectionately, Marcel Duchamp.*

---

88. Marcel Duchamp to Jacques Doucet
9 March [1926], Paris (Istria Hotel)

autograph letter
collection BLJD

Istria

Mardi 9 Mars

    Cher Monsieur Doucet

Je suis vraiment très heureux du résultat et ~~de~~ j'ai été très sensible à
l'atmosphère de sympathie qui parfumait la salle d'hier—

Vous savez *de* quel poids votre présence a aidé à la réussite et je tiens à vous
exprimer ma reconnaissance.

Un détail va vous amuser =

Sur votre conseil j'avais chargé Roché de défendre les principales
Espagnoles à 3 000.— et il m'en est resté 5— à une moyenne de 2000 =
Je ne regrette pas du tout de l'avoir fait, sachant bien que j'en trouverai
ce prix facilement. Mais j'ajoute que j'ai très bien fait de les défendre,
car, aux yeux du public, ces bonnes petites femmes se sont toutes tenues
très bien—

*"Espagnoles" refers to
a period in Picabia's
paintings devoted to
the depiction of
Spanish women (early
1920's).*

Ayant l'intention de les revendre naturellement j'ai pensé vous demander
d'abord si les amis dont vous m'aviez parlé ont assisté à la vente, auquel
cas il serait inutile d'insister—

Mais si au contraire vous voyez un ~~nouveau~~ moyen de leur signaler l'achat
possible des 5 meilleures Espagnoles (sauf le peigne brun) ou une partie,
je serai <u>enchanté</u> de m'en débarrasser.

Je ne parlerai à d'autres gens à ce sujet qu'après avoir reçu votre avis.

    Bien affectueusement à vous—

    Marcel Duchamp—

29 rue Campagne Première

▷ TRANSLATION: *Istria. Tuesday 9th March. Dear Mr Doucet, I'm really very pleased at the way things turned out and was very touched by the friendly atmosphere pervading the room yesterday. You know just how much your presence helped to make it all a success and I would like to express my gratitude to you. One small thing that will amuse you: On your advice, I had asked Roché to put up the main Espagnoles at 3,000 and I've got 5 left at 2,000 on average. I'm not at all sorry I did this, knowing I could easily get this price. But I would add that I was absolutely right to fight for them as, in the eyes of the public, these good little women held out very well. As I intend to resell them, naturally, I thought I would ask you first of all whether the friends you mentioned were at the sale, in which case there would be no point in pressing the issue. But if, on the other hand, you can think of some way of alerting them to the possible sale of the 5 best Espagnoles (except for the brown comb) or part thereof, I would be delighted to get rid of them. I won't speak to anyone else about this until I have your views. Yours very affectionately, Marcel Duchamp. 29 rue Campagne Première.*

---

89. Marcel Duchamp to Ettie Stettheimer   autograph letter
[23 August 1926], Paris   collection YCAL

29 rue Campagne Première Paris

heureusement surpris par votre lettre, honteux de ma paresse proVerbiale, je vous souhaite des "happy returns" comme à moi même puisque les lignes d'âge sont parallèles, mais aussi parce qu'il faut que 2 lignes de "quelque chose" se rencontrent pour produire amitié et quelquefois amour.

Je prends le "Paris" le 13 Octobre et vous me verrez comme je vous verrai à partir du 20 Octobre dans les rues parallèles de N.Y.

Je vais m'occuper d'une exposition Brancusi en Novembre. et lui même arrive le 15 Septembre à N.Y. Vous le rencontrerez, si vous ne l'avez déja, et l'aimerez.

Merci des nouvelles que vous me donnez des Carrie et Florine qui, au moins, sont fidèles à elles mêmes. (Portraits et doll house).

Dites leur bien mon amour ainsi qu'à votre mère.

La dernière fois que je suis arrivé à N.Y. j'avais coupé mes cheveux, cette fois ci. vous avez changé d'appartement : Vous reconnaîtrai je sans le fond de damas rouge?

Si vous avez le temps, envoyez moi votre n° de téléphone qui n'est pas encore dans le book je suppose—

D'ici mon départ je vais aller passer un mois à Monte Carlo que j'aime pour son absence de moustiques et son architecture.

"Brancusi Exhibition," Brummer Gallery, NY, 17 Nov - 15 Dec 1926. Exhibition will travel to the Arts Club, Chicago, 4-22 Jan 1927.

je dois écrire une plaquette de mon "système" et je n'aurai pas le temps de finir avant mon voyage chez vous—

Affectueusement donc à toute la famille et à bientôt les détails verbaux.

(Marcel) Duche.

Monte Carlo Bond
[cat. 49]

▷ TRANSLATION: *29 rue Campagne Première, Paris. Your letter was a very pleasant surprise: shame on my proVerbial laziness. I wish you, as I do myself, "happy returns" because age lines run parallel, but also because two lines of "something" are bound to meet to produce friendship and sometimes love. I am taking the "Paris," 13th October, and you will see me as I will see you from 20th October in the parallel streets of N.Y. I'll be taking care of a Brancusi exhibition in November and he will also be arriving 15th September in N.Y. You will meet him, if you haven't already, and will like him. Thank you for the news you sent me about Carrie and Florine, who at least do not change. (Portraits and doll's house.) Give them my love and to your mother also. The last time I arrived in N.Y. I'd cut my hair, this time you've moved apartment: will I recognize you without the red damask backdrop? If you have time, send me your telephone number which I don't suppose is in the book yet. Before leaving, I'm going to spend a month in Monte Carlo which I love for its lack of mosquitoes and its architecture. I have to write a pamphlet on my system and won't have time to finish it before setting out on my trip to you. Affectionately to all the family with verbal details following shortly. (Marcel) Duche.*

---

90. Marcel Duchamp to Constantin Brancusi   autograph letter
7 October [1926], Paris   collection MNAM

Paris 7 Oct.

　　Cher Morice

Rien de changé; je pars le 13 sur le Paris

Tes sculptures et encadrements partent sur le "Paris" mais comme frêt
　　c à d que les frais sont beaucoup moindres et ce sera plus facile à passer
　　en douane à New York. *(Les factures consulaires sont faites et la douane
　　est passée.*

Je joins ici la préface de Morand.

J'ai changé quelques détails dans l'anglais

J'emporte avec moi un paquet de photos complet— Je verrai Marthe avant
　　de partir et lui demanderai ce qu'elle t'a envoyé—

J'ai pris aujourd'hui chez Demaria. l'objectif 24 x 30.

Tout va très bien

Si tu peux. fais les photos avant que j'arrive de façon à ce que le catalogue
　　marche rondement.

Brancusi is in NY, for his exhibtion at the Brummer Gallery (see note p.155).

Paul Morand
(1888-1976), French novelist, wrote the introduction for Brancusi's catalog.

Dis à Norton qu'il vienne au bateau s'il peut_ Mais que je n'aurai rien
d'important à passer en douane en descendant puisque les caisses ne
seront délivrées que le lendemain.
Au revoir cher Morice, j'ai hâte de partir.

   Paris est idiot
   et ne fais pas d'imprudence avec la température
   Affectueusement aux Sheelers et tous_
   Marcel. Morice

Allen Norton, with whom MD planning to stay while in NY.

Morice = pet name used mutually by MD and Brancusi in their correspondence to each other.

▷ TRANSLATION: *Paris 7th Oct. Dear Morice. No change here. I'm leaving on the "Paris" on 13th. Your sculptures and frames will also leave on the "Paris," but as freight as it's much cheaper and it'll be easier to get through customs in New York. (The consular invoices are done and customs cleared.) I enclose Morand's preface. I've made a few small changes to the English. I'm taking with me a full set of photos. I'll see Marthe before I leave and ask her what she's sent you. Today I got the 24 by 30 lens from Demaria's. Everything is going really well. If you can, take the photos before I arrive so that the catalog can be done quickly. Tell Norton to come and meet the boat if he can, but that I'll have nothing big to get through customs as they only deliver the crates the following day. Farewell my dear Morice, I can hardly wait to leave. Paris is inane. And careful in the heat! Affectionately to the Sheelers and everyone, Marcel, Morice.*

14 October 1926
In Le Havre, Duchamp boards the "Paris"
headed for New York, bringing with him
some twenty sculptures by Brancusi.
When the ship arrives in New York,
a US Customs official refuses to allow the sculptures
to enter duty-free, insisting they are not works of art.
A legal battle ensues, in which Duchamp
enlists the support of his friends
in the New York art world.

---

91. Marcel Duchamp to Henry McBride   autograph letter
[between 17 November and 15 December 1926], New York   collection YCAL

Mardi
   Ci-joint une œuvre d'art = que Mr Kracke appraiser en chef m'a
donnée ce matin_ Si nous expliquons que Brancusi rentre dans la loi
américaine ça va_
Si nous discutons la'imbécillité de la loi_ ça ne va pas_
Alors mon cher Henry je passerai à 2^h ¼ à l'Hotel (Herald Square) Jeudi
avec Forbes Watson s'il est libre_
   Affectueusement
   Marcel Duchamp
at Brummer's presque all the time_

Mr Kracke, US Customs official believing Brancusi's sculpture "left too much to the imagination" to be considered art.

Forbes Watson (1880-1960), art editor New York World and regular contributor to The Arts.

Brummer Gallery, 27 E 57th Street, where MD is installing the Brancusi exhibition (see p.155).

▷ TRANSLATION: *Tuesday. Enclosed, a work of art = the one Mr Kracke, appraiser in chief, gave me this morning. If we explain that Brancusi is within the bounds of American law, things will be all right. If we argue about the idiocy of the law, things will not be all right. So, my dear Henry, I will come to the Hotel (Herald Square) at 2.15 pm on Thursday with Forbes Watson, if he is free. Affectionately, Marcel Duchamp, at Brummer's almost* all the time.

---

92. Marcel Duchamp to Constantin Brancusi
31 December 1926 [New York]

autograph letter
collection MNAM

Vendredi 31 Dec. 26.
    Bonne année!
Je pars demain Samedi pour Chicago et l'exposition ouvre le 4.__ ferme le
    18__
Les caisses seront ouvertes en ma présence Dimanche et l'oiseau de
    Steichen y est.__
— Après avoir essayé 5 ou 6 fois de *te* faire avancer par Brummer l'argent de
    tes ventes, j'ai dû renoncer et il t'écrit par le même courrier une lettre
    recommandée avec laquelle tu pourras négocier la somme totale tout de
    suite en payant 10 ou 11%__
— J'ai fait cela au cas où tu aurais besoin tout de suite
    Sinon, tu peux attendre que Mrs. Hare et Horter aient payé__
    Brummer prend 10% au dessus des 4 000__ Ce qui est très raisonnable et
    il m'a même dit aujourd'hui qu'il ne prendrait probablement rien.
    J'ai vu Madame Rumsey 2 ou 3 fois__ La commande de l'oiseau bronze
    $1500, comme Steichen est ferme. Et elle prend aussi le torse onyx
    qu'elle avait choisi pour $800.
    Donc quand l'oiseau de bronze sera arrivé ici__ je lui écrirai pour lui
    demander les $800 en plus de ses 1500 et je te paierai les 700 de
    différence__
    Veux tu être gentil et t'informer si on peut envoyer cet oiseau par le port
    de Baltimore ou de Philadelphie = (Quelle compagnie se chargerait de
    cela?)
    Je pourrais t'envoyer l'adresse d'un ami de Mme Rumsey à Philadelphie
    qui recevrait l'oiseau pour elle et éviterait les embêtements de la douane
    à New York__
    L'article dans le Dial parait le 15 Janvier.
    J'ai fait faire des photos de l'exposition Brummer par le peintre Kunioshi
    qui fait de bonnes photos pour $20.__ Je n'ai pas voulu demander à
    Sheeler.
    Ecris moi au sujet de Sheeler, j'irai lui demander des explications avant de
    rentrer à Paris__

Edward Steichen
(1879-1973), well-known American photographer owning works by Brancusi. When he attempted to import Brancusi's *Bird in Space* into US, Sept 1926, US Customs refused to classify it as art.

Earl Horter, see p.192.

Mary Rumsey
(1881-1934), heiress to the Harriman railroad fortune and widow of American sculptor Charles Cary Rumsey (1879-1922).

Yasuo Kuniyoshi
(1893-1953), Japanese-American painter, spends much time in Paris 1925 - 1928, but is at this time in NY working as a freelance photographer.

Partirai pour Paris vers le 15 Février
J'ai fait faire 250 catalogues pour Chicago— j'en rapporterai à Paris.
Je suis _invité_ au Club "Racquet Club" à Chicago. Voici mon adresse
jusqu'au 20 Janvier
      Marcel Duchamp
         Racquet Club
         1361 North Dearborn Street
         Chicago Ill.
      Au revoir, cher vieux, à bientôt d'autres bonnes nouvelles

———

Voici ce que tu toucheras en tout
Compte au 1er Janvier 1927
    Ventes chez Brummer

Oiseau Mrs Hare	2 000
Coq Horter	600
	2 600
moins 10% commission Brummer	260
	2 340

Earl Horter, see p.192.

———

avec la lettre de Brummer tu pourras négocier
cette somme à Paris   _$2 340_

Oiseau Rumsey	1 500
Frais avances faites par toi à New York	190.[15]
Voyage aller et retour New York somme convenue	500
	4 530.[15]

▷ TRANSLATION: _Friday 31st Dec '26. Happy New Year! Leaving Saturday for Chicago and the exhibition opens on the 4th, closes the 18th. The crates will be opened in my presence, Sunday, and the Steichen bird is in them. Having made 5 or 6 attempts to get Brummer to advance you the money from your sales, I have had to call it a day and he is sending you, by the same mail, a registered letter which will enable you to negotiate the overall sum straightaway by paying 10 or 11%. I have done this in case you needed it urgently. Otherwise, you can wait until Mrs Hare and Horter pay up. Brummer takes 10% over 4,000, which is very reasonable and he even told me today that he probably won't take anything at all. I've seen Mrs Rumsey two or three times. The order for the bronze bird, $1,500, like Steichen's, is definite. She's also taking the onyx torso she picked out for $800. So when the bronze bird gets here, I'll write and ask her for $800 in addition to her $1,500 and I will pay you the 700 difference. Would you mind finding out whether this bird can be sent via the port of Baltimore or Philadelphia? = (Which company would do that?) I could send you the address of a friend of Mrs Rumsey in Philadelphia_ who would be willing to receive the bird on her behalf and save all the bother with customs in New York. The article in the Dial is coming out 15th January. I had photos of the Brummer exhibition taken by the painter Kunioshi who does good photos for $20. I didn't want to ask Sheeler. Write me about Sheeler—I shall ask him to explain himself before I return to Paris. Leave for Paris around 15th February. Have had 250 catalogs made for Chicago and will bring some back to Paris. I am a guest at the Club, "Racquet Club," in Chicago. My address until 20th February: Marcel Duchamp, Racquet Club, 1361 North Dearborn Street, Chicago Ill. Goodbye then, old chap, look forward to the next bout of good news. This is what you will be paid overall. Account 1st January 1927. Sales at Brummer's. [See price list:] Bird Mrs Hare / Cock Horter / less 10% Brummer's commission / With Brummer's letter you'll be able to negotiate this sum in Paris / Rumsey bird / Cash advance you made to New York / Round trip New York agreed fare.

1 January 1927
On New Year's Day,
Duchamp takes the overnight train
from New York to Chicago. There he installs
the Brancusi exhibition at the Arts Club.
Throughout his three-week stay in Chicago,
Duchamp keeps Brancusi informed of sales through
a continuous exchange of letters.

24 January 1927
Duchamp returns to New York just in time
to assist Katherine Dreier in the installation of her
"International Exhibition of Modern Art,"
which has closed at the Brooklyn Museum
but which is scheduled to open at the Anderson
Galleries in Manhattan the following day.

26 February 1927
Duchamp boards the "Paris" (the same ship
that took him to New York four months
earlier) and returns to France.
Aboard ship with him is Julien Levy,
son of Edgar Levy, a powerful New York real
estate developer who purchased Brancusi's
white marble Bird in Space, 1923, from the Brummer
Gallery. Julien Levy will later open
a gallery in New York that features work
by both American and European Surrealists.

Paris, rue Larrey | 1927-1933

aboard ship for France, on the "Paris" | 26 Feb 1927
lives in Paris, moves into 11 rue Larrey, 7th and top floor
round trips to Mougins, Nice, Chamonix, Cannes, Hyères-les Palmiers, The Hague, Barcelona,
  Les Rousses, Geneva, Villefranche, Toulon and Hamburg—often for chess tournaments
aboard ship for USA, on the "Île de France" | 25 Oct 1933
trip to New York: Hotel Blackstone 50 East 58th Street, then 645 Madison Avenue

from 26 February 1927 to 20 January 1934

▶ MAJOR WORKS

Porte, 11 rue Larrey (wood door that operates
  two doorways, 1927)
"Opposition and Sister Squares Are Reconciled"
  (chess treatise by MD and Vitaly
  Halberstadt, cover and layout by MD,
  1932)

▶ EXHIBITIONS

**(Examples of Cubist painting with Modern Sculpture
  shown to illustrate Pr. Joseph Pigoan's lecture)**,
  Rembrandt Hall, Pomona College, Pomona, USA.
  By MD: *Nude descending the Staircase*
  — **17 Apr 1928**
Exposition de Collages, Galerie Goëmans, Paris. By MD:
  L.H.O.O.Q. (1910); *L.H.O.O.Q. (1930)*;
  Pharmacie; *Eau de voilette*; *Roulette de Monte-
  Carlo* — **March 1930**

Cubism 1910-13, De Hauke Galleries, New York. By MD:
  Nude descending a Staircase — **7 Apr - 30 Apr 1930**
L'art vivant en Europe, Palais des Beaux-Arts, Bruxelles.
  By MD: *Une glissière contenant un moulin à eau*
  — **25 Apr - 24 May 1931**
Surrealism. Paintings, Drawings & Photographs, Julien
  Levy Gallery, New York — **29 Jan 1932**
L'époque héroïque du Cubisme (1910-1914), Galerie
  Jacques Bonjean, Paris. By MD: *Mariée; Passage
  de la Vierge à la Mariée; Joueurs d'échecs*
  — **23 Apr - 14 May 1932**
**A Century of Progress. Exhibition of Painting and
  Sculpture**, The Art Institute, Chicago. By MD: *Nude
  descending the Stairs* — **1 June - 1 Nov 1933**
**Exposition Surréaliste. Sculptures-Objets-Peintures-
  Dessins**, Pierre Colle, *Paris*. By MD: *Pharmacie*
  — **7 June - 18 June 1933**

March 1927
Duchamp settles into a
small studio apartment at 11 rue Larrey.
A few weeks after his return, at a dinner party
with Germaine Everling and Francis Picabia,
he meets 24-year-old Lydie Sarazin-Levassor,
from a wealthy industrialist family.
By May, she and Duchamp are engaged to wed,
and Duchamp writes a series
of letters to his friends in America
to explain this sudden and unexpected
change in his life.

93. Marcel Duchamp to Katherine S. Dreier   autograph letter
25 May 1927, Paris   collection YCAL

Paris May 25th. 27

    I had your long letter some days ago = full of news = Splendid.
Buffalo really was a great success. Brancusi and I are delighted with the
news about Mlle Pogany. I gave Mr. Hekking's name to our lawyer who
happened to be in Paris. His word might be of great weight when the
trial comes up in October—

About the $1000.— it is perfectly all right I don't need it now. End of this
    year if not too early for you— Don't speak of %—

An important news : I am going to be married in June— I don't know
    how to tell you this, it has been so sudden that it is hard to explain—

Mlle Sarazin-Levassor is 25, she is the daughter of an important
    businessman connected with the firm Panhard-Levassor automobiles—
    She is not especially beautiful nor attractive— but seems to have rather
    a mind which might understand how I can stand marriage. All these
    "mights" and "seem" to have no disillusion when too late—

I am a bit tired of this vagabonding life and want to try a partly resting
    one— Whether I am making a mistake or not is of little importance as
    I don't think anything can stop *me* from changing altogether in a very
    short time if necessary—

I am not going to be rich— Her money is for the present hardly enough
    to make her live, and is hers—

We will have ~~to~~ 2 apartments and *I* hope to keep several hours or days for
    myself—

All this, of course, might seem foolish to another person than you.

The Wedding takes place on the 8th of June at the protestant Church—

I am keeping the little studio where I am very comfortable (I have fixed it
    as I wanted it). 11 rue Larrey—

I am not working at anything, saw the photos that Man Ray took of your
    place

"The Société Anonyme
Collection," shown at
the Albright Art Gallery,
Buffalo, 25 Feb - 20 Mar
1927.

William Hekking
(1885-1970), director of
the Albright Art Gallery,
1925-1932, acquired
Brancusi's *Mlle
Pogany II*, 1920, from
MD via the Société
Anonyme, Mar 1927.

Lydie Sarazin-Levassor
(1902-1988),
granddaughter of a
renowned French
automobile manufacturer.

Lydie moves into an
apartment of her own
rue Boussaingault,
Paris.

They are very good and you must have received them by now— Write—
and also tell me when the things are coming back from N.Y. You send
everything to Foinet

Maurice Lefèbvre-
Foinet, Paris shipping
agent.

---

94. Marcel Duchamp to Jacques Doucet   2 printed invitations with handwritten note
[26 May 1927], Paris   collection BLJD

[wedding invitation, groom]
```
       monsieur Marcel Duchamp
a l'honneur de vous faire part de son mariage avec
mademoiselle Lydie Sarazin-Levassor et vous prie
d'assister à la bénédiction nuptiale qui leur sera donnée
le mercredi 8 juin 1927, à midi précis, au temple de
l'étoile (avenue de la grande-armée).
11, rue larrey, paris V.
```

[autograph addition:]

*Ceci pour vous expliquer cher Monsieur Doucet mon silence— Puis je aller
vous voir un jour bientôt?*
> *Mes hommages à Madame Doucet*
> *et bien affectueusement à vous*
> *Marcel Duchamp—*

[wedding invitation, bride's family]
```
       monsieur et madame
Henry Sarazin-Levassor ont l'honneur de vous faire part du
mariage de mademoiselle Lydie Sarazin-Levassor, leur
fille, avec monsieur Marcel Duchamp et vous prient
d'assister à la bénédiction nuptiale qui leur sera donnée
le mercredi 8 juin 1927, à midi précis, au temple de
l'étoile (avenue de la grande-armée).
```

```
80, avenue du bois-de-boulogne
6, square du bois-de-boulogne
```

▷ TRANSLATION: [wedding invitation, groom:] *On the occasion of his marriage to Miss
Lydie Sarazin-Levassor, Mr Marcel Duchamp cordially invites you to attend the
wedding blessing to be given on Wednesday 8th June 1927, at twelve o'clock noon
precisely, at the Temple de l'Etoile (avenue de la Grande Armée). 11 rue Larrey,
Paris V.*

[autograph addition:] *Explaining hereby, dear Mr Doucet, the reason for my silence. May I come and see you some day soon? My respects to Mrs Doucet and
yours most affectionately, Marcel Duchamp.*

[wedding invitation, bride's family:] *Mr and Mrs Henry Sarazin-Levassor have pleasure in announcing the marriage of their daughter Miss Lydie Sarazin-Levassor to*

Mr Marcel Duchamp and cordially invite you to attend the wedding blessing to be given on Wednesday 8th June 1927, at twelve o'clock noon precisely, at the Temple de l'Etoile (avenue de la Grande Armée) 80 avenue du bois-de-boulogne. 6 square du bois-de-boulogne.

---

95. Marcel Duchamp to Walter Pach   autograph letter
24 June 1927, Paris   collection AAA

24 Juin 27

    Mon cher Walter ma chère Magda.

Je suis marié depuis quinze jours avec Mlle Sarazin-Levassor dont le père était dans l'affaire automobile Panhard-Levassor—

C'est une expérience charmante jusqu'ici et j'espère que cela continuera—

Ma vie n'en est en rien changée—

Je dois faire de l'argent mais pas pour deux. Espérons que quelque chance par an aidera le ménage à entretenir un bien être.

Je regrette que vous ne veniez pas en Europe— Un jour viendra où vous connaîtrez ma femme qui est vraiment très gentille

Affaires

J'ai acheté il y a quelque temps un tout petit Odilon Redon (aquarelle) 30 ^{cm} x 20 ^{cm} *environ* qui est une des dernières formules de lui; pas mystique, pas des fleurs— mais pour ainsi dire de la couleur seulement— *sans forme ni représentation*

J'avais pensé que peut-être les Bing s'intéresseraient *à* une telle chose— Si vous croyez que cela vaut la peine, je veux bien *vous* l'envoyer— J'en voudrais $500.— pour moi— ce qui ne me semble pas exagéré—

Répondez moi et je l'enverrai immédiatement si vous le voulez— Il est encadré—

    Comment allez vous? que fait Magda? Peut être irai je à N.Y. à la fin de l'année—

        Tout le monde ici va bien

        Bien affectueusement à tous trois

        Marcel.

11 rue Larrey

Paris (V)

Le petit torse de Brancusi qui plairait à Mme Bing est toujours en garde meuble de Brummer, King and Parker—

> TRANSLATION: *24th June '27. My dear Walter, my dear Magda, I have been married for a fortnight to Miss Sarazin-Levassor whose father was in the Panhard-Levassor automobile business. It's a delightful experience so far and I hope it will go on. My life is in no way changed by this. I have to make money but not for two.*

Alexander (1878-1959) and **Florence Bing**, collectors of modern art, owning several important paintings by Redon.

Let's hope that luck will come our way each year to help keep the household in good shape. I am sorry you are not coming to Europe. The day will come when you'll actually meet my wife who is really very nice. Business: I bought, some time ago, a very small Odilon Redon (watercolor), 30cm by 20cm approx., which is one of his latest formulas—not mystical, no flowers, but, so to speak, just color, without form or representation. I thought the Bings might be interested in something like this. If you think it's worth it, I'll be happy to send it to you. I would like $500 for it, for myself, which seems reasonable. Let me know and I'll send it straight away if you want it. It's framed. How are you? What is Magda up to? Maybe I'll go to N.Y. at the end of the year. Everybody is fine here. Very affectionately to all three of you, Marcel, 11 rue Larrey, Paris (V). Brancusi's small torso, which Mrs Bing would like, is still in storage at Brummer, King and Parker.

---

96. Marcel Duchamp to Katherine S. Dreier   autograph letter
12 March 1928, Nice   collection YCAL

Nice

March 12th 1928

I have been going to *the* Post Office almost every day expecting to get a letter from you— Now I am afraid that the letter has been lost—

Anyway— I just weighed myself, the result being a gain of 4 pounds in 2 months. I needed them very badly—

I am living in Nice "bachelorly"— and I enjoy every minute of my old self again—

Divorce is over— since Jan. 25th

The "wife" is also down here in St Raphael and we see each other every other week—

I received a note from the Fifth Ave. Bank, about the $100^{00} you deposited in January—

If I am right, you deposited $700 (twice $350) and $100. in January—

I am living very cheaply here.

and don't seem to care what is going to happen after September—

I play chess a lot—

Won a little international tournament in Hyères. in February.

Chess is my drug; don't you know it!

I expect to be back in Paris by April 15th

I did not hear anything about your ~~shipping~~*ment* of the paintings (Dorothea and Eilsheimius)

Please write what happened.

Also, I suppose that Stieglitz must have gotten the shipment of Picabias—

Have you heard anything about it?

MD and his wife divorce after only just over 6 months of marriage.

St Raphaël = town on the French Riviera

MD won (2 Feb) the Coupe Philidor jointly with Halberstadt and O'Hanlon.

"Dorothea and Eilsheimius" = Dorothea Dreier (1870-1923), Katherine S. Dreier's sister; Louis Eilshemius, see p.57.

Write directly to Nice Poste Restante— until April 12th
    Affectueusement
    Dee. (Vorced)

---

97. Marcel Duchamp to Alfred Stieglitz   autograph letter
30 March 1928, Nice   collection YCAL

GRAND CAFE DE LA POSTE
Place Wilson et 25, Rue Hôtel-des-Postes
- Nice -

March 30th 1928
    Dear Stieglitz
Very glad you like the pictures = You will find here an Introduction that
    Picabia had written by Miss Guinness whom you probably know in
    New York.
I hope it will do.
Picabia is writing you and very excited over your show—
Don't bother about the broken frame.— Leave it aside if you can't show
    it—
I was sorry to hear about O Keefes operations. My love to the convalescent
    and to you
        Marcel Duchamp
11 rue Larrey Paris
I will be in Paris the 15th of April.

———

Names and prices of Pictures by Picabia—
    Shipped to G. Of— *(for Alfred Stieglitz)*

1 Papilliomanie	$200⁰⁰
2 Femme aux bas noirs	$200⁰⁰
3 L'Enfer	400⁰⁰
4 Tête de mort	300⁰⁰
5 Tableau	500⁰⁰
6 Le Mousquetaire	400⁰⁰
7 Le Grand Livre	600⁰⁰
8 Cadre Moucheté	200⁰⁰
9 Femme au glacier	300⁰⁰
10 Les Chiens	400⁰⁰
11 Danseur et Caraïbe	300⁰⁰

"Picabia Exhibition," The Intimate Gallery, NY, 19 Apr - 11 May 1928.

Georgia O'Keeffe (1887-1986), American painter, wife of Alfred Stieglitz (see p.109). She underwent several operations for removal of a breast tumor, 1927 and 1928.

G. Of = George Of

98. Marcel Duchamp to Katherine S. Dreier   autograph letter
18 April 1928, Paris   collection YCAL

Paris
April 18th 1928
11 rue Larrey.
    I got both your letter and telegram in Nice just before I left__ I am
now back to Paris__

Eilsh. and Dorothea's pictures have arrived. They are still at the
customs'__ but will be delivered in a week. I will be very much
interested to see what I can do with them.

— First__ You don't seem to have ever grasped my relationship with
    Stieglitz__

I don't think, I never thought that Stieglitz was a friend of mine__ But I
    add who can I call a friend of mine? Aside from that statement I
    arranged with Stieglitz to have that show of Picabia because he used to
    like Picabia, and I thought it was the only way to show these things in
    N.Y.__ I don't really expect any financial returns from it__

Secondly__ it never was in my mind to have Stieglitz show any other
    painter through me (like Max Ernst).

In other words, the whole thing had been arranged in N.Y. with Stieglitz
    while I was there last year and I told you about it = then__

The show is to be opened end of April, according to Stieglitz's letter__

————

I received the notice from the bank about the $250.⁰⁰ Thanks.

————

I am really sorry about Walden and the whole story. In the first place
    Walden has nothing to ask *from* you.__ He has been enough of a crook
    for the last ten years, keeping the works of all *the* French artists__ and
    he is not worth a penny of pity__ I acknowledge that my sister in law
    should give him a commission although the sculpture was sold in N.Y.
    at the Brooklyn Show.

It had been impossible *for ten years* to get it back from Berlin to Paris.__
It was only a happy accident that you should be in Berlin, and had the
    kindness to ship to N.Y. etc

~~An~~

————

In other words don't pay any more attention to Walden's kicking__ You
    don't owe him anything__ and I will do my best to have the % paid to
    him by my sister in law.

Margin notes:

"Eilsh. and Dorothea"
= L. Eilshemius (p.57)
and D. Dreier (p.165).

"Picabia Exhibition,"
The Intimate Gallery
(see note p.166).

Herwarth Walden
(1878-1941), editor of
Der Sturm, gave the
Blaue Reiter its first
exh. in Berlin.

Raymond Duchamp-
Villon's *Seated
Woman*, 1914 (Yale
Univ. Art Gallery; gift of
the Société Anonyme),
shown in Brooklyn exh.

(Notice that my sister in law had forbidden *him* to sell it, in the last years, as she was so sore at him : all this to explain that his talk about 600^{00} instead of 800^{00} is pure bluff—

———

Max Ernst—
I will see Van Leer who is handling Max Ernst.— If I can get a set of 10 pictures, I will send them on to you (Lincoln Warehouse)

———

Maximilien Ernst alias **Max Ernst** (1891-1976) held his first major exhibition in Paris, at the Galerie Van Leer, 10-24 March 1926.

The cable was a wonderful news. My brother is overcome—
And I am anxious to see Brummer about what the cable meant in the end.

———

Back here, I am enjoying my studio again.
I will write soon again—
Brancusi is building his new studio— quite near the old one— it is to be ready in two months— Sends his love
          So do I
          Dee—

———————————————————————

99. Marcel Duchamp to Alfred Stieglitz   autograph letter
2 July 1928, Paris   collection YCAL

Paris 11 rue Larrey
July 2nd 1928
          Dear Stieglitz
I received your two letters and am sorry to have been so long to answer you—
Yes I think it was wonderful of you to have kept 3 of the paintings—
          Picabia is one of the few today who are not "a sure investment"—
The feeling about the "market" here is so disgusting that you never hear anymore of a thought for itself—
Painters and Paintings go up and down like Wall Street stock—
It was not exactly like that 20 years ago, and much more amusing—
Hope to arrange for Chicago, as I have to send a few more paintings to complete the show—
Of has been perfect as usual.
Lake George, I hope, is the right place for you and O'Keefe's rest—
Picabia is in Paris for a few days and I showed him your letter and the clippings = He is sending you his love—
Hope but not expect to go to New York soon—

The Stieglitz summer home, **Lake George**, NY.

My love to both of you
Marcel Duchamp
11 rue Larrey
Paris V

---

100. Marcel Duchamp to Katherine S. Dreier   autograph letter
5 November 1928, Paris   collection YCAL

Paris
Nov. 5ᵗʰ— 1928

Your 2 letters announcing the possible stop of activities in the S.A. did not surprise me— The more I live among artists, the more I am convinced that they are fakes from the minute they get successful in the smallest way.

This means *also* that all the dogs around the artist are crooks— If you see the combination fakes and crooks— how have you been able to keep some kind of a faith (and in what?)

Don't name a few exceptions to justify a milder opinion *about* the whole "Art game".

In the end, a painting is declared good only if it is worth "so much"— It may even be accepted by the "holy" museums— So much for posterity—

Please come back to the ground and if you like some paintings, some painters, look at their work, but don't try to change a crook into an honest man, or a fake into a fakir.—

This will give *you* an indication of the kind of mood I am in— Stirring up the old ideas of disgust—

But it is only on account of you—

I have lost so much interest (all) in the question that I don't suffer from it— You still do—

— Exhibitions with Brummer don't seem to take any shape.

He is going to have [a show of] my brother (40 pieces of sculpture) in December— He might ask you to lend one or two things (seated woman)— Would you mind letting him have it for the show (really very important)—

He may have another show of sculpture in February (miscellaneous) for which I would ~~come~~ *go* to America— and a show of Pascin's work if Pascin and Brummer arrange it in N.Y. (Pascin is leaving in a few days for *the* US)

— It is "verbally" understood that Brummer would pay my expenses (ocean trip and stay in N.Y. for 2 months about)—

27 sculptures are to be included in "Raymond Duchamp-Villon," **Brummer Gallery**, NY, 5 Jan - 9 Feb 1929.

Jules Pascin (1885-1930), French painter of Bulgarian origin.

But please don't see him about this because I want him to realise by
himself whether he wants me or not—
I don't care personally one way or the other.
Seeing N.Y. is always a pleasure but too expensive even if you are paid to
come over.
I will write again.— Soon
    Bien affectueusement
    Marcel Dee.
Holland was very nice— we played in the Binenhof (Knights' room)

Binnenhof = famous
square in The Hague
surrounded by
government and
Parliament buildings.

---

101. Marcel Duchamp to Katherine S. Dreier   autograph letter
11 September 1929, Paris   collection YCAL

Paris 11th of September 1929

You have all the rights to be furious, but If have been actually unable
to write : I had so many things to decide on—
    You must understand :
My attitude toward the book is based upon my attitude toward "Art," since
1918—
So I am furious myself that you will accept only partly that attitude.
It can be no more question of my life as an artist's life : I gave it up ten
years ago; this period is long enough to prove that my intention to
remain outside of any art manifestation is permanent
The second question is that, according to my attitude, I don't want to go
to America to start anything in the way of an "Art," museum of any kind.
The third question is that I want to be alone as much as possible.
This abrupt way to speak of my "hardening process" is not meant to be
mean, but is the result of a "42 years of age" Summing up—
I am a little sick— physically— my bladder is beginning to speak— So I
have to take care of myself— doctors included—
My opinion is that anything one does is all right and I ~~ruf~~ refuse to fight
for this or that opinion or their contrary
Don't see any pessimism in my decisions : They are only a way toward
beatitude—
Your life has been and is connected with the actions and reactions of so
many people that you can hardly approve of my choice between a snale
[sic: for "snail" or possibly "snake"?] and a butterfly for a disguise
Please understand, I am trying for a minimum of action, gradually—
I would never let Waldemar George write anything about me, if it were in
my power—
My brother never said a word… Yet to me—
All this is very annoying

Apparently, Dreier
suggested that
Waldemar George (see
below) write a book
on MD.

Waldemar George
(1893-1969), French art
historian, known for his
writing on Picasso, will
publish two books on
Jean Crotti (1930 and
1959).

so let's forget it—

I wrote to Dr. Fox. and sent him the photos and prices of the bird.

According to Brancusi (sick in Aix les Bains, better now), it is the same
   Bird in marble as Mrs Steichen's one— Let us hope this will succeed.

I will go to Nice in October for 2 months I hope— Chess.

10 000 apologies for this rough letter and affectueusement
   Dee—

---

102. Marcel Duchamp to Jean Crotti   autograph letter
6 February 1930, Villefranche s/Mer   collection AAA

Villefranche ^{S}/mer
6 Fev. 1930
   Cher vieux,
Je voulais te téléphoner avant de partir— J'ai fait juste avant de quitter
   Paris une Joconde pour Aragon qu'il doit exposer Galerie Goëmans—
   Aragon fait aussi une préface.
Man Ray a ~~eu~~ la 1ère Joconde—
Peut-être Zervos trouverait-il quelque chose là s'il n'est pas trop tard—
Affec^t
Je joue à Nice du 12 au 25— Fév
adressez correspondance
Poste Restante Nice
   Marcel.

"Joconde" = version of
LHOOQ [cat. 41]

Galerie Goëmans,
Paris, directed by
Belgian writer **Camille
Goëmans** (1900-1960);
"Exposition de
Collages," March 1930,
cat. preface by **Louis
Aragon** (1897-1982),
French writer and poet.

Christian Zervos
(1899-1970), French art
historian, specialist on
the work of Picasso.

▷ TRANSLATION: *Villefranche s/Mer, 6th Feb 1930. Hello old chap, I wanted to telephone you before leaving. I made, just before leaving Paris, a Mona Lisa, for
Aragon, which he's going to exhibit—Goëmans Gallery. Aragon's also doing a
preface. Man Ray has the 1st Mona Lisa. Maybe Zervos might find something
there, if it's not too late. Affectionately. I'm playing in Nice from 12th to 25th Feb
Address for correspondance Poste Restante, Nice. Marcel.*

---

103. Marcel Duchamp to Katherine S. Dreier   autograph letter
18 December 1930, Paris   collection YCAL

Paris Dec. 18th 1930
   They *usually* put together ~~sh~~ different shipments in order to save
   money on the whole— So, if on one ~~th~~ side you pay for *2* brokerages,
   on the other side you pay less freight = That big amount of money
   means everything from Paris (Packing included)— C.O.D.
As for California, all of the exhibitors accept to have you keep the pictures
   until March 1932, except Ozenfant who says that he is sorry not to have

"C.O.D." = Cash On
Delivery

Amédée Ozenfant
(1886-1966), French
painter.

been able to give better works, and wants them back in <u>March 1931</u>; So
you might bring these two pictures back with you.

The apartment is all painted in that <u>blue white</u> as near as possible of the
color we had at the 1ˢᵗ Société Anonyme East 47ᵗʰ Street—

It is very clean, very clear; the furnace <u>is</u> in the kitchen but leaves space for
the gas stove; the partition has been taken out so that you have a kitchen
opened on the infinite =

The second apartment is very nicely sectioned in 2 rooms and entrée also
white— The whole thing looks very attractive—

    Studio like open air. (light).

—————

Finally I took my book to Brussels where I have great hope to publish it.
I am waiting for the answer.

The Nouvelle Revue française felt they finally could not do it.

I̶n̶ The Brussels publisher wants to do it in 3 languages German, English
and French in the same book : Excellent idea.

- *german text*
- *English text*
- *Diagrams*
- *French text*

I intend to do 12 copies on good paper and sell them as "deluxe edition"
numbered and signed to help the publisher.

I am expecting news from you about show, lectures. etc. You probably are
very busy.

— About my brother's etchings there is no special hurry.

But could you think about starting a monthly deposit to my bank, Fifth
AVE. 530, for the Brancusi and the etchings— if the market permits it,
(in your case). You might deposit something every month half going to
my brother, half toward the Brancusi— As you wish—

Please (I forgot to tell you), have the marble bird and the soft stone piece
removed from the garden for the winter : Brancusi told me it is better
f̶o̶r̶ to avoid cold weather—

    Affectueusement
    Dee.

"apartement" at 16 place Dauphine, Paris.

"entrée" = hallway

Opposition... [cat. 57] rejected by Gallimard, (NRF) is later to be published by Ed. Lancel, Brussels, [Jun] 1932.

Yellow Bird, 1919 (Yale University Art Gallery; bequest of the Société Anonyme).

---

104. Marcel Duchamp to Henri-Pierre Roché   autograph letter
24 May 1933, Paris   collection HRHRC

24 mai 1933
11 rue Larrey
       Cher vieux
Je t'ai écrit poste Restante Arcachon il y a quelques jours et la lettre   **Arcachon**, city on the
probablement ne t'a pas eu—   French Atlantic coast.
Voici ce que je te demandais : Peux tu compléter les 1000 fr nécessaires au
livre maintenant car je crains que mon fameux héritage ne rentre pas   **"livre"** = *Green Box*
avant 2 mois, et toutes les notes à payer pour le livrc devront l'être au   [cat. 3]
fur et à mesure des progrès cà d le long de ł Juin.
Comme j'ai peur d'être à court, je te demande de m'envoyer un chèque de
5 000 au nom de Rrose Sélavy
J'ai déjà 6 noms sûrs pour les luxe ; encore 4 et ça suffira— D'ailleurs j'en
ai plus de 4 éventuels.
Ecris, je te tiendrai au courant—
       Affectueusement
       Totor

▷ TRANSLATION: *24th May 1933, 11 rue Larrey. Hello old man, I wrote to you Poste
Restante in Arcachon a few days ago and the letter probably didn't catch you. What
I was asking you is this: Can you make up the 1,000 francs needed for the book now,
as I'm afraid that my famous inheritance won't be coming in for 2 months and all
the bills for the book have to be paid as we go along i.e. within the month of June.
As I'm worried about being short, could you send me a check for 5,000 in the name
of Rrose Sélavy? I already have 6 definites for the deluxe boxes—4 more and that
will be enough. In fact, I already have more than 4 possibles. Write, I'll keep you
posted. Affectionately, Totor.*

---

105. Marcel Duchamp to Man Ray   autograph letter
21 August 1933, Cadaquès   collection HRHRC

Cadaquès
21 Août 33
       Cher Man
Nous sommes installés ici avec Mary dans une petite maison sinon   **Mary Reynolds**, née
délicieuse, au moins suffisante— Temps idéal et peseta charmante   Hubacheck (1891-
Nous avons une chambre de plus dans laquelle tu pourrais coucher— et   1950), American
nous mangeons à la maison—   bookbinder and
Dali est ici avec Gala et nous les voyons souvent—   companion of MD.
Tâche donc de venir passer quelque temps avec nous.   **Salvador Dalí** (1904-
          1989), and companion
          Gala Eluard (1894-
          1982), pseudonym of
          Helena Dmitrievna
          Diakonova, whom he is
          to marry in 1934.

Nous avons la maison jusqu'au 14 Sept. après nous partirons pour
Barcelone et rentrerons directement à Paris le 1er Octobre.
Ecris en tout cas où tu es et ce que tu fais
     Affectueusement *de tous deux*
     Marcel
Dali voudrait prendre des photos des fameuses maisons Modern Style de
Barcelone pour reproduction dans "Minotaure" et croit que tu serais
peut être intéressé de'y voir tes photos reproduites.

Photos by Man Ray to
illustrate Dali's article
"De la beauté terrifiante
de l'architecture
modern' style,"
Minotaure, Paris,
No.3-4, Dec 1933.

▷ TRANSLATION: *Cadaquès. 21st August 1933. Dear Man, Mary and I have moved
into a little house—perhaps not fabulous, but quite adequate. Weather ideal and
peseta delightful. We have a spare room where you could stay and we eat at home.
Dali is here with Gala and we see them often. Do try to come and spend some time
with us. We have the house until 14th September—after that, we're leaving for Barcelona and will go straight back to Paris 1st October. Write and tell me where you
are and what you're doing, in any case. Affectionately from both of us, Marcel. Dali
wants to take photos of the famous Modern Style houses of Barcelona for reproduction in "Minotaure" and thought you might like to see your photos reproduced there
too.*

---

106. Marcel Duchamp to Pierre de Massot   autograph letter
30 August 1933, Cadaquès   source: from André Gervais transcript

     30 Août 1933
Fixés à Cadaquès pour 1 mois, la peseta valant 2 francs et les prix étant très
bas j'ai l'impression de vivre avant guerre ; la connerie de Paris est
incommensurable.
Dali est ici— Nous nous voyons presque tous les jours ; il habite à 1 km
     du village.
Serons [à] Barcelone le 15 Sept.
Écris Casa Lopez.
     Aff^t à tous deux
     Marcel
Cadaqués
por Figueras (Espagne)

MD spends a month in
Cadaquès, where he
will not return until
1958.

MD in **Barcelona**
14-28 Sept 1933.

[allograph writing (Mary Reynolds):]
     Love Mary

▷ TRANSLATION: *30th August 1933. Not moving from Cadaquès for a month—with
the peseta at 2 francs and prices very low, it feels like life before the war. Paris is so
full of crap, it's unbearable. Dali is here. We see each other practically every day.
He's staying just 1km away from the village. We'll be in Barcelona on the 15th September. Write Casa Lopez. Affectionately to you both, Marcel. Cadaquès via
Figueras (Spain).*

25 October 1933
In Le Havre, Duchamp boards the "Ile de France"
headed for New York, to install and oversee
all details in connection with Brancusi's
second exhibition at the Brummer Gallery.

107. Marcel Duchamp to Louise and Walter Arensberg   typed letter (retained carbon)
31 October 1933, New York   collection PMA

BRUMMER GALLERY, Inc.
Works of Art
55 east fifty seventh street

New York, October 31st, 1933.
    Dear Lou and Walter :
Just arrived in New York. The Brancusi show is opening the
17th of November, and Brummer and I would like very much
to have your collection represented by "l'Enfant
Prodigue." Can you ship it as soon as possible to the
Brummer Gallery, 53 East 57th Street? Will write more
later.
Thanking you in advance for your cooperation,
Sincerely yours,

[allograph writing:]
    Marcel Duchamp
    by E.S.

Brancusi's second
show at the Brummer
Gallery, NY, 17 Nov
1933 - 13 Jan 1934:
57 sculptures shown.

The Prodigal Son, 1915,
oak sculpture (PMA,
gift of Louise and
Walter Arensberg).

108. Marcel Duchamp to Constantin Brancusi   autograph letter
2 November 1933, New York   collection MNAM

HOTEL BLACKSTONE
fifty east fifty-eighth street
New York
2 Nov__ 33
    Cher Vieux
Me voici parfaitement arrivé et installé à l'hotel choisi par Brummer__ il
est entendu qu'il paie tous mes frais__ Sois tranquille de ce côté.
Pour les prix à faire, il préfère attendre d'avoir vu les choses pour
décider__
Le catalogue est chez l'imprimeur. Pas d'avant propos, Brummer; il
n'avait rien préparé, et il pense que c'est mieux.
Nous faisons venir l'enfant prodigue de chez Arensberg, l'oiseau de Clark,
le bébé de Miss Dreier afin que toutes les collections importantes soient
représentées (aussi la Pogany de Mme Pollak).

Stephen C. Clark (1882-
1960), heir to Singer
Sewing Machine
Company, trustee of
MoMA, and owner of
Brancusi's bronze *Bird
in Space*, 1928 (MoMA,
NY).

58 numéros—

Je vais à Philadelphie incessamment.

J'ai écrit à Sheeler qui a perdu sa femme;

Vu Crowninshield qui va faire paraître un article dans Vanity Fair—

Je vois McBride demain—

Tout le monde est enthousiaste, et surtout épaté ~~que~~ qu'une chose aussi énorme puisse se faire en ce moment.

T'écrirai dès que les choses seront arrivées.

Ouverture pour la presse le 15 ou le 16

Ouverture pour le public 17 Nov.

Fermeture 13 Janvier—

     ! ! !

Tout le monde t'envoie des amitiés— la liste serait trop longue

     Affectueusement Morice

Catalogue pliant

Sheeler's wife, Katherine Shaffer, died June 1933.

Frank Crowninshield (1872-1947), editor of *Vanity Fair*.

- titre
- Vitrac
- Vitrac
- Brancusi
    cliché

- derrière
    le catalogue

Roger Vitrac (1899-1952), French Surrealist writer, author of preface to catalog.

t'en enverrai dès fini

▷ TRANSLATION: *2nd Nov '33, Hello old chap, So here I am: arrived and accommodated beautifully at the hotel of Brummer's choosing. The understanding is that he's paying all my expenses. Relax on that score. As for what prices to ask, he'd rather wait until he's seen the things before taking a decision. The catalog's at the printer's. No foreword—Brummer hadn't written anything and he thinks it better that way. We're bringing the prodigal child over from Arensberg's, Clark's bird and Miss Dreier's baby so that all the big collections are represented (also Mrs Pollack's Pogany). 58 pieces. I'll be going to Philadelphia any time now. Have written to Sheeler who's lost his wife. Saw Crowninshield who's bringing out an article in Vanity Fair. Am seeing McBride tomorrow. Everybody is very enthusiastic and above all amazed that something so huge could come off right now. Will write you as soon as the things arrive. Opening for the press 15th or 16th. Opening for the general public 17th Nov. Close on 13th January!!! Everybody sends you their best—too many of them to mention. Affectueusement, Morice. Folding catalog.* [sketch captions: *title; Vitrac; Vitrac; Brancusi negative; back of catalog.*] *Will send you some soon as finished.*

---

109. Marcel Duchamp to Constantin Brancusi   autograph letter of 12 pages
18 November 1933, New York   collection MNAM

THE BLACKSTONE
50 East 58th Street
New York
   New York
   Samedi 18 Nov. 33
      Cher vieux
Enfin je trouve un moment de tranquillité pour te renseigner.
L'exposition est vraiment très belle, et les 58 numéros flottent très
   facilement dans les 3 galeries—
La galerie a été complètement passée à la chaux et le parquet déciré donne
   assez bien un ton neutre sans cirage (passé au papier de verre et à
   l'acide!)
Tu verras par le catalogue quelles choses j'ai pu obtenir des collections et
   ça complète l'ensemble—
Hier vernissage Beaucoup de monde amis anciens et nouveaux, vraiment
   abasourdis par le poisson, félicitations sur l'arrangement— Vraiment
   beaucoup de joie dans l'air—
Remarque bien que ce n'est plus comme en 1927; la presse ne marche pas
   avant l'ouverture (en 1927 le procès avait permis cette propagande
   avant-vernissage)— Mais cette année les choses sont des œuvres d'art et
   se défendent elles mêmes— En 2 jours plus de 500 personnes sans la
   moindre réclame— Tu verras ci joint les quelques articles parus jusqu'à
   ce matin (Samedi)—
Comme je te l'ai câblé tout a été monté par l'ascenseur, sans couper le
   coq— les colonnes étaient 2^{cm} trop longues pour la galerie à cause d'un
   manque de nivellement (vieille maison) et nous avons pris la liberté de
   les raccourcir de 2^{cm} en haut.
Oiseau Rumsey.— Il est debout en place d'honneur et personne n'a
   remarqué la fêlure. Ceci pour te tranquilliser— C'est pratiquement
   invisible.
Naturellement je dois annoncer à Mme Rumsey cette mauvaise nouvelle
   mais je le ferai de façon à ce qu'elle l'accepte avec sérénité. Elle m'a
   téléphoné, elle est à Washington et viendra la semaine prochaine voir
   l'exposition.

"Oiseau Rumsey" =
Bird in Space, 1930
(private collection),
white marble sculpture
by Brancusi, owned by
Mrs Rumsey.

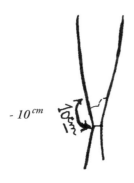

— Quant à l'assurance personne n'a
assuré— Donc je trouve cette négligence
impardonnable mais je dois ajouter que,
même assuré, vous auriez touché quelque
chose comme 4 ou 500 francs ou moins.—
ce qui n'arrangerait pas Mme Rumsey.
voilà à peu près où se trouve la fêlure.
Mais elle est beaucoup moins apparente
que mon dessin et la tige de cuivre est
absolument rigide. Rien n'a bougé.

- 10 cm

_____

Buffalo ayant prêté sa Pogany, Brummer a décidé que 2 Poganys trop
ressemblantes feraient mauvais effet et nous ~~la~~ montrons la seconde
seulement aux acheteurs éventuels— Dis moi si tu approuves—

La question poids a été très sérieuse. 24 tonnes, voilà à quoi arrive ton
exposition avec l'emballage—

Donc Brummer affolé a fait venir un ingénieur et a fait monter le mur
entre les 2 galeries pour pouvoir placer le portrait de Mme Meyer.

- 2ᵐᵉ galerie
- 1ʳᵉ marche
- 1ᵉʳ galerie à droite en entrant

Sous la ~~seconde~~ *première* marche ~~il y a~~ il a fait mettre des briques et du
ciment, de sorte que Mme Meyer repose sur la marche soutenue par le
double mur ~~de~~ mitoyen des 2 maisons—

J'ai mis ton étude anatomique à ~~len~~ la sortie de l'ascenseur. Mais
malheureusement ~~ton~~ ta photo ~~n'était~~ de la colonne en raccourci n'est
pas arrivée dans le même paquet— J'attends qu'elle arrive.

Je fais faire des photos de l'ensemble et te les enverrai la semaine
prochaine.

Dans Art News le grand journal des marchands, a paru ton oiseau (Clark)
sur la couverture. Photo faite exprès pour cela, avec une interview de
moi— La semaine prochaine un article paraîtra sur l'exposition même
avec détails— Je t'enverrai les 2 Art News en même temps.

Espoirs de vente :
Gallatin est revenu, a vu, a demandé tous les prix.

Agnes Ernst Meyer
(1887-1970), married to
wealthy NY banker and
broker Eugene Meyer Jr.
*Portrait of Agnes E.
Meyer*, 1929-1933, today
in National Gallery of
Art, Washington, DC.

Laurie Eglington,
"Marcel Duchamp Back
in America, Gives
Interview," *ARTnews*,
Nov 1933.

Albert Eugene Gallatin
(1881-1952), artist and
collector, owner of
Brancusi's *Torso of a
Girl II*, ca. 1923 (PMA).

Une Mme Guggenheimer pourrait acheter quelque chose

Madame Guggenheim (la mère de Peggy) est venue avant l'ouverture et
doit revenir—

Brummer pense que Clark achètera

D'ici quelques jours j'écrirai à Barnes pour lui demander d'aller voir sa
collection et en même temps je tâcherai de le décider à venir voir
l'exposition

Mme *E*. Meyer est venue quelques jours avant l'exposition et a demandé
qu'on lui prépare des photos de l'ensemble pour faire paraître des
articles dans différentes revues. Elle doit revenir cette semaine. Elle n'a
pas encore vu son portrait—

———

En somme impression très bonne—

Mais il y a un point très embêtant. C'est la fluctuation du change.

Pour être prudent et rester dans tes prix il faudrait compter le dollar à 13
francs ce qui fait des prix énormes en dollars.

Brummer a donc décidé de faire les prix qu'il juge bons pour tenter
l'acheteur au lieu de l'épouvanter.

Je suis de son avis sauf pour les 3 ou 4 choses à 75 000 francs que je laisse
intactes.

D'ailleurs sauf pour le portrait de Mme Meyer il y a peu de chances de
vendre ces gros prix.

Veux tu me dire par retour du courrier si tu es bien d'accord sur cette
question, car si tu n'étais pas d'accord j'aimerais le savoir très vite— ·

En résumé nous allons plus ou moins compter le dollar à 15 ou 16
francs.— selon l'importance du sujet et selon l'idée de Brummer. (Sauf
pour les grosses pièces à 75 000 francs pour lesquelles je tâcherai
d'obtenir l'équivalent en dollars au cours du jour de paiement)

Brummer à qui j'ai demandé ses conditions m'a dit =

Je prendrai 10% si le total des ventes est peu important et 15% si la vente
a bien marché.

Je pense qu'il n'y a rien à dire à cela. étant donné que ~~cela lui~~ l'ensemble
lui coûte déjà plus de 4 000 dollars, dit il— et ce n'est pas loin de la
vérité.

Il n'a donc pas l'intention de retrouver ses frais, comme tu le comprends

———

Alice Roullier naturellement m'a écrit pour *m*'inviter à faire l'exposition
à Chicago. Brummer quoique contre l'idée m'a dit d'attendre avant de
donner une réponse définitive— et m'a suggéré l'idée d'exiger une vente
certaine à l'avance si tu acceptais d'envoyer à Chicago—

Veux tu me répondre très vite sur ce point : Quelle somme *à peu près*
voudrais tu que j'exige pour consentir à faire ~~ce~~ Chicago—

Peggy Guggenheim (1898-1979), collector and gallerist, will marry Max Ernst in 1941.

Stephen C. Clark, see note p.175.

MD visits the **Albert C. Barnes** (1872-1951) collection, Merion, Pennsylvania, 3 Dec 1933.

Alice Roullier, see p.190.

This second Brancusi exhibition will never travel to Chicago.

Naturellement je saurai mettre cela en termes parlementaires mais en somme ce serait peut-être une façon de s'assurer quelques ventes.

Réponds par cable si tu veux, mais une lettre sera plus explicite et presque aussi rapide si tu regardes les bateaux.

    Affectueusement

    Morice

adresse en haut

Je suis à cet hôtel, très content

Brummer me donne $150 par mois et paie ma chambre $70 par mois en plus.

▷ TRANSLATION: *New York, Saturday 18th Nov. '33. Hello old chap, Finally got a moment's peace so I can fill you in. The exhibition is really very beautiful and the 58 pieces are floating with the greatest of ease in the three galleries. The gallery has been completely whitewashed and the dewaxed parquet gives quite a good neutral tone without the polish (rubbed down with sandpaper and acid!). You'll see from the catalog which things I've been able to obtain from various collections and that finishes off the group. Yesterday: opening. Lots of people, friends old and new, totally dumbfounded by the fish. Congratulations on the arrangement. Really a very joyful atmosphere. Note that it's nothing like in 1927. No press before the opening (in 1927 procedure permitted this pre-preview propaganda). But this year the pieces are works of art that speak for themselves. In 2 days, over 500 people without the least publicity. You'll see, enclosed, the 1 or 2 articles that have come out to date (Saturday morning). As I said in my cable, everything was mounted by the elevator, without cutting off le Coq. The columns were 2cm too long for the gallery because of the lack of levelling (old house) and we took the liberty of shortening them by 2cm at the top. Rumsey Bird: upright, with pride of place, and nobody's noticed the crack. Just for your peace of mind. It's almost invisible. Naturally I will have to break the bad news to Mrs Rumsey but I will do it in such a way that she will take it calmly. She telephoned me—she's in Washington and will come and see the exhibition next week. As for insurance, nobody took out insurance. I find this negligence unforgivable but should add that, even with insurance, you would have only got something like 4 or 500 FF or less. Which wouldn't be any good to Mrs Rumsey. [sketch: 10cm] this is more or less where the crack is. But it's a lot less visible than in my drawing and the copper rod is absolutely rigid. Everything is in place. As Buffalo leant his Pogany, Brummer decided that 2 Poganys that were too alike wouldn't look good and we're only showing the second one to potential buyers. Let me know if you approve. Weight was a serious problem. 24 tons, that's what your exhibition comes to with packing. So Brummer, in a panic, brought in an engineer and had the wall between the two galleries put in so he could find a place for Mrs Meyer's portrait.*

[sketch] *He's had bricks and cement put in, under the first step, so that Mrs Meyer is resting on the step supported by the double wall between the two houses. I put your anatomical study at the exit to the elevator. But unfortunately your photo of the shortened version of the column did not arrive in the same batch. I'm still waiting for it to arrive. I'm having photos done of the whole thing and will send them to you next week. In Art News, the dealers big journal, your bird (Clark) appeared on the cover. Photo taken specially and interview of me. Next week, an article is coming out on the exhibition itself with details. I'll send you both copies of Art News at same time. Hopeful sales: Gallatin came back, looked around, asked for all the prices. A Mrs Guggenheimer might buy something. Mrs Guggenheim (Peggy's mother) came before the opening and is to come back. Brummer thinks Clark will buy. In a few days, I'll write to Barnes to ask him to go and see his collection and, at the same time, will try to get him to come and see the exhibition. Mrs E. Meyer came a few days before the exhibition and asked us to have photos taken of the whole thing so that she can publish articles in different magazines. She should be coming back this week. She hasn't seen her portrait yet. Overall, things looking very good. But there's one thing that's a real nuisance—fluctuations in the exchange rates. To be on the safe side and keep within your prices, you'd need to reckon the dollar at 13 francs, which makes the price in dollars sky high. Brummer has decided, therefore, to price things as he sees appropriate, in order to tempt the buyer instead of frightening him away. I agree with him about everything except the 3 or 4 things at 75,000 francs which I am leaving as they are. What's more, there's very little chance of selling these heavyweight prices, except for Mrs Meyer's portrait. Can you let me know by return whether you agree on this matter, because if you didn't agree I would like to know very soon. To sum up, we are going to reckon the dollar at 15 or 16 Francs, according to the importance of the subject and to Brummer's idea. (Except for the big pieces at 75,000 francs for which I'll try to get the equivalent in dollars at the rate of exchange on the day of payment). Brummer, when I asked his terms, said: I will take 10% if total sales are not very high and 15% if sales go well. I think that's fair enough, given that the whole thing is already costing him over 4,000 dollars, he says—and that's not far from the truth. So he's not trying to cover his costs, as you can see. Alice Roullier wrote to me, naturally, to invite me to take the exhibition to Chicago. Brummer, whilst against the idea, told me to hold on before giving her a definite answer and put the suggestion to me of insisting on a sure sale in advance, were you to agree to go to Chicago. Can you give me a quick answer on this point. What amount approx. would you like me to insist on for you to agree to go to Chicago? Naturally I will put it to her in true negotiator style, but all in all it might be a way of making sure of a few sales. Let me know by cable if you like, but a letter would be more explicit and almost as fast if you take a look at the ships. Affectionately, Morice. Address above. I'm at this hotel, delighted. Brummer gives me $150 a month and pays for my hotel room, $70 a month on top.*

110. Marcel Duchamp to Constantin Brancusi
28 December [1933], New York

autograph letter
collection MNAM

> *M. Duchamp*
> *645 Madison Avenue*
> *New York*
> New York 28 Décembre
>   Cher vieux
> 2 nouvelles importantes :
> Nous avons vendu le chef à M. Behrman un ami des Meyers—
> Il n'a pas voulu s'engager à prendre le socle— mais il a payé pour le Chef
>   seul $1000— et à la fin de l'exposition il espère compléter l'achat ~~ent~~ en
>   prenant le socle avec— Ceci s'est passé par l'intermédiaire de Mlle
>   Meyer (Elizabeth je crois) avec qui j'ai passé une heure charmante à la
>   galerie et qui doit revenir avant la fermeture de l'exposition—
> 2me nouvelle— J'ai enfin vu Madame Rumsey une première fois et je lui
>   ai montré son Oiseau, elle n'a pas vu la fêlure et elle est revenue une 2me
>   fois et je lui ai montré la fêlure et lui ai conseillé de ne pas mettre l'oiseau
>   dehors à cause de l'eau qui pourrait s'infiltrer. Elle a parfaitement
>   compris que la fêlure n'enlevait aucune solidité à l'oiseau et, se voyant à
>   peine, ne changeait rien— D'ailleurs elle n'a pas fait de remarque
>   exprimant le regret d'une cassure— car en somme il n'y a pas cassure,
>   c'est comme un défaut du marbre à accentué par le transport.
> Tout ceci pour te tranquilliser—
> Elle était très gaie en général ; elle a envie d'acheter la Muse endormie et je
>   crois que je vais la décider— ces jours ci— Elle a un poste très important
>   à Washington dans le NRA (demande à Mary ce que ça veut dire).—
> ~~J'ai l'im~~ Brummer a écrit à Mme Meyer en réponse ~~au~~ à une lettre d'elle
>   et lui a parlé ~~de son~~ du prix de son portrait avec discussion du prix si elle
>   désire l'acheter— D'ailleurs je pense que la 2me visite de Elizabeth
>   Meyer est justement pour décider cette question—
> J'ai bien reçu tes rectifications de prix et tout est en ordre à ce sujet.
> J'ai déjeuné à Philadelphie (peut être t'ai je déjà dit cela) il y a 10 jours
>   environ et il est possible qu'un groupe de collectionneurs (dirigé par
>   Ingersoll et Speiser) achète une pièce importante pour le Musée de
>   Philadelphie.
> Chicago ne répond plus— je pense que c'est dans le lac— Je reviendrais
>   donc à Paris fin Janvier
>   Affectueusement
>   Morice
> J'ai fait changer les dollars en francs immédiatement = Cela fait 900
>   dollars à 16fs26 = 14.635 francs environ *pour toi* (le 10% étant déduit).

The Chief, 1924 - 1925 (today Coll. Phyllis Lambert).

"Mlle Meyer, Elizabeth": MD means Agnes Meyer, see p.178.

"NRA" = National Recovery Administration

R. Sturgis Ingersoll (1891-1973), President of the PMA, 1948 - 1963

Maurice Speiser (1880-1948), Philadelphia lawyer and collector representing Brancusi in US Customs trial.

▷ TRANSLATION: *New York. 28th December. Hello old chap. 2 important items of news: we've sold The Chief to Mr Behrman, a friend of the Meyers. He didn't want to commit himself to taking the base, but paid, for the Chief alone, $1,000. And, at the end of the exhibition, he hopes to round off the purchase by taking the base to boot. This all came about through Miss Meyer's doing (Elizabeth, I think) with whom I spent a delightful hour at the gallery and who is to come back before the exhibition closes. 2nd piece of news: I finally got to see Mrs Rumsey for the first time and I showed her her bird. She didn't notice the crack and came back a second time and I showed her the crack and advised her not to put the bird outside as it might let in water. She fully appreciated that the crack did not in any way detract from the sturdiness of the bird and that, since barely visible, it makes no difference. Actually she didn't say a word about being upset about a break, as in fact there is no break, more like a fault in the marble accentuated by the transportation. All this just to reassure you. She was altogether very jolly. She fancies buying the Sleeping Muse and I'll think I'll be able to get her to make up her mind—in the next few days. She has a very important job in Washington in the NRA (ask Mary what that means). Brummer wrote to Mrs Meyer in reply to a letter she sent him and spoke to her about the price of her portrait with possibility of negotiating price if she wants to buy it. What's more, I think Elizabeth Meyer's second visit was precisely to settle this matter. I received your price adjustments and everything is in order on this score. I had lunch in Philadelphia (maybe I told you so already) about 10 days ago and it's possible that a group of collectors (controlled by Ingersoll and Speiser) might buy an important piece for the Philadelphia Museum. Chicago has stopped replying—I think it's died a death. I'll be back in Paris end of January, then. Affectionately, Morice. I had the dollars exchanged for francs immediately. = It comes to 900 dollars at 16FF26 = 14.635 francs approx. for you (with the 10% deducted).*

Paris, rue Larrey | 1934-1940

aboard ship for France, on the "Champlain" | 20 Jan 1934
lives in Paris, returning to 11 rue Larrey
round trips to Noirmoutier Island (France) and Salzburg (Austria)
aboard ship for USA, on the famous "Normandie" | 20 May 1936
stays in West Redding (Connecticut) at Katherine Dreier's
crosses the USA: San Francisco, Hollywood, Albuquerque, Cleveland, New York
aboard ship for France, on the "Normandie" | 2 Sept 1936
Paris: again returning to 11 rue Larrey, often also 14 rue Hallé, at Mary Reynolds'
round trips with Mary Reynolds to London, Vittel, Aix-en-Provence, Montpellier, Palavas-les-Flots

from 20 January 1934 to late May 1940

▶ MAJOR WORKS

Boîte verte / Green Box (green cardboard box containing 93 notes and documents related to *The Bride stripped bare...*, Sept 1934)
Bride (aquatint by Jacques Villon and MD, after MD's painting, 1934)
Bookbinding for "Ubu Roi" (1935)
Rotoreliefs / Optical Disks (set of 6 cardboard disks, printed in color, 1935)
Cover of "Minotaure," (winter 1935, Paris; ser. 2, No.6, 1934-35)
Covers for "La Septième Face du dé" (by Georges Hugnet, Paris, May 1936)
Cœurs volants / Fluttering Hearts (cover of *Cahiers d'Art*, 1936)

Door for Gradiva (glass door, in the form of the silhouette of a couple, for entrance to Breton gallery; 1937)
Cover for "Transition" (New York; No.26, winter 1937)
Rrose Sélavy mannequin (Female wax mannequin dressed in Duchamp's clothes, for "Exposition Internationale du Surréalisme," Jan-Feb 1938)
Environment with Coal Bags and Stove (for same exhibition, Jan-Feb 1938)
Rrose Sélavy (anthology of puns by MD, published by GLM, Paris, Apr 1939)

▶ ONE MAN SHOW

Exhibition of Paintings by Marcel Duchamp, The Arts Club, Chicago. By MD: *Nude descending the Stairs No.1*; *Nude descending the Stairs No.2*; *The King and Queen traversed by Swift Nudes, 1912*;

Sonata; *The Chocolate Grinder, 1914*; *The Bachelors* [*Cimetière...*]; *Water Color Study for "The King and Queen traversed by Swift Nudes"*; *Jeune Homme triste dans un train*; *Le Passage de la Vierge à la mariée* — 5 Feb - 27 Feb 1937

▶ EXHIBITIONS

Modern Paintings from the Collection of Mr Earl Horter of Philadelphia, The Arts Club, Chicago. By MD: *Nude descending the Staircase* — 3 - 26 Apr 1934

Exposition Minotaure, Palais des Beaux-Arts, Bruxelles. By MD: *Le Roi et la Reine traversés par des nus en vitesse* — 12 May - 3 June 1934

French Painting from the Fifteenth Century to the Present Day, California Palace of the Legion of Honor, San Francisco. By MD: *Nude descending the Stairs*; *The Sonata* — 8 June - 8 July 1934 (?)

8 Modes of painting, Société Anonyme Inc. cooperating with the College Art Association, Julien Levy Gallery, New York. (Traveling exhibition through the USA). By MD: *Drawing for Big Glass* — 22 Oct - 3 Nov 1934

Modern Works of Art, Fifth Anniversary Exhibition, The Museum of Modern Art, New York. By MD: *Disturbed Balance* [*To Be Looked at...*] — 20 Nov 1934 - 20 Jan 1935

Exposition internationale du Surréalisme, Ateneo, Santa Cruz, Spain. By MD: *Farmacia*; *Espiral*; *Porqué no estornudar?* — 10 May - 24 May 1935

33e Concours Lépine, Parc des expositions, Porte de Versailles, Allée F (Stand 147), Paris. By MD: *Rotorelief* — 30 Aug - 7 Oct 1935

Cubism and Abstract Art, Museum of Modern Art, New York City (travels to San Francisco). By MD: *Nude descending a Staircase*; *The Bride*; *The Bachelors*; *Disturbed Balance* [*To Be Looked at...*]; *Six roto-reliefs* — 2 Mar - 19 Apr 1936

Exposition Surréaliste d'objets mathématiques, naturels, trouvés et interprétés, Charles Ratton, Paris. By MD: *Porte Bouteilles* [first replica]; *Why not sneeze, Rrose Sélavy?*; *La Bagarre d'Austerlitz* — 22 May - 31 May 1936

The International Surrealist Exhibition, New Burlington Galleries, London. By MD: *The King and Queen crossed rapidly by Nudes*; *Chemist's Shop*; *About a Young Sister*; *Roto Relief* — 11 June - 4 July 1936

The Twentieth Anniversary Exhibition, Museum of Art, Cleveland, USA. By MD: *Nude descending a Staircase* — 26 June - 12 Oct 1936

Fantastic Art, Dada, Surrealism, The Museum of Modern Art, New York. By MD: *Coffee mill*; *The Bride*; *The King and Queen traversed by Swift nudes*; *Pharmacy*; *The Bachelors*; *Ready-made (photo)*; *Rotating apparatus*; *Stoppages-étalon*; *Why not sneeze?*; *Monte Carlo share*; *Roto-Reliefs* — 9 Dec 1936 - 17 Jan 1937

Exhibition organized by *Orbes* review at the bar "La cachette," Paris. By MD: *La Mariée mise à nu par ses célibataires même (boîte verte)* — 12 Mar - 31 Mar 1937

Galerie Gradiva, Paris (inaugural). By MD: entry glass door — May 1937

Los Angeles. By MD: *Nude descending a staircase No.2* — 15 Oct - 15 Dec 1937

Exposition Internationale du Surréalisme, Galerie des Beaux-Arts, Paris. By MD: *Pharmacie*; *Neuf moules mâlic*; *La Bagarre d'Austerlitz*; *Rrose Sélavy et moi... (Rotary)*; *Ready made, 1914* — 17 Jan - February 1938

Témoignage, Galerie Matières, Paris. By MD: *disques optiques* — 10 May - 3 June 1938

Guillaume Apollinaire et ses peintres, Galerie de Beaune, Paris — 17 June 1938

Exposition Internationale du Surréalisme, Galerie Robert, Amsterdam, Netherlands. By MD: *La Mariée mise à nu par ses célibataires même (livre-boîte)*; *Couverture cigarettes (1936)*, photographie en couleurs du "dé" de Georges Hugnet — spring 1938

Exhibition of Collages, papiers collés and photomontages, Guggenheim Jeune, London. By MD: *Obligation* — 3 Nov - 26 Nov 1938

Contemporary Movements in European Painting, Museum of Art, Toledo, USA. By MD: *Nude descending a staircase* — 6 Nov - 11 Dec 1938

Golden Gate, San Francisco, USA. By MD: *Nude descending a staircase No.2* — 18 Feb - 2 Dec 1939

Art in our time, The Museum of Modern Art, New York. By MD: *Young Man in a Train* — 10 May - 30 Sept 1939

Some New Forms of Beauty 1909-1936, a selection of the Collection of the Société Anonyme, Museum of Modern Art, 1920. The George Walter Vincent Smith Gallery, Springfield, USA (Traveling exhibition to Hartford and New Haven). By MD: *Revolving Glass* — 9 Nov - 17 Dec 1939

Origins of Modern Art, The Arts Club, Chicago. By MD: *Young Man in a Train* — 2 Apr - 30 Apr 1940

20 January 1934
A week after the Brancusi show closes in New York,
Duchamp boards the "Champlain" and returns
to France. After settling back into his small
apartment on the rue Larrey, he writes a letter to the
Arensbergs to explain the details of a
new project he is working on.

111. Marcel Duchamp to Louise and Walter Arensberg   autograph letter
20 February 1934, Paris   collection MNAM

Paris 20 Février 1934
11 rue Larrey
    Chère Lou cher Walter
Bien rentré après traversée désagréable.   20 - 27 Jan 1934
L'exposition Brancusi a en somme bien marché; il est content.
J'espère que vous avez reçu votre enfant prodigue.

———

Je viens de commencer à mettre au point l'édition de notes, documents,   *The Bride Stripped*
    concernant mon verre "La Mariée mise à nu par ses célibataires,   *Bare...* [cat. 1]
    même"—
Je voudrais réunir toutes mes notes écrites en 1912, 13, 14 et 15 à ce sujet   *Green Box* [cat. 3]
    et les faire reproduire en fac simile (par la phototypie qui donne tout à
    fait l'impression de l'original surtout pour les notes manuscrites).
Je voudrais aussi reproduire les principaux tableaux et dessins qui ont servi
    à la composition de la "Mariée…"
Voulez vous donc avoir l'extrême obligeance de faire faire une bonne   *Chocolate Grinder*
    photo de la <u>Broyeuse</u> de chocolat (1914; celle qui a des fils collés) et me   *No. 2* [cat. 28]
    l'envoyer aussitôt; j'aimerais avoir 2 épreuves, une plus foncée et une
    plus claire pour choisir (dimension des photos 9 à 10 inches x 10 à 11
    inches <u>environ</u>; ⅔ épreuves sur papier brillant).

———

Je pense tirer l'édition à 500 exemplaires ordinaires (100 francs
    l'exemplaire). Mon intention est de réunir toutes ces photos et papiers
    coupés à leur forme originale dans une boîte en carton (environ 14
    inches x 10 inches) avec le titre sur la boîte.
Il y aurait à peu près 135 notes et une dizaine de photos.
Comme l'édition en phototypie coûte très cher, j'ai pensé demander à dix
    vrais amis s'ils consentiraient à payer $50.^{00} un exemplaire de luxe de
    cette édition—
Naturellement ce tirage de luxe serait aussi beau que possible avec j'espère
    une photo en couleurs, papier spécial boite luxueuse etc. et serait limité
    à 20 exemplaires (dont ces 10 hors commerce)

Donc je commence par vous mon Cher Walter et vous demande si vous
voulez m'aider par ces $50⁻ à réaliser cette édition‒ Si vous me
répondez oui aussi tôt que possible, je pourrai commencer
— La photo de la Broyeuse n'est pas aussi pressée que votre yes; et l'argent,
lui aussi peut attendre jusqu'à la parution en Juillet prochain‒
Voilà mon "hobby" pour le moment
Viendrez vous en Europe cet été?
j'y serai je pense, sûrement si vous venez‒
    Affectueusement à tous deux
    Marcel
11 rue Larrey Paris V

Chocolate Grinder
No. 2 [cat. 28]

▷ TRANSLATION: *Paris 20th February 1934. 11 rue Larrey. Dear Lou, dear Walter,
Back safely after unpleasant crossing. The Brancusi exhibition went well, on the
whole. He's pleased. I trust you have your prodigal child back. I have just embarked
on the task of compiling an edition of my notes and documents on my glass, "The
Bride Stripped Bare by her bachelors, even." I would like to get together all the notes
I wrote on it in 1912, 13, 14, and 15 and have them reproduced in facsimile (using
phototypography which gives a very good idea of the original especially for handwritten notes). I would also like to reproduce the main paintings and drawings
which went into the composition of the "Bride..." Would you therefore do me the
great service of taking a good photo of the Chocolate Grinder (1914, the one with
glued wires) and send it to me at once? I would like to have 2 prints, one rather dark
and one lighter so I can choose (dimensions of photos 9-10 inches by 10-11 inches
approx. gloss prints). I'm thinking of having 500 ordinary copies of the edition
printed (100 francs a copy). My plan is to put together all these photos and papers
cut to their original format, in a cardboard box (approx. 14 inches by 10 inches)
with the title on the box. There must be about 135 notes and ten or so photos. As
publishing a phototype edition is very costly, I thought of asking ten real friends if
they would be prepared to put up $50 for a copy of a deluxe edition. Naturally this
deluxe edition would be as attracive as possible with, hopefully, a color photo, special paper, deluxe box etc. and a limited run of 20 copies (including these ten not
for commercial sale). So I'm starting with you, my dear Walter, to see if you would
like to help me, for $50, to bring out this edition. If you say "yes" as soon as possible,
I'll be able to make a start. The photo of the Grinder is not as urgent as your "yes";
the money can also in fact wait until it's published in July. So that's my "hobby"
at the moment. Will you be coming to Europe this summer? I will be there, I think,
and definitely if you're coming. Affectionately to you both, Marcel. 11 rue Larrey
Paris V.*

---

112. Marcel Duchamp to Constantin Brancusi   postcard
[1 April 1934], Greece   collection MNAM

> Mon cher Maurice
> Je pense à toi et je regrette que tu ne sois pas avec moi.
> La Grèce est le pays des "Maurices"
> Je t'embrasse.
> Roger Maurice

▷ TRANSLATION: *My dear Maurice. Thinking of you and sorry you are not with me. Greece is the domain of "Maurices." Love, Roger Maurice.*

---

113. Marcel Duchamp to Henri-Pierre Roché   autograph letter
18 May 1934, Paris   collection HRHRC

> 11 rue Larrey__
> 18 mai 1934
>   Cher vieux
> Bien reçu ton mot il y a quelques jours__ Je vais m'occuper de faire transporter la cariatide à ton appartement__
> Je suis allé 3 ou 4 fois chez toi avec mon homme du pochoir : Nous avons beaucoup de mal et je dois lui refaire un calque de tous les pochoirs qu'il devra faire pour j'espère arriver à un résultat.
> Entre temps j'ai reçu mon devis de phototypie qui me semble trop élevé__ Je vais donc voir ailleurs avant de décider.
> Je pense quand même que j'aurais besoin des 5 autres mille francs car tout devra être payé dans les 2 mois qui vont suivre et j'ai peur d'être à court ; tu sais ce que sont les héritages et ces petits 5 000 fr. ne viendront peut être pas avant 3 mois.
> Donc peux tu compléter les 10 000__ avec un chèque de 5 000__ au nom de Rrose Sélavy?__
> Je t'enverrai aussitôt un reçu mais dis moi si tu considères que les nouveaux 5 000 peuvent se servir de Prométhée comme garantie, ou veux tu une autre sculpture (comme garantie) et laquelle? Merci.

Brancusi's *Caryatid*, 1914 (today in Fogg Art Museum, Harvard University, Boston).

MD is preparing stencil reproductions relating to the *Large Glass* [cat. 2] for inclusion in his *Green Box* [cat. 3].

Prometheus, 1911, marble sculpture by Brancusi purchased by MD and Roché in 1926 from the estate of John Quinn (today in PMA; Louise and Walter Arensberg Collection).

▷ TRANSLATION: *11 rue Larrey, 18th May 1934. Hello old chap, Got your letter a few days ago. I will see to having the caryatid transported to your apartment. I've been to your place 3 or 4 times with my stencil man. We're having a lot of trouble and I have to make him another tracing of all the stencils he's to make in order hopefully to achieve a result. Meanwhile, I received my estimate for the phototype which seems too expensive, so I'm going to look elsewhere before coming to a decision. I think, even so, that I'm going to need the other 5 thousand francs as it all has to be paid for in the next 2 months and I'm worried I'll be short—you know what inher-*

itances are like and this nice little sum of 5,000 might not arrive for 3 months. So
could you make up the 10,000 with a check for 5,000 in the name of Rrose Sélavy?
I'll send you a receipt straightaway but let me know whether you think Prometheus
could serve as a guarantee for the 5,000, or do you want another sculpture (as a
guarantee) and which one? Thanks.

---

114. Marcel Duchamp to Alfred Stieglitz   autograph letter
[1934], Paris   collection YCAL

> Paris V
> 11 rue Larrey
> > Dear Stieglitz
> This is my last secretion (latest).   *Green Box* [cat. 3]
> Old papers respected and framed in their original shape only.
> All about the glass you saw in Brooklyn a few years ago (which by the way
> > is broken, [hope to mend it]).
> How are you? and how is O'Keefe? Sorry to see you so rarely and when I
> > am in N.Y. not to be with you more often. The "essential" of one's life
> > amounts probably to a few hours.
> > Affectionately yours
> > M. Duchamp

---

115. Marcel Duchamp to Alice Roullier   autograph letter   **Alice Roullier,**
16 October 1934, Paris   collection Newberry Library, Chicago   chairperson of the
                                                    exhibition committee,
                                                    Arts Club of Chicago,
                                                    where Brancusi show
                                                    was held in 1927.

> 11 rue Larrey
> Paris V
> 16 octobre 1934
> > Chère Alice
> Etes vous venue à Paris cet été? Si oui, je regrette bien de ne vous avoir pas
> vue.
> Je vous envoie trois modèles du bulletin de souscription pour un livre que   "livre" = *Green Box*
> > je viens de publier sur un tableau en verre que j'ai fait il y a quelques   [cat. 3]
> > années. Ce livre est plutôt une boîte contenant des reproductions
> > photographiques de notes écrites à la main. et des photos de tableaux—
> Mon édition est payée par les "luxe" que je vends—
> Je vous demande donc si vous pouvez sans trop de tracas, me trouver un
> > ou 2 clients pour le luxe
> — Le prix de 750 francs est évidemment élevé mais il s'agit d'une édition
> > de <u>20</u> exemplaires seulement

— Je grave le nom de l'acheteur dans sa boîte et si donc vous me trouvez quelqu'un n'oubliez pas de me donner son nom et ses initiales très exacts—

Si e̊ ce n'est [pas] trop de travail, peut être pourriez vous me donner quelques adresses intéressantes à Chicago, auxquelles j'adresserais des bulletins de souscription.

Merci en tout cas mille fois chère Alice, et dites moi comment vous allez—
      Affectueusement
      Marcel Duchamp

▷ TRANSLATION: *11 rue Larrey, Paris V, 16th October 1934. Dear Alice, Did you come to Paris this summer? If so, I'm really sorry not to have seen you. I'm sending you three designs for the subscription form for a book I've just published on a glass painting I did a few years ago. This book is more like a box containing photographs and reproductions of handwritten notes and photos of paintings. My edition is being paid for by the "deluxe" boxes I sell. I'd like to ask you, therefore, if you could find, without too much trouble, one or 2 clients for the deluxe editions. The price, at 750 francs, is obviously high, but it's a series of only 20 editions. I engrave the name of the buyer on their box, so if you find anybody, don't forget to give me their exact name and initials. If it's not too much work, perhaps you could give me a few likely addresses in Chicago where I could send the subscription forms. In any case, very many thanks, dear Alice, and let me know how you are. Affectionately, Marcel Duchamp.*

---

116. Marcel Duchamp to Walter Pach   autograph letter
17 October 1934, Paris   collection AAA

11 rue Larrey
17 octobre 34
      Cher Walter, Chère Magda
Voici 4 mois que j'ai reçu votre longue lettre si intéressante. Et je n'y ai pas répondu plus tôt car il m'était impossible de prendre une décision rapide—

Je vous avais dit l'hiver dernier le manque de confiance que j'avais en Barr, plus le sentiment d'animosité contre moi (en particulier) se traduisant par des petites vexations qui m'avaient fait comprendre son étroitesse.

Ce que vous me dites ne fait par conséquent que confirmer cette impression et puisque la guerre est déclarée, je suis décidé à la lui faire à ma manière.

Je pense qu'une polémique ouverte ne ferait qu'augmenter ses partisans, car la seule arme du critique est le silence— (vous savez comme je m'amuse toujours quand des peintres se plaignent que 50 lignes leur ont

Alfred H. Barr, Jr. (1902-1981), founding director of MoMA, NY. After MD moves to NY in 1941, they will play chess often and become good friends.

été consacrées pour les engueuler— Ils oublient que c'est meilleur que
100 lignes de félicitations—)

Donc, dernièrement Horter m'a vendu son esquisse du Nu descendant…
que j'ai revendue immédiatement à Arensberg. M. Barr a écrit à mon
emballeur à N.Y. pour savoir où était ce nu, pour l'exposer au mois de
~~Jan~~ Novembre ~~da~~ au Musée moderne— J'ai immédiatement demandé à
Arensberg de refuser d'envoyer cette esquisse à l'exposition. J'ai reçu de
Barr une lettre me demandant d'exposer ce nu— je lui ai simplement
répondu d'écrire à M. Arensberg— vous verrez si Barr a cherché à
exposer une autre chose de moi— Et en tout cas, si par hasard il vous
demandait un de mes tableaux, refusez par une excuse bien anodine,
sans acrimonie—

Comme vous le dites, Derain, Picasso etc. ne témoigneront jamais par
écrit dans le sens que vous voudriez— Vous ne recevriez aucune
réponse— Car le propre de l'artiste est de manger d'abord son voisin.

Je me charge simplement de définir Barr aux gens qui me demanderont
mon avis sur lui.— Et si cela ne l'attaque pas d'une façon apparente je
suis sûr que sa malicieuse incompétence se retournera automatiquement
contre lui dans un avenir pas si lointain.

Il n'a aucune valeur personnelle, C'est un étudiant et les gens qui le paient
seront payés pour le savoir, ou le découvrir.

N'oubliez pas que la "clientèle" américaine des dix dernières années est
absolument modelée par les marchands de la rue *de* la Boétie. Il n'y a
plus aucune recherche de découverte personnelle dans le collectionneur.
Il a été, malgré lui, ou même consciemment, un spéculateur de l'ordre
des acheteurs de Rembrandt ou Raphaël et dans ce moment où l'or n'a
plus de valeur constante l'huile des tableaux garde la sienne— quitte
d'ailleurs à se tromper mais dans 50 ans seulement on le saura.

Donc cher Walter excusez mon retard à vous répondre.

J'ai travaillé tout l'été à mon "livre" qui est enfin paru. Je suis enchanté,
tous les amis le trouvent à leur goût; il ne me reste plus qu'à le vendre—
Vous l'avez sans doute vu chez Julien Levy qui en a quelques exemplaires
Par le même courrier je vous adresse quelques bulletins de souscription, au
cas où des amis à vous s'y intéresseraient.

Au revoir donc cher Walter, mes bonnes amitiés à Magda et à Raymond.
       Très affectueusement à vous
       Marcel.

Earl Horter
(1880-1940), artist and
collector from
Philadelphia, owner of
MD's *Nude
Descending No. 1*
[cat. 16] (PMA;
Arensberg Collection).

Green Box [cat. 3]

Julien Levy (1906-1981)
opened his gallery in
NY in 1931.

▷ TRANSLATION: *11 rue Larrey. 17th October '34. Dear Walter, dear Magda, It's already 4 months since I got your long letter which was so interesting. And I didn't
reply earlier because it was impossible for me to make a snap decision. I told you
last winter how I didn't trust Barr, plus his feelings of animosity towards me (in*

particular)—coming out as little tantrums—made me realize how small-minded he is. Consequently, what you tell me merely confirms my own impression and now that war has been declared, I've made up my mind to let him have it in my own way. I think an open argument would only increase support for him, and the critic's only weapon is silence. (You know how it always amuses me when painters complain somebody has written 50 lines slagging them off. They forget that it's better than 100 lines of praise.) So, recently Horter sold me his sketch of the "Nude descending"... which I immediately sold to Arensberg. Mr Barr wrote to my packer in N.Y. to find out where this nude was, so he could exhibit it in the month of November at the Modern Museum. I immediately asked Arensberg to refuse to send this sketch to the exhibition. I had a letter from Barr asking me to exhibit this nude. I replied simply that he should write to Mr Arensberg. You'll get to know if Barr has tried to exhibit anything else of mine. And in any case, if, by any chance, he asks you for one of my paintings, just say no, giving him some anodine excuse without being acrimonious. As you rightly say, Derain, Picasso, etc. will never testify to anything in writing the way you would like them to. You'd never even get a reply. For it is the artist's nature first to eat his neighbour. I will simply take it upon myself to tell people exactly what Barr is like if they ask me what I think of him. And if this does not appear to affect him, I am sure his own malicious incompetence will backfire on him in the not too distant future. He is not worth a cent. He's a student and it would pay the people who pay him to know that or to find out. Don't forget that the American "clientele" of the last ten years has been totally shaped by the dealers of the rue de la Boétie. The collector interested in coming across things for himself is a thing of the past. He has become, in spite of himself or even in full conscience, a speculator of the same ilk as buyers of Rembrandts and Raphaëls and, in these times, when gold no longer keeps its value, the oil in paintings does— and even if one makes the odd mistake, it will only come out in 50 years' time. So, dear Walter, please forgive my late reply. I've been working all summer on my book which is finally out. I am delighted, all my friends find it to their taste. All I have to do now is sell it. You've probably seen it at Julien Levy's as he has a few copies. In the same parcel, I'm sending you a few subscription forms in case you or your friends might be interested. Farewell then, dear Walter. My best wishes to Magda and to Raymond. Very affectionately to you, Marcel.

117. Marcel Duchamp to Katherine S. Dreier   autograph letter
15 December 1934, Paris   collection YCAL

Paris 11 rue Larrey

15 Dec. 1934

    I have been very lazy lately that is to say concentrating on the sale of
my box which by the way is almost a success. I hope that you have
received my card boards to have your glass repaired.

I am going to send you next week the last issue of "Minotaure" in which
Breton writes a long article about the "Mariée"— your library panel
illustrates also the article.—

The cover of the magazine is by your friend M.D.

On the other hand I am sorry to have been lazy to write you, as I had asked
Levy and Pach not to lend anything *of mine* to Mr. Barr.— So you did
and were right—

But do you remember my telling you about the arrogance of the
gentlemen. and you know that my only attitude is silence.— But please
keep that for yourself and write what you know of the show.

it is all very unimportant. In haste to catch the Europa

    Affectueusement

    Dee

Apparently, Dreier's
Green Box [cat. 3]
contained a piece of
glass that was broken
(possibly the covering
which is attached to the
inside back cover of all
deluxe editions).

André Breton, "Phare
de La Mariée," Paris,
Minotaure No.6, winter
1935, pp.45-49.

"**library panel**" = *Tu m'*
[cat. 29]

S.S. "**Europa**",
Transatlantic Line.

118. Marcel Duchamp to Alice Roullier   autograph letter
22 December 1934, Paris   collection Newberry Library, Chicago

Paris 11 rue Larrey

22 Dec. 34

    Chère Alice

Votre lettre est arrivée hier soir avec le chèque. Merci— Je craignais que
vous ne soyez très pressée d'avoir les livres (pour Christmas)— Je
m'aperçois maintenant qu'il n'y a pas de bateau (pour colis postaux)
jusqu'au 3 janvier (Champlain).—

Donc les 2 luxes et un exemplaire ordinaire que je vous prie de garder pour
vous partiront en un petit colis postal sur le Champlain— (3 Jan.)—
Pour qu'il vous arrive plus vite je le fais réexpédier par un "broker" à
N.Y. qui ira chercher le paquet en douane et vous l'adressera
"express"—

Vous l'aurez vers le 14 janvier.

Maintenant merci d'avoir si bien travaillé— C'est évidemment
remarquable à notre époque de trouver encore des amis pour les
dépenses inutiles.— Espérons qu'en ~~le~~ montrant le livre, d'autres
enthousiastes se décideront.

Deluxe and regular
editions of MD's *Green
Box* [cat. 3].

Sur 20 luxes, j'en ai vendu 10— Pas mal n'est ce pas. Les ordinaires vont plus vite et se vendent assez bien—

Je joins au paquet un numéro du "Minotaure" qui vient de paraitre et qui contient un article plus ou moins explicatif du livre par Breton.—

A ce sujet, Skira le directeur du Minotaure me demande si je connais à Chicago quelqu'un capable de "distribuer" le Minotaure—

Evidemment pas un agent de distribution ni un libraire— J'ai vaguement pensé que l'Arts Club pourrait peut être s'intéresser à la question.— Si vous voyez un intérêt quelconque à cette propagande par l'Arts Club ou par un autre moyen, écrivez-moi et j'en ferai part à Skira— (Il y a déjà 5 numéros de parus en 1933 34)— Katharine Dudley doit connaitre Skira qui allait souvent voir les Harvey— Dites lui bien mes amitiés et affections. J'ai aussi pensé que notre ami Bulliet (?) critique d'art serait intéressé de voir le Minotaure. Mais quelle est son adresse?

Voilà chère Alice, vous verra t on à Paris cet été? Comment allez vous?—

A bientôt j'espère et bien affectueusement

Marcel

Mes amitiés à Arthur Heun et mes hommages à Mme. Goodspeed

Minotaure, winter 1935, see p.194.

Albert Skira (1904-1973), editor of *Minotaure*.

The **Arts Club**, 410 North Michigan Avenue, Chicago.

Clarence J. Bulliet (1883-1952),art critic for the *Chicago Daily News* 1932 - 1952. Meets MD 1927.

Arthur Heun, (1866-1946), architect of the Arts Club of Chicago and one of its directors.

Elizabeth Fuller Goodspeed, a.k.a. Bobsy (1893-1980), president of the Arts Club of Chicago 1931 -1941.

▷ TRANSLATION: *Paris, 11 rue Larrey, 22nd Dec. '34. Dear Alice, Your letter arrived yesterday evening with the check. Thank you. I thought you might be in a hurry to get the books (for Christmas). I realize now that there is no ship (for postal parcels) until 3rd January (Champlain). So the 2 luxuries, and the one ordinary edition which I'll ask you to keep for yourself, will be coming to you in a small parcel on the Champlain (3rd Jan.) So that you will get it faster, I'm sending it on by a broker in N.Y. who will go and pick up the parcel at Customs and send it to you express. You'll have it around 14th January. Now then, thank you for your very good work. Obviously it's quite remarkable these days to find friends for unnecessary expenditure. Let's hope that when the book is shown around, other enthusiasts will come forward. Out of 20 deluxe boxes, I've sold 10. Not bad, is it. The ordinary ones go faster and are selling quite well. I've enclosed in this parcel an issue of the "Minotaure" which has just come out and contains a fairly comprehensive article by Breton on the book. On this point, Skira, the director of the "Minotaure," is asking me if I know anyone in Chicago capable of "circulating" the "Minotaure"— obviously not a distribution agent or a bookshop owner. I vaguely thought the Arts Club might be interested in the matter. If you see any interest at all on the part of the Arts Club or any other body, write and tell me and I'll let Skira know. (5 issues have already come out in 1933-34). Katharine Dudley must know Skira as he used to go to see the Harveys a lot. Give her my affectionate good wishes. I also thought that our friend Bulliet, art critic, would be interested to see the Minotaure but what is his address? So there we are, dear Alice. Will we see you in Paris this summer? How are you? See you soon I hope and very affectionately, Marcel. My best wishes to Arthur Heun and my respects to Mrs Goodspeed.*

---

119. Marcel Duchamp to Mariette Mills   big envelope
[after September 1934], Paris   collection Romain Lacroix, Paris

> **Mariette Mills,** American, lives in Paris and has salon on rue Boissonnade; MD has known her since his return from US in 1923.

Marcel Duchamp
11 rue Larrey
Paris V
     Madame Mariette Mills

———

Merci; voici des bulletins.
Il est préférable de donner mon adresse (rue Larrey 11)
L'adresse qui est sur le bulletin n'est qu'une adresse de banque.
     Bien affectueusement à tous deux
     Marcel Duchamp

> *Green Box* [cat. 3] and its subscription bulletin are both addressed: "18 rue de la Paix, Paris."

▷ TRANSLATION: *Marcel Duchamp, rue Larrey, Paris V. Mrs Mariette Mills. Thank you. Here are some forms. It's preferable to give my address (rue Larrey, 11). The address which is on the form is only a banking address. Affectionately to you both, Marcel Duchamp.*

---

120. Marcel Duchamp to André Breton*   autograph letter
[3 February 1935], Paris   source: from Yves Poupard-Lieussou transcript

11 rue Larrey
Dimanche
     Mon cher Breton
Arp me disait hier qu'il y a une grande exposition surréaliste à
     Copenhague— en ce moment.

> **Hans [Jean] Arp** (1886-1966), Alsatian artist, part of the Dada and Surrealist movement.

---

* **André Breton** (1896-1966) is best remembered today as the founder and principal spokesman of the Surrealist movement. Throughout his career as a poet and writer, André Breton remained one of Duchamp's most articulate and outspoken supporters. He and Duchamp met in the fall of 1919 at the Café Certa, a center for Dada activities in Paris. Breton said that he found the artist to be *"extremely cordial,"* with *"a face of admirable beauty."* But what he admired most was Duchamp's intelligence, which, he said, *"from the time I had heard of it, I expected to be wondrous."* During the 1920's, Breton served as an adviser to the wealthy collector Jacques Doucet (p.137), whom he immediately convinced to purchase two works by Duchamp and to commission another. Breton often seized the opportunity to write about Duchamp and his work, culminating in the first major article on the artist, "The Lighthouse of the Bride," which appeared in 1934 in *Minotaure*. Even though Duchamp could hardly be described as a Surrealist, Breton enlisted his assistance in the design and installation of nearly all of the major Surrealist exhibitions he organized. For his part, Duchamp seems to have had a great deal of respect for his younger colleague. *"Breton and I are men of the same order,"* he told an interviewer, *"we share a community of vision."* But towards the end of their lives, the two old friends grew distant, not a situation that Duchamp felt was his fault. *"He can't be approached,"* Duchamp complained a few months before Breton's death, *"He's playing the great man too much, completely clouded by the idea of posterity."*

J'ai pensé que peut être je pourrais envoyer une "boîte" à cette exposition. Si vous n'y voyez pas d'inconvénient voulez vous m'envoyer l'adresse de l'organisateur danois là bas— Aussi quelques détails si vous en avez (l'adresse de l'exposition par exemple)

————

Je n'ai pas encore de réponse au sujet du tableau ; j'en attends une avant la fin Février—

Comment allez vous?

Mes bonnes amitiés à tous deux

Marcel Duchamp

MD proposes a "**boîte**" (= *Green Box* [cat. 3]) for the "Exposition International Kubisme-Surrealisme," Copenhagen, 5 - 28 Jan 1935, organized by Bejrke Petersen with the help of A. Breton.

▷ TRANSLATION: *11 rue Larrey, Sunday. My dear Breton, Arp was telling me yesterday that there's a big surrealist show in Copenhagen at the moment. I thought I could perhaps send a "box" to this show. If you have no objection, could you send me the address of the Danish organizer over there? Also some details if you have any (the address of the exhibition, for instance). I haven't had a reply yet about the painting. I'm expecting one before the end of February. How are you? My very good wishes to you both, Marcel Duchamp.*

---

121. Marcel Duchamp to Katherine S. Dreier
5 March 1935, Paris

autograph letter
collection YCAL

Paris 11 rue Larrey March 5. 1935

This is a long time since I wrote : I have been very busy with two new ideas.

1) I want to make, sometime, an album of approximately all the things I produced.

"**album**" = future *Box-in-a-Valise* [cat. 4]

Before I do this, I want to prepare the album by making ten color reproductions of my better things.— Selling these 10 reproductions separately like color photographs (but really color "phototypie" like the one reproduced in my box) I hope to get enough money to do the complete album.

Then I will ask you to have a photograph (in black and white) made of every painting or object of mine you possess.

But this won't come before 6 months from now—

For the big glass which I intend to reproduce in color, I will make an interpretation (for the colors) from the other paintings made for it— Anyway it would be too difficult to make a color photograph of the glass in the condition it is now.

2) I am going to make a playtoy with the discs and spirals I used for my film— — The designs will be printed on heavy paper and collected in a round box.

Rotoreliefs [cat. 53]

I hope to sell each box 15 francs and [to sell] many__ (Each disc is to be seen
   turning on a Victrola).

Victrola, see p.118.

This second project is less expensive than the other and I am working very
   seriously at it. Please don't speak of this as simple ideas are easily stolen.

There we are__

_____

Now I have looked at your financial state of affairs.

I received from the Electric Company	40 fr
and from the Gaz Company	6. 85
because there was a bill of 18 f.^{15} to pay	46 f. 85

So after the moving done in September for which I paid :

moving	170 f
tips	80
Louise's time	30
	280 f

    You still owe me $280 - 46.^{85} = 233$ f.^{15}

Of course I expected Mr. Munguia to give 500 francs for the curtains but
   when I saw him not long ago, he told me that he was leaving Paris for
   Geneva in a few months and expected to sublet his apartment and sell
   the curtains to his successor in which case he would give me the 500
   francs__

If he does not rent it, he would pay me the "renting" of the curtains and
   give them back to me__

I could not say anything to such an argument except hope that he sells the
   curtains. He is perfectly honest but a bit complicated.

This anyway won't come for two months.

In the meantime I would like to give Magdeleine the storage of your
   furniture which now amounts to six months at 50 francs a month = 300
   francs plus (as she suggests rightly) a moth disinfection before
   Springtime amounting to *about* 100 francs.

Magdeleine Duchamp
(b.1898), MD's
youngest sister,
married name
Magdeleine Dagnet.

So see if you are rich and if you can send pa me part or all of these monies :
    233.^{15}
    400
    633.^{15}

I will let you know more about the developement of my ideas.__ Tell me
   what you are doing and if anything of interest is going on in N.Y.

What is your N.Y. address?
    Affectueusement
    Dee

---

122. Marcel Duchamp to Katherine S. Dreier   autograph letter
3 May [1935, Paris]   collection YCAL

3rd of May

I received your letter only today (it was written the 24th of April!!).—

I don't mind showing the "revolving glass" as long as it enables you to see it and make good photographs of it (from the front, the back the side please).

But in your letter there seems to be a little confusion :

There are <u>two different things</u> :

I   The <u>3 Stoppage étalon</u> 1913-1914. which are three panels ~~pu~~ (canvas painted dark blue with a very fine line made by a thread fallen on the canvas).— May be I put in the box the three wooden rulers which I used for your painting (Tu m')—   *Standard Stoppages* [cat. 34]

Tu m' [cat. 29]

(II) And then the revolving glass— which consists of 5 (I think) <u>glass</u> panels painted at the top *and bottom* only, like this   *Rotary Demisphere* [cat. 51]

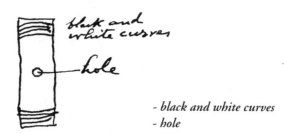

- *black and white curves*
- *hole*

The 5 panels are different each one from the other in height—

They all go on a shaft (through the hole) as shown in the next drawing :
Seen from profile

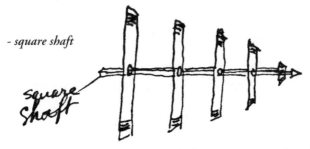

- *square shaft*

Each panel is attached to the *iron* shaft with¢ screws and rubber cushions.

———

Then the whole thing is placed on a kind of a "horse" made of iron. about
1ᵐ heigh [=high]

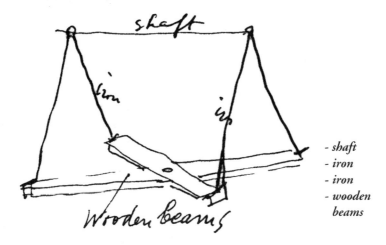

- *shaft*
- *iron*
- *iron*
- *wooden*
  beams

The horse is placed on 2 wooden beams crossing each other

———

Then on the back of the shaft there is a wheel connected with the motor
placed on the floor (back also of the machine)

- *wheel*
- *cord*
- *motor*
- *shaft*

The whole thing mounted should look more or less like this

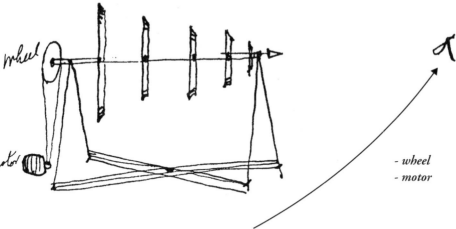

- wheel
- motor

Seen with one eye from the front 1^m or so away, the black and white lines
should continue from one glass to the next like a perfect drawing—
Something like this
Seen from front

And then last warning when they make it turn they should not make it go
too fast— please ask them to have a "resistance" put on the motor ~~so~~ to
regularize the speed at will.
All the pieces of the mounting should be in a box where the thing was placed
after unmounting it.
— I have no time now to answer your last letter, I want this to catch the very
next steamer.
Am going to write you soon—
Am in the midst of my toy which is nearing ~~its~~ completion.

Don't speak about it yet. although you may mention that I am doing a
playtoy—

Rotoreliefs [cat. 53]

I intend to put it on the market only after August when I will exhibit *it* at
a special salon (the inventors' salon called ~~he~~ le concours Lépine)
I will send you a set of the printed discs. soon.
        and a another letter
        Affectueusement
        Dee

33rd Concours Lépine,
Paris, 30 Aug - end Sept
1935.

---

123. Marcel Duchamp to Katherine S. Dreier   telegram
12 May 1935, Paris   collection YCAL

WESTERN UNION
received at Pershing Bldg.
194 Main Street, Danbury, Conn.

   NBJ2 VIA RCA
   CD PARIS MAY 12 1935 1150
     MISS KATHERINE DREIER
     WEST REDDING CONN
   USELESS EXHIBIT STOPPAGES
   923A

In reponse to Dreier's
telegram saying she
couldn't find the *Rotary
Glass Plates* [cat. 50],
only the *Standard
Stoppages* [cat. 34].

---

124. Marcel Duchamp to Katherine S. Dreier   autograph letter
20 May 1935, Paris   collection YCAL

Paris 20th May 1935

        First the revolving glass.
I don't understand your cable at all.— In your *previous* letter you said that
        you were sending <u>three</u> glass panels to the Modern Museum—

Rotary Glass Plates
[cat. 50]

And then your cable seems to indicate that you have lost trace of glass
        panels in general.
Anyway here is the story as I recall it :

<u>First</u> The Stoppages-étalon are 3 <u>canvasses</u> blue black on which only a very
        fine line is made by a thread <u>glued down</u> with varnish = At the bottom
        of each of the three *canvasses* are written these words : 3 Stoppages étalon
        1913-14.

Standard Stoppages
[cat. 34]

        — When I made the panel " <u>Tu m'</u> ", I made from the Stoppages-étalon
        3 wooden rulers which have the same profile as the threads on the
        canvas.

Tu m' [cat. 29]

<u>and then</u> in 1920 or 21 I built the "revolving glass" which has nothing to do
        with the Stoppages-étalon.

There are 5 glass panels of different length with a black and white design
at top and bottom of each glass

The 5 glasses were mounted on a *iron* chassis as I described it in my last   *Rotary Glass Plates*
letter— There also was a motor (electric) Everything was unmounted   [cat. 50]
and put in a long box, specially made for it at your place (I think 135?
Central Park West).

So ~~in~~ outside of the 5 glass panels there were the big iron chassis and the
electric motor and all the details— That made a very heavy box and it
must be in a storage— if you can't find it in your place.

———

I cabled not to exhibit the Stoppages étalon and you can't show 3 panels   *Standard Stoppages*
of glass unmounted when there should be five and a motor etc.   [cat. 34]
I hope you will find it again.

———

To go back to your letter of March 29th—
I received the 634 francs paid Magdeleine and there are a few francs left   Probably **Magdeleine**
in your favor.   **Duchamp**

About coming this year. It is utterly impossible. I am working *on* and   **Inventor's Fair**, held
finishing my playtoy and I intend to exhibit it at the inventors' fair here   annually at the
from August 30th to October 8th.   Concours Lépine in
                                                                               Paris, where MD tries
This means trying to launch it in a business like way.   to sell his *Rotoreliefs*
In ~~as~~ a week or 2, I will send you a sample of the toy.— If you show it,   [cat. 53].
don't *let* anyone take it away from you, as I want to first copyright it in
America.

All these precautions may mean nothing if I don't sell, ~~but~~
Then after that, I will start collecting photos for the album.   "album" = future *Box-
                                                                               in-a-Valise* [cat. 4]

———

It was awfully nice of you to offer me all the facilities ~~of coming~~ *to* come
to N.Y. and I thank you very much, as I really would like to go for a
while.
Maybe next year— if things lend themselves to it.

———

Villon accepts ~~to~~ your transaction :
etching vs. lithograph—
This is about all for the moment
Write soon—
    Affectueusement
    Dee

125. Marcel Duchamp to Katherine S. Dreier   autograph letter
6 September 1935, Paris   collection YCAL

Paris 6. September 1935
    Now I can find a little time to write.
My counter at the "Concours Lépine" is installed and for since it was   *Rotoreliefs* [cat. 53]
    opened I have sold 2 boxes__   *Box-in-a-Valise* [cat. 4]
This a complete failure commercialy speaking__ That is why I can write
    in peace.
I have sent the toy two or 3 days ago; you will have it before this letter.
    Anyway I had it am having it copyrighted in the USA hoping still to sell
    a few there.
— I am sorry you sent the Brancusi column back. I wish you would like it
    enough to place it somewhere in your house and enjoy it.
I don't want it back here and I don't know when I will sell it.
So if you have no desire to have it will you wire the word "no" without
    any signature and I will write immediately to Of *what* to do (I don't   Of = George Of
    know what).__
If you don't wire I will let understand that you have asked Of to bring it
    again to Redding.
Regarding the cost of transportation, it is understood that I will pay
    George Of or reimbourse [=reimburse] you__

    _____

Many thanks for offering me the studio. I don't think I can go for the
    moment__ We will have to wait for the good weather again, in order to
    work at the glass.
— I received 100 francs from the Munguias for the renting of the curtains
    and I am supposed to go and see the new tenants (Mr. Carpentier whom
    I don't know) to arrange about the the buying of the curtains.

    _____

Villon is better than ever__ So is Gaby__   **Gaby** [Gabrielle Bœuf],
Magdeleine is in the South and also th my other sister and husband (from   Jacques Villon's wife.
    Saigon)   **"Magdeleine"** =
Has Villon ever sent you the etching in exchange for yours. I mean have   Magdeleine Duchamp
    you written to him about it? I told you he liked the idea of exchanging   "my other sister and
    etchings.   husband" = Yvonne
Many thanks for the 48 wishes.   Duchamp (see p.133)
and write (if you can accept my decease [sic for «disease»] to be unable to   and Alphonse
    write)   Duvernoy, Customs
        Affectueusement   and Excise officer in
        Dee   Indochina.

---

126. Marcel Duchamp to André Breton   autograph letter
[22 September 1935], Paris   source: from Y. Poupard-Lieussou transcript

11 rue Larrey
Dimanche
    Mon cher Breton— Comme inconnu je ne vois qu'une fenêtre que
Man Ray a photographiée il y a quinze jours, datant de 1920; elle
s'appelle "La bagarre d'Austerlitz"— *(jamais reproduite que je sache)*
Vous pourriez voir la photo chez Man Ray et décider si ça va—
Un détail : j'aimerais qu'elle soit reproduite aussi grand que possible; car
c'est le seul moyen de donner une idée de l'original au pauvre lecteur.
Mais si pas possible, ça va quand même.
Quand vous aurez décidé quelque chose faites moi signe je vous
    retrouverai un après midi qui vous plaira.
        Affectueusement à tous deux
        M Duchamp

A reproduction of MD's 1921 The Brawl at Austerlitz [cat. 47], is used as the frontispiece of Breton's Au Lavoir Noir, to appear in 1936 (Schwarz cat. No. 448).

▷ TRANSLATION: *11 rue Larrey, Sunday. My dear Breton, The only unknown I can
think of is a window Man Ray photographed a fortnight ago dating back to 1920.
It's called the "The Brawl at Austerlitz" (never been reproduced as far as I know).
You could go and see the photo at Man Ray's and decide whether it will do. One
small thing; I would like the reproduction to be as large as possible as it's the only
way of giving the poor reader any idea of the original. But if not possible, still OK.
Once you've reached a decision, let me know and I'll come and meet you one afternoon when it suits you. Affectionately to you both, M Duchamp.*

---

127. Marcel Duchamp to Katherine S. Dreier   autograph letter
7 December 1935, Paris   collection YCAL

11 rue Larrey 7 Dec. 1935
    Of course, we will exchange storage for transportation of Brancusi
    column— And many thanks again.
— Play-toy— I cabled you because I wanted you to know right away that they
    are protected by copyright in USA (got the slip recently)—
As to the price, I can't sell them anymore than $1.^{25} the whole set. In the
    few places I have sent them in America (I have no special agent) that is
    the price they should be sold. But at Macy's they would sell them $3^{00}
    if they took them— meaning that they have bought <u>one set</u> on approval
    and I have not heard anything since (6 weeks ago).
So you have all liberty to sell them from $1.^{25} to $3^{00}— If people find it
    too cheap, too bad, but the cost of making it does not allow me to more
    profit.

Rotoreliefs [cat. 53]

Macy's Department Store, one of the biggest department stores in NY at the time.

They are only typographical prints on cardboard. and have no value as
originals. (Which they are evidently not, not even comparable to
etchings)

I saw Mr. John Davidson who is very lively and we had a very nice time
together

He probably will see you and tell *you* if he enjoyed his short stay in Paris.

———

Thanks for the catalogue of Hartford, I'll give *it* to Pevsner— Do you
think there is any hope of selling for Gabo and Pevsner— They need it
as much morally as substantially.

You never wrote about the fire?!!

Will you send me photographs of the garden and the island (if you have
some) and mark where you would want to put the column. I will tell you
my preference—

———

By the way will you be so kind as to have a good commercial photographer
make a black and white photo of your "window" *(French window)*
(8 *inches* x 10 *inches* about) and also a photo of the three "Stoppages-
étalon" (you know the 3 <u>canvases</u> ₹elongated on which is glued a piece
of ~~strin~~ thread) Please have the three canvases photographed on the
same plate next to each other witout any special order

Many thanks— This is for my album (next year) Affectueusement
     Dee

John Davidson
(b.1890), American
painter living in NY.

*The Abstract Art of
Gabo, Pevsner,
Mondrian and Domela,*
Wadsworth Atheneum,
Hartford, 22 Oct -
17 Nov 1935.

Naum Gabo
(1890-1977) and
Antoine Pevsner (1886-
1962), brothers and
leading Russian
Constructivist artists
then living in Paris.

Fresh Widow [cat. 44]
Standard Stoppages
[cat. 34]

"album" = future *Box-
in-a-Valise* [cat. 4]

---

128. Marcel Duchamp to Katherine S. Dreier   autograph letter
1 January 1936, Paris   collection YCAL

11 rue Larrey 1ˢᵗ January 1936
     Happy new year and many happy returns.
— Play Toy—

Many thanks for the trouble you take.— I will be thankful to you for
whatever Ann Watkins finds or decides.

For the moment I had 500 printed— but *at* any time I can have 500
printed and ready for sale in 3 weeks.

An amusing detail : I showed it to scientists (optical people) and they say
it is an new form, unknown before, of producing the illusion of volume
or relief—

So I am going to take it to a "Professor" of optics and may be have a
scientific account written by him for the Academy of Sciences, if he
decides so.

That serious side of the play toy is very interesting.

Rotoreliefs [cat. 53]

Ann Watkins,
professional name of
Anne Burlingame
(b.1881), agent for
books, plays and screen
plays, married to writer
Roger Burlingame
(1889-1967); both
friends and neighbors
of Dreier's.

— Revolving glass

    The box, as I remember it was elongated and I should say, over a yard long 2 feet wide and the same thickness—

    The 5 glass blades were piled up in the box with the motor and the iron frame (taken to pieces) I found *(at Man Ray's)* a very good photograph he took of the revolving glass in N.Y. in 1920.— ~~The~~ It will be reproduced in the album I am slowly preparing—

    That Picabia is not mine. But there is no special hurry to give it back to Picabia.

    It is much better to show it around and may be sell it for it is a nice example of that period.

    Do you think you can have the "Stoppages-étalon" photographed for my album (I am now speaking of three canvases painted with a thin coat of Prussian blue, and a very fine thread can be seen in the middle of each when you look close to the canvas. The 3 canvases are over a yard long and one foot wide (about.)

Good bye happy stay in New York—

        Affectueusement

        Dee

Rotary Glass Plates [cat. 50]

"album" = future *Box-in-a-Valise* [cat. 4]

Standard Stoppages [cat. 34]

---

129. Marcel Duchamp to Katherine S. Dreier   autograph letter
18 March 1936, Paris   collection YCAL

    11 rue Larrey

    18. March 36

        I have not been able to answer your two letters because I wanted to make up my mind about going to New York this Summer.

After adding and subtracting I came to the conclusion that I probably <u>will</u> go 15th or end of May and stay June and July— I hope to fix the glass in the course of those 2 months.

Large Glass [cat. 2]

Are you sure I won't be too much in your way if I stay at the Haven while I work— and then a few weeks in N.Y. at your studio?

Dreier's house called "The Haven."

My idea about repairing the glass is to put it between two other glasses framed in an iron frame.— (as ~~Hh~~ Roché had it done for the glass which you saw I think at his place)—

9 Malic Moulds [cat. 31]

I would glue every piece broken on to one of the glasses with an invisible glue (which I am studying) ~~et~~ and the whole thing although very heavy, would make a <u>solid</u> piece of furniture when in place.

— Now could you afford the expense of the 4 pieces of ~~g~~ plate glass necessary? ~~wo~~ I think there is one already which we can use— Will you ask the man who has the glass now, how much would cost the 3 ~~q~~ other plate glasses?

Also the 2 big frames *(one for each half)* in iron screwed and reinforced at
the four corners would be a bit of iron work? Could he get an
approximate estimate before I leave—

All this has to be decided before hand. There would not be any more
expense attached to the repairing as I would do it all myself— except
occasional help for handling the big glasses.

So please think all this over, take your information and let me know as
soon as possible.

— When do you expect to leave N.Y. for the Haven again? I am sure it
will be lovely

Affectueusement

Dee

Leave all the search in warehouses for my arrival.

---

130. Marcel Duchamp to André Breton   autograph letter
14 April 1936, Paris   source: from Y. Poupard-Lieussou transcript

11 rue Larrey

14 Avril 36

    Cher Breton, Hugnet me téléphone : vous avez vu chez Roché la
petite toile de 1911 et elle vous plait. Je ne vois aucun inconvénient à
l'envoyer à Londres comme vous le désirez— En fait je remplacerai le
dessin *(MCimetière uniformes)* qui était aux 4 chemins par cette toile,
car j'espère vendre ce dessin en Amérique.

Quant au titre, il n'y en a pas à proprement parler— Mais si vous voulez :
"A propos de jeune sœur„ cela nous éviterait "portrait" "étude" ou
quelque chose de semblable.

J'aimerais vous voir quelques instants puisque la Seine semble
infranchissable au même moment pour nous deux—

Il est possible que j'aille passer deux mois à New York; je partirais vers le
15 Mai.

Quand vous avez une occasion donnez moi rendez vous— Je vais souvent
à l'imprimerie Ramlot pour Cahiers d'Art ces 2 prochaines semaines.

    Affectueusement à tous deux

Georges Hugnet
(1906-1974), French Surrealist poet and writer.

Cemetery of Uniforms... [cat. 25], which apparently MD sells to the Arensbergs in 1936.

Little Sister [cat. 12]

▷ TRANSLATION: *11 rue Larrey. 14th April '36. Dear Breton, Hugnet phoned me:
you've seen the little 1911 canvas and like it. I have no objection to sending it to London as is your wish. In fact I will replace the drawing (Cemetery Uniforms), which
was at the 4 Chemins, with this canvas, as I hope to sell it in America. As for the
title, there isn't one strictly speaking. But if you like: "Apropos of Little Sister" which
would spare us from "portrait," "study" or the like. I would like to see you briefly as
it seems an impossibility for us both to cross the Seine at the same time. I might be
going to spend two months in New York. I would be leaving around 15th May.*

When you have time, arrange to meet me. I'll be going to Ramlot's the printers for
Cahiers d'Art review this coming fortnight. Affectionately to you both.

---

131. Marcel Duchamp to Henri-Pierre Roché   autograph letter
12 July 1936, West Redding, Connecticut   collection HRHRC

> Redding 12 Juillet '36
>   Chers enfants
> je n'ai pas répondu à ta lettre, ni écrit, car je suis devenu un vitrier qui de
>   9ʰ à 7ʰ du soir ne pense à rien d'autre qu'à réparer du verre cassé.
> Mais ça va— Encore 3 semaines et la Mariée aura retrouvé ses jambes.
> — Vers le 1ᵉʳ Aout je pars pour 2 semaines en Californie (Walter m'a très
>   gentiment invité) et je suis thrilled.
> Serai de retour à Paris vers fin Aout—
> — Pour la cage à sucre je voudrais bien qu'elle soit empaquetée de telle sorte
>   que le poids du marbre ne porte pas sur les barreaux ou le fond de la
>   cage.— (Si Barr la veut toujours).
> Je ne pense pas que le marbre de Sheeler soit spécialement intéressant. il
>   est très bien mais cassé— et je ne sais pas s'il l'a encore
> A bientôt autres nouvelles
>   Affectueusement à tous trois
>   Totor

Restoring of Large Glass [cat. 2].
The Bride Stripped Bare... [cat. 1]

Why not Sneeze... [cat. 46]; shown in Alfred Barr's exh., "Fantastic Art, Dada and Surrealism," MoMA, NY, 9 Dec 1936 - 17 Jan 1937.

▷ TRANSLATION: *Redding. 12th July '36. Dear kids, I haven't replied to your letter, nor written at all, as I am now a glazier who from 9 in the morning to 7 in the evening thinks of nothing but how to mend broken glass. But it's OK. Another three weeks and the Bride'll have her legs back. Towards 1st August I'm leaving for California for 2 weeks (Walter has very kindly invited me) and I am thrilled. Will be back in Paris toward end August. As for the sugar cage, I would like it to be packed so that the weight of the marble doesn't rest on the bars or the bottom of the cage. (If Barr still wants it.) I don't think Sheeler's marble is particularly interesting: it's all right, but broken and I don't know if he's still got it. So long until further news. Affectionately to all three of you. Totor.*

---

132. Marcel Duchamp to Constantin Brancusi   autograph letter
22 July 1936, West Redding, Connecticut   collection MNAM

> Redding 22 Juillet 36
>   Cher vieux
> Je me réveille—
> Depuis 2 mois j'ai réparé du verre cassé et je suis très loin de mes habitudes
>   parisiennes.

Que deviens tu? Ta colonne (celle de Quinn) va être mise dans le jardin de Miss Dreier; elle fera très bien.

Je pars dans 8 jours pour Hollywood.

Arensberg m'a invité à passer quinze jours chez lui et je suis enchanté.

Ɉ Serai retour à Paris fin Aout commencement Septembre.

Où seras tu?

Tu peux m'écrire un mot à New York— je le trouverai en rentrant vers le 20 Aout.

> M. Duchamp
>> Studio 910
>> Carnegie Hall
>> 56th Street and 7th Avenue
>> New York City
> Affectueusement et à bientôt
> Morice

The Endless Column, 1918 (MoMA, NY; gift of Mrs Mary Sisler), formerly in the collection of John Quinn.

▷ TRANSLATION: *Redding. 22nd July 1936. Hello old chap. Just woken up. I've spent the last two months mending broken glass. Things here a far cry from my way of life in Paris. What are you up to? Your column (Quinn's) is going in Miss Dreier's garden—it'll look very good there. I leave for Hollywood in a week's time. Arensberg has invited me to spend a fortnight at his place and I'm delighted. Will be back in Paris end August beginning September. Where will you be? You can drop me a line in New York. I'll get it when I get back around 20th August. M. Duchamp, Studio 910, Carnegie Hall, 56th Street and 7th Avenue, New York City. Affectionately and see you soon, Morice.*

August 1936
While in the United States, Duchamp takes the opportunity to travel out west and visit the Arensbergs at their home in Hollywood.
He takes with him color notes on his paintings, and arranges for photographs to be taken of those works he plans to reproduce in his *Box-in-a-Valise* [cat. 4].

2 September 1936
After just over three months in the US, Duchamp returns to France on the "Normandie."
Aboard ship, he writes to Katherine Dreier: "*this trip has really been a wonderful vacation in my past life.*"
His ship docks in Le Havre on September 7, 1936.

---

133. Marcel Duchamp to Katherine S. Dreier
29 September 1936, Paris

autograph letter
collection YCAL

Paris 29th Sept 36
It is a month now since I left and I have not been able to accomplish anything :
People have not come back to town or I have been lazy—

I am going to write to the treasurer of the "Amis de la Bibliothèque
Doucet" who might be interested in buying Verlaine.

It is a curious thing (again) : why I could be so energetic in America and
the minute I land in Europe my muscles refuse to function.

Anyway I have very pleasant memories of Redding and the glass and the
sun

I hope I was not *too* much of a nuisance—

Villon and Gaby are well and send you their love—

I have not seen Pevsner but I heard that the insurance is paying for
breaking their works in *the* transportation.

That's Something.

I have not found the time to inquire about your lithographs but I will soon
get busy

Brancusi is well and asked about you—

Man Ray is leaving for N.Y. to morrow and has a regular job with
Harper's Bazaar. He will have to stay in N.Y. 3 months twice a year.

Write soon and tell me how long you are staying at the Haven.

I left the studio in a terrible state please excuse me—

    Affectueusement

    Dee

Paul Verlaine (1844-1896), French poet. Apparently, MD trying to help Dreier sell a Verlaine manuscript.

"lithographs" = while in US, MD volunteers to arrange printing of Dreier's series of colored lithographs, *40 Variations*.

In the 1930's, Man Ray is hired as a fashion photographer by the magazine *Bazaar*.

---

134. Marcel Duchamp to Katherine S. Dreier   autograph letter
9 February 1937, Paris   collection YCAL

11 rue Larrey 9th Feb 37

    Bombshell all right.[*]

It is difficult for me to picture the whole thing from my peaceful Paris—
but your statement clarified the situation for the public.

Also it will make the public more conscious of the importance of what is
going on—

Comparing with our past times — the Matisse, the cubist and futurist
episodes — it is always good for general recognition to stir the stew
which is generally created by such episodes.

As for Man Ray, he does not want to do any further move giving
unnecessary publicity to the museum.

---

[*] Context is necessary to understand MD's letter fully. Alfred Barr's traveling exhibition *Fantastic Art, Dada, Surrealism* (opening at the MoMA, 9 Dec 1936 - 17 Jan 1937) mixes Surrealism, Bosch, Blake, and art works by the very young and the mad. Upset by the comparison, Dreier calls a press conference 19 Jan 1937 to announce that the Société Anonyme art works on loan will not go on tour. She then sends a cable to MD : "*Threw bombshell withdrew loan Société for exhibition on tour because insane and children pictures included. Ask Man Ray to do likewise by cable writing.*"

I still think that criticizing for or against is of equal value, meaning that
the amount of publicity is proportional to the number of lines written
for as well as against.
— The thing criticized always profits by any criticism (at least along the
public lines).
As long as you made it a clear statement it is perfect__ If it becomes a fight
there should be a winner__ And the win has no more to do with right
or wrong__ it is a gamble.
All this please keep to yourself and let me know the further
developments__
I received the 300 francs which I gave to Madeleine__ Many thanks
And now get ready for your trip__
    Affectueusement
    Dee

"Madeleine" =
Magdeleine, MD's
youngest sister, helped
him make arrangements
for Dreier's apartment in
Paris (see p.198).

---

135. Marcel Duchamp to Katherine S. Dreier   autograph letter
25 June 1937, Paris   collection YCAL

11 rue Larrey June 25th 1937
    I have waited to write hoping to give good news of the work in
progress. The news are good but slow__

40 Variations,
see p.211.

Naturally the printing in black of the lithograph was finished long ago__
and the 3200 prints taken to the "colorist" who expected to finish in a
month. I called him up yesterday and I am to see, in a few days, half of
the whole work cut out and ready for color-brushing.
This means that his main work consists of cutting out in the zinc foil the
areas for each color__ The actual brushing of the color does not take so
much time.
Anyway we will have to wait until August before his work is finished.

As for the port-folios__ The binder wrote me announcing that, having
miscalculated his price of 30 fr. per port folio, on account of increase of
price in materials, he would have to ask 35 fr. (instead of 30). I told him
to go ahead, knowing that it is was legitimate.__ He will be ready soon

---

Budget. In enclose the figures on separate sheet :
On one side what I received
On the other side the expenses (I have already paid many things or
deposited advances).
You will see that on account of the new price of the port-folios, I will be
lacking 1221 francs in the end. Could you send it to me before the
1st of August__

I have started the reproduction in color of 5 paintings of mine.— It will take me all summer.— Next winter I expect to attack the big glass and the Tu m'—

Received from Kiessler the wonderful article (Architectural Record) on the glass— I will use the cellophane print to decide how to make my own reproduction.

Would it be asking too much to have you write to Berenice Abbott and ask her to send you or me directly all the photos she made of the glass. (and in their original size— in fact I need them as large as the cellophane reproduction). Is there a straight view of the glass without any perspective effect in two parts or in one part?

Large Glass [cat. 2] and *Tu m'* [cat. 29]

Frederick Kiesler (1896-1966), Viennese-born architect, wrote about the *Large Glass* [cat. 2] for *The Architectural Record* (May 1937).

Berenice Abbott (1898-1990), American photographer, studied with Man Ray.

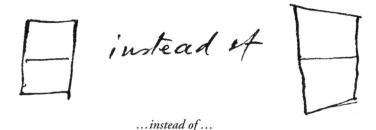

…instead of…

I am writing to Kiesler asking him also to have Berenice Abbott send me the photos— But I trust you for accuracy—

How is the Haven this year?

My regards to Mr. Penny and Cocky

Affectueusement

Dee

136. Marcel Duchamp to Frederick Kiesler   autograph letter
25 June 1937, Paris   formerly collection Lilian Kiesler

Paris V
11 rue Larrey
25 Juin 37
    Cher Kiesler
Quelle surprise vous m'avez faite! J'ai eu très grand plaisir à lire votre
    article da[ns] les 5 extraits de l'Architectural Record sur le verre—
    d'abord l'esprit de l'article, puis votre interprétation et la présentation
    de vos idées!
Je vous remercie d'avoir bien voulu regarder le verre avec une telle
    attention et d'avoir fixé des points que peu de gens connaissent.
— Je ne me rappelle pas si vous avez une boîte verte qui, en somme, est le   *Green Box* [cat. 3]
    "manuscrit" du verre.— je vous en envoie un exemplaire par ~~le~~ un
    prochain courrier— espérant qu'[en] le parcourant vous verrez combien
    vous aviez raison—
Pourriez vous demander à Berenice Abbott (je n'ai pas son adresse) de
    m'envoyer une photo~~s~~ de <u>tout</u> ce qu'elle [a] pris du verre—
j'ai besoin de grandes photos— Chaque moitié du verre faisant environ
    8 inches de hauteur

- 8 inch
- 8 inch
- 16 inch—

Y a t il des photos prises complètement de face?
En un mot tout ce qu'elle pourra m'envoyer comme documentation
    (devant et derrière) sera bienvenue.
    Merci.
    et Affectueusement à tous deux
    Marcel Duchamp

▷ TRANSLATION: *11 rue Larrey, 25th June '37. Dear Kiesler, What a surprise you gave
me! I very much enjoyed reading your article in the 5 extracts of the Architectural
Record on the glass—firstly, the spirit of the article, then your interpretation and
the way your ideas were set out. Thank you for having looked at the glass so closely
and for having put on paper points that so few people know about. I can't remember
whether you have a green box which is in fact the "manuscript" of the glass. I'll send*

you one in the next mail, hoping that when you go through it, you'll see how right
you are. Could you ask Berenice Abbott (I don't have her address) to send me a
photo of everything she took of the glass. I need large photos—each half of the glass
being about 8 inches high. [sketch] Are there any photos taken head on? In a word,
anything she can send me in the way of documentation (back and front) would be
welcome. Thanks. And affectionately to you both, Marcel Duchamp.

---

137. Marcel Duchamp to Walter Pach   autograph letter
28 September 1937, Paris   collection AAA

11 rue Larrey Paris V
28 Sept. 37
    Cher Walter
Je relis aujourd'hui votre lettre d'il y a un an (presque jour pour jour)—
    C'est vous dire ma honte de n'avoir jamais répondu.   *Sad Young Man...*
Toujours au sujet du "Jeune homme triste dans un train" = J'ai   [cat. 15]
    naturellement été bouleversé par le prix que vous aviez décidé et je n'ai
    pas voulu le discuter, vous laissant tous les droits de lui attribuer une
    valeur.
Dans votre lettre vous me réservez, sur $3500⁻, 20 % c-à-d. $700⁻ et je
    suis très sensible à votre pensée.
Pourriez vous supprimer ces 20 % et réduire à une somme variant entre
    $2 000 et 2 500 le montant de votre part?
Je me contenterais parfaitement de $100⁻ ajoutés à cette somme.
Je voudrais surtout que vous ne voyiez pas dans ma réponse tardive un
    marchandage désagréable : Je vous ai dit pourquoi j'aimerais que cette
    toile (si elle vous quitte) aille rejoindre ses frères et sœurs en
    Californie—
Je reste convaincu que ma production parce qu'elle est réduite n'a aucun
    droit à la spéculation c-à-d. le voyage d'une collection à l'autre en
    s'éparpillant et je suis certain qu'Arensberg a, autant que moi,
    l'intention d'en faire un tout cohérent.
Si donc cette lettre et ma proposition ne vous intéressent pas, oubliez les.
Si au contraire vous répondez à ma façon de voir, j'écrirai tout de suite à
    Arensberg et je doute fort qu'il refuse.

De plus puis je vous demander de faire faire une bonne photo (pas trop   *Sad Young Man...*
    foncée) 8^{inch} x 10^{inch} du "Jeune homme"— Je voudrais le reproduire   [cat. 15]
    dans l'album auquel je travaille depuis l'année dernière et qui ne sera pas   **"l'album"** = *Box-in-a-*
    terminé avant 2 ans.— Dites moi aussi combien coûte la photo—   *Valise* [cat. 4]
    naturellement.

— Comment allez vous? comment va Magda; et Raymond?— Je ne pense pas **Magda** and **Raymond**, aller à New York cet hiver.— Viendrez vous en Europe? wife and son of Walter Pach.

D'une façon ou de l'autre nous ne serons pas longtemps sans nous voir.

Au revoir, mon cher Walter, mille affections pour vous trois
   Cordialement
   Marcel

▷ TRANSLATION: *11 rue Larrey, Paris V. 28th Sept. '37. Dear Walter, I have just been re-reading today your letter of a year ago (almost to the day). I can't tell you how ashamed I am not to have replied. Still on the subject of the "Sad young man on a train" = Naturally I was flabbergasted by the price you decided on and I didn't want to argue, leaving you sole rights to price it. In your letter, you set aside for me out of $3,500 20% i.e. $700 and I am very touched by the thought. Could you cut out this 20% and reduce your share by an amount somewhere between $2,000 and $2,500? I would be very happy with $100, to be added to this amount. Above all, please do not take my late reply as some cheap way of bargaining. I have told you why I would like this painting (if it is to part from you) to go and join its brothers and sisters in California. I am still convinced that because my output is limited, my things should not be subjected to speculation, i.e. traveling from one collection to an-other and being scattered about, and I am certain that Arensberg, like myself, in-tends making it a coherent whole. If you are not interested in the proposal in this letter, forget about it. If, on the other hand, you see things the way I do, I will write to Arensberg straight away and would be very surprised if he refused. In addition, could I ask you to have a good photo (not too dark), 8-inch x 10-inch, made of the "Young man." I would like to reproduce it in the album I've been working on since last year and which won't be finished for another two years. Let me know how much the photo costs, of course. How are you? How is Magda? and Raymond? I don't think I'll be going to New York this winter. Will you be coming to Europe? It won't be long until we meet up one way or another. Farewell, my dear Walter. All my affection to the three of you. Sincerely, Marcel.*

---

138. Marcel Duchamp to Man Ray   autograph letter
25 August 1938, Paris   collection HRHRC

Paris V 11 rue Larrey
25 Août 38
  Cher Man
Je ne suis pas tout à fait sûr de ton adresse mais j'espère que tu recevras **Adon** (or Dona)
ceci— **Lacroix**, alias Donna Lecœur, Belgian poet,
D'abord j'ai reçu une lettre de Adon Lacroix que je t'enverrai quand je married Man Ray
 serai sûr de ton adresse—Toujours la même histoire— enfin tu verras. (3 May 1913); they separated 1919.
— Ensuite j'avais vu Barr et il m'avait donné l'adresse de John Abbott (film Apparently she is trying to contact Man Ray to
 director) à qui j'ai écrit au sujet des $25.^{00} que je n'ai jamais reçus pour make their divorce official.

mon film (tu m'avais dit leur avoir envoyé cette copie il y a 2 ans). Qu'est
il arrivé? je n'en sais rien. Barr m'écrit ce matin que la film Library du
Modern Museum n'a jamais reçu de film (Anemic Cinema) "they have   *Anémic Cinéma*
checked very carefully even going through the material sent them by   [cat. 52]
Man Ray" (quoting Barr's letter)
et ils n'ont rien trouvé
Dis moi vite ~~sur~~ ce que tu penses qui s'est passé▁
En même temps donne moi l'adresse d'une maison d'impression de films
où je pourrais faire imprimer un positif de l'anémic Cinémac▁   *Anémic Cinéma*
Combien approximativement ça coûtera t il (environ 10 minutes   [cat. 52]
standard *size* film) ?

─────────

Merci Que fais tu? Quand rentres tu?
Revenus de Vittel (agréable,
    Bonjour à tous deux
    Marcel

▷ TRANSLATION: *Paris V. 11 rue Larrey. 25th August '38. Dear Man, I'm not altogether sure of your address but hope this will reach you. Firstly, I got a letter from Adon
Lacroix which I will send you when I'm sure of your address. Same old story, anyway you'll see. Next, I saw Barr and he gave me John Abbott's address (film director) so I wrote to him about the $25 which I never received for my film (you told me
you sent him that copy two years ago). What happened? I haven't the foggiest idea.
Barr wrote to me this morning saying that the Film Library of the Modern Museum never got the film (Anemic Cinema) "they have checked very carefully even
going through the material sent them by Man Ray" (quoting Barr's letter) and
didn't find anything. Let me know as soon as possible what you think happened. At
the same time, give me the address of a printing house for film where I can have a
positive made of the Anemic Cinemac. And how much all this will cost approximately (about 10 minutes standard size film)? Thanks. What are you up to?
When are you coming back? We are back from Vittel (very nice) Greetings to you
both, Marcel.*

───

139. Marcel Duchamp to André Breton   autograph letter
12 January 1940, Paris   source: from Y. Poupard-Lieussou transcript

Paris
11 rue Larrey
12 Janvier 40   Breton posted as head
    Cher Breton   doctor at Poitiers pilot
                                        school (Jan - July 1939);
J'ai été désolément surpris d'apprendre votre "déplacement" à Poitiers   **Jacqueline Lamba**
quand j'ai téléphoné à Jacqueline l'autre jour. Puisse ledit lieu vous   (1910-1995) is his
acheminer rapidement vers la psychiâtrie de vos rêves!   second wife. They
                                        married in 1934 and are
                                        to separate in 1942.

Peggy Guggenheim à qui j'avais parlé du Miro que vous voulez bien vendre est venue le voir Mercredi avec moi. Elle a vu aussi le Max Ernst (huile) du coin en haut près du vitrage. et Jacqueline a pensé que vous seriez assez disposé à le vendre.

Encore Peggy a jeté un œil d'envie sur le Dali au dessus du lit.＿ Là Jacqueline a pensé que vous n'étiez pas enclin à vous en séparer.

Des trois, Peggy préfère le Dali : le côté "érotique" n'est pas *un* obstacle, le tableau ne devant pas passer de frontières＿ Si vous n'avez pas de raison sentimentale pour le garder, je vous serais reconnaissant de mentionner le prix auquel vous vous en sépareriez.

De même donnez moi un prix pour le Max Ernst

Le Miro est à 8 000 comme entendu.

Un prix global pour les 3 pourrait aussi compléter cette aventure commerciale.

J'ai mis de côté la planche (Mariée) qui manque dans votre boîte verte＿   *Green Box* [cat. 3]
Si je retourne rue Fontaine je la déposerai sur la table＿ Faites moi signe si vous venez à Paris

    Affectueusement

    Marcel Duchamp

▷ TRANSLATION: *Paris, 11 rue Larrey. 12th January '40. Dear Breton, I had a nasty surprise when I phoned Jacqueline the other day to learn of your "move" to Poitiers. May the above-said place lead you rapidly to the psychiatry of your dreams! Peggy Guggenheim, whom I'd spoken to about the Miro that you would like to sell, came to see it with me on Wednesday. She also saw the Max Ernst (oil) in the corner, high up near the windows, and Jacqueline thought that you would be rather in-clined to sell it. Once again Peggy was looking enviously at the Dali over the bed. There Jacqueline thought you would not be inclined to part with it. Of the three, Peggy prefers the Dalí: the erotic aspect is not an obstacle as the painting wouldn't have to cross any borders. Unless you have sentimental reasons for keeping it, I would be grateful if you would name the price at which you would part with it. Like-wise give me a price for the Max Ernst. The Miro is at 8,000 as agreed. A global price for the three could conclude this business venture. I've put aside the plate (Bride) that is missing from your green box. If I go back to rue Fontaine, I'll put it on the table. Get in touch if you come to Paris. Affectionately, Marcel Duchamp.*

Arcachon, Grenoble, Sanary | 1940-1942

lives in Arcachon, then Grenoble (Hôtel Moderne), then Sanary (Hôtel Dol and Hôtel
  Primavera)—to escape the occupied zone
several trips to Marseilles, Montélimar, Aix-en-Provence
aboard ship for Casablanca, Bermuda and New York | arriving 25 June 1942

from late May 1940 to 25 June 1942

▶   MAJOR WORK

Boîte en valise / The Box-in-a-Valise (miniature
  replicas and color reproductions of 69
  works by Duchamp contained in a
  cardboard box enclosed in a valise,
  1935-41)

▶   EXHIBITION

United Nation Festival, Museum of Art, Santa Barbara,
  USA. By MD: *Nude descending a Stair No.2*
  — 20 May 1942

16 May 1940
Fleeing the rapid advancement of German troops
(who have just taken over Holland),
Duchamp leaves Paris for Arcachon, a city near
Bordeaux on the south-west coast of France.
There he continues work on the assembly
of his *Box-in-a-Valise* [cat. 4].

---

140. Marcel Duchamp to Louise and Walter Arensberg   autograph letter
16 July 1940, Arcachon   collection PMA

Arcachon 16 Juillet 1940
    Chère Lou cher Walter.
Depuis ma dernière lettre, l'organisation du pays n'a pas été aussi
    désagréable que je pouvais le craindre.— Arcachon est dans la zone
    occupée, mais la vie civile continue sans que les Allemands ne s'en
    mêlent trop— Beaucoup de réfugiés de Belgique et du Nord sont partis
    et les Allemands qui viennent ici sont là "pour se reposer" (4 jours par
    paquets de 4 000 à la fois. Ils vont et viennent sans arrêt—
Je peux même travailler— j'ai un bon imprimeur et j'avance mon album—   "album" = *Box-in-a-*
Je pense rester à Arcachon jusqu'en Septembre. Il n'y a que très peu de   *Valise* [cat. 4]
    trains pour Paris, d'ailleurs réservés à la poste et aux officiels.— Les
    ponts de chemin de fer ont tous été dynamités.—
Crotti et ma sœur vivent dans notre petite villa et le temps passe
    agréablement.— Villon est à 200 Klm. d'ici mais je ne peux pas aller le
    voir (manque de trains).
Maintenant il semble plus difficile de faire des envois d'argent d'Amérique
    en France.
Nos comptes sont d'ailleurs finis pour les Brancusis. Parmi les petites
    choses que vous pourriez avoir, il y a un chèque original (dessiné et écrit   *Tzanck Check* [cat. 42]
    à la main) que j'avais fait en 1919 pour payer mon dentiste. Il serait
    enchanté de recevoir $50.^{00} pour vous le remettre.
Comme moyens d'envoi d'argent, le plus simple serait que vous
    m'envoyiez par Clipper un chèque personnel ordinaire (pas un draft
    mais un chèque comme ceux que vous employez journellement) je
    trouverais quelqu'un ici qui me donnerait, sur parole, la contre valeur
    en francs—
Quand je rentrerai à Paris en Septembre je vous enverrais "l'œuvre d'art"
    par Clipper.
Une autre chose dans le même genre est l'original de la Joconde aux   *LHOOQ* [cat. 41]
    moustaches (1919)— Pensez-vous que $100⁻ soit trop pour la dite
    Joconde.

J'aimerais bien recevoir un mot de Lou pour qu'elle me dise où en est son
   état de santé__
J'ai reçu une lettre de Béatrice à qui je réponds aujourd'hui__
   A bientôt de vos nouvelles
   Affectueusement à tous deux
   Marcel
toujours Poste Restante
   Arcachon (Gironde)
   jusqu'en Septembre.

Beatrice Wood, see
biography next page.

▷ TRANSLATION: *Arcachon. 16th July 1940. Dear Lou, dear Walter. Since my last letter, the way the country is being run has not been as unpleasant as I had feared.
Arcachon is in the occupied zone, but civilian life goes on without too much inter-
ference from the Germans. Many refugees from Belgium and the North have left
and the Germans just come here "for a rest" (4 days in batches of 4,000 at a time,
coming and going non stop). I am even able to work. I have a good printer and am
making headway on my album. I'll probably stay in Arcachon until September.
There are only very few trains to Paris, and these only for the Post Office and
officials. The railway bridges have all been blown up. Crotti and my sister are staying at our little villa and we while away the hours quite pleasantly. Villon is 200km
from here but I can't go and see him (no trains). It seems more difficult now to send
money from America to France. Anyway our accounts for the Brancusis are settled.
There are a few small things you could have, including an original check (design
and text done by hand) that I made in 1919 to pay my dentist. He would be delighted to let you take it off his hands for $50. To send money, the simplest way would
be to send me, c/o Clipper, an ordinary personal check (not a draft but the kind of
checks you use everyday) and I will find someone here who'll give me on trust the
equivalent value in French francs. When I return to Paris in September, I will send
you the "work of art" by Clipper. In the same vein, there is also the original of the
Mustachioed Mona Lisa (1919). Do you think $100 would be too much for the
Mona Lisa in question? It would be nice if Lou would drop me a line and let me
know what state of health she is in. I got a letter from Béatrice and am replying today. Look forward to hearing from you soon. Affectionately to you both, Marcel—
still Poste Restante Arcachon (Gironde) until September.*

141. Marcel Duchamp to Beatrice Wood[*]   autograph letter
17 July 1940, Arcachon   collection AAA

CAFÉ-BRASSERIE AUX SPORTS
chez Julien Moineau
59, Boulevard d'Haussez
Arcachon, le *17 Juillet*   19*40*
     Chère Béatrice
Merci beaucoup pour tes deux gentilles lettres que j'ai bien reçues— Celle
     du 24 Juin est arrivée vers le 10 Juillet— ce qui est très satisfaisant.
La vie, depuis l'occupation, s'est organisée— Nous avons très peu de
     rapports avec les Allemands. Ils s'occupent surtout de trouver et de
     prendre [de] l'essence pour leurs autos.
Arcachon est un centre de "repos" pour les troupes.—
Donc je reste jusqu'en Septembre puis retourne à Paris.
— Roché est à 200^{km} d'ici : voici son adresse
     Roché
     La Bastidette
     par Gaillac (Tarn)
Je le mettrai au courant de tes gentilles intentions.— il nous est difficile de
     bouger pour le moment
Mais cela ne va pas durer. Tous les réfugiés rentrent peu à peu à Paris ou
     dans le Nord.
Le mois d'Aout ici sera j'espère très agréable.
J'ai écrit hier à Walter et à Lou.   **Walter** and Lou[ise]
                                            Arensberg

---

* **Beatrice Wood** (1893-1998) met Duchamp in New York in September of 1916, while visiting the composer Edgard Varèse, who was in hospital recuperating from a broken leg. She and Duchamp got along so well that they "tutoyed" one another immediately (the informal address that is used primarily among friends), initiating a friendship that was to last the rest of their lives. At the time, Wood was working as an actress, but through the encouragement of Duchamp and his friends—particularly Roché (p.57) and the Arensbergs (p.50)—she began to pursue the career of an artist, beginning with a series of quickly executed sketches (which she preferred to call "scrawls") that Duchamp liked so much that he arranged for one of them to be published in a magazine edited by a friend. It was also through Duchamp's prodding that she submitted a controversial assemblage depicting a nude female figure emerging from her bath—with an actual bar of soap attached to the canvas in the position of a fig leaf—to the Independents Exhibition of 1917. With Duchamp and Roché, she edited *The Blind Man*, a magazine devoted to defending R. Mutt's submission of an ordinary white porcelain urinal for display in this same exhibition. After moving to California in the 1920's, Wood resumed her friendship with the Arensbergs, and remained in contact with Duchamp through correspondence. In the 1930's, she began a new career in ceramics, and quickly established an international reputation for her brilliant, lusterware vessels. To the end of her life (she lived to the remarkable age of 105), Wood frequently cited her friendship with Duchamp and Roché as among the most important and influential experiences of her life as an artist.

J'espère que dans le courant de l'année j'arriverai à quitter la France. et
aller vous voir en Californie—

En tout cas le "dramatique" est passé—

Je n'ai pas reçu la lettre d'Helen— Embrasse la pour moi ainsi que son
mari

Ecris de temps en temps

Mille affections pour ta nouvelle maison et ceux dedans.

Embrasse les Arensbergs pour moi et souhaitons le "à bientôt"

Affect^t Marcel

Poste Restante

Arcachon (Gironde)

Helen = Helen
Freeman, see p.308.

▷ TRANSLATION: *17th July 1940. Dear Béatrice, Thank you very much for the two
kind letters you sent to me. The one of the 24th arrived around the 10th July which
is very satisfactory. Life since the occupation has gotten organized. We have very
little contact with the Germans. They're mainly busy looking for petrol and taking
it for their cars. Arcachon is a "rest" center for the troops. So I'll be staying here until September then going back to Paris. Roché is 200km from here. His address:
Roché, La Bastidette, nr. Gaillac (Tarn). I will pass on to him your kind wishes.
It's difficult for us to move about at the moment. But this won't last. All the refugees
are gradually going back to Paris or going north. The month of August will hopefully be very pleasant here. I wrote yesterday to Walter and Lou. I hope that in the
course of the year I'll manage to leave France and come and see you in California.
In any case, the "drama" is over. I didn't get Helen's letter. Give her my love and
also to her husband. Drop me a line from time to time. Much affection for your new
house and all within it. Give my love to the Arensbergs and, let's hope, "see you
soon." Affectionately, Marcel.*

---

142. Marcel Duchamp to Walter Arensberg   postcard
30 September 1940, Sanary   collection PMA

~~Mademoiselle Jeanine Picabia~~
~~11 rue Chateaubriand~~
~~Paris~~ VIII

~~Chère Jeanine~~

30 Sept. 40

Pouvez vous faire démarches à Washington pour qu'on m'accorde
un visa (temporary visitor) de 6 mois? transmis au Consulat américain
de Marseille—

Raisons : commande ferme d'une décoration— garantie de ma subsistance
pour six mois— signature légalisée (notary public).

Ecrivez moi chez le mari d'une de mes sœurs :
Duvernoy
Villa Amandiers St Roch
Sanary (Var)
Ils recevront vos lettres d'une façon permanente__ je suis rentré chez
moi__ inutile écrire. Affect^t Marcel

Alphonse Duvernoy,
husband of Yvonne
Duchamp (see p.133).

▷ TRANSLATION: *30th Sept. '40 Can you do the necessary in Washington for them to
give me a visa (temporary visitor) for 6 months?—to be sent to the American Consulate in Marseilles. Reasons: definite commission for a decoration. guaranteed in-
come for 6 months, signed and witnessed (notary public). Write to me c/o the
husband of one of my sisters: Duvernoy, Villa Amandiers, St Roch, Sanary (Var).
You can write to me there on a regular basis. I have gone home. no use writing.
Affectionately, Marcel.*

---

143. Marcel Duchamp to Robert Desnos   postcard
21 March [1942, Sanary]   collection BLJD

21 mars__ Merci de votre carte et des nouvelles de la Sonde.__ Pouvez me
faire un plaisir : trouver un exemplaire de "Corps et biens" et me le faire
envoyer par Mary 14 rue Hallé XIV. Elle vous remboursera aussi__
C'est bien là que sont vos contre songeries n'est ce pas ? J'ai voulu les
montrer et j'aimerais les revoir.__ Aucune nouvelle de Picabia__
— Tzara est [à] Aix en P. vous le savez par Frank.
        a bientôt évidemment
        Affectueusement M Duchamp

"La Sonde,"
provisional title of
Desnos' novel *Le vin
est tiré*, 1934.

Corps et Biens, edited
by Robert Desnos (see
p.127), NRF, 1930.

Aix en Provence, South
of France.

▷ TRANSLATION: *21st March. Thank you for your card and news of "La Sonde." Could
you do something for me?—find a copy of "Corps et Biens" and send it to me via
Mary, 14 rue Hallé, XIV. She will also reimburse you. That is where your back-to-
front reveries are, isn't it? I wanted to show them to somebody and I would like to
see them again. No news at all of Picabia. Tzara is in Aix en Provence, as you will
know from Frank. See you soon of course. Affectionately, M Duchamp.*

"contre songeries" =
portmanteau word:
contrepèteries
(spoonerisms) +
songeries (reveries).

---

144. Marcel Duchamp to Robert Desnos   postcard
10 May [1942, Sanary]   collection BLJD

10 mai__ Bien reçu Corps et biens et je vais le relire sur le bateau; j'ai
retrouvé le même plaisir aux "Rrose Sélavy" qu'il y a de nombreuses
années__ Merci beaucoup__
Je pars Jeudi ou Vendredi 15 de Marseille. A Casablanca je change de
bateau et espère arriver à New York vers 20 juin.

Au revoir donc et bien affectueusement
    Marcel Duchamp

▷ TRANSLATION: *10th May. Received Corps et Biens and I'm going to read it on the boat. I enjoyed the Rrose Sélavy's just as much as years ago. Many thanks. I'm leaving Thursday or Friday 15th from Marseilles. I change ships in Casablanca and hope to arrive in New York around 20th June. So long then and very affectionately, Marcel Duchamp.*

14 May 1942
Almost exactly two years after having left Paris,
Duchamp finally departs for the United States.
A ship from Marseilles takes him to Casablanca,
where he will remain for nineteen days before
finally boarding the "Sera Pinto",
a Portuguese ship headed for New York.

move to USA: New York, 210 W 14 St | 1942-1946 chapter 9

lives in New York: staying at Robert Parker's, at Peggy Guggenheim's, and at the Kieslers'
moves within New York into 210 West 14th Street, 4th and top floor | from 2 Oct 1943
aboard ship for France, on the S.S. "Brazil" | 1 May 1946
lives in Paris, again returning to 11 rue Larrey | from 9 May 1946
trips to Bern, Chexbres, Lausanne, Chardonne, Zurich, with Mary Reynolds

from 25 June 1942 to 13 January 1947

▶ MAJOR WORKS

In the Manner of Delvaux (collage of tinfoil and
   photograph on cardboard, 1942)
Duchamp's "Compensation Portrait"
   (photograph by Ben Shahn, circa 1935-41,
   exhibited 1942)
Cover for "First Papers of Surrealism"
   (exhibition catalog, 14 Oct - 7 Nov 1942)
Sixteen Miles of String (installation for "First
   Papers of Surrealism," 14 Oct - 7 Nov
   1942)
*Window installation publicizing "La Part du
   Diable"* (by Denis de Rougemont at
   Brentano's, Fifth Avenue, New York; Jan
   1943
Allégorie de genre / George Washington
   (assemblage, 1943)
Cover for "VVV Almanac for 1943" (New York;
   No.2-3, Mar 1943)

Pocket Chess Set (leather pocket chessboard,
   celluloid, pins; 1943)
Pocket Chess Set with Rubber Glove
   (assemblage, Dec 1944)
Cover for "View" (MD number, Mar 1945,
   New York)
Duchamp at the Age of Eighty-five (anonymous
   photograph selected by Duchamp, 1945)
*Window installation publicizing "Arcane 17" by
   André Breton* (Gotham Book Mart, NY,
   19-26 Apr 1945)
*Window installation publicizing "Le Surréalisme
   et la peinture" by André Breton* (Brentano's
   bookstore, NY, autumn 1945)
Pipe for Donati (carved wooden pipe with
   standard mouthpiece, 1946)
Paysage fautif / Wayward Landscape (Seminal
   fluid on Astralon, 1946)
*Cover for "Young Cherry Trees Secured against
   Hares"* (book of poems by André Breton,
   1946)

► ONE MAN SHOWS or SEMI-ONE MAN SHOWS

Joseph Cornell, Marcel Duchamp, Laurence Vail, Art of this Century, New York. By MD: *Box-Valise*
— 30 Nov - December 1942

Through the Big End of the Opera Glass, Marcel Duchamp, Yves Tanguy, Joseph Cornell, Julien Levy Gallery, New York. By MD: *Box-Valise (No.X/XX)* — 7 Dec 1943

Duchamp, Duchamp-Villon, Villon, Yale University Art Gallery, New Haven, USA; By MD: *Three Stoppages Etalon*; *The Bachelors*; *Disturbed Balance [To Be Looked at...]*; *Revolving Glass Machine*; *Fresh Widow*; *Soins dentaires du Dr. Tzanck*; *Six Roto-reliefs*; *La Mariée mise à nu par ses célibataires, même (green box)*; *Valise*; *In advance of the Broken Arm*; *Pocket Chess Set* [not in catalog] — 1 Mar - 1 Apr 1945

Duchamp and Villon, College of William and Mary, Williamsburg, USA (Traveling exhibition to San Francisco, Meadville, St. Paul, Northfield, Orono) By MD: *The Bachelors*; *Six Roto-reliefs*; *In Advance of the Broken Arm*
— October - November 1945

Window of the bookshop La Hune, Paris. By MD: *Boîte-en-valise*; *Porte-Bouteilles*; *Rotoreliefs*; documents and photos — July 1946

► EXHIBITIONS

First Papers of Surrealism, exh. org. by André Breton and "his twine" Marcel Duchamp, Coordinating Council of French Relief Societies, 451 Madison Av., New York. By MD: *A la manière de Delvaux*; *Cimetière des Uniformes et Livrées*
— 14 Oct - 7 Nov 1942

Opening for the Benefit of the American Red Cross, Art of this Century, New York. By MD: *Sad young Man in a Train*; *Valise containing miniature reproductions of the complete works of Marcel Duchamp*
— 20 Oct 1942

Paintings, 15 Early, 15 Late, Art of this Century, New York. By MD: *Sad young Man in a Train*
— 13 Mar - 10 Apr 1943

Exhibition of Collage, Art of this Century, New York
— 16 Apr - 15 May 1943

Le Temps d'Apollinaire, Galerie Breteau, Paris. By MD: *La Partie d'Echecs* — 22 Dec 1943 - 31 Jan 1944

Abstract and Surrealist Art in the United States, Art Museum, Cincinnati, USA. Selection from MD's "Boîte-en-valise." Travels to Denver, Seattle, Santa Barbara, San Francisco — 8 Feb - 12 Mar 1944

Color and Space in Modern Art since 1900, Mortimer Brandt Gallery, New York. By MD: *Les Joueurs d'échecs*; *Le Passage de la Vierge à la Mariée*; *Boîte-en-valise* — 19 Feb - 18 Mar 1944

Art in Progress, a survey prepared for the Fifteenth Anniversary, The Museum of Modern Art, New York — 24 May - 15 Oct 1944

The Imagery of Chess, Julien Levy Gallery, New York. By MD: *Miniature Chess Board with rubber glove*
— 12 Dec 1944

Variety in Abstraction, The Arts Club, Chicago. By MD: *Drawing, 1911* — 5 - 30 Mar 1946

European Artists in America, Whitney Museum of American Art, New York. By MD: *Boîte-en-valise*; *Allégorie de genre* — 13 Mar - 11 Apr 1945

Eleven Europeans in America, The Museum of Modern Art, New York — Mar (?) 1946

Plastic Experience in the 20th Century. Contemporary Sculptures, Yale University Art Gallery, New Haven, USA — 4 Apr - 6 June 1946

Hommage à Antonin Artaud, Galerie Pierre, Paris. By MD: *poisson japonais* — 4 - 13 June 1946

1910-12, The Climactic Years of Cubism, Jacques Seligmann & Co., Inc., New York. By MD: *Nu descendant un escalier (for Carrie Stettheimer's doll's house)* — 16 Oct - 6 Nov 1946

25 June 1942
Duchamp arrives in New York and goes immediately
to the apartment of Robert Allerton Parker
and his wife Jessica Daves, where he remains for
about a month before moving into the townhouse of
Max Ernst and Peggy Guggenheim.
After settling in, he begins work on the assembly of
his *Box-in-a-Valise* [cat. 4], and writes to several
friends about finding clients to purchase them.

145. Marcel Duchamp to Man Ray
[early Fall 1942], New York

autograph letter
collection GRI

440 E 51

Cher Man Tu as gagné : tu m'as écrit avant que mon éberluement et ma paresse disparaissent.

Je t'avais écrit 2 ou 3 fois chez ta sœur à N.Y. il y a un an environ.

Je pense que tu n'as jamais rien reçu— de même que je n'ai rien reçu en France de toi. as tu écrit?—

Je ne crois pas que j'aille à Hollywood. Walter a dû t'expliquer   = Walter Arensberg

— D'un autre côté j'ai apporté du matériel pour faire 50 boîtes (tout est   *Box-in-a-Valise* [cat. 4]
fini sauf le montage et l'assemblage et la valise en cuir à faire) et je vais rester à N.Y. pour mettre en train la fabrication de ces 50 boîtes.— En fait 20 seront grand luxe avec un original et les 30 autres sans original.

Tu vois, comme les autres je viens te demander service. Crois tu pouvoir trouver un ou 2 (ou plus) acheteurs de cette boîte parmi tes amis— J'ai demandé la même chose à Walter.

Les prix approximatifs sont $200 pour les boîtes avec originaux et 100 pour les autres.

D'un autre côté si je les vends facilement (ce qui pourrait arriver) je voudrais ~~que~~ choisir parmi mes acheteurs et non pas promettre une boîte à n'importe qui—

Toi même, tu m'avais parlé de t'en garder une— Mais je ne sais pas si tu es en bon état financier?

La complication pour moi est que pour sortir même une dizaine de boîtes   *Box-in-a-Valise* [cat. 4]
il faut faire une dépense de plusieurs centaines de dollars, car si je n'achète pas tout le cuir (pour les 50) maintenant il est probable que je n'en trouverai plus dans 6 mois.

Anyway écris moi souvent quelques mots et peut être nous nous rencontrerons à Omaha

Affectueusement Marcel

Mary fait tout son possible pour venir ici.   **Mary** = Mary Reynolds

Mais il ~~est~~ lui est impossible de quitter Paris sans la permission des Allemands et son frère cherche à la faire échanger ~~pour~~ contre un diplomate allemand ici.__ Je n'ai d'ailleurs aucun détail.

Frank Brookes Hubachek, Mary Reynolds' brother, lawyer for household finance company, Chicago.

▷ TRANSLATION: *440 E 51. Dear Man, You win: you've written to me while I am still in a state of bewilderment and idleness. I did write to you 2 or 3 times at your sister's in N.Y. about a year ago. I don't think you ever got anything, the same as I never got anything in France from you. Did you write? I don't think I'll be going to Hollywood. Walter must have told you about it. On the other hand, I've brought enough material to make about 50 boxes (all finished except for mounting and assembling the leather suitcase, still to do) and I'm staying in N.Y. to get started on manufacturing these 50 boxes. In fact, 20 will be deluxe containing an original and the other 30 with no original. You see, like the rest, here I am asking you a favor. Do you think you could find one or 2 (or more) buyers for this box among your friends. I've asked the same thing of Walter. The price is approximately $200 for the boxes with originals and 100 for the others. On the one hand, if I can sell them easily (which could happen), I would like to choose between my buyers and not promise boxes to just anybody. You said you might like to keep one for yourself. But I don't know how your finances stand? The snag for me is that to produce just ten boxes, I have to spend several hundred dolllars, as if I don't buy all the leather (for the 50) now, it's likely I won't be able to find any more in 6 months' time. Anyway, write me often, just a line or two and maybe we'll meet up in Omaha. Affectionately, Marcel. Mary is doing everything she can to come over here. But it's impossible for her to leave Paris without authorization from the Germans and her brother is trying to have her exchanged for a German diplomat here. And in fact I know nothing more than that.*

---

146. Marcel Duchamp to Man Ray
[early October 1942], New York

autograph letter
collection GRI

MD rents a room in Frederick and Steffi Kiesler's penthouse apartment, 2 Oct 1942 - 1 Oct 1943.

N.Y. changement d'adresse 56 Seventh AVE. N.Y. City
   Cher Man
Merci de ta lettre à laquelle *je m'excuse* de mettre si longtemps à répondre.
Rien de bien nouveau ici. Je m'occupe du Surrealist Show qui n'aura rien de commun avec celui de Paris.
René me dit que tu as l'intention de venir à N.Y. ces temps ci.
Je ne connais pas bien Hollywood mais sauf *pour* ceux qui sont ~~oce~~ dans le cinéma la vie doit être assez monotone.
N.Y. a l'avantage d'être très varié on a un choix de milieux assez vaste; même le milieu de la tour d'ivoire que je crois le plus souhaitable.
   Enfin j'espère te voir bientôt
   Affectueusemt
   Marcel

"First Papers of Surrealism," Coordinating Council of French Relief Societies, Whitelaw Reid Mansion, NY, 14 Oct - 7 Nov 1942.

René = René Lefèbvre-Foinet.

▷ TRANSLATION: *N.Y. change of address: 56 Seventh Ave, N.Y. City. Dear Man, Thank you for your letter and sorry for taking so long to reply. Nothing much new here. I'm taking care of the Surrealist Show which will be nothing like the Paris one. René tells me you're planning on coming to N.Y. sometime soon. I don't know Hollywood very well, but, outside people in the movie business, life must be pretty monotonous. N.Y. has the advantage of being very varied, there's quite a wide choice of milieu—even the ivory tower set which I find the most desirable. Anyway hope to see you soon. Affectionately, Marcel.*

---

147. Marcel Duchamp to Alice Roullier   autograph letter
26 October 1942, New York   collection Newberry Library, Chicago

56 Seventh Avenue New York City
26 Octobre 42
    Chère Alice
Cette lettre me donne l'impression d'avoir été écrite il y a 3 mois, quand
    je suis arrivé—
Car je ne me crois pas capable d'un manque aussi simple d'effusion qu'une
    lettre quand on est sûr qu'elle arrivera à destination.—
Sans toute cette littérature, comment allez vous?— Madame Goodspeed
    m'a donné de vos nouvelles mais pas assez et j'aimerais que vous
    m'écriviez un mot sur ce que vous faites—
J'ai vu beaucoup Roché en zone inoccupée— il habite un village près de
    Montélimar et donne des leçons d'anglais et d'échecs aux enfants d'une
    école où son fils et sa femme habitent.— Sa maison à Bellevue a été
    pillée et il n'est pas rentré à Paris depuis 1940—
Moi même après avoir quitté Paris en Juin 41, j'ai passé 9 mois à Sanary
    entre Toulon et Marseille pour attendre mon visa américain—   14 rue Hallé, Paris,
Mary Reynolds entêtée comme un cheval n'a pas voulu quitter sa maison   where **Mary Reynolds**
    et son chat— Elle s'est enfin décidée il y a un mois et a passé la ligne   has been living since
    clandestinement— Elle est maintenant à Lyon où elle attend ses visas   1938.
    pour *aller* prendre le Clipper à Lisbonne.
Et maintenant pour finir un peu de business. J'ai apporté quelques
    nouvelles boîtes sur lesquelles je travaille depuis 1936 et qui
    représentent les reproductions de tout ce que j'ai fait dans ma vie— Il
    m'est difficile de faire l'article mais j'aimerais en vendre une ou deux à
    Chicago si vous trouviez les 2 acheteurs.— Il s'agit évidemment d'une
    grosse somme ($200⁻ par boîte) et l'édition est limitée à vingt boîtes.   *Box-in-a-Valise* [cat. 4]
    Ecrivez vite
    Affectueusement
    Marcel Duchamp

▷ TRANSLATION: *56 Seventh Avenue New York City, 26th October '42. Dear Alice, This letter feels like it was written 3 months ago when I first arrived, as I cannot think myself so dried up as to be incapable of writing a simple letter one knows is sure to reach its destination. So, without all this literature, how are you? Mrs Goodspeed gave me news of you but not enough and I would really like you to drop me a line and tell me what you are up to. I've seen a lot of Roché in the unoccupied zone. He's living in a village near Montélimar and giving English and chess lessons to children at a school where his wife and son are staying. His house in Bellevue was pillaged and he hasn't been back to Paris since 1940. After leaving Paris in June 41 myself, I have spent 9 months in Sanary, between Toulon and Marseilles, waiting for my American visa. Mary Reynolds, who's as stubborn as a mule, refused to leave her house and her cat. She finally made up her mind to go and crossed the line secretly a month ago. She's now in Lyons waiting for her visas so that she can take the Clipper from Lisbon. And now to finish a little business. I brought with me a few of the new boxes I've been working on since 1936 which contain reproductions of everything I've ever done in my life. It's difficult for me to sing my own praises but I would like to sell one or two of them in Chicago if you were to find the two buyers. It's a lot of money of course ($2,000 a box) and there's a limited series of twenty boxes. Hurry up and write. Affectionately, Marcel Duchamp.*

---

148. Marcel Duchamp to Alice Roullier
4 December 1942, New York

autograph letter
collection Newberry Library, Chicago

56 Seventh AVE.
N.Y. City
4 Dec. 42

Chère Alice, merci d'avoir si bien arrangé la présentation de la "boite"— Sidney Janis me dit que ce fut très réussi— Merci aussi pour le chèque et je finis hâtivement la valise que j'espère envoyer à Mrs. Paepcke dans le courant de la semaine prochaine.

L'édition de ces boites et est réduite à 20 exemplaires et j'en ai vendu 7 (tant en France qu'ici). Il en reste donc 13 et vous vous rendez compte qu'en ce moment surtout, cela ne se vend pas comme des petits pains.

Je n'attends malheureusement plus de nouvelles de France— j'essaierai d'écrire par la Suisse— mais peu d'espoir que cela arrive.

Madame Goodspeed m'a envoyé un petit mot très gentil; il est malheureusement difficile d'organiser un voyage à Chicago pour le moment— Mais l'occasion peut venir.

En tout cas si vous revenez à N.Y. tâchez qu'on se voie un peu plus longtemps.

Affectueusement chère Alice
Marcel Duchamp—
j'écris un petit mot à Mrs. Paepcke.

Sidney Janis (1897-1989), NY art dealer and writer, is to open a gallery E 57th St. 1948.

This *Box-in-a-Valise* [cat. 4] (No. VII/XX), dated "Dec. 1942," (today in Fine Arts Museums of San Francisco, Achenbach Foundation for Graphic Arts) is sold to **Elizabeth H. Paepke**, a painter in the Chicago area and wife of Walter Paepke, head of the American Container Corporation.

▷ TRANSLATION: *56 Seventh Ave. N.Y. City, 4th Dec. '42. Dear Alice, Thank you for having organized the presentation of the "box" so well. Sidney Janis told me it was a great success. Thanks also for the check and I'm rushing to finish the box-valise for Mrs Paepcke which I hope to send her in the course of the coming week. The series of these boxes is limited to 20 and I've sold 7 (as many in France as here). So there are 13 left and, as you can imagine, they're not exactly selling like hot cakes at the moment. I'm not expecting any more news from France, sadly. I'll try to write via Switzerland, but not much hope of anything getting through. Mrs Goodspeed sent me a very nice note. Unfortunately, it's difficult to organize a trip to Chicago at the moment, but there might be an opportunity one day. In any case, if you do come back to New York, try to make it so that we see each other for a bit longer. Affectionately, dear Alice, Marcel Duchamp. I'll drop Mrs Paepcke a line.*

---

149. Marcel Duchamp to Walter Pach   autograph letter
3 January 1943, New York   collection AAA

56 Seventh AVE. N.Y. City
3 Janvier 43

Chère Magda cher Walter— Je relis votre lettre du 30 Septembre à laquelle je dois répondre tous les jours depuis 3 mois.— Elle est tellement persuasive, si fortement pensée par vous que mon hésitation à répondre s'explique par l'indécision qu'elle a créée en moi.
Tout est tentant, Frida, Rivera, le Mexique, la vie comme je l'aime, les avantages matériels— et votre description de tout cela est un chef d'œuvre de diabolisme.

Malgré la tentation, j'ai décidé de ne pas bouger, la raison principale étant que j'obtiendrais très difficilement un visa de rentrée aux U.S.A. (car je ne suis que visiteur temporaire) et je ne peux pas risquer de me trouver l'éternel touriste dans ce beau pays— D'autant plus que je n'ai pas encore amassé le minimum même pour 3 mois de vie là-bas.—

J'habite dans la maison des Kiesler 56 Seventh AVE. (entre 14th et 13th Streets)— ils m'ont sous loué une grande chambre qui ressemble à un atelier, avec bain et entrée privée— au 20me étage, vue superbe, je me trouve très bien.

J'ai fait quelques valises (vous en aviez je parlé?)— Ce sont des boîtes-monographies représentant les 69 choses que j'ai faites dans ma vie (à peu près complet)— j'en ai vendu assez pour vivre jusqu'à présent.— je me suis occupé d'un surrealist show avec Schiaparelli et Breton au mois d'octobre— Peggy a ouvert sa galerie qui est un gros succès d'architecture intérieure (Kiesler fecit) et la Collection fait très bien dans ce cadre.

Enfin reçu de très bonnes nouvelles de Mary Reynolds— il y a 10 jours elle est arrivée à Madrid (comment??) et a cablé à son frère— Hier j'ai reçu

Frida Kahlo (1907-1954), and **Diego Rivera** (1886-1957), both painters.

Box-in-a-Valise [cat. 4]

"First Papers of Surrealism," see p.230.

Elsa Schiaparelli (1890-1973), famous French fashion designer, creating rather outrageous clothing.

Peggy Guggenheim's gallery "Art of the Century," designed by Frederick Kiesler, opened with a Surrealists group show, 20 Oct 1942.

un cable d'elle de Lisbonne où elle espère prendre un Clipper le
6 Janvier. Elle sera donc ici dans quelques jours si tout se passe
normalement— vous ne savez peut être pas qu'elle avait enfin quitté
Paris pour Lyon (comment??) le 15 Sept. et n'avait pu obtenir son visa
de sortie de France avant que les Allemands n'envahissent la zone libre =
je la croyais donc coincée et je craignais le camp de concentration (car
Américains et <u>Américaines</u> y sont tous maintenant)— Elle aura
quelques histoires à nous raconter!

Embrassez Frida pour moi et dites lui que si je vois la possibilité d'aller
faire un tour au Mexique je sauterai dessus— Faites bien mes amitiés à
Rivera— et si vous voyez les Paalen, Péret dites leur bien des choses—
Pour vous deux mon affectueux souvenir— Quand rentrez vous?

Affectueusement et happy New Year

Marcel

Wolfgang Paalen
(1905-1959), Austrian
Surrealist painter who
settled in Paris in the
1930's. With Breton
and César Moro, he
organized Surrealist
exh. in Mexico City
(Jan-Feb 1940).

Benjamin Péret
(1899-1959), French
poet of radical political
persuasion, lives
in Mexico during
World War II.

▷ TRANSLATION: *56 Seventh Ave. N.Y. City. 3rd January '43. Dear Magda, dear
Walter, I am just re-reading your letter of 30th September to which I've been meaning to reply every day for the last three months. It is so persuasive, so cleverly thought
out on your part that my hesitation in replying can only be explained by the inde-
cisiveness it stirred up in me. It's all so tempting, Frida, Rivera, Mexico, the kind
of lifestyle I like, material comforts, and the way you describe it all is the devil's own
work. In spite of such great temptation, I have decided to stay put, the main reason
being that it would be very difficult for me to get a return visa to the U.S.A. (as I
am only a temporary visitor) and I cannot afford the risk of ending up a perpetual
tourist in this beautiful country. Especially as I haven't even got together the minimum for spending three months there. I'm living at the Kieslers' house, 56 Seventh
Ave. (between 14th and 13th Street) They've sublet a large room to me which looks
like a studio, with bath and private entrance, on the 20th floor, superb view, very
good for me. I've made a few suitcases (did I already talk to you about that?) They
are boxed monographs representing the 69 things I have made in my life (that
about does it) I have sold enough of them to make a living so far. I took care of a
Surrealist show with Schiaparelli and Breton in the month of October. Peggy
opened her gallery and it's a huge success in interior design (Kiesler's touch) and
the Collection looks very good in the setting. Finally, had some very good news from
Mary Reynolds. She arrived in Madrid 10 days ago (what??) and wired her brother. Yesterday I got a cable from her in Lisbon and she's hoping to take a Clipper
from there on 6th January. So she will be here in a few days, if all goes according
to plan. You may not know that she finally left Paris for Lyons (what??) on 15th
Sept. and was unable to get her exit visa from France before the Germans invaded
the free zone = I thought she was trapped and feared her in a concentration camp
(for American men and women are all there now). She'll have some stories to tell!!
Give Frida my love and tell her that if I get the chance to go to Mexico, I'll jump at
it. Give my best wishes to Rivera and if you see the Paalens/Pérets give them my*

regards. Thinking of you both very affectionately. When are you coming back? Affectionately and happy new year, Marcel.

---

150. Marcel Duchamp to Man Ray   autograph letter
19 April 1943, New York   collection GRI

---

56 Seventh AVE. N.Y

19 Avril 43

    Cher Man

Je regarde ta lettre datée du 16 Février— et je n'ai aucune excuse pour
avoir tant tardé à te répondre.

Mary est arrivée par le Clipper vers le 8 Janvier et s'est installée dans un   **Mary** = Mary Reynolds
petit appartement 28 West 11th Street N.Y. où elle sera enchantée de
recevoir de tes nouvelles.

Nous avons à peu près la même vie qu'à Paris (avant 39) et j'essaie de voir
le moins de monde possible, ce qui est difficile!

J'ai fait et vendu quelques boîtes 4 ou 5 mais je sens que cela ne suffira pas   *Box-in-a-Valise* [cat. 4]
à me faire vivre—

Ce qui est vrai des boîtes serait vrai des tableaux si j'en faisais; personne
n'achète et tout le monde veut me faire croire que je pourrais vivre de
ma peinture.— Quel racket!

J'arrive à vivre comparativement à bon marché— et c'est là tout mon idéal.   Man Ray designs and
Naturellement je veux bien échanger une boîte contre un jeu d'échecs— Il   issues several limited
est possible qu'en le montrant à quelques gens je t'en vende.—   edition chess sets while
   in Hollywood.

Je te demande seulement un délai pour t'envoyer la boîte car je n'en ai
aucune faite d'avance et je les monte toutes moi même.— Où est   In 1942, Man Ray
l'artisanat de Paris??   rendered the images in
   his ***Revolving Doors***
J'attends aussi la photo des Revolving Doors.   series 1916-1917 as
Vu René Lefebvre qui m'a donné des nouvelles fraiches de Hollywood.   a series of 10 large
   canvases.
Vois tu beaucoup Walter et Lou fais leur mes amitiés naturellement.   **Walter** and **Lou**[ise]
Viendras tu à N.Y. un de ces jours? Ecris de temps en temps.   Arensberg

    peut être à bientôt

    Affectueusement

    Marcel

▷ TRANSLATION: *56 Seventh Ave. N.Y. 19 April '43. Dear Man, I have your letter in front of me dated 16th February and have no excuse for taking so long to reply. Mary arrived on the Clipper around 8th January and has moved into a small apartment 28 West 11th Street N.Y. and will be pleased to receive correspondence from you there. We lead more or less the same life as in Paris (before '39) and I try to see as few people as possible, which is difficult! I've made and sold a few boxes, 4 or 5, but I have a feeling that won't be enough to live on. What's true of the boxes*

would also be true of painting if I did any—nobody buys and everybody would have
me believe I could live off my painting. What a racket! I'm managing to live rela-
tively cheaply and that's my main priority. Of course I'd be happy to swap a box
for a chess set. I might well be able to sell some for you if I showed it to one or two
people. I just need a little time to send you the box as I don't have any made in ad-
vance and I make them all up myself. Whatever happened to the craftsmanship of
Paris?? I'm also waiting for the photo of the Revolving Doors. *Saw René Lefebvre*
who brought me recent news from Hollywood. Do you see much of Walter and Lou?
Give them my regards of course. Are you ever going to come to New York at all?
Drop me a line from time to time. See you soon perhaps. Affectionately, Marcel.

---

151. Marcel Duchamp to Man Ray   autograph letter
20 July 1943, New York   collection GRI

56 Seventh AVE.

20 Juillet 43

    Cher Man j'ai voulu finir ta boîte avant de te remercier pour le jeu   *Box-in-a-Valise* [cat. 4]
d'échecs et je sais que Mary t'a écrit et parlé du jeu en question. Il est   **Mary** = Mary Reynolds
très beau comme le premier et je cherche une occasion d'en parler à
Marshall qui malheureusement joue beaucoup plus au bridge qu'aux   **Frank J. Marshall,**
échecs.   see p.92.

J'en ai parlé à Julien qui éventuellement pourrait l'exposer l'hiver   **Julien** = Julien Levy
  prochain.

Maintenant ta boîte partira dans une semaine environ, c'est sûr.

Ton idée de la boutique m'intéresse beaucoup. La seule condition possible
  est que la boutique ne soit pas une boutique autrement q dit que tu
  vendes <u>chez toi</u> ces objets sans avoir à payer de loyer spécial = Il suffirait
  de trouver une forme de publicité adéquate pour attirer la clientèle.

Arrives tu à une décision sur ton retour à N.Y.?   A Man Ray solarization

Ici rien de nouveau qu'un été chaud. J'ai vu ta couverture pour View que   appears as the cover of
  j'ai beaucoup aimée.   June 1943 issue of *View*.

Je fais un petit film 16^{mm} en couleur de mes disques Rotorelief— j'ai   *Rotoreliefs* [cat. 53]
  emprunté une Bell and Howell— je pense faire 3 copies et par la suite
  si je peux commercialiser l'idée faire faire un technicolor en 35^{mm}

A bientôt cher Man écris et je tâcherai d'être moins paresseux—
    Affectueusement Marcel

▷ TRANSLATION: *56 Seventh Ave. 20th July '43. Dear Man, I wanted to finish your*
box before thanking you for the chess set and I know Mary has written to you and
spoken to you about the set in question. It's very fine just like the first one and I'm
waiting for an opportunity to talk to Marshall about it, though unfortunately he
plays more bridge than chess. I spoke to Julien who could possibly exhibit it next
winter. Your box will leave in about a week now, for sure. I'm very keen on your

idea of a store. But on one condition—that the store shouldn't be a store, in other words you should sell these things at home without having to pay any extra rent = it's just a matter of finding the right kind of publicity to attract customers. Have you come to a decision about your return to N.Y.? Nothing new here apart from a hot summer. I saw your cover for View *and liked it very much. I'm making a short film, 16 mm, in color, about my Rotorelief disks. I've borrowed a Bell and Howell. I plan to make 3 copies and then, if I can market the idea, have a technicolor version made in 35 mm. So long, dear Man, write me and I will try not to be so lazy. Affectionately, Marcel.*

---

152. Marcel Duchamp to Man Ray
[November 1943], New York

autograph letter
collection GRI

In October, MD moves into a studio on 14th Street and 7th Avenue which he is to rent for the next 23 years.

> 210 West 14ᵗʰ St. ⟵
> *Note ma nouvelle adresse.*
> Cher Man
> Mary me dit que tu as été invité ~~by~~ par Norlyst Gallery— Jimmy Ernst fait un gros effort pour faire valoir une formule à lui dans le picture business— Vendre à bas prix dans le voisinage de la 57ᵗʰ Street.— Sa galerie est très bien placée et très appréciée par le petit collectionneur La formule est très sympathique et je trouve que tu devrais accepter l'offre en question— Tache d'arranger l'exposition pour avoir une grande gamme de prix (très bas et très hauts)
> je passe la parole à Mary
> Mon nouvel atelier est un peu comme Paris, et je l'arrange à ma façon—
> Affectueusement Marcel

Mary = Mary Reynolds

Jimmy Ernst (1920-1984), painter and Max Ernst's son. In 1943, he opens the Norlyst Gallery, W 56th St., with girlfriend Eleanor Lust.

[allograph writing (Mary Reynolds):]

> So nice to hear from you. It would seem very strange for Picasso to get to London — Picasso Picabia? Don't worry about coming out better than others. Think what you can do for the others. We are here for better or for worse — in N.Y. I mean — but I try all the time to escape. Not so Marcel who feels sentenced for life. You sound a little bit like coming here. Hope you have a show — it will be a way to see you in spirit — and perhaps in person— Love
> Mary

▷ TRANSLATION: *210 West 14th St. NB my new address. Dear Man, Mary tells me you've been invited by the Norlyst Gallery. Jimmy Ernst is trying very hard to have a scheme of his accepted in the* picture *business—selling things cheap around 57th Street. His gallery is in a very good location and very popular with the small collector. It's a very nice scheme and I think you should accept the offer in question. Try to fix things so that you have a wide range of prices at the exhibition (very high and very low). I'll hand you over to Mary. My new studio is a bit like Paris and I'm fixing it up the way I like it. Affectionately, Marcel.*

153. Marcel Duchamp to Carrie and Ettie Stettheimer   autograph letter
18 May 1944, New York   collection YCAL

210 West 14th Street.—
New York City
18 Mai 1944

    Chère Carrie chère Ettie

Je n'ai appris que ce matin le décès de Florine : je m'excuse donc de venir
si tard vous témoigner mes sentiments de profonde sympathie en ces
jours douloureux.

Vous savez quelle admiration j'ai pour sa peinture et son attitude en
général pour comprendre à quel point j'ai été frappé par la triste
nouvelle.

Je savais qu'elle avait été très malade l'année dernière mais je n'avais pas
eu de récentes nouvelles d'elle— Virgil, il y a 2 mois déjà, ne semblait
pas alarmé par son état de santé.

Puis je faire quelque chose dans le domaine de la peinture qui corresponde
à ses dernières volontés?

Vous seriez très gentilles toutes les deux de me dire quand je peux venir
vous voir—

Je n'ai pas de téléphone mais une carte postale me dira quand vous préférez
que je vienne.

    Affectueusement à toutes deux
    Marcel Duchamp

Florine Stettheimer
died 11 May 1944.

Virgil Thomson (1896-
1989), vanguard
composer, good friend
of the Stettheimers'.

▷ TRANSLATION: *210 West 14th Street. New York City. 18th May 1944. Dear Carrie,
dear Ettie. I only heard this morning about Florine's death: I am so sorry to be so
late in expressing my deepest sympathy at this painful time. You know how much
I admire her painting and her attitude in general to understand what a blow this
sad news is to me. I knew she had been very ill last year but had no recent news from
her. Virgil, 2 months ago now, didn't seem alarmed by the state of her health. Is
there anything in the field of painting I could do that would correspond to her last
wishes? I would be grateful to you both if you would let me know when I can come
and see you. I don't have a telephone but a postcard would do to say when it would
be convenient for me to come. Affectionately to you both, Marcel Duchamp.*

154. Marcel Duchamp to Man Ray   autograph letter
23 July 1944, New York   collection GRI

> 210 West 14th St
> N.Y. City
> 23 Juillet 44
>   Cher Man
> quoiqu'inexcusable j'ai essayé de te faire transmettre par Heythum ma
>   paralysie écritoire comme explication à mon long silence :
> Nous avons passé Mary et moi d'excellents moments avec les Heythums
>   et je comprends votre amitié.
> J'arrive à vivre un peu comme à Paris, sans téléphone sans cocktails un peu
>   en ours— mais c'est la seule façon de résoudre la question sociale.
> Tu as reçu l'échiquier de poche? j'en fabrique (moi même) une
>   cinquantaine et le marché américain sera épuisé— il y a trop de main
>   d'œuvre pour vouloir se lancer dans une production importante.
> et les joueurs d'échecs ne veulent pas payer de gros prix pour un échiquier
>   de poche—
> A part cela je me suis remis à l'étude des échecs (pas très sérieusement).
> Koltanowski et moi avons un petit bureau down town où il reçoit sa
>   correspondance et il joue en ce moment une cinquantaine de parties
> Si cela t'amuse de jouer 6 parties avec lui par correspondance écris moi—
>   ou envoie les 6 coups sur une seule carte postale— cela va assez vite.
>   (3 Blancs 3 Noirs).
> Julien Levy s'est mis aux échecs sérieusement et nous jouons de temps de
>   en temps.
> Mary va bien— elle cherche la par tous les moyens à être envoyée en
>   Europe— Elle réussira, car elle est entêtée—
>   Ecris bientôt cher Man et affections de nous deux.
>   Marcel.

Mary = Mary Reynolds

Antonín Heythum
(1901-1954), Czech
stage designer, director
of the Art and
Technology Program,
California Institute of
Arts.

Pocket Chess Set
[cat. 60]

George Koltanowski
(b.1903), world
champion of blindfold
chess.

▷ TRANSLATION: *210 West 14th St. N.Y. City. 23rd July '44. Dear Man, While there
is no excuse, I tried to have Heythum convey my writing paralysis to you as an explanation for my long silence. Mary and I had an excellent time with the Heythums
and can see why you are friends with them. I am managing to live more or less the
same way as in Paris, no telephone, no cocktail parties—a bit like a badger, but it's
the only way to solve the social problem. Did you get the pocket chess set? I'm making (myself) 50 or so of them and then the American market will be exhausted. too
much labor involved to want to launch a grand-scale production and chess players
don't want to pay huge prices for a pocket chess set. Apart from that, I've gone back
to studying chess (not very seriously). Koltanowski and I have a small office downtown where he receives his mail and is playing about 50 matches at the moment. If*

you would like to play half a dozen games with him by correspondence, write and tell me, or send him 6 moves on a single postcard, it's very quick. (3 White, 3 Black). Julien Levy has taken up chess seriously and we play from time to time. Mary is fine, she's trying every possible means of being sent to Europe. She'll succeed because she's headstrong. Write me soon dear Man and affections from us both. Marcel.

---

155. Marcel Duchamp to Man Ray   autograph letter
10 August 1944, New York   collection GRI

210 W 14.

10 Août 44

   Cher Man

Mary et moi avons été passer quelques jours dans les Catskills— et j'ai eu   **Catskill** Mountains,
ta lettre en rentrant.— merci pour le chèque.   NY State.

Je t'envoie par ce même courrier l'échiquier et une Reine rouge. Si tu en casses encore dis le moi, je peux te les remplacer facilement—

J'ai peur d'un trou plus grand qui augmenterait la fragilité— Peut être des têtes d'épingles plus fines mais ce n'est pas facile à trouver.

Je vais donner la partie surréaliste à Julien pour son exposition et je lui   **Julien** = Julien Levy
prêterai aussi ton grand échiquier en bois— je lui demanderai s'il   In the exhibition "The
préfère celui en argent et t'écrirai.   Imagery of Chess,"
    Julien Levy Gallery,
Je n'envoie que mon échiquier de poche à cette exposition.   12 Dec 1944 - 31 Jan
    1945, MD will show
Dis à Heythum toutes mes amitiés ainsi qu'à sa femme— j'ai commencé   *Chess Set with Rubber*
sa boîte.   *Glove* [cat. 61].

   Affectueusement   Antonín **Heythum**,
    see previous letter.
   Marcel
    Box-in-a-Valise [cat. 4]

▷ TRANSLATION: *210 W 14. 10th August '44. Dear Man, Mary and I have been to spend a few days in the Catskills and I got your letter when we got back. Thanks for the check. I'm sending you in the same mail a chess set and a red Queen. If you break any more let me know, I can replace them for you easily. What worries me is a bigger hole as it would make them more fragile. Maybe finer pinheads but they're not easy to find. I'm going to give the Surrealist part to Julien for his exhibition and I'll also lend him your wooden chess set. I'll ask him if he'd prefer the silver one and will write you. I'm only sending my pocket chess set to this exhibition. Give my regards to Heythum and also to his wife. I've made a start on his box. Affectionately, Marcel.*

156. Marcel Duchamp to Yvonne Chastel   autograph letter
21 September 1944, New York   collection GRI

210 West 14ᵗʰ Street
N.Y. City
21 Sept 44
    Chère Yvonne

Ta lettre que j'ai gardée précieusement est datée du 24 Nov. 43— Il me
faut presqu'un an pour te répondre— J'ai fait partir aujourd'hui les 2
derniers Nos. du VVV— Il n'y en a pas eu d'autres depuis un an—
D'ailleurs tu as dû les voir à Londres—

VVV, probably No. 2-3 (Mar 1943) and 4 (Feb 1944).

T'ai je dit que j'ai envoyé Peter chez une belle sœur de ma sœur Yvonne
qui a épousé un américain à Boston— je pense qu'ils l'ont très bien reçu
car ils m'en parlent toujours quand je les vois.

Peter = Peter Lyon, Yvonne Chastel's son.

Yvonne = Yvonne Duchamp, MD's sister, see p.133.

J'espère que tu n'es pas restée trop à Londres ces mois derniers— et que ta
ferme n'est pas au sud!

Rien ici que tu ne saches par les nombreux amis communs qui sont passés
par Londres.

Je n'ai pu pas vu les Arensbergs depuis mon arrivée ici il y a plus de 2 ans.
(je les ai vus en 1936) Ils restent en Californie et je ne peux pas me payer
le luxe du voyage— Evidemment ils n'ont plus vingt ans; et je crois que
Lou ainsi que Walter d'ailleurs sont souvent malades— Ils sont très
isolés et ne voient presque personne, sauf les étrangers qui demandent à
visiter leur collection.

Lou[ise] and **Walter** Arensberg

Evidemment après Paris, New York a été pour moi un paradis; mais la
bête humaine est si bête qu'on finit par ne plus voir le paradis.

Je n'ai aucune nouvelle de France et j'aimerais que tu me dises si tu en as
ou si tu connais des gens (soldats ou civils) qui pourraient transmettre
une lettre de moi à Villon si je te l'envoyais.

Donc sois gentille et réponds moi par retour du courrier afin que je
t'envoie un mot à transmettre aux Villons sur si c'est possible.— Les
lettres ne sont permises qu'entre Amérique et les départements du
Calvados et *de* la Manche.

Je me vois ici encore pour au moins un an— car même si la guerre se
termine demain; on ne laissera pas partir les gens facilement sans
compter les difficultés de trouver une place.—

    Les burlesques sont supprimés
    Bien affectueusement Marcel et amitiés à Mesens

E.L.T. Mesens (1903-1971) Belgian collage artist and poet.

Stella quand je l'ai vu il y a six mois m'a chargé de grandes amitiés pour toi
Man est au Hollywood mais ne fait pas de cinéma— Il peint beaucoup

▷ TRANSLATION: *210 West Street, N.Y. City, 21st Sept. '44, Dear Yvonne, Your letter, which I carefully hung on to, is dated 24th Nov. 43. It's taken me almost a year to reply to you. I sent off today the two latest issues of VVV. There haven't been any others for a year. What's more, you must have seen them in London. Did I tell you I sent Peter to one of my sister Yvonne's sisters-in-law who married an American in Boston? I think they must have looked after him very well because they always talk to me about him whenever I see them. I hope you didn't stay too long in London these past months—and that your farm is not in the south! Nothing here that you haven't already heard from the many mutual friends we have stopping by London. I haven't seen the Arensbergs since I got here over two years ago. (I saw them in 1936.) They're staying in California and I can't afford the luxury of the trip. Obviously they're not so young anymore and I think that Lou is often sick and Walter, too, for that matter. They are very cut off and hardly see a soul, except for strangers asking to see their collection. Obviously, after Paris, New York was a kind of paradise for me. But the human beast is such a dumb beast that he ends up being no longer able to see paradise. I have no news from France and would be glad if you could tell me whether you have or know anyone (soldiers or civilians) who could pass on a letter from me to Villon if I sent it to you. It would be really nice of you to reply by return so that I can send you a note to pass on to the Villons if that's possible. Letters are only permitted between America and the Calvados and Manche departments. I see myself staying here for at least one more year, for even if the war ends tomorrow, they won't let people leave just like that, not to mention the difficulties of finding a passage. The Burlesques got closed down. Very affectionately, Marcel. And best wishes to Mesens. Stella, when I saw him six months ago, asked me to pass on his very warm wishes to you. Man is in Hollywood but not making movies—painting a lot.*

---

157. Marcel Duchamp to Jean Crotti   postcard
24 September 1944, New York   collection AAA

DUCHAMP
210 West 14th St.
New York City
24 Sept 44

    La poste nous annonce qu'on peut vous écrire— Voici mon adresse et vite donnez des nouvelles— Nous avons été voir tous les films de la libération de Paris— Ç'a dû être quelque chose! Ici rien de bien important. La mort de Mondrian il y a 6 mois.— Mary est désolée d'avoir quitté Paris et ne peut pas arriver à trouver un joint pour repartir. Je ne pense pas que le retour se fera de sitôt.—

    Affectueusement à tous naturellement
    Marcel
210 W. 14.
j'ai vu ton frère, Jean, il y a 2 ans.

Piet Mondrian (1872-1944), died in NY, 1 Feb.

Mary = Mary Reynolds

Jean Crotti's brother, André, is a doctor in Columbus, Ohio.

▷ TRANSLATION: *DUCHAMP. 210 West 14th St., New York City, 24th Sept. '44. The Post Office has informed us we can now write to you. This is my address and please send news quickly. We've been to see all the films about the liberation of Paris. That must have been something! Nothing special here. Death of Mondrian 6 months ago. Mary is frantic about having left Paris and can't seem to find a scam to get back. I don't think the return journey is on the cards just yet. Affectionately to one and all naturally, Marcel. 210 W.14. Jean, I saw your brother 2 years ago.*

---

158. Marcel Duchamp to Jacques and Gabrielle Villon   autograph letter
15 December 1944, New York   Estate of Marcel Duchamp, Villiers-sous-Grez

210 West 14th street
15 Dec. 44.
New York City
    Chère Gaby cher Gaston
J'ai bien reçu votre carte du 3 oct., vers le 10 Nov. et entre temps je vous
    avais aussi envoyé une carte au commencement d'Oct. et une lettre par
    Londres un peu plus tard— j'ai aussi donné de mes nouvelles par le
    sergent américain des Crottis.
J'ai vu Pach qui m'a donné quelques détails de votre vie depuis mon départ
    (par la lettre que tu lui as écrite "à la manière" de Raymond Pach).
Tout cela d nous donne beaucoup d'espoir de vous retrouver bientôt dans
    une atmosphère respirable.
Raymond a dû vous donner un aperçu de la vie ici, qui n'a rien
    "d'intéressant"— Personnellement j'ai fait quelques couvertures pour
    des livres d'amis et des revues— j'ai aussi monté mes boîtes et en ai
    vendu une douzaine environ.
A part cela, j'ai mis au point un échiquier de poche avec des épingles qui
    accrochent les pièces de cellulo et les empêchent de tomber— Malgré
    tous ces avantages je n'ai pas réussi à en faire une bonne affaire.
Mary, comme déjà dit, cherche par tous les moyens à rentrer à Paris et
    jusqu'ici n'a pu être acceptée par aucune organisation civile ou
    militaire.— Au moment de la libération elle ne tenait plus en place;
    depuis et devant l'inévitable elle s'est un peu résignée mais fait encore
    des pieds et des mains—
René Lefebvre Foinet habite Hollywood et je ne le vois que rarement.—
    Il a une boutique là bas et voit souvent les English—
Breton, depuis son arrivée ici en 1941, parle à la radio; vous avez peut-être
    entendu sa voix; il continue plusieurs fois par jour.
Bea et Francis vont bien (ont reçu de vos nouvelles) Francis prêt à partir
    en France (comme reporter plus ou moins militarisé)— il semble qu'on
    en envoie moins.

Raymond, Walter Pach's son, aged 30.

Notably *First Papers of Surrealism* (1942), *VVV* (1943), *View* (1945), *Objects of My Affection* (1945); *Yves Tanguy*, Breton's book (1945)... *Box-in-a-Valise* [cat. 4]

Pocket Chess Set [cat. 60]

Mary = Mary Reynolds

"libération" = German garrison in Paris surrenders 25 Aug 1944.

"Bea et Francis" = Not Beatrice Wood and Francis Picabia

Pach, très bien, vous ont sans doute donné des nouvelles directes par
Raymond—

Dreier aussi habite New York cet hiver; elle souffre beaucoup des pieds
(sorte de rhumatismes) mais elle a gardé toute sa tête et vous [a] acheté
un sweater pour chacun de vous que j'espère vous envoyer bientôt.

Les paquets vont être autorisés d'ici quelques temps et je vous enverrai café
chocolat, riz cigarettes mais j'aimerais bien que vous me disiez ce que
vous préférez et ce qui vous manque le plus— (lainages etc,)— je me
propose de vous faire des envois réguliers (soit à vous soit aux Crottis)
que je vous demande de partager avec les sœurs aussi.

Mary naturellement pleure Miki mais vous remercie du fond du cœur de
l'avoir eu près de vous.

Peggy Guggenheim a ouvert son musée en 1942; elle fait aussi des
expositions courantes.

Naturellement dès que vous pourrez faire des envois on organisera
facilement une exposition de tes tableaux de guerre.

Man Ray, à Hollywood, ne vient jamais ici, il va bien par correspondance.

———

Il n'est pas question pour moi de rentrer; ne rentrent que les Français en
mission militaire— il faudra je crois attendre un an au moins—
Affectueusement de tous à tous deux Marcel

Miki = probably the name of Mary Reynolds' cat.

▷ TRANSLATION: *210 West 14th Street, 15th Dec. '44, New York City. Dear Gaby, dear Gaston, I received your card of 3rd Oct. around 10th Nov. and in the meantime I also sent you a card at the beginning of Oct. and a letter via London a little later. I also sent news with the Crotti's American sergeant. I saw Pach who told me a bit about your life since I left (through the letter you wrote to him "à la manière de Raymond Pach"). All of which gives me to hope I will soon be seeing you again in an atmosphere that is bearable. Raymond must have given you some idea of what life is like here, nothing "interesting" about it. As for me, I've done a few covers for friends' books and for reviews. I've also mounted my boxes and have sold about a dozen. Apart from that, I've finished a pocket chess set with pins hooking in the celluloid pieces to stop them falling off. In spite of all these good things, I have not managed to make a good business deal out of it. Mary, as I said before, is trying everything she can to get back to Paris and, so far, has not managed to get herself taken on by any civilian or military organization. During the liberation, she got very restless. Since then, and in the face of the inevitable, she's become a little more resigned, but she's still going all out for it. René Lefebvre Foinet is living in Hollywood and I only see him occasionally. He has a shop there and is often with Brits. Breton has been on the radio since he arrived here in 1941. You might have heard his voice—he's still doing it several times a day. Bea and Francis are well (received your news): Francis ready for going off to France (as some kind of military reporter)—it seems they're sending fewer. The Pachs, fine and have no doubt sent you news directly through Raymond. Dreier is also staying in New York this winter. She has a lot of trouble with her feet (some kind of rheumatism) but she still has all her faculties and has bought you all a sweater each which I hope to send you soon. Parcels are going to be authorized in a short while and I'll send you coffee, chocolate, rice, cigarettes but I'd like you to tell me what you would like most and what you most need (woolens etc.). I volunteer to send you regular parcels (either to you or to the Crottis) which I will ask you to share with the sisters also. Mary, naturally, is mourning Miki, but thanks you from the bottom of her heart for having taken care of him. Peggy Guggenheim opened her museum in 1942. She also holds contemporary exhibitions. Ship some things over as soon as you can, naturally, and we'll easily organize an exhibition of your wartime paintings. Man Ray, in Hollywood, never comes here, is fine in correspondence. It's out of the question for me to come back—only the French on military mission are allowed back. I'll have to wait a year, I think, at least. Affectionately from all to you both, Marcel.*

---

159. Marcel Duchamp to Henri-Pierre Roché   autograph letter
17 December 1944, New York   collection HRHRC

210 West 14th Street New York City. ◄—— *mon adresse*
17 Dec. 44
  Chère Denise, cher Pierre
Après ces 2 années de silence on peut enfin échanger quelques mots. Ta carte (chez Parker) m'a tranquillisé sur votre sort et il ne reste qu'à patienter pour que les conditions s'améliorent.
Ici c'est, comme prévu, une vie de grand luxe comparée à celle que j'ai quittée en France; il est d'ailleurs inutile et peu décent d'en parler : les quelques rationnements (sucre, viande rouge) ne jouent pas dans les restaurants où on mange sans tickets.
Les amis Tanguy, Léger, Seligmann, Ernst sont fidèles au poste et travaillent; mais il n'y a plus comme aux premiers jours de l'exil de fréquentes réunions d'âmes en peine.— Chacun s'est débrouillé de son côté.
Breton est le seul que je voie assez souvent. il a parlé depuis presque 3 ans et parle encore à la radio plusieurs fois par jour; vous avez sans doute entendu sa voix.
<u>Peggy</u> Guggenheim a ouvert son musée avec sa <u>collection 30 West 57th</u> st. et fait aussi des expositions courantes.
René Lefebvre est à Hollywood dans son magasin; il vient 2 ou 3 fois par an ici et je le vois chaque fois— il est resté adorable— Quand je suis arrivé et par son entremise Lieberfield m'a donné cinq cents dollars qui m'ont d'ailleurs servi à payer Alec en partie— Lieberfield allait bien quand je l'ai vu il y a plus d'<u>un an</u>.

Denise Renard
(b.1894 or 1895) met
H.-P. Roché 1929; they
will marry in 1948.

Robert Allerton Parker
(1888-1970), American
journalist, editor and
critic, interviewed MD
shortly after he arrived
in NY, 1915.

Yves Tanguy (1900-
1955), French Surrealist
painter, and **Fernand
Léger** (1881-1955),
French Cubist painter.

Kurt Seligmann (1900-
1962), Swiss Surrealist
painter living in NY.

La peinture se vend médiocrement__ je n'en fais toujours pas__ j'ai fait
quelques couvertures pour des livres d'amis et des magazines.__

Pocket Chess Set
[cat. 60]

J'ai aussi mis au point un échiquier de poche avec des têtes d'épingles qui
accrochent les pièces de cellulo et les empêchent de tomber__ mais la
main d'œuvre est trop chère et je ne continue pas sur le plan
commercial.__ je t'en réserve un que je t'enverrai dès qu'on pourra
envoyer des paquets. Dis moi à ce sujet ce qui vous manque le plus__
j'espère pouvoir ~~fai~~ vous faire des envois réguliers bientôt.

Wols (1913-1951),
German painter and
photographer, friend of
H.-P. Roché's.

— Il y a eu une expo. Wols. dans une petite galerie l'année dernière mais ~~que~~
je crains que le résultat n'ait été médiocre.

— Mary va bien; elle ne tient plus en place et veut rentrer en France__ Mais,

Mary = Mary Reynolds

sauf aux militarisés, le gouvernement ne donne pas de passeports; même
moi ne pourrais pas rentrer comme Français; je n'ai pas d'ailleurs très
envie.

Pas vu les <u>Arensbergs</u> qui restent en Californie; ils ont donné leur
collection à l'<u>Université de Californie</u> (section Los Angeles)__

The "Deed of Gift" is
later nullified and the
collection given to PMA.

Miss Dreier va bien, habite N.Y. l'hiver et me charge d'amitiés pour vous.

Si tu sais quelque chose sur Alec__ dis moi ce qui est arrivé, quand a t il
été emmené par les Allemands et où a t il été pris__ où est la famille? sa
femme, sœur, son père?

Je t'écrirai encore bientôt mais j'aimerais répondre à tes questions (ce que
tu veux savoir)

J'attends donc ta lettre.__ je te cable en même temps que cette lettre pour
que tu n'attendes pas trop longtemps

très affectueusement à tous trois

Marcel

▷ TRANSLATION: *210 West 14th Street New York City: my address. 17th Dec. '44. Dear
Denise, dear Pierre. After these two years of silence we can finally exchange a few
words. Your card (at Parker's) reassured me as to your fate and the only thing to
do is to wait for things to improve. Here, as expected, living in the lap of luxury
compared to the life I left behind in France. Moreover it's pointless and somewhat
indecent to talk about it: rationing only on a few items (sugar, red meat) and
doesn't apply in restaurants where you don't need a ticket to eat. Our friends
Tanguy, Léger, Seligmann, Ernst all present and correct and working, but the frequent gatherings of troubled souls no longer take place like in the first days of exile.
Each one's doing his own thing. Breton is the only one I see regularly. He has been
talking for almost 3 years and still talks on the radio several times a day; you must
have heard his voice. Peggy Guggenheim has opened her museum with her collection 30 West 57th St. and also has other exhibitions running. René Lefebvre is in
Hollywood in his shop. He comes 2 or 3 times a year here and I see him each time.
he is still adorable. When I arrived, and through his doing, Lieberfield gave me five
hundred dollars which in fact meant I could pay Alec in part. Lieberfield was well*

when I last saw him more than a year ago. Painting sales are mediocre. I'm still not doing any. I did a few covers for friends' books and for magazines. I've now perfected a pocket chess set with needle heads hooking onto the celluloid pieces to stop them falling off, but labour costs are too high and I'm not going ahead with it commercially. I'll keep one for you and send it to you as soon as we are allowed to send parcels. Tell me, on this note, what you need most. I hope to be able to send you things on a regular basis soon. There was a Wols exhibition at a small gallery last year but I'm afraid it turned out to be rather mediocre. Mary is fine: she can't settle and wants to go back to France but, apart from the military, the government is not giving out any passports. Even I, as a Frenchman, can't go back—I don't feel much like it either. Not seen the Arensbergs who are staying in California. They've given their collection to the University of California (Los Angeles section). Miss Dreier is well, spends the winter in N.Y. and asks me to pass on her best wishes to you. If you know anything about Alec, let me know what happened: When was he taken by the Germans and where was he picked up? Where is the family? his wife, sister, father? I will write again soon but would like to answer your questions (what you want to know). So I'll wait for your letter. I'll wire you at the same time as sending this letter so you won't have to wait too long. Very affectionately to all three, Marcel.

---

160. Marcel Duchamp to Man Ray   autograph letter
24 December 1944, New York   collection GRI

210 West 14th St.
N.Y.
24 Dec. 44
    Cher Man je ne sais pas si je te dois une lettre— En tout cas Christmas est une bonne occasion pour écrire—
De plus View prépare un "Duchamp number" et je voudrais bien avoir ta collaboration.— Peux tu envoyer les documents (photographiques et autres) qui rappellent ~~nous~~ nos relations de 30 ans et que tu as pu rapporter de France.

As tu, par exemple, une photo de ton portrait de Rrose Sélavy?
De plus Charles Ford aimerait que tu composes une longue "caption" pour whatever document tu as sous la main— ou bien une courte note de 500 mots environ sur ce qui te passera par la tête à mon sujet.

En un mot ta collaboration est vivement souhaitée et rapidement car Ford voudrait faire son dummy dans les tout premiers jours de Janvier.
Si tu veux quelques jours de réflexion veux tu avoir la gentillesse de m'écrire par retour du courrier si tu prépares quelque chose et quand tu penses pouvoir l'envoyer.

Le n° contiendra la réimpression en anglais d'articles du Minotaure et de Cahiers d'Art— Soby, Julien Levy, Calas, Janis écrivent aussi quelque chose.— Je fais la couverture du N°

View, series V, No. 1 (March 1945).

Charles Henri Ford (b.1910), editor of *View*. Man Ray to write "Bilingual Biography," pp.32, 51.

James Thrall Soby (1906-1979), then Director of Paintings and Sculpture at the MoMA, NY.

Nicolas Calas (1907-1989), pseudonym of Nikos Kalamares, Greek-born American art historian.

Redouble mes excuses auprès de Heythum— j'ai à moitié fini sa boite et dernièrement j'ai été pris par d'autres choses— de sorte que je remets constamment la livraison de sa boîte.

L'exposition échecs chez Julien est très amusante—

Nous allons avoir une séance de simultanées à l'aveugle par Koltanowski le 6 Janvier.— Dommage que tu ne sois pas là pour tenir un échiquier

A bientôt de tes nouvelles cher Man et affectueusement de Mary et de Marcel

Box-in-a-Valise [cat. 4]
Antonín **Heythum**, see p.239.

"The Imagery of Chess," see p.240.

George **Koltanowski**, see p.239.

▷ TRANSLATION: *210 West 14th St. N.Y. 24th Dec. '44. Dear Man I don't know whether I owe you a letter. In any case Christmas is always a good time to write. What's more View is preparing a "Duchamp number" and I would like to have your collaboration. Can you send any documents (photographic or other) retracing our relationship over the last thirty years that you managed to bring back from France? For example, do you have a photo of your portrait of Rrose Sélavy? What's more Charles Ford would like you to write a long "caption" for whatever document you have to hand, or a short blurb of about 500 words on whatever comes to mind about me. In a word, your collaboration would be very much appreciated and the sooner the better as Ford wants to make his dummy right at the start of January. If you want to think it over for a few days, would you be kind enough to reply to me by return and tell me whether you are going to do something and when you think you'll be able to send it? The issue will contain a reprint in English of articles in the Minotaure and Cahiers d'Art. Soby, Julien Levy, Calas, Janis are all writing something too. I'm doing the cover for the issue. Please make my apologies to Heythum once more. I'm halfway to finishing his box and lately I've been very taken up with other things so that I keep on putting off delivering his box. The chess exhibition at Julien's is great fun. We're going to watch Koltanowski play a session of blind games in parallel 6th January. Pity you won't be there to hold a chess set. Hear from you soon, dear Man, and affectionately from Mary and Marcel.*

---

161. Marcel Duchamp to Elisa and André Breton   autograph letter
2 July 1945, New York   source: from Y. Poupard-Lieussou transcript

210 West 14th Street

2 Juillet 45

    Cher Elisa cher André

Vu ce matin Taenger : la couverture en effet est un peu sévère.

Une vraie reliure à cartons épais recouverts d'une toile vert demi foncé et c'est tout—

Je propose de faire quelque chose d'analogue àau livre de Tanguy c-à d : garder cette reliure et

— Prendre les pieds nus chaussures de Magritte

Elisa Breton, née Claro, third wife of André Breton. They met Dec 1943 and will marry 31 July 1945.

Proposed cover for an American edition of Breton's book *Le Surréalisme et la peinture* (Brentano's, NY, 1945).

André Breton's book, ***Yves Tanguy*** (Pierre Matisse Gallery, 1946), designed by MD.

— En faire une impression sanguine au lieu de noire sur papier rose au besoin (ou simplement blanc).

Cette reproduction soignée serait estampée au milieu du ex du plat et aussi estampés votre nom, le titre du livre (sans "suivi de…") et Brentano en bas.

C'est une "suggestion"—

Ayez la bonté de me répondre par avion par retour du courrier : si vous préférez autre chose que le Magritte; si vous voyez la chose différemment en un mot votre décision

Tenger semble pressé!! *Je le vois Lundi avec votre réponse.*

Tout va bien ici même la chaleur

Affectueusement Marcel

Le modèle rouge, 1935, **René Magritte**, finally reproduced on the cover.

▷ TRANSLATION: *210 West 14th Street, 2nd July 1945. Dear Elisa, dear André, saw Tenger this morning. It's true, the cover is a bit severe. A bona fide thick cardboard binding covered in semi-dark green canvas and that's all. I suggest doing something similar to Tanguy's book, i.e. keeping this binding and taking Magritte's bare-feet-shoes, to make it look more sanguine instead of black on pink paper if needs be (or white simply). This carefully produced reproduction would be embossed in the center of the page and also embossed with your name, the title of the book (without "followed by…") and Brentano at the bottom. This is my "suggestion." Be good enough to reply by airmail and by return letting me know whether you prefer something other than the Magritte or whether you envisage things differently, in a word your decision. Tenger seems to be in a hurry!! I'm seeing him Monday with your reply. Everything fine here, even the heat. Affectionately, Marcel.*

---

162. Marcel Duchamp to Henri-Pierre Roché
21 August 1945, New York

autograph letter
collection HRHRC

210 West 14th St. N.Y. City 21 Aout 45

Chère Denise cher Pierre Je relis 3 cartes de toi et la longue lettre (Post Mortems) auxquelles je me reproche tous les jours de tant tarder à répondre—

Généralités— j'ai réussi à vivre ici presque comme à Paris càd. en évitant la vie publique (expositions, cocktails parties)— Malgré cela j'ai dû aider à la confection d'un N° de "View" que Mary a dû te montrer—

— Je vois souvent James Sweeney (oui, le même qui a déjeuné au Restaurant St Marcel), qui, lui aussi, va écrire une assez longue monographie sur moi— je lui raconte toute ma vie comme à un confesseur et il y a déjà 6 mois que cela dure à raison de 2 heures par semaine!!

Sweeney est maintenant à la place de Barr, directeur du Museum of Modern Art et s'occupe activement de l'affaire.— A ce propos il

View (special issue on MD), see p.247.

James Johnson Sweeney (1900-1986) replaced Alfred Barr Jr. in Jan 1945 as director of the Painting and Sculpture Dept., MoMA, NY. Later becomes director of the Guggenheim Museum.

voudrait que tu lui racontes, si tu la sais, l'histoire : comment le
Rousseau (Bohémienne endormie) *Marembert lettre*\\ est arrivé jusqu'à
la coll. Quinn (par tes soins) en partant de Laval (où parait il la toile
donnée par Rousseau avait été roulée et oubliée par le Conseil
Municipal de Laval)— En un mot il aurait besoin du pedigree de cette
toile qui maintenant appartient au Musée— Donne lui tous les détails :
la controverse à propos de l'authenticité etc—

— Sûrement il voudrait bien acheter Adam et Eve quand les conditions
monétaires seront plus stables.

— <u>Wols</u> Très heureux de le voir "sortir"— Kay Boyle et moi d'ailleurs
pensons qu'il est beaucoup mieux pour lui maintenant de ne pas venir
aux USA où il n'y a d'avantages que pour les noms déjà faits en Europe.

— <u>Alice Roullier</u>— pas vue depuis 1 an et ½ à N.Y.— Elle allait bien— Peut
être ta carte a été perdue (ou bien la sienne?)

— <u>Walter Brewster</u>— Connais pas sauf de nom, mais Alice saurait.

— Mon verre (le tien) Sweeney avait pensé l'acheter pour le musée— Ils n'ont
rien de moi et je m'amuse beaucoup à la pensée que tous ces gens ont
attendu si longtemps pour désirer, acheter quelque chose; évidemment
maintenant les prix ont changé.

— Oui je rentrerai au printemps 46— j'aime mieux rester égoïstement ici et
aussi envoyer des paquets— <u>dis moi ce qui vous manque le plus.</u>

— Non je ne sais rien au sujet du remariage d'Indore

— René Clair est à Paris; je l'ai vu à son passage ici par hasard dans un
restaurant.

— Je crois que la collection Walter n'est que léguée et qu'ils en ont toute la
jouissance de leur vivant.

— Si tu trouves un Wrong Wrong (pas un Blindman, il y en a un ici) Ça ferait
très plaisir à Sweeney pour son livre et si tu peux t'en séparer, fais le
envoyer par l'OWI à Paris (Mary se chargera de la démarche)

— Marie Sterner vivante— l'ai vue il y a 2 mois.

— Béa j'ai vue à son exposition de céramique il y a un an ici.

— De Journo rencontré dans un bus mais n'ai pas fait d'autre effort pour le
revoir— je regrette d'ailleurs— Le même, un plus gris de moustache.

— <u>Post Mortems.</u> Naturellement l'idée est excellente— L'éxécution en est
compliquée.

Je pourrais en parler à Sweeney et sans l'engager en quoi que ce soit je
pourrais avoir son avis sur l'éxécution.

Donc dis moi d'abord si tu es d'accord de lui en parler (ce serait
évidemment le Musée de Mod. *Art* qui ferait les frais d'édition)— je lui
communiquerais ton très clair essai sur la question.

Henri Rousseau, *The Sleeping Gypsy*, 1897 (gift of Mrs Simon Guggenheim, 1939, to MoMA, NY). Rousseau urged Mayor of Laval to buy it. He refused and it disappeared until 1923 when Roché saw it at Kahnweiler's gallery and brought it to the attention of John Quinn who acquired it Mar 1924.

Brancusi, *Adam and Eve*, 1916 - 1921 (Guggenheim Museum, NY).

Kay Boyle (1902-1992), novelist married to American Surrealist painter Laurence Vail.

Alice = Alice Roullier

9 Malic Moulds [cat. 31]

Maharajah of **Indore**, see p.305.

René Clair, pseudonym of René Chomette (1898-1980), French filmmaker, directed *Entr'acte*, 1924; MD played a minor role.

Rongwrong (p.50) and *The Blindman* (p.57) are two Dada reviews edited by MD, 1917.

Béa = Beatrice Wood, "Ceramics by Beatrice Wood of California," American House, NY, 20 Mar - 18 Apr 1944.

Fondation Post-Mortems = the name proposed by Roché for an organization to collect and preserve artists' journals.

Peut être un éditeur serait mieux mais comment s'assurer du secret et le
rendement serait à longue échéance pour l'éditeur

J'attends donc ta permission de communiquer ton essai à Sweeney et aussi
écris très vite la liste de choses que tu préfères d'abord.

La paix est vraiment très sensible ici___ C'était peut être l'indifférence pour
la "guerre en Chine" mais maintenant c'est vraiment un soulagement
sincère à la pensée de paix surtout agrémenté par les chatouillements de
la bombe atomique.

> Two **atomic bombs**
> have just been dropped
> on Hiroshima and
> Nagasaki in Aug 1945.

    Affectueusement à tous trois___ il faudra que je donne quelques
leçons d'échecs à Claude quand je rentrerai___

> **Jean-Claude** (b.1931),
> H.-P. Roché's son.

    Marcel Totor

▷ TRANSLATION: *210 West 14th St. N.Y. City 21st August '45. Dear Denise, dear
Pierre, Am just rereading three postcards you sent and your long letter (Post Mortems) and I reproach myself every single day for taking so long to reply. General information: I'm managing to live here almost the same way as in Paris i.e. avoiding
public life (exhibitions, cocktail parties), in spite of which, I did have to help with
the making of an issue of "View" which Mary must have shown you. I often see
James Sweeney (yes, the one who was at the lunch at the Restaurant St Marcel),
and he too is also going to write a fairly long monograph on me. I tell him my life
story like he was my confessor and this has been going on for 6 months now for
2 hours a week!! Sweeney has now replaced Barr as director of the Museum of Modern Art and is taking a very active role in the running of the thing. On this score,
he would like you to tell him something, if you can: how did the Rousseau (sleeping
Bohemian) \Marembert letter\ end up in the Quinn collection (thanks to you)
starting off in Laval (where it seems the canvas given by Rousseau had been rolled
up and forgotten about by the Laval town council)? In short, he needs the pedigree
if possible of this canvas which now belongs to the Museum. Let him have all the
details: the controversy surrounding its authenticity etc.. He's bound to want to buy
Adam and Eve as soon as the financial situation is more stable. Wols—very glad
to see him "out." Kay Boyle and I, what's more, think that it's actually much better
for him not to come to the USA which is only any good for those who have already
made a name for themselves in Europe. Alice Roullier—not seen for 1 year and a
½ in N.Y. She was well. Maybe your card got lost (or hers did?). Walter Brewster—
don't know him except by name, but Alice would know. My glass (yours)—
Sweeney was thinking of buying it for the museum. They don't have anything of
mine and I very much like the thought that it took these people so long to have the
urge to buy anything—obviously now the prices are not the same. Yes, I will come
back in spring '46. I prefer to stay selfishly here and send parcels. Tell me what you
need most. No, I don't know anything about Indore getting married again. René
Clair is in Paris—I ran into him by chance when he was passing through here in
a restaurant. I think that Walter's collection is only bequeathed and that they have
the benefit of it for as long as they live. If you find a Wrong Wrong (not a Blindman, there is one here already), Sweeney would really like to have it for his book*

and, if you can bear to part with it, have it sent to Paris by the OWI (Mary will make the necessary arrangements). Mary Sterner—alive, saw her 2 months ago. Béa I saw at her ceramics exhibition here a year ago. De Journo I met on a bus but made no subsequent effort to see him again—sorry I didn't actually. Same as ever, mustache a little grayer. Post Mortems. Of course the idea is excellent, its execution complicated. I could speak to Sweeney about it and, without him committing himself in any way, get him to give his opinion on the execution. So tell me first of all if you are happy for me to talk to him (obviously it would be the Museum of Mod. Art who would pay the publishing costs). I could pass on to him your very clear essay on the question. Perhaps a publisher would be better, but how can we rely on confidentiality when profit would only be long term for the publisher? I will wait for your permission to talk to Sweeney, therefore, and also first make a list of your preferences. You can really feel the peace here. People were perhaps indifferent to the "war in China" but now there really is sincere relief at the thought of peace and heightened by the titillating threat of the atomic bomb. Affectionately to all three of you. I'll have to give Claude a few chess lessons when I get back. Marcel Totor.

---

163. Marcel Duchamp to Tristan Tzara   autograph letter
2 or 3 January 1946, New York   collection BLJD

210 West 14th street
New York
2 ou 3 janvier 46
    Cher Tzara

M'enlisant de plus en plus dans un retard à te répondre, j'ai rencontré Maria Jolas qui me dit avoir répondu en grande partie à tes questions colis et la question des livres chez Brentano.__ Je pense d'ailleurs que maintenant d'autres libraires vont importer les livres dont tu parles :

— VVV a eu 3 numéros en 3 ans : tu les verras sûrement

— Connais *pas* Georges Lemaître : From Cubism…

— Art of this Century est le nom de la galerie de Peggy Guggenheim__ Tout ce qu'elle a fait paraître est le catalogue de sa collection avec biographie des artisstes.

— Henry Miller est probablement le seul qui t'intéresserait mais je n'ai ni vu ni lu ses livres.__ Redis moi si tu ne veux pas que je te les envoies.

— View : tu peux voir la collection chez Mary Reynolds 14 rue Hallé 14me Gob. 3337 Elle est rentrée à Paris depuis Mars dernier. En général la littérature critique est une répétition des lieux communs des 20 dernières années

— Comme tu l'imagines, j'ai continué ici ma vie de Sanary ne consentant à faire que quelques petites sorties d'expositions forcées. D'ailleurs le

Maria, wife of Eugène Jolas (1894-1952), editor of *Transition* magazine.

Georges Lemaître (1892-1972), French writer on literature and art.

Catalog appeared 1942.

Henry Miller (1891-1980), American novelist.

groupe des exilés, d'abord compact il y a 3 ans, s'est vite changé en un "chacun pour soi" avec brouilles et engueulades coutumières.

Léger, Masson sont rentrés—

Breton est parti pour Haïti (conférences) 3 mois et il pense repartir en France après être repassé par N.Y. en Avril.

— Max Ernst restera ici jusqu'à sa naturalisation américaine (l'an cette année)

— Peggy Guggenheim parle aussi de repartir en France; mais ils sont séparés, sinon divorcés.

— Tanguy est tout à fait installé à la campagne aux environs de N.Y. et ira faire un tour en France mais je crois comme touriste.

— Je compte partir en Avril pour Paris, d'ailleurs sans grande joie— Le panier de crabes ne m'attire pas— ici au contraire l'ordinaire de la vie donne une tranquillité qui me permettrait de travailler si j'en avais envie.

A bientôt cher vieux donne de tes nouvelles
et ne m'en veux pas de ma négligence
        Affectueusement Marcel

Fernand Léger and André Masson (1896-1987), painters, returned to France late 1945.

Breton and his wife Elisa in Haiti Dec 1945 - late Feb 1946 to give lectures on Surrealism.

Max Ernst and Peggy Guggenheim are already divorced; Ernst marries American painter Dorothea Tanning 24 Oct 1946.

Yves Tanguy moved to Woodbury, Connecticut, 1940, with wife, American painter Kay Sage (1898-1963).

▷ TRANSLATION: *210 West 10th Street, New York, 2nd or 3rd January '46. Dear Tzara, As I was getting more and more bogged down being so late replying to you, I ran into Maria Jolas who told me she had, for the most part, replied to your questions about parcels and the question of books at Brentano's. I think, in fact now, that other bookshops are going to start importing the books you are talking about. VVV has had three issues in 3 years: you'll definitely see them. Don't know Georges Lemaître: From Cubism... Art of this Century is the name of Peggy Guggenheim's gallery. All she has published is the catalog of her collection with biography of the artists. Henry Miller is probably the only one you'd be interested in, but I have neither seen nor read his books. Are you sure you don't want me to send them to you? View: you can see the collection at Mary Reynolds', 14 rue Hallé, 14ème, Gob. 3337. She has been back in Paris since last March. On the whole, critical writing is just regurgitation of the commonplaces of the last 20 years. As you might imagine, I continue to live over here the life I lived in Sanary, only acquiescing to the occasional compulsory trip out for exhibitions. What's more, the group of exiles, compact in the beginning 3 years ago, rapidly turned into "every man for himself" with the usual discord and rows. Léger, Masson are back, Breton has left for Haïti (lectures) for 3 months and expects to leave for France after passing through New York in April. Max Ernst is staying here until he can be naturalized an American (this year). Peggy Guggenheim is also talking about going back to France, but they are separated if not divorced. Tanguy is all set up in the countryside just outside N.Y. and will be taking a trip to France, but as a tourist, I think. I expect to leave for Paris in April, without any great enthusiasm, in fact. The way they're all at each other's throats doesn't do anything for me. Here, on the other hand, the ordinariness of life provides a kind of tranquillity which would allow me to work if I felt like it. So long, dear boy, let me have your news and don't hold my negligence against me. Affectionately, Marcel.*

1 May 1946
Duchamp returns to France aboard the S.S. "Brazil."
In August, he and Mary Reynolds
take a vacation to Switzerland, where, in Bern,
they are houseguests of the French Ambassador
Henri Hoppenot and his wife Hélène.
They also spend a week in a small hotel overlooking
Lake Geneva in the town of Chexbres.

---

164. Marcel Duchamp to Ettie Stettheimer   autograph letter
9 August 1946, Chexbres, Switzerland   collection YCAL

    Chexbres Suisse 9 aout 46
      Chère Ettie
Faut il vous dire ma surprise quand au 3me jour du voyage on apporta un   H[enrie] **Waste**,
gros paquet dans ma cabine avec une vague indication : H. Waste.___   pen name of Ettie
Mais aussi quelle joie d'inviter Virgil et quelques amis du bateau à boire   Stettheimer, see p.139.
immédiatement ce champagne monté des eaux.___ j'en avais gardé   **Virgil** = Virgil Thomson
quelques bouteilles pour la famille qui, à mon arrivée à Paris, a sablé le
champagne à votre santé.
Tout ce qu'on raconte sur l'Europe est à peu près vrai___ je dois dire
cependant qu'il n'y a pas disette___ beaucoup de gens appauvris ou mal
payés qui se nourissent difficilement___ les prix et les salaires, et le
marché noir… vous connaissez la chanson.
A Paris les arbres sont plus verts que jamais parce que l'essence des autos
et la fumée des cheminées ne les ont pas empêchés de pousser à leur
guise pendant la guerre___
Je suis en Suisse pour 3 semaines et rentre en Aout à Paris.___   **MD in Switzerland** with
J'ai été très peiné d'apprendre la mort de Stieglitz.___ N.Y. sans Stieglitz   Mary Reynolds 29 July -
n'est plus notre N.Y___ Ayez la gentillesse de transmettre toute ma   2 Sept.
sympathie à O'Keefe qui doit être bien désemparée.   **Alfred Stieglitz** died
— En rentrant à Paris j'espère obtenir rapidement mes visas de retour. et   13 July 1946.
si tout marche bien j'espère encore arriver à temps pour l'exposition de   "Florine Stettheimer: A
Florine___   Memorial Exhibition,"
Soyez assez gentille pour m'écrire une carte postale me disant en style   MoMA, NY, opens
télégraphique si rien n'a été changé à la date et aux conditions de   1 Oct 1946.
l'exposition Florine : je n'ai rien reçu de Monroe à ce sujet.___   **Monroe Wheeler**
A bientôt donc et j'espère que l'été a été clément pour vous   (1899-1988), director of
    Affectueusement Marcel   exhibitions at MoMA,
<u>11 rue Larrey Paris V</u>   NY.

▷ TRANSLATION: *Chexbres Switzerland 9th August '46. Dear Ettie, I need not tell you my surprise when, on the 3rd day of my trip, a large parcel was brought up to my cabin bearing the vague inscription H. Waste. But also what a joy to be able to invite Virgil and some friends from the ship at once to drink this champagne risen from the waves. I kept a few bottles for the family who toasted your very good health in champagne when I arrived. Everything they say about Europe is more or less true. I must say though that there is no food shortage. A lot of people are impoverished or badly paid or don't have much to eat—prices and salaries and the black market... same old story. In Paris the trees are greener than ever because without gas from automobiles and chimney smoke they could grow to their hearts' content during the war. I am in Switzerland for 3 weeks, return to Paris in August. I was greatly saddened by the news of Stieglitz's death. N.Y. without Stieglitz will not be our old N.Y. anymore. Please be kind enough to convey my sympathies to O'Keefe who must be very distressed. Once I get back to Paris, I hope to get my return visas very quickly and if all goes according to plan, I'm still hoping to arrive in time for Florine's exhibition. Please be so kind as to drop me a postcard telling me telegraphic style whether there have been any changes in the date and terms of Florine's exhibition: I have had nothing from Monroe about it. So long then and I hope the summer has been kind to you. Affectionately, Marcel. 11 rue Larrey Paris V.*

---

165. Marcel Duchamp to Man Ray   autograph letter
25 September 1946, Paris   collection GRI

11 rue Larrey Paris V 25 Sept 46
   Cher Man
Merci pour ta lettre : je crois d'ailleurs que tu as bien fait de remettre à
   l'année prochaine ton départ pour Paris__
Non pas que ce soit invivable ici au sens matériel__ Au contraire la
   question nourriture est assez bien résolue__ Mais il te faut un coin pour
   habiter et ce n'est pas facile à trouver. Je te conseille vivement de penser
   à remettre ta maison du Pecq en état et d'amener une voiture avec toi ce
   qui te permettra une vie délicieuse à quelques minutes du centre de
   Paris__
Moi même je rentre cet automne à N.Y.__ Mais je ne pourrai avoir mon
   visa qu'en Décembre__ Raisons de quota__
J¢'ai vu Maurice Lefebvre Foinet et il est entendu que j'essaierai
   d'emporter tes quatre choses comme si elles m'appartenaient. Te
   tiendrai au courant en temps voulu__
Dis moi seulement si tu vois un inconvénient à ce que je déclare ces
   tableaux sans valeur, sans intention de les revendre etc.
      Affectueusement à Juliette et à toi
      Marcel

MD will not be able to leave, in fact, until 13 Jan 1947.

Juliet Browner (1911-1991), lived with Man Ray in Hollywood; they marry 24 Oct 1946 in a joint ceremony with Max Ernst and Dorothea Tanning.

▷ TRANSLATION: *11 rue Larrey Paris V 25th Sept '46. Dear Man, Thank you for your letter: I think you did the right thing actually in putting off your trip to Paris until next year. Not that it's intolerable in the material sense—quite the opposite, the food problem is pretty well solved. But you need a place to stay and that's not easy to find. I strongly urge you to think about getting your house in the Pecq in shape and bringing a car with you then you could have a very pleasant life just a few kilometers away from the center of Paris. I myself am going back to N.Y. this autumn. But I won't be able to get my visa until December—because of quotas. I saw Maurice Lefebvre Foinet and we've arranged that I'll try to take those four things of yours as if they were my own. Will keep you informed when the time comes. Just let me know if you have any problem with me declaring these paintings as worthless, no intention of selling etc. Affectionately to Juliette and to you, Marcel.*

---

166. Marcel Duchamp to Ettie Stettheimer   autograph letter
26 September 1946, Paris   collection YCAL

> Paris V
> 11 rue Larrey
> 26 Sept 46
>   Chère Ettie
> James Sweeney a dû vous annoncer déjà la mauvaise nouvelle :
> Mon tour de quota n'arrivera pas avant un mois ou deux et il n'y a rien à
>   faire pour tourner la loi américaine—
> Je ne puis donc en aucun cas être là pour l'exposition de Florine— j'en suis
>   d'autant plus désolé que je me faisais une fête d'aider à la présentation
>   de cette manifestation nécessaire à la mémoire du peintre qu'elle est—
> J'espère seulement que vous avez pu obtenir la forme que vous désiriez et
>   j'aimerais que vous disiez dans un petit mot comment s'est passé le
>   vernissage—
> Tout ce que je sais maintenant c'est que j'espère être à N. Y. en
>   Décembre—
> à bientôt donc quand même et encore tous mes vœux
>   Affectueusement
>   Marcel Duchamp

Exh. "Florine Stettheimer," MoMA, see p.254

▷ TRANSLATION: *Paris V. 11 rue Larrey. 26th Sept '46. Dear Ettie. James Sweeney must have told you the bad news by now: My quota won't be up for another month or two and there is no way of getting round American law. Therefore there is no way I can be there for Florine's exhibition. I am even more upset because I was really looking forward to helping set up this very necessary event in memory of the painter that she is. I only hope you managed to get the arrangement you wanted and would be glad if you would drop me a line to let me know how the opening went. All I know now is that I hope to be in N.Y. in December. See you soon all the same and once more best wishes. Affectionately, Marcel Duchamp.*

---

167. Marcel Duchamp to Man Ray
10 October 1946, Paris

autograph letter
collection MNAM

11 rue Larrey Paris V
10 Oct 46
　　Cher Man
Parmi les 4 choses qui sont chez Lefebvre Foinet l'ovale n'est pas celui
　　dont tu parles (sous verre et si je me rappelle bien gris blanc et noir)
Il a bien un ovale mais c'est une peinture avec des traits un peu comme ça :

Painting similar to Man Ray's *Tableau ton gout I*, 1929 (Collection Marion Meyer, Paris).

Donc dis moi dans une prochaine lettre si tu veux celui ci ou non car il ne
　　semble pas avoir l'autre —
2e — Il y aura une exposition surréaliste à Paris en 47 (Mars ou Avril) —
　　Et Breton a l'intention de t'inviter mais j'ai aussi pensé qu'on pourrait
　　exposer plusieurs tableaux anciens du XVIIème XVIIIme siècle en accord
　　avec le surréalisme — Et je trouve que ton Arcimboldo serait un bon
　　exemple — Si tu acceptes de le prêter éventuellement pour cette
　　exposition veux tu me le dire dans le même mot et dans ce cas je le
　　laisserais ici —
Je ne pars qu'en Décembre. Mon N° de quota est long à sortir.
　　Affectueusement
　　Marcel

"Le Surréalisme en 1947," Galerie Maeght, organized by Breton, will open 7 July 1947.

Winter, painting owned by Man Ray, no longer attributed to Italian Mannerist painter **Giuseppe Arcimboldo** (ca.1527-1593).

▷ TRANSLATION: *11 rue Larrey Paris V, 10th Oct. '46. Dear Man, Among the 4 things which are at Lefebvre Foinet's, the oval is not the one you're talking about (under glass and, if I remember rightly, gray, white and black). There is an oval but it's a painting with lines a bit like this: [sketch] So write and let me know soon whether you want this one as there doesn't seem to be another one. 2nd There's going to be a Surrealist exhibition in Paris in '47 (March or April)—and Breton is planning to invite you, but I also had this idea that we could exhibit several old paintings from XVII / XVIII Century in tune with Surrealism. And I think your Arcimboldo would be a good example. If you could see your way to lending it for this exhibition, could you let me know in the same letter and, in that case, I'll leave it here. I'm not leaving until December. My quota No. is taking a long time to come up. Affectionately, Marcel.*

---

168. Marcel Duchamp to Yvonne Chastel   autograph letter
8 or 9 December 1946, Paris   collection GRI

11 rue Larrey
8 ou 9 Dec 46
    Chère Yvonne
Merci de ta lettre et des livres bien arrivés—
L'extérieur du Lautréamont ne me rappelle rien mais la typographie
    intérieure me dit quelque chose. Ce pourrait être le premier
    Lautréamont que j'avais eu en 1912 ou environs.
En tout cas j'aimerais le garder comme un des 5 ou 6 livres qui forment
    toute ma bibliothèque.— Merci de me l'avoir donné si non redonné.
Toujours rien pour mon visa— Je vais Mardi au consulat américain pour
    leur demander s'ils peuvent me donner une date même approximative—
Ne te fais pas de bile pour la Cunard. Je pense qu'en dortoir (hommes) je
    trouverai un passage à la French Line.
Je t'écrirai de toute façon
Rien de nouveau depuis ton départ—
Un peu froid mais je trouve du charbon—
Ecris de temps en temps te mettrai au courant de mon départ—
    Affectueusement
    Marcel

Lautréamont book MD owned in 1912, probably original edition (1869) of *Les chants de Maldoror.*

▷ TRANSLATION: *11 rue Larrey, 8th or 9th Dec. '46. Dear Yvonne, Thank you for your letter and the books which I also got. The outside of the Lautréamont doesn't ring a bell but the inside looks familiar. It might be the first Lautréamont I ever had in 1912 or thereabouts. In any case, I would like to keep it as one of the 5 or 6 books that make up my entire library. Thank you for having given it to me or given it back to me. Still nothing about my visa. I'm going Tuesday to the American Consulate to ask them if they can give me a date, even an approximate one. Don't lose any sleep over the Cunard. I think that if I take a berth in a dormitory (men's), I'll get a passage on the French Line. I'll write you in any case. Nothing new since you left. A little cold but I can get coal. Write to me from time to time and I'll let you know about my departure. Affectionately, Marcel.*

New York, 210 West 14 St | 1947-1950

aboard ship for USA, on the "Washington" | 13 Jan 1947
New York: returning to 210 West 14th St, room on 4th and top floor
round trips to Endicott, San Francisco, Chicago, Milford, Los Angeles, Binghamton
back to Paris, 99 Boulevard Arago, at Henri-Pierre Roché's | 19 Sept 1950
aboard ship for USA, on the "Mauritania" | arriving 2 Dec 1950

from 13 Jan 1947 to 1 Jan 1950

▶ MAJOR WORKS

Cover for "Le Surréalisme en 1947" (catalog of the "Exposition Internationale du Surréalisme" Galerie Maeght, Paris, July - Aug 1947)
Le Rayon vert / The Green Ray (installation for same exhibition, 1947)
The Juggler of Gravity (installation realized by Matta, same exhibition, 1947)
Given: Maria, the Waterfall, and the Illuminating Gas (pencil on paper; 1947)
The Illuminating Gas and the Waterfall (painted leather over plaster relief, mounted on velvet, 1948-49)

▶ EXHIBITIONS

The Cubist Spirit in its time, The London Gallery, London. By MD: *Excerpts from the Duchamp valise*; *Photograph of a glass* — 18 Mar - 3 May 1947
American Print-Making 1913-1947, Brooklyn Museum, Brooklyn, USA. By MD: *Six Roto-reliefs* — 18 Nov - 17 Dec 1947

Painting and Sculpture by the Directors of the Société Anonyme since its foundation 1920-1948, Yale University Art Gallery, New Haven, USA. By MD: *The Chess Players*; *Sieste éternelle*; *Le Passage de la Vierge à la Mariée*; *Study for La Mariée*; *The Bachelors*; *Trois Stoppages Etalon*; *In Advance of the Broken Arm*; *Disturbed Balance [To Be Looked at...]*; *Revolving Glass Machine*; *Valise* — 5 Mar 1948
Mobiles and Articulated Sculpture, California Palace of the Legion of Honor, San Francisco. By MD: *6 Roto-Reliefs* — 2 Oct - 21 Nov 1948
The Peggy Guggenheim Collection, Twenty-fourth Biennale, Venice, Italy (traveling exhibition). By MD: *Jeune Homme Triste dans un Train*; *Boîte-en-valise* — ? 1948
Isms in Art since 1800, Rhode Island School of Design, Providence, USA. By MD: *Three Stoppages Etalon*; *The valise*; *In Advance of the Broken Arm* — 3 Feb - 9 Mar 1949
Western Round Table on Modern Art, Museum of Art, San Francisco. By MD: *Nude descending the Staircase* — 8 Apr - 10 Apr 1949

L'Art Abstrait, Les Préliminaires, Galerie Maeght, Paris.
By MD: *Pour une partie d'échecs*; *La Mariée*
(gravée par J. Villon) — 27 May - 30 June 1949

The Société Anonyme Collection of 20th Century Painting,
Institute of Contemporary Art, Boston (travels to
South Hadley, Saginaw, Washington). By MD: *The*
Bachelors; *Rotoreliefs*; *In Advance of the Broken*
Arm
— 4 June - 1 July and 6 Sept - 2 Oct 1949

Twentieth Century Art from the Louise and Walter
Arensberg Collection, The Art Institute, Chicago. By
MD: 30 works (Nos. 52 to 81) — 19 Oct - 18 Dec 1949

22 January 1947
After over nine months in Europe,
Duchamp returns to New York.
Throughout the first half of 1947, he works
on various projects relating to an international
exhibition of Surrealism being organized
by André Breton in Paris and for which Duchamp
designs the cover of the catalog.
After the opening of the show on 7 July 1947,
Duchamp writes to Breton acknowledging
receipt of some reviews that he has received
and asking for more information
about the exhibition.

169. Marcel Duchamp to Elisa and André Breton   letter
18 July 1947, New York   source: from Y. Poupard-Lieussou transcript

210 West 14th Street
18 Juillet 1947
    Chère Elisa Cher André
Bien reçu votre mot et coupure me donnant l'impression que l'expo donne
    de très bons signes de succès— C'est assez agréable d'être méprisé
    comme des jeunes "A NOTRE AGE."
J'attends le catalogue avec impatience (que Maeght j'espère a dû mettre à
    la poste!) J'aimerais beaucoup que Maeght m'envoie aussi un jeu de
    photos de toutes les salles avec des photos de détail.
— Vous allez sans doute faire un petit album-souvenir car tant de travail
    ne doit pas s'évanouir complètement en Septembre.
— Avez vous eu le temps de faire la salle des "malgré eux" et la cuisine?
Un mot quand vous serez reposé
    Affectueusement à tous trois
    Marcel

"Le Surréalisme en 1947," see p.257.

Rooms in the Surrealist exhibition.

▷ TRANSLATION: *210 West 14th Street, 18th July 1947. Dear Elisa, Dear André, I got your note and cutting which make me think the exhibition is showing signs of great success. It's rather nice to be treated with contempt like youngsters "AT OUR AGE." I can't wait to see the catalog (which Maeght, I hope, must have put in the mail!) I would really like Maeght also to send me a set of photos of all the rooms with some close-ups. You'll no doubt be making a little souvenir album as so much work should not just completely evaporate in September. Have you had time to do the "in spite of them's" room and the kitchen? A line once you've had a rest. Affectionately to all three of you, Marcel.*

---

170. Marcel Duchamp to Man Ray   autograph letter
8 November 1947, New York   collection GRI

8 Nov. 47
210 W. 14th St. N.Y
    Cher Man
Merci de tes 2 lettres, des photos, du livre d'échecs et du chèque à Roché.
— Tout s'est très bien passé et Roché m'apprend que la somme a été
    payée.
— L'idée du sein est très bonne et je crois faisable.
— j'ai trouvé un petit compteur que je vais adapter à la pendule d'échecs
    de mon ami Phillips.__ En attendant le "recording" photographique de
    la partie!
Bonjour à Juliette; n'ai aucune nouvelle de mon voyage à San Francisco
    pour Janvier. Je crois que ce sera remis à l'été prochain__
      Affectueusement à tous deux
      Marcel

▷ TRANSLATION: *8th Nov. '47. 210 W. 14th ST.N.Y. Dear Man, Thank you for your
2 letters, the book on chess and the check for Roché. Everything went very well and
Roché tells me the sum has been paid. The idea of the breast is a very good one and
feasible I think. I found a small counter which I'm going to adapt for the chess clock
belonging to my friend Phillips. Until the day of the photographic "recording" of
the game! Say hello to Juliette; I've heard nothing about my trip to San Francisco
in January. I think it'll be postponed until next summer. Affectionately to you both,
Marcel.*

"The idea of the breast"
for the cover of a
catalog: see note on
next letter.

Juliette = Juliet Browner,
Man Ray's wife.

MD invited to take part
in a symposium on
modern art in San
Francisco, which will
actually not take place
until Apr 1949.

---

171. Marcel Duchamp to Elisa and André Breton   autograph letter
8 March 1948, New York   source: from Y. Poupard-Lieussou transcript

210 West 14th Street
N.Y. City
8 Mars 1948
    Chère Elisa cher André.
après ce grand silence sans excuse, voici une offre intéressante :
John Ployardt un ami de Man Ray ~~qui~~ est venu me voir (de Californie) et
    veut faire une sorte de galerie à Hollywood, qui ne serait pas une galerie
    mais un endroit à "thèmes" (tendance nettement favorable au Surr.)__
    Mais la proposition qui vous intéresse est la suivante :
Il voudrait publier avec une quarantaine de photos et photos-montages
    faits par un de ses amis George Hunell votre poème l'~~Amour~~Union libre
    (paru̧ chez Ford). Il a trouvé un éditeur (Doubleday qui est une des plus
    grandes maisons d'édition ici) Doubleday accepte d'entreprendre cette

American artist and
patron, **John Ployardt**,
brother-in-law of
William Copley, will run
the Copley Galleries
Oct 1948 - Mar 1949.

L'union libre, poem first
published 1931
(translated as "Freedom
of Love") and
appearing in Breton's
*Young Cherry Trees
Secured Against Hares*,
published by View
Editions, NY, 1946.

publication et offre 10 % de royalties qui seraient partagées en 3 : le
photographe *Hunel*, le metteur en page (Ployardt) et vous même.
— Une édition de luxe d'abord et une édition de 15 000 (mille)
exemplaires qui seraient distribuées dans ~~to~~ les USA avec la science que
vous connaissez—
Au bas mot chacun de vous 3 devrait recevoir plusieurs 1000 dollars (peut-
être 4 ou 5) comme royalties.—
Ployardt me dit qu'il aura probablement des difficultés à obtenir la
permission de se servir de la traduction déjà existante et propose d¢'*en*
faire une spécialement pour ce livre.
Acceptez vous ces conditions ?
Si vous pouvez faire vite en me répondant cela aiderait = Faites une lettre
directe pour John Ployardt qui ~~vous~~ lui permette de commencer en
même temps que vous m'écrirez un mot pour me parler un peu de vous
et de ce qui se passe—
— Donati ma donné quelques nouvelles (Antibes, un peu de repos)— les
revues nouvelles que je n'ai pas vues—
Ici rien de bien intéressant.
Vu Maeght a son passage ici. et Drouin qui n'est pas encore reparti.— je
parle de Donati à Drouin pour une expo. à Paris— Pourrez vous faire la
même chose quand vous le verrez *(Drouin)*
       Affectueusement à tous deux
       Marcel

Enrico Donati
(b.1909), American
painter, helped MD
attach the foam rubber
breasts to the covers of
the exh. cat. *Le
Surréalisme en 1947*,
see p.257.

René Drouin (1905-
1979), joint owner with
Leo Castelli of the
Galerie René Drouin,
Paris (1939-1962).

▷ TRANSLATION: *210 West 14th Street, N.Y. City, 8th March 1948. Dear Elisa, dear
André, After this great and inexcusable silence, I have an interesting proposition.
John Ployardt, a friend of Man Ray's, came to see me (from California) and wants
to set up a sort of gallery in Hollywood, which wouldn't be a gallery but a place that
would have "themes" (with a markedly favorable bias towards Surrealism). But the
proposition concerning you is the following: He wants to publish, together with forty
or so photos and photo-mountings by a friend of his, George Hunell, your poem
"Freedom of Love" (published by Ford). He's found a publisher (Doubleday, which
is one of the biggest publishing houses here). Doubleday has agreed to take on this
publication and is offering 10% royalties to be shared in three: the photographer,
Hunel, the pagemaker (Ployardt) and yourself. A deluxe edition first of all, then a
series of 15,000 (thousand) copies which would be circulated within the USA with
the skill you are familiar with. The bottom line is that each of you should receive
several 1,000 (perhaps 4 or 5) in royalties. Ployardt tells me he'll probably have
difficulty obtaining permission to use the existing translation and suggests doing a
new one specially for this book. Do you agree to these terms? If you could hurry and
let me know, that would be helpful. Write a letter straight to John Ployardt, so that
he can make a start, at the same time as writing to me and letting me know how
you are and what's going on. I got some news from Donati (Antibes, for a little*

rest), the new journals I haven't seen. Nothing very interesting here. Saw Maeght when he was passing through and Drouin who hasn't yet left. I'm speaking to Drouin about Donati for a show in Paris. Could you do the same when you see him (Drouin)? Affectionately to you both, Marcel.

---

172. Marcel Duchamp to Man Ray   autograph letter
10 April 1948, New York   collection GRI

10 Avril 48
210 W14th St. N.Y.

    Cher Man

Merci pour ~~t~~ta lettre et mes excuses de ne t'avoir pas répondu plus tôt.—
    Excuse moi aussi auprès de Fitzsimmons que j'ai manqué, étant absent
    de N.Y. pour quelques jours chez Miss Dreier.—

Merci encore pour ton idée d'exposer les Rotoreliefs. Mais un conseil (dû   *Rotoreliefs* [cat. 53]
    à mon expérience)—

N'en montre pas plusieurs à la fois : C'est toute une construction avec
    poulies, qui te demandera un travail du diable.

Je propose plus simplement :

un moteur électrique et un rhéostat faisant tourner ~~les tout~~ disques à 35
    tours à la minute.

Le moteur par terre ou presque et le disque légèrement incliné comme un
    bureau d'écolier

- mur
- section
- moteur

une planche trouée et recouverte de velours noir avec charnières

- charnières
- velours noir

    pour qu'on ne vole pas les disques.
    Tu lèves la planche tu poses un disque et tu rabats la planche—

Etant presque horizontal nul besoin d'attacher le disque__
Tu peux même laisser assez d'espace entre la planche et le disque pour
    mettre une lampe ou 2 qui éclairent le disque de côté.__
Tu peux empiler les 6 disques sur le moteur et les changer quand
    quelqu'un de plus intéressé demande à voir tous les dessins.__
Le tout pour être vu à 10 ou 15^{cm} du sol. (le plus bas possible).
    Merci et affectueusement à tous deux
    Marcel

▷ TRANSLATION: *10th April '48. 210 W14th St. N.Y. Dear Man, Thank you for your
letter and sorry for not replying earlier. My apololgies also to the Fitzsimmons
whom I missed, being out of New York for a few days at Miss Dreier's. Thanks
again for your idea of exhibiting the Rotoreliefs. But one piece of advice (from personal experience): don't show more than one at a time. You've got to set the whole
thing up with pulleys which is a hell of a job. I propose more simply: an electric motor and a rheostat rotating the disk 35 times a minute. The motor on the ground or
almost and the disk tilting at a slight angle like a schoolboy's desk [sketch: wall; section; motor] a plate with a hole in it and covered in black velvet with hinges [sketch:
hinges; black velvet] so people won't steal the disks. You lift the plate, put in a disk
and pull the plate down again. As the disk is almost horizontal, no need to secure
it. You can even leave enough room between the plate and the disk to fit a bulb or
two to light the disk from the side. You can stack all six disks on the motor and
change them when somebody seriously interested asks to see all the drawings. The
whole thing to be seen 10 to 15 cm off the ground (as low as possible). Thanks and
affectionately to you both, Marcel.*

---

173. Marcel Duchamp to Man Ray   autograph letter
13 June 1948, New York   collection GRI

13 Juin 48
210 W 14.
    Cher Man
Tu as sans doute entendu parler d'une grande exposition internationale à
    Sao Paolo (Brésil) au mois de Septembre prochain__
Je suis chargé par Drouin qui dirige toute l'affaire de m'occuper avec Janis
    et Castelli de la sélection américaine ici__
Tendance "abstraite" ou semi "abstraite".
Dis moi où on peut trouver *ici* un tableau <u>important</u> de toi datant le plus
    tôt possible (1916-17) et à direction "abstraite" et dis moi lequel tu
    préfères envoyer.

Francisco Matarazzo Sobrinho, President of of Museu de Arte Moderna, São Paolo, asked MD, upon Maria Martins' suggestion, to help gather works for the show.

Leo Castelli, see next letter.

L'exposition voyagera probablement après Sao Paolo— Rio de Janeiro—
l'Europe?— Les Etats Unis?
  Affectueusement à tous deux
  Marcel
– *on pourra vendre—*

▷ TRANSLATION: *13th June '48. 210 W 14. Dear Man, You have no doubt heard about a big international exhibition taking place in São Paolo (Brazil) in September. Drouin, who is running the entire affair, has asked me to take care of the American selection here together with Janis and Castelli. "Abstract" or "semi-abstract" tendency. Can you tell me where one could find over here one of your important paintings going back as far as possible (1916-17) and with "abstract" leanings and which one you would prefer to send. The exhibition will probably travel after São Paolo— Rio de Janeiro, Europe? The United States? Affectionately to you both, Marcel. Good opportunity to sell.*

---

174. Marcel Duchamp to Man Ray   autograph letter
14 July 1948, [New York]   collection GRI

14 Juillet 48
  Cher Man
J'ai négligé de te répondre vite.
— A cause de la dimension *des Revolving Doors* nous avons décidé de
  prendre 2 choses de toi, l'Arc de Triomphe (Kath. Dreier) et l'"homme
  infini" chez Budworth—
Castelli s'occupe de l'envoi qui doit partir bientôt.
Viens tu à N.Y. cet été?
Que deviennent Copley et Ployardt?
  Affectueusement à tous deux et à tous les amis
  Marcel

L'Arc de Triomphe, 1923 and *L'homme infini*, 1942 (Giorgio Marconi, Milan).

Budworth, warehouse in Manhattan.

Leo Castelli (1907-1999), world-renowned art dealer, just getting involved in the buying and selling of art.

William Copley (1919-1996), artist and collector, runs the Copley Gallery with **Ployardt** (see p.262).

▷ TRANSLATION: *14th July '48. Dear Man, I have been remiss in not replying to you sooner. Because of the size of the Revolving Doors, we have decided to take two things by you, the Arc de Triomphe (Kath. Dreier) and "infinite man" at Budworth's. Castelli is taking care of the shipment which should leave soon. Are you coming to N.Y. this summer? What are Copley and Ployardt doing these days? Affectionately to you both and to all our friends, Marcel.*

---

175. Marcel Duchamp to Yvonne Chastel   autograph letter
8 January 1949, [New York]   collection GRI

8 Janvier 49.

Chère Yvonne, oui que devenons nous? J'ai un peu l'impression
d'être retiré à la campagne, dans une province éloignée; car c'est la vie
que je mène à N.Y.

Je vois peu de gens et les gens ne cherchent plus à me voir, sachant qu'ils
m'embêtent.

J'écris aux Arensbergs une fois par an et eux de même. Il y a une lassitude
générale qui je crois n'est pas seulement pour notre génération— A vrai
dire le gros du monde préfère la guerre à la paix.

Est ce que les restrictions de nourriture sont ~~aus~~ toujours aussi sévères en
Angleterre? On entend tellement d'histoires fausses.

Comme tu le sais par la radio il a beaucoup neigé en Décembre—
Maintenant il fait doux comme au printemps. Pourvu que ça dure!!

A propos j'ai cherché ton percolateur, et je n'ai jamais pu trouver la
fabrique; je suppose qu'il n'existe plus.

As tu envie de quelque chose dans ce genre ou autre chose que tu peux
avoir vu dans les reclames de revues?

Dis le moi je te l'enverrai.

Veux tu du café ou du thé, du riz—

Peut on envoyer facilement en Angleterre?

Voila ma chère Yvonne Rien comme toujours; les échecs, le plus possible :
au moins les joueurs d'échecs ne parlent pas—

Très heureux pour Penrose. Et Mesens? Y a t il à Londres la même débacle
en peinture qu'ici?

Ecris de temps en temps

tu es une des rares personnes à qui on puisse parler librement—

Affectueusement

Marcel.

Roland Penrose (1900-1983), English artist, author and collector.

▷ TRANSLATION: *8th January '49. Dear Yvonne, Yes indeed, what have we been up
to? I feel rather like I've retired to the country, in some remote province, for that's
what my life is like in N.Y. I see few people and people don't try to see me anymore
as they know they bore me. I write to the Arensbergs once a year and they do the
same. There is a general weariness which, I think, is not confined to our generation.
To tell the truth, most people prefer war to peace. Is food rationing still as severe in
England? You hear so many things that aren't true. As you will know from the radio, it snowed a lot in December. It's mild now, like in springtime. Long may it
last!! By the way, I looked for your percolator, but never found the manufacturers.
I expect it doesn't exist anymore. Would you like something like it or anything else
you might have seen in advertisements in magazines? Just tell me and I'll send it*

to you. Do you want any coffee, tea, rice? How easy is it to send things to England? Well there you are, my dear Yvonne. Nothing as usual. Chess as much as possible: at least chess players don't talk. Very pleased for Penrose. And Mesens? Is there the same collapse in painting in London as there is here? Do write from time to time. You are one of the few people one can speak freely to. Affectionately, Marcel.

---

176. Marcel Duchamp to Henri Hoppenot   autograph letter
29 January 1949, New York   collection BLJD

Henri Hoppenot
French ambassador to Switzerland, lives with his wife, Hélene, in Bern. Mary Reynolds knew their daughter, Violaine.

210 West 14th Street
29 Janvier 49
    Cher Henri
Voici ce que j'ai trouvé comme littérature au sujet du Webster wire
    recorder. Le modèle mentionné sur le prospectus forme valise— Mais ils
    ont un autre modèle qui n'est *pas* fait pour être transporté facilement—
    Entre nous l'effet n'est pas fait— et s'appelle "table model"
    Ce dernier est moins cher : 134⁹⁵ (et c'est exactement le même
    mécanisme).
— De plus je connais un exportateur qui me dit pouvoir obtenir 20% sur
    le prix marqué.
Si vos désirs prenaient corps, avertissez moi et je vous ferai envoyer tous
    les recorders du monde.
Webster ne fait pas le ruban, il fait seulement le fil— Les recorders sur
    ruban sont fabriqués par d'autres maisons.
— Votre paquet (la lanterne magique) attend patiemment dans mon
    atelier—
        Mes affections pour Hélène et pour vous
        Marcel
J'ai toujours 10 dollars à vous—

▷ TRANSLATION: *210 West 14th Street, 29th January '49. Dear Henri, Here's what I've found in the way of literature on the Webster wire recorder. The model mentioned in the prospectus is in the form of a suitcase. But they have another model not made for being moved around easily. Between you and me, it doesn't achieve the desired effect—it's called "table model." This latter is cheaper (and the mechanism is exactly the same). What's more, I know an exporter who says he can get 20% off the official price. If your desires take shape, let me know and I'll have all the recorders in the world sent to you. Webster doesn't make the ribbon, just the wire. Tape recorders are made by other firms. Your parcel (the magic lantern) awaits patiently in my studio. My affections to Helen and to you, Marcel. I still have 10 dollars of yours.*

177. Marcel Duchamp to Louise and Walter Arensberg   autograph letter and two plans
8 May 1949, New York   collection PMA

N.Y. Sunday morning—
8th May 49
     Dear Lou dear Walter
Went to Philadelphia Friday morning. Kimball showed me the whole
     museum in the morning ; We were invited to lunch by Ingersoll and
     went back to the museum after lunch for more discussion.
Here are all the points discussed :
Generally speaking K. is ready to give you complete satisfaction even
     though he might give you the impression of bargaining on space.
— Precolumbians. By "Americans" he meant Sheeler, Marin, etc.— not the
     precolumbian sculpture— As stated before, he still thinks the Fulcroom
     is the best place to show it.
— Area offered— As you will see in my drawings, the red pencil area
     represents what he offers on the 1st floor and on the second floor
     (both)— That area contains 9 big windows and ample space for the
     collection I think.
The only problem is how to divide the space : K. agrees to divide it as you
     please : low and high ceilings according to size of the rooms— No too
     small rooms.
Windows. On the first floor, the 3 windows in Sect. 7 and in Rm 1699 come
     from the ceiling to about 8 ft. from the floor and give a very good
     daylight.
On the second floor, the 3 windows come down to the floor (in fact they
     are the same windows continuing below onto the first floor (sect.7)
First floor Sect. 7
     The rooms already built in the lower corner of the building with low
     ceiling have no daylight at all— The disposition and size of these rooms
     can be changed.
Second floor. Sect. 7. Only *the* four walls (brick) of the building, a roof, but
     no ceiling, a cubic space to utilize as you please with the 3 big windows.
Flooring. K. Will put any kind of flooring you want (cork, parqueting etc.)
     and agrees to the idea of resilience.
     ———

     The only change I would suggest (and I did not dare propose it myself) is
     to try to get (instead of Rm 1699) the symmetrically located Rm in
     Sect. 6, immediately connected with your part of section 7 (first floor),
     marked(A)in my drawing.
     I did not want to ask him [for] this change because the Rm(A)is now
     occupied by things belonging to a permanent collection (I believe) but

Fiske Kimball
(1888-1955), Director of
the PMA, 1925 - 1955.

John Marin (1870-
1953), American
painter, discovered by
Stieglitz.

"red pencil area" = see
diagonal hatching on
sketch.

I don't see why these things could not be shifted to the Rm. 1699 which
is of the same size— You ought to make that proposition—

Vestibule. on first floor (Sect. 7).

That vestibule can be very useful for drawings and small sculpture.

Library. K. ~~tok~~ took me to the Phila. Library where the Director, Mr. Price
showed me how they treat small libraries— In the case of the Elkin (?)
library they have furnished a big room to make an exact reproduction of
the original library in the Elkin home, with the original furniture,
carpets, boiseries etc.

They even have made photographic enlargements of the view on the Elkin
gardens through the windows, giving the whole room the original
atmosphere—

Also K. spoke of giving a special room for the continuation of your work.

Eli Kirk Price (1860-1933), President of the PMA, 1926 - 1933.

"boiseries" = wood panelling.

Enclosure 1 (sketch redrawn according to MD's plan):

Sect. 6

Brick wall

Sect. 7

Brick

no partitions

no ceiling built yet

tall windows to the floor

hoist

The whole space vacant, you can dispose of it as you please.

Brick

Brick

Second floor

As you said, K. has a convincing tone of voice— Nevertheless, I think that
if you insist on a definite plan you will obtain what you want.

The difficulty will be how to divide the space offered so that it does not
look like an ordinary museum collection.

The way Gallatin has arranged his collection is very attractive— although
not completely what you would like : Several small low ceiling rooms
with electric light and a large high ceiling room with the 3 big windows,
for the large paintings.

A. E. **Gallatin** (see p.178) gave his entire collection of modern art to the PMA in 1943.

Could you have a photostat made of the blue prints (only the sect. 7 and
6 of 1st and 2nd floor) for me to study more exactly and go back to Phila.

Enclosure 2 (sketch redrawn according to MD's plan):

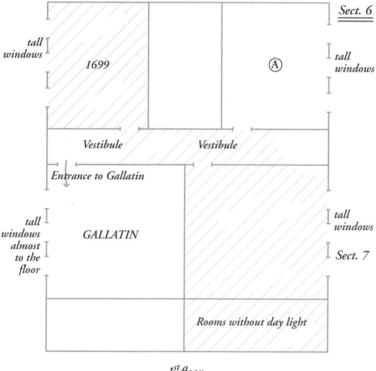

1st floor

Kimball proposes the red pencil aera *(section 7 and 1699)* on the first
floor— plus half of section 7 on the 2nd floor (see my drawing of
the 2nd floor)

and see where the partitions are exactly placed (my drawings are not exactly like the blue print).

———

All in all there is a good air of permanency in the building and in the offer— But you have to see it when you go to Chicago before the final decision.

An exhibition of the Arensberg collection is planned at the Art Institute of Chicago for the fall of 1949 (see note on next letter).

    Affectueusement à tous deux
    Marcel

---

178. Marcel Duchamp to Henri-Pierre Roché   autograph letter
9 May 1949, New York   collection HRHRC

210 W. 14th St.
9 Mai 49
    Malgré toutes les démonstrations amicales de la galerie Maeght je préfère ne pas exposer la "jeune sœur" qui ne s'explique pas toute seule.   *Little Sister* [cat. 12]
Dans un ensemble elle aurait sa place avec d'autres 1911— La vraie raison est aussi que j'ai de moins en moins envie de cabotiner et de me prêter au petit jeu parisien (et New-Yorkais) de la bourse à la peinture. Toute cette charlatanerie de goût me ferait presque oublier qu'il existe autre chose qu'une profession plus ou moins lucrative— c'est aussi pour cela (beaucoup) que je vis loin de l'article ~~paris~~ de Paris—
Pour la valise, je ne suis pas non plus d'accord mais je ne peux rien; ils trouveront toujours une valise à exposer s'ils le veulent—

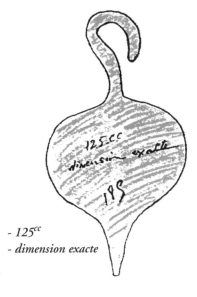

- *125^{cc}*
- *dimension exacte*

Puis je te demander le petit service suivant : Walter Arensberg a cassé son ampoule "Air de Paris"— je lui ai *Paris Air* [cat. 43]
promis de la remplacer—
Pourrais tu aller dans la pharmacie qui est au coin de la rue Blomet et la rue de Vaugirard (si elle existe encore, *c'est là que j'avais acheté la première ampoule*) et acheter une ampoule comme celle-ci : 125$^{c.c.}$ et de la même dimension que le dessin; demande au pharmacien de la vider de son contenu et de resouder le verre à la lampe— Ensuite faire un paquet et me l'envoyer ici.
— Si pas rue Blomet ailleurs, mais autant que possible la même forme, merci

Voyage en Calif. très épatant; la table Ronde amusant et 12 jours chez
  Walter à revoir tous les vieux tableaux qui se portent de mieux en mieux
Vu Béa à Ojaï— Maison étonnante, travaille beaucoup, quelle énergie—
Pourquoi ne demandes tu pas à Janis de faire quelque chose avec tes
  Hirschfields ? te les garder en dépôt ou te les vendre; et te donner un
  reçu.—
Il y aura une exposition de la Collect. Arensberg à Chicago (Institute) en
  Oct. prochain avec catalogue important. Les Arensbergs y viendront.—
Villon grand succès ici chez Carré.
Comment vont Denise et Jean-Claude? et la maison de Sèvres
    Viens ici bientôt.
    Affectueusement à tous
    Marcel
*Vu Copley en Calif. Il a fermé boutique après avoir dépensé 70 000 dollars
en un an.— Peu de chances pour la Nuit Espagnole. Mais peut-être plus
tard.*

▷ TRANSLATION: *210 W. 14th St. 9th May '49. In spite of all the show of friendship
on the part of the Maeght gallery, I prefer not to exhibit the "young sister" which
cannot be understood in isolation. In a group, she would have her place with other
1911's. The real reason is that I feel less and less like playing to the gallery and of
this Parisian (and New York) stock-exchange-to-painting-game. All this phoney-
ness about taste could almost make me forget that something other than just a profession where one makes money—more or less—actually exists. That's also why
(mainly) I live far away from Paris the genuine article. As for the suitcase, I'm not
happy about it either but nothing I can do: They'll always find a suitcase to exhibit
if they want to. May I ask you the following favour. Walter Arensberg has broken
his ampoule, "Paris Air." I've promised him I'd replace it. Could you go into the
pharmacy on the corner of rue Blomet and the rue de Vaugirard (if it's still there,
that's where I bought the first ampoule) and buy an ampoule like this one: 125 c.c.
and the same measurements as the drawing. Ask the pharmacist to empty it of its
contents and seal the glass with a blow torch. Then wrap it up and send it to me
here. If not rue Blomet, somewhere else—but, as far as possible, the same shape and
size. Thanks. [sketch caption: 125cc exact measurement]. Trip to California surprisingly pleasant: Round table fun and 12 days at Walter's looking at all the old canvases which look better all the time. Saw Béa at Ojaï. Amazing house, works
enormously, so much energy. Why don't you ask Janis to do something with your
Hirschfields?—Keep them for you in a safe deposit or sell them and give you a receipt. There will be an Arensberg Collection exhibition in Chicago (Institute) next
October with significant catalog. The Arensbergs will be there. Villon a great success*

MD participated in "The Western **Round Table** on Modern Art," San Francisco Mus. of Art, 8 - 10 Apr 1949.

Béa = Beatrice Wood moves in 1948 to Ojai, a picturesque town and artists' community, north-west of LA.

Morris Hirshfield (1872-1946), Polish-born painter whose work Roché admires and collects.

"20th Century Art from the L. & W. **Arensberg Collection**," Art Institute of Chicago, 19 Oct - 18 Dec 1949.

Villon shows 17 paintings, Louis Carré Gallery (see p.275), NY, 26 Apr - 14 May.

Denise, wife, and **Jean-Claude**, son of Roché.

La Nuit Espagnole, see note on next letter.

here at Carré's. How are Denise and Jean-Claude? and the Sèvres house? Come over soon. Affectionately to all, Marcel. Saw Copley in Calif. He shut up shop after spending 70,000 dollars in a year. Not much hope for "Spanish Night." But maybe later on.

---

179. Marcel Duchamp to Henri-Pierre Roché   autograph letter
29 May 1949, New York   collection HRHRC

210 W. 14^(th) St. N.Y.C.

29 Mai 49

Merci de tout ce dérangement.

Oui l'ampoule doit avoir la dimension que je t'ai donnée parce que c'est la   *Paris Air* [cat. 43]
dimension de l'original (cassé). Celles qui sont dans les valises sont des   *Box-in-a-Valise* [cat. 4]
réductions, comme toutes les reproductions (en général).

Fais t'en faire une par la même occasion—

Tu pourrais l'envoyer par quelqu'un de confiance qui voyage, si tu *en* vois   *La Nuit Espagnole,*
un parmi les touristes américains. Ce n'est pas tellement urgent—   1922 (Ludwig Museum,
  Cologne), painting by
Tu recevras un jour du mois prochain la visite de William Copley, celui   Francis Picabia shown
qui voulait acheter la Nuit espagnole. Malheureusement il n'achète plus   Galerie Drouin, Paris,
ayant dépensé tout son argent disponible dans l'aventure désastreuse   4 - 26 Mar 1949.
d'une galerie à à [sic] Hollywood.
  The **Copley** Galleries
Il vient à Paris avec l'intention de peindre tranquillement et veut éviter les   close 1949.
gens pour commencer au moins.

C'est un très brave type.

T'écrirai plus longuement—

     Affectueusement

     Totor

▷ TRANSLATION: *210 W. 14th St. N.Y.C. 29th May '49. Thank you for all your trou-ble. Yes, the bulb must be the same size that I gave you because that's the size of the original (broken). The ones in the box-valises are miniatures, like all reproductions (in general). Have one made for yourself at the same time. You could send it with some trustworthy person traveling over, if you see one among the American tourists. It's not terribly urgent. You'll be getting a visit, one day next month, from William Copley, the one who wanted to buy Spanish Night. Unfortunately, he's no longer buying as he's spent all his disposable cash in some disastrous affair involving a gal-lery in Hollywood. He's coming to Paris with the intention of painting in peace and wants to keep away from people, to begin with at least. He's a really great guy. Will write you at greater length. Affectionately, Totor.*

180. Marcel Duchamp to Jacques and Gabrielle Villon   autograph letter
15 June 1949, [New York]   Estate of Marcel Duchamp, Villiers-sous-Grez

15 juin 49

Chère Gaby cher Gaston

Bien reçu et si rapidement le catalogue et ta lettre.

Le catalogue est pour Dreier qui fait, elle aussi, son catalogue de la Soc. Anonyme et a besoin de quelques dates exactes. Je te les renverrai d'ici une quinzaine de jours. Merci.

Le Baudelaire c'est pour Arensberg— quand j'étais chez eux il y a un mois, j'ai découvert que leur épreuve du Baudelaire (le plus simple sans socle) est la reproduction parue je crois dans "Architectures"— Ils m'ont donc demandé de trouver une épreuve de la gravure— Tu n'en as plus et tu ne pourrais pas en trouver une je pense— Si oui dis le moi, sinon envoie l'autre épreuve (avec socle) et dis moi combien elle coûte. Pour éviter les embêtements d'envoi par l'office des changes, peut être attends de trouver un voyageur (250 000 cette année paraît il) qui la prendrait sans complications. Sinon demande à Lefebvre Foinet de me l'envoyer— comme tu préfères.

Ton exposition a eu tout le succès désiré. Toutes les critiques sans exception ont été longues et de très bon aloi. Le public aussi, tous les gens que j'ai vus attendaient cette exposition, sachant très bien la nécessité de "montrer" ici, après tout ce qu'ils avaient lu—

Carré est content; j'ai dîné avec eux l'avant veille de son départ; et je ne doute pas qu'il "réussisse" ici, dans le genre Brummer—

Mon voyage en Californie très épatant— 6 jours à San Francisco; je me suis trouvé pour la première fois de ma vie devant un micro, et ce dans une langue étrangère. Tu vois le bafouillage; mais sans aucune importance; la publication de la conférence se fera en Octobre après corrections et mise au point des âneries dites. (ci joint photos de la conférence).—

Puis 12 jours chez les Arensbergs à Hollywood— Arrêt au retour en Arizona chez Max Ernst. Tout ça en avion.

D'accord pour la gravure de la Mariée naturellement (Skira). Rien de nouveau au Musée de Modern Art : ils sont insensés de lenteur et d'insouciance—

Le cheval de Raymond? Probablement Dr. Sandborg à Amsterdam. je l'ai vu ici il y a un mois.

Affectueusement à tous deux Marcel

j'oublie : je voudrais faire cadeau à Arensberg du livre sur Raymond— En existe t il encore?

Louis Carré Gallery exh. **catalog**, see p.273.

The catalog **Dreier** is preparing is *Collection of the Société Anonyme* (New Haven, Yale University Art Gallery, 1950) to which MD contributes 33 separate artists' biographies.

Villon's etching, *Baudelaire avec socle*, 1920, is actually a rendering of Raymond Duchamp-Villon's sculpture, *Baudelaire*, 1911.

Louis Carré **exhibition**, see p.273.

Louis Carré (1897-1977), Director of Louis Carré Gallery, NY.

"The Western Round Table," see p.273.

Probably an example of the hand-colored **collotype** of MD's *Bride* [cat. 23] by Villon, 1937.

Willem Sandberg, a curator at the Stedelijk Museum, Amsterdam.

Walter Pach, *Raymond Duchamp-Villon Sculpteur (1876-1918)*, Paris, Povolozky, 1924.

▷ TRANSLATION: *15th June '49. Dear Gaby, dear Gaston, Got the catalog and your letter and so quickly. The catalog is for Dreier as she is also making her own catalog for the Société Anonyme and needs some exact dates. I'll send them back to you in a fortnight or so. Thanks. The Baudelaire is for Arensberg. When I was at their place a month ago, I discovered that their proof of the Baudelaire (the simplest one with no base) is the reproduction that came out, I think, in "Architectures." They asked me, therefore, to find a proof of the engraving. You haven't got any more and wouldn't be able to find one, as far as I know. If you can, let me know and send the other proof (with base) and tell me how much it costs. To avoid any shipping problems with the Exchange Control Regulation, wait perhaps until you find somebody traveling over (250,000 this year, it seems) who would take it without any complications. Otherwise, ask Lefebvre Foinet to send it to me—as you prefer. Your exhibition had all the desired success. All the critics without exception covered it at length and with well-deserved praise. The public too, all the people I saw had all been waiting for this exhibition, very aware of the necessity to "show" here, after all they'd read. Carré is pleased. I had dinner with them two days before he left and I have no doubt he will be a success here, Brummer style. My trip to California really amazing—6 days in San Francisco. I found myself, for the first time in my life, in front of a microphone and in a foreign language to boot. You can imagine what gibberish, but no matter. The conference proceedings will come out in October when corrections have been made and the nonsense spoken tidied up. (Photos of the conference enclosed.) Then 12 days at the Arensbergs in Hollywood. Stop on the way back at Max Ernst's. All this by plane. OK about the engraving of the Bride, of course (Skira). Nothing new at the Museum of Modern Art—they are insanely slow and indifferent. Raymond's horse? Probably Dr Sandborg in Amsterdam. I saw him here a month ago. Affectionately to you both, Marcel. I was forgetting: I would like to give Arensberg a copy of the book on Raymond. Is it still in existence?*

---

181. Marcel Duchamp to Jean Suquet   autograph letter
9 August 1949, New York   collection Jean Suquet, Paris

9 Août 49
210 West 14ᵗʰ Street
New York City
     Mon cher Suquet,
Excusez mon retard à répondre; je rentre d'un petit tour à la campagne.
Suis tout à fait d'accord pour votre projet.
Et comme vous le dites, "en poète" est la seule façon de dire quelque chose.
Evidemment, je suis le dernier à pouvoir vous aider; tout au plus pourrai-
     je dire oui ou non et j'aurai beaucoup de plaisir à lire votre "mon
     miroir".
La déformation gauche-droite est plus sensible dans un écrit sur soi que
     dans la réflection de la glace.

Jean Suquet (b.1928), will eventually go on to write several books on the *Large Glass*, notably *Miroir de la Mariée* (Paris, Flammarion, 1974) and *Le grand verre rêvé* (Paris, Aubier, 1991).

Suquet's "project," put to him by Breton, is "to write a book about you and your work to appear in K editions" (first letter from Suquet to MD, 15 July 1949).

Mary Reynolds me dit que vous avez pu consulter la boîte verte chez elle. Dites-moi ce qui vous manque.

Affectueusement à vous et à Breton.

Marcel Duchamp.

▷ TRANSLATION: *9th August '49, 210 West 14th Street, New York City. My dear Suquet, Forgive my late reply. I am just back from a short trip to the country. You have my full agreement for your project. And as you say, "as a poet" is the only way to say anything. Obviously I am the last person who could help you: at best, I'd be able to answer yes or no and I would really enjoy reading your "my mirror." The left-right distortion is more noticeable in something written on oneself than in the reflection in the mirror. Mary Reynolds tells me you were able to consult the green box at her place. Let me know if there's anything you don't have. Affectionately, Marcel Duchamp.*

18 October 1949
Duchamp takes an overnight train from New York to Chicago to attend the opening of the Arensberg Collection at the Art Institute of Chicago. He stays only a few days and, on the train back to New York, writes to the Arensbergs about the exhibition.

---

182. Marcel Duchamp to Louise and Walter Arensberg   autograph letter
21 October 1949, on the train from Chicago to New York   collection PMA

Friday 21
on the train back to N.Y.

Dear Lou dear Walter

I had a very pleasant time in Chicago and must tell you that the collection, in these new surroundings, stands out like a block apart from the already classic Impressionists, Bonnard etc which the modern section of the Museum is made of.

You will have an approximate idea of the placing from the map I joint here—

6 small and 4 rectangular large rooms. One special room with only Brancusi sculpture and one special room where all and only my things are shown with a great deal of spacing—

The Picassos together on a large wall.

The double Braque shown at right angle with the wall so that you can see both sides—

All the rooms are lighted from an entirely luminous ceiling (ground glass) which gives evenly distributed daylight or electric light.

That even distribution of the light is very becoming to the paintings and sculpture (as compared with the ordinary spotlighting).

In fact you are not conscious of the source of light.

"20th Century Art from the Louise and Walter Arensberg Collection," opens 19 Oct 1949.

See reproduction of the "**map**" on last page of illustration section.

The walls are dim white thick cloth crackelled by time and do not carry
   any decorative intention.

The general effect was that all the paintings had been cleaned and in the
   case of the "Portrait" hung in your dining room, all the colors stood out
   as though the painting had been painted yesterday.

Probably *Portrait
Father* [cat. 6]

The conclusion is that you must see the collection in that presentation
   which naturally is an "Exhibition" presentation.

It will help you enormously to discuss the other problems and you will
   have all kinds of ideas about the possible final arrangements.

I saw Sam Marx yesterday morning with Rich and Kath. Kuh, all
   enthusiastic about having the collection in Chicago—

— Space : They showed me a space in the museum where they the have 2
   cathedral portals, almost full size—

Samuel A. Marx (1885-
1964), architect, art
collector, trustee of the
AIC (Art Institute of
Chicago).

Daniel Catton Rich
(1904- 1976), Director
of the AIC, 1943 - 1958.

Katharine Kuh
(1904-1994) curator of
20th Century Art at the
AIC, 1943 - 1959.

That space (200 ft x 58 ft and 28 feet high) would be sectioned in 2 or 3
   floors— and divided into large and small rooms, holding more than
   easily the whole collection— This remodeling would cost,
   approximately, between 200 000 and 300.000 dollars—

The next step is to have the trustees agree to raise that sum—

If you are coming in November, Rich will have already spoken and worked
   out the possibilities of raising the funds (which, according to Sam Marx,
   is not difficult).

As you said in your letter, Chicago is certainly a student center. In the 3
   days I was there, I saw flocks of students, and a big lecture was given in
   the rooms where the collection is shown—

A period of 20 years could be easily agreed upon during which the
   collection would be permanently shown in its ensemble—

The point I insist on, is that you must see your collection flying on its own
   wings.

I had to go through the usual lemon squeezing of the newspaper men but
   I enjoyed it and the notices were all decent and enthusiastic.

Sam Marx invited to dinner last night with Bobsy Goodspeed and Alice
   Roullier— His apartment and collection show his great love for what we
   also like.

I have no feeling toward or against Minneapolis— I only feel that
   remoteness and Cosmopolitanism are two very important factors— and
   I feel that Chicago is better, geographically, than Minneapolis.

The Arensbergs are
also considering the
idea of donating their
collection to the
Minneapolis Museum
of Art.

I also feel that a promise to raise funds and to keep their word from the
   Chicago people can be trusted.

   Affectueusement à tous deux
   Marcel

183. Marcel Duchamp to Henri-Pierre Roché   autograph letter
14 November 1949, New York   collection HRHRC

210 W. 14th St.

14 Nov 49

    Cher Totor

L'ampoule est bien arrivée mais elle est encore chez Sweeney qui n'a pas
eu le temps de m'inviter à venir la chercher. Tous mes mercis "sans
voir"__ D'ailleurs je te dois des tas de lettres et j'ai un mal de chien à
écrire.__

J'ai été invité à Chicago et j'y ai passé 3 jours très agréables__ L'expo
Arensberg est vraiment remarquable__ je t'envoie le catalogue par poste
ordinaire (10 ou 12 jours)__ Vu le brave Brewster, Alice, Bobsy
Goodspeed. Dans l'expo. Arensberg, Brancusi a une salle entière pour
ses choses, et moi aussi une salle pour les miennes__

D'accord pour te vendre une ou 2 choses de mon lot d'anciennes toiles__
Mais je ne me les rappelle pas, et j'attends les photos pour tâcher de me
les remettre en mémoire.__ De plus je te dois toujours $300⁻ pour
l'urinal (te rappelles tu?)__ Dis moi toi même ce que tu veux payer__ je
ne pense pas qu'il y aura une "grande demande" malgré les bons
conseillers qui regrettent que je ne peins plus__

Je vis de plus en plus loin de la 57th St__ et je joue beaucoup aux échecs
sans bons résultats (excepté un petit tournoi cet été où j'ai gagné mes 6
parties, mais vraiment les adversaires étaient faibles).

Jean Claude va certainement te battre si tu ne t'entraînes pas.

Comment va Denise?

Ta notice sur Bruce va paraître dans le catalogue de Yale (Soc. Anonyme)
qui paraîtra l'été prochain__

T'écrirai bientôt, dès que j'aurai reçu les photos__

    Affectueusement à Denise Jean Claude et toi

    Totor

Replacement of *Paris Air* [cat. 43] MD asked Roché to send, see p.272.

"20th Century Art from the L. & W. Arensberg Collection," see p.273.

Alice = Alice Roullier

Probably miniature versions of *Fountain* [cat. 38] MD made for his *Box-in-a-Valise* [cat. 4], which Roché sold (through MD) to Maria Martins (p.286).

"57th St" = home of Brummer, Guggenheim, Sidney Janis, Julien Levy and Jacques Seligmann... Galleries.

Roché's entry on American painter **Patrick Henri Bruce** (1881-1936), for the Société Anonyme catalog.

▷ TRANSLATION: *210 W. 14th St. 14th Nov. '49. Dear Totor. The ampoule arrived
safely but is still at Sweeney's who hasn't yet had time to invite me over to fetch it.
My "unseeing" thanks to you. What's more, I owe you stacks of letters and I have
a devil of a job writing. I was invited to Chicago and spent 3 very enjoyable days
there. The Arensberg exhibition is absolutely remarkable. I'm sending you the catalog by ordinary mail (10 to 12 days). Saw Brewster, grand chap, Alice, Bobsy
Goodspeed. In the Arensberg exhib. Brancusi has a room all to himself for his
things and so do I for mine. OK on selling you one or 2 things out of my lot of old
canvases. But I can't bring them to mind, and am waiting for the photos to jog my*

memory. What's more, I owe you $300-for the urinal (remember?). You tell me just how much you want to pay. I don't think there'll be a "great demand" in spite of the wise counsellors who are sorry I don't paint any more. I live further and further away from 57th St. and play chess a lot without great success (apart from a small tournament this summer where I won my 6 games, but the opponents really were weak). Jean Claude will certainly beat you if you don't get in training. How is Denise? Your announcement on Bruce is coming out in the Yale catalog (Soc. Anonyme) coming out next summer. Will write soon, as soon as I get the photos. Affectionately to Denise, Jean-Claude and yourself, Totor.

---

184. Marcel Duchamp to Henri-Pierre Roché   autograph letter
18 December 1949, New York   collection HRHRC

> 210 W. 14.
> N.Y.C.
> 18 Dec 49
>   Cher Totor
> je rentre de Chicago pour la 2eme fois; j'ai vu les Arensbergs venus de
>   Californie pour voir leur collection dans une lumière complètement
>   différente— T'ai je dit que j'ai été frappé par la fraîcheur et le bon état
>   (technique) de la plupart de mes toiles— vues dans cette forte lumière
>   de musée—
> — J'ai parlé à Walter des [sic] mes tableaux de jeunesse et je lui envoie les
>   photos aujourd'hui de toutes les toiles (sauf celles de Mary
>   naturellement) mais y compris les tiennes— Y vois tu un inconvénient?
>   et dis moi si 500 dollars est un prix qui te convient <u>au cas où</u> ils
>   exprimeraient le désir d'en acheter.
>   Affectueusement
>   Totor

Mary = Mary Reynolds

▷ TRANSLATION: *210 W. 14. N.Y.C. 18th December '49. Dear Totor, Back from Chicago for 2nd time. I saw the Arensbergs who came over from California to see their collection in a completely different light. Did I tell you that I was struck by how fresh most of my canvases looked and in what good condition (technical), seen under the strong museum lighting? I spoke to Walter about the paintings I did in my youth and am sending him today the photos of all the canvases (except the ones of Mary, naturally) but including yours. Do you have any objection? And let me know if you are happy with 500 dollars in case they express the wish to buy. Affectionately, Totor.*

185. Marcel Duchamp to Elisa and André Breton   autograph letter
25 December 1949, New York   source: from Y. Poupard-Lieussou transcript

210 West 14th St.
New York 11. N.Y.
25 Déc. 49
    Chère Elisa cher André
Ce ne sont plus des mois *maintenant* mais des années qui passent sans que
je vous donne signe de vie. Il est clair que vous savez à peu près tout de
moi, puisque je reste fidèle à mon inaction externe; celle-ci
s'accompagne malheureusement d'une tendance à la pétrification
spirituelle dûe à l'actuelle connerie médiocre décidément déclarée
d'utilité publique.
Autrement, je viens de lire le texte de Jean Suquet sur la Mariée et je lui
écris aujourd'hui même combien j'ai eu de plaisir à retrouver tous mes
"détails de jeunesse" oubliés pour la plupart =
Il a fait un travail de Romain, plein d'exactitude et de clairvoyance et je
suis sûr que la publication de ce texte sera une pour beaucoup de gens
une mise au clair de mes pseudo-obscurités, en même temps qu'une
condamnation de toutes les monographies qu'on me promet de temps à
autre, ici.
Etais chez Donati l'autre soir et il m'a parlé de votre angoisse présente.—
Si on trouvait une revue américaine sans tendance trop définie (littéraire
en général) qui pourrait publier une "lettre de Paris" sur la critique des
activités européennes (tout ce qui vous plairait d'écrire) vous sentez vous
le courage d'envoyer une fois par mois (je suppose) 3 ou 4 pages qui vous
seraient payées convenablement.— Dites moi ce que vous pensez de
l'idée et quelle somme vous considérez une rémunération désirable.
Y a t il dans votre collection des tableaux dont vous vous sépareriez sans
chagrin? je pourrais les proposer sur photo à des musées ou à des
collectionneurs.
Enfin, racontez moi quelque chose bientôt
    Toutes nos affections à tous deux et à Aube qui devrait s'appeler
    Rosée (déjà)—
    Marcel

Suquet's initial work on *The Bride Stripped Bare...* [cat. 1], 1949-1956, written under the general title "Psyché d'une mariée mise à nu," is not published at the time. Suquet sends 40 pages of this (with a second letter, 12 Dec 1949). Only "Le Signe du Cancer" appears in *La Nef*, Paris, numéro spécial *(Almanach Surréaliste du demi-siècle)*, Mar-Apr 1950.

Aube Breton (b.1935), daughter of A. Breton and Jacqueline Lamba. Pun on the names *Aube* meaning "dawn" and *Rosée* meaning "dew."

▷ TRANSLATION: *210 West 14th St. New York 11. N.Y. 25th Dec. '49. Dear Elisa, dear André, It's no longer months now but years that have gone by since I last gave you any sign of life. Clearly you know more or less everything about me as I remain constant in my outward inaction, which unfortunately is accompanied by a tendency towards spiritual stultification due to the current bloody mediocrity firmly established as something for the public good. Apart from that, I've just read Jean Suquet's text on the Bride and I'm writing to him this very day to say what a joy it was to rediscover all those "details of [my] youth," forgotten for the most part. He has worked like a Trojan, with great precision and lucidity and I'm sure that publication of this text will shed light on my pseudo-obscurity for many people, while at the same time serving as a condemnation of all the monographies that have been promised to me at one time or another over here. Was at Donati's the other evening and he spoke to me about your current anxiety. If we found an American journal that didn't have too definite a bias (literature in general) that could publish a "letter from Paris" on the criticism of European activities (whatever you would want to write), could you bear to send, once a month (I assume), 3 or 4 pages for which you would be decently paid? Let me know what you think of the idea and what you would consider desirable remuneration. Are there any paintings in your collection which you could part with painlessly? I could propose them in photo form to museums or collectors. Anyway, let me have some news soon. All our affection to you both and to Aube who should be called Rosée (already), Marcel.*

---

186. Marcel Duchamp to Jean Suquet   autograph letter
25 December 1949, New York   collection Jean Suquet, Paris

> 210 West 14th street
> New York 11, N.Y.
> 25 Déc. 49
>   Cher Suquet,
> Bien reçu votre lettre et presque en même temps le long texte qui m'a rempli de joie. Vous savez sans doute que vous êtes le seul au monde à avoir reconstitué la gestation du verre dans ses détails, avec même les nombreuses intentions jamais exécutées. Votre travail de patience m'a permis de revivre une longue période d'années au cours desquelles furent écrites les notes de la boîte verte en même temps que le verre prenait forme; et je vous avoue que, n'ayant pas relu ces notes depuis très longtemps, j'avais perdu complètement souvenir de nombreux points, pas illustrés sur le verre, qui m'enchantent encore.
> Une chose importante pour vous est que vous sachiez combien je dois à Raymond Roussel qui m'a délivré, en 1912, de tout un passé "physico-plastique" dont je cherchais déjà à sortir. Une représentation au théâtre Antoine d'"Impressions d'Afrique" à laquelle j'assistais avec Apollinaire et Picabia, en Octobre ou Novembre 1912 (je vous serais reconnaissant de vérifier la date) fut une révélation pour nous trois; car il s'agissait vraiment d'un homme nouveau à ce moment-là. Encore aujourd'hui, je considère Raymond Roussel d'autant plus important qu'il n'a pas fait école.
> Naturellement, mon cher Suquet, faites reproduire tout ce que vous jugerez nécessaire à votre texte si lumineux.

Raymond Roussel (1877-1933), French vanguard writer. In June 1912, MD saw a play adapted from his novel, *Impressions d'Afrique* (Paris, Lemerre, 1910).

"Avoir l'apprenti dans le soleil", si je me rappelle exactement la phrase accompagnant la silhouette du cycliste montant une côte, faisait partie d'une courte série de courts textes dans une boîte à plaques photographiques (1912 ou 1913?); je suis heureux que vous ayez pu en voir un exemplaire (il y en a eu seulement trois) chez Villon qui en sait bien d'autres sur mon compte. Naturellement, servez-vous de l'apprenti si vous le jugez digne.

To Have the Apprentice... [cat. 27]

Box of 1914 [cat. 54]; Villon's example seen by Suquet and later lost.

Un point important aussi que vous avez senti très exactement porte sur l'idée que le verre en fin de compte n'est pas fait pour être regardé (avec des yeux "esthétiques"); il devait être accompagné d'un texte de "littérature" aussi amorphe que possible qui ne prit jamais forme; et les deux éléments verre pour les yeux, texte pour l'oreille et l'entendement devaient se compléter et surtout s'empêcher l'un l'autre de prendre une forme esthético-plastique ou littéraire. Après tout, je vous dois la fière chandelle d'avoir mis à nu ma mise à nu.

Très cordialement,
Marcel Duchamp.

▷ TRANSLATION: *210 West 14th Street, New York 11, N.Y. 25th Dec. '49. Dear Suquet, Received your letter and, almost at the same time, the long text at which I was over-joyed. You no doubt know that you are the only person in the world to have put to-gether the gestation of the glass in all its detail, including even the numerous intentions which were never executed. Your patient work has enabled me to relive a period of long years during which the notes were written for the green box at the same time as the glass was taking shape. And I confess to you that, not having read these notes for a very long time, I had completely lost all recollection of numerous points not illustrated on the glass and which are a delight to me now. One impor-tant point for you is to know how indebted I am to Raymond Roussel who, in 1912, delivered me from a whole "physicoplastic" past which I had been trying to get out of. A production at the Antoine theater of "Impressions d'Afrique" which I went to see with Apollinaire and Picabia in October or November 1912 (I would be grateful if you would check the date), was a revelation for the three of us, for it really was about a new man at that time. To this day, I consider Raymond Roussel all the more important for not having built up a following. Naturally, my dear Suquet, have reproduced whatever you deem necessary to your brilliantly lucid text. "To have the apprentice in the sun," if I remember the exact caption accompanying the silhouette of a cyclist going up a hill, part of a short series of short texts in a box of photographic plates (1912 or 1913?)—I'm glad you've been able to see one (there are only three) at Villon's who knows plenty more about me. Use the apprentice, naturally, if you think it worthy. Another important point which you so very accu-rately sensed concerns the idea that the glass in actual fact is not meant to be looked at (with "aesthetic" eyes). It should be accompanied by a "literary" text, as amor-phous as possible, which never took shape. And the two elements, glass for the eyes, text for the ears and understanding, should complement each other and above all prevent one or the other from taking on an aesthetico-plastic or literary form. All in all, I am hugely indebted to you for having stripped bare my Bride stripped bare. Most sincerely, Marcel Duchamp.*

---

187. Marcel Duchamp to Suzanne Duchamp and Jean Crotti   autograph letter
31 December 1949, New York   collection AAA

210 W. 14.
31 Dec. 49.
    Chère Suzanne cher Jean
Il y a déja quinze jours, j'ai vu Ardinger d'Inter Ocean et il a promis
d'écrire à Buenos Aires pour savoir si la Banque est toujours en
possession des Gemmaux <u>en bon état</u>; il doit me faire parvenir la
réponse que je te ferai suivre immédiatement.
L'avocat Tremaine (il y a plus d'un mois) m'a aussi promis de faire ta
proposition 450 dollars. Il m'a dit que, vraisemblablement (et je
suppose pour ne pas se compromettre vis à vis de la douane) l'affaire se
ferait (si elle se fait) par mon entremise : tu m'enverrais le verre et une
fois en ma possession (douane payée par moi) je lui vendrais 450 et il me
rembourserait la douane en plus.__ mais ne t'emballe pas ce ne sont que
des possibilités
Merci Suzanne, du paquet de photos qui m'ont fait grand plaisir.
Non, je ne fais pas de catalogue de mes choses mais ces photos peuvent être
utiles__
C'est drôle que tu ne te rappelles pas ce grand portrait à l'huile de profil,
avec si je me rappelle bien un dessous au noir et blanc; une grande toile
plus d'1ᵐ

dans le genre du portrait de Marcel (neveu de Clémence) dont tu pourras
voir la photo chez Mary; j'ai à peu près la certitude que cette toile a été
faite à Blainville vers 1902 comme le dessin que tu m'envoies (quelle est
l'année exacte du départ pour Rouen?)

Autre chose : j'écris une notice biographique sur Emile Nicolle pour le
catalogue Yale j'ai déja demandé à Gaston ses souvenirs

Ardinger probably an agent of Inter Ocean shipping company.

Gemmaux, term given to technique of working in glass invented and patented by Jean Crotti. A work in this medium is apparently lent in 1949 to an Exh. of modern art, Museu de Arte Moderna in São Paolo, (see p.265).

Clémence has been in service with Duchamp family. (She committed suicide 18 Dec 1925.)

Mary = Mary Reynolds

Departure in 1905

Emile Nicolle (1830-1894), still life painter and engraver, maternal grandfather of MD. The Emile Nicolle entry is signed by MD only.

Dis moi ce que tu sais du grand père; je signerai la notice de nos 3 noms, **Gaston** = Jacques
Gaston, toi et moi.   Villon

————

je vais aller cette semaine à l'Argent Gallery et faire envoyer tes aquarelles à
Columbus—

————

Jean Inter Ocean a changé d'adresse :
        39 Broadway

————

à bientôt autres nouvelles
      affectueux 1950
      Marcel

▷ TRANSLATION: *210 W.14. 31st Dec. '49. Dear Suzanne, dear Jean, I saw Arlinger
from the Inter Ocean a fortnight ago now and he promised to write to Buenos Aires
to find out whether the Bank is still in possession of the Gemmaux and in good condition. He's to let me know their reply which I will forward to you instantly. The
lawyer, Tremaine, (over a month ago now) also promised me he would make your
offer of 450 dollars. He told me that, most likely (I suppose so as not to compromise
himself regarding customs) the deal would go through (if it goes through at all)
through me: you would send me the glass and once in my possession (customs paid
by me), I would sell it to him 450 and he would pay me back the customs duties on
top. But don't get too carried away. These are only maybe's. Thank you, Suzanne,
for the set of photos which I was very glad to receive. No, I'm not making a catalog
of my things but these photos could be very useful. Funny you don't remember this
large oil portrait in profile, the sketch, if I remember rightly, done in black and
white —a big canvas, more than 1m [sketch]—same kind of thing as the portrait of
Marcel (Clémence's nephew) of which you can see a photo at Mary's. I'm practically certain that this canvas was done at Blainville around 1902 like the drawing
you're sending me. (What is the exact year of departure for Rouen?) One more
thing: I'm writing a biographical entry on Emile Nicolle for the Yale catalog and
have asked Gaston for his recollections. Tell me all you know about our grandfather. I'll sign the entry with our three names, Gaston, you and myself. I'm going to
the Argent Gallery this week and will have your watercolors sent to Columbus.
Jean, Inter Ocean has moved to 39 Broadway. Hope to hear from you soon. An
affectionate 1950, Marcel.*

188. Marcel Duchamp to André Breton   autograph letter
10 January 1950, [New York]   source: from Y. Poupard-Lieussou transcript

10 Janvier 1950

Cher André

Vite un mot en réponse à votre longue lettre qui m'a fait très plaisir—

Voici :

Holtzman un peintre plus ou moins abstrait mais qui a d'autres préoccupations veut faire une revue, sorte de forum sans couleur bien définie et surtout pas une défense de l'art abstrait; tout ce que je sais de lui est plutôt sympathique et les noms des gens à qui il a demandé des articles sont très différents les uns des autres. Donc il vous propose un article d'environ 3 000 mots et si vous n'avez pas un sujet préféré, il serait heureux si vous consentiez à écrire quelque chose sur un thème comme "Science et Surréalisme" ou un thème analogue— Sans d'ailleurs aucune exigence— il acceptera avec enthousiasme tout ce que vous écrirez et ne tripotera pas—

3 000 mots $30— C'est peu— mais il dit que si votre article est assez long pour couvrir 2 numéros— ce qui ferait environ 6 000 mots et $60— il est tout à fait d'accord—

Il est entendu d'ailleurs que si vous n'en écrivez que 4 000 vous recevrez 40 dollars— etc.

D'autre *part* Maria m'écrit qu'elle a trouvé à Rio des possibilités d'articles pour vous et elle va vous écrire.

Merci surtout mon cher André pour avoir déclenché cette curiosité, chez de jeunes types, à comprendre ce que 30 ans de voisinage esthétique de misérables teinturiers m'avaient déjà découragé d'entreprendre.

— Pour la reproduction du petit tableau de jeunesse, entendu— Comme titre je propose : Courant ~~sur~~ d'air sur le pommier du Japon.

J'attends ~~la lettre~~ l'article de Carrouges— J'ai de lui une lettre très gentille et il faut que je lise "la Colonie pénitentiaire". J'ai dit à Suquet ce que je devais à Roussel. Kafka n'était pas né pour la France en 1912.

Affectueusement à tous deux

Marcel

Harry Holtzman (1912-1994), American abstract painter and writer, edits journal *trans/formation: arts, communication, environment.*

Maria, artist's name of **Maria Martins** (1894-1973), Brazilian sculptor who knew MD in the 1940's and about whom Breton had written.

Japanese Apple Tree [cat. 11]

On **Carrouges**'s article, see note on next letter.

"La colonie pénitentiaire", first translation into French of *In der Strafkolonie* by **Franz Kafka** (1883-1924), appeared only in 1938 (in a journal under the title "Au bagne"). The second, published in book form (1945), is used by Carrouges in his analysis.

▷ TRANSLATION: *10th January 1950. Dear André, In haste, a line in reply to your long letter I was so pleased to receive. So: Holtzman, a more or less abstract painter but who also has other preoccupations, wants to start a journal, kind of forum with no set flavor and above all not in defense of abstract art. As far as I know, he seems very nice and the people he has asked for articles are all very different from each other. So he's asking you for an article of about 3,000 words and if you don't have any preference for a particular subject, he would be pleased if you would agree to write something on a theme like "Science and Surrealism" or something similar—with* *no pressure whatsoever—he'll eagerly accept whatever you write and won't fiddle with it. 3,000 words $30. It's not much, but he says that if your article is long enough to cover 2 issues, which would be 6,000 words and $60, he's perfectly happy with that. In fact the arrangement is that if you only write 4,000 you'll get 40 dollars etc. In addition, Maria tells me in her letter that she has found possibilities of articles for you in Rio and is going to write to you. Thanks above all, my dear André, for having awakened among young guys the curiosity to understand what 30 years of living in aesthetic proximity with wretched dyers had already discouraged me from taking on. As for the reproduction of the small painting from my youth, OK. As its title I suggest: Draft on the Japanese Apple Tree. I'm waiting for Carrouges's article. I got a very nice letter from him and I must read "The Penal Colony." I told Suquet all I owed to Roussel. Kafka wasn't born for France in 1912. Affectionately to you both, Marcel.*

---

189. Marcel Duchamp to Michel Carrouges   autograph letter
6 February 1950, New York   source: from André Gervais transcript

210 West 14th Street
New York City
6 Février 1950
    Mon cher Carrouges,
J'ai reçu longtemps après votre lettre le texte que j'ai lu plusieurs fois.
Si je suis redevable à Raymond Roussel de m'avoir permis, dès 1912, de
    penser à autre chose qu'à une peinture rétinienne (André Breton vous
    éclairera sur ce terme car nous l'avons discuté ensemble), je dois avouer
    n'avoir pas lu le Pénitencier, et seulement la Métamorphose il y a fort
    peu d'années.
Seulement pour vous dire les événements circonstanciels qui m'ont
    conduit vers la Mariée.
J'ai donc été émerveillé par le parallélisme évident que vous avez
    clairement établi.
Les conclusions auxquelles vous êtes amené dans le domaine "signification
    intérieure" me passionnent, même si je n'y souscris pas (au moins en ce
    qui concerne le Verre).
Mes intentions de peintre, qui d'ailleurs n'ont rien à faire avec le résultat
    profond dont je ne peux être conscient, étaient dirigées vers les
    problèmes d'une "validité esthétique" obtenue principalement dans
    l'abandon du phénomène visuel, tant au point de vue rapports rétiniens
    qu'au point de vue anecdotique.

"**Text**" = *Franz Kafka et Marcel Duchamp* by **Michel Carrouges** (1910-1988) first appears as an article in *Le Mercure de France* (1 Jan 1952), then as a chapter of his book, *Les machines célibataires* (Paris, Arcanes, 1954).

The Metamorphosis (1937) and *The Penal Colony* (1941), Franz Kafka.

The Bride Stripped Bare... [cat. 1]

Large Glass [cat. 2]

Quant au reste, je puis affirmer que l'introduction d'un thème de base
expliquant ou provoquant certains "gestes" de la mariée et des
célibataires, ne m'est jamais venue à l'esprit. Mais il est probable que
mes ancêtres m'ont fait "parler", comme eux, de ce que mes petits-fils
diront aussi.
>   Célibatairement à vous
>   Marcel Duchamp.

▷ TRANSLATION: *210 West 14th Street, New York City, 6th February 1950. My dear
Carrouges, I received, long after your letter, the text which I have read over several
times. I am indebted to Raymond Roussel for having enabled me, as early as 1912,
to think of something other than retinal painting. (André Breton will enlighten you
on this term as we discussed it together.) I must confess that I have never read The
Penal Colony and that I only read The Metamorphosis just a few years ago. Simply
to let you know the circumstantial events which led me to the Bride. So I was
amazed at the evident parallelism you clearly establish. The conclusions you are led
to draw in the domain of "inner significance" I find passionately interesting, even
if I don't agree with them (at least as far as the Glass is concerned). My intentions
as a painter, which actually have nothing to do with the deep result which I cannot
be conscious of, were directed towards problems of "aesthetic validity" principally
achieved through abandoning the visual phenomenon from the point of view of retinal relationships as from the anecdotal point of view. As for the rest, I can confirm
that the introduction of a basic theme, explaining or provoking certain "gestures"
on the part of the bride and the bachelors, never occurred to me. But it's likely that
my ancestors made me speak, as they did, about what my grandchildren will say
too. Bachelorly yours, Marcel Duchamp.*

---

190. Marcel Duchamp to Louise and Walter Arensberg   autograph letter
8 July 1950, New York   collection PMA

210 W. 14th St.
8th July 1950
>   Dear Lou dear Walter
Many thanks for your letter— I am very proud to become Vice President
of the Francis Bacon Foundation—
Went to Philadelphia on Wednesday and found Fiske Kimball at his
desk— We reviewed every proposition he had made and went and
looked at the rooms.
In a letter, he sent you on Dec. 14th 1949 he offers 20 rooms (3 very large
ones) on 3 floors—

The Arensbergs make
MD Vice President of
the Francis Bacon
Foundation,
organization they
founded to continue
W. Arensberg's literary
work on Francis Bacon.

Here is the detail :

(Take your small blue prints) :

1st floor__ Rooms marked   16115

16112

16111

1715

1711

1721

1751

1753

Rm 1721 is large and has the 3 windows to the ceiling.

Second floor__ The second floor is not yet built up inside__ In other words, you have an area of 75 feet (with the 3 windows from floor to *ceiling* by 85 feet. (except the rooms marked 2719 and 2729 which are not built either)

Between these two floors there is a mezzanine comprising ~~two~~ 2 long galleries (each 80 ft x 20) and divided I think into several rooms.

As far as space goes, you have ample room for everything, pre-Colombian sculpture included.

According to F.K.'s estimate, there are 1400 running feet as against 1100 in Chicago.   **F.K.** = Fiske Kimball

— The side lighting of the 3 high windows on the 1st and second floors makes an impression quite different from the usual cubicle effect of museum galleries, in general.

— as I said before, the second floor not being built inside, would lend itself to any disposition of rooms you may desire__ and I think this should be taken up seriously since, according to F.K., they would make the division of the space to suit what the rooms are to contain.

— I leave it to you to discuss whether the Pre-Colombian sculpture should be put in another part of the Museum__ But I think that, in the space offered, you may very well find several rooms to present it beautifully and by itself.

— I did not mention the question of time__ as you will take care of it much better than I would have.

— But F.K. is all keyed up again and ready to see your points with sympathy.

— Walter Pach was very generous : he sent me a cheque for $500⁻ immediately and the picture was shipped Wednesday (the 5th)

— Yes I agree with Walter about <u>no</u> sales and (almost \?\) no loans.

— I received a letter from the photographer in Venice. He mentions the size of the <u>transparent film</u> in <u>color</u> (<u>positive</u>) : 10 x 7 inches which is a good size.

He also speaks of the possibility to make a colored print on paper of 1^m (40 inches high) which is the actual size of the painting.

I answered, asking for the price of this second item and as soon as I know it I will place the final order of the 2 things.

Hope you won't get tired reading this long letter.

Affectueusement à tous deux

Marcel

MD has ordered a color transparency of his painting *Sad Young Man*... [cat. 15] from the Guggenheim Collection in Venice.

---

191. Marcel Duchamp to Henri-Pierre Roché   autograph letter
17 July 1950, New York   collection HRHRC

210 W. 14th
17 Juillet 1950

Merci de ta lettre du 14 Juillet avec la carte de Mary à toi, vraiment révélatrice de l'etat nerveux dans lequel elle est, et aussi de sa faiblesse.

Je décide de ne pas partir car de deux choses l'une, ou bien elle ne connaît pas son état et ma venue serait un choc dangereux pour son moral. ou bien elle peut encore guérir si ce sont vraiment des colibacilles.

Voici le point important : Je n'ai jamais prononcé le mot cancer; Mais crois tu qu'il y a là une terrible possibilité— Ou bien sais tu quelque chose négatif ou positif de ce que les docteurs ont dit? n'hésite pas à me le dire.

De plus si tu ne sais pas, pourrais tu t'arranger pour communiquer avec Franz Thomassin Hotel Bellevue *Souillac* qui est avec Mary depuis La Preste.

Lui en sait certainement plus long

— Mais si tu communiques avec lui fais le sans que Mary le sache— Un télégramme est dangereux car il le recevrait probablement en présence de Mary.

Le plus simple peut être serait de lui écrire une lettre ordinaire et de lui demander de te téléphoner à St Robert ou à Paris et tu lui parlerais de cette idée de cancer qui me turlupine.

J'ai écrit à son frère à Chicago le mettant au courant et lui demandant d'être prudent dans ses lettres pour ne pas alarmer Mary si elle ne croit pas être en danger—

Le tout est de mourir sans le savoir, ce qui d'ailleurs se passe toujours ainsi. Mais éviter les appréhensions et les souffrances physiques.

Affect— Totor

Mary Reynolds has been experiencing kidney problems since Apr 1950.

Dr. Franz Thomassin runs a private clinic at La Preste in the Pyrenees.

Mary Reynolds' brother Frank Brookes Hubacheck, see p.230.

▷ TRANSLATION: *210 W. 14th 17th July 1950. Thanks for your letter of 14th July with the card Mary sent you, really revealing about the state her nerves are in at the moment, and also how weak she is. I have decided not to go because it comes to the same thing: either she is not aware of her condition and my coming would be a blow to her morale, or she can still get better if it really is coli bacilli. The thing is this: I have never actually said the word cancer, but do you think such a dreadful thing is a possiblity? Or do you have any idea, either negative or positive, of what the doctors have said? Don't hesitate in telling me. In fact, if you don't know could you manage to get in touch with Franz Thomassin, Hotel Bellevue, Souillac, who has been with Mary since La Preste? He will certainly know more. But if you do get in touch with him, don't let Mary know. A telegram is dangerous because he might well receive it while Mary is there. The simplest thing would be to send him an ordinary letter asking him to telephone you in St Robert or in Paris and then talk to him about this idea of cancer which is plaguing me. I've written to her brother in Chicago putting him in the picture and asking him to be cautious in his letters so as not to alarm Mary if she doesn't think she is in danger. The main thing is to die without knowing anything about it, which is in any case what always happens. But avoiding anxiety and physical suffering. Affect. Totor.*

---

192. Marcel Duchamp to Louise and Walter Arensberg   autograph letter
7 September 1950, New York   collection PMA

210 W. 14th
7th Sept 1950
      Dear Lou dear Walter
I went to Philadelphia today and came back with the feeling that your idea
      of having the whole ground floor + 2 mezzanines was the better
      solution—
My only objection was that I thought the windows started 15 ft f above
      the ground— They actually start only 7 feet above the ground. hardly
      above eye level— The rooms are flooded with daylight— and even
      under the windows the wall is quite well lighted.—
I am sending you the tracings I made with the indication of length, width
      and height of every room—
The first solution : The whole ground floor, including the big central room
      which is not built yet (only the four walls). + the 2 mezzanines.
      (being understood that the Gallatin Collection is removed upstairs).

Gallatin Collection, p.271.

The second solution : The large space upstairs with 3 windows to the ground
      + the 2 mezzanines and a large room (ground floor) with 3 windows
      (starting 7 feet from ground) and maybe the big central room, not built
      yet.
— In both solutions you get the same amount of space.

— But after reconsidering my first idea *(in my last letter)*, I now prefer the first solution that is (removal of Gallatin upstairs) the whole ground floor and the 2 mezzanines.

— Of course the next step is for you to see it.

Fiske Kimball tells me that the Jubilee opening is for the 3rd of November

— ~~He~~ As he knows your taste for Jubilees in general, he suggests that you choose to come before or after the opening, as he seems to have put Zeagrosser in charge of the whole organization "jubilaire". And he will have all his time for you, when you come.

I, on the other hand, am going to Europe for a month— my old friend Mary Reynolds is dying of uremia and her brother has asked me to go and see her— There is very little hope of saving her— her kidneys are too far gone— This was a great shock—

I am leaving on the Queen Mary Sept 14th and have reserved my passage back on the 24th of October (also Queen Mary)— If you have time before the 14th of Sept. (next Thursday) ~~will y~~ please give me your first reaction to the tracings and you can always write to me in Paris— as a permanent address I will be probably at the Crotti's

> ^c/o Jean Crotti
> 5 rue Parmentier
> Neuilly ^s/Seine (Seine)

of course I would like to be here when you come East.

If November is not too late, I surely will be back then—

Anyway let me know the developments.

You never told me about the time limitations in the Philadelphia proposals.

Are there any?

I did not ask Kimball about it.

> Affectueusement et à bientôt
> Marcel

P.S. as I am scared of the Parisian crocodiles, I keep my going as mute as possible— Keep it for yourself at least for a few days—

"Masterpieces in America," PMA, 3 Nov 1950 - 11 Feb 1951.

Carl Zigrosser (1891-1975), curator of Prints at the PMA 1941-1963.

In fact at Roché's (99 bd. Arago), then at Mary Reynolds' (14 rue Hallé), then at a hotel (108 rue Saint-Lazare).

14 September 1950
Realizing that Mary Reynolds' condition is steadily worsening, Duchamp departs for Paris aboard the "Queen Mary." With Duchamp at her side, Mary Reynolds dies in her apartment on 30 September 1950. After just over two months in Paris, he returns to New York, writing a letter to Man Ray aboard ship to relate the sad news.

193. Marcel Duchamp to Man Ray   autograph letter
1 December 1950, on board ship returning to US from Paris   collection GRI

[letterhead crossed out in pen:]

~~Grand Hotel~~
~~TERMINUS SAINT LAZARE~~
~~108, Rue Saint Lazare~~
~~Paris~~

1ᵉʳ Dec. 50
en bateau, revenant aux U.S.A.
    Cher Man
Tu a su certainement que j'étais allé à Paris pour voir Mary mourir avec
    un minimum de souffrance—
La même pensée de rage que j'ai toujours eue depuis le début de sa
    maladie, me poursuit car elle même, par une sorte de suicide
    inconscient, s'est refusée à toute intervention chirurgicale quand
    peut être il aurait été temps encore—
Rien de tel qu'<u>une seule</u> mort pour mettre à jour la connerie du reste des
    humains—
        écris
        Affectueusement à tous deux
        Marcel

▷ TRANSLATION: *1st Dec. '50. aboard ship, returning to USA. Dear Man, You will
have heard that I went to Paris to see Mary die with minimal suffering. The same
rage in my head that I've had ever since the beginning of her illness hounds me now
for she herself, in a kind of subconscious suicide bid, refused to have any kind of sur-
gery when there perhaps would still have been time. Nothing like the death of one
person to bring home to you the senselessness of all the rest of the bloody human
race. Write to me. Affectionately to you both, Marcel.*

New York, 210 West 14 St | 1950-1953

chapter 11

New York: returning to 210 West 14th St, room on 4th and top floor
round trips to Syracuse and Cazenovia, for chess tournaments

from 1 January 1950 to early 1954

▶ MAJOR WORKS

Not a Shoe (galvanized plaster, 1950)
Feuille de vigne femelle / Female Fig Leaf
(galvanized plaster, resembling mold of a
vagina, 1950)
Objet-Dard / Dart-Object (galvanized plaster,
with inlaid lead rib, resembling a phallus,
1951)
Poster-catalog for "Dada: 1916-1923" exhibition
(Sidney Janis Gallery, New York, 15 Apr -
9 May 1953)
Moonlight on the Bay at Basswood (pen, pencil,
talcum powder and chocolate on paper,
21 Aug 1953)

▶ ONE MAN SHOWS or SEMI-ONE MAN SHOWS

Marcel Duchamp, Amici della Francia, C. Vittorio
Emanuele, 31, Milan, Italy. By MD: *La Mariée mise
à nu par ses Célibataires, même (Green Box)*
— **23 Jan - 5 Feb 1952**
Duchamp, Frères & Sœur, œuvres d'art, Rose Fried
Gallery, 40 East 68 St, New York. By MD: *Chess
Players, drawing, 1911; Drawing for Jules
Laforgue's "La Siesta," 1912; Drawing for the
Large Glass; Reseaux de Stoppages-Etalon, 1914;*

*The Bachelors, watercolor, 1915; Boîte-en-valise,
1911; Knight, drawing, 1951* — **25 Feb - March 1952**
Marcel Duchamp - Francis Picabia, Rose Fried Gallery,
New York. By MD: *Objet-dard; Feuille de vigne
femelle; Boîte-en-valise; Rotoreliefs; Green Box*—
7 Dec 1953 - 8 Jan 1954

▶ EXHIBITIONS

20th Century Old Masters, Sidney Janis Gallery,
New York. By MD: *Chess Players*
— **27 Feb - 25 Mar 1950**
**An exhibition commemorating the 30th Anniversary of the
Société Anonyme**, Museum of Art 1920, Yale
University Art Gallery, New Haven, USA. By MD:
The Bachelors — **30 Apr 1950**
**Challenge & Defy, Extreme examples by XX century
artists, French & American**, Sidney Janis Gallery,
New York. By MD: *Fountain (first replica)*
— **25 Sept - 21 Oct 1950**
Masterpieces in America, Museum of Art, Philadelphia,
USA. By MD: *Nude descending a Staircase*
— **3 Nov 1950 - 11 Feb 1951**
Climax in 20th Century Art 1913, Sidney Janis Gallery,
New York. By MD: *Wheel* [first replica]; *3
Stoppages Etalon* — **2 Jan - 3 Feb 1951**

The Peggy Guggenheim Collection, Kunsthaus Zurich, Switzerland. Travels to Brussels and Amsterdam — 1951 - 1952

75 œuvres du demi-siècle, Knocke-le-Zoute, Albert Plage, Belgium. By MD: *A regarder d'un œil (photo)*; *Eau de Voilette (photo)* — 15 July - 9 Sept 1951

Brancusi to Duchamp, Sidney Janis Gallery, New York. By MD: *Femme au tub*; *Tête d'Homme (Chauvel)* — 17 Sept - 27 Oct 1951

L'œuvre du XXe siècle, Peintures, Sculptures, Musée National d'Art Moderne, Paris. By MD: *La Mariée*; *Nu descendant un escalier* — May-June 1952 (Travels under title Twentieth Century Masterpieces to the Tate Gallery, London — 15 July - 17 Aug 1952)

In memory of Katherine S. Dreier (Her own collection of Modern Art), Yale University Art Gallery, New Haven, USA. By MD: *Tu m'* — 15 Dec 1952 - 1 Feb 1953

Le Cubisme (1907-1914), Musée National d'Art Moderne, Paris. By MD: *Les Joueurs d'échecs*; *A propos de petite sœur*; *Formes maliques* — 30 Jan - 9 Apr 1953

Dada, Sidney Janis Gallery, New York. By MD: *Tu m'*; *A regarder d'un œil, de près...*; *La Joconde*; *Dr. Tzanck*; *Fountain (replica)*; *La Bagarre d'Austerlitz**; *Fresh widow*; *Apolinère enameled**; *A Bruit secret**; *L.H.O.O.Q.**; *50 cc air de Paris**; *Pliant de voyage**; *(* = from the boîte-en-valise)* — 15 Apr - 9 May 1953

The classic tradition in Contemporary Art, Walker Art Center, Minneapolis, USA. By MD: *The Bachelors* — 24 Apr - 28 June 1953

Inaugural exhibition of the Art Center, Forth Worth, USA. By MD: *Tu m'* — October 1953

194. Marcel Duchamp to Louise and Walter Arensberg   autograph letter
16 January 1951, New York   collection PMA

> New York Jan. 16. 1951
>   Dear Lou dear Walter,
> I received your long letter some days ago, I think just after returning from
>   Phila. where I saw Fiske who told me the news with ecstacy [sic]!__
> As you remark in your letter, the non-sequitur Fiske is some times hard to
>   follow but after a few hours with him, I heard all I wanted to know.
> First of all, the period of 25 years is really comforting.
> We went through the space reserved for the collection, and, as you and he
>   are not especially inclined to have the floor raised, we might drop the
>   question for the moment.
> But I suggested opening two small doors, one from each of the 2 window-
>   rooms into the central big room__ That central big room (not in use
>   now) is only opening on the entrance hall and on the back galleries__
>   I feel necessary to be able to go from the 2 window-rooms in the central
>   room directly without having to go around the corner__ Fiske saw the
>   point and suggested that the 2 doors be opened in a corner instead of
>   the center of the panel (not to spoil the hanging space).
> — This also brings back a remark I made to him, that I am sure that you
>   would be pleased if he were not too impressed with the "theme of
>   symmetry" in hanging the pictures,
>   and that a "gentle disorder" would be preferable to a geometric
>   "balancing" in the disposition of the paintings.
> Some times, he could put 2 pictures above one another.
> — I have no special feeling about my own things.
> In fact Fiske is going to make a miniature dummy of the placing with
>   small pieces of card board representing each painting in its respective
>   proportion, and show you this miniature hanging of the whole
>   collection.__ That will, to a certain extent, help us to get an accurate
>   preview of the show.
> — I had already spoken, some time ago, to Miss Dreier. and she is perfectly
>   willing to give the glass to Phila__ I announced it to Fiske who accepted
>   promptly__
> — It is true that time is getting short and I think you are wise to have the
>   fragile things sent over immediately.
> At the same time, I think that you ought to keep with you a large group
>   of the works you like best (the ones easily transported) instead of
>   emptying the house completely when you know that remodeling of the
>   rooms in Phila will take nearly a year.

Los Angeles, 27 Dec 1950, Arensberg and **Fiske Kimball** signed an agreement turning over Arensberg Collection to PMA.

Large Glass [cat. 2] is to be officially accepted by the museum 24 Nov 1952.

— The important point is that you both get in fine shape around Springtime
and come up to Phila to see the space and decide about some final points.
The "Nude" is holding its own among the masterpieces of the Jubilee,
says I.

Nude Descending No. 2 [cat. 17], "Masterpieces in America," see p.292.

— The door to be opened on the North side would not have any balcony like
the one they will open on the South side—

Affectueusement à tous deux

Marcel

---

195. Marcel Duchamp to Louise and Walter Arensberg   autograph letter
28 January 1951, New York   collection PMA

210 W. 14. N.Y.C.

28. Jan. 1951

Dear Lou, dear Walter,

Thank you for your letter describing the confusion due to that press
indiscretion :

Some one sent me a clipping of the Tribune at about the same time, a
week or 10 days ago.

— Yesterday I went to Philadelphia to attend one of jubilations, an afternoon
dedicated to museum directors (Sir Phillips Handy, National Gallery
London, Francis Taylor, Finley.)— It was what it should be but I liked
better the tea-party at Kimball's afterwards.

— In addition to the glass, Miss Dreier is about to give to Philadelphia quite
a number of paintings and sculpture from her own collection— I
announced it to Kimball who, delighted, is going to Milford in the early
Spring to arrange with her.

— While in Paris, I tried to see my old friend Dr. Dumouchel but he does
not live in Paris anymore— so I wrote to him and asked him if he would
be willing to sell the portrait I made of him in 1910 (reproduced in black
and white in the "Valise").

A few days ago I received an answer telling me that he would accept if, as
I told him, the portrait were to go in your collection.

Now, as a tentative price, I spoke of $860⁻ representing about 300.000
francs.

Not knowing at all how you feel about this transaction, I nevertheless
submit it in case you see some sense in it.

Among the paintings of 1910, The Chess Players you just bought and this
portrait are the 2 important ones.

The portrait is very colorful (red and green) and has a note of humor
which indicates my future direction to abandon more retinal painting.

News of the Arensberg Collection gift to the PMA is scooped by the California press.

Sir Phillips Handy, Director of the National Gallery, London.

Francis Henry Taylor (1903-1957), Director of the Metropolitan Museum of Art, NY, 1939 - 1954. The Met is also negotiating with the Arensbergs to secure the donation of their collection.

David Edward Finley, Director of the National Gallery of Art, Washington DC.

Raymond Dumouchel, a medical student when MD painted his *Portrait Dumouchel* [cat. 5]; friend of MD's from Lycée Corneille, Rouen.

Box-in-a-Valise [cat. 4]

Chess Players [cat. 14] Arensberg bought from Walter Pach.

— In his introduction of the speakers yesterday Sturgis Ingersoll announced R. Sturgis Ingersoll,
the gift of the collection in terms of great appreciation__ see p.182.
Affectueusement à tous deux
Marcel
P.S. Love to Sophie and Helen.

---

196. Marcel Duchamp to Pierre de Massot   autograph letter
28 January 1951, New York   source: from André Gervais transcript

210 West 14th St.
28 Janvier 1951
New York
      Cher Pierre
je relis ta lettre du 21 Décembre (!), ce qui accentue mon retard, ...
D'abord la collection Arensberg a été offerte au (et acceptée par le) Musée Arensberg - Kimball
      de Philadelphie qui en prendra progressivement possession dès cette agreement, see p.297.
      année__
On pourra donc photographier à gogo. Massot requesting
Dis moi si tu la sais, quelle liste de reproductions tu penses mettre dans le photos of MD's work
      livre__ for book he is planning.
Je pourrai ainsi savoir s'il existe déjà une photo blanc et noir.
D'un autre côté, je travaille (méditativement) à une reproduction en
      couleurs du Grand Verre__ c'est à dire non pas une photo en couleurs *Large Glass* [cat. 2]
      mais les moyens typographiques d'obtenir plusieurs centaines ou
      milliers d'exemplaires__
Mais ceci va me prendre une petite année__
Le reste de la vie va. Je trouve toujours qu'on est moins harcelé par la
      mauvaise humeur ici qu'à Paris. **Eliza Robertson**
            Affectueusement à Robbie et à toi a.k.a. Robbie, wife of
            Marcel Pierre de Massot.

▷ TRANSLATION: *210 West 14th St. 28th January 1951. New York. Dear Pierre, I am
just re-reading your letter of 21st December (!) which is making me even later...
Firstly, the Arensberg Collection has been offered to (and accepted by) the Philadelphia Museum which will gradually take possession of it as from this year. So we'll
be able to take photos to our hearts' content. Tell me, if you know, which list of reproductions you're thinking of putting in your book. This way I can find out whether a black and white photograph exists. On the other hand, I'm working
(meditatively) on a reproduction in color of the Large Glass, i.e. not a color photo
but the typographical means of obtaining several hundred or several thousand copies. But this is going to take me almost a year. Otherwise life OK. I always find that
one is less harassed by bad moods here than in Paris. Affectionately to Robbie and
to you, Marcel.*

197. Marcel Duchamp to Henri-Pierre Roché   autograph letter
18 March 1951, New York   collection HRHRC

210 W. 14. N.Y.C.

18 Mars 51

Cher Totor

Bien reçu ta lettre du 8 mars ; et tu fais bien d'arrêter de fumer si ç'a une telle action sur ton cœur—

Je devrais moi même me réarrêter mais j'ai repris de plus belle sur le bateau en revenant.

Vu Fautrier qui, entre nous, n'est pas un personnage <u>agréable</u> à fréquenter— Sa facilité à décider péremptoirement sur toutes choses avec un œil sur son nombril, rend les mieux intentionnés indécis.

Laisse Madeleine Castaing exposer la machine optique — sans le verre dessus naturellement — et demande lui d'éviter toute publicité "autour"—

———

On pourrait faire faire un couvercle en "plastic", pour remplacer celui en verre cassé ; est ce facile à Paris? si non je [v]errais ici, donne moi le diamètre exact et aussi la profondeur si ce n'est pas une demi-sphère complète

— J'ai téléphoné au Sherry-Netherland et quoique je n'aie pas pu en parler à Lieberfield la téléphoniste l'a sonné pendant 2 minutes— Donc il habite toujours là et c'est bien 781 Fifth—

J'ai aussi entendu dire qu'il était divorcé, déjà—

K.S. Dreier me dit qu'elle regrette mais n'avait jamais eu l'intention de te faire faire un travail physique (simplement un coup de téléphone) Tout cela sans importance. Elle te remercie de ta lettre.

Affectueusement

Totor

Jean Fautrier (1898-1964) French painter and member of "Art informel" group in Paris.

Rotary Demisphere [cat. 51]

▷ TRANSLATION: *210 W.14.N.Y.C. 18th March '51. Dear Totor, Received your letter of 8th March and you're right to give up smoking if that's what it's doing to your heart. I should stop again myself but I started again more than before on the boat coming back. Saw Fautrier who, between you and me, is not very nice to know. The ease with which he makes peremptory judgments about everything, keeping one eye on his navel, makes even those with the best of intentions feel dubious. Let Madeleine Castaing exhibit the optical machine—without the glass on top, obviously, and ask her to avoid all "surrounding" publicity. We could have a "plastic" cover made to replace the broken glass one. Is this easy in Paris? If not, I'll see here.*

Give me the exact diameter and also the depth if it's not a full demisphere. I tele-
phoned the Sherry-Netherland and although I didn't get to speak to Lieberfield, the
telephonist called him for 2 minutes, so he's still staying there and it is in fact 781
Fifth. I also heard he'd got divorced, already. K.S. Dreier tells me she's sorry but she
never meant to make you do physical work (just a telephone call). All that of no
matter. She says thank you for your letter. Affectionately, Totor.

---

198. Marcel Duchamp to Louise and Walter Arensberg   autograph letter
19 April 1951, New York   collection PMA

210 W. 14th St.

19th april 51

    Dear Lou dear Walter

I understand perfectly your position on "loans" and I think that you made
    the right decision.

Received your big envelope with the Calas articles— If his imagination
    has a fascinating facet, he might introduce too much "selfishness" in an
    interpretation of texts and his congenital limitations with the English
    language can't be tolerated in your research.

You probably have received by now a copy of the letter Fiske Kimball sent
    to Miss Dreier (after his visit to Milford)— Well! That's that.

Of course I understand that Phila does not want everything in her
    collection but I suspect that F.K. and the Trustees hardly like anything
    she has, including the glass as well.

This is <u>strictly confidential</u> : ~~It is in my hun~~ I have a hunch that broken
    glass is hard to swallow for a "Museum"—

Please never mention it to anyone.

— Without saying the word : "appropriation" I asked him about the
    arrangement of the rooms for the collection and he told me that they
    were making the architectural drawings to be presented for adequate
    appropriation.

This is a little vague but I feel that the museum does not want to forget
    anything before asking as it probably would be difficult to get a
    supplement (if necessary) afterwards—

    Affectueusement à tous deux

    Marcel

Dumouchel is back home and Lefebvre-Foinet will take the picture today or
"yesterday"— Soon now, we will hear of the actual shipping—

"**research**" of the
Francis Bacon
Foundation, trying to
prove "Shakespeare"
was written by Bacon.

F.K. = Fiske Kimball
Large Glass [cat. 2]

Portrait Dumouchel
[cat. 5]

199. Marcel Duchamp to Louise and Walter Arensberg   autograph letter
2 May 1951, New York   collection PMA

210 West 14th St.
N.Y.C.
May 2nd 1951
    Dear Lou dear Walter
Two days ago I received word from Dumouchel that the painting is in the
    hands of Lefebvre-Foinet and will be shipped immediately.
The money arrived safely and unless there is a small difference in the
    operation of exchange, I owe you $40⁰⁰ out of the $900 you sent me—
I received a long letter from Miss Adler. I am very touched by the interest
    and the care she takes of my paintings and I am going to answer
    immediately.
By the way the inscription she asks me to rewrite and translate is the
    dedication I wrote to another friend of mine, Dr. Tribout to whom
    I gave the "Baptême" around 1910—
        ~~att~~ AU CHER TRIBOUT CARABIN
           J'OFFRE CE BAPTÊME
           M. D.
Carabin is the slang word for "medical student"—
Tribout died in 1937 or 1938.

———

The lack of desire to dicuss at all terms, in the case of the Dreier collection,
    (on the part of F.K.) corroborates my inner feeling that nothing ~~that~~ *of*
    what she offered was good enough for the Phila Museum—

———

I am sorry that you can't come East for the moment, but hope that you
    will find ~~a~~ propitious conditions to come in the near future.
        Affectueusement à tous deux
        Marcel

Mary Ann Adler
(d.1952), Arensbergs'
paintings restorer, lives
on North Las Palmas
Avenue, Hollywood.
She wrote a long,
3-page, single-spaced
typewritten letter to
MD, 24 Apr 1951, about
restoration of pictures
by MD in Arensberg
Collection.

Baptism [cat. 10]

Ferdinand Tribout
(d.19 June 1935), son of
a piano maker in Rouen
and friend from MD's
youth.

F.K. = Fiske Kimball

200. Marcel Duchamp to Louise and Walter Arensberg   autograph letter
22 July 1951, [New York]   collection PMA

210 W. 14th St.
New York
    22nd July 51
["Dear Lou" = cut off on manuscript] dear Walter,
[M]any thanks for your letter : I am so happy that Dumouchel arrived and
    in good health, although very durty [sic].

Portrait Dumouchel
[cat. 5]

Miss Adler will have no difficulty to clean it, as there is nothing else but good oil paint (<u>Behrendt colors</u>, the German make she certainly used to know about) and it had been varnished with "<u>Vernis mastic cristal</u>" Lefranc__ All this information may help her__

Most important is your reaction to it__ It is a definite 1910 painting in technique; yet the "halo" around the hand which is <u>not</u> expressly motivated by Dumouchel's hand is a sign of my subconscious preoccupations toward a metarealism__ It has no definite meaning or explanation except the satisfaction of a need for the "miraculous" that preceded the cubist period.__

Your comparison between the chronological order of the paintings and a game of chess is absolutely right... but when will I administer check mate ? or will I be mated ?

Affecteusement à tous deux Marcel

PS. Hope Miss Baker will get the con‖ [cut off on manuscript]

Carol Baker is one of Arensberg's assistants.

---

201. Marcel Duchamp to Louise and Walter Arensberg   autograph letter
15 August 1951, [New York]   collection PMA

Aug. 15th 1951

Dear Lou dear Walter

You will find on a separate sheet the list of what I remember approximately having purchased for you between 1935 and 1940__

My memory is so vague that I am afraid the memorandum is full of inaccuracies, in the dates as well as in the prices.

Nevertheless you can with a clear conscience declare these purchases and prices__ The State of California could evidently get more exact data from the Customs House. But they won't bother__

— I was sure that Dumouchel could be surprisingly fresh after Miss Adler's shower.__ and I am delighted.

— Also very happy to hear that after your third visit to the hospital you feel completely well now.

— Could Sam Little send me a print of the "King and Queen (oil over your mantel)? Richter wants it for an article__ or if you have another print *of King and Queen* in your files that would do.

Thanks and affectueusement à tous deux

Marcel

Because of a "use tax" on works of art purchased outside the State of California, the Arensbergs are asked to account for all purchases made from 1935 onwards.

Portrait Dumouchel [cat. 5]

Sam Little, photographer used by the Arensbergs while living in California.

Hans Richter (1888-1976), German painter and filmmaker, author of *Dreams that Money Can Buy* (1944) in which MD played a minor role.

King and Queen... [cat. 19]

[enclosure:]

Between 1935 and 1940

Brancusi	The Kiss		See *The Louise and*
	Penguins	about $400.‾ each	*Walter Arensberg*
	Chimera		*Collection*, PMA, 1954.
	Fish (from Peggy Guggenheim)		
Braque	Violin and pipe. *oil*	about 16,000 francs	
	at an auction sale in Paris 1937 (?)		
Calder	Mobile	about $300.‾	
Chirico	The Poet and his Muse. oil	about $250.‾	
Duchamp	The artist's father— oil	about $500.	= *Portrait Father* [cat. 6]
	Two seated figures— oil	about $250.	= *Baptism* [cat. 10]
	The Bush— oil	about $300	= *The Bush* [cat. 9]
	Study for the Virgin water color	$150	= *Virgin No. 2* [cat. 21]
1940?	The Bride oil (Julien Levy)	$3500.‾	= *Bride* [cat. 23]
	Why not sneeze? Ready made	$300	= *Why not Sneeze...* [cat. 46]
Duchamp Villon	Head of a horse— bronze	?	
	Portrait of Prof. Gosset— plaster	?	
Ernst Max	Garden Plane Trap— oil	about $300.	The Ernst painting is
Kupka	Fugue in 2 colors— oil	about $400	dated in pencil "1938" by
Magritte	The six elements— oil	about $500	Arensberg on the letter.
Roy Pierre	Metric system oil	about $600	
Villon Jacques	Abstraction— oil	about $300	

---

202. Marcel Duchamp to Louise and Walter Arensberg   autograph letter
18 August 1951, [New York]   collection PMA

18ᵗʰ August 1951

Dear Lou dear Walter

I received your second letter re"use tax"—

I have a Chicago catalogue and made the list I sent from it.

Now in that list only two items seem to be subject to the "use" tax.

1° Braque, Violin and pipe which was purchased at an official auction sale in Paris, I guess in 1937. I am practically sure that the bid was 16000 francs but don't remember the rate or exchange at that date

2° The "Bride" bought from Julien Levy and the simplest fr to make sure   *Bride* [cat. 23]
about dates and price would be to write to him— I can do that, if you want— or here is his address :

      Julien Levy

      Hemlock Ridge

      Bridgewater

      Conn.

All the other items were bought from the artist or from an individual
collection (six elements Magritte from Breton— ~~Mlle~~ Penguins,
Chimera Brancusi from my collection.) The rest from the artists.
Let me know if you need more help—
I am leaving Friday the 24th of August for 10 days; I am playing in the
N.Y. State Tournament in Syracuse and will be back in N.Y. the 5th of
September.
my address in Syracuse :

> Chess Tournament
> Syracuse University
> Syracuse N.Y.
> Affectueusement à tous deux
> Marcel

P.S. Your catalogue has not arrived yet. But I will return it as soon as I get
it. Without any notes—

NY State Chess Championship Tournament, where MD gets 50% result and is satisfied.

Art Institute of Chicago catalog, see p.273.

---

203. Marcel Duchamp to Henri-Pierre Roché   autograph letter
20 September 1951, New York   collection HRHRC

210 West 14th St.
N.Y.C.
20 Sept '51
> Cher Totor

Je relis ta lettre du 21 Juillet et je pense que tu vas rentrer bientôt de
St Robert— reposé si Villefranche ne t'a pas appelé trop souvent—
Entendu pour 1952 à N.Y. rencontre avec les Maharadjas.—
Aperçu Lieberfield il y a 3 mois chez Carré
> qui voulait aussi arranger quelque chose dans ce sens—
— Maria me dit que Brancusi n'est pas représenté dans la liste des invitations
françaises (Cassou) pour la Biennale de São Paolo (Brésil)— Elle te serait
infiniment reconnaissante si tu pouvais savoir si cette absence est dûe au
refus de Brancusi ou bien si on l'a oublié.— Demande-le-lui, et si tu es
bien avec Cassou demande lui sa version—
Pourrais tu me rendre un petit service : m'acheter et m'expédier par la
poste 2 petits flacons de vernis Mastic Cristal. Comme celui que tu avais
acheté lors de mon passage à Paris— je joins ici l'étiquette pour que tu
ne sois pas obligé de faire du "guessing"— je dois vernir les tableaux que
Janis a— et expose en ce moment—

Maharajah of Indore, Yeshwant Holkar, owns at this time 3 Brancusi *Birds in Space.*

1st Bienal Internacional de São Paulo organized by Maria Martins, 1951.

Jean Cassou (1897-1986), Director of Musée National d'Art Moderne, Paris (1945-1965), and art historian.

Mastic Cristal = Brand name of varnish MD uses in paintings.

Peut être as-tu vu un M. Sanouillet qui écrit une thèse sur Dada
(Sorbonne); il est professeur à Toronto (Canada) et est à Paris en ce
moment ou à Montélimar (son pays d'origine); tu pourrais, si tu
préfères, lui confier les 2 flacons en question, car je dois le voir à son
passage à ~~Paris~~ N.Y. en Octobre—
Comment va tous?
    Affectueusement à eux et à toi
    Totor

Michel Sanouillet
(b.1924), met MD in
NY May 1951: will
publish first collected
writings of MD in 1959
(see p.356).

▷ TRANSLATION: *210 West 14th St. N.Y.C. 20th Sept '51. Dear Totor, Re-reading your
letter of 21st July, I think you must soon be coming back from St Robert—rested if
you didn't get too many calls from Villefranche. OK for 1952 in N.Y. meeting with
the Maharadjas. Caught sight of Lieberfield 3 months ago at Carré's who also wanted to fix up something like this. Maria tells me that Brancusi does not appear on
the list of invitations from France (Cassou) for the São Paolo Biennale (Brazil).
She would be immensely grateful to you if you could find out whether this is on account of a refusal on the part of Brancusi or whether they forgot him. Ask him and,
if you're on good terms with Cassou, get him to give you his version. Could you do
me a small favor: buy me and send me by post 2 small bottles of Mastic Cristal varnish. Like the one you bought when I last came to Paris. I enclose the label to spare
you any "guessing." I have to varnish the paintings Janis has—and is showing at
the moment. You might have met a certain M. Sanouillet who is writing a thesis
on Dada (Sorbonne). He is professor at Toronto (Canada) and in Paris at the moment or in Montélimar (his home town). You could, if you prefer, give the two bottles in question to him, as I am to see him when he passes through N.Y. in October.
How is everyone? Affectionately to them and to you, Totor.*

---

204. Marcel Duchamp to Katherine S. Dreier   autograph letter
15 January 1952, [New York]   collection YCAL

Jan. 15th '52.

    The circus continues : Tomorrow an interview appears in the Art
Digest as a forerunner f of the show— I will send it to you— Rose Fried
told me today that "Life" is interested and will probably interview me a
little later—
Also the "Talk of the Town" in the New Yorker might ask me a few
questions at the time of the show.
All this to show *you* how my peaceful life has been changed into a publicity
machine.
I received from George Hamilton a "delighted" letter telling *me* how
happy he was to lend his drawing for the show.
— I wonder how you feel since your last tapping— and hope that your
energy is still building up.

"A MD Profile," *Art
Digest* (16 Jan 1952).

Rose Fried (1896-1970)
shows, at her NY
gallery 40 E 68th St.,
"Duchamp Frères &
Sœur: Œuvres d'Art,"
25 Feb - 31 Mar 1952.

Winthrop Sargeant,
"Dada's Daddy," *Life*
(28 Apr 1952).

George Heard
Hamilton (b.1910),
Professor of Art History
at Yale University, on
the curatorial staff of
the Yale University Art
Gallery, 1936-1966.
Drawing lent is *Eternal
Siesta* [cat. 13].

I told you that I wrote to your sister Mary— Poor Mary, it must have been
a terrible shock as really nothing indicated such a sudden denouement.
— especially that she did not know about the ~~sleeping pills~~ heart pills.
Is she with you?

— Today I was at Rose Fried's and she and Glarner were hanging her new
show "Coincidences"— very good title and good examples of
Malevitch, Rothchenko etc.

— Hoping to receive a little note from you telling me the last news of your
village. I am sending you my best wishes from my village—

Affectueusement

Dee

Mary Elizabeth Dreier
(1875-1963), Katherine
Dreier's sister.

"dénouement" = end,
outcome of a plot...

Fritz Glarner (1899-
1972), American Swiss-
born abstract painter.

"Coincidences," Rose
Fried Gallery.

---

205. Marcel Duchamp to Louise and Walter Arensberg   autograph letter
4 February 1952, [New York]   collection PMA

Feb. 4. 1952

Dear Lou dear Walter

It has been a long time since I wrote, probably because I have been more
busy than I usually am.

Rose Fried, a small gallery here, is having a show of the Duchamp family
and since December she and I have been planning the show which will
include 3 brothers and one sister.

(Duchamp frères et sœur

œuvres d'art)

= Duchamp brothers
and sister / works of
art, see p.306.

Of course the gallery is too small to undertake a large showing and we have
to reduce to 4 or 5 items the representation of each member of the
family—

In my case, for example, I show only small drawings and the boîte-en-
valise—   *Box-in-a-Valise* [cat. 4]

Villon   3 oils
Duchamp-Villon 4 bronzes
Suzanne   3 oils

But the point of the story is that the art magazines are very keen about the
idea of "a family of artists"— and I have to go through interview after
interview—

Life will have 4 pages in color

Art News— Art Digest...— Maybe the New Yorker—

In the catalogue I intend to reproduce on "my page" your glass   *Glider...* [cat. 30]
(Watermill)

The show will open Feb. 25th and I will send you the catalogue

— I hope you have been well all this time and that your worries about the
Californian tax are over—

— Have heard nothing from Philadelphia. What do you know about the
appropriation and the preparations for the rooms.
They are a bit slow to my taste.
> Hope to hear from you soon
> Affectueusement à tous deux
> Marcel

---

206. Marcel Duchamp to Helen Freeman   autograph letter
12 February 1952   collection PMA

Helen Freeman (1886-
1960), actress and one
of Beatrice Wood's
closest friends. Moved
to California in the
1920's and later married
the writer Edwin Corle.

> Enfin chère Helen je peux répondre à toutes vos lettres et

manuscrits— parce que je suis définitivement convaincu que je ne suis
pour rien dans tout cela : peintures et vos pensées évoquées par ces
peintures—

"manuscrits" = Notes
on the Work of Marcel
Duchamp by a
Contemporary, written
in 5 parts, 1949-1951,
unpublished.

Si au point de vue strictement chronologique je suis le même individu que
le peintre de ces peintures, l'écoulement linéaire du temps (1912-1952)
n'est pas une justification de l'identicité de M.D. 1912 avec M.D. 1952.
Au contraire je crois qu'il [y] a dissociation constante, si cette dissociation
n'est pas empêchée par des considérations et des acceptations
superficielles du principe d'identité.
Mon grand intérêt à lire ce que vous avez écrit n'est en rien basé sur un
écho intérieur qui me guide vers cet intérêt—
J'ai lu ce que vous avez écrit exactement comme "étranger à la chose"— et
de *ce* fait mon intérêt est plus valable.
— Vous même avez écrit ces mots sans intention de sens, de syntaxe,
d'explication— Vos mots sont par rapport au langage à peu près comme
le fumet d'une nourriture par rapport à son goût—
— Redescendant sur la terre, je viens de recevoir une lettre de Fiske
Kimball me demandant d'aller à Philadelphie
— J'irai Lundi 18, pour voir les projets d'aménagement de la collection—
Voulez vous le dire à Lou et à Walter par téléphone, car dans ma dernière
lettre il y a quelques jours, je n'~~e savais~~ avais pas reçu l'invitation.
> Très affectueusement chère Helen
> Marcel

Lou[ise] and Walter
Arensberg

▷ TRANSLATION: *At last, dear Helen, I can reply to all your letters and manuscripts
because I am convinced, once and for all, that all this—paintings and the thoughts
these paintings evoke in you—has nothing to do with me. If, from a strictly chronological point of view, I am the same individual as the painter of these paintings, the
linear passage of time (1912-1952) is not a justification of the identicality of M.D.
1912 with M.D. 1952. On the contrary, I think there is constant dissociation, if this*

dissociation is not prevented by superficial thinking and acceptance of the principle of identity. The great interest I have in reading what you have written in no way comes from an echo inside me guiding me to this interest. I read what you've written exactly like a "stranger to the matter" and, on account of this, my interest is more valid. You yourself wrote these words without intention of meaning, syntax or explanation. Your words are to language something like what the aroma of food is to its taste. Coming back down to earth, I've just received a letter from Fiske Kimball asking me to go to Philadelphia. I'll go Monday 18th to see how they plan to set out the collection. Could you let Lou and Walter know by telephone as, in my last letter a few days ago, I hadn't yet received the invitation. Very affectionately, dear Helen, Marcel.

---

207. Marcel Duchamp to Marcel Jean
15 March 1952, New York

autograph letter
present whereabouts unknown

Marcel Jean (1900-1993), French Surrealist artist and writer.

210 West 14th St. New York

15 Mars 1952

    Cher Marcel Jean

Ci joint le résultat de mon citron pressé. J'espère m'être rappelé assez
    exactement les dates et circonstances dont vous avez besoin— Je me
    réjouis à l'avance de lire votre long travail— et vous remercie de
    m'envoyer les 4 premiers chapitres avant la parution de l'ouvrage entier.
    N'hésitez pas à me poser d'autres questions si elles peuvent vous être
    utiles—
Il est seulement curieux de constater combien la mémoire est fragile même
    pour les époques importantes de la vie—
C'est d'ailleurs ce qui explique la fantaisie heureuse de l'histoire.
    Affectueusement à vous
    Marcel Duchamp

Marcel Jean is in the process of writing his *L'Histoire de la peinture surréaliste* (Paris, Seuil, 1959), translated by Simon Watson Taylor, *History of Surrealist Painting* (NY, Grove Press, 1960).

▷ TRANSLATION: *210 West 14th St. New York, 15th March 1952. Dear Marcel Jean, Enclosed the outcome of my racking my brains. I hope I have recalled fairly accurately the dates and circumstances you needed. I am really looking forward to reading your lengthy work and would be glad if you could send me the first 4 chapters before the overall work comes out. Feel free to ask me further questions if this can be any use to you. Isn't it strange to realize how fragile the memory is even when it comes to important periods in life. That actually accounts for the blissful fantasy that is history. Affectionately to you, Marcel Duchamp.*

208. Marcel Duchamp to Louise and Walter Arensberg   autograph letter
27 March 1952, New York   collection PMA

210 W. 14th St. N.Y.C.

27th March '52

    Dear Lou dear Walter

I feel very guilty to have brought so much trouble in your life by the loan
    to Sweeney's show__

First of all let me thank you "du fond du cœur" for having made it possible
    to have two of my things in the exhibition.

Then, I am also very sorry to have misunderstood or misinterpreted the
    "legal ownership"__ I thought I was merely repeating what Fiske had
    told me in Philadelphia__ Evidently I was wrong.

As for lending in general, I am in complete agreement with your decision
    as I always was__ The risk is too great and not worth being taken when
    the works have been restored with the care Miss Adler gave to it.

The exhibition at Rose Fried's had its "succès d'estime familiale"__
    People like a change, used as they are to one man, group or school
    shows__

Received from Beatrice some time ago a letter telling me how happy she
    was to have spent a few moments with you__ She asks me when I will
    come and <u>live</u> in Ojai (?)

I can't imagine myself playing chess with the Prophets in Ojai!

    Hope you both are well.

    Affectueusement à tous deux

    Marcel

Margin notes:

Sweeney's exhibition "L'Œuvre du XXème Siècle," for Musée d'Art Moderne, Paris, 4 May - June 1952.

"du fond du cœur" = from the bottom of my heart

F.K. = Fiske Kimball

"Duchamp Frères & Sœur," see p.306.

"succès d'estime familiale" = critical family success

Ojai (California), where Beatrice Wood lives.

209. Marcel Duchamp to Henri-Pierre Roché   autograph letter
11 April 1952, [New York]   collection HRHRC

11 avril '52

    2 mots en hâte, et en réponse à ta lettre du 7 Avril, très détaillée,
    merci__

Je suis d'avis d'attendre pour exposer ces tableaux anciens__ Suspens donc
    tes démarches à ce sujet.__ on verra plus tard__

Le jeu de la vente est vraiment un jeu de marchands et ni toi ni moi ne
    savons y faire__

Les acheteurs de mes tableaux dans le passé ont toujours passé outre à la
    dénigration savante des marchands ~~vis~~ ce qui veut dire que peu de gens
    ont acheté, ce qui veut dire que je n'ai pas de "marché" au sens
    "marchand" du mot__

Un point seulement m'intéresserait : Chicago (Catton Rich et Katherine   D.C. Rich and K. Kuh, see p.278.
Kuh) cherche un bon tableau de moi pour l'Art Institute de Chicago—
je te propose de ~~te~~ réfléchir à l'idée de leur vendre ton verre un bon prix   *9 Malic Moulds* [cat. 31]
~~qui ser~~ à condition que tu gardes le verre ta vie durant—
C'est une combinaison qui a beaucoup d'avantages. et la somme serait
   payée tout de suite ou en tout cas selon l'arrangement que tu préfères—
Je ne connais pas autre chose de moi qui puisse faire figure importante
— je crois que tu obtiendrais la somme que tu désires si tu as déjà pensé à une
   somme—
Rose Fried t'écrit dans ce sens et elle serait l'intermédiaire avec Chicago
   qui l'a chargée de cette mission : trouver un beau Dchp.
     Affectueusement
     Totor
j'avais téléphoné au Savoy Plaza et la téléphoniste m'a dit que Bouboule
était à N.Y. quoiqu'il n'ait pas répondu au téléphone

▷ TRANSLATION: *11th April '52. A very quick line, and in reply to your letter of 7th April, very detailed, thanks. I am of a mind that it is better to wait to exhibit these old canvases. Please put all you are doing on this subject on hold. We'll see about it later. The sales game is a dealer's game and neither you nor I know how to go about it. People who have bought my paintings in the past have always risen above the erudite backbiting of the dealers, meaning that few people bought, meaning I have no "market" for the dealers i.e. in the "commercial" sense of the word. Just one thing I was interested in: Chicago (Catton Rich and Katherine Kuh) is looking for a good painting of mine for the Art Institute of Chicago. I suggest you think about selling them your glass for a good price on condition that you get to keep the glass for the rest of your life. There are many advantages to this strategy and the money would be paid immediately or else by whatever arrangements suit you. I don't know of anything else of mine that would make an impression. I think that you could get the price you want for it if you have a price in mind. Rose Fried is going to write to you about this and she will be the go-between with Chicago who have given her this mission: find a good Duchamp. Affectionately, Totor. I phoned the Savoy Plaza and the telephonist told me that Bouboule was in N.Y., although he didn't answer the telephone.*

---

210. Marcel Duchamp to Henri-Pierre Roché   autograph letter
26 April 1952, [New York]   collection HRHRC

26 avril 52
     Tu ne sembles pas cher Totor, avoir très bien compris ma pensée au
   sujet du verre—
Sachant combien tu l'aimes, je t'ai proposé comme condition sine qua non
   de le garder tant que tu vivras tout en l'ayant vendu au Musée de

Chicago qui pourrait trouver la proposition faisable (peut être pas)—
Une ~~son~~ vente semblable a eu lieu dans la collection K. Dreier— Le
musée Guggenheim (art non figuratif) a acheté en 1948 ou 49 un très
beau Kandinsky 1ère manière et l'a payé 15 000, tout en lui laissant la
jouissance de ~~le g~~ l'avoir chez elle.—

Wassily Kandinsky, *Circles on Black*, 1921 (Guggenheim Museum, NY), in 1946 purchased from Dreier who retained lifetime ownership.

L'autre côté de la question est qu'à un moment donné toi (je crois) et moi
avions pensé que tu pourrais le léguer au Musée qui recevrait la Coll.
Arensberg— Mais à cela je m'oppose maintenant car tu n'as pas le droit
de priver Denise et Jean-Claude d'une somme aussi importante.

Roché's wife and son

— D'un 3eme côté si ce sont eux qui sont obligés de ou qui désirent le
vendre tu sais, comme moi à quels ~~blo~~ bandits ils auront à faire.
— Enfin 20 000 pourrait très bien être le prix que Chicago paierait— mais
là encore je crois qu'un intermédiaire (marchand) est nécessaire pour
obtenir ce résultat— Les américains aiment avoir une personne
responsable entre l'artiste et eux.— je ne suis pas d'~~avai~~ avis de traiter
avec ~~Xxxxxxxx~~ [word ultra crossed out] qui te roulera comme dans un bois
(please déchire cette lettre)— tandis que j'ai toute confiance en Rose
Fried—
Si nous envisageons 20 000, je crois que Rose Fried se contenterait de
2 500— et si tu insistes pour que j'aie quelque chose je proposerais 5 000
pour moi et le reste pour toi.

———

Je t'en prie évite toutes les expositions et manifestations à mon sujet— je
voudrais garder ma tranquillité— L'expo famille m'a montré le danger
de sortir son nez—

— Life magazine vient de sortir le numéro où ils m'ont consacré 4 pages en
couleur et 6 en noir (Dada's Daddy)— Si l'article ne paraît *pas* dans le
Life de Paris, dis le moi je t'enverrai un numéro— (Daté ici 28 avril
52)—

Life Magazine article, see p.306.

— Ecris à Lieberfield au Savoy Plaza (Fifth avenue *and* 58th *Street*) je suis à
peu près sûr qu'il habite là. La téléphoniste me l'a dit— et quant à ton
chèque de lui, il n'y a pas péril en la demeure—
— Sweeney doit avoir déjà accroché son expo—
    une autre fois nous parlerons de tes derniers 5—
    Affectueusement Totor

Sweeney's exhibition, see p.310.

▷ TRANSLATION: *26th April '52. You don't seem, my dear Totor, to have quite understood my thoughts on the glass. Knowing how much you like it, I proposed the sine
qua non condition to you that you could keep it as long as you live while having sold
it to the Museum of Chicago who might find this proposal feasible (and might not).
A similar sale took place in the K. Dreier collection. The Guggenheim Museum
(non-figurative art) bought in 1948 or 49, a very nice Kandinsky 1st manner and
paid 15,000 for it, while still letting her have the enjoyment of it at home. The other*

side of the coin is that, at one time, both you (I think) and I thought you could be-
queath it to the Museum which is going to be given the Arensberg collection. But I
am very much against this idea now as you do not have the right to deprive Denise
and Jean-Claude of such a large sum of money. Thirdly, if they have to sell it them-
selves or should they wish to, you know as well as I what kind of bandits they'll have
to deal with. Anyway 20,000 could quite well be the price Chicago would pay, but
then again I think a go-between (dealer) would be needed to get that price. The
Americans like to have somebody in charge between the artist and themselves. I am
not of a mind to deal with [name crossed out] *who would swindle you good and prop-*
er (please tear up this letter) whereas I completely trust Rose Fried. If we aim for
20,000, I think Rose Fried would settle for 2,500 and, if you insist that I have some-
thing, I would propose 5,000 for me and the rest for you. Please avoid all exhibitions
and demonstrations involving me. I want to live my life in peace. The family exhi-
bition taught me how dangerous it is to set foot outside. Life Magazine has just
brought out the issue where they have 4 pages on me in color and 6 in black (Dada's
Daddy). If the article doesn't come out in the Paris Life, let me know and I'll send
you one. (Dated here 28th April 52.) You can write to Lieberfield at the Savoy
Plaza (Fifth avenue and 58th Street) I'm pretty sure he's staying there—the tele-
phone operator told me he was. And as for his check to you, it's not a matter of life
and death. Sweeney must have set up his show by now. Another time we'll talk
about your last 5. Affectionately, Totor.

---

211. Marcel Duchamp to Louise and Walter Arensberg   autograph letter
6 May 1952, New York   collection PMA

210 W. 14ᵗʰ St. N.Y.C.
May 6. 1952

    Dear Lou dear Walter

Miss Dreier died already a month ago, as you know, after a slow and long
   illness (dropsy) which the doctors declared incurable several months
   before the fatal issue—

   Katherine Dreier died 29 Mar 1952, at age seventy-four.

It is really a hard experience to be unable to show your feelings to some
   one in complete ignorance of the inevitable character of the situation.
   Fortunately we all have in us a curious animal belief in eternity, as
   though Time would stop in our personnal case.—

I am one of 3 Executors of her will in which she gives all her private
   collection to non profit organizations without specific mentions— The
   executors are in charge of designating the organizations to which her art
   works will go—

— I received from Fiske Kimball a letter in which he expresses the desire
   to see the Big Glass in Philadelphia and I am writing to him today,
   telling him that it was Miss Dreier's intention to offer the glass to
   Philadelphia.

   Large Glass [cat. 2]

This I am sure will please you as it pleases me.

I will try to ~~her~~ *have* the rest of the collection presented in one or 2 rooms in a Museum under her name instead of breaking it up—

The Merrilds were here and delivered your message— I know that you are taking care of yourselves and hope that your general health is good.

I will send you the catalogue of the Paris-London show as soon as I receive it. The show was to open on the 4th of May— in Paris—

> Affectueusement à tous deux
>
> Marcel

Kund Merrild (1894-1954), Danish-born painter living with his wife Else in Los Angeles.

Sweeney's show, p.310.

---

212. Marcel Duchamp to Fiske Kimball   autograph letter
6 May 1952, New York   collection PMA

> 210 W. 14th St.
> New York
> May 6. 1952

> Dear Fiske Kimball

Many thanks for your 3 letters to which I reply a little late—

It is my intention to have the Executors of Miss Dreier's will (I am one of them) make an offer of the "Big Glass" to the Philadelphia Museum. Miss Dreier always had it in mind, and she actually spoke to me about it, only a few weeks before she died.

— I feel confident that I am carrying [out] her wish.

Walter and Lou, I am sure, will be as pleased as I am to see the final grouping *of my things* take actual shape in Philadelphia.

it would be hypocritical to say that my "farther" ego was not pleased by the Life Magazine article.

> affectueusement
> Marcel Duchamp

Large Glass [cat. 2]

Walter and **Lou**[ise] Arensberg

Life **Magazine article**, see p.306.

---

213. Marcel Duchamp to Henri-Pierre Roché   autograph letter
7 May 1952, New York   collection HRHRC

> 210 W. 14.
> 7 Mai '52

> Cher Totor

Je t'ai câblé "oui" pour l'idée de Carré de faire une petite expo. chez lui vers le 20 Mai.

Trois ou 4 choses maximum me semble la meilleure idée.

— Le verre

— La machine optique

— Les petits joueurs d'échecs (chez Villon)

— Les disques optiques (si vous pouvez installer un système pour les faire

Exh. is never to materialize at Galerie Carré, Paris, as far as it is known: works MD proposes to show are all in France at the time: *9 Malic Moulds* [cat. 31], *Rotary Demisphere* [cat. 51], *Chess Players* [cat. 14], and an example of the *Rotoreliefs* [cat. 53].

tourner ~~a~~ à 30 tours à la minute)—
Ça suffirait bien
Peut être 20 Mai est un peu tôt, ça dépendra de l'ouverture de l'expo
Sweeney— Donne m'en des nouvelles. Ça devait ouvrir le 4 Mai??

Sweeney's exhibition, see p.310.

— on pourrait ajouter une boîte en valise sous vitrine— (comme chez
Rose Fried

Box-in-a-Valise [cat. 4]

J'ai chargé Rose Fried d'entamer des pourparlers "gratuits" avec Chicago
au sujet du verre— de sorte que si tu vois cet été Daniel Rich et
Katherine Kuh (de Chicago) à Paris, tu sauras qu'ils sont prévenus des
possibilités (Prix 20 pour eux, conditions viagères etc.)— Tu pourras en
discuter librement avec eux s'ils le jugent à propos—

9 Malic Moulds [cat. 31]

— Le grand verre Dreier ira très vraisemblablement à Philadelphie
rejoindre la coll. Arensberg.
— Quant au reste de sa collection j'ai l'intention (en grand secret) de
l'offrir à Duncan Phillips (*Phillips* Memorial de Washington) ~~pou~~ car
j'espère obtenir de lui qu'il lui donne une salle ou 2 ~~avec~~ sous le nom de
Coll. K.S. Dreier

Duncan Phillips (1886-1966), important early collector of modern art from Washington DC, who opened his collection to the public in 1921.

— je préférerais cette solution à une dispersion—
~~a aucun~~ Tiens moi au courant
Affectueusement
Totor

▷ TRANSLATION: *210 W. 14. 7th May '52. Dear Totor, I wired you "yes" to Carré's idea of holding a small exhibtion at his place around 20th May. Three or 4 things maximum seems the best idea to me. The glass. The optical machine. The little chess players (at Villon's). The optical disks (if you can fix up a system to make them rotate at thirty times a minute). That will be plenty. Perhaps 20th May is a little early, it'll depend on the opening of the Sweeney exhibition. Fill me in on this. Wasn't it supposed to open on 4th May?? We could also include a box-in-a-valise in a glass case (like at Rose Fried's). I've asked Rose Fried to start "free" negotiations with Chicago about the glass, so if you see Daniel Rich and Katherine Kuh (of Chicago) in Paris this summer, you'll know they are aware of the various possibilities. (Price 20 for them, lifetime conditions etc.) You could discuss it with them freely if they consider it appropriate. Dreier's large glass will most likely go to Philadelphia where the Arensberg collection is. As for the rest of her collection, I plan on giving it (in utmost secrecy) to Duncan Phillips (Phillips Memorial Washington) as I'm hoping I can get him to give it a room or 2 in the name of K. S. Dreier Collection. I would prefer this solution to everything being scattered all over the place. Keep me posted. Affectionately, Totor.*

214. Marcel Duchamp to Henri-Pierre Roché   autograph letter
[early July 1952, New York]   private collection, Paris

> Cher Totor
>
> Enrico Donati t'apportera ce papier. Aide le car il n'aura probablement
> que peu de temps et ça t'amusera peut être de présider à
> l'agrandissement de quelques unes de mes choses— Voici une liste ~~des~~
> de celles que je crois plus importantes :
>
> ___
>
> Liste des principales choses à agrandir à grandeur originale :
>   <u>Grand Verre</u>   (se servir de la photo ci jointe et non pas du celluloïd dans   = *Large Glass* [cat. 2]
>   la boîte) 3^m hauteur environ
>   <u>Roi et Reine</u>   1^m hauteur environ (boîte)   = *King and Queen...* [cat. 19]
>   <u>Nu descendant...</u>   1^{m}10 haut environ (boîte)   = *Nude Descending No. 2* [ca
>   <u>Mariée</u>   0^{m}85 haut. environ (boîte)   = *Bride* [cat. 23]
>   <u>Verre Roché</u>   voir chez toi les dimensions (boîte)   = *9 Malic Moulds* [cat. 31]
>   <u>Tu m'</u>   3^m longueur environ (boîte)   = *Tu m'* [cat. 29]
>   <u>Glissière</u> vue de dos   (photo en noir dans la boîte) 1^{m}20 haut. environ   = *Glider...* [cat. 30]
>   Broyeuse de chocolat <u>1914</u>   0^{m}65 haut. environ (en couleurs dans la   = *Chocolate Grinder No. 2* [ca
>   boîte)
>   Tu peux en choisir d'autres qui t'amuseront Carte blanche et merci
>   Affectueusement
>   Totor

▷ TRANSLATION: *Dear Totor, Enrico Donati will deliver this note to you. Help him as*
he probably won't have much time and you might enjoy presiding over the enlarge-
ment process of a few of my things. Here is a list of what I think are the most im-
portant ones. List of main things for enlargement to original size: Large Glass (use
photo enclosed and not the celluloid one in the box) 3m high approx.; King and
Queen, 1m high approx. (box); Nude Descending, 1m 10 high approx. (box);
Bride, 0m 85 high approx. (box); Roché's Glass, see dimensions at your place
(box); Tu m', 3m long approx. (box); Glider, seen from behind (black photo in the
box), 1m 20 high approx.; Chocolate Grinder 1914, 0m 65 high approx. (in color
in the box). You can pick out any others you please. Carte blanche and thanks.
Affectionately, Totor.

215. Marcel Duchamp to Henri-Pierre Roché   autograph letter
15 July 1952, New York   private collection, Paris

210 W. 14.
N.Y.C.
15 Juillet 52
    Cher Totor
Je réponds point par point à la lettre de Donati qui vraiment se donne
    beaucoup de mal pour l'expo. en Octobre.
1) Oui vous pouvez ajouter à la liste que je t'ai envoyée la machine à faire   *Rotary Demisphere* [cat. 51]
    dormir, le verre (moules malic), le tableau chez Villon (joueurs d'échecs)   *9 Malic Moulds* [cat. 31]
    et une ou 2 toiles maximum époque fauve.   *Chess Players* [cat. 14]
2) je t'enverrai demain le négatif du grand verre (photo blanc et noir) avec   **Paul Facchetti**, owner
    lequel Facchetti peut faire un bon agrandissement à 3^m de haut.   of the Studio Paul
                                                                                    Facchetti, Paris.
3) Si Breton veut prêter son Washington très bien_ et aussi si ce n'est pas
    trop compliqué d'obtenir le "jeune homme triste" de Peggy à Venise.   *Genre Allegory*
                                                                                    [cat. 59], in Breton's
4) Catalogue_ En même temps que le ~~catalo~~ négatif tu recevras 2 ou 3   collection at this time.
    photos de moi pour choisir   *Sad Young Man...*
    je ne tiens pas à ce que cette lettre soit reproduite dans le catalogue_ Elle   [cat. 15]
    n'ajouterait vraiment rien.
5) Reproduction(s) en couleurs si le budget le permet mais pas essentiel.
6) je crois que vous avez tous les droits de reproduction puisque les
    reproductions seront faites d'après des reproductions de la boîte (qui
    m'appartient). Pour éviter toute ambiguité, mentionnez que les
    reproductions auront été faites d'après les reproductions de la boîte-en-   *Box-in-a-Valise* [cat. 4]
    valise._ ~~il~~
    Il serait aussi bon de mentionner que les tableaux de la coll. Arensberg
    appartiennent maintenant au Philadelphia Museum of Art (Coll. Louise
    and Walter Arensberg)
    Le grand verre : (collection K.S. Dreier)   *Large Glass* [cat. 2]
        En hate affectueusement
        Totor

▷ TRANSLATION: *210 W.14 N.Y.C. 15th July '52. Dear Totor, I'll reply point by point
to Donati's letter: he really is going to a lot of trouble over the show in October. 1)
Yes, you can add to the list I sent you: the machine to send you to sleep, the glass
(malic molds), the painting at Villon's (chess players) and one or 2 canvases maximum from the Fauvist era. 2) I'll send you the negative of the Large Glass (black
and white photo) from which Facchetti can make a good enlargement 3m high. 3)
If Breton wants to lend his Washington that's fine—and also if it's not too complicated to get the Sad Young Man from Peggy in Venice. 4) Catalog—at the same
time as the negative, you'll be receiving 2 or 3 photographs of me to choose from. I'd
rather this letter were not reproduced in the catalog—it really wouldn't add any-*

thing. 5) Reproduction(s) in color, budget permitting but not essential. 6) I think you have full reproduction rights as the reproductions will be carried out according to those in the box (which belong to me). To avoid all ambiguity, mention that these reproductions will have been carried out according to those in the box-valise. It would also be good to mention that the paintings from the Arensberg Collection now belong to the Philadelphia Museum of Art (Louise and Walter Arensberg Collection); The Large Glass (K.S. Dreier Collection). In haste, affectionately, Totor.

---

216. Marcel Duchamp to Jean Crotti
17 August 1952, [New York]

autograph letter
collection AAA

style télégraphique
pour correspondance
en retard.
210 WEST 14TH STREET
NEW YORK 11, N.Y.

17 Aout 52

Cher Jean chère Suzanne

Tu as dû te demander ce que je faisais après m'avoir envoyé ta longue lettre sur l'expo Sweeney!

Sweeney exh., p.310.

Tout à fait d'accord avec toi— Sans oublier que Sweeney a dû organiser toute cette expo. En 3 6 semaines (avant l'ouverture), je sais qu'il n'a pas pu faire autre chose que de l'à peu près, et malheureusement trop suivre son goût (qui n'est d'ailleurs pas mauvais)

"DADA 1916-1923," Sidney Janis Gallery, NY, 15 Apr - 9 May 1953

je me rappelle que dans mes conversations avec lui à ce sujet, je lui avais suggéré l'idée de donner au moins un petit panneau (tout petit) à Dada qui est d'une des manifestations certaines des 50 derniers années.— Il n'en a rien fait, naturellement.

A ce propos Janis organise un expo Dada pour Mars ou Avril 1953— Il me charge de l'organisation des idées de cette expo.— et du côté ~~fran~~ parisien je voudrais avoir ton Clown sur verre (fait à N.Y.?) Si tu veux l'envoyer tout de suite par le fils de Marthe Pelletier qui part pour N.Y. sur le Queen Mary du 3 sept., peut être auras tu encore le temps. En tout cas ce n'est pas pressé— je trouve que c'est mieux de l'envoyer par quelqu'un—

The Clown, 1916 (Musée d'Art Moderne de la Ville de Paris).

Au fait Rose Fried pourra le ramener ~~av~~ à son retour en Octobre.

Si tu pense à autre chose de la même époque, dis le moi—

Merci pour les articles de Suisse *et* de Carrouges à qui je n'ai pas encore écrit.

Michel Carrouges, see p.287.

La sœur de Katherine Dreier, Mary Dreier, m'a donné pour toi et Gaby 2 châles espagnols très beaux comme souvenir— je te les fais apporter

Gaby = Gabrielle Villon

par Rose Fried (elle part le 12 Sept., te dirai le bateau une autre fois)—
Vous déciderez Gaby et toi lequel va à qui.— Tu remercieras Mary
Dreier après réception

   Miss Mary Dreier 24 West 55th St. New York.

Tu me demandes mon opinion sur ton œuvre, mon cher Jean— C'est bien
long à dire en quelques mots— et surtout pour moi qui n'ai aucune
croyance — genre religieux — dans l'activité artistique comme valeur
sociale.

Les artistes de tous temps sont comme des joueurs de Monte Carlo et la
loterie aveugle fait sortir les uns et ruine les autres— Dans mon esprit
ni les gagnants ni les perdants ne valent la peine qu'on s'occupe d'eux—
C'est une bonne affaire personnelle pour le gagnant et une mauvaise
pour le perdant.

Je ne crois pas à la peinture en soi— Tout tableau est fait non pas par le
peintre mais par ceux qui le regardent et a lui accordent leurs faveurs;
en d'autres termes il n'existe pas de peintre qui se connaisse lui même
ou sache ce qu'il fait— il n'y a aucun signe extérieur qui explique
pourquoi un Fra Angelico et un Leonardo sont également "reconnus".

Tout se passe au petit bonheur la chance— Les artiste qui, durant leur vie,
ont su faire valoir leur camelotte sont d'excellents commis-voyageurs
mais rien n'est garanti pour l'immortalité de leur œuvre— Et même la
postérité est une belle salope qui escamote les uns, fait renaître les autres
(Le Greco), quitte d'ailleurs à changer encore d'avis tous les 50 ans.

Ce long préambule pour te conseiller de ne pas juger ton œuvre car tu es
le dernier à la voir (avec de vrais yeux)— Ce que tu y vois n'est pas ce
qui en fait le mérite ou le démérite— Tous les mots qui serviront à
l'expliquer ou à la louer sont de fausses traductions de ce qui se passe par
delà les sensations.

Tu es, comme nous tous, obnubilé par une accumulation de principes ou
anti-principes qui généralement embrouillent ton esprit par leur
terminologie et, sans le savoir, tu es le prisonnier d'une éducation que
tu crois libérée—

Dans ton cas particulier tu es certainement la victime de l'"Ecole de Paris",
cette bonne blague qui dure depuis 60 ans (les élèves se décernant les
prix eux même, en argent)

A mon avis il n'y a de salut que dans un ésotérisme— Or, depuis 60 ans
nous assistons à l'exposition publique de nos couilles et bandaisons
multiples— L'épicier de Lyon parle en termes entendus et achète de la
peinture moderne—

Les musées américains veulent à tout prix enseigner l'art moderne aux
jeunes étudiants qui croient à la "formule chimique"—

Tout cela n'engendre que vulgarisation et disparition complète du <u>parfum</u>
<u>originel</u>.

Ceci n'infirme pas ce que je disais plus haut, car je crois au parfum originel
mais comme tout parfum il s'évapore très vite (quelques semaines,
quelques années maximum) ; ce qui reste est une noix séchée classée par
les historiens dans le chapitre "histoire de l'art"—

Donc si je te dis que tes tableaux n'ont rien de commun avec ce qu'on voit
généralement classé et accepté, que tu as toujours su produire des choses
entièrement tiennes, comme je le pense vraiment, cela ne veut pas dire
que tu aies droit à t'asseoir à côté de Michel-Ange—

De plus, cette originalité est suicidale, dans ce sens qu'elle t'éloigne d'une
"clientèle" habituée aux "copies de copistes", ce que souvent on appelle
la "tradition"—

Une autre chose, ta technique n'est pas la technique "attendue"— Elle est
<u>ta</u> technique personnelle empruntée à personne— par là encore, la
clientèle n'est pas attirée.

Evidemment si tu avais appliqué ton système de Monte Carlo à ta
peinture, toutes ces difficultés se seraient changées en victoires. Tu
aurais même pu créer une école nouvelle de technique et d'originalité.

Je ne te parlerai pas de ta sincérité parce que ça est le lieu commun le plus
courant et le moins valable— Tous les menteurs, tous les bandits sont
sincères. L'insincérité n'existe pas— Les malins sont sincères et
réussissent par leur malice mais tout leur être est fait de sincérité
malicieuse.

En 2 mots fais moins de self-analyse et travaille avec plaisir sans te soucier
des opinions, la tienne et celle des autres
    Affectueusement
    Marcel

[added left margin of second page:]
    Suzanne te reste i̶l t-il des dessins ou aquarelles Dada que tu voudrais
    exposer ? Donne les à Rose Fried

▷ TRANSLATION: *17th August '52. Dear Jean, dear Suzanne, You must have been
wondering what I was up to after having sent me your long letter about the Sweeney
show! Agree with you entirely—not forgetting that Sweeney had to organize this
whole exhibition in 6 weeks (before the opening). I know that he could only do
something fairly approximate and unfortunately go too much by his own taste
(which actually isn't bad). I remember that in my conversations with him on this
subject, I put the idea to him of giving Dada a little plaque (just a little one) as it
is one of the definite movements of the last 50 years. He didn't do anything of the
sort, naturally. On this score, Janis is organizing a Dada show for March or April
1953. He's having me take care of the organization of ideas in this show and, on
the Parisian side, I would like to have your Clown on glass (done in N.Y.?) If you*

want to send it straightaway with Marthe Pelletier's son on the Queen Mary 3rd
September, you might still have time. In any case, there's no rush. I think it's better
to send it with somebody. In fact Rose Fried could bring it over when on her way
back in October. If you think of anything else from the same era, let me know.
Thanks for the articles from Switzerland and those by Carrouges to whom I have
not yet written. Katherine Dreier's sister, Mary Dreier, has given me 2 very beauti-
ful shawls for you and Gaby as a souvenir. I'm sending them to you with Rose Fried
(she leaves 12th September, will let you know which boat later). You and Gaby can
decide who takes which. You can thank Mary Dreier once you've received them:
Miss Mary Dreier, 24 West 55th St. New York. You were asking my opinion on your
work of art, my dear Jean. It's very hard to say in just a few words, especially for me
as I have no faith—religious kind—in artistic activity as a social value. Artists
throughout the ages are like Monte Carlo gamblers and the blind lottery pulls some
of them through and ruins others. To my mind, neither the winners nor the losers
are worth bothering about. It's a good business deal for the winner and a bad one
for the loser. I do not believe in painting per se. A painting is made not by the artist
but by those who look at it and grant it their favors. In other words, no painter
knows himself or what he is doing. There is no outward sign explaining why a Fra
Angelico and a Leonardo are equally "recognized." It all takes place at the level of
our old friend luck. Artists who, in their own lifetime, have managed to get people
to value their junk are excellent traveling salesmen, but there is no guarantee as to
the immortality of their work. And even posterity is just a slut that conjures some
away and brings others back to life (El Greco), retaining the right to change her
mind every 50 years or so. This long preamble just to tell you not to judge your own
work as you are the last person to see it (with true eyes). What you see neither re-
deems nor condemns it. All words used to explain or praise it are false translations
of what is going on beyond sensations. You are, as we all are, obsessed by the accu-
mulation of principles or anti-principles which generally cloud your mind with
their terminology and, without knowing it, you are a prisoner of what you think is
a liberated education. In your particular case, you are certainly the victim of the
"Ecole de Paris," a joke that's lasted for 60 years (the students awarding themselves
prizes, in cash). In my view, the only salvation is in a kind of esotericism yet, for
60 years, we have been watching a public exhibition of our balls and multiple erec-
tions. Your Lyons grocer speaks in enlightened terms and buys modern painting.
The American museums want at all costs to teach modern art to young students
who believe in the chemical formula. All this only breeds vulgarization and total
disappearance of the original fragrance. This does not undermine what I said ear-
lier, since I believe in the original fragrance, but, like any fragrance, it evaporates
very quickly (a few weeks, a few years at most). What remains is a dried up nut,
classified by the historians in the chapter "History of Art." So if I say to you that
your paintings have nothing in common with what we see generally classified and
accepted, and that you have always managed to produce things that were entirely
your own work, as I truly see it, that does not mean you have the right to be seated
next to Michelangelo. What's more, this originality is suicidal as it distances you

*from a "clientele" used to "copies of copiers," often referred to as "tradition." One
more thing, your technique is not the "expected" technique. It's your own personal
technique, borrowed from nobody. And there again, this doesn't attract the clientele. Obviously, if you'd applied your Monte Carlo system to your painting, all these
difficulties would have turned into victories. You would even have been able to start
a new school of technique and originality. I will not speak of your sincerity because
that is the most widespread commonplace and the least valid. All liars, all bandits
are sincere. Insincerity does not exist. The cunning are sincere and succeed by their
malice, but their whole being is made up of malicious sincerity. In a word, do less
self-analysis and enjoy your work without worrying about opinions, your own as
well as that of others. Affectionately, Marcel.*

*Suzanne, do you still have any Dada drawings or watercolors that you would
like to show? Give them to Rose Fried.*

---

217. Marcel Duchamp to Henri-Pierre Roché   autograph letter
7 April 1953, New York   collection HRHRC

210 W. 14.

7 avril 1953

　　Cher Totor

O.K. pour les 24 que je tiens à ta disposition pour acheter ce dont tu
　　pourrais avoir envie ici.

— Mon <u>petit</u> verre de la coll. Dreier (à regarder d'un œil, de près. etc__)   *To Be Looked at...*
　　a été complètement démoli dans le transport de New Haven à N.Y.   [cat. 32]
　　(Museum of Mod. Art à qui je l'ai <u>donné</u>)__

Le Museum l'a fait réparer magnifiquement et nettoyer en même temps.
　　Le restaurateur a dû employer une colle invisible entre les morceaux de
　　verre cassé.

Veux tu que je lui demande le nom de la colle en question__

Avec cette colle, on pourrait démonter le cadre en fer du ~~moi~~ "Cimetière"   *"Cimetière" = 9 Malic*
　　et après avoir nettoyé les 2 côtés du verre cassé__ coller les morceaux   *Moulds* [cat. 31]
　　soigneusement.__ De plus il faudrait je crois cimenter (avec un mastic
　　très fort[)] les 3 verres dans l'intérieur du cadre__ et s'assurer que les
　　verres extérieurs *(surtout celui du dos)* touchent au moins en beaucoup
　　d'endroits et de ce fait consolident l'ensemble.__

Après consultation avec l'expert du Louvre dont tu me parles; je crois
　　qu'on pourrait décider quelque chose.

— Si le verre devait voyager, il serait essentiel qu'il arrive en parfaite forme
　　"pour les siècles à venir."

— J'attends ton article NRF

— Les 34 dollars m'ont été payés par Janis qui a dû transmettre à Lefebvre Foinet l'avis.

Tout pour le moment
Affectueusement à tous
Marcel Totor

"Souvenirs sur Marcel Duchamp," H.-P. Roché, *Nouvelle Revue Française* (June 1953).

▷ TRANSLATION: *210 W. 14. 7th April 1953. Dear Totor, OK for the 24 which I'm keeping for you so that you can buy whatever you might fancy over here. My small glass from the Dreier collection (to be looked at with one eye, close up etc.) got completely demolished during transportation from New Haven to N.Y. (Museum of Modern Art to which I have given it). The Museum had it repaired magnificently and cleaned at the same time. The restorer must have used invisible glue between the pieces of broken glass. Would you like me to ask him for the name of the glue in question? With this glue, we could take the iron frame off the "Cemetery," clean both sides of the broken glass and then very carefully stick the pieces back together again. In fact, I think we would need to cement (with very strong putty) the three glasses inside the frame and ensure that the outside glasses (especially those at the back) touch, in many places at least, thus consolidating the whole. After discussing things with the Louvre specialist you've been telling me about, I think we can come to a decision. If the glass had to travel, it would be vital for it to arrive in perfect condition "for centuries to come." I'm waiting for your article NRF. I got 34 dollars paid to me by Janis who must have passed on the chit to Lefebvre Foinet. All for now. Affectionately to all, Marcel Totor.*

---

218. Marcel Duchamp to Robert Lebel
7 April 1953, [New York]

autograph letter
private collection, Paris

Robert Lebel (1901-1986), expert on old master paintings, will write the first monograph and cat. rais., *Sur Marcel Duchamp*, Trianon Press, 1959.

7 avril 1953
Cher Lebel
Merci de votre lettre et de sa belle humeur =
"A propos de jeune Sœur" n'est pas ce que je prefère voir photographier.
   Le verre que Roché possède aussi me serait plus agréable <u>si vous le trouvez photogénique</u>
Si non prenez la "petite Sœur" et merci.
— J'attends le questionnaire avec impatience— Marcel Jean a transcrit avec une minutie étonnante toutes les pensées de la boîte verte et aussi mes faits et gestes.
Vous pouvez vous appuyer sur ses notes sans crainte.
      Cordialement à tous
      Marcel Duchamp

Little Sister [cat. 12]

9 Malic Moulds [cat. 31]

MD replies 20 June 1953.

▷ TRANSLATION: *7th April 1953. Dear Lebel, Thanks for your letter and the very good humor it brings. "Apropos of little sister" is not what I'd most like to see photographed. I would be happier with the glass in Roché's possession if you find it photogenic. If not, take the "little sister" and thanks. I can't wait to see the questionnaire. Marcel Jean has transcribed with amazing fastidiousness all the thoughts that went into the Green Box and also my life story. You can rely on these notes completely. Sincerely to all, Marcel Duchamp.*

---

219. Marcel Duchamp to Henri-Pierre Roché
15 May 1953, [New York]

autograph letter
collection HRHRC

15 Mai '53
    Cher Totor

J'ai reçu et lu en grande partie Jules et Jim et avec plaisir, très prenant dans son style volontairement simplifié— aussi naturellement l'autobiographie ajoute son mordant— Le prix Claire Belon a dû *aussi* être un bon déjeuner—

Enfin, continue, mais sans passer par l'Acad. Fr—

Janis voudrait exposer ton "Verre"— je lui ai dit que d'abord *il faut* le remettre en parfait état (nettoyage et mastiquage dans le cadre en fer)— il participerait a vraisemblablement aux frais mais d'un autre côté cela lui donnerait un droit de pourcentage sur la vente éventuelle = Donc à réfléchir—

Il est probable que Sweeney te verra au mois de Juin et vous parlerez vraisemblablement du verre pour le Musée Guggenheim. Offre lui une option de quelques mois pour éviter les ennuis que tu as eus avec Adam et Eve—

    Affectueusement à tous
    Totor

Roché's *Jules et Jim* (Paris, Gallimard, 1953) won the Claire Belon prize, 16 Apr 1953.

"Acad. Fr" = Académie Française

9 *Malic Moulds* [cat. 31]

Brancusi's *Adam and Eve*, p.250.

▷ TRANSLATION: *15th May '53. Dear Totor. I have received and read most of Jules et Jim and really enjoyed it, very compelling in its deliberately simplified style, also the autobiography gives it extra bite. The Claire Belon prize must have been a good lunch as well. Anyhow, carry on, but don't go through the French Academy. Janis would like to exhibit your "Glass." I told him that first of all it has to be restored to perfect condition (cleaning and puttying in the iron frame). He'll probably contribute financially but, on the other hand, that would entitle him to royalties on sales=so needs some thought. There's a good chance Sweeney will see you in June and will probably talk to you about the glass for the Guggenheim Museum. Give him an option of a few months so as to avoid the problems you had with Adam and Eve. Affectionately to you all, Totor.*

220. Marcel Duchamp to Constantin Brancusi
3 June 1953, New York

autograph letter
present whereabouts unknown

210 West 14th Street
New York
U.S.A.
3 Juin 1953
    Cher Morice

Tu seras sans doute étonné d'avoir de mes nouvelles ; je ne vais pas mal et
j'espère que tu vas bien.

De plus voici un projet qui j'espère te tentera :

Sweeney a été nommé directeur du Musée Guggenheim (Sœalomon) à la
place de la Baronnesse Rebay l'année dernière après la mort de Salomon
Guggenheim.

Sweeney a complètement changé l'esprit et l'organisation en supprimant
le titre "<u>non figuratif</u>" que la Baronnesse avait suivi à la lettre.

Dans une conversation, l'autre jour, Sweeney m'a demandé s'il y aurait
une chance que tu acceptes de faire une exposition aussi complète que
possible à ce musée Guggenheim__

Je lui ai répondu que tu pourrais peut être y consentir si moi j'acceptais de
te représenter dans la présentation de l'exposition.

De plus il serait entendu que tu serais <u>invité</u> à faire le voyage de New York
passer le temps qu'il te plaira et t'occuper de la mise en place avec moi.

J'ai aussi dit à Sweeney que tu te chargerais toi même de la maquette du
catalogue avec tes photos ; on pourrait au besoin le faire imprimer à
Paris si tu voulais.

En tout cas réfléchis__ Sweeney sera à Paris la semaine prochaine entre le
7 et le 14 Juin et <u>ira te voir</u> pour t'expliquer plus longuement la
proposition.

J'espère que tu seras tenté par le voyage et moi serais vraiment ravi de
revivre avec toi les bonnes heures de 1927 et 1933
    Affectueusement
    Marcel Duchamp
    Morice.

Hildegard Rebay von Ehrenwiesen a.k.a. Hilla Rebay (1890-1967), was replaced by Sweeney in 1952 as director of I he Solomon R. Guggenheim Museum, originally Museum of Non-Objective Art, which she helped Solomon R. Guggenheim to found.

The proposed Brancusi retrospective will take place at Guggenheim Museum two years later, 25 Oct 1955 - 8 Jan 1956.

▷ TRANSLATION: *210 West 14th Street. New York. U.S.A. 3rd June 1953. Dear Morice,
You will no doubt be surprised to hear from me. I'm not too bad and hope you are
well. What's more, I have a project which I hope will appeal to you: Sweeney has
been appointed director of the Guggenheim Museum (Salomon) in place of Baroness Rebay after the death of Salomon Guggenheim last year. Sweeney has completely changed the ethos and way things are organized by dropping the "non-figurative"
classification the Baroness adhered to the letter. While we were talking the other
day, Sweeney asked me if there was any chance you might be willing to hold an ex-*

hibition at this Guggenheim museum showing as many of your works as possible. I told him you might possibly be persuaded if I were to agree to set up the exhibition on your behalf. Furthermore, you would naturally be invited to make the trip to New York all expenses paid and spend as long as you wanted setting up the exhibition with me. I also told Sweeney you would take care of the dummy for the catalog yourself with your photos. We could even have it printed in Paris if you prefer. Think about it anyway. Sweeney will be in Paris next week between 7th and 14th June and will go to you to go through his proposal with you at greater length. I hope you'll be tempted by the trip and I, for my part, would be frankly delighted to relive the good times we had together in 1927 and 1933. Affectionately, Marcel Duchamp, Morice.

---

221. Marcel Duchamp to Constantin Brancusi   autograph letter
22 September 1953, New York   collection MNAM

> 210 West 14th Street
> New York
> 22 Septembre 53
>   Cher Morice
> Sweeney, rentré ici, a toujours l'espoir de faire une exposition de toi au   See letter 220.
>   Musée Guggenheim cet hiver.
> Si tu n'es pas encore décidé, laisse moi te dire que cette exposition offre
>   toutes les garanties que tu peux exiger.— Je te promets d'être là et de
>   m'occuper de tout si tu ne viens pas en Amérique.   Brancusi planning a
> — Est-ce que tu ne devrais pas venir à Pittsburgh cet hiver?— on pourrait   trip to **Pittsburgh** as
>   faire coïncider les deux choses—   collector Daniel T.
>   Thomson has offered
> Enfin réfléchis et dis moi ce que tu veux faire   to cast at his foundry
>   à bientôt peut-être et affectueusement   his *Grand Coq*.
>   ton Morice

▷ TRANSLATION: *210 West 14th Street. New York. 22nd September '53. Dear Morice. Sweeney is back here and still holding out hope of having an exhibition of your work at the Guggenheim Museum this winter. If you are still undecided, let me reassure you that, with this exhibition, you have every guarantee you could possibly require. I promise I'll be there and will take care of everything if you don't come to America. Aren't you supposed to be coming to Pittsburgh this winter? We could have the two events coincide. Anyway think about it and let me know what you want to do. See you soon then maybe and affectionately, your Morice.*

222. Marcel Duchamp to Beatrice Wood   autograph letter
23 September 1953, New York   collection AAA

210 W. 14th St. N.Y.C.

23 Sept. 53

Chère Béa.

Merci et grand merci pour m'avoir donné des nouvelles précises sur la
santé de Lou et le résultat de l'opération.   **Lou[ise] Arensberg** is
                                                               operated on for cancer.

Quelle grande tristesse de voir nos plus chers amis touchés par
l'inévitable ; car le choc d'un accident mortel ne contient pas l'élément
d'espoir sur lequel une maladie lente même inéluctable permet de
spéculer—

En même temps la science d'aujourd'hui est trop catégorique pour
permettre cette spéculation et l'agonie lente d'un être à qui on ne peut
pas dire la vérité est une torture faite de la trahison silencieuse
implicite—

J'ai *passé* par ces moments et je sais combien Walter doit en souffrir après   **Walter** = Walter
une vie de complète communion entre Lou et lui—   Arensberg

Dis lui tout cela car je ne peux pas le lui écrire—

Merci chère Béa et affectueusement à tous deux

Marcel

▷ TRANSLATION: *210 W. 14th St. N.Y.C. 23rd Sept. '53. Dear Béa, Thanks and a big
thank you for giving me precise news about Lou's health and the outcome of the operation. How deeply sad to see those dearest to us affected by the inevitable, for the
shock of a fatal accident does not contain that element of hope that a long illness,
even if inescapable, allows us to speculate on. By the same rule, today's science is
too categorical to allow such speculation and the slow agony of a person to whom
one cannot tell the truth is a kind of torture made up of the betrayal implicit in our
silence. I've been through it and know how much Walter must be suffering after the
life of such complete communion he and Lou shared. Tell this to him for I cannot
write to him. Thank you, dear Béa and affectionately to you both, Marcel.*

223. Marcel Duchamp to Louise and Walter Arensberg   autograph letter
29 October 1953, New York   collection PMA

210 West 14th St. N.Y.C.

Oct. 29. 1953

Dear Lou dear Walter,

I was in Philadelphia again, two days ago and I saw the rooms prepared
for the collection—

They are completely finished except for some details in the electric
lighting— and they are beautiful, white, clear—

The 3 large rooms (two with daylight) are connected by ~~th~~ several doors
and the long mezzanine adds a great deal of space for hanging— Also
the outdoor terrace with a door from one of the rooms gives a pleasant
feeling to the whole arrangement—
I asked Kimball when he expected to have the grand opening and he was
completely non committal—
What is your feeling and have you any ideas you want ~~to~~ me to give them.
It seems that until March they have other large exhibitions— But I think
March could be a good time even if you don't want to send everything—
Kimball tells me that Lou is home and feels better. This is good news—
But let me hear directly from you and tell me if I should undertake
anything with the Philadelphians.
      Affectueusement à tous deux
      Marcel

---

224. Marcel Duchamp to Man Ray   autograph letter
29 October 1953, New York   collection Attilio Codognato, Venice

210 West 14th St. N.Y.C. Oct. 29th 1953
      Cher Man
Mon silence ne m'empêche pas de penser souvent à toi…   "Marcel Duchamp,
Rose Fried (6 East 65th Street New York) organise une petite expo de   Francis Picabia," **Rose**
      Picabia et moi en Décembre   **Fried Gallery**, NY, 7
                                                                Dec 1953 - 8 Jan 1954.
j'ai pensé qu'on pourrait y joindre un exemplaire du moulage "Feuille de   *Female Fig Leaf*
      vigne femelle".   [cat. 62], edition of 10
                                                                plaster casts executed
Si ça n'est pas trop compliqué veux tu lui faire envoyer directement un ou   by Man Ray in 1951
      2 exemplaires par Lefebvre Foinet (ou par un voyageur éventuel) et dis   (Schwarz cat. 536b).
      moi quel prix tu demandes <u>pour toi</u> (au cas où ils seraient vendus)—
      je te demande de faire vite car le temps presse
Copley me dit qu'il y a une meilleure patine que celle du moulage que tu
      m'as envoyé. T'en ai je jamais remercié?
      Affectueusement à Julie et à toi   **Julie** = Juliet Browner,
      Marcel   Man Ray's wife.

▷ TRANSLATION: *210 West 14th St. N.Y.C. Oct 29th 1953. Dear Man, My silence does
not mean I don't think of you often. Rose Fried (6 East 65th Street New York) is
organizing a small exhibition of Picabia and myself in December. I thought we
could include a copy of the cast "Female fig leaf." If it's not too much hassle, could
you have sent directly to him one or 2 copies through Lefebvre Foinet (or with someone who might be traveling) and let me know what price you're asking for yourself*

(in case they are sold)? Please act quickly as time is of the essence. Copley tells me there is a better patina than the one on the cast you sent me. Did I ever thank you for it? Affectionately to Julie and to you, Marcel.

---

225. Marcel Duchamp to Walter Arensberg   telegram
[26 November 1953, New York]   collection PMA

WESTERN UNION

1953 NOV 26 PM 4 12

LA312

L.NA249 NL PD=NEW YORK NS 26=

WALTER ARENSBERG

=7065 HILLSIDE AVE HOLLYWOOD CALIF

=JE NE SAIS LES MOTS POUR DIRE LA STUPEUR QUI MA SAISI EN RECEVANT AFFREUSE NOUVELLE STOP CHER WALTER MEME SI VOUS AVIEZ ACCEPTE L'INEVITABLE STOP AU MOMENT MEME ON MEURT LA MORT D'UN ETRE CHER TOUTE MON AFFECTION

=MARCEL=

Louise Arensberg dies 25 Nov 1953.

▷ TRANSLATION: *I have no words to express my shock on hearing the awful news stop dear Walter even if you have accepted the inevitable stop at the time one dies the death of a loved one all my affection Marcel.*

---

226. Marcel Duchamp to Man Ray   autograph letter
30 November 1953, New York   collection Attilio Codognato, Venice

210 West 14th St N.Y.C
30 Nov 53
    Cher Man
Merci de ta longue lettre :
j'exposerai mon exemplaire comme tu le suggères— Mais envoie quand même 2 autres par les amis du 11 ou 12 Déc. au cas où il y aurait une vente.

Que veux tu dire : 7 000 francs pour la patine? Est ce pour les galvaniser? ou pour une autre forme de patine?

Ici br *copper* "plating" couterait environ $25.00 mais je ne tiens pas à le faire : je préfère les vendre comme "Moulages peints"—

— Ça ne va pas très bien le N° de Flair parce que ça coute un prix fou même fait en France.—

Quels sont ces documents dont tu parles car Fleur Cowles a payé $750.00 pour la maquette. qui, donc lui appartient.

Quand *même* si l'édition n'a pas lieu tu pourrais ravoir tes documents

Original *Female Fig Leaf* [cat. 62] still in MD's possession at this time.

Fleur Cowles, author, painter and, from 1950, editor of *Flair* magazine.

~~Dis moi~~ Donne moi une liste et je *lui* en parlerai⎯

———

Verrai Dorothy Miller à l'occasion et lui parlerai
  A bientôt d'autres nouvelles
  Affectueusement à tous deux
  Marcel

Dorothy Canning
Miller (b.1904), wife of
Holger Cahill (1887-
1960), former director
of the WPA Art Project,
curator at MoMA, NY,
most faithful disciple of
Alfred Barr, Jr.

▷ TRANSLATION: *210 West 14th St N.Y.C. 30th Nov '53. Dear Man, Thank you for your long letter. I will exhibit my copy in the way you suggest. But send me 2 others anyway via our friends of 11th and 12th December just in case we make a sale. What do you mean: 7,000 francs for the patina? Is that to galvanize them or for a different kind of patina? Here "copper plating" would cost around $25 but I'm not so bent on doing it, I'd rather sell them as "painted casts." The issue of Flair is not doing too well because it costs a bomb even made in France. What are these documents you're talking about?—because Fleur Cowles paid $750 for the dummy which therefore belongs to her. Even so, if the publication doesn't happen, you could have your documents back. Give me a list and I'll speak to her about it. Will be seeing Dorothy Miller at some point and will speak to her. Will write soon. Affectionately to you both, Marcel.*

---

227. Marcel Duchamp to Walter Arensberg
3 December 1953, New York

autograph letter
collection PMA

210 West 14th St. New York
Dec. 3rd 1953
   Dear Walter
I could not write you any sooner⎯ I felt that you don't want to see anyone
   or hear any of the polite expressions of sorrow which irritate more than
   help.
Beatrice has let me know step by step Lou's fatal journey and I don't want   **Beatrice** = Beatrice Wood
   to mention the torments you had to go through in the last year.
But you Walter have to face a new reality and do you want to face it?
Do you feel the uselessness of accepting the new living conditions in which
   her absence will beat like a deafening drum?
All these questions remain unanswered when they are formulated in words
   like these.
The answer must come of itself, unformulated, by breathing again for her
   and give the final form to the work that she and you started together.
When I wrote you, about a month ago, I really hoped that there might be
   enough time to open the rooms in Philadelphia and let her know that
   one of her dreams had become a reality.

I understand now how useless it was to even hope for that.

I don't expect you to write for some time : Words are too much of a passe-partout approximation and never carry the subtleties of our thoughts.

"passe-partout" = all-purpose

All I want you to know is that I think of Lou and you

>Affectueusement
>
>Marcel

New York, 327 East 58 St | 1954-1959

lives in New York, with Teeny moves into 327 East 58th Street, top floor, Max Ernst's former apt
apartment 210 West 14th Street becomes MD's studio
round trips to Philadelphia, Cincinnati, East Hampton, Paris, Peterboro (New Hampshire),
  Houston, Mexico, Binghamton, Washington, Amherst (Massachusetts)
spends one or two months every spring or summer in Cadaquès (Gerona, Spain) | from 1958
round trips to Paris, French Riviera, Pittsburgh, Boston, Lisbon, Le Tignet (Alps) and London

from early 1954 to Nov 1959

▶ MAJOR WORKS

Coin de chasteté / Wedge of Chastity
  (galvanized plaster and dental plastic,
  Jan 1954)
Jaquette / Jacket (draft for a catalog cover,
  1956)
Waistcoat (waistcoat with buttons bearing
  letters, New York, spring 1957)
Verrou de sûreté à la cuiller / The Locking Spoon
  (metal spoon fixed to a door lock, 1957)
Self-Portrait in Profile (torn paper, 1957)
L'Equilibre (drypoint on celluloid, Aug 1958)
*Eau & gaz à tous les étages / Water & Gas on
  Every Floor* (lettering on blue plate, 1958)
Layout for "Sur Marcel Duchamp" (for the first
  monograph on MD by Robert Lebel, 1959)
Poster after "Self-Portrait in Profile" (for the
  exhibition "Sur Marcel Duchamp,"
  May 1959)
*Les Délices de Kermoune / The Delights of
  Kermoune* (watercolor and collage of pine
  needles on paper, 1958)

Interior Lighting (gold-plated zinc block, on
  which is engraved the sketch of a note
  from the Green Box, June 1959)
Du Tignet / From Tignet (pencil on paper,
  1959)
Cols alités / Bedridden Mountains (ink and
  pencil on paper, 1959)
Première Lumière (etching, Aug 1959)
With My Tongue in My Cheek (plaster on
  pencil and paper, mounted on wood,
  1959)
Torture-morte / Still Torture (painted plaster
  and flies on paper background, 1959)
Sculpture-morte / Still Sculpture (marzipan
  and insects on paper background, 1959)
Couple of Laundress's Aprons (two potholders,
  male and female, cloth and fur, 1959)
Tiré à 4 Épingles (etching, 1959)

▶ ONE MAN SHOWS or SEMI-ONE MAN SHOWS

**Jacques Villon, Raymond Duchamp-Villon, Marcel
  Duchamp**, The Solomon R. Guggenheim Museum,
  NY (travels to Houston). By MD: *The Artist's
  Father*; *The Chess Players*; *Nude Descending a*

Staircase No.1; Portrait of Chess Players; The
Sonata; Yvonne and Magdeleine Torn in Tatters;
The Bride; The King and Queen surrounded by
Swift Nudes; Nude Descending a Staircase No.2;
Le Passage de la Vierge à la Mariée; Chocolate
Grinder II; Why not sneeze Rrose Sélavy?
— 8 Jan - 17 Feb 1957
(On the occasion of Lebel's book publication in
English), Sidney Janis Gallery, New York. By MD:
Nu no.3; The Bride; First Study for Cemetery
— 6 Apr - 2 May 1959
Sur Marcel Duchamp (for the publication of Lebel's
book in French), La Hune bookshop, Paris
— 5 May - 30 May 1959

▶ EXHIBITIONS

Regards sur la peinture contemporaine, Musée Galliera,
Paris. By MD: Le Printemps; Pour une partie
d'échecs — 21 Jan 1955
Pérennité de l'Art Gaulois, Musée Pédagogique, Paris.
By MD: A propos de jeune sœur; Deux nus: un fort,
un vite; Machine optique [not in catalog];
Cimetière des uniformes et livrées [not in catalog]
— 18 Feb - March 1955
Objekt eller Artefakter verklig helten for verklig AD,
Galerie Samlaren, Stockholm
— February - March 1955
Le Mouvement, Galerie Denise René, Paris. By MD:
Rotative Demi-Sphère — 6 Apr - 30 Apr 1955
Le Mouvement dans l'Art contemporain, Musée
Cantonal des Beaux-Arts, Lausanne, Switzerland.
By MD: Machine optique; Rotoreliefs; 2 Nus, un
fort, un vite — 24 June - 26 Sept 1955
Twentieth Century Painting from Three Cities: New York,
New Haven, Hartford, Wadsworth Atheneum,
Hartford, USA. By MD: The Bachelors
— 19 Oct - 4 Dec 1955
Cubism 1910-1912, Sidney Janis Gallery, New York. By
MD: Nu Descendant un escalier, n°1; Nu
Descendant un escalier, n°2 — 3 Jan - 4 Feb 1956
Dada..., Yale University Art Gallery, New Haven, USA.
By MD: Les Célibataires; In Advance of the Broken
Arm; Boîte-en-valise — January 1956
Surrealism & its Affinities, the Mary Reynolds Collection,
The Art Institute of Chicago — 1956
Retrospective Dada [1916-1922?], Galerie de l'Institut,
Paris. By MD: Rotative demi-sphère; Projet pour

Rotative demi-sphère; L.H.O.O Q; Porte-
Bouteilles — 13 Mar - 12 May 1957
Bosch, Goya et le Fantastique, Bordeaux, France. By MD:
Obligation pour la roulette de Monte-Carlo
— 20 May - 31 July 1957
Dessins Cubistes, Galerie Le Bateau Lavoir, Paris. By
MD: Deux Nus, un fort, un vite — 4 June - 4 July 1957
The disquieting Muse: Surrealism, Contemporary Arts
Museum, Houston, USA. By MD: The Bachelors
— 9 Jan - 16 Feb 1958
The 1913 Armory Show in retrospect, Amherst College,
Amherst, USA. By MD: Nude Descending a
Staircase — 16 Feb - 17 Mar 1958
50 ans d'Art Moderne, Palais International des Beaux-
Arts, Bruxelles. By MD: Le Passage de la Vierge à la
Mariée; Broyeuse de chocolat n°2; Réseaux de
Stoppages étalon — 17 Apr - 21 July 1958
Dada: Dokumente einer Bewegung, Kunstverein für die
Rheinlande im Westfalen, Düsseldorf, Germany
(travels to Frankfurt and Amsterdam). By MD:
Roue de bicyclette; In Advance of the Broken Arm;
Fontaine; Boîte-en-valise; Manuscript; La Mariée
(gravée par J. Villon) — 5 Sept - 19 Oct 1958
Old Masters of Modern Art, Hackley Gallery, Muskegon,
USA. By MD: The Bachelors — Oct - Nov 1958
Le Dessin dans l'Art Magique, Galerie Rive Droite, Paris.
By MD: Boîte-en-valise — 21 Oct - 20 Nov 1958
Art and the found object, traveling exhibition circulated
by the American Rockefeller Federation of Arts,
Reception Center, Time Life Building, New York.
Travels to Williamstown (Massachusetts),
Bloomfield Hills (Michigan), Chicago (Illinois),
South Bend (Indiana), Montreal (Canada),
Poughkeepsie (New York).
By MD: Roue de bicyclette; Bottle Dryer; In
Advance of the Broken Arm — 12 Jan - 6 Feb 1959
Mostra Surrealista Internazionale, Libreria Schwarz,
Milan, Italy. By MD: Feuille de vigne femelle;
Boîte-en-valise — 27 Apr - 16 May 1959
Dessins surréalistes, Galerie le Bateau Lavoir, Paris. By
MD: Nous nous cajolions — 5 June - 11 July 1959
Vente de solidarité au profit de Benjamin Péret, Hôtel
Drouot, Paris. By MD: Gilet pour Benjamin Péret
— 24 June 1959
On the occasion of Lebel's book publication, I.C.A.,
London — September 1959

16 January 1954
Duchamp marries Alexina ["Teeny"] Sattler Matisse
(1906-1995). They move into an apartment at
327 East 58th Street (formerly occupied
by Max Ernst), while Duchamp retains his studio
at 210 West 14th Street.

228. Marcel Duchamp to Walter Arensberg   autograph letter
23 January 1954, New York   collection PMA

Jan 23. 1954
210 W. 14th St
N.Y.C
    Dear Walter

Thursday 21st I received your large envelope with all the documents and I
telegraphed Fiske to announce my coming to Phila Friday.   Fiske = Fiske Kimball
It turned out that Fiske was coming to N.Y. on Friday (22nd) and I
arranged by telephone to meet him in N.Y., which I did.
(After seeing him I received a copy of his letter to you dated Jan. 21st)

From my conversation with him he seems to have finally grasped the
reasons of your dissatisfaction and will change his previous propositions
to the following new ones :

I__ No mention at all of a "Modern Museum" (and that you should insist
upon)

II The Collection opening won't be connected with anything else.

III This opening should take place as early as possible.
    I suggested that if there are difficulties to ~~be~~ get ready in a month or 2,
    they could easily be ready by the end of April or May__
    Even June would be a good moment__ But not wait until October.

IV The objections based on the readiness of the catalogue fall of themselves
    if the catalogue need not be ready for the opening__
    A good catalogue could hardly be ready by October anyway__ So why not
    work at it with great care and spend all the time necessary to make it a
    "monument".
    As for the visitors on the opening day they could have a black and white
    printed listing of all the works without any reproductions or literature.

V The objections based on the lack of time to obtain adequate publicity do
not hold water, for this kind of a show is not a "produit de beauté" which   "produit de beauté" =
needs heavy advertising. On the contrary a few press releases will start   cosmetic product
the ball rolling and "Life" has already arranged with Phila to start on the
project of a long article with color plates to appear at the time (or
probably after as they always do) of the opening date.__ "Life" needs two

PMA want to have the
Gallatin and Arensberg
Collections displayed
in adjoining rooms,
thus constituting a
"Modern Museum."

months for the color plates alone, although they are not made in
Europe—

— The "Art News Annual", if they want to run a long survey of the
Collection, comes out in November.

— These are the 2 important items of "dignified" publicity and the
opening date (May or June) would "cooperate" perfectly with the "Life"
article and the "Art News Annual"—

VI. The framing of the pictures can be simplified as indicated in one of Fiske's
letters.

I have seen Sweeney's framing at the "Guggenheim" and approve of it
completely.

It would be simple enough to keep the good frames and use the "strip
system" to replace the inadequate frames, without loss of time.

VII As to editing the catalogue of the 20th Century painting and sculpture
Fiske said that he has asked Clifford to submit a number of pages and
have you decide.— I know Clifford and like him very much but I don't
know about his writing.

Soby also would be a good choice for editing— in my opinion. I can't
think of anyone in particular whom I like better than those two.

After all it is primarily a question of translating into words the inner tenor
of the Collection in all its aspects, more than a general dissertation on
modern art.

I don't like Shapiro's approach to art in general— because he uses art to
write about Shapiro. He is a funny kind of a poet.

———

This is a résumé of my conversation with Fiske yesterday— Hope that he
will keep his promise to open before Summer, without any "Modern
Museum" strings attached.

———

VIII Another point concerning myself alone is that I would like to postpone
the showing of my large glass— I have to do some repairing on it and I
am afraid I might not be ready in time.—

Moreover, to avoid any misunderstanding I think that every painting or
sculpture shown at the opening should belong strictly to the collection.

IX— Another mere piece of news is that I married last Saturday Teeny
Matisse, the ex-wife of Pierre :

"En vieillissant, l'ermite se fait diable"—

Affectueusement
Marcel

Henry Clifford (1904-1974), curator of Paintings at the PMA 1942 - 1964; writes Arensberg catalog introduction.

Soby = James Thrall Soby

Meyer Shapiro (1904-1996), Professor of Art History at Columbia University.

Large Glass [cat. 2]

Alexina Sattler a.k.a. **Teeny** (1906-1995), ex-wife of Pierre **Matisse**, marries MD 16 Jan 1954

Literally = "Growing old, the hermit would be devil." English saying, "The devil would be monk."

229. Marcel Duchamp to Walter Arensberg
27 January 1954, [New York]

autograph letter
collection PMA

Walter Arensberg dies
29 Jan 1954, 2 days after
this letter (and just
over 2 months after his
wife's death).

210 W. 14.

Jan. 27. 54

Dear Walter

In haste, in answer to your telegram :

Kahnweiler, in my opinion, is too much one-sided—

By this I mean that, having discovered cubism in Picasso, Braque, Gris, never considered anything else <u>as worthy</u> of his attention.

Even though he is capable of general views, I don't see how he could "faire justice" to your collection, without having seen it in its setting, { or from photographs =

I don't see anyone better than Soby

—————

Please don't show this letter

Affectueusement

Marcel

**Daniel-Henry
Kahnweiler** (1884-
1979), famous Paris
dealer of Cubist art,
discussed as candidate
to write Arensberg Coll.
catalog introduction.

"faire justice" = do
justice

Soby = James Thrall
Soby

---

230. Marcel Duchamp to Suzanne Duchamp and Jean Crotti
31 January 1954, [New York]

autograph letter
collection AAA

[MD's personal stamp:]

*style télégraphique
pour correspondance
en retard.*
**210 WEST 14TH STREET
NEW YORK 11, N.Y.**

31 Janvier 54

Chère [sic] Jean chere Suzanne

Lou est morte il y a un mois et Walter est mort avant hier—

—————

Je suis marié depuis le 16 Janvier avec Teeny Matisse; pas encore d'enfant— sauf les 3 ready made.

Louis XVI et St Marcel

Affectueusement à tous deux

Marcel

See letters 225 and 229.

"3 ready made" =
Teeny's 3 children,
Paul, Pierre-Noël and
Jacqueline, all born in
the 1930's.

"St Marcel" = 16 Jan,
MD's wedding day also
his saint's day; Louis
XVI in fact guillotined
21 Jan 1793, not 16 Jan.

▷ TRANSLATION: [stamp:] *telegraphic style for late correspondence. 210 West 11th Street, New York 11, N.Y.* [letter:] *31st January 1954. Dear Jean, dear Suzanne, Lou died a month ago and Walter died day before yesterday. I have been married, since 16th January, to Teeny Matisse. No children yet, except for the three* ready made. *Louis XVI and St Marcel. Affectionately to you both, Marcel.*

---

231. Marcel Duchamp to Pierre de Massot   autograph letter
31 May 1954, New York   source: from André Gervais transcript

210 West 14th St.
31 Mai 1954
New York
    Cher Pierre
Merci de ta bonne lettre qui m'arrive après mon retour à N.Y. après appendicite et pneumonie. Tout cela du passé déjà.

Vers le 25 Juin je pense retourner à Cincinnati pour me faire enlever la prostate.

J'espère qu'après cela la Nature me laissera un peu tranquille.

Je suis marié depuis le 16 Janvier avec Teeny Matisse l'ex femme de Pierre Matisse et je suis très heureux.

Si la chance s'en mêle nous espérons pouvoir aller à Paris en Novembre (ou fin Octobre). Tout cela évidemment sans certitude.

Pourrais tu m'envoyer le livre de Carrouges sur les machines célibataires et me dire combien ça coûte je t'enverrai l'équivalent en dollars par chèque.
    Donc peut être à bientôt
    grand'affectueusement
    Marcel

MD operated on 18 Apr 1954 for appendicitis.

MD operated on for an enlarged prostate 24 June 1954, Cincinnati.

Pierre Matisse (1900-1989), Henri Matisse's son, owner and director of a successful gallery in NY since 1932.

Trip to Paris (staying at Roché's apartment) 14 Nov 1954 - 3 Feb 1955.

Michel Carrouges's book published 1954, see p.287.

▷ TRANSLATION: *210 West 14th St. 31st May 1954, New York. Dear Pierre, Thank you for your kind letter which has reached me on my return to New York following appendicitis and pneumonia. All that's in the past now. I expect to return to Cincinnati around 25th June to have my prostate removed. I hope that after that Nature will leave me be for a while. I've been married, since 16th January, to Teeny Matisse, ex-wife of Pierre Matisse, and am very happy. If luck's on our side, we hope to be able to go to Paris in November (or end October). Though this is not for certain, obviously. Could you send me Carrouges's book on the bachelor machines and let me know how much it costs and I'll send you the money in dollars by check. So see you soon maybe. Much affection, Marcel.*

---

232. Marcel Duchamp to Henri-Pierre Roché   autograph letter
5 July 1954, Cincinnati   collection HRHRC

Cincinnati 5 Juillet '54
    Cher Totor
le bulletin de libération :
J'ai quitté l'hopital hier et me repose à la campagne près de Cincinnati pour permettre à la croûte de mon rabotage *de* se former et disparaître.
Cela va durer jusqu'au 12 Juillet et nous rentrons à N.Y. le 12 au soir__

MD's operation almost 2 weeks earlier (see note on previous letter).

Transmets je te prie ~~le~~ ces détails par téléphone à la famille___

je t'avoue que c'est un plaisir nouveau et immenses de pisser comme tout
le monde (un plaisir que je ne connaissais pas depuis 25 ans)   *See letter 101.*

L'opération elle même m'a laissé complètement froid car je n'ai *eu* aucun
après-effet et n'ai fait aucune fièvre___ (anesthésie : ponction
lombaire)___ Je suis sorti de la table d'opération à 1^h après midi et à 7^h
du soir je fumais ma pipe___!!

Tout ceci pour te renseigner sur les bons côtés de l'opération intra-
urétrale___

J'espère que tu vas profiter de ton séjour en Corrèze pour te remettre à
neuf aussi___

En Octobre (vers le 11) ouverture de la coll. Arensberg à Philadelphie___

J'y vais bientôt pour installer mon Grand Verre (Dreier) dans une des   *Large Glass* [cat. 2]
salles importantes de la coll. Arensberg.

    Affectueusement de nous deux à tous

    Totor

▷ TRANSLATION: *Cincinnati 5th July '54. Dear Totor, Liberation bulletin: I came out
of hospital yesterday and am resting in the country near Cincinnati to let the scab
form after my scrape and disappear. This will be until 12th July and we're going
back to New York on the 12th in the evening. Please let the family know these details
by telephone. I must admit that being able to pee just like everybody else is a new-
found and immense pleasure (one I haven't known for 25 years). The operation itself was something of an anticlimax as I had absolutely no after effects and no
temperature. (anesthetic: lumbar puncture). I got up from the operating table at 1
o'clock in the afternoon and at 7 o'clock in the evening I was smoking my pipe!! All
this just to fill you in on the good sides of having an intra-urethral operation. I hope
you're going to make the most of your stay in Corrèze and come back as good as
new yourself. In October (around 11th) opening of the Arensberg collection in Philadelphia. I'll be going there soon to set up my Large Glass (Dreier) in one of the
main rooms of the Arensberg collection. Affectionately from the two of us to all of
you, Totor.*

---

233. Marcel Duchamp to André Breton   autograph letter
31 August 1954, New York   source: from Y. Poupard-Lieussou transcript

210 West 14th st. New York
31 aout 54
    Cher André
Drôle d'année en effet pour un homme qui n'a jamais été malade ni
    marié___
J'avance d'ailleurs que les 2 choses s'avalent sans peine et vous
    "réassurent" pour un moment___

Granell que je connais bien a été aussi gentil que possible et m'a envoyé votre lettre de Puerto Rico après m'avoir manqué à New York.

— Figurez vous que Carrouges a dû m'envoyer ses "Machines célibataires" il y a au moins quelques mois et que je ne l'en ai jamais avisé— Il me reste encore à les lire (j'ai demandé à Wittenborn de me les faire venir) Quand je les lirai (3 semaines environ) je pourrai vous envoyer quelques mots dessus si j'en trouve à dire, sans savoir quel genre de débat vous entreprenez.

A ce sujet pouvez vous me faire envoyer le texte de Jean Reboul s'il existe en forme imprimée.

— Le musée de Philadelphie ouvrira ses salles de la Collection Arensberg vers le 15 octobre et ils y ont joint mon grand verre Me voilà tranquille pour 25 ans!

— Teeny vous envoie ainsi qu'à Elisa ses bons souvenirs et dit qu'elle a aussi, en dehors des empreintes, le beau livre manuscrit que vous avez fait en 1940 avec Tanguy à New York

Nous "espérons"?? venir fin Octobre à Paris quoique rien n'en soit absolument sûr.

"on se verra donc avec plaisir" Vous savez peut être que Jacquie vient de se fiancer avec un Français et va probablement habiter Paris— Teeny très contente.

Espérons donc à bientôt
  Affectueusement à tous deux
  Marcel

Eugenio Fernandez Granell (b.1912), Spanish Surrealist painter.

George Wittenborn (1905-1974), NY book dealer.

Jean Reboul writes "Machines célibataires, schizophrénie et lune noire," *Journal intérieur du cercle d'études métaphysiques*, Toulon, June - July 1954.

Large Glass [cat. 2]

Elisa, A. Breton's wife, see p.248.

Yves Tanguy by André Breton (see p.248), book design by MD.

27 Dec 1954, Teeny's daughter, *Jacqueline*, marries Bernard *Monnier*, Paris financial analyst.

▷ TRANSLATION: *210 West 14th St. New York. 31st August '54. Dear André, Funny year indeed for a man who's never been ill or married! I dare to say that both things are easy to swallow and are "reassuring" for a while. Granell, whom I know well, has been as kind as can be and sent your letter on to me from Puerto Rico having missed me in New York. Would you believe that Carrouges must have sent me his "Bachelor machines" at least several months ago and that I never even let him know? I've yet to read them (I've asked Wittenborn to have them brought over to me). When I've read them (in about 3 weeks or so), I'll be able to drop you a line about them, without knowing what kind of a debate you're getting into. On this score, could you send me Jean Reboul's text if it exists in print? The Philadelphia Museum will open its rooms containing the Arensberg Collection around 15th October and they've included my Large Glass so I'll be all right for the next twenty five years! Teeny wishes to be remembered to you and to Elisa and says that she also has, in addition to the handprints, the beautiful manuscript book you did in 1940 with Tanguy in New York. We're "hoping"?? to come to Paris end October though nothing definite. "So look forward to seeing you!" You may have heard that Jacquie has just got engaged to a Frenchman and is probably going to live in Paris. Teeny very happy. So see you soon, let's hope. Affectionately to you both, Marcel.*

234. Marcel Duchamp to Henri-Pierre Roché   autograph letter
31 August 1954, New York   collection HRHRC

327 E. 58th St
31 Aout 54
    Cher Totor
Je ne sais pas si j'ai répondu à ta lettre du 10 Juillet. Pardonne moi mes
    répétitions.
— J'ai encore été à Philadelphie Lundi dernier et tout est en place : le Grand   *Large Glass* [cat. 2]
    Verre de Katherine Dreier est placé au beau milieu d'une énorme salle de
    la coll. Arensberg; soutenu par deux colonnes d'aluminium de 6^m de
    haut_ Ç'a été une opération de haut-fourneau pour le monter_ Mais
    je suis très touché par la gentillesse des directeurs qui m'ont consulté
    pour les moindres détails_ Inutile d'ajouter que la coll. Arensberg est
    présentée avec beaucoup d'air, dans une dizaine de salles_
    Brancusi est seul dans une grande salle avec une vingtaine de ses choses.
    Si tu urines assez facilement sans douleur, ne pense pas à une opération_
        Tu as la chance de n'avoir aucun rétrécissement (conséquence de chaude
        pisse!) et ta prostate est vraisemblablement de dimension normale.
— Teeny et moi avons en effet l'intention d'aller passer deux mois environ en   **Teeny** = Teeny Duchamp
    France si nous en voyons la possibilité financière_ fin Oct_ à fin
    Décembre
    Le premier point et le plus important est l'endroit où habiter pendant ce
    séjour.
    Tu me dis que Jean Claude habitera Arago cet hiver_ Y aurais tu par
    hasard une petite chambre à louer dans l'appartement qui pourrait nous
    abriter sans déranger tes projets pour ces deux mois?

[end of letter missing]

▷ TRANSLATION: *327 E. 58th St. 31st August '54. Dear Totor. I don't know whether I
replied to your letter of 10th July. Please forgive me if I repeat myself. I went back
to Philadelphia again last Monday and everything is in place: Katherine Dreier's
Large Glass is right in the middle of an enormous room at the Arensberg collection;
held up by two aluminium columns 6m high. It was an enormous feat getting it up
there! But I'm really touched by how kind the directors have been who have consult-
ed me about every slightest detail. Needless to say the Arensberg collection is hand-
somely spaced out, in ten or so rooms. Brancusi is on his own in a big room with
twenty or so of his things. If you can urinate fairly easily and painlessly, don't en-
tertain an operation. You are fortunate not to have any shrinking (consequence of
the clap!) and your prostate is probably the normal size. Teeny and I do indeed
plan to go and spend about two months in France if we can manage it financially—
end Oct. until end December. The first and most important point is a place to stay*

during this trip. You say that Jean Claude will be in Arago this winter: Would you by any chance have a small room to let in your apartment where we could shelter without disrupting your progress for these two months?

---

235. Marcel Duchamp to André Breton   autograph letter
4 October 1954, New York   source: from Y. Poupard-Lieussou transcript

210 West 14th St. New York

4 Octobre 54.

    Cher André

D'abord, vous remercier de m'avoir fait parvenir le texte de Jean Reboul ; Jean Reboul, see p.340.
entretemps aussi j'ai reçu le livre de Carrouges. Michel Carrouges, see p.287.

La question de savoir si Carrouges se sert de sa formation surréaliste pour
en faire profiter "l'Eglise" n'appartient pas à ma "juridiction", car je ne
le connais pas et j'ai lu très peu de ses écrits.

Son idée de grouper sous une même appellation les différentes machines à
mythe érotique trouve sa justification tout le long du livre : il y a un
rapprochement évident entre les intentions des différents auteurs
considérés.

"Machine célibataire", en ce qui concerne "La Mariée…", terme décrivant *The Bride Stripped Bare...* [cat. 1]
un ensemble d'opérations, n'a pour moi que l'importance d'un titre
partiel et descriptif et non pas celle d'un titre à thème
intentionnellement mythique.

Dans la Machine Célibataire un désir érotique en action est "ramené à" sa
"projection" d'apparence et de caractère machinisés.

De même la Mariée ou le Pendu femelle est une "projection" comparable
à la projection d'une "entité imaginaire" à 4 dimensions dans notre
monde à 3 dim. (et même dans le cas du verre plat à une re-projection
de ces 3 dimensions sur une surface à 2 dim.).

A l'aide de la boîte verte Carrouges a mis à jour le processus sous-jacent
avec toute la minutie d'une dissection sub-mentale. Inutile d'ajouter
que ses découvertes, si elles forment un ensemble cohérent ne furent
jamais <u>conscientes</u> dans mon travail d'élaboration parce que mon
inconscient est <u>muet</u> comme tous les inconscients ; que cette élaboration
portait plus sur la nécessité <u>consciente</u> d'introduire l'"<u>hilarité</u>" ou au
moins l'humour dans un sujet aussi "sérieux".

La conclusion de Carrouges sur le caractère athée de la "Mariée" n'est pas
déplaisante mais je voudrais seulement ajouter qu'en termes de
"métaphysique populaire" je n'accepte pas de discuter sur l'existence de
Dieu— ce qui veut dire que le terme "athée" (en opposition au mot
"croyant") ne m'intéresse même pas, non plus le mot croyant ni
opposition de leurs sens bien clairs :

Pour moi il y a autre chose que <u>oui</u>, <u>non</u> et <u>indifférent</u>— C'est par exemple l'absence d'investigations de ce genre.

———

Et maintenant le texte de Reboul m'a appris à quelles réactions le Verre peut amener un esprit "armé de clairvoyance pseudo-scientifique"; je dis "pseudo" car la psychiatrie emploie des procédés analogues à ceux de l'artiste, procédés par lesquels l'interprétation peut délirer à souhait.
C'est une façon de vous dire que j'aime son analyse descriptive de la "Mariée"… et surtout son paragraphe sur les "ready mades"
— J'aime aussi son diagnostic de mon cas particulier de schizophrénie— Très ignorant de la gravité de mon cas, je ne suis pas autrement alarmé, ayant déjà passé une bonne partie de ma vie dans cette brume derrière le verre.
De plus j'ai quand même à ma disposition le <u>thermomètre</u> des échecs qui enregistre assez exactement mes écarts d'une ligne de pensée strictement "syllogistique"—
Voilà cher André à peu près tout ce que je puis vous dire de ces lectures
Mettez moi au courant des débats dans Medium—
Toujours peut être Teeny et moi viendrons à Paris vers le 15 Nov.   Teeny = Teeny Duchamp
Affectueusement à tous les 3
Marcel

▷ TRANSLATION: *210 West 14th St. New York, 4th October '54. Dear André, First of all to thank you for sending the Jean Reboul text. Meantime I've also received Carrouges's book. The question of whether Carrouges uses his Surrealist training for the benefit of "the Church" does not fall under my "jurisdiction" as I don't know him and have read very little of what he has written. His idea of grouping together, under the same heading the different machines of erotic myth, finds justification all the way through the book. There are clearly similarities between the different authors considered. "Bachelor machine" talking about the "Bride," term describing a set of operations, has no more importance for me than a partial and descriptive title, and not that of a title with an intentionally mythical theme. In the Bachelor Machine, an erotic desire in the act is "brought back" to its apparent and mechanized "projection." In the same way, the Bride or the Hanged female* ["Pendu femelle"] *is a projection comparable to the projection of an "imaginary entity" in 4 dimensions, in our world in 3 dimensions (and even the case of the flat glass has a re-projection of these 3 dimensions on a 2 dimensional surface). With the help of the green box, Carrouges has brought to light the underlying process with the meticulousness of a sub-mental dissection. No need to add that his findings, even if they form a coherent whole, were never conscious when I was working out my strategy because my sub-conscious is dumb like all subconsciouses and that my strategy had more to do with the need to introduce some "mirth" or at least humour into such a "serious" subject. Carrouges's conclusion on the atheistic character of the "Bride" is not displeasing but I would just like to add that in terms of "popular metaphysics," I refuse to get involved in arguments on the existence of God—which means that the term "atheist" (as opposed to the word "believer") is of no interest to me at all, no more than the word believer or the opposition of their very clear meanings. For me, there is something other than yes, no and indifferent—the absence of investigations of this sort, for instance. Then Reboul's text taught me what kind of reactions the Glass can provoke in a mind "armed with pseudo-scientific lucidity." I say "pseudo" because the psychiatrist uses procedures very similar to those used by the artist, according to which you can make up whatever interpretation you like. By this I mean I like his descriptive analysis of the "Bride" and especially his paragraph on the "ready mades." I also like his diagnosis of my particular case of schizophrenia. Quite ignorant of the seriousness of my case, I am not unduly alarmed, having spent most of my life in this mist behind the glass. What's more, I have at my disposal the chess thermometer which keeps quite a precise record of whenever I stray from a strictly "syllogistic" line of thought. So there you are, dear André, about all I can tell you about my reading. Fill me in on the debates in Medium. Teeny and I might perhaps still come to Paris around 15th Nov. Affectionately to all three of you, Marcel.*

---

236. Marcel Duchamp to Robert Lebel   autograph letter
26 February 1955, New York   private collection, Paris

327 East 58th Street N.Y.

26 Fev. 55

    Cher Lebel

Je ne sais pas où vous êtes__ mais je n'ai eu aucune sensation de votre
    présence à N.Y. quand je suis rentré il y a quinze jours.

Nous avons dû nous croiser d'une façon ou de l'autre, ou dans des
    dimensions différentes.

Je reçois de Skira tout ce paquet et une lettre explicative. Je vous propose
    donc de téléphoner à Roché (Observatoire 12 50) à Sèvres *S et O* (2 rue
    Nungesser et Coli) et lui demander s'il a reçu les clichés de Skira__

Si à ce moment vous vous êtes déja entendu avec Fawcus 19 Rue Rousselet
    qui est le représentant et l'éditeur que Copley doit commanditer pour
    votre livre, peut être pourriez vous lui suggérer de mettre au <u>point déja
    le format</u> du livre comprenant les 2 reproductions en couleur et faire
    tirer (à part) le <u>nombre nécessaire</u> de reproductions en couleur sur les 2
    planches de Skira__

"**S et O**" = Seine et Oise (around Paris).

Arnold Fawcus, English publisher, owns Trianon Press and publishes Lebel's book on MD, 1959.

A aucun prix ne laissez les planches en couleur passer aux mains de Losfeld— Je me sens trop responsable ~~vers~~ vis à vis de Skira pour risquer de ne jamais revoir ces planches.
> Affectueusement à tous deux
> Marcel Duchamp

Eric Losfeld (1922-1979), French publisher, founder of Arcanes Editions, 1952, and Terrain vague, 1955.

▷ TRANSLATION: *327 East 58th Street, N.Y. 26th Feb. '55. Dear Lebel, I don't know where you are—but I did not get the feeling you were in N.Y. at all when I got back a fortnight ago. We must have crossed, one way or another, or in different dimensions. I've received from Skira this whole parcel and a covering letter. I suggest then you telephone Roché (Observatoire 12 50) in Sèvres S and O (2 rue Nungesser et Coli) and ask him whether he's received the negatives from Skira. If by now you have already reached an agreement with Fawcus, 19 rue Rousselet, who is the representative and editor that Copley is to commission for your book, maybe you could suggest deciding on the format of the book straightaway, including 2 color reproductions and have the necessary number of color reproductions printed on Skira's 2 plates. On no account let these color plates fall into Losfeld's hands. I feel too duty-bound to Skira to run the risk of never seeing these plates again. Affectionately to you both, Marcel Duchamp.*

---

237. Marcel Duchamp to Guy Weelen
26 June 1955, New York

autograph letter
present whereabouts unknown

327 East 58th St.
New York
26 Juin 55
> Cher Weelen
Désolé que vous ayez perdu mon premier papier :
Mes souvenirs sur l'apparition d'une roue de bicyclette montée sur un tabouret de cuisine dans mon atelier en 1913, sont trop vagues et ne peuvent que se transformer en réflexions a posteriori

Bicycle Wheel [cat. 33]

Je me rappelle seulement que l'ambiance créée par ce mouvement intermittent avait quelque chose d'analogue à la danse d'un feu de bois ; c'était comme une révérence au côté inutile d'une chose généralement utilisée pour d'autres buts.
En fait c'était un ready made "avant la lettre" car le mot ne m'est venu qu'en 1914.

"1914" = actually 1915

J'ai probablement accepté avec joie le mouvement de la roue comme un antidote au mouvement habituel de l'individu autour de l'objet contemplé.
> En hâte cordialement à vous
Marcel Duchamp

▷ TRANSLATION: *327 East 58th St. New York, 26th June '55. Dear Weelen, Sorry to hear you lost my first paper. My recollections as to the apparition of a bicycle wheel mounted on a kitchen stool in my studio in 1913 are too vague and can only be treated as a posteriori reflections. I only remember that the atmosphere created by this intermittent movement was something analogous to the dancing flames of a log fire. It was as if in homage to the useless aspect of something generally used to other ends. In fact, it was a ready made "before the event" as the word only came to me in 1914. I probably accepted the movement of the wheel very gladly as an antidote to the habitual movement of the individual around the contemplated object. In haste, sincerely yours, Marcel Duchamp.*

---

238. Marcel Duchamp to Robert Lebel   autograph letter
4 August 1955, East Hampton   private collection, Paris

East Hampton
4 Aout 55
    Cher Lebel
Bien reçu "Chantage" que j'ai lu comme je lis Platon càd à grande allure—
    Nevertheless il m'en reste beaucoup collé à ma matière grise.
Pour le livre avec Fawcus j'ai obtenu de Philadelphie une promesse
    "morale" d'acheter un <u>certain</u> nombre d'exemplaires, tout cela à
    déterminer quand les prix de gros et de détail seront établis—
Dites à Fawcus (par téléphone) que j'attends sa réponse au sujet de ces prix
    pour continuer mes pourparlers avec le Musée de Philadelphie
et bonne chance pour les dernières (les plus difficiles) lignes de votre livre
    Affectueusement de nous deux à vous deux
    Marcel Duchamp

Robert Lebel, *Chantage de la beauté*, Paris, Ed. de Beaune, 1955.

▷ TRANSLATION: *East Hampton, 4th August '55. Dear Lebel, Received "Chantage" which I read the way I read Plato i.e. very fast. Nevertheless, much of it has managed to stick to my gray matter. As for the Fawcus book, I got a moral promise out of Philadelphia that they would buy a number of copies—all this to be determined once the prices, wholesale and retail, have been worked out. Tell Fawcus (by telephone) that I'm waiting for his reply about these prices so that I can continue negotiations with the Philadelphia Museum and good luck for the last lines (the most difficult ones) of your book. Affectionately from the two of us to the two of you, Marcel Duchamp.*

239. Marcel Duchamp to Jehan Mayoux
8 March 1956, New York

autograph letter
source: from André Gervais transcript

Jehan Mayoux (1904-1975), French Surrealist poet.

327 East 58th Street

New York, 8 mars 1956

   Cher Mayoux

Merci de m'avoir fait parvenir votre étude dans Bizarre que j'ai lue avec
   "étonnement" car votre analyse implacable du texte de Carrouges m'a
   éclairci sur bien des points que j'avais laissé passer par manque de
   "technique analytique"—

Je suis un grand ennemi de l'écriture critique car je ne vois dans ces
   interprétations et ces comparaisons avec Kafka et autres que l'occasion
   d'ouvrir un robinet de mots dont l'ensemble est du Carrouges ou
   quelquefois sa traduction très libre pour faire valoir une idée Carrouges.

— Évidemment toute œuvre d'art ou littéraire, dans le domaine public, est
   forcément le sujet ou la victime de telles transformations— et ceci va
   beaucoup plus loin que le cas particulier Carrouges. Tous les 50 ans, El
   Greco est révisé et adapté au goût du jour, en plus ou en moins. Il en va
   de même de toutes les œuvres qui survivent.

Et ceci m'amène à dire qu'une œuvre est faite <u>entièrement</u> par ceux qui la
   regardent ou la lisent et la font survivre par leurs acclamations ou même
   leur condamnation.

— Autant que je me rappelle ce que j'ai écrit dans la lettre parue dans
   Medium, je refuse de penser aux clichés philosophiques remis à neuf par
   chaque génération depuis Adam et Eve, dans tous les coins de la
   planète—. Je refuse d'y penser et d'en parler parce que je ne crois pas au
   langage. Le langage, au lieu d'exprimer des phénomènes subconscients,
   en réalité crée la pensée par et <u>après</u> les mots (je me déclare
   "nominaliste" très volontiers, au moins dans cette forme simplifiée).

Toutes ces balivernes, existence de Dieu, athéisme, déterminisme, libre
   arbitre, sociétés, mort, etc., sont les pièces d'un jeu d'échecs appelé
   langage et ne sont amusantes que si on ne se préoccupe pas de "gagner
   ou de perdre cette partie d'échecs"—.

En bon "nominaliste", je propose le mot Patatautologies qui, après
   répétition fréquente, créera le concept de ce que j'essaie d'exprimer par
   ce moyen exécrable : le sujet, le verbe, le complément... etc.

— J'étais à Paris l'année dernière— mais je suppose que vous n'y venez pas
   souvent—

   Peut-être la prochaine fois
   Très cordialement à vous
   Marcel Duchamp

Mayoux wrote articles in *Bizarre* (May and Oct 1955) condemning Carrouges's book, *Les Machines Célibataires*.

See letter 235.

▷ TRANSLATION: *New York, 8th March 1956. Dear Mayoux, Thank you for sending me your study in Bizarre which I read with "wonder" as your unrelenting analysis of Carrouges's text enlightened me on a number of points that I had overlooked for want of "analytical technique." I am a great enemy of critical writing as all I see in these interpretations and comparisons with Kafka and others is just an opportunity to open up the floodgates of words which, overall, amounts to Carrouges or at times a translation of Carrouges—very free to make his ideas look good. Obviously any work of art or literature, in the public domain, is automatically the subject or the victim of such transformations and this is not just confined to the case of Carrouges. Every fifty years, El Greco is revised and adapted to the tastes of the day, either over-rated or underrated. The same goes for all surviving works of art. And this leads me to say that a work is made entirely by those who look at it or read it and make it survive by their acclaim or even their condemnation. As far as I remember what I wrote in the letter that appeared in Medium, I refuse to think of the philosophical clichés rehashed by each generation since Adam and Eve in every corner of the planet. I refuse to think about it or to talk about it because I don't believe in language. Language, instead of expressing subconscious phenomena, in reality creates thought through and after words (I readily declare myself a "nominalist," at least in this simplified form). All this twaddle, existence of God, atheism, determinism, free will, societies, death etc. are the pieces of a game of chess called language and are only entertaining if one is not concerned about "winning or losing this chess match." As a good "nominalist," I propose the word Patatautologies which, after frequent repetition, will create the concept I have been trying to express by the execrable means of subject, verb, complement etc. I was in Paris last year, but I suppose you don't go there often. Maybe next time. Most sincerely yours, Marcel Duchamp.*

---

240. Marcel Duchamp to Henri-Pierre Roché   autograph letter
5 June 1956, New York   collection HRHRC

327 East 58th St.
New York
5 Juin 1956
    Cher Totor

Nous avons reçu ton ~~lettre~~ *livre* et je l'ai avalé avec avidité. Que te dire sinon qu'il a la fraîcheur de toutes les jeunes années et semble avoir été écrit par l'homme que tu étais il y a cinquante ans.

Le tour de force consiste à n'avoir pas gâté l'explosion par des considérations ou un style trop adultes.

Dis moi comment le premier public l'a accepté.

———

Reçu de Fawcus une lettre annonçant le départ de l'édition du livre sur moi avec ton texte et ceux de Breton et de Lebel— Mais verra ce jamais le jour?

H.-P. Roché, *Deux anglaises et le continent* (Paris, Gallimard, 1956).

Z… est OK— je crains seulement qu'il ne soit un peu cavalier en
affaires— à toi de te défendre— Pas de valise pour le moment— Elles
sont en douane française depuis un an!! et je commence à croire que je
vais tout perdre dans cette affaire.

T'ai déjà donné mon avis sur les Brancusis— Lui peut demander ce qu'il
veut et les gros prix ont toujours été son principe—
Je trouve plus "relaxing" de se contenter de ne pas toujours obtenir le
maximum si on veut vendre.
15^m 18^m 20^m sont pour moi des prix suffisants.

<u>Autre chose!</u> :

Teeny depuis notre séjour à Paris en Arago rêve de posséder mon verre
qu'elle a vu tous les matins en se réveillant— Comme tu le sais elle n'a
rien de moi—
Donc voici la proposition :
Si le verre vient en Amérique pour l'exposition des 3 frères, au Texas et
chez Guggenheim à N.Y. pourrais tu considérer de vendre à Teeny le
verre après les 2 expositions pour la somme de 14^m dollars.
Comme nous avions décidé momentanément 21^m à diviser en trois ⅔
pour toi et ⅓ pour moi. Tu recevrais ta part (⅔) = 14^m
D'ailleurs elle l'achèterait pour <u>ne pas</u> le revendre—
Pour te payer elle vendrait un Rouault et un des ~~ses~~ Miros de sa collection
afin de faire la somme.
— Elle aimerait seulement avoir dès maintenant une promesse définitive
pour pouvoir entreprendre la vente du Rouault (qui ne se vend pas
comme des petits pains)
— Elle pourrait selon ton désir laisser l'argent ici ou te le faire parvenir
(tout ou partie)
Réfléchis et dis nous ton impression
C'est tout pour le moment
Nos félicitations au jeune marié.
  Affectueusement à tous trois de nous deux
  Totor

"en Arago" = at Roché's
place, 99 Bd. Arago,
where MD and Teeny
stayed Nov 1954-Feb 1955.

9 Malic Moulds [cat. 31]

"Three Brothers
Exhibition" is called
"Les Duchamps" at
Musée des Beaux-Arts
de Rouen, 15 Apr -
1 June 1967 (as it also
includes MD's sister
Suzanne) and
"Raymond Duchamp-
Villon / Marcel
Duchamp" at the Musée
National d'Art
Moderne, Paris, 7 June
- 2 July 1967.

"Groom" is H.-P.
Roché's son, Jean-
Claude, who marries
Monique Potin in the
summer of 1956.

▷ TRANSLATION: *Dear Totor. We received your book and I devoured it. What can I
say except that it has all the freshness of our youth and feels like it was written by
the man you were fifty years ago. The trick is not to spoil the explosion with reflections or a style that are too adult. Let me know what the first readers make of it.
Received from Fawcus a letter saying that the edition of the book on me with your
text and that of Breton and Lebel had been sent off. But will it ever see the light of
day? Z…is OK. my only fear is that he may be somewhat cavalier in business—*

you'll have to stand your ground. No suitcases for the time being. They have been with French customs for a year!! and I'm starting to think that I'm going to lose everything in this affair. Have I already told you what I think about the Brancusis? Brancusi can ask whatever he likes and high prices have always been his policy. I find it more "relaxing" to be satisfied with not always getting the top price when you want to sell. 15,000, 18,000, 20,000 are all acceptable prices to me. One more thing!—It's been Teeny's dream, since staying in Arago on our trip to Paris, to own my glass which she saw every morning as she woke up. As you know, she has nothing of mine. So here is my proposition: if the glass comes to America for the 3 brothers exhibition in Texas and at the Guggenheim in N.Y., would you consider selling the glass to Teeny after the 2 exhibitions for the sum of 14,000 dollars? As we had at one point fixed on 21,000 divided by three, 2/3 for you and 1/3 for me. You would receieve your share (2/3) = 14,000. Moreover she would be buying it not to resell it afterwards. To pay you she would sell a Rouault and one of the Miros in her collection to meet the sum. She would just like to have a definite promise now so that she can undertake the sale of the Rouault (which won't exactly sell like hot cakes). She could, as you wish, leave the money here or send it to you (all or in part). Think it over and let us know what you think. That's all for now. Our congratulations to the groom. Affectionately to the three of you from the two of us, Totor.

---

241. Marcel Duchamp to George Heard Hamilton
10 July 1956, New York

autograph letter
collection YCAL

George Heard Hamilton, see p.306 and p.354.

327 East 58th Street
New York
July 10th 1956
Tlph. Plaza 11658
    Dear George
I just received an SOS letter from Pevsner asking me to intervene in
    respect to the lending of my portrait by him which the University
    apparently has declined on account of the fragility of the work.
Pevsner tells me that he is evidently more than interested in the welfare of
    the piece and that if there is any kind of "accroc" he will be on hand to
    repair it.
The show is an important retrospective one man show and he is very
    anxious to have this piece.
Could you in any way have "no" change to "yes"? I would be very grateful
    to you as I consider him a rare artist.
I also wish that I could see you whenever you come to N.Y.
If you telephoned, Teeny and myself would love to have Polly and you for
    dinner

Antoine Pevsner, requests *Portrait of Marcel Duchamp*, 1926 (Yale University Art Gallery) for his retrospective exh. at Musée National d'Art Moderne, Paris, Dec 1956 - Mar 1957.

"accroc" = snag

Teeny = Teeny Duchamp

Polly, George Heard Hamilton's wife.

Please do—
 Affectueusement à tous deux
 Marcel Duchamp

---

242. Marcel Duchamp to George Heard Hamilton   autograph letter
15 October 1956, New York   collection YCAL

327 East 58th St.
New York
Oct. 15th 1956
 Dear George
Many thanks for your photo of the "Table servie" (Still Life) by Villon and
 for your willingness to lend also the "Femme assise" by R.D.V.
You will receive shortly the official request from the Guggenheim and
 Houston Museums.
I am very flattered to be asked for my prose. Here it is : a piece I wrote in
 1916, which has never been published (except in my boîte-en-valise)—
 Hope it can be reproduced as is, since it was intended to have not
 beginning and no end.
— The title is on the back and I don't mind if it is typographed at the top
 of the prose (to avoid printing complications)
 Affectueusement de nous deux à tous trois
 Marcel Duchamp

Jacques Villon,
Déjeuner; **La Table
servie**, 1941, and
Raymond Duchamp-
Villon, *Seated Woman,*
1914 (both Yale
University Art Gallery).

"prose" = copy of
*Rendez-vous
Dimanche* [cat. 55].

Box-in-a-Valise [cat. 4].

---

243. Marcel Duchamp to Suzanne Duchamp and Jean Crotti   autograph letter
8 December 1956, New York   collection AAA

327 E. 58.
N.Y.
8 Dec. 56
 Cher Jean chère Suzanne.
En hâte voici :
Pas de valise prête avant 3 mois—
Le prix sera 100 000 francs pièce— au public et 70 000 au marchand.
Tu peux prendre des commandes, sans délai de livraison.
Pour l'expo Dada, peut-être Roché prêtera son exemplaire.
— J'attends Lebel et lui parlerai de photos pittoresques (?) pour Pierre
 Cailler
— Sûr je t'autorise à mettre la photo du croquis aquarelle 1903

Box-in-a-Valise [cat. 4]

"Retrospective Dada,"
13 Mar - 12 May 1957,
Galerie de l'Institut,
Paris.

Pierre Cailler, Swiss
publisher.

— Aussi je tâcherai de faire rapporter les Documents Dada de Jean par Lebel__

Jean = Marcel Jean

Ça c'est rapide__
et affectueux de nous deux
Marcel

▷ TRANSLATION: *327 E.58, N.Y. 8th Dec. '56. Dear Jean, dear Suzanne, In haste: No suitcase ready before 3 months. The price will be 100,000 francs apiece for the general public and 70,000 for dealers. You can start taking orders, but no deadline for delivery. As for Dada exhibition, perhaps Roché will lend his. I'm expecting Lebel and will talk to him about picturesque photos for Pierre Cailler. Sure I authorize you to include the photo of the watercolor sketch 1903. Also I will try to have Jean's Dada Documents returned by Lebel. That's quick for you. And affectionately from us both, Marcel.*

---

244. Marcel Duchamp to George Heard Hamilton   autograph letter
12 March 1957, New York   collection YCAL

327 East 58th Street
New York
March 12. 1957
    Dear George
Djuna Barnes has asked me to help her dispose of the M.S. writings of the Baroness Freytag Von Loringhoven (?)__ who died around 1935 in Paris.
Djuna would like to will them to Yale along with some of her own M.S. (Nightwood etc.) and also some illustrations she herself designed for some of her books__
If you find this feasible could you give me the name of the curator in charge of the M.S. department and she would then write a direct letter to arrange the gift.
    Amicalement à vous
    Marcel Duchamp

Djuna Barnes (1892-1982), American writer and journalist, author of *Nightwood*, 1936.

Elsa von Freytag-Loringhoven, see p.121. Her manuscripts will eventually be donated to the University of Maryland at College Park.

---

245. Marcel Duchamp to Robert Lebel   autograph letter
[circa 17 April 1957], Mexico   private collection, Paris

Hotel IXTAPAN *(pour 8 jours) et des bains radio-actifs*

   Cher Lebel

Après 3 jours de cirque à Houston où j'ai joué mon rôle de pitre artistique
aussi bien que possible, nous sommes au Mexique et j'y retrouve toute
la bonne petite saleté nécessaire à un Européen-né.

A part cela vu et revu Copley qui était très inquiet à cause du livre.

Il paraît que votre manuscrit est perdu!! Dites moi si vous l'avez retrouvé
et si Fawcus a commencé.

Copley est bien décidé à signer le contrat de participation (quelque chose
comme $6 000⁻) avec Fawcus mais je lui ai fait ajouter dans ce contrat
la stipulation de dead line (31 Dec 57).

Il semble tout à fait d'accord et surtout rasséréné après mon assurance que
tout avait été réglé définitivement par vous et moi à votre passage à N.Y.
(Luxe, Super luxe etc).

Il m'a promis de ne rien changer à nos plans.

Donc mettez-moi au courant vers le 10 Mai (date de ma rentrée à N.Y.)
de la mise en marche.

De mon côté j'ai déjà commandé les 15 photos du verre à Schiff et je en
rentrant je les colorierai et les monterai prêtes à être collées à l'intérieur
de la couverture du livre comme convenu.

   Hasta luego

   Marcel Duchamp

(margin notes)

5 Apr 1957, MD, guest speaker at American Federation of Arts annual convention, **Houston**, Texas, delivered lecture "The Creative Act."

John D. Schiff photographed the *Large Glass* [cat. 2] in front of a window in K. Dreier's property in Milford (Conn.), 19 Oct 1948.

▷ TRANSLATION: Hotel IXTAPAN *(for a week) and radio-active baths. Dear Lebel, After 3 days of the circus in Houston where I played my role as the artist-clown as well as I could, we are in Mexico where I can find just the right dose of dirt a born European needs. Apart from that, seen Copley and seen Copley again: he was very worried about the book. It seems that your manuscript has been lost!! Let me know if you've found it and if Fawcus has made a start. Copley has made his mind up to sign the participation contract (something like $6,000) with Fawcus but I got him to add into this contract the stipulation of a deadline (31st December 1957). He seemed in total agreement and above all his mind at rest after I reassured him that you and I had sorted everything out once and for all when you passed through N.Y. (Deluxe, Super-deluxe etc.) He promised he would make no changes to our plans. So fill me in around 10th May (date I return to N.Y.) about things getting under way. For my part, I've already ordered the 15 photos of the glass from Schiff and when I get back I'll color them and mount them ready for them to be stuck on the inside cover of the book as agreed. Hasta luego, Marcel Duchamp.*

246. Marcel Duchamp to Richard Hamilton   autograph letter
15 May 1957, New York   collection Richard Hamilton, Oxon, England

Richard Hamilton (b.1922), English Pop artist.

327 East 58th Street
New York
May 15th 1957
    Dear Richard Hamilton
It is almost a year now since I received your letter and the diagram of the glass—
I was very pleased to see how well you had deciphered the notes of the green box and by your idea of making a translation.
But having worked in the past with several people and nothing having ever materialized, I became discouraged.
Lately I have been in touch with a student in Yale University, who undertook the translation of some 25 "papers" in the green box.
This student, Henry Steiner, is a pupil of Professor George Heard Hamilton, Art History in Yale, curator of the "Société Anonyme" Collection in Yale and an old friend of mine.
George Hamilton to whom I showed your diagram and your letter expressed the desire to work with you on the publication of a translation—
I am giving him your address and you will hear from him shortly—
    Cordialement à vous
    Marcel Duchamp

Diagram of the cogs of the *Large Glass* [cat. 2] appears in R. Hamilton's typographic edition of the Green Box (p.368).

Green Box [cat. 3]

Henry Steiner, graphic designer in the Graphic Arts Dept, Yale University, designs *Marcel Duchamp: from the Green Box*, trans. by **George Heard Hamilton** (New Haven, The Readymade Press, 1957).

---

247. Marcel Duchamp to Henry McBride   autograph letter
15 April 1958, New York   collection YCAL

327 East 58th St.
New York
April 15th 1958
    Dear Henry
Do you remember anything about an article of yours in the Herald (or the Sun) around 1915, 16, or 17 about me.
Someone in Paris is preparing a bibliography of "études" on my very august person.
Where could I find it in the archives of what paper?
around these years.
We saw and loved "Endgame" of Beckett?
A bientôt
    et affectueusement à vous
    Marcel Duchamp

Unsigned **article** must be interview in *NY Tribune*, 12 Sept 1915.

"Someone in Paris" = Robert Lebel preparing *Sur MD* (p.323) or Yves Poupard-Lieussou, bibliography of *Marchand du Sel* (see p.356).

Samuel Beckett (1906-1989), Irish bilingual novelist and playwright; MD saw premiere of *Endgame*, NY, 28 Jan 1958.

248. Marcel Duchamp to Patrick Waldberg   "pneumatique" letter
[18 June 1958], Paris   collection BLJD

Patrick Waldberg (1913-1985), American-born French writer, living in Paris. Wrote several books on Surrealism.

58 r. Mathurin Régnier
Mercredi
    Cher Patrick
Malheureusement Jeudi 26 ne va pas pour dîner :
Mais—
Jeudi 26, 5^h ½ à Montparnasse, <u>Select</u> par exemple, si Beckett et toi
    peuvent!
Donc pas de réponse et entendu—
Autrement propose quelque autre endroit et heure et jour——
    Affectueusement de nous deux
    Marcel

▷ TRANSLATION: *58 rue Mathurin Régnier, Wednesday. Dear Patrick, Unfortunately Thursday 26th is no good for dinner. But: Thursday 26th, 5.30 in Montparnasse, Select, for example, if Beckett and you can make it! So no reply and deal. Otherwise, suggest some other day, time and place. Affectionately from us both, Marcel.*

---

249. Marcel Duchamp to Robert Lebel   autograph letter
21 October 1958, New York   private collection, Paris

21 Oct. 58
327 E. 58
    Cher Lebel
Oui la gravure du petit Benoit (Picabia "Equilibre") est un original sur celluloïd (1958) mais vraiment sans importance.

Pierre-André Benoit (1921-1993), owner and editor of publishing house, P.A.B., Alès, France.

— Surtout ne remaniez pas toute la mise en page du cat. rais. pour cet "item"—

"cat. rais." = catalogue raisonné, see p.323.

Ou alors je vous enverrai tous mes doodles journaliers faits en attendant un n° de téléphone—
— Si vous l'avez le *(le cellulo)* regardez en miroir ou en transparence vous pourrez à peine y lire Et qui libre?

Et qui libre, 1958, drypoint by MD to illustrate a 1917 poem by Picabia, *L'Equilibre* (P.A.B., Alès, France, 1958).

— Entre nous je perds le genre d'enthousiasme que j'ai eu à Paris pendant quelques semaines—
L'indifférence profonde de Fawcus, cette sorte de bouillonnement en surface continuera probablement mê probablement [sic] même après la parution et je me demande si M. Weber ne subira pas cette contagion avant de signer au bas de la page.

Weber, French distributor (for editors).

— Braziller est il repassé par Paris après mon départ?— J'attends des instructions de Fawcus avant d'aller le voir— (là encore, quelle indifférence?!) quelle beauté d'indifférence!

Georges Braziller, NY publisher.

Cordialement

M. Duchamp

▷ TRANSLATION: *21st Oct. '58. 327 E.58. Dear Lebel, Yes, the engraving by young Benoit (Picabia, "Equilibre") is an original on celluloid (1958) but really insignificant. Whatever you do, don't do over the entire page layout of the catalogue raisonné for that "item." Or else I could send you all the doodles I do all day while waiting for a telephone number. If you look at it (the celluloid) in the mirror or a transparency you can just make out "Et qui libre?"* [literally: "Who is free?"; phonetically: "Equilibrium"] *Between you and me, I'm losing the kind of enthusiasm I had in Paris for a few weeks. Fawcus is deeply indifferent and this latheriness will probably continue even after publication and I wonder whether Mr Weber won't also become contaminated before signing on the dotted line. Did Braziller pass through Paris again after I left? I'm waiting for instructions from Fawcus before going to see him. (Here again, so indifferent! how beautifully indifferent!) Sincerely, Marcel Duchamp.*

---

250. Marcel Duchamp to Marcel Jean
25 October 1958, New York

autograph letter
present whereabouts unknown

327 East 58 N.Y.C.

25 Oct. 1958

Chère Lily, cher Marcel Jean

Nous avons bien reçu les merveilleuses photos et nous les regardons 3 fois par jour, après les repas.

Lily, wife of Marcel Jean

Marcel Jean took photos of the *Large Glass* [cat. 2] on recent trip to Philadelphia.

J'ai même à vous demander la permission de reproduire celle du Grand Verre (votre futur frontispice) dans un livre que Sanouillet arrange de mes "écrits" chez Losfeld (!)

Michel Sanouillet, ed., *Marchand du Sel: écrits de Marcel Duchamp* (Paris, Le Terrain Vague, 1958).

Ce serait reproduit (15 cm x 24 cm) sur papier cristal et plié en deux (hors texte à l'intérieur de la couverture)— *si* vous me donnez la permission— avec naturellement mention du Maître-photographe.

Tout cela demande donc votre autorisation.

La chambre du 327 E 58 nous a demandé de vos nouvelles dès notre rentrée le 3 Oct.; j'ai répondu que vos néphrètes allaient mieux.

"néphrètes" = colic Marcel Jean suffered from on recent trip with his wife.

Affectueusement à tous deux

Marcel Duchamp

Dear Marcel and Lilly,
The photos of the glass have given us <u>great</u> pleasure. They are the <u>best</u> I've ever seen and I am so delighted to have them.

(and what a good "scaler" you are Lilly)
    Many thanks to you both
        Teeny

▷ TRANSLATION: *327 East '58 N.Y.C. 25th Oct. 1958. Dear Lily, dear Marcel Jean, The marvelous photos have arrived and we look at them 3 times a day, after meals. I would even like to ask your permission to reproduce the one of the Large Glass (your future frontispiece) in a book that Sanouillet is organizing of my "writings" at Losfeld's(!) It is to be reproduced (15cm by 24cm) on crystal paper and folded in two (inset on the inside cover)—if you give me permission to do it—with a reference, naturally, to the Master photographer. All this requires authorization from you. Room 327 E 8 has been asking for news of you since you got back 30th October, so I told them your bouts of colic weren't as bad. Affectionately to you both, Marcel Duchamp.*

---

251. Marcel Duchamp to Robert Lebel   autograph letter
15 November 1958, New York   private collection, Paris

327 E. 58 NYC.
15 Nov. 58
    Cher Lebel
Merci de m'avoir envoyé l'interview qui devrait certainement faire l'affaire si le livre paraissait incessamment. Elle sera, autrement, oubliée bien vite.
je n'ai pas encore pu obtenir de Fawcus, après au moins 3 lettres, une phrase positive me disant si oui ou merde le roulage typographique est commencé (au moins)__
Janis m'a dit qu'il adapterait son calendrier d'expositions à nos exigences de parution.
Encore faut il le prévenir un mois à l'avance.
— j'ai résolu le problème Péret : je vous envoie par avion, par même courrier, un gilet fantaisie pour lequel j'ai "aidé" les 5 boutons à épeler PERET__ le tout "signé et daté"__
"N'oubliez pas que le 31 Décembre 1958 nous donnons congé à Fawcus pour dénonciation de contrat."
    Affectueusement de tous à tous deux
    Marcel Duchamp

Interview by Alain Jouffroy, recorded between 23 Sept and 2 Oct, published in *Arts*, Paris, 29 Oct - 4 Nov 1958.

Waistcoat [cat. 63] for Péret (Schwarz cat. 554b, 1958), made for auction in aid of Benjamin **Péret**.

▷ TRANSLATION: *327 E. 58 N.Y.C. 15th Nov. '58. Dear Lebel, Thanks for sending me the interview which should certainly do the trick, were the book about to appear imminently—an interview which would, otherwise, be very soon forgotten. After at least 3 letters, I still haven't managed to get one single positive word out of Fawcus telling whether the bloody typography run has begun to roll (at least). Janis told me he would adapt his timetable of exhibitions to our publication needs. We'd still need*

to give him a month's warning. I've solved the Péret problem: I'm sending you by
air mail, in the same mail, a fancy waistcoat on which I helped the buttons to spell
PERET—the whole thing "signed and dated." "Don't forget that on 31st December
we're giving Fawcus his notice for breech of contract." Affectionately from all to you
both, Marcel Duchamp.

---

252. Marcel Duchamp to Man Ray   autograph letter
26 November 1958, New York   collection MNAM

327 East 58th St.
N.Y.C.
26 Nov. 58
    Cher Man
L' American Fed. of Arts veut organiser une exposition d'objets (Art in the
    found Object) et heureusement évitera l'interior decoration—
Roy Moyer qui s'occupe de cette exposition (qui doit faire le tour des USA
    pour un an)— me demande si tu as le Métronome et le fer à repasser—
Aussi je te demande si tu as encore ~~le~~ mon bottle dryer—
Pourrais tu faire envoyer par Lefebvre Foinet ces 3 objets <u>Air freight</u> à
    l'adresse suivante :
    ROY MOYER
    American Federation of Arts
    1083 Fifth AvenUE
    New York City

Frais à mon compte chez Lefebvre Foinet; je me ferai rembourser ici.
En tout cas réponds moi par retour du courrier ce qui est available de ces
    3 objets—
L'expo ouvre en Janvier à N.Y. (Life and Time Magazine Bldg.—).
P.S.— Dis à Lef. F. de mettre des évaluations très basses pour éviter ~~les~~ la
    douane américaine. $10 pour mon bottle dryer
Si tu l'as perdu, peut être en acheter un au Bazar de l'Hotel de Ville—
Affectueusement à tous deux
    Marcel

"Art in the Found Object," organized by Roy Moyer, American Federation of the Arts, Time-Life Building, 12 Jan - 6 Feb 1959.

Man Ray's **metronome** is *Indestructible Object* and his iron with nails is called *Cadeau.*

Lef. F. = Lefèbvre-Foinet

Readymade (bottle dryer) [cat. 35]; Man Ray sends 3 different sizes.

▷ TRANSLATION: *327 East 58th St., N.Y.C., 26th Nov. '58, Dear Man, The American*
Fed. of Arts wants to organize an exhibition of objects (Art in the Found Object)
and, thankfully, will steer clear of interior design. Roy Moyer, who is organizing
this exhibition (which is to go around the USA for a year) is asking me if you have
the Metronome and the iron. I would also like to know whether you have my bottle
dryer. Could you send these 3 objects by Lefebvre Foinet, Air Freight, to the follow-
ing address: ROY MOYER, American Federation of Arts, 1083 Fifth Avenue, New

York City. Expenses charged to me at Lefebvre Foinet, I will be reimbursed here. In any case, send a reply by return saying what is available out of these three objects. The exhibition opens in January in N.Y. (Life and Time Magazine Bldg.) P.S. Tell Lef.F. to put a very low value on them to get round American customs. $10 for my bottle dryer. If you've lost it, maybe buy another one at the Bazar de l'Hôtel de Ville. Affectionately to you both, Marcel.

---

253. Marcel Duchamp to Marcel Jean   autograph letter
2 or 3 December 1958, New York   present whereabouts unknown

327 E. 58 N.Y.C.

2 ou 3 Déc. 58

    Cher Marcel Jean

J'ai fini la lecture édifiante du Ms. ci-joint et je vous dois beaucoup d'admiration pour la diversité et l'accuracy de votre histoire américaine du Surréalisme__ en plus, gai à lire et très bien lié avec les chapitres précédents.

Alors à quand les premières épreuves?__ Je parie que vous sortirez avant le livre de Lebel!

P. A. Benoit (d'Alès, Gard) m'envoie la mise en page d'une plaquette minuscule (comme toutes ses plaquettes) d'une lettre que j'ai écrite à Tzara en 1930 et cette plaquette est illustrée d'une gravure sur celluloïd par Tzara!!

J'ai, comme je crois vous l'avoir dit, envoyé votre photo du verre à Sanouillet qui l'a fait déjà clicher à Paris__

Donc 1959 verra naître nos best sellers!!

    Affectueusement de nous deux à tous deux

    Marcel Duchamp

"Ms" = Manuscript of Marcel Jean's *Histoire de la peinture surréaliste*, see p.309.

Lebel, *Sur Marcel Duchamp*, see p.323.

Pierre-André Benoit sends MD *Lettre de Marcel Duchamp (1921) à Tristan Tzara* (Alès [Gard], 1958). See letter 58.

Large Glass [cat. 2]

▷ TRANSLATION: *327 E. 58. N.Y.C. 2nd or 3rd Dec. '58. Dear Marcel Jean, I have finished what was edifying reading of the enclosed manuscript and you have my great admiration for the diversity and accuracy of your American History of Surrealism—what's more, a lively read that links up very nicely with previous chapters. So, when'll these first proofs be ready? I bet you'll be out before Lebel's book! P.A. Benoit (Alès, Gard) has sent me the layout for a minute edition (like all his editions) of a letter I wrote to Tzara in 1930 and it's illustrated with an engraving on celluloid by Tzara!! I sent, as I think I told you, your photo of the glass to Sanouillet who's already had it printed in Paris. So 1959 will be the year of both our best sellers!! Affectionately from both of us to both of you, Marcel Duchamp.*

254. Marcel Duchamp to Pierre-André Benoit   autograph letter
5 December 1958, New York   source: from André Gervais transcript

327 East 58th St.
New York
5 Dec. 58
    Cher P.A.B.
La gravure de Tzara et votre présentation me plaisent beaucoup :
— Titre à l'extérieur comme je l'indique (inutile de mettre LETTRE   See letter 58.
    DADA \?\
— La date de la lettre entre parenthèses sur la couverture extérieure et aussi
    au début de la lettre
— Mentionner "celluloïd par Tzara" *1958* sous la gravure.
    C'est tout, merci et bonne chance
        Cordialement à vous
        Marcel Duchamp
P.S. important
    après réflexion, cette lettre a dû être écrite en 1921 et non en 1920 puisque   Letter in fact written, it
    je parle de <u>Man Ray à Paris</u>. et que Man Ray est arrivé à Paris pour la   seems, ca. Oct 1922.
    première fois en Juin 1921.
    Voulez vous recouper avec Tzara et Man Ray

▷ TRANSLATION: *327 East 5th St. New York. 5th Dec. '58. Dear P.A.B., I like Tzara's engraving and your presentation of it very much. Title on cover as shown by me (no need to put DADA LETTER \?\). The date of the letter in brackets on the outside cover and also at the top of the letter. Put in "celluloid by Tzara" 1958 beneath the engraving. That's all. Thanks and good luck. Sincerely yours, Marcel Duchamp. P.S. Important: after due thought, this letter must have been written in 1921 and not in 1920 because I talk about Man Ray in Paris and Man Ray arrived in Paris for the first time in June 1921. Would you like to double-check with Tzara and Man Ray?*

255. Marcel Duchamp to Juliet and Man Ray   autograph letter
6 February 1959, New York   collection MNAM

327 East 58.
N.Y.C.
6 Fev. 59
    Cher Man chère Julie   **Julie** = Juliet Browner,
Non; pas de catalogue à l'exposition "Art and the Found Object"__   Man Ray's wife
Ci joint la carte que tu as sans doute reçue.__ L'exposition fait le tour des
    U.S. en un an.

Merci pour le bottle dryer et dis moi si tu as eu des frais— qu'au moins je te les rembourse.

Readymade (bottle dryer) [cat. 35]

— Reçu une carte annonçant l'exposition d'Amsterdam mais pas de catalogue

— Ci joint ce que tu pourrais mettre dans ton catalogue pour Paris et Londres.

— Larcade, de la galerie Rive Droite, me dit Copley dans une lettre, t'a acheté quelque chose et semble prêt à continuer— Mon impression de lui, à Paris, avait été très sympathique.

Jean Larcade, Director of the Galerie Rive Droite, Paris.

A bientôt d'autre nouvelles et affectueusement à tous deux de Teeny et moi

Marcel

Teeny = Teeny Duchamp

▷ TRANSLATION: *327 East 58, N.Y.C., 6th Feb. '59, Dear Man, dear Julie, No, no catalog at the exhibition "Art and the Found Object." Enclosed, the invitation which you'll have no doubt received. The exhibition is going around the U.S.A. for a year. Thank you for the* bottle dryer *and let me know if you had to pay anything so that I can at least pay you back. Got a card announcing the Amsterdam exhibition but no catalog. Enclosed things you could put in your catalog for Paris and London. Larcade, from the Rive Droite Gallery, according to a letter Copley sent me, bought something of yours and seems ready for more. When I saw him in Paris, I thought he seemed really nice. Hope to hear from you soon and affectionately to you both from Teeny and me, Marcel.*

---

256. Marcel Duchamp to Robert Lebel
7 April 1959, [New York]

autograph letter
private collection, Paris

Pas d'adresse
7 Avril 1959
       Cher Lebel
The deed is done.
Présentation réussie
Succès janissaire

Arnold = Arnold Fawcus

Le principal est qu'Arnold doit <u>signer</u> demain "avec" Grove Press pour 2500 exemplaires américains, à paraître fin Septembre.

Grove Press publishes American edition of Lebel's *Sur Marcel Duchamp* (translated by George Heard Hamilton).

Ecrivez maintenant Poste Restante Cadaquès (Gerona) où nous serons Dimanche prochain.

J'ai, sur votre conseil insisté sur "~~pas~~ aucune peinture" seulement des dessins pour la Hune.
       Affectueusement
       Marcel

La Hune, bookshop in Paris to premiére Lebel's book in an exhibition beginning 5 May 1959.

▷ TRANSLATION: *No address, 7th April 1959. Dear Lebel,* The deed is done. *Presentation a success. Janissian victory. The idea is that Arnold is to sign tomorrow "with" Grove Press for 2,500 American copies to appear end September. Write now Poste Restante Cadaquès (Gerona) where we will be next Sunday. I have, on your advice, insisted on "no paintings," only drawings for La Hune. Affectionately, Marcel.*

---

257. Marcel Duchamp to Suzanne Duchamp   autograph letter
12 October 1959, [New York]   collection AAA

HOTEL DAUPHIN
Broadway at 67th Street
New York 23, N.Y.

12 Oct. 59

Chère Suzanne

Je me sens incapable d'écrire quelque chose de spécial pour un catalogue dans le sens sérieux du mot et je te demande de comprendre pourquoi je ne me sentirais pas à l'aise avec le conservateur et l'inspecteur général.

En revanche si tu veux encore te servir de la fameuse lettre que j'avais envoyée à Jean, je crois que, même incohérente, elle aura peut-être une certaine chaleur

Renvoie la moi car je l'ai perdue et peut-être en retouchant un peu tu pourras t'en servir.

N'avons pas eu le temps d'aller chez "Maud chez elle"— Nous venons enfin de trouver un appartement dans lequel nous entrons le 1ᵉʳ Nov. (28 West 10ᵗʰ St.)— écris toujours au Dauphin pour le moment.

Affectueusement de nous deux
Marcel

"Jean Crotti" show,
Palais Galliera, Paris, 11
Dec 1959 - 11 Jan 1960.

See letter 216.

Jean = Jean Crotti,
Suzanne's husband,
died 30 Jan 1958.

▷ TRANSLATION: *12th Oct. '59, Dear Suzanne, I feel incapable of writing something special for a catalog in the serious sense of the word and ask you to understand why I would not feel at ease with the curator and the chief inspector. On the other hand, if you want to use the famous letter I sent to Jean again, I think that, while incoherent, there might be a certain warmth about it. Send it back to me as I've lost it and maybe by touching it up a bit, you could use it. We've had no time to go and see "Maud at home"—we've only just found an apartment, at last, and are moving in on 1st Nov. (28 West 10th St.). Write c/o the Dauphin still for now. Affectionately from us both, Marcel.*

New York, 28 West 10 St | 1959-1964 chapter 13

moves within New York to 28 W 10th Street, 1st floor | Nov 1959
*round trips to New Haven, Atlanta, Hempstead, Paris, Philadelphia, Stockholm, Amsterdam,
London, Detroit, Boston, Palm Beach, Cleveland, Baltimore, Utica, Rome, Naples, Taormina,
Palermo, Puteaux, Rouen, Milan, Nice, Pasadena and Waltham*

from Nov 1959 to 20 Apr 1964

▶ MAJOR WORKS

*Environment for "Surrealist Intrusion in the
Enchanters' Domain" exh.* (Nov 1960)
Anagram for Pierre de Massot (gouache on
black paper; Jan 1961)
Signed Sign (paint on masonite, "Hotel Green
Entrance," 1963)
A Poster Within a Poster (poster for MD's
Retrospective, Pasadena, 1963)

▶ ONE MAN SHOWS or SEMI-ONE MAN SHOWS

Marcel Duchamp, Bokkunsum, Stockholm
— 7 May 1960
Dokumentation über Marcel Duchamp,
Kunstgewerbemuseum, Zurich, Switzerland
— 30 June - 28 Aug 1960
Duchamp, Picabia, Schwitters, The Alan Gallery,
New York. By MD: *Bottle Dryer; Feuille de vigne
femelle; Rotorelief; Objet Dard; Boîte-en-valise;
Tablier de blanchisseuse* — 7 Jan - 2 Feb 1963

Marcel Duchamp, Galerie Buren, Stockholm. By MD:
*Cœurs volants; Rotorelief; Young Cherry trees
Secured against Hares; Feuille de vigne femelle;
Eau & Gaz; Cykelhjulet; Fresh widow; Trois
stoppages etalon; Flasktorkaren; A Bruit Secret;
Peigne; Fontaine; In Advance of the Broken Arm;
Pliant de voyage; Air de Paris; Why not sneeze?;
Ur Grona Asken; Ur Boîte-en-valise*
— 7 Apr - May 1963
By or of Marcel Duchamp or Rrose Sélavy, a retrospective
exhibition, Art Museum, Pasadena, USA
— 8 Oct - 3 Nov 1963

▶ EXHIBITIONS

Multiplication d'objets, Société d'Art Saint-Germain-
des-Prés (Edouard Loeb), Paris. By MD:
Rotoreliefs — 27 Nov - 19 Dec 1959
Exposition Internationale du Surréalisme, Galerie Daniel
Cordier, Paris. By MD: *Autoportrait (With my
Tongue in my Cheek)* — 15 Dec 1959 - 29 Feb 1960

Bamberger's Store (window), Newark, USA. By MD: *Nude Descending a Stair No.3*; *Study for the Chess Players (charcoal)*; *Study for the Virgin (watercolor)* — 1 Feb - 15 Feb 1960

Kinetische Kunst, Kunstgewerbemuseum, Zurich, Switzerland. By MD: *Rotoreliefs (ed. MAT)* — May - June 1960

National Institute of Arts and Letters, New York. By MD: *Artist's father*; *Chocolate Grinder No.2*; *Passage de la Vierge à la Mariée* — 25 May 1960

Les Sources du XXe siècle, Musée National d'Art Moderne, Paris. By MD: *Sonate*; *Les Joueurs d'échecs*; *Nu descendant un escalier n°2* — 4 Nov 1960 - 23 Jan 1961

Surrealist Intrusion in the Enchanter's Domain, exh. directed by André Breton and MD, D'Arcy Galleries, New York. By MD: *Pharmacy*; *Wedge of chastity* — 28 Nov 1960 - 14 Jan 1961

Surréalisme et Précurseurs, Palais Granvelle, Besançon, France. By MD: *Pharmacie*; *Rotorelief*; *Boîte-en-valise*; *La Mariée (gravée par J. Villon)*; *Moulin à café (gravé par J. Villon)* — 1961

The World of Dada, Museum of Modern Art, Rhode Island School of Design, USA. By MD: *Bicycle Wheel*; *Bottlerack*; *Rotoreliefs*; *In Advance of the Broken Arm*; *Boite en valise*; *Roulette de Monte-Carlo*; *Rotoreliefs*; *The Green Box* — 18 Jan - 19 Feb 1961

Paintings from the Arensberg and Gallatin Collections of the Philadelphia Museum of Art, The Solomon R. Guggenheim Museum, New York — 6 Feb to ? 1961

L'oggetto nella pittura, Galleria d'arte Schwarz, Milan, Italy. By MD: *Tabliers de blanchisseuse*; *Rotorelief* — 1 Mar - 15 Mar 1961

Bewogen Beweging, Stedelijk Museum, Amsterdam. By MD: *Reconstructie van het Fietswiel*; *Duplicaat van de Rotary glass - plaques*; *Schijven met woordspelingen*; *Reconstructie van decor van het atelier, 11 rue Larrey, Paris*; *Draaiende halve bol*; *12 rotoreliefs*; *2 valises*— 10 Mar - 17 Apr 1961 Exhibition travels to Moderna Museet, Stockholm

under the title **Rörelse I Konsten**; includes the first replica of the *Large Glass* — 16 May - 10 Sept 1961

The Art of Assemblage, The Museum of Modern Art, New York (travels to Dallas and San Francisco). By MD: *Bicycle Wheel*; *Bottle Dreyer*; *Comb*; *With Hidden Noise*; *Apolinère Enameled*; *Fountain*; *Tu m'*; *LHOOQ*; *Paris Air*; *Fresh Widow*; *Why not sneeze?*; *The green box*; *Boite-en-valise* — 2 Oct - 12 Nov 1961

L'œil, Galerie d'Art, Paris. By MD: *A propos de jeune sœur*; *Deux nus, un fort et un vite*; *Boîte verte*; *Machine optique*; *Rotoreliefs* — 23 May - 30 June 1962

Kunst von 1900 bis heute, Museum des 20. Jahrhunderts, Vienna. By MD: *Studie zum König und Königin von schnellen Akten umgeben*; *Kofferschachtel*; *Flaschenständer* — 21 Sept - 4 Nov 1962

Collages et objets, Galerie du Cercle, Paris. By MD: *Obligation pour la roulette de Monte-Carlo*; *Porte-bouteilles* — 24 Oct - 17 Nov 1962

Collages Surréalistes, Galerie Le Point Cardinal, Paris. By MD: *Pharmacie*; *Anémic Cinéma (8 disques)*; *Autoportrait* — 2 Dec 1962 - 12 Jan 1963

1913 Armory Show, 50th Anniversary Exhibition, Munson-Williams-Proctor Institute, Utica, USA (travels to New York City). By MD: *The King and Queen surrounded by Swift Nudes*; *Portrait of Chess Players*; *Nude descending a staircase No.2*; *Nude (watercolour)* — 17 Feb - 31 Mar 1963

La Grande Aventure de l'art du XXe siècle, Château de Rohan, Strasbourg, France. By MD: *A propos de jeune sœur* — 8 June - 15 Sept 1963

Patamostra, Galleria Schwarz, Milan, Italy — 3 Mar - 13 Mar 1964

Le Surréalisme: Sources-Histoire-Affinités, Galerie Charpentier, Paris. By MD: *La Mariée mise à nu par ses célibataires, même (copie de Ulf Linde)*; *Feuille de vigne femelle*; *Boîte verte*; *Boîte-en-valise*; *Coin de chasteté* — 24 Apr to ? 1964

---

258. Marcel Duchamp to Richard Hamilton   autograph letter
19 May 1960, New York   collection Richard Hamilton, Oxon, England

N.Y.C.

May 19. 1960

> Dear Richard
>
> Many thanks for the pages—
>
> I did not find anything to correct on your text and I sent it to George = I
> think it is exactly what most readers don't but should know.
>
> My corrections on the pages : NONE.
>
> — Naturally the black dots go with the white ones
> — I adore the hand colored pages!
>
> For the wasp you should use a half tone photograph and superimpose
> the text
>
>> Affectueusement de tous deux à tous deux
>>
>> Marcel

MD forwards to George
Hamilton proofs for
Richard Hamilton's
typographic edition of
the *Green Box* (p.368).

---

259. Marcel Duchamp: open letter to numerous acquaintances   typed letter
9 June 1960, [New York]   collection MNAM

MARCEL DUCHAMP
28 West Tenth Street - New York City

June 9, 1960

> **Dear** [name of correspondent]
>
> I have had a lifelong interest in chess and have great
> faith in its cultural and intellectual values.
>
> I have become a Voting Member of the American Chess
> Foundation, a tax exempt, educational organization whose
> work is described in the enclosed brochure.
>
> Upon invitation, I have accepted the chairmanship of its
> "Arts Conmittee [sic] for American Chess".
>
> The purpose of my Committee is to enlist the support of
> people in the world of art : artists, art patrons,
> gallery owners and museum directors, in order to make
> possible a greater degree of American participation in
> international chess events.
>
> I hope and anticipate that this Committee will obtain, as
> gifts, an impressive collection of paintings — old and
> new — which will be exhibited and sold, with the proceeds
> going to the Foundation. Those who make art contributions
> to this Committee will be able to avail themselves of the
> valuable tax-deductibility feature of the gift.

I believe and dare hope that you will be sympathetic to
this purpose and will respond favorably to my request
that you join as a member of my Committee and help me
carry out its purposes. Your membership on this Committee
will not require atttendance at meetings.
Do please let me hear from you.
    Sincerely,
    Marcel Duchamp
    Marcel Duchamp

---

260. Marcel Duchamp to Man Ray   autograph letter
11 June 1960, New York   collection MNAM

28 West 10th St.
New York
11 Juin 60
    Cher Man
Je suis dans le chess business maintenant, missionaire en quête d'argent
    pour les échecs—
    Autre chose :
Sidney Wallach que tu connais à New York est le Director de la Chess
    Foundation (not Federation) et c'est avec lui que je "travaille"—
Il m'a demandé de lui trouver un artiste qui accepterait de faire une
    maquette (dessin ou plaster cast, or otherwise) d'un trophée pour
    récompenser le gagnant d'un match annuel entre 2 forts joueurs— (aux
    USA.)
Le mécène qui fait le don *annuel* d'une somme pour ce match offre aussi
    $600⁻ à l'artiste qui lui fera la maquette en question, quitte après à la
    faire fondre en métal (frais en plus naturellement)—
J'ai donc pensé à toi si cela t'intéresse— Tu es complètement libre surtout
    d'éviter le "Stéréotyped trophy"—
Nous partons le 29 Juin directement pour Cadaques (Juillet et Aout—
Ecris ici avant ou à Cadaques (Gerona) SPAIN suffit comme adresse.
Pour la maquette si cela t'intéresse écris directement à
    Sidney Wallach
    381 Fourth Avenue
    New York City
Affectueusement de nous deux à vous deux
    Marcel

Sidney Wallach, Director of American Chess Foundation.

▷ TRANSLATION: *28 West 10th St. New York. 11th June '60. Dear Man, I'm in the* chess business *now, a missionary raising funds for chess. Something else: Sidney Wallach whom you know in New York is the Director of the* Chess Foundation (not Federation) *and he's the one I'm "working" with. He's asked me to find him an artist who would be willing to make a model (drawing or* plaster cast, *or otherwise) of a trophy to reward the winner of an annual match between two very good players (in the USA). The sponsor, who makes an annual donation of a sum of money for this match, is also offering $600 to the artist who will make him the model in question, even have it cast in metal (plus costs, naturally). I therefore thought of you if it's of any interest. You are entirely free above all to avoid the* "Stereotyped trophy." *We are leaving on 29th June and going straight to Cadaques (July and* August. *Write to me here before or in* Cadaques (Gerona), SPAIN *will do for the address. About the model, if you're interested write directly to Sidney Wallach, 381 Fourth Avenue, New York City. Affectionately from the two of us to the two of you, Marcel.*

---

261. Marcel Duchamp to André Breton   autograph letter
20 October 1960, [New York]   source: from Y. Poupard-Lieussou transcript

[printed envelope:]
D'ARCY GALLERIES
1091 Madison Avenue, New York City

[letterhead: printed drawing by Arshile Gorky, Peggy Guggenheim's stationery]
20 Oct. 60
    Cher André
Suis chez Bonnefoy
Tout marche bien__
La question du titre se pose encore un peu
Je propose avec l'avis de Julien
    Surrealist Intrusion into the Domain of the Enchanters Domain
Domaine me semble plus simple et plus direct et sonne mieux (pour moi)
    en anglais que Realm__
Décidez rapidement et répondez rapidement
S.V.P.
et surtout allez mieux et écrivez votre texte please
    Affectueusement
    Marcel
P.S. En tout cas l'inversion (into the Enchanters' Domain) est moins
    plaisante que "into the Domain of the Enchanters"
après examen rapide de la maquette Tarnaud, Bonnefoy et moi ne savons
    pas comment remplir les Cadres (tableau synoptique) dans chaque
    Enchanteur__

[margin notes:]

Maurice Bonnefoy, Director of d'Arcy Galleries.

"Surrealist Intrusion in the Enchanters' Domain," D'Arcy Galleries, NY, 28 Nov 1960 - 14 Jan 1961. MD's "carrot," French tobacconists' sign, printed in relief on the catalog cover (Schwarz cat. 576).

Claude Tarnaud (b.1922), French poet, with **Bonnefoy** forms group "La révolution la nuit."

Y̶-a̶ Devons nous attendre des indications de vous?
o̶u̶ b̶i̶e̶n̶ Donnez les en tout cas— pour les 8 enchanteurs "Couples"

	Sites	Poètes	Artistes	Couples	
Opale					

surtout nous a inquiétés—
— Pas de place pour Maria dans le catalogue
Est ce intentionnel? Nous aurons vraisemblablement une sculpture d'elle dans l'expo *prêtée par le* Musée d'art Moderne.
Je propose de reproduire cette sculpture sans texte à la fin du catalogue sur une page

L'Impossible, **Maria Martins**, included in the show (lent by MoMA, NY) is finally reproduced on the last page of the catalog.

▷ TRANSLATION: *20th Oct. '60. Dear André, Am at Bonnefoy's place. Everything going fine. The question of the title still not quite settled. I propose going along with Julien's idea, Surrealist Intrusion into the Domain of the Enchanters. Domain seems to me simpler and more direct and sounds better (to me) in English than Realm. Please come to a decision quickly and let me know quickly and most of all get better and write your text* please. *Affectionately, Marcel. P.S. In any case the inversion (into the Enchanters' Domain) is less pleasing than "into the Domain of the Enchanter." After glancing quickly at the Tarnaud model, Bonnefoy and I don't know how to fill in the boxes (synoptic table) in each Enchanter. Should we wait for instructions from you? Send them anyway, for the 8 enchanters. "Couples"* [sketch] *particularly worried us. No room for Maria in the catalog: is this intentional? We will probably have one of her sculptures in the exhibition lent by the Museum of Modern Art. I suggest reproducing this sculpture with no text at the end of the catalog on a single page.*

---

262. Marcel Duchamp to Richard Hamilton   autograph letter
[26 November 1960]   collection Richard Hamilton, Oxon, England

Dear Richard
We are crazy about the book.
Your labor of love has given birth to a monster of veracity and a crystalline transsubstantiation of the French green box— The translation, thanks above all to your design, is enhanced into a plastic form so close to the original that the Bride must be blossoming ever more.
Many thanks for the first copy just received and I will go to Wittenborn's next week and after taking my 8 copies will see to it that George Hamilton receives his.

MD receives
A Typographic Version by R. Hamilton of MD's *Green Box* translated by G.H. Hamilton, London, Percy Lund, Humphries & Co., 1960

The ideal solution for the British television's good intentions would be to have you and Terry come to Cadaqués (sent by B.T.) during July or August when we hope to be there.

Terry Hamilton (d.1962), wife of Richard.

B.T. = British Television

At least this gives *you* something to work on in a direction we all would like.

Teeny and I send our best love to Terry and yourself and I will let you know later about the reception of the book in USA.

Teeny = Teeny Duchamp

Affectueusement Marcel Duchamp

---

263. Marcel Duchamp to André Breton   autograph letter
27 November 1960, New York   source: from Y. Poupard-Lieussou transcript

28 West 10th St
New York
Dim. 27 Nov 60
        Cher André
Ce petit mot à la veille du vernissage de l'exposition (Lundi 28 Nov.)
Tout va bien

Exh. "Surrealist Intrusion," p.367.

Le catalogue (Intrusion) est fini et je vous en enverrai un exemplaire dès demain.

Nous travaillons dur, Tarnaud, Bonnefoy et moi depuis 10 jours à l'aménagement dans salles avec de petites "inventions" qui doivent se contenter d'une certaine timidité mais dont la formule générale au moins ne répète pas celles des expositions surréalistes précédentes.

J'espère que Tarnaud vous fera une description complète bientôt.

Vous recevrez aussi une double feuille jointe à l'Intrusion donnant le détail des exposants et choses exposées.

        Bientôt d'autres nouvelles après l'ouverture en hâte
Affectueusement à Elisa et à vous même
Marcel Duchamp

Elisa, Breton's wife.

▷ TRANSLATION: *28 West 10th St, New York. Sun. 27th Nov. '60. Dear André, Just a note on the eve of the opening of the exhibition (Monday 28th Nov.) All is well. The catalog (Intrusion) is finished and I'll send you a copy tomorrow. Tarnaud, Bonnefoy and I have been working hard for 10 days on setting up rooms with one or two small "inventions" which have to remain rather shy but at least the general formula doesn't duplicate that of previous Surrealist events. I hope Tarnaud will give you a full description soon. You will also receive a 2-page brochure, attached to Intrusion, giving details of exhibitors and things exhibited. More news to follow, after opening, in haste affectionately to Elisa and yourself, Marcel Duchamp.*

264. Marcel Duchamp to André Breton   autograph letter
1 December 1960, New York   source: from Y. Poupard-Lieussou transcript

28 West 10th St
New York
1er Dec. 60
Cher André

Le vernissage a eu le succès prévu et la presse nous est sympathique— *(et réciproquement)*

Vous recevrez dans quelques jours des articles qui doivent paraître Dimanche prochain (4 Dec.) dans le N.Y. Times et l'Herald Tribune et aussi dans Time Magazine du 12 Dec.

Pour vous donner quelque idée de l'aménagement, je vous énumère ici.

Vernissage seulement : une cartomancienne (professionnelle qui a été occupée toute la soirée).

A demeure :
- 3 poules blanches (vivantes) dans un placard transformé en poulailler
- Un rayon de soleil couchant (ou levant).
- Une bande de magnétophone spécialement enregistrée : une petite fille faisant de pénibles exercices de piano dans la maison voisine.
- Projection au plafond d'un tarot (Arcane 17)
- Un Tuyau d'arrosage serpentant négligemment dans toute la galerie.
- Chemin de fer électrique dans une vitrine sur la rue—
- Chaque tableau porte son *petit* drapeau (nationalité de l'artiste).
- Une glace entre presque tous les tableaux
- 4 pendules (une dans chaque pièce) avec des heures différentes
- Une paire de chenêts avec du bois légèrement brûlé sans cheminée
- Une machine à écrire style 1900
- Un grand bocal de pharmacie (vert rouge, jaune)
- La carotte de tabac à l'extérieur
- Paquets de cigarettes collés sur une vitre intérieure
- Appareil de poinçonnage d'entrée à l'usine.

Tarnaud, en dehors des traductions qu'il a dû faire en vitesse pour le catalogue, nous a beaucoup aidé pour l'aménagement.

On parle aussi de faire suivre l'exposition à Chicago, Millwaukee, Minneapolis et même Rio.

Dites-nous comment vous allez—

Nos affections pour Elisa et vous même

Affect^t

Marcel

Je mets à la poste demain ~~le~~ un catalogue par avion—
(en attendant que vous receviez un paquet de 30 qui viendront moins vite).

Marginal notes:

Exh. "Surrealist Intrusion," p.367.

John Canaday, "Nostalgia and the Forward Look: Duchamp Surveys Surrealism and Dali Forges Ahead in All Directions," *NY Times* (4 Dec 1960); "Surrealistic Sanity," *Time* (12 Dec 1960).

Arcane 17, autobiographical novel by André Breton (NY, Brentano's, 1944).

Elisa, Breton's wife.

▷ TRANSLATION: *28 West 10th St., New York. 1st Dec. '60. Dear André, The opening met with expected success and the press likes us (it's mutual). You will receive, in a few days' time, articles which are due to come out next Sunday (4th Dec.) in the N.Y. Times and Herald Tribune and also in Time Magazine 12th Dec. To give you some idea of how it was set up, here is a list. Opening only: a fortune-teller (professional, who has been taken up the whole evening). Permanently: 3 white hens (alive) in a cupboard made into a hen house; a ray of sunshine at sunrise(or sunset); a reel of tape recorded specially with a little girl doing painful exercises on the piano in the house next door; a tarot card (Arcane 17) projected onto the ceiling; a hosepipe nonchalantly snaking its way through the entire gallery; electric train set in a shop window on the street; each painting carries its own little flag (nationality of the artist); a mirror between practically all the paintings; 4 clocks (one in each room) all showing different times; a pair of firedogs with some wood slightly burnt without chimney; a 1900-style typewriter; a large pharmacy jar (green red, yellow); the tobacconists' sign (carrot) outside; cigarette packets stuck onto a window inside; clocking-on machine like at a factory entrance. Tarnaud, apart from the translations he had to do at great speed for the catalog, helped us a great deal setting things out. There's also talk of taking the exhibition to Chicago, Milwaukee and even Rio. Let us know how you are. Our affections to Elisa and yourself. Affectionately, Marcel. I'm sending a catalog to you tomorrow by airmail (until you get a packet of 30 which will take longer).*

---

265. Marcel Duchamp to André Breton   autograph letter
11 December 1960, New York   source: from Y. Poupard-Lieussou transcript

28 West 10th st.
New York
11 Dec 60

    Cher André Permettez-moi de ne pas ergoter sous forme d'"explications et justifications"—

Simplement je regrette maintenant d'avoir accepté de m'occuper de cette exposition.

    Toujours tout aussi affectueusement <u>à vous et à Elisa.</u>

PS[1] — Je puis vous assurer que l'oreille ne sera pas itinérante, ni moi non plus d'ailleurs.

PS[2] — Goldwater, le directeur du Musée d'Arts primitifs à New York, me demande si vous accepteriez de faire une exposition de votre collection (ou une partie d'icelle) à ce Musée très beau, je trouve. Au cas où vous accepteriez d'en parler au moins, il (Goldwater) vous enverrait la demande officielle.

Breton, angered by the inclusion of Dalí (artist he earlier exiled from the Surrealist group) in the exhibition, sent MD a letter in protest, it seems.

Elisa, Breton's wife.

Robert Goldwater (1907-1973), author of *Primitivism in Modern Painting* (NY, Harper & Brothers, 1938), also teaches art history at the Institute of Fine Art, NY University.

▷ TRANSLATION: *28 West 10th St. New York. 11th Dec. '60. Dear André, Allow me not to prevaricate in the form of "explanations and excuses." Simply that I now regret having agreed to organize this exhibition. Always as affectionately to you and Elisa. P.S.1 I can assure you that the ear will not go wandering off and neither will I for that matter. P.S.2 Goldwater, the director of the Museum of Primitive Arts in New York is asking me if you would agree to holding an exhibition of your collection (or part thereof) at this, I find, very beautiful museum. Were you to agree to discuss it at least, he (Goldwater) would send you the official request.*

---

266. Marcel Duchamp to George Heard Hamilton   autograph letter
16 December 1960, New York   collection YCAL

28 W. 10.
N.Y.C.
16. Dec. 60
      Dear George
Thanks for your letter and Norman Dolph's letter—
We will talk about it when we see you here, before Christmas (!)
(a detail : <u>No hole</u> in the center of my discs!! a complication I am afraid.)   *Rotoreliefs* [cat. 53]

Someone organizing a show on "Movement" in Stockholm wants to   *Rotary Glass Plates*
   "reconstruct" in plastic a model of my "Rotative" at Yale and he wants   [cat. 50] for exhibition
   some exact measurements of it   "Bewogen Beweging,"
                                                                           Stedelijk Museum,
                              Could you, if it is not too much ~~of a~~ bother   Amsterdam, 10 Feb -
                              measure :   14 Apr 1961, organized
                                                                           by Pontus Hulten; also
                              1) Length and width of largest glass   travels to Moderna
                              2) Length of the central bar holding all the Museet, Stockholm,
                              glasses   "Rörelse I Konsten,"
                              Those 2 measures should be sufficient with a 16 May - 9 Sept 1961.
                              good photo <u>which they have</u>.
      A bientôt donc et affectueusement
              à tous deux de nous deux
              Marcel

267. Marcel Duchamp to Man Ray   autograph letter
6 March 1961, New York   collection MNAM

28 West 10th Street
N.Y.C.
6 Mars 61
    Cher Man
Bien pris possession il y a quelque temps déjà de ton échiquier avec
    personnages pour la vente aux enchères qui aura lieu à Parke-Bernet le
    18 Mai.__
Donne moi un titre et l'année pour le catalogue s.v.p.__
Une chose importante que je voudrais savoir c'est si la'echiquier
    t'appartient ou appartient à Rive Droite.
Mon idée est de préparer cette vente en obtenant d'avance des "bids"__
Rive Droite nous a donné comme prix minimum $2850.⁻ mais si la chose
    t'appartient, je peux te demander de réduire ce prix de base pour ne pas
    être obligé de le reprendre à la vente s'il n'atteignait pas 2850.⁻
Pour moi $1500.⁻ serait un prix de départ beaucoup plus
    "sympathique"__
    Dis moi ce que tu en penses__

——————

P.S. Reçu ta lettre ce matin__ Bravo pour la "cup"__
Pour la "feuille de vigne" d'accord en principe et dis moi ce que je dois
    normalement demander. et sous quelle forme__ une édition de
    combien?
    Affectueusement de nous deux à vous deux
    Marcel

Man Ray submits a **chessboard** with wood mannequins attached entitled *Knights of the Square Table*.

Galerie Rive Droite, Paris, in 1961 issues an edition of 10 casts in bronze of the *Female Fig Leaf* [cat. 62].

Female Fig Leaf [cat. 62]

▷ TRANSLATION: *28 West 10th Street. N.Y.C. 6th March '61. Dear Man, Safely in my possession for some time now your chess set with characters for the auction taking place at Parke-Bernet 18th May. Give me a title and the year for the catalog please. Something important that I would like to know is whether the chess set belongs to you or belongs to Rive Droite. My idea is to lay the foundations for this sale by obtaining "bids" in advance—Rive Droite has given us a minimum price of $2,850 but, if the thing belongs to you, I can ask you to lower the starting price so as not to have to take it back if it didn't get $2,850. I think $1,500 would be a much "friendlier" starting price. Let me know what you think. P.S. Got your letter this morning. Well done about the "cup." As for the "fig leaf," OK in principle and let me know what I should ask and in what form—an edition of how many? Affectionately from us both to you both, Marcel.*

268. Marcel Duchamp to Man Ray — autograph letter
23 March 1961, New York — collection MNAM

28 West 10th
23 Mars 61
Cher Man
Merci des bons renseignements pour la vente. Je pense qu'au moins on pourra "défendre" ~~l'echi~~ les Knights of the Square Table à partir de 1500— et que ça ira beaucoup plus haut.

Pour la feuille de vigne, enchanté d'avoir un exemplaire et je voudrais une commission de $1000— si tu peux l'obtenir
Dis moi franchement si c'est trop (ou pas assez??)
Pas poli

Female Fig Leaf [cat. 62], Galerie Rive Droite edition. See note on previous letter.

Je suis en train de jouer la partie par cable avec Amsterdam et au 12me coup j'ai obtenu une partie que je crois satisfaisante après un début difficile
Te tiendrai au courant
Affectueusement à Julie et à toi de Teeny et de moi
Marcel

Julie = Juliet Browner, Man Ray's wife.

▷ TRANSLATION: *28 West 10th. 23rd March '61. Dear Man, Thanks for the useful information about the sale. I think that the "Knights of the Square Table" will be able to hold their own at 1,500 at least and that it'll probably go much higher. As for the fig leaf, delighted to have one and I would like $1,000 commission—if you can get it. Tell me straight if it's too much (or too little??) No politeness. I'm in the throes of playing a match by cable with Amsterdam and on the twelfth move I got a match which seems satisfactory after a difficult start. Will keep you posted. Affectionately to Julie and to you from Teeny and from me, Marcel.*

269. Marcel Duchamp to Man Ray — autograph letter
11 April 1961, New York — collection MNAM

28 W. 10
N.Y.C.
11 Avril 61
Cher Man
Teeny a vu ton échiquier monté (The Knights of The Square Table) et est enchantée; les gens de Parke-Bernet veulent le reproduire dans le catalogue de la vente = Nous pourrons donc t'envoyer une photo dans quelques ~~jour~~ temps.

Teeny a compté 30 pièces + le mannequin.

Elle demande si c'était ton intention de supprimer le Roi et la Reine des
Blancs — qui manquent. (simplement pour vérifier)＿ Si George Marci
a une photo dis lui de nous l'envoyer.

Nous avons environ 90 items d'excellente qualité＿

Vente le 18 Mai — chez Parke-Bernet

Preview et réception à la galerie Cordier et Warren le 9 Mai.

— Nous nous occupons maintenant de la publicité.

    C'est tout pour le moment

    Affectucusement de nous deux à Julie et à toi

    Marcel Duchamp

▷ TRANSLATION: *28 W.10. N.Y.C. 11th April '61. Dear Man, Teeny has seen your chess set all set out and is thrilled; the people from Parke-Bernet want to reproduce it in their sales catalog = So we'll be able to send you a photo in a little while. Teeny counted 30 pieces + the model. She is asking whether you intentionally took out the white King and Queen that are missing (just to make sure). If George Marci has a photo tell her to send it to us. We have around 90 items of excellent quality. Sale 18th May at Parke-Bernet. Preview and reception at the Cordier and Warren gallery 9th May. We're working on the publicity now. That's all for the time being. Affectionately from us both to Julie and to you, Marcel Duchamp.*

---

270. Marcel Duchamp to Suzanne Duchamp   autograph letter
24 October 1961, New York   collection AAA

28 W. 10 New York

24 Oct. 61

    Chère Suzanne

Bien reçu ta lettre＿ Vu aussi Jackie qui te rapportera 4 catalogues =
L'exposition est <u>presque</u> choquante＿ Beaucoup de gens trouvent ça
dégoûtant.

Tu es très bien accrochée, avec Jean sur un panneau.

— Peut être as tu pu lire Canaday dans le N.Y. Times de Paris＿
reproduisant quelquefois son article dans le N.Y. Times de N.Y.
(17 Oct. 61).＿

J'ai fait une petite interview à la Voix de l'Amérique qui passera (Radio)
France III 19^h mercredi 1er Nov. (Ici New York)＿

    Merci des nouvelles et affect^t

    Marcel

merci si tu pouvais récupérer mes 2 planches chez Leblanc

Love from Teeny

▷ TRANSLATION: *28 W.10, New York, 24th Oct. '61. Dear Suzanne, Got your letter. Saw Jackie also who's going to bring you 4 catalogs. = The exhibition is almost shocking. Many people find it disgusting. You're very nicely exhibited, with Jean, on a panel. You might have been able to read Canaday in the Paris N.Y. Times, which sometimes reproduces his article that appears in the N.Y. Times of New York (17 Oct. 61). I gave a little interview on The Voice of America which will go out (Radio) France III 7pm Wednesday 1st Nov. (New York). Thanks for news and affectionately, Marcel. Would be glad if you could retrieve my two planks from Leblanc's. Love from Teeny.*

---

271. Marcel Duchamp to Man Ray   autograph letter
27 March 1962, New York   collection MNAM

28 West 10th St.
N.Y.C.
27 Mars 62
     Cher Man
J'ai vu Schwarz (Milan) de passage à New York il y a quelques jours et dans
     le cours de la conversation je lui ai promis l'exemplaire de "Feuille de
     vigne femelle" qui n'est pas signé et que tu dois avoir, d'après une lettre
     de Larcade ce matin.
Cette promesse est une grosse erreur de ma part car Teeny m'a engueulé
     pour avoir fait cette promesse et tient beaucoup à avoir cet exemplaire.
Il paraît que toute l'édition est vendue et qu'il n'y en a plus.
Crois tu que Larcade pourrait en faire tirer un exemplaire de plus ou bien
     vois tu une autre solution pour satisfaire Teeny et Schwarz?—
Peut-être une 2me édition??
Dis moi aussi si Schwarz est venu te voir et s'il a pris l'exemplaire en
     question car Larcade me dit qu'il a dit à Schwarz que pour lui cet
     exemplaire était $900⁻
Tu vois dans quel pétrin je suis!!
Donne moi une idée et merci
     Affectueusement à tous deux de nous deux
     Marcel

Arturo Schwarz (b.1924), Italian art dealer and scholar, will show MD's work in his Milan gallery in the 1960's and go on to author the most complete MD catalogue raisonné.

Female Fig Leaf [cat. 62]

Teeny = Teeny Duchamp

▷ TRANSLATION: *28 West 10th St. N.Y.C. 27th March '62. Dear Man, I saw Schwarz (Milan) passing through New York a few days ago and in the course of the conversation I promised him the "Female fig leaf" that is not signed and which you must have, according to a letter from Larcade this morning. This promise was a big mistake on my part as Teeny gave me hell for having made this promise and is totally bent on having this copy. It seems that the entire series has been sold and that there are none left. Do you think Larcade could have another copy made or can you think* *of any other solution for Teeny and Schwarz? Maybe a second series?? Let me know also whether Schwarz has been to see you and whether he's taken the copy in question as Larcade told me that he told Schwarz he thought this copy was $900. See what a spot I'm in!! Help me come up with something and thanks. Affectionately to the two of you from the two of us, Marcel.*

---

272. Marcel Duchamp to Robert Lebel   autograph letter
18 October 1963, New York   private collection, Paris

28 West 10th St.
N.Y.C.
18 Oct 63
    Cher Robert
Bien rentrés de Pasadena après une semaine de libations et de freeways.
Ci joint le catalogue qui comme vous le verrez vous a tété copieusement.
En tout cas la vie commence à 76 ans avec a one-man show.
— Ci joint aussi 2 catalogues avec des "petites phrases" pour vos addenda.
— Les sœurs n'écrivent pas beaucoup. J'espère en vous pour me dire les
    développements du "procès" s'il y en a
Je retourne à Pasadena le 2 Novembre pour 3 jours de <u>télévision Française</u>.
    Jean Marie Drot m'y a donné rendez vous, car Philadelphie a été vidé.
Ecrivez un peu
    Affectueusement de nous deux à tous
    Marcel Duchamp

MD in California 6-14 Oct for his first major retrospective exh., "Marcel Duchamp, A Retrospective Exhibition," Pasadena Art Museum, 8 Oct - 3 Nov 1963.

French filmmaker, **Jean-Marie Drot** interviews MD; film later released as a video cassette, "Marcel Duchamp: A Game of Chess," Home Vision, 1987.

▷ TRANSLATION: *28 West 10th St. N.Y.C. 18th Oct. '63. Dear Robert, Safely back from Pasadena after a week of drinking and freeways. Catalog enclosed which, as you will see, has milked you copiously. In any case, life begins at 76 with a one-man show. Also enclosed 2 catalogs with some "little sentences" for your addenda. The sisters don't write much. I put my hopes in you to update me on events in the "trial" if there are any. I'm going back to Pasadena 2nd November for 3 days of French television. Jean Marie Drot set up our meeting there as everyone has left Philadelphia. Please write. Affectionately to all from us both, Marcel Duchamp.*

---

273. Marcel Duchamp to Robert Lebel   autograph letter
30 October 1963, New York   private collection, Paris

28 West 10th St.

N.Y.C.

30 Oct. 63

    Cher Lebel

J'ai parlé à George Staempfli des 2 Renoirs.

Il est intéressé et ira à Paris en Décembre pour les voir et les emporter s'ils
    lui plaisent__

Il m'a demandé naturellement si vous consentiriez à me donner une
    authentification en règle, ce qui évidemment simplifierait ses
    possibilités de vente.

Dites moi si vous acceptez de m'envoyer ici ce papier, étant bien entendu
    que sur le prix de vente un % vous sera reservé.

Dites moi aussi quel % vous plairait?

Pour la description des tableaux il serait bon (si vous êtes obligé de le
    mentionner) de les déclarer appartenant à moi ou à Jean Crotti, comme
    vous jugerez préférable__

Il est aussi sous entendu que j'espère ne pas faire exploser un cas de
    conscience chez vous.

Je retourne à Pasadena pour 3 jours, me faire téléviser par Jean-Marie Drot
    et son équipe.

    A bientôt de vos nouvelles et affectueusement de nous à vous 2

    Marcel Duchamp

P.S. Avez vous reçu mon catalogue (Pasa)?

George Staempfli (1910-1999), American art dealer.

Film by J.-M. **Drot**, see note on previous letter.

Pasadena catalog, see previous letter.

▷ TRANSLATION: *28 West 10th St. N.Y.C. 30th Oct. '63. Dear Lebel, I've spoken to
George Staempfli about the 2 Renoirs. He's interested and will go to Paris to see
them and take them with him if he likes them. Naturally he asked me if you would
consent to giving me some formal authentication which would obviously simplify
sales possibilities for him. Let me know whether you would agree to sending this paper to me here, on the understanding of course that a percentage of the sales price
would go to you. Let me know what percentage you would like. As for the description
of the paintings, it would be good (if you have to mention it at all) to declare them
as belonging to me or to Jean Crotti, whichever you deem preferable. Hoping, of
course, not to spark off a crisis for your conscience, that goes without saying. I'm
returning to Pasadena for 3 days to be televised by Jean-Marie Drot and his team.
Look forward to your news soon and affectionately from the two of us to the two of
you, Marcel Duchamp. P.S. Did you receive my catalog (Pasa)?*

274. Marcel Duchamp to Robert Lebel
8 November 1963, New York

autograph letter
private collection, Paris

28 W. 10.
N.Y.C.
8 Nov. 63
    Cher Lebel
Rentré pour la seconde fois de Pasa. où je suis allé me faire photographier par Jean-Marie Drot dans un bain de salive—
Trouve votre lettre, merci : j'ecris immédiatement à Lefebvre-Foinet pour savoir s'il fait encore garde-meubles ou m'indiquer l'adresse d'un garde-meubles pas cher.
et dès qu'Yvonne sera rentrée à Neuilly vers fin Novembre, elle fera enlever les toiles de Crotti (qui attendront probablement *longtemps* l'approbation du "lait") plus une centaine de toiles de Suzanne ce qui videra l'atelier et permettra de faire faire les travaux en Dec. et Janvier.
Avez vous fait enlever les tableaux du litige par le nouveau restaurateur?

———

Avec le catalogue Pasa, je vous avais envoyé un catalogue Iolas pour Takis dans lequel j'avais une "petite phrase"— je crois que l'autre "petite phrase" était celle du catalogue Man Ray chez Ekstrom (demandez à Man Ray).
Staempfli sera à Paris vers le 4 Déc. et verra les Renoirs, au besoin les emportera
Dites moi NON (sans autre explication) si je ne peux pas compter sur un certificat en règle pour ces Renoirs— vous faut il des photos?
    Toutes mes affections au président du concile
    Marcel Duchamp

"Pasa." = Pasadena Film by J.-M. **Drot**, see p.377.

Yvonne Duchamp, MD's sister, see p.133.
Following the death of their sister, Suzanne, 11 Sept 1963.

Pasadena catalog, p.377.
Alexander Iolas (1908-1987), gallerist in NY from 1945, then in Paris from 1964.
"little sentences" = aphorisms of MD's published as epigraphs of catalogs for exhibitions of **Takis** (Galleria Schwarz, Apr-May 1962) and **Man Ray** (Cordier & Ekstrom Gallery, Apr-May 1963).

▷ TRANSLATION: *28 W. 10 N.Y.C. 8th Nov. '63. Dear Lebel, Back from Pasa. for the second time where I went to be photographed by Jean-Marie Drot in a bath of saliva. Find your letter, thanks. Am writing to Lefebvre-Foinet immediately to find out if he still does storage or can give me an address of someone not too expensive and as soon as Yvonne gets back from Neuilly toward end November, she'll have all the Crotti canvases taken away (they'll probably have to wait a long time before meeting with the approval of the "milk") and also a number of Suzanne's canvases which will empty the studio so that work can be done on it in Dec. and January. Have you had the paintings in the dispute taken away by the new restorer? Along with the Pasa catalog, I sent you an Iolas catalog for Takis in which I had a "little sentence." I think the other "little sentence" was in the one in the Man Ray catalog at Ekstrom's (ask Man Ray). Staempfli will be in Paris around 4th Dec. and will*

"milk" = may be a pun on the *crème de la crème* or possibly a reference to the French expression, *ça se boit comme du petit lait*, meaning "to lap it up," anticipating the reaction of the critics.

see the Renoirs, if needs be take them away. Just say NO to me (without further explanation) if I can't count on a formal certificate for these Renoirs. Do you need photos? All my affection to the President of the Church Council, Marcel Duchamp.

New York + Neuilly-sur-Seine | 1964-1968

lives half the year in Neuilly-sur-Seine: 5 rue Parmentier (spring and summer)
lives the other half of the year in New York: 28 West 10th Street, 1st floor (autumn and winter)
spends every summer in Cadaqués, staying a month or two
round trips to Milan, Florence, Livorno, Rome, Bergamo, London, Saint Louis (Missouri), Mexico,
 Rome, Hanover and Minneapolis
moves his studio to a new location: 80 East 11th Street, 4th floor, room 403 | around Christmas 1965
round trips to London, Amsterdam, Monte-Carlo, Rouen, Buffalo, London, Genoa and Barcelona

from 21 April 1964 to October 1968

▶   MAJOR WORKS

Edition of 13 replicas of MD's sculptures and
 readymades (Galleria Schwarz, 1964)
Bouche-Evier (lead mould of a sink-stopper,
 1964)
Un robinet original révolutionnaire
 (copperplate, June 1964)
L'horloge de profil / The Clock in Profile (pliage
 and "pop-up" on flat cardboard sheet,
 1964)
Shaved L.H.O.O.Q. (playing card of the Mona
 Lisa for dinner invitation, 1965)
Cover for "Not Seen and/or Less Seen..."
 (Cordier & Ekstrom gallery cat., NY, 1965)
Series of 8 lithographs of different details of the
 Large Glass (summer 1965)
Homage to Caissa (wood chessboard,
 Jan 1966)
Etant donnés 1° la chute d'eau, 2° le gaz
 d'éclairage... / Given: 1.The Waterfall;
 2.The illuminating Gas (mixed-media
 installation, 1946-66)

Manual of Instructions for the Assembly of
 "Etant donnés..." (black vinyl binder
 containing manuscript notes, photo prints
 and drawings, 35 pages, 1966)
"A l'Infinitif" or *The White Box* (box of 79
 facsimile notes, published by Cordier &
 Ekstrom, New York, 1967)
Poster for the "Éditions De et Sur MD" (Galerie
 Givaudan, Paris, 8 June - 30 Sept 1967)
Morceaux choisis (selected details after
 Cranach, Rodin, Ingres, Courbet... for a
 series of 9 lithographs on love, Mar 1968)
Cheminée anaglyphe / Anaglyphic Chimney
 (Stereoscopic drawing, Sept-Oct 1968)

▶   ONE MAN SHOWS or SEMI-ONE MAN SHOWS

Omaggio a / Hommage à / Homage to Marcel Duchamp,
 Galleria Schwarz, Milan, Italy (travels to Bern,
 London, The Hague, Eindhoven, Krefeld,
 Hanover). By MD: 108 works
 — **5 June - 30 Sept 1964**

Not seen and/or less seen of/by Marcel Duchamp/Rrose Sélavy 1904-64 (Mary Sisler Collection), Cordier & Ekstrom, Inc., New York (Travels to Houston, Waltham, Baltimore, Milwaukee, Minneapolis, and in Australia: Auckland, Wellington, Christchurch, Hobart, Melbourne, Sydney, Brisbane, Adelaide, Perth). MD's retrospective: 90 works + 35 miscellanea — 14 Jan - 13 Feb 1965

Marcel Duchamp Readymades, Galleria Gavina, Rome — June 1965

Marcel Duchamp, Museum Hans Lange, Krefeld, Germany — 19 June - 1 Aug 1965

Marcel Duchamp, Early Drawings, Late Graphics, Rare Editions, Galleria Schwarz, Milan, Italy. Retrospective of 61 items — 4 Dec 1965 - 3 Feb 1966

The Almost Complete Works of Marcel Duchamp, Arts Council at the Tate Gallery, London. Retrospective of 244 items — 18 June - 31 July 1966

Marcel Duchamp between 1912 & 1928 'A l'infinitif', Cordier & Ekstrom, Inc., New York — 14 Feb - 4 Mar 1967

Les Duchamps: Jacques Villon, Raymond Duchamp-Villon, Marcel Duchamp, Suzanne Duchamp, Musée des Beaux-Arts, Rouen, France (travels to Paris). Retrospective of 82 works — 15 Apr - 1 June 1967

Marcel Duchamp, Galleria d'Arte La Bertesca, Genoa, Italy — June - July 1967

Ready-Mades et Editions de et sur Marcel Duchamp, Claude Givaudan, Paris — 7 June 1967

Marcel Duchamp disegni dal 1902 al 1910, Galleria Solaria, Milan, Italy — 7 Nov - 10 Dec 1967

The Large Glass and related works, Biblioteca Comunale, Milan, Italy (cfr. volume completo, incisioni I e II stato) — 7 Nov - 5 Dec 1967

► EXHIBITIONS

8 ans d'agitation, Galerie Daniel Cordier, Paris. By MD: Couple de tabliers — 10 June 1964

Nieuwe Realisten, Gemeentemuseum, The Hague, Netherlands. By MD: Roue de bicyclette; Porte-bouteilles — 24 June - 30 Aug 1964

1908-1928, Galleria Schwarz, Milan, Italy. By MD: Ruota di bicicletta, 1913; Fontana, 1917 (Ready-made Aiutato, Edizione Galleria Schwarz, 1964) — 17 Oct 1964

Ten Years of Activities 1954-1964, a Collection of The Galleria Schwarz Catalogs, Galleria Schwarz, Milan, Italy — 1965

Chef d'œuvre du mois: Chapeau de paille? 1921 (Hommage à Francis Picabia), Galerie Louis Carré,

Paris. Exhibit: L'Œil Cacodylate (M.D. signataire) — 4 Nov - 4 Dec 1964

3 générations, Sidney Janis Gallery, New York. By MD: Roue de bicyclette — 24 Nov - 26 Dec 1964

The Peggy Guggenheim Collection, Arts Council at the Tate Gallery, London (traveling exhibition). By MD: Sad Young Man in a Train — 31 Dec 1964 - 7 Mar 1965

Kinetische Kunst uit Krefeld, Gemeentemuseum, The Hague, Netherlands (travels to Eindhoven). By MD: 12 Rotoreliefs (ed. MAT) — 3 Feb - 14 Mar 1965

Pop Por, Pop Corn, Corny, Galerie Jean Larcade, Paris. By MD: Boîte-en-valise — 29 June - 14 Aug 1965

Réhabilitation de l'objet, Galerie Breteau, Paris. By MD: Porte-bouteille — November 1965

Parke Bernet Galleries, New York. By MD: Nu sur nu — 14 Oct 1965

Licht und Bewegung, Staatliche Kunsthalle, Baden-Baden, Germany. By MD: Rotative Plaques Verre; 10 Rotoreliefs — 3 Dec 1965 - 9 Jan 1966

XIe exposition internationale du Surréalisme, L'Œil, Galerie d'Art, Paris. By MD: Why not Sneeze; Fresh widow; Torture morte — 7 Dec 1965 - 1966

Hommage à Caïssa, Cordier & Ekstrom, New York — 8 Feb - 26 Feb 1966

USA, Nouvelle Peinture, Musée des Beaux-Arts, Lyon, France — 12 Feb - 26 Feb 1966

Cinquantenaire de Dada, Galerie Krugier et Cie, Geneva. By MD: Nos. 7 to 26 — 15 Feb - March 1966

Première Biennale de Peinture, Hôtel de Ville, Puteaux, France. By MD: Les joueurs d'échecs — 15 June - 10 July 1966

Sotheby and Co., London. By MD: Objet Dard — 23 June 1966

Cinquant'anni Dada, Dada in Italia, 1916-1966, Civico Padiglione d'arte contemporanea, Milan, Italy. 19 items — 24 June - 30 Sept 1966

Dada: Ausstellung zum 50 Jahrigen Jubilaum, 1916-1966, Kunsthaus, Zurich, Switzerland. By MD: Nu descendant un escalier; Tu m'; Boîte-en-valise; LHOOQ; Maquette de Fountain; Liste de contrepèteries; Boîte verte (exemplaire de Brancusi) — 8 Sept - 17 Nov 1966 Travels to Paris: Dada, exposition commémorative au cinquantenaire 1916-1966, Musée National d'Art Moderne — 30 Nov 1966 - 30 Jan 1967

Labyrinthe, phantastische Kunst vom 16. Jahrhundert bis zur Gegenwart, Kunstverein, Berlin (Travels to Nuremberg and Baden-Baden). By MD: Boîte-en-valise — October - November 1966

Peggy Guggenheim, Moderna Museet, Stockholm (traveling exhibition) — 26 Nov 1966 - 8 Jan 1967

Painters of the Section d'Or, The alternative to Cubism, Albright-Knox Art Gallery, Buffalo, USA. By MD: *The King and the Queen* — 27 Sept - 22 Oct 1967

Sammlung Marguerite Arp-Hagenbach, Kunstmuseum Basel, Switzerland. By MD: *Boîte-en valise n°XIX/ XX* — 4 Nov 1967 - 7 Jan 1968

Dal Dada al Surrealismo, Galleria Narciso, Turin, Italy. By MD: *Apollinère*; *Chèque Tzank*; *LHOOQ*; *Obligation pour la Roulette de Monte-Carlo*; *Gilet pour Benjamin Péret*; *Les Joueurs d'échecs (engraving No.VII/XXV)*; *Allevamento di polvere (photo Man Ray)* — 26 Nov 1967 - 5 Jan 1968

1er Salon International du Livre sur l'Art et de Bibliophilie, Musée d'Art Moderne de Paris. By MD: *The Large Glass and related works* — 21 Nov-10 Dec 1967

Table d'Orientation pour une sculpture d'aujourd'hui, Galerie Creuzevault, Paris. By MD: *A Bruit Secret* — 22 Nov 1967 - mid-Jan 1968

I maestri del Surrealismo, Museo d'Arte Moderna, Turin, Italy — December 1967 - January 1968

Polly imagists, Cordier & Ekstrom, Inc., New York. By MD: *Pollyperruque* — 5 Dec 1967 - 6 Jan 1968

Le Surréalisme est-il un art érotique? Galerie Saqqarah, Gstaad, Switzerland. By MD: *Coin de chasteté*; *Objet dard*; *Feuille de vigne femelle*; *Mona Lisa*; *Boîte-en-valise* — 28 Dec 1967 - 15 Mar 1968

Ars Multiplicata, Vervielfältigte Kunst seit 1945, Wallraf-Richartz Museum in der Kunsthalle, Köln, Germany. By MD: *Rotorelief*; *1 Buch über die Ready-Mades*; *Il reale assoluto*; *13 Ready-Mades*; *The Large Glass and related works*; *9 Radierungen* — 13 Jan - 15 Apr 1968

Doors, Cordier & Ekstrom, Inc., New York. By MD: *Entrance Door for Gradiva (replica)* — 19 Mar 1968

Dada, Surrealism and their heritage, The Museum of Modern Art, New York (travels to Los Angeles and Chicago). By MD: *The Bride*; *The Passage from Virgin to Bride*; *Bicycle Wheel*; *Chocolate Grinder No.1*; *Bottlerack*; *Nine Malic Molds*; *The Bride Stripped Bare by her Bachelors, even*; *Traveler's Folding Item*; *Tu m'*; *Fresh Widow*; *Rotary Glass Plates*; *Why not sneeze?*; *Rotoreliefs* — 27 Mar - 9 June 1968

Parke Bernet Galleries, New York City. By MD: *Paysage aux arbres* — 3 Apr 1968

Presentation at Editions Alecto, London. By MD: *Morceaux choisis* — 6 June 1968

275. Marcel Duchamp to Arne Ekstrom
24 July 1964, Cadaquès

autograph letter
collection Niki Ekstrom, New York

Arne Ekstrom
(1908-1996), Director
of the Cordier &
Ekstrom Gallery, NY.

Cadaquès (Gerona)
2~~5~~4 Juillet 64
Cher Arne

Teeny et moi avons l'idée suivante pour la couverture du catalogue :

Je ne sais pas si vous avez vu chez Schwarz dans la galerie au 2me étage une
reproduction photographique en couleurs, grandeur nature, d'une porte
de la rue Larrey Paris, porte qui est à la fois ouverte et fermée.
Cette porte d'ailleurs existe encore.

Door Larrey... [cat. 58]
shown in "Omaggio a
Marcel Duchamp,"
Galleria Schwarz,
Milan, 5 June - 30 Sept
1964.

— Je voudrais m'en servir
comme couverture (de
devant) pour le
catalogue mais en
dépassant un peu en
haut et en bas la
dimension du catalogue
Pasadena.

Cover MD proposes for
his forthcoming exh. at
Cordier & Ekstrom
Gallery, NY (see p.386).

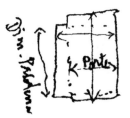

- *Dim. Pasadena*
- *Porte*

Derrière *et dedans*, le catalogue serait de mêmes dimensions que le
Pasadena

Pasadena = Pasadena
catalog, p.377.

Si l'idée vous plaît. je demanderai à Schwarz la transparence qui lui a servi
à faire son "grandeur nature"__ mais je ne lui en ai pas encore parlé.

Répondez moi à Cadaquès afin que j'en confère avec Richard qui arrive *ici*
à la fin Juillet.

Richard = Richard
Hamilton

Quelques nouvelles s.v.p.

Etes vous à N.Y?

Affectueusement pour Parmenia et vous même de Teeny *aussi*
Marcel Duchamp__

Parmenia Migel
(1908-1989), wife of
Arne Ekstrom, ballet
historian and author.

P.S. En plus ~~un~~ il y aurait une couverture plastique transparente avec
inscriptions adéquates__

▷ TRANSLATION: *Cadaquès (Gerona), 24th July '64. Dear Arne, Teeny and I had the
following idea for the cover of the catalog: I don't know if you saw at Schwartz's, in
the gallery on the 2nd floor, a photographic reproduction in color, life-size, of a door
in the rue Larrey, Paris, a door which is at the same time open and shut. This door
actually still exists. I would like to use it as a cover (front) for the catalog, but overshooting slightly, top and bottom, the size of the Pasadena catalog. [sketch captions:
Pasadena catalog dimensions; Door] Back and inside of the catalog would have the
same dimensions as the Pasadena one. If you like the idea, I will ask Schwarz for
the transparency he used to make his "life-size" photograph—but I haven't men-*

tioned it to him yet. Reply to me in Cadaquès so that I can confer with Richard who gets here end July. Some news please! Are you in N.Y.? Affectionately to Parmenia and yourself from Teeny too, Marcel Duchamp. P.S. In addition, there will be a transparent plastic cover with appropriate inscriptions.

---

276. Marcel Duchamp to Douglas Gorsline
28 July 1964, Cadaquès

autograph letter
collection Ronny van de Velde, Antwerp

Douglas Gorsline (1913-1972), American painter and illustrator, teacher of drawing at National Academy of Design, NY.

Cadaquès (Gerona)
Spain
July 28. 1964
    Dear Gorsline
Your letter found me here where we are enjoying the best weather.

Contract on replicas of 13 readymades, issued 1964.

In Milan I have just made a contract with Schwarz, authorizing him to make an edition (8 replicas) of all my few readymades, including the porte bouteilles.

"porte-bouteilles" = Readymade (bottle dryer) [cat. 35]

I have therefore pledged myself not to sign anymore readymades to protect his edition.

But signature or no signature your find has the same "metaphysical" value as any other readymade, even has the advantage to have <u>no</u> commercial value.

We will be back in Paris around Sept. 20 until Sept. 30— N.Y. Oct. 1st

Maybe I will see you in Neuilly—
    Cordialement
    Marcel Duchamp

---

277. Marcel Duchamp to Arne Ekstrom
16 August 1964, Cadaquès

autograph letter
collection Niki Ekstrom, New York

Cadaques (Gerona) Spain
16 Aout 64
    Cher Arne
Je suis désolé que vous n'aimiez pas mon idée de la "porte" comme couverture du catalogue.

Door Larrey... [cat. 58]

Je trouve d'abord que l'exposition n'est pas marquée dans le catalogue comme l'exclusive exposition de la coll. S. mais (beaucoup plus important!) comme une collection de choses "not seen or less seen" depuis 60 ans— pas nécessairement devant aller dans une collection X ou Y.

"coll. S." = Mary Sisler's collection of MD works, will form the basis of MD exhibition at the Cordier & Ekstrom Gallery.

— Une autre idée à exploiter pour vous est la possibilité d'acheter cette porte pour la collection— Car c'est moi qui l'avais fait faire et elle

n'appartient pas à l' "architecture" de la maison ou de l'atelier, 11 rue
Larrey. Paris V.

— De plus Isabelle Waldberg (Mme. Patrick Waldberg) qui habite là
maintenant acceptera certainement de me laisser l'emporter en la
dédommageant pour la remplacer par une copie faite par un menuisier.

— Enfin le fait que nous aurons la très bonne transparency de Schwarz à
notre disposition diminuera les frais d'autant

Richard à qui j'en ai parlé est aussi convaincu que l'idée est importante et
en directe relation avec le "NON VU" = il dit aussi que, avec la
couverture plastique stapled et le dépassement d'un centimètre en haut
et en bas maximum, il n'y aura pas de problèmes de "bending or
breaking".

— En plus de la transparency je voudrais que la reproduction de la porte
soit "embossed" légèrement c. à d. que les lignes principales
apparaissent en léger relief— ce qui n'entraine pas de grands frais mais
devrait faire une "belle couverture"

Ce travail de la couverture seul pourrait peut être être fait en Italie— Car
j'ai bien reçu les 3 repro. en couleurs tout à fait remarquables.

———

Reçu de Parmenia son poème en ballet d'échecs qui est très beau. Merci
chère Parmenia.

———

Et maintenant autre chose :

Gabrielle Picabia et la fille de Picabia (Jeannine) m'ont donné les photos
ci jointes de 2 Picabias qu'elles voudraient vendre (pour elles
2 Millions AF *$4 000 environ* et 4 Millions AF *$8 000.¯ environ*
respectivement.)

Ci joint les photos et les renseignements— Ce sont de bons Picabias qui
pourraient vous intéresser pour une spéculation éventuelle—

Dites moi seulement si vous voulez "considérer" ou pas— et je
transmettrai votre réponse sans vous nommer même.

———

Voilà— cher Arne— Richard et moi travaillons au texte du catalogue et il
vous mettra directement au courant.

Répondez nous assez vite, car Richard repart le 1ᵉʳ Sept.

Mais quand *même* je pense repartir par Londres au début d'Octobre pour
N.Y—

> Affectueusement de nous deux à vous deux
> Marcel Duchamp

Isabelle Waldberg, née
Margaretha Farner
(1911-1990), Swiss
sculptor, ex-wife of
Patrick Waldberg.

Richard = Richard
Hamilton

Final catalog to appear
with cover of MD's
choice, "Not Seen and/
or Less Seen of/by
Marcel Duchamp/
Rrose Sélavy 1904-
1964: The Mary Sisler
Collection," Cordier &
Ekstrom Gallery, NY,
14 Jan - 13 Feb, 1965
(Schwarz cat. 616).

Parmenia = Parmenia
Ekstrom

Cécile Picabia, a.k.a.
Jeannine Picabia
(b.1913), daughter of
Francis Picabia and
Gabrielle Buffet.

Richard Hamilton
writes introduction for
Ekstrom catalog.

▷ TRANSLATION: *Cadaques (Gerona), Spain. 16th August '64. Dear Arne, I am really sorry you don't like the idea of the "door" for the cover of the catalog. It seems to me, first of all, that the exhibition is not defined in the catalog as the exclusive exhibition of the S. collection but (far more importantly), as a collection of things "not seen or less seen" for 60 years not necessarily having to go in X or Y collection. Another idea for you to exploit is that of buying this door for the collection. For I'm the one who had it made and it doesn't belong to the "architecture" of the house or the studio, 11 rue Larrey, Paris V. Furthermore, Isabelle Waldberg (Mrs Patrick Waldberg), who lives there now, would certainly let me take it away if I paid for having it replaced with a copy made by a carpenter. Also, the fact of our having the Schwarz transparency at our disposal will reduce expenses considerably. Richard, with whom I've discussed this, is also convinced that the idea is an important one and directly related to the "NON SEEN." He also says that with the plastic cover stapled on and overshooting by a centimeter top and bottom maximum, there would be no problems of "bending or breaking." As well as the transparency, I would like the reproduction of the door to be lightly "embossed" i.e. so that the main lines appear slightly in relief, which would not imply huge costs but should make a "good cover." This particular work on the cover could perhaps be done in Italy, as I have received the 3 color reproductions and they are absolutely remarkable. Parmenia sent me her poem which is a chess ballet and very beautiful. Thank you, dear Parmenia. And now something different: Gabrielle Picabia and her daughter, Janine, gave me the enclosed photos of 2 Picabias which they would like to sell (they're asking 2 million old francs—about $4,000—and 4 million old francs—about $8,000 dollars—respectively). Enclosed: photos and the details. They are good Picabias which could be of interest to you for speculation, possibly. Just let me know whether you wish to "consider" or not and I'll pass on your reply without even mentioning your name. So, there we are, dear Arne. Richard and I are working on the text of the catalog and will keep you posted directly. Send us your reply fairly soon as Richard is leaving 1st Sept. Although I do expect to leave for N.Y. via London beginning of October. Affectionately from us both to you both, Marcel Duchamp.*

---

278. Marcel Duchamp to Arne Ekstrom   autograph letter
6 September 1964, Cadaquès   collection Niki Ekstrom, New York

Cadaques
Gerona
6 Sept 64
     Cher Arne
Merci pour votre lettre du 31 Aout. *(et aussi confirmation du cable).*
— J'espère donc avoir une réponse et peut être une épreuve en couleurs de
     SEPA avant notre départ d'ici qui <u>est avancé au 15 Sept.</u>

En effet Jean-Marie Drot (Radio telévision française) a obtenu un prix, je crois, au Festival de Bergamo (Italie) Television— ~~et il me d~~ avec le film qu'il a tourné avec moi à N.Y—

Il me demande d'aller à Bergamo le 19 Sept.

Nous passerons donc 2 jours à Milan (Bergamo est à 50 kms.) et rentrerons à <u>Neuilly le 21 au soir</u>, comme prévu.

Dès le 22 ou 23 Sept. je me mettrai en rapport avec Isabelle Waldberg qui vit avec "la porte" et si je peux faire vite je vous ferai expédier à N.Y. la porte par Delamare.

Il n'y aura à payer à Isabelle W. que le remplacement de cette porte par un menuisier de quartier— Vous tiendrai au courant—

— Les histoires de mère à fils et réciproquement sont vraiment à rendre fou— Votre solution me semble la meilleure simplification—

———

Donc nous restons à Neuilly jusqu'au <u>9 Oct.</u>— Nous serons chez Richard à Londres le 9 au soir et travaillerons ensemble le 10 et le 11—

Le 12 nous prenons *à Londres* l'avion du matin et serons à N.Y. le 12 vers 5^h de l'après midi.—

A bientôt donc autres nouvelles
et affectueusement de nous deux à Parmenia et vous même
Marcel.

Gran Premio Bergamo for Jeu d'échecs avec Marcel Duchamp, interview filmed in Pasadena, LA and NY in Nov 1963.

Door Larrey... [cat. 58]

Isabelle W. = Isabelle Waldberg

Richard = Richard Hamilton

Parmenia = Parmenia Ekstrom

▷ TRANSLATION: *Cadaques, Gerona, 6th Sept. '64. Dear Arne, Thank you for your letter of 31st August (and also confirmation about the cable). I hope, then, to have a reply and perhaps a color proof from SEPA before our departure from here which has been brought forward to 15th Sept. Actually Jean-Marie Drot (French television and radio) has won a prize, I think, at the Bergamo (Italy) Television Festival— with the film he shot with me in N.Y. He has asked me to go to Bergamo 19th Sept. So we'll spend 2 days in Milan (Bergamo 50 km away) and return to Neuilly the evening of 21st, as planned. I will get in touch straightaway—from 22nd or 23rd— with Isabelle Waldberg who lives with "the door" and, if I'm quick, I'll send it to you in N.Y. with Delamare. Isabelle Waldberg will only need to be paid the cost of having a replacement of the door made by a local carpenter. Will keep you posted. Mother-son relationships and vice-versa really drive you crazy. Your solution seems to me the best way to simplify things. So we'll be staying in Neuilly until 9th Oct. We'll be at Richard's in London the evening of 9th and we'll be working together 11th and 12th. On the 12th, we're taking the morning flight in London and will be in N.Y. on the 12th around 5 o'clock in the afternoon. Look forward to more news soon and affectionately from us both to Parmenia and yourself, Marcel.*

279. Marcel Duchamp to Pierre Cabanne
17 March 1967, New York

autograph letter
collection David Fleiss, Paris

Pierre Cabanne (b.1921), French art critic, author of several essays on Cubism, on Picasso and also of a famous interview-book of MD: *L'ingénieur du temps perdu*, 1967, Fayard.

28 West 10th Street
New York City
17 Mars 67
  Cher Pierre Cabanne
Merci de l'exemplaire de notre livre, bien arrivé et bien lu—
J'ai lu d'ailleurs l'écho que l'Express en a fait.
"J'en suis béat"—
Nos entretiens je crois tombent à pic pour l'expo. au Musée d'art moderne
et j'espère que notre éditeur n'oubliera pas sa promesse de nous en faire
  partager les résultats—
Je serai à Neuilly le 5 Avril, après une dizaine de jours à Monte Carlo
  Cordialement et à bientôt
  Marcel Duchamp

"Marcel Duchamp, Raymond Duchamp-Villon" at the **Musée National d'Art Moderne**, 7 June - 2 July 1967.

▷ TRANSLATION: *28 West 10th Street, New York City, 17th March '67. Dear Pierre Cabanne, Thank you for the copy of our book, arrived and read safely. I also in fact read what "l'Express" had to say about it. "My cup runneth over." Our interviews are, I think, very timely in terms of the exhibition at the Museum of Modern Art and I hope our publisher won't forget his promise to share the proceeds with us. I'll be in Neuilly on the 5th April, after ten days or so in Monte Carlo. Sincerely and see you soon, Marcel Duchamp.*

---

280. Marcel Duchamp to Pierre de Massot
8 August 1967, Cadaquès

autograph letter
collection BLJD

Cadaquès (Gerona) Espagne
8 Aout 67
  Cher Pierre
Merci de ta carte Roseraie.
Naturellement j'ai bien reçu et avalé ton Breton Septembriseur.
Merci et regrets de ne pas t'en avoir écrit.
  Affectueusement à tous deux de nous²
  Marcel

André Breton ou Le septembriseur, Paris, Éric Losfeld, le Terrain vague, 1967.

▷ TRANSLATION: *Cadaquès (Gerona), Spain. 8th August '67. Dear Pierre, Thank you for your Roseraie card. Naturally, I devoured your Breton Septembriseur as soon as I got it. Thanks and sorry for not having written to you about it. Affectionately to you two from us², Marcel.*

---

281. Marcel Duchamp to Man Ray   postcard
[9 August 1967, Cadaquès]   collection MNAM

> Merci de tes cartes et vœux.
>
> J'aime beaucoup l'éloge à la paresse!
>
> — Espère que tu iras mieux à ton retour d'Angleterre et qu'on te verra ici
> en Sept.— Nous rentrons à Paris le 17 Sept.— Tu pourrais avoir notre
> appart^t du 15 au 30 Sept. Marcel

Probably reference to Paul Lafargue, Le droit à la paresse, 1880.

▷ TRANSLATION: *Thanks for your card and good wishes... I really like the eulogy to sloth! Hope you will feel better when you get back from England and that we'll see you here in Sept.—We're going back to Paris on the 17th Sept.—You could have our apartment from 15th to 30th Sept. Marcel.*

---

282. Marcel Duchamp to Rose Fried   autograph letter
11 August 1968, Cadaquès   collection AAA

> CADAQUES (GERONA)
> Spain
> Aug. 11 1968
>   Dear Rose
> Thank you for your letter of July 18th and the enclosed letter.
> But don't count on me to write an article on anything—
> — it is absolutely impossible for me to do it but I could help you with
> some talks with you in New York after Oct. 15th.
> Bravo for your trip to India : I want to hear all about it when we see you
> again in October.
>   Affections from us both and Regrets!
>   Marcel Duchamp

Rose Fried has written to MD asking him to write "an article with the flavor of time," on Rose Fried's "activities in art," for Studio Magazine.

---

283. Marcel Duchamp to Pierre de Massot   autograph letter
[1 October 1968, Neuilly]   collection BLJD

1 October 1968 = morning of Marcel Duchamp's death.

> Mardi matin
>   Cher Pierre
> Porte Maillot
> prendre Rue de Chartres
> Place Parmentier
> Tourner autour de la Bibliothèque et tout droit après l'avenue du Roule
> 5 minutes en tout
>   à Vendredi vers 1^h
>   Marcel

▷ TRANSLATION: *Tuesday morning. Dear Pierre, Porte Maillot, take rue de Chartres, place Parmentier, go around the library then straight on after the avenue du Roule, 5 minutes in all. See you Friday around 1 o'clock, Marcel.*

2 October 1968
Duchamp dies at the age of 81,
in his Neuilly apartment, within only
a few hours of he and Teeny having had dinner
with Robert Lebel, Man Ray, and their wives.

---

284. Teeny Duchamp to Richard Hamilton   telegram
2 October 1968, Paris   collection Richard Hamilton, Oxon, England

> 13 2 0947
> TS 15/105 LN FO46 X-F867 4521 PARIS 422044
>   RICHARD HAMILTON 25 HURSTAVE LONDONN6
> MARCEL DIED LAST NIGHT SUDDENLY AND PEACEFULLY
>   TEENYN
> COL 25 LODONN6 TS 15/105 LN+

---

285. Teeny Duchamp to Pierre de Massot   typed letter
14 October 1968, Paris   collection BLJD

> **Paris, Oct. 14 1968**
>   **Dear Pierre,**
> **Merci pour votre lettre et d'avoir si bien compris.**
> **J'ai du faire connaitre hier encore un voeux qui**
>   **malheureusement va déplaire à beaucoup de gens ... mais**
>   **c'est seulement pour six petit mois.**
> **Aidez moi à faire connaître ce que suit :**
>   **Je demande que pendant six mois il n'y ait**
>   **aucune manifestation ou hommage à Marcel.**
>   **Dimanche**
>   **le 13 octobre**
>   *Alexina Duchamp*
> **Je pars samedi. Passez avant quand vous pouvez. J'ai**
>   **quelques petits souvenirs pour vous ('Only' pratiques car**
>   **il ne gardez pas d'autres).**
>   **Amitiés**
>   *Teeny*

"souvenirs pratiques" =
in fact, Teeny is to give
him MD's overcoat.

▷ TRANSLATION: *Paris, Oct. 14th 1968. Dear Pierre, Thank you for your letter and for being so understanding. Yesterday, I once more had to reveal a wish that unfortunately will displease a lot of people...but it's only for six short months. Please help me to make known the following: I ask that for six months there be no manifestations or tributes to Marcel. Sunday, 13th October, Alexina Duchamp. I'm leaving Saturday. Come by before whenever you can. I have a few souvenirs for you. ("Only" practical ones as he didn't keep any others). Best wishes, Teeny.*

index of MD's works | cited or evoked

In compiling this index, systematic classification, by alphabetical or chonological order, was rejected as useless to the reader trying to find his way through the heterogeneous jungle of the Duchamp production (in which works include other works, replicas are to be considered as new originals, the same title can apply to totally different works, a single work may carry different titles, etc).

Moreover, this substantial index has been an opportunity to reflect the diverse interests and activities of Marcel Duchamp as outlined in our "Preamble" (p.12).

MD's works have therefore been grouped according to the following eight self-explanatory categories:

1. Major Works (Large Glass, Green Box, Box-in-a-Valise); 2. Oil Paintings (up to 1912); 3. Works Related to the Large Glass; 4. Smaller Works on Glass (also related to the Large Glass); 5. "Readymades" and Dada Works (1913-1924); 6. Optical Experiments (1919-1935); 7. Other writings and publications; 8. Miscellanea.

For each work, the reader will find: the abbreviated title used in the sidenotes; the complete original title; the nickname, where applicable; and a brief description of the work.

(MODEL)

cat.oo **Abbreviated title**
Original title, as used in the Box-in-a-Valise + other denominations, as they appear in the letters
English translation of the complete title, when necessary
Schwarz cat. reference[1] ("Sch.") + short description
• See page 000.

MAJOR WORKS

cat. 1 **The Bride Stripped Bare...**
La mariée mise à nu...:
either *"Large Glass"* or *"Green Box"*
• See pages 187, 209, 224, 281, 287, 342.

---

1. *Catalogue raisonné of Marcel Duchamp*, by Arturo Schwarz, Delano Greenidge ed., 1997.

---

cat. 2 **Large Glass** ☞ *see ill.*
La mariée mise à nu par ses célibataires, même
also called: *"Grand verre," "Big glass," "Large Glass"*
The Bride Stripped Bare by Her Bachelors, Even *(Large Glass)*
Sch. 404: glass, 277.5 x 175.8 cm, 1915-1923
• See pages 31, 45, 54, 64, 69, 92, 102, 189, 207, 209, 213, 213, 287, 297, 299, 301, 313, 314, 316, 317, 336, 339, 340, 341, 353, 354, 356, 359.

cat. 3 **Green Box** ☞ *see ill.*
La mariée mise à nu par ses célibataires même
generally called *"Boîte verte"*
The Bride Stripped Bare by Her Bachelors Even *(Green Box)*
Sch. 435: box containing 94 notes and documents, 33.2 x 28 x 2.5 cm, 1934 (300 copies)
• See pages 173, 187, 189, 190, 192, 194, 196, 197, 214, 218, 354.

index of names

This index catalogs names of magazines, institutions and people.

The reader will find some biographical information on many of these in sidenotes (and footnotes) where the page number is given in bold.

Names of correspondents only feature here when quoted in letters to other people. To conclude research on each name, the reader therefore needs to consult the Index of Letters (by correspondent), p.405.

The authors humbly hope not to have wrongly identified people only referred to in the letters by their first name. (Gaby = Duchamp or Picabia, Mary = Reynolds or Dreier, Walter = Pach or Arensberg, Yvonne = sister, mistress or sister-in-law, etc.)

index of letters | by correspondent

A list of the 48 correspondents featured in this volume is given below in alphabetical order. Page numbers refer to the different letters addressed to each of them.

also
to the future of
Barbara
Obalk

printed by **Die Keure** Bruges | bound by **Splichal** Turnhout

Box-in-a-valise [cat. 4]

Green Box [cat. 3]

The Large Glass [cat. 2]

Nude Descending No. 2 [cat. 17]

Tu m' [cat. 29]

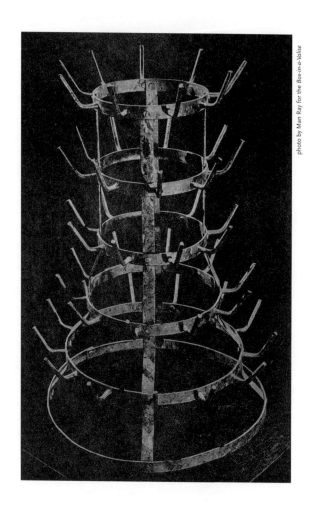

Readymade (bottle dryer) [cat. 35]

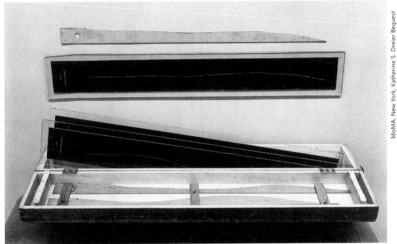

Standard Stoppages [cat. 34]

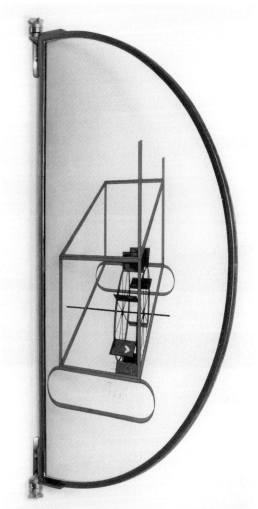

Glider... [cat. 30]

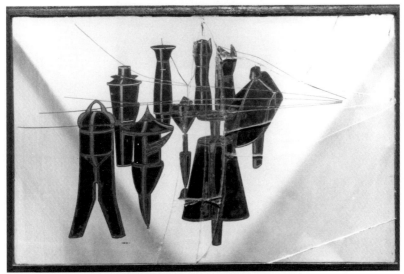

9 Malic Moulds [cat. 31]

Paris Air [cat. 43] **and** *Fountain* [cat. 38]

Female Fig Leaf [cat. 62] **and** *Pocket Chess Set* [cat. 60]

Rotary Glass Plates [cat. 50]

Rotary Demisphere [cat. 51]

Rotoreliefs [cat. 53]

Some French Moderns... [cat. 56]

Ronny van de Velde, Antwerp

Reprinted with permission from the series of articles in the New York Sun and the New York Herald, 1915–1922, by Henry McBride.

Printed, copyrighted, 1922, by Rrose Sélavy.

Société Anonyme Inc.,
19 East 47th Street
New York City.

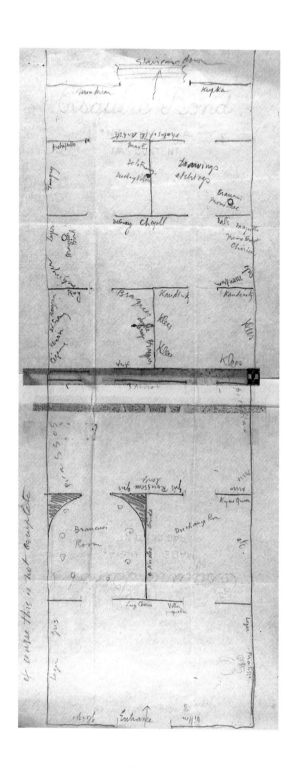

map, enclosure of letter 182